WEST and NON-WEST

NEW PERSPECTIVES

an Anthology

edited by *VERA MICHELES DEAN*
and *HARRY D. HAROOTUNIAN*

 HOLT, RINEHART and WINSTON, Inc., New York

Contemporary Civilizations Series

The Editors

VERA MICHELES DEAN, general editor of the Contemporary Civilizations Series, was born in St. Petersburg, Russia. She came to the United States in 1919, receiving her M.A. from Yale University and her Ph.D. from Radcliffe College in international law and international relations. She served on the staff of the Foreign Policy Association, 1928 to 1961, first as research associate, then as research director and editor, and is now professor of international development at the Graduate School of Public Administration, New York University. From 1954 to 1962 she was director of the Non-Western Civilizations Program at The University of Rochester.

Mrs. Dean is author of several books on world affairs, among them Builders of Emerging Nations, The Nature of the Non-Western World, and New Patterns of Democracy in India. Among other honors, she has received the Legion of Honor from the French government for her contribution to world understanding.

HARRY D. HAROOTUNIAN received his Ph.D. in history at the University of Michigan in 1957. After teaching history at Oklahoma State University and at Pennsylvania State University, he joined the faculty of The University of Rochester in 1959, where he is now associate professor of history. A specialist in Asian studies, Professor Harootunian spent 1962–63 in Japan on a Fulbright fellowship doing research on Japanese intellectual history. He has written a number of articles which have appeared in Korean Survey, Journal of Asian Studies, and Pacific Historical Review. Professor Harootunian was coordinator of the Non-Western Civilizations Program directed by Mrs. Dean.

The format for this book was designed by Robert Sugar.

The cover and art work were prepared by Frank Haines.

This book was made possible by funds granted by Carnegie Corporation of New York to the Non-Western Civilizations Program of The University of Rochester. That Corporation is not, however, the author, owner, publisher, or proprietor of this book, and is not to be understood as approving by virtue of its grant any of the statements made or views expressed therein.

Preface

The most exciting and forward-looking trend in the social studies since World War II has been the enlargement of the curriculum to include materials on non-Western civilizations. American students are now being introduced to new dimensions of the world we live in—dimensions which are fully as important to the future of mankind as the study of outer space or nuclear energy.

Until very recently, however, effective teaching about the non-West has been handicapped by a lack of up-to-date, readable materials. While there has been vast research in the field of non-Western studies, most of the publications resulting from this research have been too specialized to meet the needs of high school students or students at the freshman-sophomore college level. WEST AND NON-WEST: NEW PERSPECTIVES helps to fill this need by providing a collection of writings carefully selected from the works of a broad range of authorities—historians, political scientists, economists, sociologists, scientists, novelists, and playwrights.

The book is divided into three parts:

Part I, *The Development of the West*, provides historical perspective by giving the reader an overview of the evolution of the Western world.

Part II, *The Development of the Non-West*, focuses on the areas that lie outside the Western world. Here the great forces that have influenced or shaped the twentieth century—colonialism, democracy, nationalism, and communism—are analyzed in terms of their impact on the non-West. The social, political, economic, and psychological transformations these forces have brought about are viewed through the eyes of expert observers.

Part III, *The Interaction of West and Non-West*, deals with the potential advantages and the complex problems that arise from contacts between various cultures: the challenges of cooperation among peoples of diverse levels of political, economic, and social development; the lessons learned from the experience of diplomats, economists, foreign aid experts, the Peace Corps, and international civil servants; and the prospects of advancement for peoples of ancient civilizations on the threshold of modern technology through partnership between the rich and the poor lands of the world.

The plan of this anthology, and the selection of the works included in it, were developed in two contexts: in the Non-Western Civilizations Program of The University of Rochester, in which Professor Harry D. Harootunian participated, and in courses and summer institutes for

iii

secondary school teachers of social studies held under the auspices of the Program.

To my colleagues at The University of Rochester, and to the social studies teachers who worked with us, I want to express my warmest appreciation for eight years of stimulating work together.

Vera Micheles Dean

Contents

[3] *Impact of Communism*

[4] *Impact of Democracy*

[5] *Social and Psychological Adjustments*

[6] *Political Adjustments*

[7] *Economic Adjustments*

PART I

THE
DEVELOPMENT
OF
THE WEST

Introduction

SINCE WORLD WAR II, citizens of the United States have suddenly been introduced to a new dimension in international affairs, the dimension of areas outside the confines of Western civilization. These areas, Asia, Africa, the Middle East, we knew, of course, existed on the map. Some of us had worked or taught or served there as doctors, or teachers, or missionaries: in India or Egypt, China or Nigeria. But for the majority of Americans these areas were a *terra incognita*. Even for those who had had personal experience in what, for lack of a better term, we call the non-Western world, the customs, traditions, way of life, and ideas of the many and varied peoples of Asia, Africa, and the Middle East seemed strange and often difficult to understand.

The sense of strangeness was due in large part to our feeling that the conditions we now see in non-Western countries are the result of situations basically different from our own. Tribal power struggles, backward agriculture, extreme poverty in villages where most of the population lives, lack of adequate food and opportunities for education, puzzle us, worry us, and even frighten us. We see nothing in common between these experiences and ours. But are these aspects of the non-Western world really new to the West—or are they only new to Americans? Are we trying to look at the peoples of the non-Western countries in terms only of our own experience, which is in fact unique and has not been shared by any other Western nation?

If we look at the way in which the Western world developed, what do we see? We find that in Western Europe, too, there were tribes during what are now called the Dark Ages. These tribes—the Goths, the Vandals, the Huns—invaded and broke up the Roman Empire. Then they struggled with each other for territory, for resources, for power. We find that it took several centuries for these tribes to organize themselves into what we call nations—England, France, and others. And we find that it was not until the middle of the nineteenth century that the German tribes, whose descendants were by that time grouped in small states, joined in establishing modern Germany in 1871, or that Italy's city states coalesced into a nation in 1861.

We find that the peoples of Europe lived in great poverty before and during the Middle Ages, and that medieval villages were not very different from the villages we see today in Asia, the Middle East, and Africa. Then as now, villagers, once freed from various forms of serfdom through changing conditions, sought new occupations and greater freedom in newly-arising cities. There they began to acquire education and apply new ideas, to make use of science, and later, with the development of technology, to start the Industrial Revolution.

As their economic conditions changed, people began to demand greater freedoms: political freedom, the freedom to speak, write, and think as they saw fit, and the freedom to follow whatever religious concepts they believed in. With the spread of these new freedoms came the overthrow of, or constitutional limitations on, authoritarian monarchs such as Charles I and Louis XVI. Gradually, too, came the establishment of parliaments where all citizens were represented, not merely the rich and powerful.

Nor did the Western Europeans seek political freedoms only. They also wished to obtain social and economic improvements, again not only for the rich and powerful, but for the least among them. They carried out not only political and religious, but also social and economic revolutions which, in the twentieth century, brought about the acceptance of the "welfare state" in Western Europe as well as the United States.

But while all these far-reaching changes were taking place inside Western nations, their governments, in the name of national interests, continued to clash with each other in Europe and all over the globe, as all sought to win new territories, new resources, new strategic bases, and new prestige in Asia, Africa, the Middle East, and Latin America.

An important result of this struggle was the acquisition of colonies, which, since World War II, have been rapidly achieving independence. These former colonies, for the first time in one hundred, or two hundred, or three hundred years, as the case may be, are now free to start out on their own process of developing new political, economic, and social conditions. Judging from the experiences of Western Europe, it is not fair to expect them to issue forth full grown from the moment of birth like Athena from the head of Zeus. To understand the traumas and difficulties many of the emerging nations must pass through before they reach full maturity, let us look briefly at the way in which the Western world developed as described in the following selections. Then we shall see that perhaps we have a great deal more in common with these nations than we had previously thought.

HENRI DANIEL-ROPS

The Church
in the Dark Ages

When we read about armed strife between the many tribes of the
Congo, or study the problems that President Kwame Nkrumah of
Ghana has had to face in seeking to integrate the chiefs of the
Ashanti tribes into a nation-state, we are apt to think that these
events are completely alien to the experience of Western societies.
But the story of the Dark Ages, told here by the French church
historian Henri Daniel-Rops, helps us to see the tribal struggles of
Africa and other areas in historical perspective.

As in Africa today, Western Europe, four centuries after Christ,
was overrun by tribes whose very names spelled frightening cruelty
—Vandals, Huns, Goths, Alemans, and others—who are generically
described as Barbarians. These tribes fought with each other but,
though each acting in its own interest, succeeded in overthrowing
the once glorious, well-ordered, skillfully administered Roman Empire. Eventually what brought order out of the resulting chaos was
the synthesis between the old order and the new effected by the
single force of the early church. The Church provided a universal
system which rose above tribal conflicts, and it grew in strength and
influence during the Middle Ages until the impact of the Reformation and the Renaissance began to erode its political domination.

Henri Daniel-Rops, a Jesuit, is director of the journal Ecclesia.
He is a member of the French Academy and the author of over
seventy books, among them Jesus and His Times, 1954. The following selection is from Volume Two of his monumental History of
the Church of Christ.

Chapter 2

The Barbarian Holocaust and the
Pillars of the Church

Barbarism

ONE winter's night, when the air was misty with hoar-frost, an astounding noise set the guards at the watch-posts on the alert. A jumbled mass of people was milling about on the right bank of the Rhine; there was a sound of raucous shouting, a clatter of war chariots, the stamping of a thousand feet. Weapons gleamed in the moonlight. It was very cold. Had the hour which Rome had dreaded for so long come at last? The Roman legionaries and their Frankish allies—but a thin curtain of troops—hurried to their battle positions. The river was already choked with swimming horses and with rafts filled with men, and armed warriors were clinging to floating tree trunks. The great Barbarian onslaught began. Vandals, Alans, Suevians, and a whole conglomeration of greedy tribes had discovered the weak spot in the Roman defences, the sector of the frontier which was almost unguarded. What could the wretched defenders do? Swept from their posts, massacred where they stood, they quickly surrendered. And, when day dawned, the sleeping Empire was already in the power of the Barbarian hordes. Wave upon wave of tribesmen was rolling across its territories, and henceforth no one would be able to stop them any more.

Such is the picture, romantic, if one fancies it so, and yet strictly historical, in which the event of incalculable importance known as "the Great Invasions" is often portrayed. It occurred on the night of 31st December 406, at the approaches to Mainz. This Barbarian tide—the "ethnic waterspout" as Ferdinand Lot has called it—swept over the whole of northern Gaul, devastated it, and occupied it. But nothing would be more false than to reduce the Barbarian entry into the Empire to the scale of this one tragic scene. That entry had its roots in the distant past, and it developed in many different ways. The Rhine crossing was only one episode among many, and was certainly not the most important one.

The Roman world had had dealings with these formidable hordes for a long time past. From time to time their pressure forced breaches in her frontiers, but over the centuries they had always been overpowered in the end. The name by which they were known, "Barbarians," which had been given them by the Greeks, had a ring of scorn to it—the scorn felt by the civilization of the city and the state towards the civilization of the tribe. And, ever since the dreadful period when, about one hundred years before our era, Marius had been unable to stop the first big Germanic raids until they reached the shores of the Mediterranean, the Teutons at Aix-en-Provence (102) and the Cimbri at Verceil (101), all the politicians at Rome had never lost sight of what they well knew to be the Empire's greatest threat. Caesar had been flung into Gaul to bar the advance of the Suevian Ariovistus (57), and his genius had seen clearly that, in order to stop the pressure on the frontiers, it was necessary to carry the fight right into Barbarian territory itself, into the lands from which the hordes obtained their fighting men. Augustus had followed his uncle's example. But after the disaster of Varus, and the loss of the legions in the Hercynian forest (nine years after Caesar), Roman policy had tended to go on the defensive; the "wisdom" of Tiberius and of Hadrian, which their contemporaries eulogized so, stupidly abandoned the project of occupying Germany, Central Europe, Caledonia, and Ireland, although such a project was still perfectly possible. Henceforth Rome relied only on powerful fortifications—as if the Great Wall of China or the Maginot Line could make good human weakness—on the *limes* and the legions in the frontier barracks to bar the way to all attacks. She accepted the sight of a swarming mass of unreliable peoples beyond her frontiers, whom only respect for her war-engines held in check.

During the third century the situation had altered. Certain changes had taken place within the complex mass of differing Barbarian tribes. Without disappearing completely, the petty groupings of Germanic peoples were absorbed into large military confederations: Franks, Vandals, Alamans, Goths, Saxons. In the same way, at the other end of the Empire, the Parthians, successors of the Persians, had their ranks closed again by the powerful Sassanid dynasty (227). From this time forward the Barbarian threat was a permanent one. There were some tragic episodes, as, for example, in 258, when the Alamans and the Franks had swept over Gaul, northern Italy, and Spain, or in 378, when the Goths had wiped out the Roman army at Adrianople and killed the Emperor Valens. However, in the main, the Barbarian peril did not seem very serious to the average Roman citizen until the time of the death of the great emperor, Theodosius (395). Of course the frontiers had to be shortened a good deal, the Decumate Fields (the future Grand Duchy of Baden) were abandoned to the Alamans, and the Dacian territories to the

Goths; but after the clean sweep under the Illyrian emperors, did not people feel fairly confident? After all, these Barbarians were all so eager to come and enrol under the Roman eagle!

This was the most serious aspect of the situation; but everyone was so used to it that not the slightest attention was paid to it. For three hundred years now, slowly at first, then with increasing momentum, the Barbarians had been infiltrating into the *Imperium*. It had all started with the acceptance of individual Barbarians into the army, mainly in the auxiliary corps, or as contracted labour in the agricultural colonies. Subsequently, under the title of *foederati*—Federates—the Romans had recruited soldiers of all races, Germans, Arabs, Asians, and even Negroes, in complete racial units, in order to lighten the burdens of military service and the field duties of the decadent descendants of the soldier-labourers. The senior command of these units, which was initially confined to Romans, passed little by little into the hands of Barbarians, who were adorned with Latin titles. In this way whole tribes, still under the orders of their chiefs, and retaining their customs, language, and methods of war, were installed along the whole length of the frontiers, replacing the thinning legions and the missing farmers. And, during the civil wars which had been so frequent over the past three hundred years, the rival factions often made simultaneous appeal to the Barbarian armies in order to gain or to maintain power.[1]

This situation, serious enough in itself, was accompanied by a barbarization of the entire Roman world. One or two emperors were dimly aware of the dangers of this. In 375 Valentinian and Valens had promulgated a law forbidding marriages between Romans and Barbarians, on pain of death. All the evidence shows that very few people obeyed them: mixed marriages multiplied, even at Court! After all, what law could prevent the kind of morbid fascination which the wholesome violence of the Barbarians exercised on a senile society like the Roman?[2] What law could alter the eternal rule of history, which ordains that those who hold authority end by wielding power? How could these Germanic generals, into whose hands the might of Rome had been allowed to fall, fail to play a decisive role in an epoch when ambition of every kind had

---

[1] When, in 394, Theodosius defeated his rival, Arbogast, at the second battle of Aquileia, his army included Goths, Alans, Iberians from the Caucasus, and even Huns, and among his generals was Stilicho the Vandal, the future defender of the Empire, and Alaric the Goth, who was to capture Rome fifteen years later. Arbogast, on his side, had an army of Franks and Alamans. How complex Roman politics had become. . . .

[2] There are innumerable proofs of this fascination: the most astonishing is the story of Honoria, the daughter of the Empress Galla Placidia, who sent a ring to Attila and a love-letter asking him to marry her!

free scope? From the end of the fourth century all the protagonists in important political affairs are Barbarians, more or less Romanized, of course, but no longer desiring to hide their origin. There is Stilicho, a Vandal who assumed the responsibilities of the Empire after the death of Theodosius with such heroism; Aetius, a semi-Barbarian, the son of a Pannonian German and a Latin mother, and the future conqueror of Attila; the generals Victor, Magnentius, Sylvanus, and Sebastianus were, despite their Roman names, all Barbarians, and, among those whose names do not disguise their racial origin are Merobaud, Dagalaif, Bauto, and Ricimer. . . . Were these men faithful to Rome? The majority of them were. Stilicho and Aetius sacrificed their lives in obedience to this loyalty. But they were also tempted to play their personal hand in the imbroglios of a policy that was entirely without morality; between the general who served the emperor and the rebel who dreamt of seizing the Empire, there was often nothing but the flimsy barrier of a satisfied vanity or assuaged greed. Several of the outstanding episodes which fall under the general heading of the Invasions—the adventure of Alaric is one of these—are indeed simply the results of a reversion to ancient loyalties. And since it was hard to tell where treason began or where it ended, why prevent a Barbarian from the Empire summoning help from Barbarians beyond its frontiers, if he was in need of troops?

For, on the other side of the frontiers, the mass of invaders at the ready went on growing. A reservoir of excellent warriors existed there. New tribes were continually joining the old; all the time the pressure grew. Since the revolutions of the third century, the Barbarians, now better organized, had become more conscious of their own strength. Right from the North Sea to the Caspian it was as if a succession of wild beasts was poised, all ready to spring. The greater part of these Barbarians were Germans, a branch of the Aryans which had originated in the foggy lands around the Baltic, and which was now, after much wandering, coming together again. For the most part they were tall, strong, aggressive, greedy folk, organized nearly everywhere into highly disciplined tribal communities in which the "principle of chieftainship" operated rigidly. About the year 400 the Barbarian map looked rather like this: the federation of the Franks stretched the whole length of the Rhine, from the North Sea to the Main, and was bounded, from the basin of the Weser as far as the Elbe, by the Saxons, and, between the Elbe and the upper Main, by the Lombards; a little farther south were the giant-like Burgundians, who had come originally from Brandenburg, and whose territory adjoined the lower reaches of the Rhine around Mainz. The Alamans, momentarily checked by the victories of the Emperor Julian in 357, were henceforth installed in the former Roman territories known as the Decumate Fields; known as prodigious raiders, they were among the most dangerous of the Barbarians. This left the Marcomans in Bohemia and the Rugians and the Herulians in the surrounding areas. These were less important. In contrast to this two stronger Germanic federations were drawn up along the Danube. The Vandals occupied the area extending as far as present-day Austria. Tacitus had already described them as a vicious people, familiar with all the tricks of warfare. Beyond them were the Goths, who had arrived in the region sixty-five years before from their original home around the Vistula. Henceforth they were to be masters of Dacia, the ancient bastion of Trajan. They were divided into two groups: "the brilliant Goths" or Ostrogoths, who faced the Sea of Azov, and the "wise Goths" or Visigoths, who faced the Empire. And, in the rear, behind this line-up of peoples, others were waiting and pressing forward: Angles and Jutes in what is now Denmark; Skirians in Galicia, Norwegians, Geats, and Swedes in Scandinavia, and, on the Russian plains, Slavs and Wends in the north, Quads and Gepidae in the south, and Alans on the shores of the Black Sea. Meantime, way back in the infinity of the Asiatic steppes, sprawled the Ural-Altaic tribes, shifting, intermingling with one another, getting ready for the future. It was the thrust of these yellow-skinned folk which was to set the drama in motion. The most famous of them were the Huns.

Such is the general picture of the Barbarian world at the moment when the drama of the fifth century was about to begin. But in considering it in this global fashion, there is a risk of making numerous errors of interpretation. Even if the Huns, whose case is a peculiar one, are not included among them, considerable differences existed between the different elements of which this enormous Barbarian puzzle was composed. Physically, even, these peoples were not much alike, though they were all more or less fair-haired. One could not mistake a "blue-eyed Saxon, his hair shaved high off his forehead, in order to make his features appear longer" for a Sicambrian, with his enormous shock of unkempt hair falling down his back, nor the skinny Herulian, "with bluish cheeks, pallid as seaweed," for the ruddy complexioned Burgundians, gigantic in stature, who were over six feet tall! Morally and psychologically, too, the dissimilarities were very great. Whilst the Burgundians were well-meaning, cheerful brutes, free from malice, the Alamans were considered violent and avid for plunder, and the Alans had a reputation for implacable cruelty that the Vandals—whose name has become proverbial—often contested with them. Christian writers like Salvianus recognize that they possessed certain virtues: they were loyal, well disciplined, chaste, and, in their dealings with one another, upright. They had a civilization of a sort which we can only begin to uncover. During their wanderings in the Russian plains they had learnt the secrets of a strange art from the Scythians and the Sarmatians, and they produced a polychrome jewellery decorated with animal designs which still fascinates us today. Above all, many of them had already acquired the distinctive stamp of Rome or Greece in varying degrees and in varying ways, sometimes up to the point of being permeated by it.

This is a fact which must never be forgotten when considering the Barbarian invasions; these peoples had at least a vague understanding of classical civilization, which was often of long-standing, and the majority of them admired it. As early as the second century the kingdoms of the Marcomans had been considerably Romanized, and perhaps Trajan and Marcus Aurelius had been mistaken in dismembering this buffer state. The Franks in the Belgian districts and the Goths on the Lower Danube had already had a good deal of intercourse with the Graeco-Roman world, with its diplomats, and, particularly, with its merchants. The Jutes' adaptation of the "Grecian style" as a model for their decorative badges, the Scandinavian use of Roman coins, the religious conversions among the Goths are all evidence of the numerous contacts and influences. Moreover Rome's habit of bringing young Barbarian princes to Court, in order to guarantee the execution of treaties signed with their peoples, made the Barbarian nobility well acquainted with the Empire, with its civilization, and with its weaknesses. Alaric, Theodoric, and even Attila himself had been "hostages" of this type. These Barbarian chieftains, whom we tend to group together as all of a kind, as savages in charge of savage hordes, could speak Latin, and often Greek, and knew how to appreciate the good things of civilization. This only incited them the more to steal its fruits for themselves. They were queer people, these chieftains, on the fringes of two worlds, one on its deathbed, the other in its birth pangs. In the depths of their hearts they were Barbarians, yet they were fascinated by the venerable lure of Rome. . . . So we find Alaric, the Visigoth conqueror, a scion of the "divine" race of the Balthungs, demanding nothing more as a ransom of war, on his seizure of Athens, than the right to spend a day walking through the streets of the wonderful city, saluting Phidias' statue in the Parthenon, having the Platonic dialogue of *Timaeus* read to him, and listening to the *Persians* at the theatre; but when he marched on Rome in 410, he reverted once again to his ancestral loyalties. He threw the imperial badges denoting his rank into the Rubicon, robed himself once more in the dyed-red furs of the Gothic horseman, and put on the bronze, two-horned Gothic helmet—this was the kind of leader to whom the immediate future belonged.

Therefore, whether one is considering the decadent Romans, obsessed by the healthy violence of the Barbarians, or the Romanized Barbarians in the service of Europe, or the Barbarians who were fascinated by the splendour of Rome, even while they hated her,[3] there is always the same impression of ambiguity and overlap. Suddenly the very notion of Barbarism is enlarged and freed from its historical framework of a few murderous raids and bloody intrigues. *Barbarism*: was it not the characteristic of a world where the past and the future mingled in the melting-pot? Of a world where the old, civilized values no longer had healthy roots, but in which the new elements were not yet sufficiently assimilated to contain any humanity? In these circumstances of tragic disequilibrium, the decadence of the civilized Romans and the violence of the invaders complemented and attracted each other. It was indeed the entire Western world which was in a state of Barbarism, a state which was to last for six hundred years, the time necessary for the painful birth pangs of a new civilization. As for the Germanic tribes which threw themselves upon the Empire during the fifth century, they were merely the means which history used to effect an inevitable change.

The Stages in the Drama

Nothing would be more erroneous than to see the Great Invasions as a gigantic and concerted attack by Barbarism as a whole against civilization as a whole. Though alliances existed between certain Germanic peoples for the undertaking of specific operations, there was never any united plan amongst them, no unanimity of purpose, nor any deep feeling of community of race or interest. Even the name "German" was not used by the tribes themselves; it had been given them by the Gauls and was intended to signify simply "neighbours." Each of the acts in the drama was based on motives which were nearly always of an episodic nature; this does not mean, however, that there were not certain profound and decisive causes behind the phenomenon as a whole.

The actual origin of the disturbance which was to impel the tribes to assault the Empire at the beginning of the fifth century must be sought in the conditions of Barbarian life itself—in the petty divisions of the tribal system, and in the perpetual quarreling. Ever since the Romans had been aware of this sea of Germanic peoples, they had seen it periodically tossed by tempests, whose significance, however, eluded them. The inborn Germanic taste for wandering, for indulging in pillaging expeditions, the custom of *vendetta* between tribes, the rivalries among individual chieftains—these were all explanations for these perennial outbursts. Shortly after the middle of the fourth century, southern Russia, and the lands across the Danube, were the centres of a

---

[3] There is one exception to this: Attila, King of the Huns. From this stems his exceptional role in history. . . .

series of disturbances which were soon to burst upon the West. The great Germanic wave which had been flowing from the Baltic towards the south for more than a century was halted by another wave of peoples advancing from the Asian steppes. They had a power such as had never been known before. They were the Huns, the same terrible Hiang-Now who had been the scourge of China for the past several hundred years. Now that they had been chased from their familiar hunting-grounds by the heroism of the Han emperors, and thrown out of their old territories as a result of the construction of the Great Wall, they were turning round and heading westwards. One by one the Sarmathians from the lower Volga, then the Alans, then the Ostrogoths, then the Visigoths, had been driven back by their cavalry squadrons. The Great Invasion at the beginning of the fifth century was no less than the direct consequence of the Mongol attack, which co-ordinated and channelled in a single purpose the unstable forces which made up the Germanic world.

The necessity of leaving their threatened lands; the pell-mell flight before a dreaded peril; the lure of the fine, rich, sunny lands of the West; the desire to be like their kinsmen already installed in agricultural colonies or as *foederati*; the burning love of war and conquest which was ingrained in the Germanic soul; and too, without question, that poetic sense of adventure, directed by splendid young heroes into a world of enchantment, of victories and catastrophes, such as that immortalized in the epic poem of the *Niebelungen*, eight centuries later—all these were causes of the Barbarian onslaught on the Empire. But parallel with these there are others too attributable not to the aggressors but to the Empire itself; Court intrigues amounting to actual treason, such as the action of Rufinus, the leading minister, in flinging the Barbarians upon Italy, or, possibly (it was generally suspected to be the case, at all events) that of Count Boniface, in throwing Africa open to Genseric's Vandals; personal rivalries among the "Roman" generals, Barbarians themselves, with but a bare veneer of Roman civilization; the help of tribes already installed inside the imperial boundaries; more subtly, the moral connivance of a section of the civilized people themselves, and that kind of fatal invitation which utter feebleness holds out to brute force, almost begging it to reduce it, and to finish it off. Just as a human body, worn by age, attracts sicknesses, so the Empire, at the turn of the fifth century, attracted the Barbarians.

They came. They came not simply as men had been accustomed to see them come of old—as regiments of soldiers, more or less—but as whole tribes, with their womenfolk, their children, their wagons, their bundles of belongings, their reserve cavalry, their herds, and their flocks. The word "invasion," which brings to mind primarily the entry of an army into a specified area, is something of a misnomer here. The term which exactly describes the phenomenon is the German *Völkwan-derung*, i.e. a migration of peoples. The situation which the Mediterranean world had known several years before our era begins, when the Aryan invaders, the Greeks and the Latins, had led the assault on the ancient empires, was partially repeated at the end of the fourth century. Not repeated exactly, however; it was just one more wave thrown up by the great Aryan sea, the last, up to the present day, that history has known—one cannot say that it is the last she will ever know.

      •   •   •

Exactly how did these terrible events develop in practice? Here again it is a mistake to oversimplify. The Barbarians certainly did not storm into every province that they invaded with burning brands in their hands and their swords wet with blood. Every shade of behaviour can be seen amid the complex jumble of the acts of this occupation, ranging from more or less obvious sympathy with the occupied to actions that gave rise to frightful suffering. . . . In current usage the word "barbarian" has become synonymous with "ferocious savage"; in reality it is not so simple as this. In this decisive epoch, when the world was beginning to take on a new guise, violence only played the role that nature assigned to it; for men's societies, as well as for men themselves, birth and death are usually accompanied by grievous travail.

      •   •   •

. . . It is easy enough to regard all its elements with equal contempt —the Barbarians, these savages, and the fifth-century Romans, these incompetent decadents. But do not moments exist when the powers which determine events are stronger than human wills? The two protagonists in the drama each assumed their role with all the means of which they were capable, and in that fundamental uncertainty which is the characteristic of human destinies.

And then, although the fifth century was an epoch of chaos and degradation, it was also a time of vital preparation. From its filth and blood the future was growing. From this terrible melting-pot—much later on—was to come the civilization which is our own. The really great events of this century—the halting of Attila, for example—have had an enormous effect on the destinies of the Western world, greater by far than the Roman wars or the expeditions of Alexander. We are the descendants of this age of chaos, or, more accurately, of the order which came out of that chaos.

For an order did indeed emerge from it. It did so because, in the very bosom of this doomed society, a power remained which was capable of giving a meaning to the drama, of bringing order out of disorder, of

integrating the Barbarians into civilization and of using their youthful
energies to restore the world to vigour and health. This power, to which
the West owes its salvation, was the Church.

• • •

Giving the Drama a Meaning

If we want to assess the importance of the role which the Church
played in this age when the fate of everything was hanging in the
balance, two factors have to be taken into consideration: in the practical
sphere, the position held by her supporters during the worst periods of
the ordeals; in the spiritual, the decisive influence which she exercised
on the actual interpretation of events. When these are assessed against
one another, one asks oneself whether the latter point is not the essential
one. What men most need, in order to make their earthly lives worth
while, is a feeling, or at least an instinct, of the end towards which they
are striving. A society which loses this sense of purpose, which understands neither the whys nor the wherefores of events, can only fluctuate
between frenzy and despair. It moves in a kind of Hamlet-like anguish.
The greatest service which Christianity was to render to the men of the
fifth century—or, at any rate, to the more intelligent among them—was
to give a meaning to their drama, and not to abandon them, lonely and
distraught, on the edge of an abyss beyond which they could see no
further.

• • •

It remains true that, to any far-sighted observer, unhampered by
prejudice, conditions seemed of necessity to be preparing for a fusion
between the newcomers and the old inhabitants of the West. The problem now was to know whether an area of agreement could be reached
with the Barbarians, so that both elements could work together for a
revival of the Roman Empire and a rejuvenation of civilization. It is in
these terms that we see the problem today; it is wonderful indeed that,
buried to the hilt as they were in the welter of uncontrolled events
around them, some fifth-century men, some Christians, realized it too.

The reaction of these men appears to have been as follows. Since the
cataclysm of the Invasions had not in fact marked the end of the world,
the Church could not shut herself away, fruitlessly mourning the past.
Her profound understanding of the drama, which we have already
noticed, impelled her to adopt a different attitude. On the level of lofty
speculation, where his genius ranged so happily, St Augustine had
shown, in his *City of God*, that it was necessary to progress beyond the
moribund Empire and to conceive a new world. Although he was himself

so deeply attached to everything Roman, he sensed that it had to be replaced—Rome was "unworthy of the name of State"—she had proved disloyal to the true justice that was Christ's. His disciple, Orosius, who was much younger than Augustine and had therefore concrete experience to guide him—time, in matters like this, led to a good deal of modification in men's positions—was to take for granted the idea of including the Barbarians in an enlarged, transformed *Romania*, which would be a new empire. He was to develop his master's thesis and envisage a kind of confederation of Christian nations under the authority of the Pope, an idea which Otto III was to attempt to realize much later on. Twenty-five years after Orosius, Salvianus, in holding up the Germans to the Romans as models of virtue, was not merely yielding to the declamatory inclination of the preacher and the polemicist; if he passed humbly over to the Barbarians it was in order to call on Catholic society to reject the rotten elements from the old world and to create a better state of things, a new way of life. Unquestionably it did not do to take too swift a plunge in this direction and it was wisest to take the time factor into careful consideration; for instance, Paulinus of Pella, the Bordeaux nobleman, had good cause to repent bitterly of "collaborating" too early with the Visigoths, but what was still an extremely dangerous course in 417 was, by 460, almost the accepted state of things: in politics truth is often a matter of the moment. . . .

Thus Christian feeling towards the Barbarians evolved until it came to consider fusion desirable. Why? Firstly because the Church has always had a realistic appreciation of political exigencies, all the more so since, for her, these exigencies are not the essential, since the Kingdom of God is not here on earth. In the midst of the general disorder the Barbarians constituted a live force: why should the Church refuse to make use of it? Moreover had not the collapse of the Empire made a clean sweep of things, in wiping out the old enemy, Graeco-Roman paganism? Then again the Catholic hierarchy well knew that, as the old order disintegrated, its own role grew more important, for it now appeared as the leading force making for order: the bishops established that, in many cases, they were indispensable to the Barbarians. Finally—and this is the over-riding reason—these men whose souls were aflame with the zeal of their apostleship could not help having a passionate desire to win the souls of the invaders for Christ, which would mean, in this case, winning them for civilization too. Such were the feelings of those who held the responsibilities of the Church in their hands. This does not mean that there existed, as Ozanam has noted, with rather generous romanticism, a systematic plan for the conversion of the Barbarians: Catholicism decided to take them under her wing and to conquer them solely by virtue of that deep and radiant urge which, since her origins, had impelled her to spread the Good News through every land. And since she possessed, at one and the same time, an unparalleled spiritual power, a unique organization, and a universality which prolonged in men's eyes the old and now defunct universality of Rome, she succeeded in this most audacious of enterprises—the conquest, the conversion, of the Barbarians.

HENRI PIRENNE

Medieval Cities

For Americans who, whether joyously or reluctantly, are becoming accustomed to life in a country of megalopolises—vast cities linked by throughways stretching in uninterrupted array along both east and west coasts—it is hard to realize that cities were little known to Western Europeans until the end of the Middle Ages. Up to that time a predominantly agrarian society had been composed of three major classes—churchmen, princes and nobles who were also warriors, and peasants—which can be compared to three of the four castes of India: Brahmins (priests), Kshatriyas (princes and warriors), and Sudras (peasants). When towns began to be built, a fourth class, the bourgeoisie (literally, those who lived in bourgs or towns) emerged, comparable to India's Vaishyas (merchants). This new middle class became the spearhead of Europe's great revolutions in England and France.

Today, the rapid transformations which are taking place in non-Western countries are nowhere so strikingly evident as in the vast urban centers which have sprung up overnight wherever ancient agrarian economies have come in contact with modern technology—from Tokyo to Calcutta, from Cairo to Lagos. Both the positive and the negative aspects of urban life with which we are familiar in the West stand out even more dramatically in non-Western countries, where urban centers, with their neon lights, amenities and amusements, their economic opportunities and political ferment, offer a startling contrast to the arduous and barren life of backward villages and remote jungles.

Knowledge of what the emergence of city-life meant to Western peoples prepares us to understand the problems and opportunities non-Westerners face in their new urban centers. The author of this selection, Henri Pirenne, born in Belgium in 1862, lectured at the University of Liège, and in 1886 became a professor of medieval

and Belgian history at the University of Ghent. During World War
I he was arrested and deported to Germany as one of the leaders of
Belgium's passive resistance. In 1922 Pirenne was invited to deliver
a series of lectures in the United States, and out of these lectures
grew the book quoted here. Pirenne's other works include a seven-
volume History of Belgium; An Economic and Social History of
Medieval Europe; *and* Mohammed and Charlemagne, *1954.*

Cities and European Civilization

THE BIRTH of cities marked the beginning of a new era in the internal
history of Western Europe. Until then, society had recognized only two
active orders: the clergy and the nobility. In taking its place beside
them, the middle class rounded the social order out or, rather, gave the
finishing touch thereto. Thenceforth its composition was not to change;
it had all its constituent elements, and the modifications which it was
to undergo in the course of centuries were, strictly speaking, nothing
more than different combinations in the alloy.

Like the clergy and like the nobility, the middle class was itself a
privileged order. It formed a distinct legal group and the special law it
enjoyed isolated it from the mass of the rural inhabitants which continued to make up the immense majority of the population. Indeed, as
has already been seen, it was obliged to preserve intact its exceptional
status and to reserve to itself the benefits arising therefrom. Freedom,
as the middle class conceived it, was a monopoly. Nothing was less
liberal than the caste idea which was the cause of its strength until it
became, at the end of the Middle Ages, a cause of weakness. Nevertheless to that middle class was reserved the mission of spreading the idea
of liberty far and wide and of becoming, without having consciously desired to be, the means of the gradual enfranchisement of the rural
classes. The sole fact of its existence was due, indeed, to have an immediate effect upon these latter and, little by little, to attenuate the
contrast which at the start separated them from it. In vain it strove to
keep them under its influence, to refuse them a share in its privileges, to
exclude them from engaging in trade and industry. It had not the power
to arrest an evolution of which it was the cause and which it could not
suppress save by itself vanishing.

For the formation of the city groups disturbed at once the economic
organization of the country districts. Production, as it was there carried

From *Medieval Cities* by Henri Pirenne. Copyright 1925 by Princeton University
Press; copyright renewed 1952.

on, has served until then merely to support the life of the peasant and supply the prestations due to his seigneur. Upon the suspension of commerce, nothing impelled him to ask of the soil a surplus which it would have been impossible for him to get rid of, since he no longer had outside markets to call upon. He was content to provide for his daily bread, certain of the morrow and longing for no amelioration of his lot, since he could not conceive the possibility of it. The small markets of the towns and the burgs were too insignificant and their demand was too regular to rouse him enough to get out of his rut and intensify his labor. But suddenly these markets sprang into new life. The number of buyers was multiplied, and all at once he had the assurance of being able to sell the produce he brought to them. It was only natural for him to have profited from an opportunity as favorable as this. It depended on himself alone to sell, if he produced enough, and forthwith he began to till the lands which hitherto he had let lie fallow. His work took on a new significance; it brought him profits, the chance of thrift and of an existence which became more comfortable as it became more active. The situation was still more favorable in that the surplus revenues from the soil belonged to him in his own right. The claims of the seigneur were fixed by demesnial custom at an immutable rate, so that the increase in the income from the land benefited only the tenant.

But the seigneur himself had a chance to profit from the new situation wherein the development of the cities placed the country districts. He had enormous reserves of uncultivated land, woods, heaths, marshes and fens. Nothing could be simpler than to put them under cultivation and through them to profit from these new outlets which were becoming more and more exigent and remunerative as the towns grew in size and multiplied in number. The increase in population would furnish the necessary hands for the work of clearing and draining. It was enough to call for men; they would not fail to show up.

By the end of the eleventh century the movement was already manifest in its full force. Monasteries and local princes thenceforth were busy transforming the idle parts of their demesnes into revenue-producing land. The area of cultivated ground which, since the end of the Roman Empire, had not been increased, kept growing continually greater. Forests were cleared. The Cistercian Order, founded in 1098, followed this new path from its very origin. Instead of adopting for its lands the old demesnial organization, it intelligently adapted itself to the new order of things. It adopted the principle of farming on a big scale and, depending upon the region, gave itself over to the most remunerative form of production. In Flanders, where the needs of the towns were greater since they themselves were richer, it engaged in raising cattle. In

England, it devoted itself particularly to the sale of wool, which the same cities of Flanders consumed in greater and greater quantity.

Meanwhile, on all sides, the seigneurs, both lay and ecclesiastic, were founding "new" towns. So was called a village established on virgin soil, the occupants of which received plots of land in return for an annual rental. But these new towns, the number of which continued to grow in the course of the twelfth century, were at the same time *free* towns. For in order to attract the farmers the seigneur promised them exemption from the taxes which bore down upon the serfs. In general, he reserved to himself only jurisdiction over them; he abolished in their favor the old claims which still existed in the demesnial organization. The charter of Lorris (1155) in the Gatinais, that of Beaumont in Champagne (1182), that of Priches in the Hainault (1158) present particularly interesting types of charters of the new towns, which were also to be found everywhere in neighboring countries. That of Breteuil in Normandy, which was taken over in the course of the twelfth century by a number of localities in England, Wales, and even Ireland, was of the same nature.

Thus a new type of peasant appeared, quite different from the old. The latter had serfdom as a characteristic; the former enjoyed freedom. And this freedom, the cause of which was the economic disturbance communicated by the towns to the organization of the country districts, was itself copied after that of the cities. The inhabitants of the new towns were, strictly speaking, rural burghers. They even bore, in a good number of charters, the name of *burgenses*. They received a legal constitution and a local autonomy which was manifestly borrowed from city institutions, so much so that it may be said that the latter went beyond the circumference of their walls in order to reach the country districts and acquaint them with liberty.

And this new freedom, as it progressed, was not long in making headway even in the old demesnes, whose archaic constitution could not be maintained in the midst of a reorganized social order. Either by voluntary emancipation, or by prescription or usurpation, the seigneurs permitted it to be gradually substituted for the serfdom which had so long been the normal condition of their tenants. The form of government of the people was there changed at the same time as the form of government of the land, since both were consequences of an economic situation on the way to disappear. Commerce now supplied all the necessaries which the demesnes had hitherto been obliged to obtain by their own efforts. It was no longer essential for each of them to produce all the commodities for which it had use. It sufficed to go get them at some nearby city. The abbeys of the Netherlands, which had been endowed by their benefactors with vineyards situated either in France or on the banks of the Rhine and the Moselle where they produced the wine needed for their consumption, began, at about the start of the thirteenth century, to sell these properties which had now become useless and whose working and upkeep henceforth cost more than they brought in.

No example better illustrates the inevitable disappearance of the old demesnial system in an era transformed by commerce and the new city economy. Trade, which was becoming more and more active, necessarily favored agricultural production, broke down the limits which had hitherto bounded it, drew it towards the towns, modernized it, and at the same time set it free. Man was therefore detached from the soil to which he had so long been enthralled, and free labor was substituted more and more generally for serf labor. It was only in regions remote from commercial highways that there was still perpetuated in its primitive rigor the old personal serfdom and therewith the old forms of demesnial property. Everywhere else it disappeared, the more rapidly especially where towns were more numerous. In Flanders, for example, it hardly existed at all after the beginning of the thirteenth century, although, to be sure, a few traces were still preserved. Up to the end of the old order there were still to be found, here and there, men bound by the law of mortemain or subject to forced labor, and lands encumbered by various seignorial rights. But these survivals of the past were almost always simple taxes and he who paid them had, for all that, full personal liberty.

The emancipation of the rural classes was only one of the consequences provoked by the economic revival of which the towns were both the result and the instrument. It coincided with the increasing importance of liquid capital. During the demesnial era of the Middle Ages, there was no other form of wealth than that which lay in real estate. It ensured to the holder both personal liberty and social prestige. It was the guaranty of the privileged status of the clergy and the nobility. Exclusive holders of the land, they lived by the labor of their tenants whom they protected and whom they ruled. The serfdom of the masses was the necessary consequence of such a social organization. There was no alternative save to own the land and be a lord, or to till it for another and be a serf.

But with the origin of the middle class there took its place in the sun a class of men whose existence was in flagrant contradiction to this traditional order of things. The land upon which they settled they not only did not cultivate but did not even own. They demonstrated and made increasingly clear the possibility of living and growing rich by the sole act of selling, or producing exchange values.

Landed capital had been everything, and now by the side of it was made plain the power of liquid capital. Heretofore money had been sterile. The great lay or ecclesiastic proprietors in whose hands was concentrated the very scant stock of currency in circulation, by means of either the land taxes which they levied upon their tenants or the alms which the congregations brought to the churches, normally had no way of making it bear fruit. To be sure, it was often the case that monasteries, in time of famine, would agree to usurious loans to nobles in distress who would offer their lands as security. But these transactions, forbidden otherwise by canonical law, were only temporary expedients. As a general rule cash was hoarded by its possessors and most often changed into vessels or ornaments for the Church, which might be melted down in case of need. Trade, naturally, released this captive money and restored its proper function. Thanks to this, it became again the instrument of exchange and the measure of values, and since the towns were the centers of trade it necessarily flowed towards them. In circulating, its power was multiplied by the number of transactions in which it served. Its use, at the same time, became more general; payments in kind gave way more and more to payments in money.

A new notion of wealth made its appearance: that of mercantile wealth, consisting no longer in land but in money or commodities of trade measurable in money. During the course of the eleventh century, true capitalists already existed in a number of cities . . . These city capitalists soon formed the habit of putting a part of their profits into land. The best means of consolidating their fortune and their credit was, in fact, the buying up of land. They devoted a part of their gains to the purchase of real estate, first of all in the same town where they dwelt and later in the country. But they changed themselves, especially, into money-lenders. The economic crisis provoked by the irruption of trade into the life of society had caused the ruin of, or at least trouble to, the landed proprietors who had not been able to adapt themselves to it. For in speeding up the circulation of money a natural result was the decreasing of its value and by that very fact the raising of all prices. The period contemporary with the formation of the cities was a period of high cost of living, as favorable to the businessmen and artisans of the middle class as it was painful to the holders of the land who did not succeed in increasing their revenues. By the end of the eleventh century many of them were obliged to have recourse to the capital of the merchants in order to keep going. In 1127 the charter of St. Omer mentioned, as a current practice, the loans contracted among the burghers of the town by the knights of the neighborhood.

But more important operations were already current in this era. There was no lack of merchants rich enough to agree to loans of considerable amount. About 1082 some merchants of Liège lent money to the abbot of St. Hubert to permit him to buy the territory of Chavigny, and a few years later advanced to Bishop Otbert the sums necessary to acquire from Duke Godfrey, on the point of departing for the Crusades, his château of Bouillon. The kings themselves had recourse, in the course of the twelfth century, to the good services of the city financiers. William Cade was the moneylender to the King of England. In Flanders, at the beginning of the reign of Philip Augustus, Arras had become preeminently a city of bankers. William the Breton describes it as full of riches, avid of lucre and glutted with usurers:

> Atrabatum . . . potens urbs . . . plena
> Divitiis, inhians lucris et foenore gaudens.

The cities of Lombardy and, following their example, those of Tuscany and Provence, went much further in carrying on that commerce which the Church vainly sought to oppose. By the beginning of the thirteenth century, Italian bankers had already extended their operations north of the Alps, and their progress there was so rapid that a half century later, thanks to the abundance of their capital and the more advanced technique of their procedure, they had everywhere taken the place of the local lenders.

The power of liquid capital, concentrated in the cities, not only gave them an economic ascendancy but contributed also towards making them take part in political life. For as long as society had known no other power than that which derived from the possession of the land, the clergy and the nobility alone had had a share in the government. The feudal hierarchy was made up entirely on the basis of landed property. The fief, in reality, was only a tenure and the relations which it created between the vassal and his liege lord were only a particular modality of the relation which existed between a proprietor and a tenant. The only difference was that the services due from the first to the second, in place of being of an economic nature, were of a military and political nature. Just as each local prince required the help and counsel of his vassals so, being himself a vassal of the king, was he held on his part to similar obligations. Thus only those who held land entered into the direction of public affairs. They entered into them, moreover, only in paying through their own person; that is to say, using the appropriate expression, *consilio et auxilio*—by their counsel and help. Of a pecuniary contribution towards the needs of their sovereign there could be no question at an epoch when capital, in the form of real estate alone, served merely for the maintenance of its possessors. Perhaps the most striking character of the feudal State was its almost absolute lack of finances. In it, money played no role. The demesnial revenues of the prince replenished only his privy purse. It was impossible for him to increase his resources by taxes, and his financial indigence prevented him from taking into his service revocable and salaried agents. Instead of functionaries, he had only hereditary vassals, and his authority over them was limited to the oath of fidelity they gave him.

But as soon as the economic revival enabled him to augment his revenues, and cash, thanks to it, began to flow to his coffers, he took immediate advantage of circumstances. The appearance of bailiffs, in the course of the thirteenth century, was the first symptom of the political progress which was going to make it possible for a prince to develop a true public administration and to change his suzerainty little by little into sovereignty. For the bailiff was, in every sense of the term, a functionary. With these revocable officeholders, remunerated not by grants of land but by stewardships, there was evinced a new type of government. The bailiff, indeed, had a place outside the feudal hierarchy. His nature was quite different from that of the old justices, mayors, or castellans who carried on their functions under an hereditary title. Between them and him there was the same difference that there was between the old serfholds and the new freeholds. Identical economic causes had changed simultaneously the organization of the land and the governing of the people. Just as they enabled the peasants to free themselves, and the proprietors to substitute the quit-rent for the demesnial *mansus*, so they enabled the princes, thanks to their salaried agents, to lay hold of the direct government of their territories. This political innovation, like the social innovations with which it was contemporary, implied the diffusion of ready cash and the circulation of money. This is quite clearly shown to be the case by the fact that Flanders, where commercial life and city life were developed sooner than in the other regions of the Netherlands, knew considerably in advance of these latter the institution of bailiffs.

The connections which were necessarily established between the princes and the burghers also had political consequences of the greatest import. It was necessary to take heed of those cities whose increasing wealth gave them a steadily increasing importance, and which could put on the field, in case of need, thousands of well equipped men. The feudal conservatives had at first only contempt for the presumption of the city militia. Otto of Freisingen was indignant when he saw the communes of Lombardy wearing the helmet and cuirass and permitting themselves to cope with the noble knights of Frederick Barbarossa. But the outstanding victory won by these clodhoppers at Legnano (1176) over the troops of the emperor soon demonstrated what they were capable of. In France, the kings did not neglect to have recourse to their services and to ally them to their own interests. They set themselves up as the protectors of the communes, as the guardians of their liberties, and made the cause of the Crown seem to them to be solidary with the city franchises. Philip Augustus must have garnered the fruits of such a skilful policy. The Battle of Bouvines (1214), which definitely established the sway of the monarchy in the interior of France and caused its prestige to radiate over all Europe, was due in great part to military contingents from the cities.

The influence of the cities was not less important in England at the same era, although it was manifest in a quite different way. Here, instead of supporting the monarchy, they rose against it by the side of the barons. They helped, likewise, in the creation of parliamentary government, the distant origins of which may be dated back to the Magna Charta (1215).

It was not only in England, furthermore, that the cities claimed and obtained a more or less large share in the government. Their natural tendency led them to become municipal republics. There is but little doubt but that, if they had had the power, they would have everywhere become States within the State. But they did not succeed in realizing this ideal save where the power of the State was impotent to counterbalance their efforts.

This was the case with Italy, in the twelfth century, and later, after the definite decline of the imperial power, with Germany. Everywhere else they had not succeeded in throwing off the superior authority of the princes, whether, as in Germany and France, the monarchy was too powerful to have to capitulate before them, or whether, as in the Netherlands, their particularism kept them from combining their efforts in order to attain an independence which immediately put them at grips with one another. They remained as a general rule, then, subject to the territorial government.

But this latter did not treat them as mere subjects. It had too much need of them not to have regard for their interests. Its finances rested in great part upon them, and to the extent that they augmented the power of the State and therewith its expenses, it felt more and more frequently the need of going to the pocketbooks of the burghers. It has already been stated that in the twelfth century it borrowed their money. And this money the cities did not grant without security. They well knew that they ran great risks of never being reimbursed, and they exacted new franchises in return for the sums which they consented to loan. Feudal law permitted the suzerain to exact of his vassals only certain well defined dues which were restricted to particular cases always identical in character. It was therefore impossible for him to subject them arbitrarily to a poll-tax and to extort from them supplies, however badly needed. In this respect the charters of the cities granted them the most solemn guaranties. It was, then, imperative to come to terms with them. Little by little the princes formed the habit of calling the burghers into the councils of prelates and nobles with whom they conferred upon their affairs. The instances of such convocations were still rare in the twelfth century; they multiplied in the thirteenth; and in the fourteenth century the custom was definitely legalized by the institution of the Estates in which the cities obtained, after the clergy and the nobility, a place which soon became, although the third in dignity, the first in importance.

Although the middle classes, as we have just seen, had an influence of very vast import upon the social, economic and political changes which were manifest in Western Europe in the course of the twelfth century, it does not seem at first glance that they played much of a role in the intellectual movement. It was not, in fact, until the fourteenth century that a literature and an art was brought forth from the bosom of the middle classes, animated with their spirit. Until then, learning remained the exclusive monopoly of the clergy and employed no other tongue than the Latin. What literature was written in the vernacular had to do solely with the nobility, or at least expressed only the ideas and the sentiments which pertained to the nobility as a class. Architecture and sculpture produced their masterpieces only in the construction and ornamentation of the churches. The markets and belfries, of which the oldest specimens date back to the beginning of the thirteenth century— as for example the admirable Cloth Hall of Ypres, destroyed during the Great War—remained still faithful to the architectural style of the great religious edifices.

Upon closer inspection, however, it does not take long to discover that city life really did make its own contribution to the moral capital of the Middle Ages. To be sure, its intellectual culture was dominated by practical considerations which, before the period of the Renaissance, kept it from putting forth any independent effort. But from the very first it showed that characteristic of being an exclusively lay culture. By the middle of the twelfth century the municipal councils were busy founding schools for the children of the burghers, which were the first lay schools since the end of antiquity. By means of them, instruction ceased to be furnished exclusively for the benefit of the novices of the monasteries and, the future parish priests. Knowledge of reading and writing, being indispensable to the practice of commerce, ceased to be reserved for the members of the clergy alone. The burgher was initiated into them long before the noble, because what was for the noble only an intellectual luxury was for him a daily need. Naturally, the Church immediately claimed supervision over the municipal schools, which gave rise to a number of conflicts between it and the city authorities. The question of religion was naturally completely foreign to these debates. They had no other cause than the desire of the cities to control the schools created by them and the direction of which they themselves intended to keep.

However, the teaching in these communal schools was limited, until the period of the Renaissance, to elementary instruction. All who wished to have more were obliged to turn to the clerical establishments. It was from these latter that came the "clerks" who, starting at the end of the twelfth century, were charged with the correspondence and the accounts of the city, as well as the publication of the manifold Acts necessitated by commercial life. All these "clerks" were, furthermore, laymen, the cities having never taken into their service, in contradistinction to the princes, members of the clergy who by virtue of the privileges they enjoyed would have escaped their jurisdiction.

The language which the municipal scribes employed was naturally, at first, Latin. But after the first years of the thirteenth century they adopted more and more generally the use of national idioms. It was by the cities that the vulgar tongue was introduced for the first time into administrative usage. Thereby they showed an initiative which corresponded perfectly to that lay spirit of which they were the pre-eminent representatives in the civilization of the Middle Ages.

This lay spirit, moreover, was allied with the most intense religious fervor. If the burghers were very frequently in conflict with the ecclesiastic authorities, if the bishops thundered fulsomely against them with sentences of excommunication, and if, by way of counter-attack, they sometimes gave way to decidedly pronounced anti-clerical tendencies, they were, for all of that, none the less animated by a profound and ardent faith. For proof of this is needed only the innumerable religious foundations with which the cities abounded, the pious and charitable confraternities which were so numerous there. Their piety showed itself with a naïveté, a sincerity and a fearlessness which easily led it beyond the bounds of strict orthodoxy. At all times, they were distinguished above everything else by the exuberance of their mysticism. It was this which, in the eleventh century, led them to side passionately with the religious reformers who were fighting simony and the marriage of priests; which, in the twelfth century, spread the contemplative asceticism of the Beguines and the Beghards; which, in the thirteenth century, explained the enthusiastic reception which the Franciscans and the Dominicans received. But it was this also which assured the success of all the novelties, all the exaggerations and all the deformations of religious thought. After the twelfth century no heresy cropped out which did not immediately find some followers. It is enough to recall here the rapidity and the energy with which the sect of the Albigenses spread.

Both lay and mystic at the same time, the burghers of the Middle

Ages were thus singularly well prepared for the role which they were to play in the two great future movements of ideas: the Renaissance, the child of the lay mind, and the Reformation, towards which religious mysticism was leading.

J. BRONOWSKI and BRUCE MAZLISH

The Western
Intellectual Tradition

Western civilization as we know it today was shaped by four major revolutions: 1. the revolution in scientific ideas which ushered in 2. the Industrial Revolution; 3. the Puritan Revolution in England; and 4. the French Revolution. These four revolutions brought about the growth of modern technology and created conditions for the establishment of democratic institutions in the West—institutions whose emergence, in turn, is deeply influencing the development of the non-Western world.

In the second half of the twentieth century, non-Western peoples are telescoping these four revolutions—which, in the West, were spread over several centuries—into a few decades or even years. If we are to understand the meaning of contemporary revolutions in Asia, Africa, and the Middle East, we must first recall the experiences of the peoples of Western Europe, the United States, and Canada.

These experiences are brilliantly portrayed in the selections below, drawn from a book in which a scientist and a historian have pooled their talents. The scientist, Jacob Bronowski, born in 1908 in Poland, was trained as a mathematician at England's Cambridge University. During World War II he did statistical research on the economic effects of bombing, and wrote the British report, regarded as a classic, on The Effects of the Atomic Bombs at Hiroshima and Nagasaki. He is now a practicing scientist in his post of Director General of Process Development in Britain's National Coal Board, and the author of many books, among them Man Without a Mask: Biography of William Blake, 1943; and Science and Human Values, 1959.

The historian, Bruce Mazlish, is a member of the faculty at the

Massachusetts Institute of Technology, where he is in charge of a humanities program called "Modern Western Ideas and Values." He also teaches a course in the philosophy of ideas. His articles and reviews have appeared in such periodicals as Review of Politics and Journal of Philosophy.

Chapter 7
The Scientific Revolution[1]

. . . historians recognize that the unfolding of scientific thought between 1500 and 1700 was critical in the creation of modern civilization. This recognition, which has been reached only recently, is itself the result of the powerful impact of science on the life of our generation. Science has made the world over in the twentieth century, root and branch—intellectually and physically. In doing so, it has transformed our understanding of the past as radically as our expectation of the future. Physically, we live in a new and changing world. And intellectually we see the world differently, so that the processes of nature and even of history have a different logic for us.

In short, the Scientific Revolution between 1500 and 1700 was in the first place an intellectual revolution: it taught men to think differently. Only later was this thought put to a new practical use, in the Industrial Revolution about 1800 which gave our civilization its outward character. But the Scientific Revolution in itself mainly implied a basic change in the way in which people pictured the world. This was the profound change "from a world of things ordered according to their ideal nature, to a world of events running in a steady mechanism of before and after."[2]

I

The view of how the world works which was held before 1500 was quite different from ours. The difference is so great that it is difficult to

"The Scientific Revolution" from *The Western Intellectual Tradition* by J. Bronowski and Bruce Mazlish. Copyright © 1960 by J. Bronowski and Bruce Mazlish. Reprinted by permission of Harper & Row, Publishers, Inc., New York; Hutchinson & Company, Publishers, London.

[1] Footnotes from *The Western Intellectual Tradition* selections have been edited to refer only to the material reprinted here. Ed.

[2] J. Bronowski, *The Common Sense of Science* (London, 1951), *passim*. The philosophy underlying the development of science is examined in this book.

think oneself back into the earlier view. Indeed, the most difficult of all historical tasks is to think as another civilization thought: to find its explanations reasonable and its view of the world natural.

We must grasp from the outset that a medieval painter was not merely ignorant when he made the figure of Christ larger in his picture than perspective would allow.[3] A medieval traveler was not unobservant when he described what is obviously an elephant as an animal with five feet, one of which the animal uses like a hand. To us, the traveler's tale is ridiculous, because to us the elephant fits into the order of mammals and the unfolding of evolution; we see its connections with the horse and the tiger, with the whale and with man. But to medieval men, the world had a different set of inner connections; it was organized differently, as it is still organized differently today for other civilizations than ours. Today also, the primitive man who says that he *is* his totem animal, is not merely ridiculous;[4] and the islander who has a name for every kind of tree, but no general word for tree, is not merely ignorant. They are living in a different conceptual system of nature.

The conceptual system of nature which dominated the Middle Ages had been formed, or better had been welded together, by St. Thomas Aquinas about 1250. At that time, the works of Aristotle were already known to Arab thinkers, and had been translated by them from Greek into Arabic. By this roundabout path, Aristotle's system in physics and in medicine spread also to the West, and his works were translated into Latin. The great work of St. Thomas Aquinas was to join together the system of nature of Aristotle with Christian theology and ethics, and so to shape a single outlook for the next 300 years.

The Western rediscovery of Aristotle about 1250 was thus, as it were, a first revival of Greek learning. And there were isolated enthusiasts for classical knowledge at that time; Emperor Frederick II, whom his admiring age called *stupor mundi et emmutator mirabilis*, was one. But in general, the discovery of Aristotle did not bring Greek thought and literature to the West whole. It brought only a first thin and single strand of humanism: an interest in the working of nature. Nature was still conceived, as it had been before 1250, to be kept going from moment to moment by a miracle which was always new and always renewed. But after 1250, men began to be interested in the form of the miracle; they wanted to know to what order, to what hierarchy it conformed.

All things in nature were thought then, as they are now, to be compounded from a number of fundamental elements. The number which

---

[3] Cf. Lewis Mumford, *Technics and Civilization* (New York, 1934).

[4] Cf. Ernst Cassirer, *An Essay on Man* (Anchor Books ed., New York, 1953), p. 110.

Aristotle had accepted, and which became general, was four. The elements were air and fire, water and earth.

The elements were held to follow what we should want to call laws; but it would be wrong to think of their pattern of movement as if it had, or was meant to have, the exact sequence which we now seek in a natural law. The elements did not so much obey a law as express and follow their own ideal natures. The elements of water and of earth moved downward when they could, because they were striving to reach their own natural centers. The elements of air and of fire moved upward, again in order to reach their natural centers. . . .

The striving of the elements to reach their true centers kept the world going. A piece of soil, for example, although it was not wholly earth, was mainly so; and therefore it strove to return to the earth. Each element had as it were a will of its own, and this will drove it to seek to fulfill its own essence. These strivings, these movements, kept nature going, not as a machine but as a hierarchy: a hierarchy in which each element was looking for its own fulfillment of itself. If ever that universal fulfillment were reached, nature would achieve completion; the universe would stand still and, in standing still, become God's perfect handiwork, no longer restless but fixed for ever.

II

In the system of the four elements, the heavenly bodies were not made of matter, in the earthly sense. In them, the elements of air and fire were dominant in a purer form, and indeed made a fifth element, the ether; so that the heavenly bodies were of a higher order than the earth, and it was reasonable that they should stay overhead. The thought which Newton had in his mother's garden in 1666, that the planets might be held in their orbits by a force of the same kind as that which draws the apple to the ground, was not possible to the Middle Ages; and this for two reasons. One reason is that they did not conceive the forces which act on the elements in this way: they did not see the starry sky as a machine. But the other reason, which is more often overlooked, lay deeper. It was that the Middle Ages could not have conceived the planets to be made of the same stuff as an apple.

The medieval picture of the movement of the heavenly bodies was also taken from the Greeks: from Claudius Ptolemy, an astronomer who belonged to the exiled school of Greek scientists in Alexandria in the second century of our era. This picture put the stars, which do not seem to move, on a fixed sphere round the earth. Between the earth and this fixed outer sphere there were thought to be, layer by layer, seven other spheres, each with its center at the earth. Each of these seven spheres carried what was then called a planet. That is, one sphere carried the moon and another carried the sun; beyond these, one sphere carried Mercury, one carried Venus, another carried Mars, another Jupiter, and another Saturn.

The motions which the planets carried out in their revolving spheres were complicated. For the planetary paths, when they are seen from the earth, go forward and then loop back on themselves from time to time. At long intervals, even these loops turn backward, so that at times two planets for a time seem to interweave their paths. . . .

Ptolemy described the paths of the planets, with their strange loops, by the rolling of one circle on one or more other circles. To the Greeks, and again to the medieval followers of Aristotle, the circle was in some mystic way a perfect path, and it was natural to build up other paths from circles. The circle was felt to be the path which a natural object would tend to describe of itself. By contrast, to the Greeks and to the medieval followers of Aristotle, the straight line was an unnatural path: Aristotle had supposed that an arrow, in order to go on flying on a straight path, had constantly to be pushed by the air from behind. This mistaken view was one of the main obstacles to the development of a realistic mechanics so long as Aristotle was accepted as an authority.

The curves which Ptolemy pictured, traced by circles riding on circles, give reasonable agreement with the timetable of the planets. It is, in fact, possible to build up most curves in this way, as epicycles made by circles riding on circles, if one uses enough different circles. The awkwardness of Ptolemy's system in the Middle Ages was that, in order to fit the improving observations, it called for more and more circles. Domenico Maria Novara, who taught Copernicus in Italy, was one of several astronomers who criticized the system of Ptolemy for its complication.[5]

Some of these critics saw that the complications of Ptolemy were unavoidable so long as the earth was thought to be fixed and all observations were traced back to the earth. The German astronomer Johann Müller, who used the Latin name Regiomontanus, had challenged the assumption that the earth must be taken as the center of the heavens, and he quoted the doubts of some Greek astronomers against it, early in the fifteenth century.[6] Regiomontanus died young, but others shared his doubts. When Leonardo da Vinci wrote in his notebooks, "The sun does not move," he was voicing the advanced opinion of others as well as his own.

---

[5] Cf. Edwin Arthur Burtt, *The Metaphysical Foundations of Modern Physical Science* (London, 1949), p. 42.

[6] Cf. Leonardo Olschki, *The Genius of Italy* (New York, 1949), pp. 374–375.

III

The astronomical system of Ptolemy could not be overthrown merely by criticism. If it was to be displaced, then something else had to be put in its place; another system was needed. This system was formulated with admirable precision by the Polish astronomer Nicolas Copernicus.

To us, the system of Copernicus is coherent and satisfying; and we are tempted now to think it easier to conceive intellectually than the system of Ptolemy. But this was not so at the time, for several reasons.[7]

First, the motion by which Copernicus replaced the single motion of the sun is not easy: for it is made up of two separate motions of the earth. According to Copernicus, the earth swings round the sun once in a year, and at the same time the earth turns on its own axis once every day. This spin of the earth round itself outraged many ideas of mechanics which were then held—and which some people still hold. For example, if the earth is spinning under it, why does a stone fall straight? Why do things not fly off the spinning earth?

Second, the system of Copernicus did not chime with some of the detailed observations of astronomy. For example, it implied that the stars lie along different directions when seen at different times of the year. And this had not been observed then, and was not observed for another 200 years.

Third, the system of Copernicus offended the medieval sense that the universe was an affair between God and man, in the way that the Bible pictured it from the sixth day of Genesis. This fear of outraging religious tradition made Copernicus delay the printing of his work, as 300 years later it made Charles Darwin delay writing *The Origin of Species* for many years. Copernicus published his book, *Revolutions of the Heavenly Bodies*, only in the year of his death, 1543, and tradition has it that he held the first copy in his hands on his deathbed.

These objections made it certain that Copernicus could not expect to persuade the run of traditional minds of his time. Instead, he addressed himself to what he called the mathematicians. The mathematicians would appreciate the order and the essential simplicity of his vision. Copernicus had already announced to them in 1530 that he would show "how simply the uniformity of motion can be saved." Mathematicians could appreciate that, at the least, the new system reduced the number of circles which rolled in the epicycles of Ptolemy. Copernicus, of course, was not able to get rid of the epicycles altogether, because he still insisted on looking for uniform motion in a circle, and did not realize that the paths of the planets are ellipses.

---

[7] Cf. Burtt, *op. cit.*, pp. 23–25.

In a sense, then, Copernicus was appealing to the aesthetic judgment of his fellow mathematicians. This aesthetic appeal masks a complex and important idea, which underlies all the intellectual advances since the Scientific Revolution. And it is a humanist idea. Copernicus, who was born in 1473, had had a characteristic humanist education, in law, in medicine, and in the classics, first in his native Poland and then in the Italian universities. He had been encouraged in part by the pope, who wanted to reform the irregularities of the calendar which had been accumulating, uncorrected, since Julius Caesar introduced it in 46 B.C. At bottom, Copernicus rejected the system of Ptolemy on the same ground on which other humanists rejected the work of the Schoolmen: because it lacked beauty and unity. . . .

Thus, one thought which moved Copernicus, and which has moved scientists ever since, is that nature has a unity, and that this unity expresses itself in the simplicity which we find in her laws when we have them right. The assumption that the laws of nature ought to be simple is usually justified by scientists as a useful working rule of procedure, and is quoted in the form in which William of Ockham had stated it long before, that we should not multiply hypotheses. But the demand for simplicity truly goes much deeper than this, and expresses a longing to find a unity in nature. There is, in fact, no criterion of what is simple, other than the demand for the greatest measure of unity. To take a modern example, Einstein and other searchers for a unified field theory have said that such a theory is simpler than the separate theories of gravitation and of electromagnetism which it combines. But when we look at a unified field theory, we find that the combination is simple only in the sense that it is presented in linked and coherent formulas; the formulas themselves are more complex than ever.

•   •   •

IV

Copernicus had not expected to interest nonspecialists in his vision of the heavens, but two cosmic accidents ensured that he did so. In 1572, a new star blazed in the familiar constellation of Cassiopeia. This star was observed by the pioneer of accurate observation, the Danish astronomer Tycho Brahe. For two years the new star was brighter than any other star in the sky; and for a time it was so bright that it could be seen in daylight.

Then, at the end of the century another new star appeared, once again dazzling and disturbing the accepted order of the heavens. This new star was observed with care by the astronomer Johann Kepler. . . .

These celestial happenings are remarkable, for they were both supernovae, that is, explosions of old stars; and supernovae are fairly rare in any one galaxy. In the whole of recorded history, there have been only three supernovae in our galaxy. The first of these, the supernovae which is now in Crab Nebula, exploded in the sky on July 4, 1054, but no Western watcher has left a record of it; it was recorded only in China and Korea. The other two supernovae were those which have just been described, and flared up in the heavens as if providentially at the time when Copernicus had challenged the accepted vision of astronomy among professionals.

These events, of course, made an especially deep impression in an age when all men, and particularly educated men, believed that their personal fate was written in the sky. Almost everyone then believed in astrology; it was treated, as nothing else was, as an exact science; and it was, in fact, necessary in order to cast a true horoscope, to know the positions of the planets precisely at any time. There was, therefore, a real interest among astrologers in an exact knowledge of the planetary movements, and in a system of astronomy which would describe them accurately. Kepler, who did more than any other man to establish the system of Copernicus in sound detail, made his living in part by casting horoscopes. And Pope Paul III, to whom Copernicus dedicated *The Revolutions of the Heavenly Bodies*, "never appointed a consistory without having one of his astrologers calculate a favorable 'conjunction.' "[8]

Kepler, even more than Copernicus, was carried away by the mystery of mathematics, by the strange relations between numbers and by the complex properties of natural space. His books have such titles as *Mysterium Cosmographicum* and *Harmonice Mundi*. He writes again and again that *Natura simplicitatem amat* ("Nature loves simplicity") and *Amat illa unitatem*.[9] He listened seriously for the harmony of the spheres: he tried to relate the speeds of the planets to the musical intervals, not as a piece of magic fancy but in strict mathematics—nothing less satisfied him. He tried to fit the five regular solids, which had been known since antiquity, into the orbits of the planets. And his mathematics was excellent; he was the first mathematician to go beyond the five regular solids which the Greeks had known, by discovering the two star-shaped regular solids which go by his name.

At the same time, Kepler had learned from his work under Tycho Brahe (who was never converted to the system of Copernicus) to take more accurate observations of the whereabouts and the movements of the planets than had been taken before. Working restlessly through Brahe's and his own figures, and seeking always for the arrangement that

---

[8] Leonardo Olschki, *The Genius of Italy* (New York, 1949), p. 380.

[9] Cf. Burtt, *op. cit.*, p. 46. The reader will find a more popular but graphic account of these matters in Arthur Koestler, *The Sleepwalkers* (London, 1959).

would fit them, as he was convinced, into the system of Copernicus, Kepler found three laws to describe the motions of the planets. He published these in 1609 and in 1619.

The first of Kepler's laws is, in a sense, the most revolutionary, for it breaks with the tradition of movement in a circle which had been taken for granted since the time of the Greeks. Instead, Kepler discovered that each planet moves on an ellipse, and that the sun lies at one focus of this ellipse. The second law describes the varying speed at which a planet travels along its ellipse: the line from a planet to the sun sweeps out equal areas in equal intervals of time. The third law relates the movement of one planet to another: the year in which a planet rounds its orbit is such that the square of the year is proportional to the cube of the average distance of that planet from the sun.

With the discovery of these laws, exact, compact, and remarkable, the paths of the planets were mapped once and for all. In his life's work (he lived from 1571 to 1630), Kepler had established the system of Copernicus in these formulas beyond challenge. There was no further step to take until the three laws could be shown themselves to be parts of a single unity, a single law holding each planet to the sun. Almost everything was ready for that step, taken roughly fifty years later by Isaac Newton. But only *almost* everything was ready. What Copernicus and Kepler had made ready were the facts and the mathematical relations. What was still lacking before Newton could go to work was a practical understanding of the mechanics of motion.

V

If the planets run as a machine runs, then they must be moved and controlled by mechanical forces. The laws which these forces obey must be laws of mechanics. These celestial laws might, of course, be different from the laws of mechanics which are obeyed by forces on earth. The Middle Ages would have taken it for granted that they are different. By the year 1600, however, minds which had been shaken by the new stars and the new speculations found it natural to ask whether the laws of mechanics in the sky might not be the same as the laws of mechanics on earth. At the least, they found it natural to ask, with more persistence than had been used before, what precisely are the laws of mechanics on earth.

A central question in mechanics, because it was a question of fact and not of theory, asked at what rate an object falls to the ground. Aristotle had said that a heavy object falls faster than a light one, and St. Thomas Aquinas had followed him in this as in other opinions. The opinion had not gone quite unchallenged after Aquinas. . . .

. . . however, the established view until the seventeenth century remained that of Aristotle, that heavier objects fall faster than light ones. Then, about 1600, the accepted view was challenged and defeated rather quickly. The story goes that it was defeated by Galileo, who is said to have dropped two cannon balls of unequal masses from the Leaning Tower of Pisa, and to have shown that they reached the ground together. Alas, there is little evidence for this story: if cannon balls were dropped from the Tower of Pisa, they were not dropped by Galileo, and it is unlikely that they reached the ground triumphantly together.[10]

It is, in fact, foolish to suppose that the doctrine of unequal rates of fall proposed by Aristotle was as brazenly out of step with the facts as this, and might have been overthrown at any time in 2000 years simply by dropping two unequal masses. Objects which are dropped from any height, if they are unequal, also meet unequal resistance from the air, and they do not, therefore, fall equally fast. On the contrary, if the new mechanics claimed that they should, then the old mechanics could point to the fact that they did not. Deeper thinking was needed to challenge Aristotle, and more subtle experiments. One reason why such experiments had been difficult hitherto, and why all experiments in mechanics were difficult, was that there did not exist until this time any reliable clockwork to measure the passing of time in small intervals.

The work of Galileo, therefore, begins rightly with a more searching discovery: how to measure small intervals of time. This is the robust approach which marks off Galileo from his contemporaries, and makes him a first leader of practical science and pioneer of the empirical method. Copernicus and Kepler were theoretical minds: Copernicus appealed to mathematicians, Kepler to the courtly interest in astrology which then drew educated men. By contrast, Galileo was grounded in the practical outlook of the trading republics of northern Italy; he appealed particularly to the interest of Venice in navigation and in gunnery. He spent his most active years, from 1592 to 1610, at the University of Padua, which was under the protection of the Republic of Venice.

This was the age of Mediterranean commerce and, fanning out from the Mediterranean and the Atlantic coast, of the voyages of discovery by Italians, by Spaniards, and by Englishmen. Until the sixteenth century, the records of earlier travelers had been treated as curiosities. For example, Marco Polo had written a book about his travels in the East in 1298; yet, it was not until the sixteenth century that an Italian cosmographer Paolo Toscanelli, who was a friend of Christopher Columbus,

---

[10] Lane Cooper, *Aristotle, Galileo, and the Tower of Pisa* (Ithaca, 1935), deals with the evidence concerning Galileo's supposed dropping of weights from the Tower of Pisa, and disproves the whole story. Another familiar story about Galileo is corrected in Edward Rosen, *The Naming of the Telescope* (New York, 1947). . . .

used Marco Polo's book seriously as a source for geographical and navigational information.

Astronomy was now an important aid to navigation; but astronomy is not complete without accurate means of keeping time. For example, the latitude of a ship at sea can be found simply by observing the astronomical heavens; but the longitude can be found only if we know what time it is on some fixed longitude—say, on the longitude of Greenwich. For lack of a clock which could keep time at sea, navigators had to guess their longitude by what they called "dead reckoning" until well into the eighteenth century.

When Galileo Galilei was born, in 1564, there was not even a clock which could keep time accurately on land. The medieval clocks were not designed to be precise instruments which would run uniformly day in and day out. Medieval clocks were, in the first place, monastery clocks, whose purpose was to divide the day of prayer into equal parts or canonical hours, from the first matins to the evening vespers and the last complin. The day that was so divided ran essentially from dawn to dusk, and it was, therefore, a different day in summer and in winter. The clocks of the Middle Ages were a convenient means for dividing a day, but not for measuring time in any absolute sense. And these clocks were not capable of measuring time absolutely; they were clockworks, but they had no means of control to make them run uniformly—they had no escapement.

Galileo was not yet 20 when, as he reports, he noticed the regular swing of a lamp during a service in the cathedral at Pisa in 1583. How could he test its regularity? Galileo put his finger on his pulse, and he observed that the swinging pendulum and the beating pulse kept equal time. He had established an underlying uniformity in nature, on which many clocks run to this day: the uniform motion of a pendulum, which keeps virtually the same time whether it swings in a large or a small arc.

Galileo was not the first to guess that a pendulum keeps almost perfect time; it had been guessed by Leonardo, a hundred years earlier. And Galileo did not strictly prove his guess: that was done mathematically by Christian Huygens a hundred years later. What Galileo did was to use the pendulum. He probably made it a basic means for measuring time in experiments in mechanics, and thereby he brought time and the clock into the practical business of carrying out experiments on earth. This was many times more useful than any demonstration on the Leaning Tower of Pisa.

Galileo was, therefore, able to measure the fall of objects through quite small distances: more precisely, he measured the time which they take to roll down a slope. He was able to show that, whatever the slope, a ball rolls in such a way that the total distance it has gone from rest is proportional to the square of the time it has been traveling. For counting time in this way, of course, the beats of a pendulum are ideal. And Galileo proved his law to be true whatever the mass of the ball: Aristotle was defeated, as it were by the way. As a result of his work, Galileo was able to show, between 1604 and 1609, that a thrown or falling object travels to earth along a parabola.

The Paris school of philosophers had produced arguments long before to cast doubt on Aristotle's mechanics. For example, they had asked the following question. Suppose that three equal balls are dropped together; then it is clear that they will fall steadily side by side. Suppose now that two of these balls are joined; surely all three will continue to fall side by side. Is it then, they asked, not clear that a single ball, and an object made of two balls joined together, will fall side by side? And does it, therefore, not follow that Aristotle is wrong in believing that heavier objects fall faster than light ones?

Now these elegant but abstract speculations, and the arguments on the Leaning Tower, were at an end. Galileo had done more than compare the fall of one object with another: he had formulated a precise law which governs the fall, in a form which was mathematically beautiful and convincing. His practical ingenuity with the pendulum and his mathematical skill in writing the law combined to give his work a finality which nothing before had reached. Galileo had perfectly joined logic to experiment.

At the same time, Galileo's work also implied a breach with Aristotle's belief that an arrow is kept in flight only so long as the air pushes it. This belief also had been doubted long ago by Jean Buridan and Nicholas of Oresme in Paris. Now Galileo proved it false by experiment. He proved that a mass which is moving will go on moving until some force acts to stop it. This demonstration was equally important in the development of the new mechanics.

VI

About the year 1609, Galileo had news from Holland that people there had put two lenses together and had been able to see distant objects as if they were close at hand. Galileo had worked in optics, and this and the information he obtained enabled him to make a telescope for himself. He went on improving the telescope, and he also made what we should now call a compound microscope.

Galileo showed his telescope in Venice and at once created a sensation. Its usefulness to the merchant seamen there, for example, to identify distant ships, was patent.

But Galileo used the telescope more spectacularly to look into the sky with fresh, sharp eyes. He saw the craters of the moon, the spots on the sun, the phases of Venus, and what later turned out to be the rings of Saturn. The heavens were suddenly opened and transformed.

Characteristically, Galileo later proposed a still more subtle use of the telescope. Early in 1610, he had observed that Jupiter has four moons, and that they change their positions from one side of the planet to the other in a rapid and complex sequence. Therefore, Galileo proposed that a table of the positions of the moons of Jupiter should be made, to show where they will be at any time on any future night. In this way, it would be possible to read the time simply by looking at the moons of Jupiter through the telescope. Jupiter was to be turned into a divine clockwork, and the mariner at sea would be able to fix his longitude simply by looking at its face.

This suggestion did not turn out to be very practical, but it is revealing. It shows again how important a part the clock played in Galileo's thought, and in the ambitions of the merchant seamen of his time. Galileo's thought, here as elsewhere, was practical: no one else could have turned the casual observations of a lens grinder in Holland into a reasoned scheme for telling the time at sea.

The telescope was hailed with equal enthusiasm when Galileo went to Rome in 1611. Nevertheless, there began to be some critical voices. Some of Galileo's academic colleagues from the University of Padua refused to look through the telescope. Their ground was an absolute and, as it were, pious faith in Aristotle. The telescope might indeed reveal things which the eye did not see. But it revealed them, said the critics, by the agency of the devil: it was a form of conjuring and therefore at bottom an illusion.

This is in itself a puzzling objection. But under it there surely runs a deeper uneasiness. Scholastic and clerical minds were growing uneasy at the erosion by the new science of the evidence of the senses in the visible world. The Bible and Aristotle had expressed what seemed to that generation to be the evidence of the senses. Now Copernicus, Kepler, and Galileo were turning the visible world into a shadow play: the sun did not move, the earth did, the sky held hidden visions. The Scientific Revolution was creating an invisible world behind the world, and those of an older generation were afraid of it, as in our lifetime many people have become afraid of the invisible world of atoms and genes.

From this time, Galileo became embroiled with the Holy Office because he publicly avowed the system of Copernicus. The new sky that he had uncovered made him impatient with the astronomical conservatism of the church. Meanwhile, the work of Copernicus had become an issue in theology, and in 1616 it was condemned "until corrected."

The events which followed have been disputed, but are now well established. Galileo was instructed by Cardinal Bellarmine that the theory of Copernicus was contrary to Scripture and was not to be taught or defended. Cardinal Bellarmine seems to have been as friendly as his office allowed, and he had been one of those who had acclaimed Galileo's work with the telescope. There is no certainty from the Vatican records that Galileo was forbidden altogether to write about the system of Copernicus. Indeed, in 1620 the authorities decided to make only minor corrections in Copernicus' book, after which it became allowed reading.

In 1625, Galileo began to write a *Dialogue on the Two Principal World Systems*, in which their merits were argued at a sort of Renaissance court. The *Dialogue* did not openly advocate the system of Copernicus, but it put the arguments in favor of Ptolemy into the mouth of a man, Simplicius, who clearly did not have the respect of the author. In a way, then, the *Dialogue* was a subtly offensive form of siding with Copernicus; and it was certainly a popular and effective form. After some awkwardness, it was printed in Florence early in 1632. Within six months, the printer of the *Dialogue* was ordered to stop its sale; and two months later Galileo was called to Rome for trial, in spite of the protests of his protector and of his doctors.

A principal accusation against Galileo was that he had flouted the specific prohibition laid on him in 1616 not to discuss the Copernican system at all. No original of this prohibition exists in the Vatican records. What does exist is a copy which has not been witnessed. This copy may have been a forgery, which may have been smuggled into the record after 1616 by an enemy who was not content with the mild rebuke which Cardinal Bellarmine had given Galileo then. In the face of this document, Galileo had little defense. The pope had been one of his admirers in 1611, but he now thought that he recognized himself as the foolish figure in the *Dialogue*. Galileo was threatened with torture; ill and nearly 70, he was forced to recant in abject terms. Legend has it that he ended his recantation with the words *eppur si muove* ("and yet it moves"). But he was a broken man, was treated with great harshness and, when John Milton visited him under house arrest near Florence in 1638, he was blind. He died in 1642, and the pope insisted that any monument to him must contain no words which would "offend the reputation of the Holy Office."[11]

---

[11] *Galileo's Dialogue on the Great World Systems*, in the Salusbury translation, revised, annotated and with an introduction by Giorgio de Santillana (Chicago, 1953), is the best edition, with a brilliant historical introduction by Professor de Santillana. See further the same author's *The Crime of Galileo* (Chicago, 1955). Also to be consulted for Galileo's writings is *Discourses and Opinions of*

VII

The humiliation of Galileo is a climax in the Scientific Revolution. It makes it clear also why the Revolution petered out in Italy. In the same way, the contempt of Luther for the system of Copernicus[12] had early strangled the Revolution in Germany: in 1596, Kepler, who was a Protestant, had had to take refuge with the Jesuits. The climate in which the Scientific Revolution flourished when Galileo died, in 1642, was England in revolt against a dictatorial king; and in that year Isaac Newton was born in England.

The book in which Copernicus had put forward his system was called *Revolutions of the Heavenly Bodies.* Since then, the word "revolution" has come to be used in a social and political sense, which has grown out of this astronomical use.[13] The new science saw revolution as the natural movement of events, in which the old is constantly turned over and replaced by the new. The long allegiance of the Middle Ages to established authority was over.

Chapter 9
The Puritan Revolution

III

. . . The Puritan, first among modern revolutions, was the least consciously prepared for by any body of systematic ideas: political, religious, or social. Indeed, so much was this the case that the Puritans, once in

---

Galileo, tr. with an introduction and notes by Stillman Drake (New York, 1957). The reader should also consult Galileo's *Dialogues Concerning Two New Sciences,* trans. by H. Crew and A. De Salvio (New York, 1952), which presents his fundamental discoveries in mechanics.

12 Preserved Smith, *Erasmus* (New York, 1923), p. 618.

13 See further *Oxford English Dictionary,* the word "Revolution." Sigmund Neumann, in his article "The International Civil War," *World Politics* (April, 1949), declares that, as used by Galileo, revolution "connoted a *natural* phenomenon outside of human control. . . . In transferring this *scientific* observation into the field of human history, the Renaissance meant to recognize in revolution 'the power of the stars,' i.e. the interference of super-human forces within world affairs" (p. 336).

"The Puritan Revolution" from *The Western Intellectual Tradition* by J. Bronowski and Bruce Mazlish. Copyright © 1960 by J. Bronowski and Bruce Mazlish. Reprinted by permission of Harper & Row, Publishers, Inc., New York; Hutchinson & Company, Publishers, London.

power, were at a loss to know what government to install in the absence of the king. They had not intended a revolution; and they had always assumed the coexistence of king and Parliament. . . .

. . . So overlapping are the civil and ecclesiastical spheres in the seventeenth-century polity that a real separation of them is impossible; nevertheless, the issue first in importance in our judgment is the constitutional issue. The generally accepted view of government was in terms of a "balanced polity." In sum, this meant that the king's powers were limited by the so-called "law of nature," by the common law, as administered in the courts, and by the rights of Parliament. Head of the commonwealth, the king was not absolute in his powers but constrained by the rights of his subjects, the latter protected by law and in Parliament.

Between them, James and Charles brought this view of government into jeopardy. In theory, they arrogantly asserted the divine right of kings. In practice, they destroyed an independent judiciary and thus the appeal to law; they eroded property rights by "forced loans" and extraparliamentary taxes; and they threatened personal rights by arbitrary and illegal arrests. Therefore most Englishmen wanted quite simply to restrict the king's despotic rule and to restore the "balanced polity." Even at the outbreak of civil war, the Houses claimed to fight in the cause of preserving the king's just prerogative, the privileges of Parliament, and the liberties of the subject.

On the other hand, it must be admitted that Parliament itself was asserting greater rights than it could claim by tradition. Charles was correct in his estimate of affairs in 1629 when he remarked that the House "hath of late years endeavoured to expand their privileges by setting up general committees for religion, for courts of justice, trade and the like." However, the demands of Parliament, though large, were specific; they wanted an increased say in economic, foreign, and religious affairs. In the Grand Remonstrance of 1641 (which was carried only by a majority of 11), they indicated with pride what they had wanted and what they thought they had secured. . . .

In two areas—financial and administrative—the king was at a disadvantage in asserting his prerogative. He could raise large sums of money, consistently, only through Parliament; thus, he was constrained by the gentry who controlled Parliament. And he could assert his administrative power locally only through the local gentry—the justices of the peace and sheriffs and vicars—who resented attempts of a central government to filch away their authority.

Only in one area—the religious—did the king have a centralized, relatively efficient, and powerful organization to do his bidding: the Anglican Church. And it was here, in his area, as we shall see, that his assertion of right touched off the Puritan Revolution. To understand the background of the events we shall describe, we must therefore recall the religious situation in general.

The Anglican Church was a product of the Reformation. The constant issue, therefore, after the break with Rome, was: how far should the church be reformed? . . . under Elizabeth's reign, a group known as the "Puritans" arose who wished a further degree of change in the English Church than the queen was prepared to institute. Led by Thomas Cartwright, they at first concentrated on changing the method of governing the church; unsuccessful in this arena, they turned to preaching and to the indoctrination of the people with new views and attitudes.

There were many sort and shades of "Puritans," but they all shared the basic Calvinist ideas, especially of predestination. In common, too, they had the desire either to "purify" the usage of the established church from stains of popery or to worship by forms so "purified" in separate congregations. Within their ranks, however, there was what might almost be called a "trend to the left." Thus, there were Episcopalian, Presbyterian, and Independent or Congregationalist Puritans, with the latter trailing off into Separatists. The Presbyterians wanted a system of church government on the model of Geneva, with an ascending hierarchy of "elders" (the Greek for "elder" is *presbyteros*) in control; a similar system of church government existed in Scotland. The Independents wished each congregation to be legally independent of every other, with no ecclesiastical authority higher than the individual church; they were prepared, however, to remain within the established church. Those who wished to separate from the established church, its state control and financial support, were known as Separatists.[1] United in their desire to change the established church, the Puritans thus split into two major groupings: those who stressed reform of church structure and ceremonies and those who stressed liberty of conscience.

Against all the Puritans, Charles and his Archbishop of Canterbury, Laud, pressed a campaign in favor of order and uniformity in the Church of England. In the realm of theory, the attack was made on the doctrine of predestination. In the realm of practice, the attack was made in such terms as the insistence on altars in the east end of all churches, and the repression of Puritan "lecturers." The aim was to harry the opposition into conformity. The assertion of royal ambitions in the matter of religion took on the same tone as assertion of prerogative in matters of state. . . .

---

[1] For all questions of Puritan terminology, consult . . . M. M. Knappen, *Tudor Puritanism* (Chicago, 1939), and especially Appendix II, "Terminology."

Was the Puritan Revolt not only a constitutional-religious controversy but also a class conflict, waged in religious terms? . . .

In any synoptic view, the various motives—political, religious, economic, and social—must all find their place. However, the stress must be put, in our judgment, . . . on the political and religious "opinions and ideas." Indeed, the Puritan Revolt was not a "social war" exactly because it lacked a systematic and theoretical ideology of classes, which would have made men conscious of their social and economic interests. These interests existed, of course, but they were dwarfed in men's minds by other interests and only found their expression indirectly, in religious and constitutional guise.

This is understandable. Men have been wont, since 1517, clearly and consciously to fight about religion. In the seventeenth century, the conflict around political and constitutional issues also became open and acknowledged; it was an age of "reasoned dissent" in politics and religion. It was only in the late eighteenth and nineteenth centuries, however, that economic and social conflict became consciously motivated and provided with an ideology.

In the seventeenth century, therefore, a man's economic and social position was normally expressed not as such, but as a religious and political position. Emphatically, this does not mean that the religious and constitutional issues were unimportant or mere "fronts." Nor does it mean that an Anglican cavalier or a Puritan merchant was a hypocrite. It simply means that Puritans and Cavaliers thought of themselves more as religious-political groupings than as economic-social ones; their "ideology" expressed this dominant orientation of mind. And it behooves the historian, while discerning other aspects of the conflict, to realize that this cast of mind determined that the Puritan Revolt would be primarily a religious-political and not an economic-social struggle.

IV

•   •   •

Laud's "restless spirit" led him to try to introduce Anglican (i.e., "popish") elements into the externals of worship in Scotland, as well as to curb the Puritan preachers. The Scots retorted with a Covenant and a resort to arms. The result, in 1639, was the so-called Bishops' War, for Charles, with his sense of divine right and his high-flown pride, backed his archbishop. "So long as this Covenant is in force," Charles declared, "I have no more power in Scotland than a Duke of Venice, which I will rather die than suffer." His words were prophetic.

Rapidly now, the chain of events uncoiled. Charles had to call Parliament into session to finance his Scottish wars. Annoyed at its demands,

Charles dissolved the first Parliament of 1640. He was soon forced to call another in the same year; this was the famous Long Parliament, under whose auspices the Puritan Revolt broke out.

The Long Parliament first impeached Charles' favorite, Strafford, and, when this failed, took the irregular step of sending him to the block by attainder. Next, it abolished Laud's favorite courts of Star Chamber and High Commission. To gain time, Charles accepted these and other curbs on his authority, while he tried to gather troops with which to overawe Parliament. His attempt to arrest arbitrarily five leaders of Parliament, at the beginning of 1642, however, misfired.

The failure of this attempted coup d'etat was the signal for the outbreak of civil war. Charles, who had sent his queen abroad with the crown jewels (to buy arms and ammunition), moved north. He planned to gather his friends about him and to get possession of Hull, an east coast port where he could land French troops from the Continent and which was also an arsenal of arms (collected for the Scottish war).

Charles approached Hull from a little cathedral town, called Beverley, where everybody was in his favor. He expected, therefore, to be warmly received in Hull. The Lord mayor and the commander of the garrison, however, held a conference and decided to shut the gates to Charles; significantly, Hull was a big clothing-export town. This action, like the shots at Lexington in the American Revolution, was the first open act of defiance which set off the Puritan Revolution.

V

Parliament, from the beginning, held certain long-term advantages: it controlled London and thus the wealth of the capital; it could raise taxes by assessment on the countries and levy customs duties on the ports; and it commanded the fleet. But it was divided in its leadership and ambivalent in its desires. Many of those who wished to limit the king's prerogative had no desire to extend that of Parliament and the people; and they certainly had no active desire to go to war if the king could be "treated" into cooperating with Parliament. Thus, at first, the prosecution of the war dragged on the Parliamentary side, and it was only the political genius of Pym which forged a real weapon of war against the king.[2]

The initial advantages on the side of the king were his unquestioned authority and leadership over his forces; his military leaders, such as Prince Rupert, who had had training and experience in Continental

---

[2] For Pym's critically important role in the early stages of the rebellion, see J. H. Hexter, The Reign of King Pym (Cambridge, 1941).

warfare; his gentlemen horsemen, who could make excellent cavalry; and the intangible though important "divinity that doth hedge a king." In one sense, however, the very professional training of his officers made them less flexible than the Parliamentarians in meeting the special conditions of English civil war.[3]

The total effect of these factors was that the Parliamentary forces got the worst of it at the outset of the war. Gradually, however, they improved their position and by 1644, at Marston Moor, severely checked the king's forces. "New-modeled" by Parliament in 1645, unified and with regular pay, they effectively defeated the king at Naseby and Langport in that year.

The inspiring personality and military leader in the Parliamentary army was, of course, Oliver Cromwell. He had raised his own troops— the Ironsides—on a new principle: conviction in the cause for which they were fighting. Amalgamated into the Eastern Association, or league of counties, they eventually also became the core of the New Model Army; their leader, the dominating figure in the military forces of Parliament.

> • • •

Two things distinguished Cromwell's background; he was brought up in a Puritan atmosphere (his own spiritual conversion occurred when he was 28) and he belonged by birth to the English ruling class.[4] The latter fact did not necessarily mean great wealth; it did mean local power in the county. Cromwell, himself, experienced great vicissitudes of fortune, at one point having to sell his own lands and become a tenant farmer. In 1636, however, he became heir to his maternal uncle and took possession of a considerable estate and income. Thus, in spite of shifts, Cromwell's position as a country gentleman remained assured.

> • • •

There were two main motives to Cromwell's objection to the government of Charles I. The first was that if Charles could tax his subjects as he willed, their property was not safe. Cromwell, therefore, opposed Charles' exercise of authority on the ground that it was unjust and with-

---

[3] C. V. Wedgwood, in her little book, *Oliver Cromwell* (New York, 1956), pp. 42–43, has some illuminating comments on the special conditions of warfare in the English setting.

[4] For Cromwell's social position, cf. . . . . Wedgwood, *Oliver Cromwell*. The prime source for Cromwell is W. C. Abbott, *Writings and Speeches of Oliver Cromwell*, 4 vols. (Cambridge, 1937–1947), which has largely replaced Thomas Carlyle's *Letters and Speeches of Oliver Cromwell.* . . . Wedgwood gives good bibliographies on Cromwell and should be consulted for further works.

out restraint. The second motive for Cromwell's resistance to Charles' government was a positive one and much more powerful. He believed that there should be freedom of conscience in religion in England. In short, Cromwell was a confirmed Independent. It was this which distinguished him from the "Cavaliers" around Charles I.

●   ●   ●

. . . He believed firmly that God had chosen him, Cromwell, to lead His people out of the wilderness. Therefore, he attributed all victories in battle to God rather than to his own strategy and tactics. . . .

●   ●   ●

Those who were, and are, unsympathetic to Cromwell saw in the disguise of "poor worm" a proud and haughty hypocrite. It is our belief, however, that Cromwell really felt himself a "poor worm" in the sight of God; any pretension to power and might on his part was only as the humble instrument of an all-powerful God. Difficult as it may be for us to enter sympathetically into such a frame of mind, it is even more difficult to avoid the conclusion that the Puritan Revolution (like Luther's, which preceded it by over a hundred years) was led by a religious spirit who drew sustenance from what he believed to be intimate converse with God.

VI

The execution of Charles I, in 1649, was the work of the Army. Cromwell at first opposed the desire to bring Charles to account for his evil doings but later consented and took a leading part in pressing on the trial of the king. The general abhorrence of the Puritan Revolt during the next 150 years resulted from this execution, which scandalized even those who carried it out.[5] In fact, when Cromwell tried to implicate every important family in England by making one member of it sit on the bench of judges, only half of the "judges" showed up.

Charles never accepted the jurisdiction of the court which tried him. How could he who believed in the divine right of kings do so? In 1629

---

[5] One ought, however, to remember that the execution of Charles I followed such punitive actions of his as imprisoning Sir John Eliot in the Tower, where he died in 1632, William Prynne, a barrister, Henry Burton, a divine, and John Bastwick, a physician, "to be fined £5,000 apiece, to lose their ears, and to be imprisoned for life for attacks on the bishops and on ecclesiastical innovations," Sir Charles Firth, *Oliver Cromwell and the Rule of the Puritans in England* (Oxford, 1953), p. 22. Unless one thinks of the king as really being divine, his execution was a judicial (though extreme) punishment of one man by other men. The psychological importance of executing a king is, of course, another matter.

he had declared that "Princes are not bound to give an account of their actions but to God alone," and he repeated this idea at his trial in 1649. In addition, he made a reasoned attack on the Puritans which explains why their Commonwealth was not accepted by the bulk of Englishmen. Charles said: "It is not my case alone, it is the freedom and liberty of the people of England; and do you pretend what you will, I stand more for their liberties. For if power without law may make laws, may alter the fundamental laws of the kingdom, I do not know what subject he is in England that can be sure of his life, or anything that he calls his own." How ironic to see Charles accusing the Puritans of exactly the tyranny that they had charged against him! Yet, he was right. Charles' tyranny had helped bring about the Puritan Revolt. The arbitrary and illegal government of Cromwell and the Army was to cause the English people to turn back to the Stuarts in the Restoration of 1660.

•   •   •

VII

The significance of the revolt, of course, stretches outside the years 1640 to 1660. For example, the voyage of the Pilgrim Fathers in 1620 was one Puritan response to the Stuarts, played out in another country, while the 1640 revolution was another, acted out at home. The 1620 exodus, therefore, is integral to the perspective which permits seeing the depth of the Puritan movement.

The profound impact of the Puritan Revolt on subsequent American and English history hardly needs underlining. The effect of the Revolution on the European continent, however, was relatively slight because, unlike the Jacobins of the French Revolution, the Puritans did not "universalize" their message. Nevertheless, the Puritan Revolt was one of the most influential and boldest movements in modern history, for despite everything that had been said about liberty of the subject and freedom of the people, no one had ever cut off a king's head until 1649.

The weapon which accomplished that act was also something new in history—the first mass, democratic army. The origins of the New Model Army—the name suggests its novelty of conception—really dated from the Irish Rebellion of 1641.[6] At that point, Parliament realized that to give Charles I an army with which to crush the rebellion meant that their own resistance would also be overawed. Therefore, Parliament resorted to the revolutionary move of taking into its own hands the control of the Army. This step marked an assertion of new right by Parliament

---

[6] C. H. Firth, *Cromwell's Army* (London, 1912), is the standard book.

rather than a defense of old privilege against Charles. It also marked a break in the tradition linking crown and army.

At first, as we have suggested, the Parliamentary army fought a losing battle because it lacked a moving spirit, unified leadership, and a military genius. The Parliamentary support secured by Pym, the emergence of Cromwell and his small group of "Ironsides" (the name given to Cromwell by Prince Rupert after the battle of Marston Moor) corrected this defect. A "new" spirit animated Cromwell's troops. They were all godly men who fought, not for pay or through compulsion, but because of belief; to paraphrase Hooker, "one and the self-same people were the Church and the Army." As the soldiers themselves declared, "We were not a mere mercenary Army, hired to serve any Arbitrary power of a State, but called forth and conjured, by the severall Declarations of Parliament, to the defence of our owne and the people's just rights and liberties." Eventually, around this nucleus arose the New Model Army, uniformly clothed in russet coats, its officer ranks open to anyone with talent, numbering about 22,000 and enjoying an annual budget of about 1½ million pounds a year.

•   •   •

The rule of Cromwell and his major generals was based on force, represented by the Army (although, it must be remarked, the Army was really no less representative than Parliament), and not on the people's consent. It was, in fact, a dictatorial regime, opposed by the majority of the nation. One legacy of this crude military rule was to strengthen the English hatred of a standing army. Another consequence was to erode the ground from under the Puritan rule and to bring it to an end in 1660.

Nevertheless, as an innovation in modern history, the New Model Army must be numbered among the achievements of the Puritan Revolt. It introduced for the first time an army composed of ordinary citizens, fighting for ideological reasons and taking a part in politics. As such, it may be considered the fulfillment of the trend started in the Peasants' Revolt of 1525. From another point of view, it is the forerunner of the mass, democratic armies which have so strongly characterized modern times.

IX

The major accomplishment of the Puritan Revolt was in the area of religion, but it also and necessarily drew after it major political consequences. Actually, that accomplishment—the idea of a free church—was the work of only a small segment of the Puritans: the Independents. It

was they who maintained the notion of a free church against the Presbyterians and against thinkers like Hooker who believed in a single union
of state and church.

The belief in a free church entailed the belief in tolerance, which the
Presbyterians also denied. The Independents, in fact, demonstrated tolerance (although limited) at work during their own tenure of power,
the Protectorate. Under Cromwell, all creeds and doctrines were publicly tolerated except Anglicanism and Roman Catholicism. And the
adherents of these creeds, although denied the right to public worship,
were not forced into attendance at other forms of worship by fines or
punishment, as had previously been the case in England.

The tolerance achieved by the Independents was only a partial victory.[7] It lapsed again in 1660, and it was not until the Toleration Act of
1689 that the nonconformists again won the legal right to exist and to
worship publicly. As individuals, however, the members of the free
churches did not win rights of full citizenship until the repeal of the
Test and Corporation Acts (which also operated against Catholics) in
1828. Nor did they gain the right of admission to Oxford and Cambridge until 1871.

Clearly, the history of toleration is a long and slow one. . . . It is to
the credit of the Puritan Revolt that it marks another notable point in
the evolution of religious toleration.

The free church was also unlike the intolerant state church in another
way: it was a voluntary group. It represented the free association of individuals in a society, prepared to accept other freely gathered groups.
As such, it became the model of social organization on which England
developed. According to the economic historian George Unwin, "The
expansion of England in the seventeenth century was an expansion of
society and not of the State. Society expanded to escape from the
pressure of the State."[8] Thus, English colonization was originally undertaken by freely formed companies of gentlemen adventurers, such as
that sponsored by Sir Walter Raleigh, or by the Puritan connections
who took the lead in the Providence Island and Saybrook ventures.[9] And

---

[7] Toleration, of course, was neither complete nor all the work of the Puritans. For
example, the Cambridge Platonists should also be mentioned in the history of
toleration, as paving the way within the Anglican Church for what is known as
"latitudinarianism." For the early history of toleration in England, from the beginning of the English Reformation to the death of Elizabeth, see W. K. Jordan,
The Development of Religious Toleration in England (Cambridge, 1932). Two
later volumes carry the story to 1660.

[8] George Unwin, *Studies in Economic History* (London, 1927), p. 341.

[9] The Massachusetts and Virginia Companies are sufficient testimony of the great
power of privately formed companies; they were able to lay the foundations of
future growth in America.

further, as Ernest Barker points out, "Lloyds and the London Stock Exchange [were] both originally associations based on the social life of city coffeehouses in the eighteenth century."[10]

The religious idea of a freely associated group also served as the model for political organization. It could lead to the formation of political parties, or partial associations, and, to cite Barker again, "Parties, after all, are social formations: The Whig party began its life in a city inn."[11] The result was that the armed conflict of Roundheads and Cavaliers died down to the party bickerings of Whigs and Tories.

To view government as an affair of parties was not necessarily to tie it to any particular form of government. Thus there was no theoretical requirement for the Puritans to be antimonarchical. It is true that they beheaded a king, installed a republic, and introduced into England its first written constitution, the Instrument of Government. But all this was the result of historical circumstances rather than of doctrinal necessity. The events which followed the Restoration in 1660 showed that the system of party government was conveniently adaptable to the monarchical as well as to the republican form of government.

The idea that the state was composed of various parties rather than fixed in a single monolithic unity had as its complement the notion of the limited state. One of the Army documents, probably the work of Ireton, uses the image of committing "our stock or share of interest in this kingdom into this common bottom of Parliament." Thus, instead of the state being Hobbes' Leviathan, it was a "limited" company whose ends were the maintenance of peace and order. Neither the free play of religion nor of politics was to be overborne by the government.

Furthermore, it was only natural that, abhorring the whole mechanism of ecclesiastical discipline and conformity, many of the Puritans turned away from a strict state regulation of economic matters. In the case of Lilburne, for example, we know that he was debarred from entering the wool trade by the Merchant Adventurers' monopoly power. Thus a belief in freedom of economic enterprise took its place alongside a belief in religious and political freedom as a legacy of the Puritan Revolt.[12]

---

[10] Ernest Barker, *Principles of Social and Political Theory* (Oxford, 1951), p. 28.

[11] *Ibid.*, pp. 28–29.

[12] For Lillburne's debarment from the wool trade, see William Haller, *Liberty and Reformation in the Puritan Revolution* (New York, 1955), pp. 267–274. It must be emphasized, however, that not all of Puritanism's associations were with liberty; it was primarily the Independent branch of Puritanism which was affiliated with the various freedoms we have mentioned. Cf. A. S. P. Woodhouse's introduction to *Puritanism and Liberty* (Chicago, 1951), p. 53.

X

Yet, with all its accomplishments, the Puritan Revolt was rejected in 1660 by almost all the English people. After about 40 years of continuous strife—parliamentary and military—Charles I's son, Charles II, came back to England. He returned without the firing of a shot or the striking of a blow—and to a population which initially did not care for him. He was not particularly an attractive king. He was too much absorbed in the luxurious life of his court and in his numerous mistresses. He was suspected of being, and probably was, in secret, a Roman Catholic. Indeed, the only obvious benefit that he conferred upon his country was that, within a short time of his return to London, the influence of French literature and drama made itself felt within England.

Why did the English people accept the restoration of Charles II and throw away the fruits of victory, achieved at so much cost of blood and labor? Why, in the political and religious settlement which followed Charles' return, did England revert, more or less, to the state of affairs existing before the Civil War?

The answer appears to lie in the combined constitutional-religious nature of the 1640 revolt. At that time, the majority of the English nation—Presbyterian as well as Independent—opposed the king's despotic assertion of right against Parliament. The English people were largely united in their desire to insist on their political liberties. On this basis, the Puritan Revolt began.

But events led to the seizure of power by an army which, composed of Independents, placed religious liberty above political freedom. Cromwell and his followers were open in their assertion that the liberty of the "people of God" was more important than the civil liberty of the nation. This permanent limitation on the potential sovereignty of the people, in the interest of a minority, was acceptable neither to the left nor the right of the forces which had opposed Charles—neither to the Levelers nor to the Presbyterians. Thus it was these groups which combined with the Royalists in 1660 to secure the peaceful restoration of Charles II to England.

In the reaction against the Puritan tyranny, the English nation went too far in restoring autocratic power to the king. The result was that political and religious liberties had once again to be vindicated in 1689.

In itself, therefore, the Puritan Revolt had failed. Yet, it bore within itself the ashes whence might arise a new phoenix. As we have attempted to show, there were involved in the ideas and events of 1640–1660 a desire for tolerance, the belief in a free church within a free state, and the conception of a limited state. These beliefs—in religious, political, and economic individualism—the Puritan Revolt developed and extended from their origins in the Reformation and handed on to modern times in dramatic and unforgettable terms.

Chapter 17
The Industrial Revolution

I

THE Industrial Revolution took place in England and not on the continent of Europe, in part because, even when it began, England was already a society with a relatively advanced industry, by the standards of the time. Hitherto, this had been a village or cottage industry; and for the first half of the eighteenth century England basked in a last Indian summer of village industry and pleasant overseas trade. The summer faded, trade grew more competitive and the needs of industry harsher and more pressing about 1760.

It might be thought that the sharp upswing of industry at that time derived from the work of the great scientists of Newton's age. And it is indeed true that the new industries could not have gone forward without the tradition of experiment and invention which had grown in England. But this tradition was not carried on, and the industrial inventions were not made, by the established scientists in such professional bodies as the Royal Society. For the established scientists and the professional bodies had already become arid and academic. They had been browbeaten by the success of Newton's system, and as a result, science had come to mean to them something abstract and speculative—a set of theories which must be universal and mathematical.

Because the Royal Society was now dominated by this intellectual snobbery, the fine technical work of the eighteenth century was done outside it. It was done by rather unorthodox men, many of them nonconformists, who had therefore been excluded from the universities and had learned their applied science at first hand, in their own trades. And they came to form their own societies, which we shall discuss separately.

Men such as these made the practical inventions on which the Industrial Revolution depended; and yet, even their inventions were not

"The Industrial Revolution" from *The Western Intellectual Tradition* by J. Bronowski and Bruce Mazlish. Copyright © 1960 by J. Bronowski and Bruce Mazlish. Reprinted by permission of Harper & Row, Publishers, Inc., New York; Hutchinson & Company, Publishers, London.

the core and crux of that revolution. For the essential change which the Industrial Revolution brought was not in machines but in method. The Industrial Revolution was only incidentally a change in industrial techniques; it was more profoundly a change in industrial organization.[1]

To appreciate this change, we must look first at the organization of village industries as they existed in England before 1760. Some of these industries, such as the woolen industry, went back to the Middle Ages; others, such as the making of needles, had been advanced by technical innovations made in the inventive Elizabethan age. Their organization had one thing in common: it was divided into small units.

It is, of course, plain that only those industrial processes which produce raw materials—such processes as the mining of coal, the smelting of iron, and the making of glass—are necessarily large-scale processes. When these raw materials are turned into goods, i.e., secondary products like nails, the scale of the processes needed is only as large as the goods themselves. There is nothing inherent in the production of nails or of hats or of woolen cloth which requires it to be done in a factory in the presence of several hundred people. And in fact, nails and hats and woolen cloth were well made in the homes of villagers for centuries. They were made as toys are still made in Germany and Japan and as the parts of watches are made in Switzerland. A Swiss watch is an instrument of great precision, and we therefore think of it as made in a modern factory, all glass and chromium. In fact, however, what is important in the manufacture of the watch is that it is made of many parts, and these parts lend themselves to being made separately by people in their own homes. Watchmaking was run in this way, as a highly subdivided home industry, in Islington in London in the eighteenth century.[2]

The cardinal change which the Industrial Revolution brought was to move many of these industries from the home into the factory. Within two generations, roughly between 1760 and 1820, the customary way of running industry changed. Before 1760, it was standard to take the work to villagers in their own homes. By 1820, it was standard to bring everyone into a factory and have them work there.

This change was not brought about by any single factor: for example, it was not simply brought about by new inventions. Like all the great movements of history, it has no single explanation. It was the result of the interplay of many factors, some small in themselves, whose cumulative weight combined to overbalance the traditional way of making things so that it became modern industry.

---

[1] Cf. T. S. Ashton, *An Economic History of England: The 18th Century* (London, 1955), pp. 105–117. This is a fundamental work, to be constantly consulted; it includes a number of useful statistical tables.

[2] Cf. *ibid.*, p. 103.

II

It will be well to look at the influences at work in one industry; and we choose one of the key industries in the world before 1760, the making of woolen cloth. Characteristically, this was carried out in many steps. Sheep were reared and then shorn; the wool was cleaned and combed. It was then spun into thread, and the thread went to the individual weaver, who had a weaving frame in his own home and wove the cloth on it. In principle, the weaver was a private manufacturer; that is, in principle he bought the thread, he owned his frame, and he sold the cloth himself.

This detailed procedure suffered from two drawbacks. First, not all parts of it were equally mechanized. The weaver's frame was an effective machine, but the spinning wheel was not. Anyone could spin who had the minimum sense of touch needed to draw an even thread and, as this needs little skill, spinning was therefore only a minor occupation of women—as the word "distaff" still reminds us. A weaver at work could keep many hands spinning: as Defoe described the Yorkshire villages of weavers, "Hardly any thing above four years old, but its hands are sufficient to it self." Second, there was little money in spinning, with its low productivity, and those who could gave it up whenever possible, in order to do the necessary work of house and farm. It was a seasonal occupation, which was dropped at seed and harvest time, and was therefore a bottleneck at the mercy of its occasional workers.

Another handicap in the organization of the woolen industry was economic. In principle, the weaver was his own master: he bought the thread, he owned the frame, and he sold the finished cloth himself. But he had little to fall back on if times were bad, and he got into debt. He had to borrow, that is to say he had to ask for credit, from the man from whom he bought either the raw wool or the spun thread. The only security he could offer for the loan was his weaving frame. In practice, therefore, even in the seventeenth century many weavers were in effect merely workmen for the wool merchant to whom their frames were mortgaged.[3]

The wool merchant commonly had his headquarters in a small town around which the weavers' villages were clustered. The weavers would come into town on a given day, often a Friday, and sell their pieces of woolen cloth: there still stand some of the market halls in which this was done, for example the Piece Hall in Halifax. With the money, the weaver would buy fresh wool; but if times were bad and there was a surplus of cloth, he would have to ask the merchant to keep the cloth and would have to get wool on credit against it. In this way, the owner-

---

[3] Cf. *ibid.*, p. 207.

ship of the wool, the weaving frame, and the finished cloth tended all to fall to the one merchant. Thus, in a practical sense, the weaver became a workman for wages—the uncertain wages made up of the difference between what he got for his cloth and what he paid for his wool.

This relationship became common in many industries: the woolen industry of Yorkshire, the cotton industry of Lancashire, nail and needle making around Birmingham, the making of gloves and stockings, and hats, and many others. It became convenient for the merchant to send his agents into the working homes, to take the raw material there and to bring back the finished goods. He now had an investment in these homes, and needed to keep a sharp eye both on the tools and on the materials there.

He had to keep a sharp eye also on the return on his investment. The tools were in effect his, but he could not command the number of hours that the workman spent at them. In good times, the weaver wanted to work as little as was enough to earn the family's keep, but the merchant wanted him to make as much cloth as he could—for 12, 14, 16 hours a day. In bad times, the weaver wanted to work long hours in order to earn the family's keep, but the merchant wanted him to stop.[4]

In short, the organization of village industry had been appropriate to an age in which the cottager was truly his own master. It was not appropriate to an age in which he was becoming, under whatever disguise, a wage earner working for a central merchant. When the cottager was his own master, his output was controlled by the market. Once he became a workman, his output must be controlled by the investing merchant. The factory system was formed by this complex of pressures.

The early factories were organized in a number of different ways. In some, for example, the worker still brought his own tools—he did this in the Sheffield steel industry down to the present century—just as a skilled fitter brings his own tools today. Whatever the detailed organization, however, the factories turned out to have several advantages. They gave the owner control of the materials and the working hours. They enabled him to rationalize operations which needed several steps or several men. They made it possible to use new machines which could be worked by unskilled women and even children under supervision. And they allowed these machines to be grouped around a central source of power.[5]

III

•　　　•　　　•

The market that he [Arkwright] and other industrialists had in mind was in large part overseas. The pathos of the Industrial Revolution was

---

[4] Cf. *ibid.*, pp. 205–206.
[5] Cf. *ibid.*, pp. 115–117.

that it did not see a market among its own workers for the new output which they were producing. Machines were first brought in to break the bottlenecks in industry; these bottlenecks were in unskilled processes such as spinning; and therefore the processes and the workers first brought into the factories were unskilled. It was not new that women and children should spin for long hours; Defoe had found just this in the Yorkshire villages in the 1720's, and had reported frankly that if they did not, the family must "fare hard, and live poorly." What was new was the setting: child labor was moved from the village home into the stony and brutal discipline of the factory.

These factories first used water power, and therefore they were built in the wild river valleys of such lonely counties as Derbyshire; only here could the streams be counted on to run full even in the summer. . . .

These things began to change only when the steam engine took the place of water power in the factory, at the beginning of the nineteenth century. Then the factory moved to the source of labor, to the town; for power now—that is, coal—was no dearer in the town than in the country. And steam power was more massive and more dependable than water power, so that it could run heavier and more elaborate machinery. With the coming of the rotary steam engine, weaving also became a factory industry, and in time the more important factory industry.

V

With the entry of steam, coal and iron became the backbone of industry. Great advances had already been made in the working of iron, and were now made in engineering it. Until some date after 1700, iron ore could be reduced in the blast furnace only with charcoal. Wood to make charcoal remained plentiful in France, but it was scarce in England; and the scarcity prompted technical invention. The natural raw material to use in England was coal. It was, therefore, a constant ambition to reduce iron ore with coal, and several inventors had hit on the notion of first ridding the coal of its gases and turning it into coke.

•   •   •

VI

The great drive in the Industrial Revolution was for a new organization of production: the factory system. This drive directed, and in turn was directed by, a number of technical inventions. The interplay of method and machines, of economics and techniques was constant and mutual. From it, rather than from any single cause, the Industrial

Revolution grew. Like every historical movement it grew organically, cell by cell.

A major condition for its growth was a change in the economic climate of England. We are accustomed today to the idea that industry is financed by shareholders, who can choose to put their money into any one of many competing enterprises. We forget that this is quite a modern idea: it was almost unknown before the eighteenth century. The Industrial Revolution could only gather momentum when investment in industry—general as well as personal investment—became a familiar way for people to use their savings.

In the earlier age of Queen Elizabeth, inventors (and speculators in invention) had tried to protect their forms of manufacture by getting exclusive rights from the crown to exploit them. These monopolies did little to stimulate those to whom they were granted, and they became a positive bar to progress, and a scandal, in the years between the death of Elizabeth and the rise of Cromwell. Indeed, there is some ground for believing that the grant of long-standing patents slowed down the speed of development of some new ideas (for example, that of the steam engine) even in the Industrial Revolution itself.[6]

The Elizabethan inventor who wanted a monopoly had been trying to protect the money that he and others were investing in the invention. The inventor's great difficulty was to find backers with money. There was at that time no established habit of putting one's savings into investment. On the contrary, all forms of investment (except lending money to governments) were regarded by the church as usury. For this reason, banking and money-lending were often in the hands of non-Christians. They had often begun life as goldsmiths and tracers in luxuries, and they usually lent money to those who had a taste for luxuries.

In England, a wider class of savings began to accumulate after 1688, when political conditions became stable and overseas trade could flourish. These savings were used by the new king to finance his Continental wars, and in this way a public debt was established, and it became usual for merchants and landowners to have a share in the national debt and to draw interest from it. The Bank of England was founded in 1649 as part of this movement to finance government spending from the savings of all.

The movement to invest the savings which now accumulated grew, and would have grown faster had there not been a setback to it after 1711. In that year, a large company was set up to trade with the South Seas, and it offered such wild returns (indeed, it offered to displace the Bank of England as the main holder of government bonds) that it

---

[6] Cf. *ibid.*, p. 107.

started a wave of speculation. Owners of capital were in fact looking for somewhere to invest it, but there was as yet no real source of new wealth for them: there was no Industrial Revolution yet. The boom of 1720 was expanding into a vacuum, and when it collapsed, it left behind great bitterness among those who had lost money in it. As a result, laws were passed which made it illegal to found joint stock companies. These laws turned out to be a severe handicap later in the century, when the solid expansion of industry needed capital.

In one way and another, however, capital did now flow into the market. One condition for this was the progressive fall in the rate of interest. We can trace this fall most clearly in government loans, which had to pay as much as 8 per cent before 1700, but which by 1727 were paying only 3 per cent. As the rate of interest fell, it became profitable to undertake long-term work, such as the sinking of mines, the building of factories, and the construction of toll roads. When interest is high, the lender can get a quick return and therefore does not want to sink money into long-term projects which will only give a return over twenty or thirty years. But when interest is low, he cannot expect a quick return, and he is therefore encouraged to make solid investments which will give a return in the future.[7]

The expansion of credit and the general stimulus to investment was a major factor in the progress of the Industrial Revolution. The revolution would have been impossible without a new attitude by all owners of capital to the investment of money. Factory owners financed their own expansion, of course, by ploughing back their profits year by year. But they could not have expanded as they did, often they could not have begun at all, if they had not been able to find backers with money from outside their family circle. Financial skill was needed to start a new industry, and some of those who claimed to be inventors were in fact, like Richard Arkwright, skillful above all in finance and in industrial organization.

VII

We have also in the agriculture of the time an important movement —often called an agricultural revolution—characterized by the introduction of new methods in farming. Viscount Townsend introduced the

---

[7] The relation between savings, the rate of interest and industrial expansion is well put by T. S. Ashton, *The Industrial Revolution* (Oxford, 1948). This admirable little book is recommended as a balanced and compact account of the main development of the Industrial Revolution. It also has a short but adequate bibliography, to which we refer the reader.

rotation of root crops with grass and grain crops, and was called "Turnip" Townsend for his pains. Robert Bakewell brought scientific methods into cattle breeding. His work, coupled with other improvements, had such good effect that the average weight of oxen sold at Smithfield increased from 370 pounds in 1710 to 800 pounds in 1745.[8] There were other agricultural innovators such as Jethro Tull, Arthur Young, and Coke of Holkham. One result of their work was that farmers were enabled, probably for the first time in the history of the world, to keep their cattle alive through the winter. This, in turn, brought an increase in manure; and an increase in manure brought greater agricultural fertility and yields.

The whole period is a fascinating complex of cross-currents, influencing and flowing into the tide of the Industrial Revolution. For example, there was a new enclosure movement at the end of the eighteenth century. This was the second great enclosure in English history. The point of the first enclosure movement in the sixteenth century had been to make the land carry more sheep for the wool trade; and Thomas More in *Utopia* had complained that "the sheep eat the men." Now the second enclosure movement was carried out by country landlords who wanted to grow food on the common land. Unhappy as it was, it helped to create efficient large holdings, and was in this respect like the movement to factories. At the same time, in addition to farm production it affected the supply of labor and the rise of population.

In the course of this movement (running from 1760 to 1850), over 6 million acres of common land were enclosed.[9] This made possible the growing of large, scientifically cultivated crops, and so formed almost an eighteenth-century TVA program—without the social benefits. The landlords in effect stole the common land, though they claimed (and in the long run rightly) that "a better income [for everyone] could be drawn by improved methods of exploitation."[10] One result of the enclosure movement was that it also helped to destroy village industry. For the home worker had only been able to make ends meet by grazing his few animals on the common land and getting his fuel there. Now the enclosure of the commons drove him from the village into the industrial towns, where he formed a source of cheap labor.

8 J. H. Plumb, *England in the Eighteenth Century* (Harmondsworth, 1950), p. 82.

9 This figure is especially impressive when one remembers that the total area of Great Britain is only about 95,000 square miles, of which only about 58 per cent is arable or pasture land.

10 Paul Mantoux, *The Industrial Revolution in the Eighteenth Century*, rev. ed., tr. by Marjorie Vernon (New York, 1927), p. 190. This is the standard work on the whole subject of this chapter.

VIII

Food and population were linked in the thought of the eighteenth century. We know today that after 1760 the English population rose by leaps and bounds. At the time, however, no one could tell whether population was going up or down; until the first official census in 1801, everyone was merely guessing. An important authority, Richard Price, in his *Essay on the Population of England* in 1780, believed that the villages were being depopulated. Oliver Goldsmith wrote a famous poem, *The Deserted Village*, whose theme is enclosure and the resulting depopulation. They and others supposed that the population of England as a whole was falling; and Goldsmith in *The Deserted Village* intoned,

> Ill fares the land, to hastening ills a prey,
> Where wealth accumulates, and men decay.

Other observers thought that population was increasing, but drew equally pessimistic conclusions from this belief. Arthur Young, for example, in his *North of England*, thought that population would now outstrip food production. Thomas Malthus turned this into a general law, and when he wrote his *Essay on Population . . .*, the rising population and rising distress in England seemed indeed to prove his point.[11]

Statistics have now shown that Malthus was right in believing that population was increasing. But his forecast of mass starvation was falsified by the unexpectedly large productive capacity of the new agriculture and, indirectly, of the factory system which yielded an industrial surplus large enough to open up the agricultural lands of North America. (To a small measure, it was falsified also by birth control; indeed, Malthus himself had advocated "moral restraint" as a solution.)

Even now, we do not really understand the factors responsible for the large increase in population, today often called the demographic revolution. We do know that the death rate fell, and that this did much to cause the surging upward of population. But was the death rate reduced directly by the Industrial Revolution? The economic historian Max Weber casts doubt on this explanation. "The growth of population in the West made most rapid progress from the beginning of the eighteenth century to the end of the nineteenth. In the same period China experienced a population growth of at least equal extent —from 60 or 70 to 400 millions. . . . This corresponds approximately with the increase in the West."[12] There was, we know, no Industrial Revolution in China at this time.

---

11 See *ibid.*, p. 354.
12 Max Weber, *General Economic History*, tr. by Frank H. Knight (New York, 1927), p. 352.

In short, we know little more than that population increased and that in England it shifted northwest.[13] Recent work in economic history has, in fact, tended to show that the industrial workers were newcomers, "an additional population which was enabled to grow up by the new opportunities for employment which capitalism provided."[14]

We also know that these people tended to be concentrated in towns, for a distinctive feature of the Industrial Revolution was the great increase in urban living. In turn, this crowding into new towns created new problems of sanitation. And we see the interconnections of all these factors when we remember that a famous medical report, written by Dr. Percival of Manchester in 1796, led to the first modern factory legislation.

Obviously, without going into further details, the Industrial Revolution was more than a change in the system of production; it was also a revolution in the conditions of life for entire sections of society. The main industrial growth was in wool and cotton textiles, and in the complex linkage of iron, coal, and steam.[15] The main social development was in the creation of a new locus for an increasing number of people—the factory and the city. More and more, men spent their working hours in the factory and their leisure hours in the crowded streets and tenements of the city.

These tremendous changes in the conditions of life had profound repercussions in the thought of the time. In addition to the newly created proletariat, an older class had become more important: the middle class, their power visible in the Reform Bill of 1832, which, in effect, first gave the middle class a voice in public voting and affairs. A new man, the Captain of Industry, became a hero. Most important for our purposes . . . these people had new ideas and values. A new sensibility entered into and began to change the arts, the literature, and the thought of the period.[16] The Industrial Revolution changed Western man from head to foot; and thence more deeply from head to heart.

---

[13] The English people were free to move because serfdom no longer existed, by the eighteenth century, in England, as it did on the Continent. One result of this movement in England was the destruction of local ties and loyalties, with the worker often drifting rootlessly in his new urban surroundings.

[14] Cf. *Capitalism and the Historians*, ed. by Friedrich A. Hayek (Chicago, 1954), and a review of it by H. Stuart Hughes in *Commentary* (April, 1954).

[15] Some idea of the industrial increase in these fields can be given by the figures of raw cotton imports in Great Britain and of pig-iron output. In cotton, we have 1 million pounds in 1701, 3 million in 1750, 4,760,000 in 1771, 5,300,000 in 1781, 11½ million in 1784, and 32 million in 1789. In pig-iron output, we have 68,000 tons in 1788, 126,000 in 1796, and 250,000 in 1804. (All figures from Mantoux, *op. cit.*, pp. 259 and 313.)

[16] See J. Bronowski, *The Common Sense of Science* (London, 1951), Chap. 1, for a discussion of the new sensibility. . . .

Chapter 22

The French Revolution and
Its Napoleonic Sequel

III

A STRIKING feature of the French Revolution is its detailed recapitulation in the realm of action of the trends in thought. . . . Montesquieu and his ideal of an aristocratic government; Voltaire and the Physiocrats, with their notion of an enlightened despotism; Rousseau and the democratic and totalitarian implications of his rule by the general will: these political theories all worked themselves out in the course of the Revolution and its aftermath. Starting in 1789 and culminating in 1794, there was a movement of ideas to the "left." Concurrent with this was a movement of men; and we witness an emigration from France of nobles, after the failure of Montesquieu's views, and then of the upper bourgeoisie, after the failure of Physiocratic monarchical ideas.

Let us follow in some detail how the first of these three theories turned out in practice. The initial phase of the Revolution was, as the French historian Lefebvre points out, "an aristocratic revolution."[1] It involved an attempt by the nobles to assert, or regain, control of the state. For in spite of its social and tax privileges, the nobility had lost political power. Government officials, not the nobles, administered the rural areas, and it was said that France was governed by thirty intendants: although by 1789 the intendants were all noble, their ostensible loyalty was still to the state.[2]

The nobility itself was not homogeneous; it was divided into court and provincial nobles and into nobles of the sword and of the robe. The nobles of the robe were entrenched in the Parlements, a type of French law court, which claimed the right to pass on the king's edicts and to register them. The parliamentarians tended at first to give a lead to the nation. In order to protect their own tax-free position, they ad-

[1] Cf. Georges Lefebvre, The Coming of the French Revolution, tr. by R. R. Palmer (Princeton, 1947), especially Part I.

[2] Cf. Alexis de Tocqueville, The State of Society in France Before the Revolution of 1789, tr. by Henry Reeve (London, 1888), for a full statement of the nobility's loss of real power in eighteenth-century France.

vanced the idea that taxation should only be with the consent of the
nation. Dissolved in 1770, the Parlements became martyrs to the cause
of freedom; popular pressure on the king forced their recall. By the
1780's, the Parlements had linked themselves with the provincial estates
in opposition to the king. Powerful in the provincial estates, they assumed that they would control an Estates General and, through it, the
king.

When, in 1788, the king demanded registration of a new tax to solve
his financial difficulties, the Paris Parlement refused. To protect its
members against royal reprisal, it condemned administrative arrest and
declared that a natural right of all Frenchmen was liberty. Louis XVI
is reported to have said that if the Parlements had their way, France
would be "an aristocracy of magistrates."[3] Nevertheless, Louis was
forced to yield, and, in the hope of obtaining money, he agreed to the
calling of the Estates General.

Having conquered the king, the Parlements immediately lost the
nation. Throwing aside the veil of disinterested love of freedom, the
Parlements proposed that the Estates General should be constituted as
in 1614, the last date of its meeting, with each of the three orders voting as an order; it was obvious that the clergy and the nobility would
vote together against the third estate.

When the third estate asserted itself in opposition to the other two
estates, it took over from the nobility or aristocracy valuable lessons in
resistance. The aristocratic class, in its opposition to the king, had developed means of communication through salons, cafés, and agricultural societies, had organized political groups which exchanged correspondence and instructions, had enunciated declarations of fundamental
laws, and had asserted the principle that taxation could only be levied
by consent.[4] All of these lessons were taken to heart by the third estate,
when, following Abbe Sieyès' advice, it became the "nation."

IV

The failure of the "aristocratic revolution" opened the way to an
attempt at enlightened despotism. The nobility had been unable to lead
the nation because it refused to give up social privileges in return for
political power. . . .

Worse, the nobility had lost faith in itself and in its principles;
Montesquieu had been superseded, even among the nobility, by more

---

[3] Lefebvre, *op. cit.*, p. 30.
[4] *Ibid.*, *op. cit.*, pp. 33–34.

"enlightened" thinkers. Thus, in 1789, at the meeting of the Estates General, there was no forceful exponent of the aristocratic point of view, with the possible exception of Cazalès, the son of an adviser to the Parlements. Almost all the really talented nobles—Lafayette, Mirabeau, Talleyrand—had passed over into the camp of the third estate.[5] In a sense, therefore, the aristocratic revolution had gone by default.

Outstanding among the "other-class" leaders was Mirabeau. The son of the famous Physiocratic thinker, the Marquis of Mirabeau (who styled himself the "friend of man" but was the enemy of his child, shutting him up for a time in prison), the younger Mirabeau pursued a dissolute, passionate life. He was active but aimless until 1789. Rejected by his fellow nobles of Provence as a delegate to the Estates General, he then offered himself to the third estate and was successfully elected. It was Mirabeau, the noble, who dramatically replied to the king's command for the third estate to disperse: "We will not leave except by force of the bayonet."

Having thus identified himself with the third estate and asserted its right, Mirabeau proceeded to embrace the cause of the king. The Spanish philosopher Ortega y Gasset had made the penetrating observation that "All revolution, inexorably—whether red or white—provokes a counterrevolution. The politician is he who anticipates this result, and makes at the same time, by himself, the revolution and the counterrevolution. The Revolution was the Assembly, which Mirabeau dominated. It was also necessary to dominate the Counterrevolution, to hold it in his hand. He needed the King."[6] A political realist, Mirabeau . . . focused on practical issues, and opposed drawing a Declaration of Rights out of thin air. He declared: "We are not savages recently arrived from the banks of the Orinoco to form a society. We are an old nation, perhaps too old for our time. We have a preexisting government, a preexisting king, preexisting prejudices. It is necessary, as far as possible, to accommodate all these things to the Revolution and to attenuate the suddenness of the change."

It was Mirabeau who led the second phase of the Revolution—the bourgeois revolution—and attempted to consolidate the victory in a hybrid of constitutional monarchy and enlightened despotism. He advised the king to accept the National Assembly and a constitution; he advised the Assembly to allow the king an absolute veto over its future

---

[5] Lafayette and Talleyrand, unlike Mirabeau, had been elected by their respective orders, the nobility and the clergy; this did not prevent them, however, from supporting the position of the third estate.

[6] Jose Ortega y Gasset, "*Mirabeau, o el politico*," *Obras Completas*, 6 vols. (Madrid, 1950), Vol. III, p. 619. This brilliant essay should be consulted in its entirety, if possible; unfortunately there is no English translation.

actions. Mirabeau's idea was that the king would use the royal veto and the royal power in the interests of the people.[7]

Like Voltaire and the Physiocrats, Mirabeau preferred reform to a freedom which might degenerate into license.[8] He did not trust the mob. He realized, in a remarkable flash of prophecy, that the Revolution was to a large extent a continuation of old-regime trends, but in an accelerated form. He wrote to the king: "The idea of forming a single class of all the citizens would have pleased Richelieu; this equality of the surface facilitates the exercise of power. Several successive reigns of an absolute monarchy would not have done as much for the royal authority as this one year of revolution." So it was imperative, in Mirabeau's view, that the heightened power provided by equality be in the hands of a royal authority, backed by the bourgeoisie.

Mirabeau's policy was the realistic acknowledgment of existing power in France as well as of the demands voiced in the *cahiers*, or instructions, drawn up for the delegates to the Estates General. French opinion of 1789 was not antimonarchical, and there were no voices raised at the time in favor of a republic. Why should there be, when the king, by calling the Estates General, seemed to be inaugurating the reign of reform? In accord with this frame of mind, the French Constitution of 1791 set up a limited monarchy, controlled by the middle class through a restricted suffrage. It was not until August 10, 1792, that a democracy was established with universal suffrage, and not until September 22 that the monarchical form was abolished and a republic proclaimed.

Why did Mirabeau's ideas fail? It is easy to say why Mirabeau as a person came short of his goal. He was distrusted because of the ill repute of his past life and of his financial connection with the king. Nevertheless, he maintained a form of control over the Assembly by his matchless oratorical abilities; it was primarily Mirabeau who introduced the parliamentary rhetoric which was the source of power until the coming of Bonaparte. But Mirabeau's premature death, at the age of 42, on April 2, 1791, ended the one force which could hold together the bourgeoisie and the monarchy.

The main obstacle to the success of Mirabeau's ideas—both during his life and after—was Louis XVI. His personality was pivotal to the entire French Revolution. His vacillation between force and concession

---

[7] His enemies accused him of supporting the royal veto because he was in the pay of the king. Mirabeau, from 1790 on, was in the pay of the king; he received a salary of 300 pounds per month, and his debts of 10,000 pounds were paid for him. But his ideas were not for sale, and Mirabeau favored the royal veto for genuine political and not for venal reasons.

[8] Was it that, while rejecting his father, Mirabeau retained his ideas? [See] Tocqueville, . . . on the idea that "the French aimed at reform before liberty."

undermined any consistent policy. When he disowned the third estate, Louis ended the possibility of a peaceful revolution. By attempting to crush the Estates General, he provoked the decisive intervention of the Paris mob. Louis XVI caused Bastille to be the point of no return.

It was Louis XVI who made both enlightened despotism and constitutional monarchy impossible solutions for France. This is a point worth insisting upon; it was the same flaw of personality which faced Plato in Sicily when the prince whom he attempted to form into a philosopher-king turned out to be unworthy. The French Revolution was primarily a social revolution against the aristocratic hierarchy; the vacuum caused by Louis' refusal to play the part assigned him led to a republic. Condorcet's ingenious proposal, that an automation of a king be substituted for the real puppet, was not enough.

As late as July 13, 1791, Robespierre had said: "As for the monarch, I have never been able to share the terror with which the title of king has inspired almost all free peoples . . . I should not fear royalty; not even the hereditary nature of the royal functions in a single family."[9] But Louis had already demonstrated, by his attempt at flight on June 20, 1791, that he was not willing to stand in alliance with the bourgeoisie. Alone against the mob, the moderate Monarchicals gave way step by step to the Feuillants, the Feuillants to the Girondists, and eventually the Girondists to the Jacobins, led by the same Robespierre who had earlier been willing to accept an hereditary monarch.[10]

V

It was now time for the theories of Rousseau to be put into practice. The other *philosophes* had unintentionally done their part in undermining monarchical principles by accustoming the people to question the origins of sovereignty and authority. Rousseau went further and

[9] Quoted in A. Aulard, *The French Revolution: A Political History, 1789–1804* (New York, 1910), pp. 309–310.

[10] The first breach in the moderate position occurred when the advocates of a bicameral legislature (with either an hereditary or elective upper chamber) and an absolute royal veto, the Monarchicals or Anglophiles as they were called, were voted down by the majority of their own so-called party. Headed by Mounier, and with men like Lally-Tollendal and Clermont-Tonnerre in its ranks, this group of moderate monarchists gave up its parliamentary opposition and took to emigration; Mounier, for example, left France around 1789. This amputation from the patriot party in turn left the remaining moderates (who, under the leadership of Lafayette and Barnave, rejected an upper chamber because the nobility might regain its power therein) weakened in the face of the radicals who wished to push the Revolution further.

directly placed the authority of government in the hands of the people. The satire of the *philosophes* had corroded the foundations of the monarchy and prepared for its easy toppling; Rousseau laid the cornerstone on which a government of the people, or a government of the general will, could be constructed. The great question was whether the democratic or totalitarian implications of Rousseau's political philosophy would come to the fore.

It was the military invasion of France by Austria and Prussia, to support the king, which settled the issue. The conflict, starting in 1792 as a war of defense (although it was France that declared war), rapidly turned into a war of conquest and propagation of revolutionary principles. At home, the war led to a republic and, eventually, to a military dictatorship. In the beginning there seemed some possibility that Lafayette, the hero of two revolutions, might convert his position as head of the militia and general of the French armies into a dictatorship. At least this was the fear of Robespierre, who cited Cromwell as an example of the danger of military dictatorship of the republic. "I would rather see a popular representative Assembly, with the citizens free and respected, under a King, than an enslaved, degraded people under the rod of an aristocratic Senate and a dictator. I love Cromwell no more than Charles the First."

But Lafayette was not the man to play at Napoleon. He lacked political genius or realism, and contented himself with cutting a romantic and generous figure. Further, he sincerely believed in freedom and, with Barnave, headed the Feuillant party which sought a constitutional monarchy. His effort to "save" the revolution for the upper bourgeoisie failed when he could not persuade his troops, in August, 1792, to march against the more extreme revolutionaries, who were in power. Fleeing to Belgium, Lafayette took with him any chance of the Feuillants succeeding in their aim. His removal as commander of the French troops also marked the end of aristocratic leadership of the Revolution; henceforth, the French *levées en masse* were to be led by new "revolutionary" generals.

The totalitarian implications of Rousseau's doctrines now began to appear in full force. Robespierre, taking advantage of the dismay and confusion produced by the revolutionary war without, and the civil war within, instituted "government by terror." His strategy was constantly to accuse his opponents of being in the pay of Pitt and the English.[11] His tyrannical methods Robespierre justified as the reign of virtue advocated by Rousseau. The "incorruptible" leader of the French Re-

---

[11] See Albert Mathiez, *The French Revolution*, tr. by Catherine Alison Phillips (New York, 1929), p. 360.

public in 1793 even went beyond his philosophical predecessor and expounded the totalitarian principles of "a revolutionary government":

> The theory of the revolutionary government is as new as the Revolution itself, from which this government was born. This theory may not be found in the books of the political writers who were unable to predict the Revolution. . . . The goal of a constitutional government is the protection of the Republic; that of a revolutionary government is the establishment of the Republic. The Revolution is the war waged by liberty against its foes—but the Constitution is the regime of victorious and peaceful freedom. . . . Under Constitutional rule, it is sufficient to protect individuals against the encroachments of the state power. Under a revolutionary regime, the state power itself must protect itself against all that attack it.[12]

In theory, the revolutionary government was checked by the natural rights of individuals, which even the central government might not violate. These natural rights soon gave way in the face of raison d'état and of "cruel necessity" (to recur to Cromwell's phrase). Free speech and press and freedom of person—all were violated in the time of the Terror on the grounds of public safety. And Robespierre, who headed the Committee of Public Safety, merely formulated the theory to describe the reality.

When would the "revolutionary government" give way to "constitutional rule?" Only when the revolution was complete and all its foes defeated. To insure this outcome, Robespierre insisted, resort must be had to a reign of terror. One of the most competent present-day students of the Terror has stated that "In the circumstances no government could have maintained itself without very severe measures of repression. The Terror, after all, was inevitable."[13]

According to the best evidence, about 20,000 people were direct victims of the guillotine and another 20,000 died in the prisons or were executed without trial. To this total of 40,000 dead, we must add the imprisonment, at one time or another during the Terror, of about half a million Frenchmen. Yet apparently this new type of state repression, which was most active in the area of the Vendée and the war frontier, did assist the military success of the Republic.

---

12 Maximilien Robespierre, "Report on the Principles of a Revolutionary Government," Introduction to Contemporary Civilization in the West, 2 vols. (New York, 1946), Vol. I, p. 1089.

13 Donald Greer, The Incidence of the Terror During the French Revolution (Cambridge, 1935), pp. 115 and 137. Even so judicious a historian as Georges Lefebvre has asserted that the Terror institutionalized justice and prevented massacres (such as the one of September, 1792, in which over 1,000 victims were claimed). In our view, however, a justification of the Terror on the grounds of raison d'état merely opens once again the question whether any raison d'état justifies state action.

Was the Terror also a class weapon, a tool for the achievement of social or economic ends? The answer appears to be in the negative; the Terror, on sober consideration, was a political weapon. The social revolution had already been accomplished by the bourgeois Assembly.[14]

The other major political innovation created by the French Revolution was government by "clubs and committees." Real power in Revolutionary France resided, not in the legislature, but in the machinery of the Jacobin clubs.[15] These had their origin in the literary societies, or *societés de la pensée*, and in the secret societies, such as the Freemasons, which existed before the Revolution. The source of the Jacobin Club was the Breton Club, formed during June, 1789, to serve as a center for representatives of the third estate. The Breton Club members quickly discovered that, in order to succeed in their fight against the king and the other two orders, it was necessary to mobilize public opinion from outside the Assembly. This they did through the formation of the Society of the Friends of the Constitution, which became better known as the Jacobin Club, named after the Convent at Paris in which its meetings took place.

·   ·   ·

Both in their origins and in their careers, the Jacobin Clubs were middle-class bodies, whose members had standing in their local communities. According to one authority, there were probably about 500,000 enrolled Jacobins in France, or about 2.2 per cent of the French population.[16] Almost all were from the more prosperous levels of society. With the fall of the old government hierarchy, the Jacobins necessarily had to take over the task of local administration and government.

Within the Jacobin societies, two groups formed. One, outside the Assembly, was headed by Robespierre; it was this group which appropriated to itself the name of Jacobin. The other group was led, initially, by a journalist named Brissot, who was a member of the 1791 Assembly; these Brissotins, as they were at first called, split away from the Jacobins after the formation of the republic, and then became known as Girondists. Eventually led by Danton, the Girondists fought for power against Robespierre and the Jacobins. The victory of Robespierre marked the

---

[14] Cf. *ibid.*, pp. 1, 14, 81, 85, and 87.

[15] This was conclusively demonstrated by the elections of 1791 to the Legislative Assembly. On the basis of a restricted suffrage, the Feuillants gained 264 seats to the Jacobins' 136; 345 representatives considered themselves as independents. The parliamentary victory of the Feuillants, however, was misleading; without support in the clubs (which had organized the political activity of the country), the Feuillants remained, as Crane Brinton says, a "mere parliamentary caucus."

[16] See Crane Brinton's detailed study, *The Jacobins* (New York, 1930), especially pp. 40–43.

final point of the trend to the "left"; the limits to which philosophic theory might be tried in practice had been reached.

VII

Robespierre's "revolutionary government" had successfully established the Republic at home and protected it from its foes abroad; his execution on the 10th of Thermidor (July 28, 1794) marked the transition to "constitutional rule." The constitutional government of 1795–1799 which followed, known as the Directory, strongly affirmed the individualistic, bourgeois nature of the Revolution. It abolished the Terror and attempted to institute government by law; it began work on the revision of the law codes; it repealed the law of the Maximum; it attempted to solve the financial problem and to bring economic stability to France.

Unable, however, to maintain itself securely against the unregenerate followers of Robespierre, on one side, and the returned royalists, on the other, the Directory turned increasingly to the army. The Directors were forced to suppress a royalist uprising in Paris on October 5, 1795, by employing Napoleon Bonaparte and a "whiff of grapeshot"; it used General Hoche to chastise the royalist forces in the Vendée and Brittany. It was Bonaparte again who closed down Babeuf's club, the Society of Equals; and it was Bonaparte's nominee, General Augereau, who prevented a rightist coup d'état on September 4, 1797. These episodes showed that there could be no stable settlement in France unless the government could either conciliate or suppress the radicals and the reactionaries; and the Directory by itself could effectively do neither.

It was again the war which, having first brought the totalitarian implications of Rousseau to the fore, now brought forth the solution to the Directory's problems: Bonapartism. In the person of Napoleon, we have a new version of the condottiere. This comparison is lent color by Napoleon's Italian ancestry and his affectation of Roman attitudes and modes. Napoleon was like that other condottiere, Cesare Borgia, in his astuteness and Machiavellism. Unlike his prototype, however, he covered over his naked self-interest and desire for personal gain with a cloak of revolutionary ideology.

The secret of Napoleon's greatness was that he linked the doctrine of self-interest with the ideology of revolution, and turned the power which their fusion gave him to his own egoistic ends. To the French, Napoleon preached the bourgeois Directory's doctrine of self-interest. We detect the new note in Napoleon's first proclamation to the army in Italy of March 27, 1796:

Soldiers, you are naked, ill-fed: the Government owes you much, it can give you nothing. Your patience, and the courage which you have shown in the midst of these rocky crags, are admirable; but they have won you no glory; no glamour clings about you. I wish to lead you into the most fertile plains of the world. Rich provinces, great cities, will be in your power; you will find honor, glory, and riches there. Soldiers of Italy! do you lack courage or constancy?

With Napoleon, the French revolutionary army took on some of the loutishness of the old mercenary armies. But the revolutionary note was not forgotten. To the countries he entered, Napoleon held out the gains of the Revolution. For example, he promised the peoples of Italy that they "should be counted among the free and powerful nations" and reminded them that before his coming they had been "divided, and bent down by tyranny." Then, without the assent of the Directory, Napoleon set up Cisalpine and Ligurian republics in Italy.

A conquering hero abroad, Napoleon returned to France in 1799 to give it the same "liberty" he had proclaimed elsewhere. In the "Proclamation to the French People," delivered immediately after the successful coup d'état of the 19th Brumaire against the Directory, Napoleon declared: "On my return to Paris, I found division among all authorities, and agreement on just one fact, that the constitution was half destroyed and could not save liberty. Every party came to me, confided to me their designs, imparted their secrets, and requested my support; but I refused to be the man of any party." Then, having established himself as being the representative of France, a man "above party," Napoleon gave a lurid, and fictitious, account of the coup d'état and concluded, in a masterly hash of contradictory verbiage: "Conservative, protective, and liberal ideas have resumed their sway."[17]

Nevertheless, in spite of the logically contradictory nature of Napoleon's conservative and liberal ideas, and of his appeal to self-interest and revolutionary idealism, the *historical* logic of his position was accurate. Napoleon had profoundly sensed the needs of his time; he seemed to embody its dialectic spirit. It was this political genius of Napoleon which led Hegel to proclaim Napoleon as a "world historical figure."

In the judgment by Hegel, we have a recurrence of the Renaissance admiration for the brutally successful man by the great thinker. The new element is Hegel's glorification of the hero, not only as a superior man, but as the embodiment of historical forces. . . .

We have encountered this sort of man before in Mirabeau. Napoleon followed him in the attempt to combine the revolution and the counterrevolution in one policy. He endeavored to achieve a balance of social

---

[17] From Napoleon, "Proclamation to the French People" (1799).

forces while at the same time doing away with any governmental division of powers which might check or balance his own. Napoleon's method of achieving unchecked power was through direct appeal to the people in a plebiscite; thus, like Hitler later, he claimed to embody the general will.

His method of achieving the balance of social forces was continuously to play off against one another the bourgeoisie and the workers, the liberals and the royalists, in a masterly game of opportunistic politics. He held out to the bourgeoisie the promise of stability and order, to the lower classes of France the lure of national glory and power, to the liberals the slogans of equality and fraternity, and to the rightists a revival of Catholicism and of unity and authority in the government. On top of all this, he attempted to create "new men," dedicated to Bonapartism; he inserted a "marshal's baton in every soldier's knapsack," established the Legion of Honor, and set up a new, upstart nobility.

Napoleon recognized that the broad mass of Frenchmen were generally satisfied with the social reforms of the Revolution, and that the desire was for stability and order. Thrusting political liberty to one side, Napoleon used alternating force and conciliation to achieve his ends. He secured a measure of domestic peace by pacifying the Vendée; he initiated fiscal reform and set up the Bank of France; he ordered a legal code (embodying a conservative interpretation of the Revolution's social gains) drawn up, which influenced all Europe and has lasted until today; and he tried to heal the religious wounds of France by effecting a concordat with the pope.

Unlike the enlightened *philosophes* and bourgeois of the Revolution who had seen in religion the enemy of all reform, Napoleon regarded religion as a mainstay of the state. The only difference between his view and that of the old-regime supporters was in the nature of that state. For Napoleon, the state was the centralized, nationalistic state enhanced by the Revolution and based on the social dominance of the bourgeoisie. Religion was merely one more social force to be used in maintaining this Bonapartist state. As Napoleon commented: "For my part, I do not see in religion the mystery of transubstantiation but the mystery of social order."[18]

---

[18] Quoted in Pieter Geyl, *Napoleon For and Against,* tr. from the Dutch by Olive Renier (New Haven, 1949), p. 360. This is a splendid book of historiography, treating the various treatments of Napoleon with a very critical eye. For a good general survey of the Napoleonic period, see Geoffrey Bruun's volume in "The Rise of Modern Europe" series, *Europe and the French Imperium* (New York, 1938); like Brinton's book, it has an exhaustive bibliography.

Nevertheless, like Mirabeau, Napoleon failed in his effort to achieve a stable synthesis of the revolution and the counterrevolution. In his case, of course, the reasons were somewhat different from those that defeated Mirabeau. One cause of Napoleon's failure was his political illegitimacy. Louis XVI could have held the French nation together, as the embodiment of legitimate authority. Napoleon was forced to do so by means of his charismatic personality. In fine, Napoleon was never accepted either by the liberals or the royalists in France. The first considered him as the betrayer of the Revolution, and the latter thought of him as the impediment to the rightful Restoration. Thus, Napoleon did not so much enjoy their support as dexterously thwart their opposition; this, however, was not a firm basis for extended political rule.

If Napoleon was like a Renaissance condottiere in his political illegitimacy, he was also like one in placing personal ambition above the needs of his people. There is some justice in saying that Napoleon was Machiavelli's Prince come to renewed life and to increased success; and the very success of Napoleon proves the fundamental weakness in the Prince. It is as if we hear the voice of Machiavelli again in Napoleon's letter to his brother Joseph, King of Naples, in 1808: "I wish the Naples mob would attempt a rising. As long as you have not made an example, you will not be their master. Every conquered country must have its uprising." The thin covering of Napoleon's politics, provided by Revolutionary slogans, is pierced by his candid conception of the people as a conquered beast to be ridden by a master.

The basic flaw in Napoleon's attempt to bring domestic stability to France was that it conflicted with his grandiose personal ambition for empire. Napoleon was not really interested in the welfare of the French people, but only in governing them so that he might use them and the nation as a tool to realize his plans. Napoleon was a condottiere who combined with this role the attributes of Marlow's Tamburlaine, and was constantly "overreaching" himself. Or, to use the terms of nineteenth-century romanticism, Napoleon was filled with the spirit of endless striving toward an unreachable, infinite goal. Upon the altar of his lust for power, Napoleon sacrificed the synthesis of revolution and counterrevolution which he might have effected in France.

VIII

The French Revolution had destroyed the old regime in France: Napoleon, in turn, had used the momentum of the Revolution to conquer much of Europe. Between them the Revolution and Napoleon changed both the map and the mind of the Western world. By carrying the concept of the nation in arms, the slogans of liberty, equality, and fraternity, the legal code, and the whole paraphernalia of revolutionary reforms into all the conquered countries, the Revolution and Napoleon toppled not only the feudal structure of Europe, but undermined the foundations of the monarchical system as well. Then, by awakening the spirit of nationalism, in reaction to French aggression, the Revolution and Napoleon laid out the lines upon which the changed European nations might grow.[19]

The result was a "new world," with its roots deep in the fecund soil of the old Europe. The ideas of the philosophes, often distorted and twisted almost out of all recognition by the pressure of events, served to mold a new version of society, but in the process the French Revolution may be said to have partially exhausted these ideas. The result was that the minds of men were prepared to receive new thoughts and philosophies. . . . In sum, the French Revolution had not introduced the millennium, but instead had solved some of the old problems and raised new ones in their place. . . .[20]

---

[19] For example, by his famous *Reichshauptdeputationschluss* of 1803, Napoleon fused more than 300 German principalities and free cities into less than 100 and made Bismarck's "blood and iron" unification of 1870 possible.

[20] The argument whether the Revolution was a success or failure is an inexhaustible and unanswerable one. As to the question whether Napoleon was a fulfillment or a miscarriage of the Revolution, that argument has also occupied the attention of a great number of historians of the French Revolution. (Cf., for example, Peter Geyl, *op. cit.*, and Geoffrey Bruun, *op. cit.*). Napoleon himself helped create the legend which pictured him as the son of the Revolution who consolidated its gains. Writing his *Memorial de Sainte-Hélène* to justify his policy in the eyes of posterity, Napoleon contended that he had maintained equality, restored order, and brought peace; whatever war he had indulged in had been forced upon him by English imperialism. Even then, Napoleon added, his conquests had merely brought the blessings of the Revolution to other countries.

Napoleon's critics have retorted that he destroyed freedom and set up tyranny in its place, corroded the glorious doctrine of equality where he could, ruled France for his own benefit, set up his family as little kings all over Europe, and, in general, perverted and corrupted the aims and ideals of the Revolution.

ELIE KEDOURIE

Nationalism

Nationalism, which is having such a powerful impact on the former colonial territories, did not emerge in Western Europe until the end of the Middle Ages. Until that time people had thought of themselves as owing allegiance to their feudal lords or to the Church, not to a sovereign "state" which did not exist as we know it today.

Though nationalism triumphed throughout Western Europe in the nineteenth century, it had once seemed a heresy to those who believed in an all-embracing realm under the aegis of the Church. George Bernard Shaw portrayed this feeling in his play Saint Joan, where the French bishop of Beauvais, Peter Cauchon, says: "But as a priest I have gained a knowledge of the minds of the common people; and there you will find another dangerous idea. I can express it only by such phrases as France for the French, England for the English, Italy for the Italians, Spain for the Spanish. It is sometimes . . . narrow and bitter . . ." (Today nationalism is thought of once again as "narrow and bitter" by those who favor the supranational community of nations, represented by the United Nations and the Specialized Agencies, and supranational regional organizations such as the European Common Market.)

As Bishop Cauchon indicates, it is not easy to describe nationalism. Some think of it in terms of geography; others of race, or language, or religion. At its worst it can degenerate into violent racialism, as it did in Germany under the Nazis. At its best it represents a dedicated love of one's fatherland or, as the French say, of one's patrie; it is patriotism.

Nations may lack contiguous territory, like Pakistan; or for centuries even a geographic home, like Israel. Nations may have a single language or religion, but they may also include several races, languages, or religions, like India, the United States, the U.S.S.R., and the multiracial countries of East Africa. In essence, what makes a nation is a sense of common interests and traditions, a sense of belonging to a given people. President Gamal Abdel Nasser of Egypt has described it as a sense of "national identity"; the French philosopher Ernest Renan speaks of "the soul of a nation."

In this selection Professor Elie Kedourie, who teaches politics and public administration at the London School of Economics and Political Science, analyzes the growth and principal ingredients of nationalism in the West. Mr. Kedourie was born in Iraq and is now a British citizen.

Chapter 6
Nationalism and Politics: I

AT THE time when the doctrine [of nationalism] was being elaborated, Europe was in turmoil. The Revolution had succeeded in destroying the Monarchy and the traditional social order in France. Not only its example and influence, but its actions and policies carried the disturbance outwards from France in ever-widening ripples. "By sending us as deputies here," Danton said in the Convention of 1792, "the French nation has brought into being a grand committee for the general insurrection of the peoples." Napoleon, who followed, completed the destructive action of the Revolution. In a short career, of less than twenty years, he laid low the fabric of international order in Europe. Things which had not been thought possible were now seen to be indeed possible and feasible. Revolutions could succeed, empires be overthrown, and frontiers changed. A man, a handful of men, by resolution, audacity, and ruthlessness could raise masses of other men to decide the fate of governments and the frontiers of states. So much turbulence and so much violence from 1789 to 1815 could not fail to have far-reaching consequences. It revived old enmities and created new ones; classes of society which had never dreamt of exercising power tasted of it by proxy, and would never again relapse into obedient tameness; hopes were kindled, passions aroused which were impossible to extinguish. The Congress of Vienna tried to restore the European system disrupted by the Revolution and by Napoleon; the great Powers, the position of which the Congress recognized and consecrated, were England, Prussia, Austria, Russia, and France, the same states, that is, whose interlocking policies had made possible a balance of power before 1789. It was now thought that the system could again be set up, and the dance resumed where it had been so rudely disturbed.

But, of course, the dance could not be resumed, at least not to the same tune. Too much had happened in the meantime, and too much was still happening. Not only could the Revolution not be unmade, but Revolution as a possible kind of political action would henceforth always be present in the European consciousness as a promise and a threat. Alfred de Musset, who mirrors in his work the unease and the latent violence of the generation which grew to maturity in the aftermath of the Napoleonic era, expressed the matter well when he said in his *Confession d'un Enfant du Siècle* (1836) that Napoleon parodied king-

From *Nationalism* by Elie Kedourie. Copyright © 1960 by Elie Kedourie. Rev. ed., Frederick A. Praeger, 1961.

ship and destroyed it. In the past, de Musset wrote, it happened that individual kings showed that countenance of terror which incited the people to fall on them and tear them like savage dogs; but it was only during the Revolution and the Empire, he observed, that all the pillars of society, without exception, the kings, the nobles, the Church, manifested all at the same time that loss of nerve, those fatal signs of fear which irrevocably lost them everything. Napoleon had come and gone; the victorious Powers tried to ensure that he would never return, and to undo all that he did, but the kind of policy Napoleon pursued was a standing example to anybody who had ambition and ability to imitate him, and Napoleonic traditions would always have an appeal to those sections of European society which his opportunism had, at different times, led him to court and favour. One feature, in particular, of Napoleonic policies is highly pertinent to the later spread of nationalism. While still a general, serving under the Directory, in 1796–7, Bonaparte invaded Italy and occupied Venice; the better to tame the Venetian Senate, he sent emissaries to the Ionian Islands, then under Venetian rule, among them a "distinguished man of letters" whose duty was to "manufacture manifestoes" in order "to stir up the shades of Sparta and Athens," to raise up the inhabitants against their masters by reminding them of the ancient glories of Greece, and exhorting them to resuscitate these glories. As Emperor, Napoleon continued the same tactics. Quarrelling with the Habsburg Emperor in 1809, he issued a proclamation to the Hungarians saying: "You have national customs and a national language; you boast of a distant and illustrious origin: take up then once again your existence as a nation. Have a king of your choice, who will rule only for you, who will live in the midst of you, whom only your citizens and your soldiers will serve. . . . Meet therefore in a National Diet, in the manner of your ancestors . . . and let me know your decisions." When he decided to invade Russia he enlisted the aid of the Poles in his enterprise, by promising to restore the Polish state, and by actually setting up the Grand Duchy of Warsaw. "Show yourselves worthy of your forefathers," he said to a Polish deputation, "they ruled the House of Brandenburg, they were the masters of Moscow, they took the fortress of Widdin, they freed Christianity from the yoke of the Turks." He set up the Kingdom of Italy, and his coadjutor Murat, whom he made King of Naples, at the last minute, to escape the retribution of the Allies in 1815, attempted to gain Italian support against Austrian arms by proclaiming the unity and independence of Italy. The Austrian commander in Italy might exhort the Italian to pay no heed to these chimeras: "What makes a people happy?" he asked. "It is not to form an extensive and populous nation. It is good laws, the preservation of ancient traditions, and a thrifty administration." But even though Napoleon was defeated, and the old masters reinstated, the hopes of political power which he had aroused in so many would not be forgotten; should favouring circumstances ever arise, the hopes could again be fanned into a flame.

This was one reason why, in spite of the efforts of the victorious Powers, Europe in 1815 could not take up once again the way of life .interrupted in 1789. There were others. At the same time as this upheaval was taking place in the political habits of the continent, its social structure was being radically transformed. The Industrial Revolution, accompanied by a prodigious increase in population, was gradually penetrating everywhere, transforming methods of production, disturbing traditional social relations and creating vast urban agglomerations. New wealth was being created and new social classes were coming to the top who would, sooner or later, claim and obtain their share of political power. To the new classes politics presented themselves in a guise different from that familiar to the absolute monarchs and the nobility in whose hands lay the destiny of Europe in the eighteenth century. To these, the countries they ruled were a personal and family concern; their family relations and combinations extended all over Europe regardless of linguistic and religious differences, or of international frontiers, and they were as powerful a factor as any in deciding the fate of a country or a province. In contrast to them, the new social classes had no such ties to claim their attention and loyalty. That German-speaking lands should be parcelled out among a multitude of kings, princes, and other lesser sovereignties may have seemed natural to some of the negotiators at Vienna in 1815; the claims they were accustomed to deal with were dynastic and familial, reinforced or weakened by military preponderance or inferiority; once, therefore, the Napoleonic structure was demolished, they found it reasonable to revert to the earlier systems. But what had seemed before 1789 an established order of things, began increasingly to look an absurd anachronism. If Napoleon was able to arrange and rearrange at will the map of Europe, then no ancient prescription, no dynastic tie, had any claim to stand in the way of more rational and natural arrangements.

Europe after 1815 then was destined to a long period of unrest. The victors did their best to ensure that the settlement they devised would be lasting, but the turmoil bequeathed from revolutionary and Napoleonic times, and the inexorable social changes, acting separately or jointly, always threatened, and in the end overthrew the 1815 settlement. Those who opposed it did so on the ground that it took no account of the wishes of the peoples, that rulers were imposed on subjects who had not been consulted, and that territories which were naturally one were artificially separated. The two grievances were entwined with each other, both of them indeed the outcome of philosophical speculations which had preceded and accompanied the French Revolution. Of course this is not to say that every nationalist and every libertarian in revolt against the arrangements of the Congress of Vienna was competent to explain on what metaphysical grounds he believed that men had the right to decide who was to govern them, and that humanity was divided, naturally, into nations. These ideas became the commonplaces of radicalism on the continent, and young men, university students, in Italy, Germany, and Central Europe found it reasonable to believe in these things, and heroic to be enrolled in a secret society dedicated to Liberty and Nationality. Joseph Mazzini (1805–1872), son of a worthy Genoese family, destined by his parents to a respectable professional career, came, in the 1820's, while still a student, to be enrolled in the secret society of the Carbonari, to dabble in conspiracy, and handle subversive prints, to carry out secret missions on the orders of persons quite unknown to him, and as to whose real aims he was completely ignorant, eventually to be picked up by the police, and sent to gaol in a fortress, thereafter to spend a lifetime of poverty and exile, always engaged in feeble conspiracy and wordy exhortation. . . . Why should a young man of respectable family, in comfortable circumstances, . . . expose himself to the unwelcome attentions of authority? He was living under a government which, as governments go, was not really intolerable: it did not levy ruinous taxation, it did not conscript soldiers, it did not maintain concentration camps, and it left its subjects pretty much to their own devices. It was perhaps somewhat obscurantist and cumbersome but, as Mazzini himself says, it had not sufficient capacity for tyranny. It is not here that we must seek for an explanation of young Mazzini's behaviour. It is rather to be found in Mazzini himself, in a spiritual restlessness which he shared with his generation, which made him and his fellows dissatisfied with things as they were, and prodigiously eager for change. The generation which was born during the Empire, de Musset said, was "passionate, pale, restless." They had been nurtured in constant commotion, and lived in daily expectation of change, eager for new excitements, and sceptical of stability and rest. . . .

The restlessness of this generation surrounded those legendary times of the Revolution and the Empire with a haze of glory, and the political methods which they introduced had now the glamour and headiness of the forbidden. Extra-legal action became infinitely seductive, and conspiracies, riots, infernal machines were invested with an efficacy for which doctrine, not experience, provided the warrant. "Insurrection," say the *Instructions for the members of Young Italy*, the secret society which Mazzini founded in 1831, "—by means of guerilla bands—is the true method of warfare for all nations desirous of emancipating themselves from a foreign yoke. . . . It forms the military education of the people, and consecrates every foot of the native soil by the memory of some warlike deed." "Guerilla warfare," we read in the *Rules for the Conduct of Guerilla Bands*, which he composed, "opens a field of activity for every local capacity; forces the enemy into an unaccustomed method of battle; avoids the evil consequences of a great defeat; secures the national war from the risk of treason, and has the advantage of not confining it within any defined and determinate basis of operations. It is invincible, indestructible." This is a rousing and a heady doctrine, but neither then nor later did it lead to success. Conspiracies and agitations by students and ex-students led to nothing much. Italian independence was achieved by the persistent ambition of the House of Savoy and the muddled policies of Napoleon III who thought it worth while to go to war with Austria on its behalf; German unity was the work of Bismarck, who was not a nationalist, but a promoter of Prussian interests; Balkan nationalisms could show results only because they were adopted by the Russian State which sought thereby to encroach on the Ottoman domain; Arab nationalism has found resonance and extension as a result of British policies which sought to prosecute a long-standing rivalry with France, and to eliminate the influence of other great Powers from the Middle East; and it was Japan's help and encouragement which enabled Indonesian and Burmese nationalists to set up a political and military organization whereby to wrest control, in the chaos following the Second World War, from the old imperial Powers. Where nationalists found no Power effectively to espouse their cause their conspiracies and insurrections very often came to nought. This is what happened to the Hungarians in 1848, to the Poles in their risings in 1831, 1846, and 1863, and to the Armenians of the Ottoman Empire at the end of the nineteenth century.

But the restlessness was the work not only of the revolutionary legend; it proceeded from a breakdown in the transmission of political habits and religious beliefs from one generation to the next. In societies suddenly exposed to the new learning and the new philosophies of the Enlightenment and of Romanticism, orthodox settled ways began to seem ridiculous and useless. The attack was powerful and left the old generation bewildered and speechless; or if it attempted to speak, it merely gave voice to irritated admonition, obstinate opposition, or horror-stricken rejection, which only served to widen the rift and increase the distance between the fathers and the sons. . . .

This violent revolt against immemorial restraints, this strident denunciation of decorum and measure, was inevitably accompanied by powerful social strains which may explain the dynamic and violent character of nationalist movements. These movements are ostensibly directed against the foreigner, the outsider, but they are also the manifestation of a species of civil strife between the generations; nationalist movements are children's crusades; their very names are manifestoes against old age: Young Italy, Young Egypt, the Young Turks, the Young Arab Party. When they are stripped of their metaphysics and their slogans—and these cannot adequately account for the frenzy they conjure up in their followers—such movements are seen to satisfy a need, to fulfill a want. Put at its simplest, the need is to belong together in a coherent and stable community. Such a need is normally satisfied by the family, the neighbourhood, the religious community. In the last century and a half such institutions all over the world have had to bear the brunt of violent social and intellectual change, and it is no accident that nationalism was at its most intense where and when such institutions had little resilience and were ill-prepared to withstand the powerful attacks to which they became exposed. This seems a more satisfactory account than to say that nationalism is a middle-class movement. It is the case that the German inventors of nationalist doctrine came from a class which could be called the middle class, and that they were discontented with the old order in which the nobility was predominant. But the term middle class is closely tied to a particular area and a particular history, that of Western Europe. It presupposes and implies a distinct social order of which feudalism, municipal franchises, and rapid industrial development are some of the prominent features. Such features are not found in all societies, and it would therefore be misleading to link the existence of a nationalist movement to that of a middle class. In countries of the Middle and the Far East, for instance, where the significant division in society was between those who belonged to the state institution and those who did not, nationalism cannot be associated with the existence of a middle class. It developed, rather, among young officers and bureaucrats, whose families were sometimes obscure, sometimes eminent, who were educated in Western methods and ideas, often at the expense of the State, and who as a result came to despise their elders, and to hanker for the shining purity of a new order to sweep away the hypocrisy, the corruption, the decadence which they felt inexorably choking them and their society.

This breakdown in the transmission of political experience explains why nationalist movements run to extremes. Political wisdom is not to be gathered in the drab, arid world in which we actually live, it is to be culled from books of philosophy. . . . Literature and philosophy gave entrance to a nobler, truer world, a world more real and more exciting than the actual world; and gradually the boundary between the world of imagination and the world of reality became blurred, and sometimes disappeared altogether. What was possible in books ought to be possible in reality. The reading of books became a political, a revolutionary, activity. Thus, many a young man found himself advancing from the composition of poems to the manufacture of infernal machines; thus, in the intoxication of a poetic dream, Adam Mickiewicz found himself imploring God to bring about universal war in which Poland might once again secure independence. Politics could indeed be exciting, as exciting as the wonderful speculations of Schelling and Fichte. Mean provincial towns where nothing ever happens, dusty libraries, prosaic lecture-rooms became the stage of an absorbing secret game, a game of hide-and-seek, in which nothing was as it seemed, and everything took on the glowing colours of romance. Such are the delights of conspiracy. Occasionally, of course, the drabness would break in, and there would be policemen, arrests, prison, or exile. The enclosed, secret universe of plot and conspiracy would begin to exercise an obsessive compulsion of its own, from which escape was hopeless; what started as a poetic dream would be enacted with inexorable logic as a living nightmare, in which pistols did really go off, and dynamite did really explode; where men were caught up in a web of suspicion and treason, and today's executioner became tomorrow's victim. . . .

The musings of the young men dwelt on two grievances: that governments were not popular, and that they were not national. It could, of course, be reasonably argued that governments were not popular because they were not national, that because governments were controlled by foreigners, they could not minister to the welfare of the ruled. The converse of this could also be argued, namely, that once governments became national, they would come under the control of the citizens and become agencies for their welfare. This notion that national government meant popular government was made plausible by the settlement of 1815. The victorious Powers not only restored dynasties to their thrones, ignoring "national" boundaries and "national" units, as these came to be understood by European radicals, but they also declared their enmity to the principles proclaimed by the Revolution. They proscribed representative institutions and restored privileges abolished by the Revolutionaries. It was thought to follow therefore that if the 1815 settlement were overthrown, then not only would nations assume their natural sovereign rights, but also that democratic ideas would triumph, and that these sovereign nations would practise Liberty, Equality, and Fraternity. War would then disappear, for all these nations would be, *ipso facto*, pacific and just. These commonplaces of nationalist thinking in the first half of the nineteenth century can be followed in Mazzini's writings. A nation, he writes, "is a larger or smaller aggregate of human beings bound together into an organic whole by agreement in a certain number of real particulars, such as race, physiognomy, historic tradition, intellectual peculiarities, or active tendencies." Nations, Mazzini believed, exist according to a divine design which evil governments have disfigured. "They have disfigured it," he says, "by their conquests, their greed, and their jealousy even of the righteous power of others." "We are not only conspirators," he writes in a note on the organization of Young Italy, the secret society he founded, "but believers. We aspire to be not only revolutionists; but so far as we may, regenerators." "The peoples," he also wrote, "will only reach the highest point of development of which they are capable when they are united in a single bond. . . . Young Italy recognizes therefore the universal association of the peoples as the ultimate aim of the endeavours of all free men. . . . Before they can become members of the great association," however, "it is necessary that they should have a separate existence, name and power. Every people is therefore bound to constitute itself a nation before it can occupy itself with the question of humanity."

But of course it was not, it could not be, as simple as that, if only because of another commonplace nationalist attitude: "Avoid compromises," lays down Mazzini, "they are almost always immoral as well as dangerous." For if there is a divine plan which divides humanity into nations, which evil governments have disfigured, there must be no truck with evil. The relation between a country and its foreign ruler must always take the shape of a "desperate struggle." "Desperate struggle" is not kind to political liberties, and a hatred of compromise can easily turn into a hatred of those who may be suspected of compromise. It is a well-known feature of recent history that nationalist parties kill members of their own nationality whom they suspect of an inclination to compromise, and in some cases a greater number of these than of the foreigners against whom the struggle is waged fall to the assassin's bullet. . . . The grievances of the subject areas were national grievances; they were ruled by a government alien in language and religion. But their chequered history since independence suggests that national freedom is no guarantee against oppressive and iniquitous government. New ruling classes replaced the evicted Ottomans, and found extreme difficulty in ruling humanely and effectively. Neither did the formation of these national states conduce, as Mazzini hoped, to international peace. It may, of course, be argued, as the poet Wordsworth argued, that native oppression is preferable to foreign oppression. "The difference between inbred oppression and that which is from without is *essential*," he observed in *The Convention of Cintra* (1809), "inasmuch as the former does not exclude from the minds of the people a feeling of being self-governed; does not imply (as the latter does, when patiently submitted to) an abandonment of the first duty imposed by the faculty of reason." The argument is plainly sophistical, but it does recognize, by implication, as Mazzini's does not, the truth established by experience, namely, that the triumph of the national principle does not necessarily entail the triumph of liberty.

A variant of Mazzini's argument has found great vogue in recent decades in Asiatic and African countries. This variant depends on an economic interpretation of history. It is to the effect that European Powers in search of markets and cheap raw materials have imposed their direct domination or indirect influence on these areas overseas and have thus distorted their political development, stunted their economies and insulted the human dignity of their inhabitants. It is also widely argued that the liberation of these countries from European rule makes possible the creation of free societies which would bring fulfilment and contentment to their citizens. But the economic foundation on which this theory rests serves to make the domination of Europe overseas seem both tentacular and intangible. For the domination, it is argued, does not always rest on naked force: the sinister power of money holds in its grip countries outwardly independent, and rulers seemingly patriotic; and full independence with all its blessings will only come when indirect as well as direct domination will have disappeared. This variant exhibits with particular clarity the fallacy of associating national independence with efficient, humane, and just government. It is manifestly not European domination which created poverty, technical backwardness, overpopulation, or habits of despotism in Asia and Africa—it is these rather which made possible European rule overseas; and it is not the departure of European rulers—after so brief a dominion—which will change the nature of these territories, transform their poverty into wealth, or suddenly create probity in judges, moderation and public spirit in statesmen, or honesty in public servants. The truth is that good government depends as much on circumstances as on a desire for freedom and there are regions of the globe which may never know its blessings. But it is characteristic of doctrines such as self-determination to disregard the limits imposed by nature and history, and to believe that a good will alone can accomplish miracles.

In fact, it is these countries which most clearly show that nationalism and liberalism far from being twins are really antagonistic principles. In these countries, constitutionalism is unknown. Their political tradition is either a centralized despotism, which, as a method of government, has shown itself extraordinarily resilient and durable, or a fragmented tribalism which has withered and fossilized as it has come in contact with European rule. In the first case, the central mechanism of power is all-important, since to get hold of it is to acquire mastery over the whole of society. Machiavelli remarked in *The Prince* that a conqueror might easily gain possession of a country like France, but find it very troublesome to keep, since it contained many divergent interests and sectional loyalties, not easily reconciled or subdued. A state like the Ottoman Empire, on the other hand, would be most difficult to conquer, but once conquered the subjects would be submissive and quite easy to govern: "The Turkish Empire," as he says, "is governed by a sole Prince, all others being his slaves. Dividing his kingdom into sandjaks, he sends thither different governors whom he shifts and changes at his pleasure. The King of France, on the other hand, is surrounded by a multitude of nobles of ancient descent, each acknowledged and loved by subjects of his own, and each asserting a precedence in rank of which the King can deprive him only at his peril." Once, therefore, the Sultan's army is defeated "no cause of anxiety would remain, except in the family of the Prince, which being extirpated, there would be none else to fear." The same explanation holds for the success and frequency of coups d'état in despotisms, as well as for the phenomenal spread of nationalism in them in modern times.

In such countries, if the official classes, or a significant number among them, are converted to nationalism, they may easily take over and mould the state in the image of their doctrine. In such a situation the doctrine operates to make despotism more perfect and more solidly anchored. Old-fashioned despots had neither the means nor the inclination to obtain the internal assent of their subjects; for them, external obedience was enough. But since the essence of nationalism is that the will of the individual should merge in the will of the nation, nationalist rulers in Oriental despotisms seek internal as well as external obedience. Such obedience they are now more than ever in a position to obtain, thanks to modern techniques of bureaucratic control and mass communications. The Indian poet Tagore in his *Nationalism* (1917)—a book concerned not with nationalism but with European influences on Eastern government—describes and bemoans in language, the nostalgic exaggeration of which is itself testimony to the powerful and disturbing impact of Western ideas and techniques on Oriental society, the contrast between the old dispensation and the new: "Through all the fights and intrigues and deceptions of her earlier history India has remained aloof. Because her homes, her fields, her temples of worship, her schools, where her teachers and students lived together in the atmosphere of simplicity and devotion and learning, her village self-government with its simple laws and peaceful administration—all these truly belonged to her. But her thrones were not her concern. They passed over her head like clouds, now tinged with purple gorgeousness, now black with the threat of thunder. Often they brought devastation in their wake, but they were like catastrophes of nature, whose traces are soon forgotten." Now, he continues, it is different; the government of British India "is an applied science and therefore more or less similar in its principles wherever it is used. It is like a hydraulic press, whose pressure is impersonal and on that account completely effective. The amount of its power may vary in different engines. Some may even be driven by hand, thus leaving a margin of comfortable looseness in their tension, but in spirit and method their differences are small. Our government might have been Dutch, or French, or Portuguese, and its essential features would have remained much the same as they are now. Only perhaps, in some cases, the organisation might not have been so densely perfect, and therefore, some shreds of the human might still have been clinging to the wreck, allowing us to deal with something which resembles our own throbbing heart." Tagore concedes that all governments have something of the mechanical in them, but the difference between modern government on Western lines and government in the old style is like that between the hand-loom and the power-loom: "In the products of the hand-loom the magic of man's living fingers finds its expression and its hum harmonises with the music of life. But the power-loom is relentlessly lifeless and accurate and monotonous in its production."

•   •   •

Nationalist politics find scope, not only where foreigners rule a particular country, but also in regions of mixed population. One such region is Central and Eastern Europe. Here the German-speaking group is one of the most important. This group occupied not only the territory now known as Germany and Austria, but extended still further. German populations remained as residues of the conquests of the knightly Orders who advanced east in the Middle Ages; Germans had also settled later as colonists to people empty provinces and to introduce crafts and manufactures; so that in the nineteenth century scattered German settlements extended from the Gulf of Finland and the Baltic down to the Adriatic, and from the Bohemian mountains to the steppes of Russia. According to nationalist doctrine, all these Germans ought to form one nation and belong to the same state. Such an ambition could not but raise the most awkward problems, as appeared soon enough in the Revolution of 1848. This Revolution occurred almost simultaneously in the early spring of 1848 in Berlin, Vienna, and some of the smaller German states, and almost immediately met with a complete, if short-lived, success. In the first flush of their triumph, the revolutionaries decided to convoke an Imperial German Parliament at Frankfurt to reform the political state of Germany, to give it a new democratic constitution, and to prepare some measure of union, so that the grievous harm which, the nationalists held, resulted from the division of German lands among so many rulers, could be undone. A thorny issue came soon to confront the Frankfurt Parliament. Poland was partitioned between Russia, Austria, and Prussia. The Poles of Prussian Poland, taking advantage of the Revolution, asked for a measure of autonomy in the areas where they predominated. But among them lived a minority of Germans, and if autonomy were granted to the Poles, those Germans would have to live under a local government administered by Poles, and the Frankfurt Parliament had to indicate its view on the matter. There ought, really, to have been no doubt at all, since national freedom was one of the principles vindicated by the Revolution of 1848—and the Poles were universally recognized as a nationality. But when the matter came to be raised in the Frankfurt Parliament there was great opposition to these Polish pretensions. Jordan, a delegate from Berlin, sitting on the left, exclaimed: "Are half a million Germans to live under a German government and administration and form part of the great German Fatherland, or are they to be relegated to the inferior position of naturalized foreigners subject to another nation of lesser cultural content than themselves?" It was wrong to acquiesce in the Polish demands, for, he said, "it was necessary to awaken a healthy national egotism without which no people can grow into a nation." "Mere existence," he asserted, "does not entitle a people to political independence: only the force to assert itself as a state among the others."

The same problem arose with regard to Bohemia. Bohemia was part of the Habsburg Empire which was represented at the Imperial German Diet established by the Congress of Vienna. Representatives from Bohemia were therefore invited to the Frankfurt Parliament. The Czechs, however, who were the majority in Bohemia, refused to send representatives, for they pointed out that the Frankfurt Parliament claimed to represent the German nation, and they themselves were not Germans. The Germans of Bohemia, of course, sent their own representatives. But, if a state comprising the whole German nation were to be set up, would Bohemia remain outside this state, and with Bohemia a part, an integral part, of the German nation? No, it was contended; for though Bohemia was full of Czechs, it was part of the German Fatherland: "We must adhere," said the old nationalist Arndt, "to the principle that what has been ours for a thousand years . . . must remain ours . . . we must protect those Germans even if greatly outnumbered by the Czechs; and deputies from Bohemia, however few, must be deemed fully to represent the country." The leaders of the Czechs, in answer to these pretensions, organized a Slavonic Congress which met in Prague and issued a manifesto to the nations of Europe, in which they vindicated the equal rights of all nationalities. "Nature," they proclaimed, "in and for herself draws no distinction between nations as though some were noble and others ignoble; she has not called any one nation to dominate over others, nor set aside any nation to serve another as an instrument for that other's ends. An equal right on the part of all to the noblest attributes of humanity is a divine law which none can violate with impunity."

Nationalism, then, does not make easy the relations of different groups in mixed areas. Since it advocates a recasting of frontiers and a redistribution of political power to conform with the demands of a particular nationality, it tends to disrupt whatever equilibrium had been reached between different groups, to reopen settled questions and to renew strife. Because their claims are uncompromising nationalists must always cast about for opportunities to reopen an issue which, for the time being, they might consent to consider closed. Far from increasing political stability and political liberty, nationalism in mixed areas makes for tension and mutual hatred. The assertion of German nationality in 1848 was found to involve the necessity of Czechs and Poles never acquiring a comparable national status. In later years, after Bismarck had founded the Reich, the claim to bring into one national state all the Germans in Central Europe continued to be expressed, and was known as Pan-Germanism; and it was, of course, with Pan-German arguments that Hitler justified his dealings with Austria, Czechoslovakia, and Poland. The German question in Central and Eastern Europe is, however, only one of the many questions created, in a way, by nationalist doctrine. But in what sense can one speak of political problems being created by the spread of a doctrine? Doctrines do not create mixed areas, or the relation of superior and inferior, or of dominant group and subject group. These, certainly, were the realities of Central and Eastern Europe: a medley of races, languages, and religions under imperial rule. This situation was the result of no doctrine—but, if a doctrine such as nationalism does capture the intellectual and political leaders of one group, and they proceed to act according to its tenets, then the same doctrine must spread to other groups, who will feel impelled, in the face of threatening claims, to adopt it for their own use. Historic quarrels are revived, old humiliations recalled, and compromises disowned. It is a chain reaction, a vicious circle. It is in this sense that one may speak of nationalism creating a problem in Central and Eastern Europe.

It has sometimes been argued that since nationalism seeks to preserve a particular national language and culture, nationalist demands may be satisfied and nationalists may be disarmed by an imperial government conceding autonomy in cultural matters to the different nations under its rule. Thus, the Austrian Social Democrats, Otto Bauer and Karl Renner, anxious to preserve the unity of Austria-Hungary, and to transform it into a socialist state, imagined schemes whereby national groups, whether concentrated in one particular territory or scattered throughout the whole Empire, should have their cultural affairs managed by their own national institutions, while economic and political matters would be managed by a single supra-national government. But such attempts to stem the tide of nationalist discontents are seldom successful, since nationalists consider that political and cultural matters are inseparable, and that no culture can live if it is not endowed with a sovereign state exclusively its own. Such attempts only result in artistic, literary, and linguistic matters becoming the subject of acrimonious political disputes, and in being used as weapons in the nationalist struggle. In fact, cultural, linguistic, and religious autonomy for the different groups of a heterogeneous empire is practicable only when it does not rest upon, or is justified by, nationalist doctrine; such autonomy remained possible in the Ottoman Empire for several centuries—the arrangement being known as the *millet* system—precisely because nationalism was unknown, and broke down when the doctrine spread among the different groups of the Empire. The *millet* system broke down because such limited autonomy could not satisfy nationalist ambitions, while at the same time, limited as it was, it came to seem to the ruling institution dangerously disruptive of the Empire. These factors always render cultural autonomy by itself a precarious and illusory settlement of nationalist demands.

JOHN U. NEF

Cultural Foundations
of Industrial Civilization

When we in the twentieth century use the phrase "civilization," as in our discussions of Western or non-Western civilizations, we mean the whole complex of ideas, values, and institutions of a given society or group of societies. John U. Nef, American professor of economic history, points out in this selection that the phrase "civilization" is of recent origin. It cannot be traced back beyond the mid-eighteenth century.

At that time, in the wake of the cruel and devastating religious wars of the seventeenth century, this phrase came to be used to describe the improvement of manners between human beings, the practice of decency and seemliness, the condition of being "civil" to others in spite of political or religious differences. There was a revulsion against "atrocities" among men and nations, and a resulting attempt to impose limitations on the use of violence. This new outlook on violence, Professor Nef contends, is an important aspect of Europe's modern history. Henceforth cruel physical treatment was not accepted as inevitable. The qualities of civilization as thus defined "gave birth to the novel concept of universal humanity that transcends nations, races and even forms of religious worship."

Dr. Nef, born in 1899, and an authority on the sixteenth century, is professor of economic history at the University of Chicago, with which he has been associated since 1929. He is the author of several books in English and French, among them The United States and Civilization, 1942, and War and Human Progress, 1950. The volume from which this selection is taken was compiled from the second series of Wiles lectures at Queens University, Belfast.

Chapter 3
The Origin of Civilization

2. *Limitations on Violence Before Modern Times*

WHAT HELD societies back from the total use of force for the sake of conquest until after the sixteenth century was not mainly any written or unwritten renunciation of total war as an instrument of policy, or any nice feelings about the baseness of the deliberate infliction of physical pain. It was the establishment of absolute authority by armed conquest. The immediate world, subject to conquest, *could* then be conquered, because the weapons were not powerful enough, as they have now become, to destroy a large portion of the life of this planet. The most striking example perhaps was the peace within the ancient Roman Empire. Rome attained for a period of almost three centuries virtually complete dominion over the countries of the Mediterranean basin and over Europe as far as the Rhine and the Danube. The Roman peace resulted from the principle of total conquest, implemented by a series of total victories, in which the conquered were made subject peoples. This process culminated in 146 B.C. with the Roman victory over Carthage in the third Punic War. The peace within the frontiers of the Empire was not a peace of free men. For all the laws established by the Romans, with their genius as lawmakers, it was a peace of enslaved peoples.

The spread of Christianity through Europe, which began in the era of the Roman peace, produced a new kind of unity, spiritual in origin. Until the times of the Crusades, which began at the end of the eleventh century, when the papacy was growing more powerful politically than it had ever been before, this unity was not founded on force. But it was only a partial unity. With the growth of the power of the papacy from the mid-eleventh to the thirteenth century, the Church was in a position to extend its authority in an effort to restrict armed conflicts. The canon law, elaborated during that period of great ecclesiastical strength and prestige, set limits to war by defining a just war, by prohibiting the use of certain weapons, such as the crossbow, which Christians might legitimately use in fighting fellow Christians, and by making it illegal to wage war on certain days, in certain places, and in respect of certain persons. (For instance, priests were forbidden to take part in fighting.)

From *Cultural Foundations of Industrial Civilization* by John U. Nef. Cambridge University Press, 1958.

These measures were not entirely ineffective. At the beginning of the nineteenth century, when many Europeans looked back with deep distrust on the age of faith in the twelfth and thirteenth centuries, one of them, the Comte de Saint-Simon, an apostle of modern progress, wrote a pamphlet on ways of preventing a recurrence of the Napoleonic wars. He turned to medieval Europe for guidance. As long as an allegiance to the sovereign principle of religious unity and universal government through the Church subsisted, he remarked, "there were few wars in Europe and these wars had little importance."

An impression had grown up in some quarters fifty years before the time of Saint-Simon, that the later Middle Ages were marked by a remarkable improvement among the Europeans in their personal and political relations, that men and women became much less brutal and rude. On the eve of the religious wars, from 1519 to 1555, much of Europe was under the political sovereignty of the Emperor Charles V. The Scottish historian William Robertson was among the first to attempt a general account of conditions under Charles V's rule. He wrote with enthusiasm of the "improvement in policy and manners which the Europeans" had then attained. A reader of the long introduction in which these words appear gets the impression that between the early eleventh and the early sixteenth centuries, the Europeans had taken the major steps in the advance from what Robertson calls "barbarism" to what he calls "refinement."

•   •   •

How far does the new historical knowledge acquired since Robertson wrote support his thesis that Europe advanced from "barbarism to refinement" during the five centuries preceding the Reformation? There had been, certainly, immense improvement in material wealth. Early sixteenth-century Europe—with its hundreds of towns (many dependent for economic existence on the surrounding country for distances of scores of miles), with its industrial machinery driven by horse, wind and water power, with its cathedrals and monasteries, town halls, princely palaces and mansions of the nobility and of rich merchants, with its extensive international trade in luxury wares, in wines and even in some heavy commodities such as salt and wrought iron—was a sophisticated world compared with early eleventh-century Europe. In the interval the Europeans had developed codes of law and methods of administration, both lay and ecclesiastical, accompanied by appropriate conventions and forms which facilitated political and judicial as well as economic relationships.

But had there been any notable movement towards tenderness in the ways human beings treated each other in their daily lives? Had there been any lessening of the brutal treatment of enemies and non-combatants in war? Those are not questions which Robertson attempts to answer. If he had had at his disposal the vastly increased material since made available by historical research, he could hardly have answered confidently with a glowing affirmative. By comparison with the customs familiar to us in our childhood before the First World War, the manners of our Christian ancestors in Europe in the relatively peaceful times which impressed the Comte de Saint-Simon were far from tender.

The waging of relentless war, pursued with fiendish cruelty beyond the battlefields, was never outlawed even by the medieval Church when people outside the Roman Catholic community were involved. Killing, as well as dying for Christ, and killing in most terrible ways were accepted instruments of Church policy, sanctioned by the papacy in the Crusades.

During the previous five hundred years the heathen invaders of Western Europe—in the ninth and tenth centuries the Arabs, the Magyars and the Norsemen—had set sorry examples in waging war—burning peaceful villages and slaughtering women and children. It is possible therefore to represent the Europeans, in the efforts which followed to conquer the Holy Land, as having replied in what they convinced themselves, in the heat of long marches, hunger and battles, was the only language that unchristian peoples could understand. But alas for this interpretation, there seem to have been numerous occasions in which they went beyond their teachers. According to Steven Runciman, the latest thorough historian of the Crusades, the Christian armies in the Near East outdid their adversaries when it came to what we Americans and Europeans were brought up to regard as atrocities against civilians. This was true even of the first Crusade which had begun with so much genuine religious enthusiasm. In the struggles that followed the Crusades in Europe itself, the same language of pitiless slaughter which, in the name of religion, had once been at least officially reserved for heathen enemies in war, was extended to persons born Christians who were judged to have strayed from orthodoxy.

The relatively peaceful conditions that impressed the Comte de Saint-Simon in thirteenth-century Europe, rested to no small degree on the immense authority and power of the medieval papacy. They rested partly on the way in which the belligerent instincts of the Europeans had been directed temporarily by the Church in the direction of the heathen inhabitants of the Near East. They did not rest on the voluntary acceptance of a principle of limited war, based on civil laws and customs. They did not rest upon tender manners, upon the actual practice in lay life of love and charity. Although the ideals of love and charity had been given an incomparable spiritual strength by the Saviour, they had hardly passed beyond the boundaries of the city of God, partly realized long after Saint Augustine's time in the monasteries and churches. What the religious attempted to do, and could only do most imperfectly, was to shut themselves off from the temporal instincts and desires that are an integral and inevitable part of material existence in the actual world of sense experiences. Theirs was an heroic effort to redeem their fellow human beings from their sins by acts of renunciation and self-abnegation. This was something different from trying to infuse charity and love into the thoughts and actions to which natural instincts and desires give rise and so to temper the violence which human beings inflict on one another.

Once the religious unity enforced by a strong papacy was undermined—as it was already to a considerable extent in the fourteenth century, with the great schism, with the rival popes—warfare in Europe again became endemic. The ferocity of rival armies shows how thin and ineffectual under stress the rules of chivalry, which we associate with medieval knighthood, could become. Let us take almost at random a selection from Sir John Froissart's story of the Hundred Years War. He is describing the siege of Ghent carried on by an army from the adjacent country of Flanders. Ghent was one of the most advanced towns of the fourteenth century in its economic prosperity, and the whole area in which this fighting took place may almost be called in an economic sense, the heart of medieval Europe, because it was for a time the greatest centre of the most important of medieval industries, the textile industry.

> As soon as the earl [of Flanders] arrived at the square before the church, and found that the men of Ghent had retreated into it, he ordered the building to be set on fire; large quantities of straw and faggots were brought, and being placed all round the church and lighted, the flames soon ascended to the roof. The destruction of the Ghent men was now inevitable; for if they stayed in the church they were sure to be burnt, and if they attempted to sally out they were as sure to be slain, and thrown back into the fire. John de Launoy, who was in the steeple, perceiving that he must soon be destroyed, for the steeple itself was beginning to take fire, cried out to those below, "Ransom! Ransom!" and offered his coat, which was full of florins; but they only laughed at him, and said in reply, "John, come and speak to us through the windows, and we will receive you. Make a handsome leap, John, such as you have forced our friends to take this year." John thought for a moment, and then, preferring being slain to being burnt, leaped out of the window; however, both these disasters happened to him; for his enemies received him as he fell upon the points of their

spears, and after hacking him to pieces, flung him back into the flames. Of the 6000 men—of which, to say the least, the army under Rasse de Harzelle and John de Launoy consisted—not more than 300 escaped; the rest were either slain in the field or in the town, or burnt in the church.

This is hardly an inspiring example of limited warfare, or of the respect which near neighbours felt for each other as fellow Christians when they took to fighting. With many such examples before us, we are led to the conclusion that it was less the inadequacy of the will to kill, than the inadequacy of the means, with small armies and backward weapons, that prevented a widespread holocaust among the Christian peoples themselves during the later Middle Ages.

Such solidarity as existed in medieval Europe rested ultimately upon the existence of a single Church and the practice of a single worship. And, in the very age of Charles V, the age which Robertson set out to describe in his history, the idea of religious unity which the Church represented was shattered. What John Donne was to write two generations later concerning experience as a whole was true for the central part of experience which the Christian religion still occupied after the Reformation.

> 'Tis all in peeces, all cohaerence gone;
> All just supply, and all Relation. . . .

How could the authority of the Church be invoked to limit war, when large groups of Europeans numbering millions, some sustained by powerful monarchs as in Great Britain and in Sweden, set up churches of their own in opposition to the Roman Catholic Church? For men and women with deep Christian convictions in each group, the men and women of the other groups became heretics, their leaders antichrists. The same view that had prevailed among the Crusaders in their attacks on the infidel was now applied to fellow Europeans, to members of the same nation, of the same town, even of the same family. Violence of every kind was rendered possible with the sanction of the very institution—the Church—which, in the name of the Founder, had made efforts to limit war among men.

When the religious wars broke out in full force in the fifteen-sixties, the Europeans were not equipped with means of extermination at all comparable to those at our disposal today. Yet during the previous seventy years, since the battle of Fornovo in Italy, when horse-drawn artillery was first brought into action, there had been something of a revolution in the methods of waging war. Artillery and smaller firearms had become the decisive weapons. It was much easier to kill in large numbers and at a considerable distance than it had been in the Middle

Ages. The defensive strength of knights in armour had been obliterated. Again, with changes in methods in agriculture, mining and manufacturing, wealth had increased, and it was possible to put much larger armies into action—numbering 30,000 and sometimes even 50,000 men. The human target was enlarged at the same time that the effectiveness of the means of hitting it was much augmented.

When the Emperor Charles V renounced his numerous titles in 1555 and 1556 and retired to the monastery at Juste, there had not been established any general restraints on violence, either in domestic or in public relations, such as existed in the Europe and the North America of our childhood. There had been no apparent diminution in the cruelty, the messiness and the ugly violence with which, under what was regarded as provocation, men got rid of their neighbours. Unless some new ways were discovered for keeping fighting within bounds, now that both the will to fight and the means of fighting had increased in power, the elements were present for a general slaughter. Such a slaughter almost took place in Germany and the rest of central Europe during the Thirty Years War. It is estimated that about a third of the population was wiped out by warfare and its consequences in famine, exposure and massacre.

There had always been humane men like Montaigne who were shocked and saddened by the brutality of their contemporaries. There were on the eve of the Reformation men like Erasmus and Thomas More who hoped something could be done to introduce greater decency into the conduct of life, who sought a temporal world in which violence would have a less prominent place. What we miss in all these "humanists" of the Renaissance is any sense that the deliberate infliction of bodily suffering beyond the field of battle is so grievous an abuse of power that it lies beyond the bounds of accepted conduct. What we miss in Montaigne, writing as he was in the shadow of the French religious wars, is the idea that the human conscience ought never to resign itself to the commission of "atrocities," the idea that unrestrained violence lies beyond the bounds which a decent community, even of independent states and of different religious practices, can ever accept. The word atrocity, as a term for condemning the cruel and heinous conduct of a people, hardly seems to have existed in English before the late eighteenth century. It is this human conscience that we find expressed in Bernanos, in the shock he received from the Spanish Civil War, when he was told by some Spanish officers that it was more Christian to kill than to die for Christ.

It was after the times of Montaigne, then, that a change occurred in the outlook of the Europeans concerning violence. The idea developed that murder and rape were evil in themselves, not simply at the Day of

Judgement, but here and now in the temporal world, even when the victim is a black man, an infidel, an atheist or a heretic. That idea became almost universal during the nineteenth century, if not before, among a substantial part of the peoples who were descendants of those Europeans who were caught in the sixteenth century in the religious wars. For our grandfathers and fathers in countries such as France, Belgium, Switzerland, Great Britain, the British Dominions and the United States, the kinds of cruel physical treatment which Montaigne reported in his letter, which had been common from time immemorial, together with the cruel physical treatment of minorities, were not accepted as inevitable. Public opinion everywhere was trusted by condemning them to reduce their incidence. That is why atrocity stories made such an impression, and aroused such indignation, in France, England and the United States during the First World War. The outlook on the taking of human life had profoundly changed since the sixteenth century. In the times of Thomas More, which is to say at the Reformation, capital punishment could be inflicted in England for almost innumerable offences, including even petty theft. Only a year ago Parliament attempted to abolish the death penalty for any offence whatsoever.

The new outlook on violence, the new sense of human responsibility for decent conduct in this world, seems to be a part of the modern history of Europe. What relation had this improvement in the treatment of man by other men to the coming of industrialism? Before we consider that question, we must seek the origins of the change. We must try to determine the place of the late sixteenth and early seventeenth centuries in bringing it about.

In doing so we must not neglect the contribution of the Christian and even the pagan, which the Europeans inherited at the time of the religious wars. Without a knowledge of the solidarity that existed and was developed among them in the Christian society of the Middle Ages, without a knowledge of the learning and the culture they derived from the ancient Greco-Roman world and the societies of the Near and even the Far East, without perhaps the influence of the relatively decent manners which seem to have prevailed in China during the Sung dynasty (960–1279), the spiritual basis of this modern humaneness is unintelligible. But we have already said something similar about modern science. It is unintelligible without the science of the Renaissance, the science of the Middle Ages, of the Arabs, and especially of the ancient Greeks, of men such as Democritus and Euclid. The history of man's search for the good and the beautiful, and of his efforts to improve human manners, since the age of the Emperor Charles V, does not account at all adequately for the coming of more humane practices concerning violence, any more than the history of thought since Gilbert and Galileo accounts at all adequately for the coming of modern science. But in these lectures we are concerned with the efforts that distinguish modern times from past ages. Were changes comparable to those which revolutionized natural science taking place in faith, in art, in laws, customs and manners, during the decades that followed the beginning of religious wars in Europe?

When we turn for guidance concerning the changes in the outlook on violence to our forebears of the eighteenth century, who tried to see history as a whole rather than as a series of disconnected specialties, we get the impression that fundamental improvements, which we miss in connection with the Europe of Charles V, had occurred two centuries afterwards. We get the impression that a remarkable growth had taken place in the humanity men expressed and felt over killing and torture. We get the impression that the Europeans had found a new conscience before the union of coal and iron, before the union of steam power with manufactures and transport. We get the further impression that the changes in men's hearts and minds had had perhaps more tangible effects in the domestic and the political conduct of the Europeans by the mid-eighteenth century, than the development of a new technology and of new sciences had had upon their industrial life.

If the word atrocity is novel, so is the word civilization. Historical researchers, who have given the matter their attention, have not been able to trace it back beyond the mid-eighteenth century. Perhaps the first writer to use it in a published work was the Marquis de Mirabeau. It occurs in his *L'Ami des Hommes ou Traité de la Population*, which was published in 1757. It has been established that the word had in the beginning, and for some fifty years afterwards, a different meaning from the meanings which Gobineau, Spengler, Toynbee and others have now helped to give it. In another work of Mirabeau's, *L'Ami des Femmes ou Traité de la Civilisation*, which exists only in manuscript, he tells what he meant by it.

> The civilization of a people [he wrote in 1766] is to be found in the softening of manners, in growing urbanity, in politer relations and in the spreading of knowledge in such ways that decency and seemliness are practiced until they transcend specific and detailed laws. . . . Civilization does nothing for society unless it is able to give form and substance to virtue. The concept of humanity is born in the bosom of societies softened by all these ingredients.

"Civilization" clearly included the "refinement," whose coming Robertson identified with the later Middle Ages. But it covered much more. It embraced most of those virtues which enable men to turn their passions towards humane ends which can be achieved only through gentleness. What most of the persons who first used the word seem to have meant by it was a combination of spiritual and moral qualities, at least partly realized in the lives of human beings in society. Among these qualities were decency, propriety, honesty and tenderness, moderation and self-control in speech, in conduct and even in thought. These ingredients, as Mirabeau suggested, gave birth to the novel concept of a universal humanity that transcends nations, races and even forms of religious worship. Europeans coined and employed a new word, because they were describing conditions in the temporal world which they believed were novel.

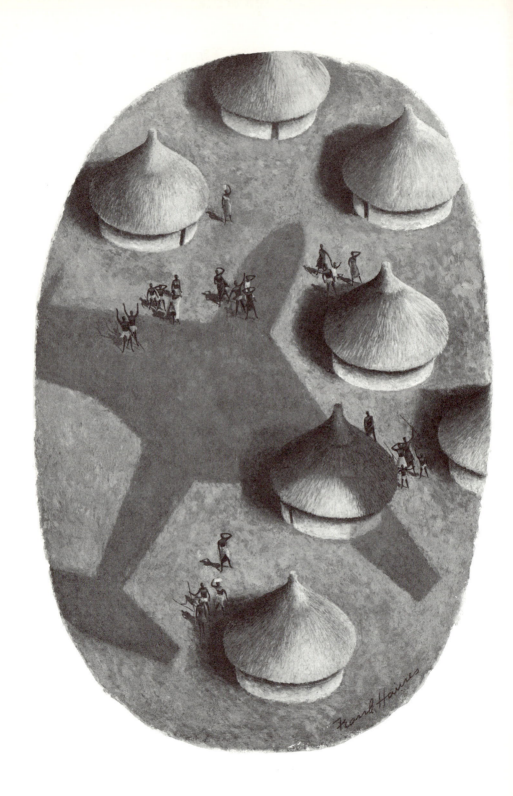

PART II

THE
DEVELOPMENT
OF
THE NON-WEST

Introduction

IN CONTRAST to the peoples of the West, those of the non-Western world did not come in contact with modern science, which set the stage for the Industrial Revolution of Western Europe, until late in the nineteenth century—and some not until the 1950's. This time lag in technological development explains many of the significant differences we see today between the non-Western peoples and those of the West. It also accounts for the complex problems that must be solved if the resulting gap in economic and social development, and hence also in political development, is to be, if not closed, at least gradually narrowed in years to come.

For the basic difference between Western and non-Western countries in the twentieth century is not to be measured in terms of the intelligence of their individual citizens, or of their capacity for creating workable political, economic, and social institutions. Although many arguments to the contrary have been made by some Westerners who believe that white people enjoy an ingrained intellectual superiority over people of color, these arguments, based on the concept of superior and inferior races, have been disproved not only scientifically, by anthropologists and psychologists, but even more impressively by the actual experience of non-Westerners over millennia of history.

It is no diminution of the magnificent spiritual and artistic achievements of Westerners to recognize that accomplishments of comparable and even greater brilliance have been contributed by Indians, Chinese, Japanese, and others in Asia; by Mesopotamia, Assyria, Egypt, and ancient Palestine in the Middle East; by the Mayas and pre-Colombian peoples of Latin America; and by "the lost kingdoms" of Africa. To give a few examples, we have only to consider the high levels attained in medicine, astronomy, and mathematics by the Hindus and Arabs; in literature, sculpture, and music by the Hindus, who also excelled in town-planning and town-building; in the arts by the Chinese and the Japanese, as well as by the Africans; in architecture by the Chinese, the Hindus, the Egyptians, and the Muslims of India and the Middle East; in engineering and the skills of administration by the Chinese, Hindus, Japanese, and too many other non-Western peoples to mention them all here. We must also acknowledge that the great religions and philosophies of the world had their origin in the non-Western world—Hinduism and Buddhism in India, Islam in Arabia, Christianity and Judaism in Palestine, Confucianism and Taoism in China. Only those who do not know history can assume that in the future the peoples of color are inherently incapable of acquiring and applying the scientific ideas and the techniques which have made it possible for Western peoples to master many of nature's forces, to improve step by step man's living conditions, and to promise still greater gains in the future, based on the West's belief in continuing progress. The American Anthropological Association has expressed this view in a resolution adopted by unanimous vote, which stated: "The basic principles of equality of opportunity and equality before the law are compatible with all that is known about human biology. All races possess the abilities needed to participate fully in the democratic way of life and in modern technological civilization."

The question is often asked why the non-Western peoples did not acquire command of science and technology in the same period of history as Westerners. To this question no completely satisfactory answer can be given. Some believe that leading non-Western peoples, notably those of India and China, having reached not one but several peaks in their long history, had entered periods of stagnation or decline, marked by civil strife, at the very time when Western peoples, emerging from the bonds of medievalism and spurred to new ideas by the Renaissance and the Reformation, were ripe for daring innovation and creative endeavor. Others contend that non-Western peoples had been intellectually trammeled by their respective religious beliefs and by priestly hierarchies which were arrayed against secular ideologies and institutions, as was the West for a long time during the Middle Ages.

Many observers, however, believe that in modern times the greatest single obstacle to modernization of non-Western peoples has been the colonial rule of Western powers. These powers brought to their colonies law and order, public health and a measure of education, but they also opposed industrialization, blocked the road to the training of technically skilled personnel, permitted, and in some cases openly encouraged, racial discrimination, and by such methods delayed the entrance of non-Western nations into the modern world. Those who hold this view point out that Japan and Russia, who remained free of Western encroachments on their territories, had entered the early stages of industrialization by the end of the nineteenth century.

Whatever view one may take of the time lag between West and non-West, today the emerging nations, having achieved political independence from colonial rule, are determined to create their own political institutions, to modernize their economies, and to carry out social reforms within the framework of their particular traditions and the limits of their own resources. This they hope to do with the help of the aid they can obtain from the technologically advanced countries of the West and of the Soviet bloc, as well as from international organizations. They are painfully aware of the time lag that separates them from the West, and are in a hurry to close the gap which, in their minds, is the most pressing issue that confronts them in the second half of the twentieth century—far more pressing than the problems and tensions of the cold war between the West and the Communist bloc.

It was not until nationalist movements in colonial territories brought about the withdrawal, voluntary or involuntary, of Western rule, that the non-Western peoples were free to focus their attention on their own problems, and to deal with them according to their own ideas.

If the West's experience is a guide, democratic political institutions in non-Western countries may be expected to follow—not precede—the economic transition from primitive agriculture to an industrial society. The economic conditions created by that revolution spurred the rise of a new middle class of traders and bankers, the "third estate," as contrasted with the clergy and the aristocracy who had dominated society in the Middle Ages, and of the "fourth estate" of intellectuals. The third and fourth estates formed the bourgeoisie, which brought about the downfall of monarchy, curtailed the power of the aristocracy, and took over political power at mid-nineteenth century, until it was itself challenged in Britain,

France, Germany, by the new rising class of factory workers, the "proletariat," acclaimed by Marx and Engels in *The Communist Manifesto.*

As expanding industrialization demanded more and more educated personnel and skilled workers, social status became less and less important, a once stratified society grew increasingly mobile and flexible, and all groups of the population came to share political power on the basis of the principle "one man, one vote." Thus increasing economic opportunities continuously enlarged the scope of political equality and social advancement.

A similar process of change is now taking place in the non-Western world, but at a faster pace and under some markedly different circumstances. In the era of astronauts and jet planes, of radio and television, of rapid communications around the globe, and of continuous exchanges of ideas in all kinds of international forums, notably the United Nations, political transformations are proceeding not at the pace of oxcarts but often at that of jet speed. Because of this very speed, the non-Western countries are not repeating the development of Western nations step by step. They are attempting to telescope revolutions that lasted several centuries in the West into a few decades or even a few years.

The transformations required to bring peoples just emerging from the equivalent of Europe's medieval period into the modern world involve harsh decisions about priorities in economic development and social changes, as well as about the character of political institutions capable of translating development and change from dreams into realities.

The selections presented in Part II give a sampling both of the problems faced by non-Western peoples as they cope with their telescoped revolutions, and of the various ways in which they may find new answers to these problems. These selections show that the achievement of freedom from colonialism is not a universal panacea, and that nationalism can spell danger as well as promise. For the newly emerging nations neither communism nor Western democracy may be the key to the future, but both may offer some elements that the new nations can use in creating their own particular institutions. These nations are beset by a wide range of difficulties, from "population explosions" in some, to shortages in most of food, or raw materials, or technical skills, or managerial talents, or financial resources, or all of these at once. Changing societies suffer from far-reaching psychological maladjustments. Education does not keep pace with the needs of still backward economies. National aspirations are often defeated or disappointed by lack of means to fulfill them, at home and abroad.

The picture that emerges from these selections has many dark aspects. To some observers it spells misery today, civil strife and wars tomorrow. Others, however, taking the long view, remind us that throughout history progress has always involved readjustments which are often painful, but without which there can be no adaptation of societies to changing conditions.

HARRY D. HAROOTUNIAN

The Impact of Colonialism, Nationalism, and Communism

MODERN colonialism, a product of Europe's nineteenth-century drive to seize territorial possessions beyond the continent for a variety of economic, social, political, and religious reasons, ultimately transformed the lives of the peoples of the colonized areas. This transformation was essentially expressed in economic terms. Peoples who had experienced to a greater or lesser degree economic self-sufficiency (that is, producing for themselves all that was necessary for their kind of existence) were forced, through the introduction of new products, to abandon a simple subsistence economy for a complex economy of exchange.

This transformation also led to the emergence of new social classes within the colonial territories. The traditional stratification of society no longer offered suitable standards of behavior and action, and the existing social structure no longer fulfilled the function it had been designed to serve.

The penetration of a new kind of economy, illustrated by the establishment of towns, mill-factories, plantations, and mines, required a continuing source of abundant and regular labor which the traditional social structure was ill-prepared to provide. The by-products of increasing industrialism—new social classes (middle class, wage-earning laborers,) and, soon, social mobility—tended to create a 'new society' whose members were no longer oriented toward traditional social and cultural values. Since these newly formed groups were in constant contact with the European rulers and traders, they often sought to model themselves after the European pattern. Although they succeeded in absorbing decisive elements of the new civilization, they paid a high price for their success. Forced to make almost impossible adjustments to swift and brutal changes, these new groups ultimately found themselves suffering from a general rootlessness, alienated from the society they knew best.

In contrast to the painful social adjustments experienced by peoples subjected to colonialism, the European aristocracy of wealth—represented by the planter, industrialist, merchant, and financier—enjoyed the best of two worlds. Often, but not always, it became aligned with the traditional aristocracy of the area over which it ruled. The resulting social disparity between ruler and ruled, however, was modified gradually by the economic transformation produced by the impact of the West. Traditional economic behavior gradually gave way to more modern institutions in which labor and capital, and no longer the landowning aristocracy, became the dominant elements. This passage from a traditional to a modern society was not accomplished without rancor and enormous difficulty, for in most colonial areas the two societies co-existed side by side, producing an unresolved conflict between two kinds of life which, at bottom, were oriented in different directions.

The first stages of the so-called colonial revolution were mirrored in subtle intellectual changes. Through such agencies as Christian missions, colonial schools, and treaty ports, the colonized peoples received their first introduction to the outside world, to Western ideas, ways of living, concepts, and techniques. The new classes, those most affected by this cultural exposure, were ultimately caught in a dilemma from which there appeared to be no escape. On the one hand, they were emotionally committed to the traditional assumptions by which their society had from time immemorial rationalized its existence in space and time. On the other hand, they were drawn intellectually to the values of Western science and technology, which more often than not were incompatible with traditional beliefs. Intellectuals in India, China, and Japan, for example, desperately attempted to find some sort of synthesis or symbiosis in which traditional ideas could be adjusted to accommodate new knowledge and information.

This attempt, however, proved to be no solution at all, for it was discovered by many who sought it that no intelligible relationship could be established in which the component elements could exist without affecting each other. What usually occurred in the end was the gradual abandonment of traditional beliefs, especially among the generation of those who grew up under colonialism. Thus, the African student found it intellectually impossible to avow tribal religious practices, and believed he was obliged to choose either Islam or Christianity in order not to appear a savage. Japanese newspapers in the 1870's and 1880's admonished people to abandon old styles of dress and behavior in order to show they were indeed civilized and avoid possible embarrassment before Europeans. Even the more sophisticated religions such as Hinduism, Islam, and Buddhism were penetrated by the waves of modernization and were forced to recognize that religion alone cannot exclusively regulate the lives of all human beings. The "Westernized" intellectuals, those most sensitive to the insoluble dilemma between tradition and modernity, could not help feeling alienated from their society since they no longer had any formal respect for traditional concepts which usually gave way before new intellectual alternatives. In short, the traditional world-view, one in which the way things were seemed eternal, was shaken, and society, which once promised the security of stability and comfort, disappeared, leaving only the disoriented and alienated individual in a situation which he neither understood nor fully accepted.

Although these changes were felt in one form or another by all social groups, the loss of cultural absolutes and norms of behavior was felt most intensely by the intellectuals. Their ultimate answer to the problems raised by colonialism was to resort, paradoxically, to a Western concept—nationalism, a concept which embraced both the aspiration for identity and the desire for action.

What were the realities, sentiments, and ideas that jointly forced non-Western intellectuals to make this choice? First, there was the question of racialism, or what has been called "the racial moat." While the nineteenth-century European experience could provide the ideological scaffolding for the practice of racial superiority, it is probably more correct, as Hannah Arendt suggests in *Origins of Totalitarianism*, that racial policies resulted from the direct confrontation between white and non-white. In any case, the colonists came to constitute a superior caste. They possessed all the levers of economic and political control, and while this control was invariably justified or masked by recourse to some notion of racial superiority or higher civilizing principle, it is nevertheless true that both white and non-white were constantly aware of the pragmatic basis of European superiority—advanced military technology. Moreover, in extreme cases, such as the Belgian Congo before 1908 and South Africa today, racism was translated into a systematic policy of brutal oppression in the first case and attempt at complete *apartheid* (apartness) in the second. Whether it was expressed in a well-formulated policy or showed itself in countless indirect measures, such situations created an invisible but veritable "racial moat" which no native could ever hope to bridge.

The Europeans, for their part, chose to separate, indeed insulate, themselves behind this invisible barrier, refusing not only to accept the indigenous population in their own society (i.e., in clubs, or hotels, or homes), but also to have any significant contact with the native group. Generally, the European community was physically separated from the native population, as in the case of the Chinese treaty ports, or on the other side of town, as in the case of British-Indian society. For the most part, the civilizations and languages among which they lived, with few outstanding exceptions, remained unknown to the immense majority of Europeans who worked in a colonial territory. Many Europeans, especially those stationed in the tropics, purposely sought to maintain their foreign identity, for they refused to establish themselves with any degree of permanence in view of their ultimate plans to retire to the home country. This temporary state of existence—this living out of a suitcase—lasted in many cases for a lifetime, during which the colonists clung tenaciously in ideas, interests, and relations not to the society in which they had to serve, but to the European country from which they came. This anomalous situation brought neither new ideas nor new sentiments, except possibly the latent racism which became a way of life that was not always clearly rationalized.

Thus, if colonial society is viewed in terms of the elements of which it is composed, the Europeans appeared as a new caste, superimposed on the traditional class structure, living apart physically and psychologically. The poorest white was considered superior to the wealthiest and most accomplished native. This kind of social stratification remained most strongly fixed in those territories where the Europeans formed a considerable part of the population, for example Algeria, which they considered an integral part of the home country. In such situations, the white immigrants could, if the native population were numerically small, drive them back and in some cases partly eliminate them or, if the native population constituted a strong numerical majority, subject them to repressive legal measures.

The second situation arising from the colonial impact was the "crisis of identity." The colonial people, seeking to understand the new developments, tended to imitate the white ruler and even, in some cases, to identify their vague aspirations with European nations in order to discover what they really were. One of the most significant developments resulting from the colonial experience was the search for identity among the colonized, especially after the old ways had been discredited. This quest was usually expressed in terms of Western ideas. The crisis of identity and the subsequent search for a new one reached its maximum intensity among intellectuals who, despite their hopes, dreams, and aspirations, despite whatever material and intellectual successes they had achieved, were ultimately forced to confront the invisible racial moat.

This crisis apparently resulted from a recognition or discovery on the part of the intellectual that he was not a part of the dominant minority, no matter how well he quoted English verse or wrote French prose. Owing to this enforced recognition that he was a "native" no matter what he did, the intellectual responded first by investing his own discredited culture and race with a new superiority, and then by developing a hatred which finally exploded in the desire for revolution, the expulsion of all foreigners, and the demand for complete self-rule. The crisis, which varied from one area to another, led the non-Western intellectual to swing wildly, as if he were suspended on a cultural pendulum, from indiscriminate imitation to xenophobic repudiation. Something like this crisis may have been experienced by the European intellectuals and bourgeoisie during the eighteenth century when they sought social status and political representation, but the comparison ends here since Europe's middle class did not have to overcome a racial barrier.

Given this situation, the non-Western intellectual had only a

limited range of choices, the most attractive of which was the psychological return to tradition. But even this return was invariably
expressed in terms of European ideas. The return was not to a
tradition of the immediate past, but usually to a more distant time
which neither history nor memory could possibly confirm. Holding
the past at arm's length, the non-Western intellectual conceived
of this distant age not just as a vague tradition or secular conformity, but as a distinct national experience, an asylum in which all of
his hopes, exultations, and aspirations could find expression.

In this quest for roots, aided often by the historical and archae-
ological researches of European scholars into his country's past,
the intellectual persuaded himself that the European judgment of
his culture was false, and that the true value of his race or civilization was both unappreciated and misunderstood. Motivated by the
intolerance of youth, the non-Western intellectual forged a past
epoch, created the myth of a golden age anterior to European
colonization which, for some inexplicable reason, had been lost in
the rubble of time. Among a few West African peoples, for example, there was enough of a demonstrable pre-colonial past to
make possible a persuasive case for past achievement, but this
process has been carried to great lengths of historical incredibility
in areas whose conscious awareness of political, social, and economic
development began with the coming of the European. The irony
of this indiscriminate historical reconstruction is that it was usually
accompanied by a desire to conserve and even spread the acquisi-
tions of modernity. What this meant, in concrete terms, was that
the non-Western intellectuals sought desperately to accommodate
elements of an inherited or manufactured past, without which, they
believed, they could not retain their identity, to technological devices imported from the West. This effort to conserve and to modernize was expressed by the pouring of new ideas into old moulds,
with the result that the moulds were bound to crack. In spite of
this fascination with the past, real or imagined, the primary orientation of the non-Western intellectual was always to the future, for
the past merely served as the necessary link to a future in which all
historical aspirations would be realized. The past, in short, furnished
the historical and geographical crucible for the development of
nationalism in the present.

The third aspect of the colonial situation which inspired the
non-Western intellectuals to embrace nationalism involved ideolo-

gies. While nationalism provided the non-Western world with the impulse for change, it was unable to offer a blueprint detailing the kind of political, economic, and social order that would emerge in the future. For this reason nationalism—the quest for identity—was compelled to seek aid in imported universalistic and egalitarian ideologies imported from the West.

Ever since the French Revolution, Europe had been moved by stirring, although often betrayed, ideas of the emancipation of all men, the inalienable right of the individual to determine his own destiny, and the sovereignty of the nation-state—ideas which unleashed unprecedented national and liberal movements that ultimately transformed the continent of Europe. While the echoes of these ideas were heard in the non-Western world only in the twentieth century, they became, when linked to the propelling force of nationalism, the foundations of a revolutionary theory of action. Moreover, the liberal and egalitarian ideas that had developed in Europe and the United States in the eighteenth century served still another function. The national experiences which had given expression to these ideas offered the non-Western intellectual concrete examples of political systems founded on universalistic principles—suffrage, parliamentarianism, and the distribution of power. The Indians and the Nigerians, for example, found in Great Britain a model to emulate, while the Chinese sought to reproduce the American variety of federalism.

Finally, in discussing imported ideologies, it would be difficult, indeed impossible, to ignore the impact of Marxism and communism. More than any other ideology, Marxism anticipated the struggle against colonialism and the emancipation of colonial peoples. The Communists, more successfully than any other organized group, were able to exploit the nationalist sentiments of many non-Western people in their struggle against the forces of colonialism. With nationalists seeking independence, the Communists often formed a community of interest, sometimes called a united front, until the common enemy—Colonialism plus Capitalism—was expelled. Once independence was achieved, the Communists shed their nationalist cloak and challenged the new leaders for supremacy. When communism could not find a climate favorable to its claims, it resorted to coalition governments as in Indo-China, the Ivory Coast, Algeria, and Burma. It should be pointed out that communism has failed in those areas, such as India, where it was unable to identify its interests with those of the nationalists.

Communism has also had other appeals for non-Western peoples. The Russian Communists have shown, by their own example, that it is possible for an economically underdeveloped area to achieve, through communism, the highest levels of technological competence. Their propaganda, championing "national self-determination" and "social justice," as expressed in Lenin's repudiation of Russia's treaties with Western powers which he regarded as unequal, has proved a further attraction for non-Western nations. Moreover, experience has shown that the Communist organizational principle of "democratic centralism" has been an effective basis for political action among politically inexperienced peasants and workers. It is also true that the Communists have expended great energy, effort, and expense to train in the Soviet Union and elsewhere party cadres in methods of organization, political action, indoctrination, propaganda, and guerilla warfare. All of these factors, and more, have combined to give the Communist image the appeal of authority, especially among non-Western peoples who are seeking practical short cuts to political, economic, and social development.

To these doctrines of egalitarianism and revolt imported from the West was added the idea of a nation-state, whose primary purpose was to give these sentiments and concepts a permanent framework. To be sure, the non-Western world has never suffered from the absence of some form of political organization. Among the many varied political systems of past ages, some were based, as in several sub-Saharan tribes, on an extended form of kinship; others, as in India under the Mogul dynasty, or in North Africa under the Ottoman Empire, on the domination of an alien group; and still others, as in Japan and Morocco, on an imperial or royal office endowed with charismatic powers.

None of these systems, however, were organized as a national, territorial state. The sentiment of a unified community, located on a definite territorial base, was another inheritance from Europe.

The conquest and colonial administration of many non-Western areas destroyed the traditional divisions of petty kingdoms, feudal states, and tribes, and established new boundaries. For example, Senegal, Madagascar, Algeria, and Indo-China were, for the most part, created by French administrative arrangements; India, despite its geographical unity, was, under British rule, for some time merged with Burma to form one jurisdictional unit, and what we now call Indonesia was little more than a loose aggregate of islands possessing different cultures before the Dutch brought them all under a single administration. The consequences of this regrouping were naturally far-reaching, for in the process the colonial countries usually destroyed the "internal frontiers" (the traditionally accepted boundaries), placed diverse groups who had little in common with each other into permanent contact, and obliged them for purposes of administrative convenience to live together.

These new frontiers, generally established as administrative links in the chain of colonial bureaucracy, constituted the crucible within which the idea of a nation could grow. Yet it was usually not enough simply to equate a territorial base with nationhood, for the formation of national sentiment owed as much to the recognition of a common past, linguistic similarities, and the like as it did to defined boundaries. Vietnam was virtually a nation; Madagascar, possessing linguistic and cultural unity, had greater potential to become a nation than either the Congo or the states of French West Africa, with their far-flung and innumerable peoples; Hinduism, despite the existence of several languages, formed and held India together; and Islam was used as the foundation stone of the state of Pakistan. But it would be equally mistaken to suggest that religion, race, or language are sufficient of themselves to form nation-states, for it still remains for Islam and Arabism to create a clearly defined national complex. A territorial base is essential for national existence for we know now that a nation is something more than a race, a common belief, or a historical unity.

It is within the context of nation-building that non-Western peoples have expressed their aspirations and their understanding of the European inheritance. The tendencies leading to xenophobia, "inferiority complexes," the yearning for a real or imagined past, must all be viewed as a non-Western response to the colonial experience. Europe, by its example, unwittingly furnished an idea, an indeterminate directive—nationalism, and since the Western powers failed to work out a political preventive to check the impact of this new force, nationalism turned against the Europeans with such might that they were unable to resist and restrain its attack.

The nationalist movement which surged over Europe in the nineteenth century was a response to a dimly perceived need to solve problems of a new world born of the disintegration of feudalism and the sweeping changes of the Industrial Revolution. Nationalism, in short, promised an easy method of achieving political reorganization based on cultural identity. In the twentieth century, with the decline of older institutions and the upheaval caused by new ones, nationalism eventually reached the non-Western world. But there it came in a different guise. Whereas in Europe nationalism provided the instrument for political renewal, in the non-Western areas it was first of all a formula of adaptation to, and reaction against, foreign domination, and only after independence, of new political construction.

Today, the peoples of the non-Western world are no longer content to remain passive subjects of the colonial system. While the struggle for national independence still continues, we can detect a gradual slowing of its pace. For as the goal of independence is won, there is a sudden awareness of problems which nationalism is ill-prepared to resolve. The obsessive dream for independence has not always proved adequate preparation for the often harsh realities of nationhood which must be met by new ideas and new methods.

[1]

Impact
of Colonialism

STEWART C. EASTON

The Twilight of European Colonialism

In the past, and even today, one of the most difficult tasks in writing about world affairs is to describe colonialism. Like the elephant of the fable, described in such different ways by the blind men who touched it, colonialism looks very different depending on whether it is described by colonial administrators, or by the colonial peoples they administered, or by Western critics of colonialism, particularly Americans nurtured in the tradition of anti-colonialism since the days of the American Revolution.

Dr. Easton in this selection writes about colonialism in 1959, before the Congo and a number of other nations of Africa and Asia had achieved independence. Although he recognizes the contributions made by the colonial powers to the development of their colonies, he writes as a critic of their attitudes toward the peoples they ruled.

British-born, Dr. Easton attended Oxford University and the University of Ottawa, and received his M.A. and Ph.D. in history from Columbia University. He is the author of several other books, among them The Western Heritage: From the Earliest Times to the Present, 1961.

Chapter 18

Contrasting Policies of the Four Western Powers

British Colonial Policy and the Challenge of Nationalism

Now, if we adopt the point of view that the Westerners, the white men, are the natural leaders of mankind, and that it is their civilization, their outlook that must be made to prevail, that there is a white man's burden in Africa, it follows that the correct policy of the Westerners indeed is

120

to save the black Africans from themselves, and not to leave their continent until the African has been truly educated on the Western model and has adopted Western civilization to such a degree that he will not slip back into the condition from which the white man rescued him.

But this is not a conceivable goal for a colonial power. There can be no guarantee that the African will be willing and able to establish a parliamentary democracy on Western lines, capable of enduring into the definite future. Ghana achieved independence but was not westernized. The main task of replacing the old tribal society with something faintly akin to Western forms of government and social organization remains one for Ghanaians themselves to carry out. The European cannot do it for them. No other African country will be westernized before independence; the utmost that it can achieve will be a small facility in handling Western institutions, a facility which it may or may not develop more thoroughly for itself. The European can have no certainty on the matter and cannot institute safeguards, either to secure his own position or to ensure that the African after independence will behave according to the conventions established in the West to meet Western needs and aspirations. In the end the European must allow his former charges to shift for themselves.

The weakness in British colonialism in recent years has been twofold: a failure in historical insight and a certain moral blindness at the human level. In both of these areas, the French, in spite of many other failures, have shown themselves in recent times manifestly superior. It is quite true to say, to quote *Round Table . . .* that "the cosmic movement of the age is towards ever closer interchange between the 'races' of the world," and that "nationalism" is the "way of mutual defiance, the way ultimately of war." But it is sheer arrogance for the European to tell that to the African. The European has lived through his nationalist era, and is now looking for new institutions to fit his belated recognition of interdependence. But the African and other inhabitants of the British dependencies have never known that age. They have been kept in subjection to an alien power. It may be that they will spend only decades, not centuries, in their nationalist epoch; but they must be permitted to live through this epoch, however short it may prove to be. They cannot be compelled to leap forward into a future only dimly envisaged by the European, least of all by the nationalistic British. The more the British and other colonial powers refuse to recognize the essential justice of African aspirations and attempt to keep them down in the supposed interests of law and order . . . the stronger these aspirations are certain to grow. It is not at all unreasonable that the African should wish to be rid of the colonial power which has ruled him for so many years. Certainly, no European nation has ever been willing to subject itself to alien rule, or even to any significant diminution of its own sovereign rights. The excuse given by these rulers for their rule is that it is in the interests, the true interests, of the ruled. But who decides that? The colonial ruler necessarily; and it appears to be an insuperable task, at least for the British, to realize that a decision made by them, and not by the African, offends the dignity of the African.

It is, of course, not easy for the European, so sure of his own dignity, to recognize that the tribal African can have a dignity as a human being. To the European the African remains a child who must be disciplined, not an adult human being who has the right to make his own decisions. True, many Africans do not wish to make their own decisions; they are willing to be led. If the European is presently the leader, then they will follow and obey him. But is this reliance on others not also true of some Westerners? In any event, it is certainly not true of all Africans. Africans followed their tribal leaders because they recognized their authority, hallowed by tradition. Colonial rulers tried and succeeded in superimposing their authority on the tribal leaders, who gradually became their servants. The average African, accustomed to obeying authority, and rarely seeing the representative of the colonial ruler, did not feel that his former condition was greatly changed by the coming of the European. But some Africans began to recognize that the chief was no longer the chief because of custom and tradition, but because his power was bolstered by the colonial ruler; and the democratic ideas of the Westerner that legitimate rule must be based on consent percolated down into them. If they could themselves gain the consent of their fellow Africans, then it was their right to rule them—it was no longer the traditional right of the chiefs, still less the right of the foreigner, whose position, to him, rested solely on the possession of superior force. To the colonial ruler his own position was legitimate, the right of conquest, the right of long occupation, a right conferred by treaty with chiefs, who pretended to, and were perhaps entitled to, speak for their subjects. But no African can be expected to recognize such a right. How can he be expected to recognize a right of conquest when the conquered is himself?

So the Westerners in the political sphere necessarily undermined their own authority, as they had already undermined that of the chiefs. But the British are too often unwilling to accept the consequences of their policy.

If this analysis is correct, it follows that the British should be looking for and encouraging the emergence of African leaders who demonstrably enjoy the confidence of the Africans, and that these men should be assisted, even trained, for the responsibility they will some day enjoy— that they, if any one, should be led to think of the white man as their elder brother who will help them some day to stand on their own feet. If an atmosphere of mutual respect and confidence is built up between the British and the African leaders, and if the African leaders have some admiration for Western institutions and a determination to try to adapt them to their own culture, if they are persuaded of the value of Western technical knowledge and the role of Western finance in helping to develop their countries, this is as much safeguard as the colonial ruler will ultimately attain.

But in actual fact the British have not been interested in working with the nationalists. They have preferred to choose as their favorites the moderate conservative Africans; and their treatment of nationalists has almost invariably been such that they have engendered ill will rather than the good will that is essential if they are to hold the confidence and trust of these groups while the colony is being prepared for independence. First they have tried to work with a substantial middle class, merchants and professional men. This class has been given the franchise; its members have been nominated to legislative and executive councils. But these men represent only their class and themselves. As soon as the franchise qualifications are lowered, this middle class is repudiated by the new electorate. So its members retire to private life, to rail bitterly against the Africans who have supplanted them, and sometimes against the British who have betrayed them. Their talents are thus lost to the future political life of the colony, unquestionably to its disadvantage, since education is still too rare a possession to be thus wantonly wasted.

•   •   •

REPRESENTATIVE GOVERNMENT—OFFICIAL, EXECUTIVE AND ELECTED LEGISLATURE

Parliamentary democracy may not be a form of government particularly suited to Africans. But it is a possible form of government, and it is the one to which Africans in British colonies have become accustomed. It is therefore incumbent upon the British to see that it is given a chance to work. A government has to hold the confidence of the legislative assembly, or it cannot function. The British have used the device of keeping the Executive firmly under official control, while allowing the elected legislative assembly the right to debate, to discuss and vote on the budget and to legislate. This so-called representative government has a long if not honorable history. It bears some resemblance to English government in Tudor times, and is the kind of government that was used in colonial Canada before the Durham Report in the early nineteenth century. It has always caused unending tensions between the executive and legislative powers—tensions which are built into the system and are made bearable in modern times only because of the knowledge that it is a transitional stage in the progress toward self-government. Under this system it is obvious that the executive must have the right to legislate if the assembly refuses to do so, and it must have the right to disallow legislation and to pass the budget whether or not it is approved. Thus the assembly becomes simply advisory. If the governor and Executive Council accept the advice, or if there is even a presumption that they will do so, the assembly will feel that it is perhaps performing a useful service. But if, as so often happens in the colonies, the elected assembly is at variance with the Executive on fundamental questions, it is certain that the elected element will constantly try to create difficulties for the government until its demands are acted upon.

Parliamentary democracy of the British type needs a strong party system. If a representative government were to be permanent, and there were to be no advance toward self-government, a party system would not be necessary. The representatives would give their advice as individuals and be listened to accordingly. But a semi-responsible or responsible government cannot function in the absence of a party system. It is possible for a coalition made up of different parties to rule responsibly, although governments will be no more stable than the system of party alliances which lie at its base. The British tradition is for rule by a major party, and it discourages coalitions of minor parties. There can be little doubt that the newly independent states need governments as strong as can be obtained through the electoral process. It would therefore seem reasonable that the British give support and encouragement to the rise of major parties. They should then be happy when one emerges which has mass support and is obviously capable of governing when they have left.

But it must be said once more that exactly the opposite has been true —hence the prevalence of the Gandhi cap. This situation has been due to the British distrust of the judgment of the electorate, and its fear of those they please to call demagogues and agitators. It seems impossible for them to understand that nationalism is bound to involve agitation against themselves, and that nationalism is a perfectly genuine emotion in their colonies. They become injured and self-righteous when criticized; they know that their rule is truly best for the colony and it is almost sacrilege to them when any criticism is made, however small and however justified. They think that their colonial subjects ought to be happy and grateful that they have been ruled so long by such an enlightened people; those whom they characterize as agitators, they say, are biting the hand that fed them. If the agitators enjoy the support of the people of the colony, it can be only because the people are compelled to support them by intimidation, or because the people are so immature that they do not appreciate the benevolence of their masters, or both. According to the British, the agitators prey upon African emotions, and the poor African is helpless against their appeal. Nevertheless, whether intimidated or not, the Africans sooner or later have to be granted the vote; and they use it to return the nationalist agitators to office. There is nothing whatever that the British can do to arrest this process.

If the British were truly at heart democrats, and if they wanted nothing better than to hand over their government to the leaders who have demonstrated that they have support from the people, then it is clear that a different policy would have been adopted from the beginning. If the leaders, in the British view, were capable sometime of undertaking the tasks and responsibility of government, then they should be encouraged in their ambitions, and trained and educated for their future responsibilities. They should be encouraged to watch the House of Commons at work, special courses should be made available to them in England or in the colonial university colleges, as every political leader in the French territories has served his apprenticeship in the French Chamber. The African potential leader should mix in government circles, be welcomed at Government House, perhaps be made familiar with the work of government departments. The British do make the last named possible by nominating the leader to the Executive Council; but they do not do so until the colony is well on the road to self-government and after the African politician has suffered the usual vicissitudes of the would-be leader, and passed through the stages of being an agitator (quite possibly a detainee), paid the customary fines for seditious libel, and finally won the election in spite of British efforts to hold him back. Meanwhile he will have seen his collaborating contemporaries nominated to the Council.

THE CRUCIAL IMPORTANCE OF UNIVERSAL SUFFRAGE

It is quite true that the various national congresses are radical and anti-colonial and that it is their radicalism and anti-colonialism that win them votes. It is also true that the prison camp is a sure passport to political success, and that some intimidation of quiet fellow Africans will be involved in the rise of nationalists to power. But why not recognize the fact? The truly essential need if the country is ever to become self-governing is that the party which is to rule should have the support of the people it will rule. To tinker with transitional safeguards and with what the London *Economist* calls "fancy franchises" is to ensure the ultimate rise to power of the most radical, not the least radical—and it is not impossible that this party will gain power only because of its radicalism, not its fitness to rule.

If, on the other hand, universal franchise had already been granted at the representative stage, when the Executive Council was made up of a majority of officials, then there could be no doubt about who really did represent the people. A few members of the majority party could undertake responsibilities in the government, and as soon as possible thereafter semi-responsible government and a full ministerial system would be granted—again with free elections under universal franchise. The members and their party would not necessarily be repudiated by the electorate as nominated members are. If they were rejected by the electorate, at least a second party would have had to come into existence to defeat them, and such a party would be equally ready to take over the government. Leaders of all parties would not have felt that the British were trying to keep them out of office and away from responsibility. There would have been no need for any party to have adopted a policy based solely on anti-colonialism, since the British themselves would have been the chief anti-colonialists. It is indeed quite possible that they would have adopted constructive programs. By standing in the way of the advance of political parties and their leaders through the attempt to institute safeguards and hold on to untenable positions, the British failed to secure the real good will of the colonial leaders but ensured instead that their initial programs would be radical and anti-colonial, and too often constructively sterile, while achieving none of their professed aims. . . .

If this analysis is correct, there is no halfway point between responsibility held by officials, and responsibility held by the colonial peoples themselves. There is no reason why Britain and other colonial powers should not rule through officials as long as they are willing to accept the consequences, and until there are at least some natives sufficiently well educated and capable of leading their fellows, who emerge into prominence. Then the decision must be made to open the road to self-government. The leaders will probably already have formed their party. The party should be given full encouragement and full freedom of speech and assembly, subject only to the maintenance of public order. The stage of representative government under universal franchise should then be inaugurated, but the officials would still be in the majority in the councils. The rulers, however, would make it clear that this stage would last for a definitely limited period, and new elections would be held at a fixed time afterward. The next stage would be semi-responsible government by an elected majority in both councils, with the governor retaining only a few powers, as is the policy in many colonies now. The beneficial consequences of such an orderly progress would be numerous. The natives would truly feel that Britain is anxious to relinquish power to them at as early an opportunity as possible. Their present feeling is, in spite of British public pronouncements on the matter, that the best way to gain self-government is to create disturbances, and the best way for a native to win respect in his community is to become a martyr. Nehru, Makarios, Nkrumah, Azikiwe, Bustamante, Nyerere, Kenyatta, Mboya, Banda, all have felt the displeasure of the British in one form or another. The first five lived to become elected ministers at the head of their responsible governments, the sixth is almost certain to become prime minister of his territory, and who shall say that the British will not one day have to come to terms with even the two last named and that the terms will be dictated, not by the British, but by the Africans?

The second great advantage to be gained from early universal suffrage is that the natives who will ultimately rule the colony will probably be those who have gained prior experience in government, and not those who have spent most of their talents before holding office in criticizing the regime and trying to gain further political concessions. Moreover, the electors themselves will have gained experience by observing that their votes are meaningful, that it is their business to choose governments that will be of benefit to them. If the governments they have put into office do not deliver, they can turn them out. Thus they will gain experience in the workings of democracy. They may come to recognize that it is they who are the ultimate masters in a democratic system.

The ultimate success of a parliamentary democracy depends upon the working of parties, preferably two parties, one of which will form the Government and the other the Opposition. This is far more important than trying to make certain that the government when in office will not misbehave itself, and trying to temper its radicalism. There are few parties in the world which have not been more radical before they held office than when they became the majority party in the government. Quite contrary to most British official opinion, the majority of Africans, in particular, are very reasonable people, and they have an intuitive understanding of the principle of government by consent. Like everyone else, they are sobered by responsibility. The radical African parties have been made radical by British or settler opposition, rather than from any special taste for radicalism. Hindered from holding legitimate public meetings and from expressing their opinions against their colonial masters in print, and not recognizing in any way the legitimacy of colonial rule over them, they, like other human beings in similar circumstances, become frustrated, and their views become the more extreme with constant thwarting. Provocative words naturally tend to become violent deeds. The law is brought into operation against them; and since they alone are its victims, the law to them becomes tyranny. None of these things is in the least unnatural; but the British seem unable to appreciate the truly provocative nature of the obstacles they oppose to native aspirations.

.   .   .

The French Community

If we consider the strange history of the French Community since it was established in 1958, what is most striking is the extraordinary spirit of give and take between European and African, the recognition by the French ruler of the humanity and dignity of the African, and the willingness of the French to face the full consequences of this recognition. . . .

The Community is a concept that is utterly alien to British tradition and thought. The Mother of Parliaments is a much older and more sacred institution than the French Chamber and Senate; and the British have never given any consideration to the possibility of African representation in the British Parliament. At one time a number of leading British statesmen agreed to make the experiment of admitting Maltese to the British Parliament, but eventually, as we have seen, the idea fell through. The inhabitant of the British colonies may be British in language and culture, but he is not regarded as a black Englishman. The French, on the other hand, for a long time tried, with astonishing success in individual instances, to make the French African into a true Frenchman. When, however, they perceived that the assimilation policy was not approved by the Africans, they gradually abandoned it under the pressure of events, though retaining some elements in the old policy that seemed capable of being used fruitfully. The African now is expected to remain fully an African, but imbued with French culture and speaking the French language in addition to his own; and he is expected to feel almost as much at home in France as in Africa. Thus he loses nothing of his Africanism but adds to it what he has gained from association with France.

Until the mid-1950's the theory of full democracy that has been in French bones since the French Revolution was at variance with the supposed needs of French colonial policy. The latter in essence did not differ much from that of the other colonial powers. The system of the double college ensured that there should be representation of the European residents in Africa in the French Parliament and in the Assembly of the French Union; but even this was intended to ensure representation of French interests rather than to perpetuate French rule. Settlers never ruled any French African territory. There were always more Africans than settlers representing the French colonies in the French Parliament, even though elected by a restricted franchise. Faced with the problem of how to ensure acceptable African representatives, the French colonial administrators used their position to influence the election and to prevent the rise of radical political parties; however, finding themselves unable to prevent the growth of parties, they accepted the fact and learned to live with them. Indeed, the Africans have shown themselves much more adept at forming effective political parties than their masters have been—perhaps because the party was the principal instrument for obtaining concessions from the French and the only one that could be effectively used. The isolated individual was early perceived to be powerless and usually unable to resist the blandishments of his masters.

In the early 1950's the French system of interference with elections was weakening. With the *loi-cadre*, theory finally triumphed over the supposed requirements of colonial policy. Universal franchise was granted, and elections henceforth were free, save in isolated instances where the governors disagreed with French policy and used their power to thwart it. Their attitude brought parties based on popular consent into office. Most of the remaining powers of the French were gradually handed over to the Africans, the culmination being the referendum of September 28, 1958 [establishing the French Community]. Although again the French administration in some areas used its influence to ensure a Yes vote, all the votes were so heavily in favor of Yes that there can be no doubt that a Yes vote represented the popular will, save in Guinea, where the vote, of course, was for No. This astonishing preponderance of Yes votes needs some explanation.

The explanation, in the opinion of this writer, lies in the studied policy of the French since the Brazzaville Conference of 1944. This policy resulted in the emergence of political parties and representative African leaders who were encouraged and aided not by colonial administrators as much as by the very system of the *Union française*. This policy led, by logical steps designed for the purpose they achieved, to full self-government, under native African rule. Before everything else comes the explicit recognition of the social and political equality of the educated African leaders—a class which has always felt itself frustrated under British rule, owing to the refusal to concede social equality. This recognition was symbolized in the seating of African members in the French Parliament. It did not matter that their power was limited, since their numbers were so small, and that their votes for a long time were without political significance and were not sought by any of the parties save the Communists. Even when the Africans learned to pull their full weight in the coalition governments of the postwar period in France and their votes became necessary to secure the confirmation of a particular government in office, nothing of any vital significance was gained in comparison with the concession of the original principle that Africans could sit side by side with their colleagues in the French Parliament, debate, talk, sit in committees, even preside over them. When African affairs were discussed, their views were sought after, and they were listened to with respect and politeness. Never were they given the slightest indication that they were members of an "inferior race." Every African leader of importance today gained some experience of politics in the French Parliament in the era of the *Union française*. There he learned how French government works, how to debate, how to form political combinations, how to make his influence felt. African conditions may not be at all similar to those prevailing in France, and it may well be that the French system is not at all suitable as a model for Africa, but the French offered freely what they had, and the Africans learned. The leaders may have been a very small fraction of the African population, but these were the men who counted and will count in this generation. Thus it was possible for the French to turn over the governments in Africa to these leaders, even while the British were still trying to persuade Africans to play a responsible part in government, with the aid of restricted franchises, electoral colleges, Houses of Chiefs, and the like.

Moreover, even in the long years when political advance was almost infinitesimal, the elected African leaders, sitting in the French Chamber, were always aware of the difficulties of passing appropriate legislation, and there was always hope that with a new combination of parties forming a government and a majority in the Chamber, the requisite legislation would be passed. The African leaders could influence it by their lobbying and voting; there was nothing more that disturbances in Africa could achieve. The few disturbances which took place in French territories were directed against the local administration rather than against French government. The war in Algeria became necessary for Algerian nationalists because they knew that, with French settlers so influential in French government and Parliament, their own wishes would never receive fair consideration in France. No such problem arose in sub-Saharan Africa, where settler influence soon became negligible in the postwar period. . . .

. . . When the wave of nationalism was reaching gale force in some territories and was a mere breeze in others, the French turned over the governments to the educated leaders and left the government to them. The result has been, in human terms, that it is difficult, as Adlai Stevenson discovered, to find any Africans who hate the French. When there are riots in the new republics, Africans from both sides take refuge in the homes of Frenchmen; there is no killing of Frenchmen, no terrorism directed against them—and in almost every African government there are Frenchmen sitting as Cabinet ministers and members of the Assembly, freely elected by the Africans. . . .

. . . The African states will seek their own alignments, and France will have to agree gracefully to the weakening of her ties with her former colonies. But it must be conceded that in spite of the weakness of postwar French governments, in spite of the slow political advances of the decade following the war, and the machinations of French governors in the colonies, the French have succeeded in the one field where the British most conspicuously failed. If now France can solve at last the problem of Algeria, as she is making serious efforts to do at the time of writing, she still has a fighting chance of retaining the respect, and even the affection, of her former African subjects. And she will have fulfilled at least some aspects of the "civilizing mission" that she set herself and of which, out of deference to the susceptibilities of the newly civilized, she has spoken ever more rarely, as the mission grew closer to accomplishment.

Belgian Congo

. . . The Belgians have undoubtedly created conditions, at least in the urban centers, which have favored the rise of an African middle class . . . the situation is seriously complicated by the fact that the capital and largest city in the Congo is situated in an area peopled so largely by a powerful tribe which looks to unity with its fellow-tribal members across the River Congo in the Congo Republic. . . . As long as political advancement was withheld from the Congolese, the only practicable policy for the Bakongo leaders in Leopoldville was to make the best of the existing situation. But now . . . the Bakongo in Leopoldville feel that they should be permitted to secede from the rest of the Belgian Congo. . . . Thus independence in association with the rest of the Belgian Congo holds no charm for them, and they do not regard it as independence at all but a continuing servitude. . . .

The Belgian Congo differs from British colonies . . . in that the Belgians in the Congo were never given any political rights, nor have they acquired, like the British in Kenya, a right to hold land in perpetuity, whatever the changing conditions of the times. . . . But neither can the Africans exercise . . . influence, as the French African deputies could exercise at least some influence in France. . . .

. . . In the days before the January, 1959, reforms were announced, the only political parties were tribal and not national. There did not seem to be any point in organizing national political parties when there were no nation-wide elections. The only elections that did take place were local, and these lent themselves more to competition between traditional and tribal groupings. . . . The organization of parties has now suddenly become a free-for-all. . . .

. . . The Congo could be one of the greatest of African nations as it is already the richest in Black Africa; but without doubt it presents the most difficult task of statesmanship in the colonial world. . . .

Portuguese Africa

There remains little to say about the Portuguese system. Angola and Mozambique, close as they are to the Union of South Africa, may for a considerable time to come remain firmly in Portuguese control; the Portuguese have shown no signs of realizing that there is a problem. The retirement or death of Premier Salazar will perhaps have few visible consequences in Africa in many years; but it could be, as with the death of Stalin, that the years will reveal a softening of the authoritarian regime of Portugal. . . .

. . . If the Portuguese were seriously to consider granting any measure of self-government to their provinces, the *assimilado* system, of which they make so much, could be utilized more effectively by encouraging more Africans to accept the status, and granting them not only social and cultural but political privileges. Such a concession would be publicized as giving effect to policies always intended to be applied to Africans, and as representing no departure in principle from the Portuguese colonial tradition. If more governmental tasks were progressively to be devolved onto African *assimilados*, effective power could be retained in Portuguese metropolitan hands; but the onus of oppressive administration would be shared with Africans. The lot of the non-*assimilado* African might not be improved for a long time to come, but at least a way would be opened for the gradual assumption by Africans to rule on their continent. In time the asperities of Portuguese rule would surely be softened as native Africans grew to feel responsibility for the lot of their fellow Africans. This, at all events, would seem to be the direction in which Portuguese policy will move, if at all.

Conclusion

. . . It seems clear that the phase of imperialism and colonialism is now nearing its end. Only the Portuguese system is as yet apparently untouched by the waves of nationalism that have been sweeping the world in increasing force since the end of World War II; and only in the countries where Europeans have made their permanent homes is there any doubt that self-government and independence under native rule will come within at most the next twenty years. . . .

The trend, it now seems certain, is irreversible. The tide of European expansion reached its peak and then receded. The first phase of the task of the Europeans to bring their technique and forms of government to the peoples who had been living in more static societies has now been accomplished. This phase required domination of the societies, while the second phase calls for cooperation on an equal basis. . . . All change is painful; yet it happens to be a law of life. We human beings did not make the law. We cannot make the sun stand still. We can, with Canute, command the waves to keep their distance, but the waves do not obey our command. It is our human task to cooperate with the change and adapt ourselves to it. History does not forgive those who are blind and do not see, any more than she forgives those who dig in their heels and stand still.

The study of modern colonialism is above all the study of the adaptation of the colonial powers to the phenomenon of change. The British, with their gift for improvisation and tactical flexibility, might have been considered especially suitable for this kind of operation, and up to a point they may be said to have fulfilled their task with credit. They perceived that their charges were restive and that concessions would have to be made. Thus they adapted themselves to the reality of the new facts confronting them. But their besetting weaknesses, complacency, lack of imagination, and excessive empiricism, were their undoing. They did not recognize that the situations in their different colonies arose from the same cause. Each colony to them presented a special unique problem of its own. Thus disturbances had to be created by the natives in each colony separately, and the British were constantly being put into a position where they appeared to be bowing before the storm, instead of firmly grasping the initiative; being unceremoniously bundled out of their colony instead of withdrawing in accordance with a preconceived plan. The plan existed, but vaguely, so loosely formulated that it could never be applied clearly at any given time. The British never recognized that the natives had a real case against them. They continued to believe that the natives were privileged in being ruled by them; it was impossible for them to see that the natives, in their own view, were not especially favored and that certainly most of them were not grateful. Their complacency in this respect was reinforced by the fact that many were indeed grateful and did feel themselves privileged. But the British did not recognize that this gratitude bestowed upon them no right for the future. The future had to be considered solely on its own merits. If the British were willing to discuss matters freely, then all would be well. If not, gratitude for past and present favors would not suffice. Without question, the British government and the settlers did much and are still doing much for Kenya and Rhodesia. But, in the African view, these facts do not mean that they can dictate the Africans' future. If the Africans wish to retreat into the barbaric condition from which the British rescued them, then even that must be permitted them. In the long run the British will not be able to prevent them. If the Africans consent to partnership with the British, the choice will be made by Africans and British, but not by the British alone. This is a lesson, it would seem, that the British have still to learn. The African, having grown to manhood, must be permitted his freedom to choose. On the one side there is no debt to be paid; on the other, no compulsion that may properly be exercised. The rights of the father have ceased with the infancy of the child.

So with the other colonial powers. The French and Belgians no less than the British doubt that the child has in truth grown up. But the French, at least, have been more willing to recognize both the right of the child to his freedom and the fact that his further education should be left to his own brothers. . . . The Portuguese remain convinced that it is possible to keep their children in their proper place and arrest development of all but a few, by well-tried and effective measures. They may find themselves mistaken.

Thus the century moves on into its seventh decade. Colonialism, already in its twilight, moves on toward its appointed end. It will soon be a phase of history to be studied only by historians, and its passing governmental forms, captured in this book as they passed, will no longer be of anything but historical interest to students of government.

WILLIAM G. CARLETON

Leninism and the Legacy of Western Imperialism

It is often assumed in the United States that anti-colonialism—which is also an expression of anti-Westernism since it was the Western powers which acquired colonies in Asia, Africa, the Middle East, and Latin America—has been due largely to the influence of communism, as expressed in the writings of Lenin and Stalin. It is true that Lenin vigorously opposed colonialism and regarded

Russia as a "colonial" country, not in the sense that it was ruled by a Western power but in the sense that its backward agrarian economy depended heavily on the West for its manufactured goods—as did those of the non-Western colonies—and declared that Russia was thus on their side. Yet the revolts against colonialism in the non-Western world drew their inspiration in the first instance from the American Revolution—from the ideas of Jefferson and Washington—long before Lenin came on the scene. Nor has communism, contrary to the misgivings of many Westerners, made notable inroads in the newly emerged nations, except in the case of North Korea and Communist China, which were never colonized by the West, and North Vietnam.

The reasons why communism has not gained as much from the decline of Western imperialism as had been expected both in Washington and Moscow are explained by Dr. William G. Carleton, professor emeritus of political science at the University of Florida. Professor Carleton, a frequent contributor to various magazines, notably The Yale Review, is currently engaged in a study of politics as an art.

ONE OF THE most curious paradoxes of our time is the way the West, while resisting the Communist powers, has itself been intellectually impressed by the Marxist interpretation of history, particularly twentieth-century history. Early in this century the high priests of Marxism made ambitious prophecies about what the forces of historical determinism had in store for us during the century, but we are now far enough along to see that history in practice is not working out according to their predictions. What is odd is the persistence on the part of non-Marxist Westerners in believing the Marxist myths.

When communism triumphed in backward Russia and failed to come to power in industrially-advanced Germany, this was contrary to Marxist prophecy. However, at the time of the Bolshevist Revolution, Lenin believed that a Communist world revolution was in the making, a revolution which would result in an international proletarian society. But this revolution miscarried after the First World War and again after the Second World War. The international proletarian society does not exist.

Communism has appeared only in a national form, and the various countries which have gone Communist have done so at different times and under different circumstances. In Russia and in China, communism came largely as the result of indigenous national revolutions. In others,

From The Yale Review, Vol. LI, June 1962, No. 4. Copyright © Yale University Press, Inc.

as in the Eastern European satellites, it has been imposed by Soviet imperialism.

Today, Communist countries differ from one another in history, conditions, cultures, stages of revolutionary development, and degrees of Marxist "orthodoxy" or "revisionism." Westerners, swayed by the Marxist myth, persist in exaggerating the solidarity of the Communist countries. Where there is "solidarity," as in the case of the Warsaw Pact countries, it is the solidarity of satellitism, a far cry from proletarian brotherhood.

Moreover, we in the West are still much impressed, consciously or unconsciously, by the Marxist doctrine of "capitalist imperialism." This emphasis on imperialism was largely Lenin's contribution to Marxism. Leninism holds that "dying capitalism" is kept alive by the economic exploitation of the colonial peoples, that these peoples will develop a great hatred for their masters and will eventually rise up against "the bourgeois imperialists," oust them, establish Communist societies of workers and peasants, and join the international proletarian society.

It is, of course, now apparent to all that the sweep of the anti-imperialist revolutions in Asia, the Middle East, and Africa is one of the most momentous and far-reaching facts of our time. It is also true that the Soviet system has marked attractions for peoples emerging from colonialism. These peoples do not have indigenous capital-supplying classes in sufficient numbers to finance industrial revolutions through private enterprise alone. They are impressed by Russia's industrial achievements, and they tend to regard the totalitarian economics of the Communists—curtailed consumption, forced savings, the regimentation of labor and collective capital into the heavy-goods industries—as an available, a sure, and a relatively self-reliant way to get an industrial revolution in a hurry.

However, most of the new nations are not adopting communism. They dislike totalitarian dictatorship and the police state, they fear satellitism, and the advanced industrial countries are helping them achieve modernization and industrialization through less drastic methods. Instead, most of the new societies are moving in the direction of mixed economies, which combine privatism, collectivism, and welfarism in varying proportions.

Nevertheless, Westerners are still haunted by the prophecies of Lenin. This is reflected in the still rather general feeling that in the contest of East and West the Communists have a "natural" advantage among the underdeveloped peoples. Westerners too often exaggerate the appeal of totalitarian economics to the underdeveloped peoples and minimize the desire of these peoples for liberty and democracy. Many Westerners see Marxist influence in the government financing of some of the basic industrial developments in the new societies, although such financing arises from indigenous necessities which would exist even if there had never been a Communist revolution in Russia or China. In addition, coming out of a sense of guilt, Westerners fear that the colonial peoples, having built up hostility to the Western governing powers during the pre-revolutionary and the revolutionary periods, will carry over that hostility into the post-revolutionary period, that the West for years to come must suffer the consequences of its "sins of imperialism."

The truth is the opposite. One of the most important advantages the West has in its contest with the Communist powers comes out of the fact that Western countries for a long period of time and until very recently ruled the colonial peoples of Asia and Africa. In spite of inherent contradictions, Western imperialism during its long sway planted Western concepts of liberty, democracy, and genuine education as distinguished from indoctrination. It modified Asian and African cultures in a Western direction. It left countless imprints of Western civilization. British or Dutch or French ways, more or less interwoven with indigenous ways, became the local and the familiar ways. The new societies in Asia and Africa cannot escape that impact, and most of their leaders do not wish to escape it. In India or Malaya or Egypt or Ghana or Nigeria, a Russian is a "foreigner" in a way an Englishman can never be, just as in Latin America the Russians and the Chinese are aliens in a sense that Spaniards—and even North Americans—are not.

Today, communism is a greater threat in Latin America than it is in most of the new countries recently carved from the old Dutch, French, and British empires in Asia and Africa. Yet most of Latin America has not been under European rule for well over one hundred years. Latin Americans cannot blame their troubles on political imperialism, and unlike contemporary Africans and south Asians they cannot pin their hopes for remedial measures on national independence, for they have had that for generations. Therefore, the most impatient among them increasingly look to new economic and social systems for relief. However, the actual implementing of adequate foreign-aid programs in Latin America (long overdue) and the basic pull of Western culture there will probably prove decisive for the West in the battle with communism.

It is highly significant that the one country (and a most important one it is) which seems to affirm the Leninist pattern—Red China— was never a political colony of a Western power. At a late stage of Western imperialism, large parts of China became economic spheres of influence of various European countries. These spheres were exploited economically, but imperialist governments were never established and the Western powers escaped political responsibilities. Their legal and political systems did not permeate the country. They did not build roads, schools, and clinics as they did in their political colonies. In not a single one of these economic spheres into which China was divided did any European culture penetrate in the way British culture penetrated India, Pakistan, Ceylon, Burma, and Malaya. (In Latin America, too, for the past century the advanced industrial countries have enjoyed immense economic advantages without political, social, and educational responsibilities.)

But in most of the new countries which have emerged from the old Dutch, French, and British empires—where imperialism was political, where it lasted long enough to penetrate culturally, where the governing power met its social and educational responsibilities to a reasonable degree, and where resistance to the national independence movements was not overprolonged or unusually violent—the Communist expectations are not being borne out.

The anti-imperialist revolutions have now been with us long enough to be put into something like true historical perspective. The process of a typical anti-imperialist revolution seems to run as follows.

First comes the long period of revolutionary agitation, with growing animosity toward the governing power. For the most part the revolutionary agitation is led by those who have been educated not in Moscow but in Britain, France, or some other Western country. Indeed, it is this Western education which has largely imbued the leaders with the idea of nationalism for their homeland.

The base of the national revolution gradually broadens. The conflict intensifies. At this stage many of the leaders pass through a more or less Marxist phase. They think of Marxism as a tool for winning the national struggle; they cooperate with out-and-out Communists; they flirt with communism's totalitarian economics as an available method for the rapid industrialization of their country once independence is achieved.

Passive resistance, non-cooperation, sabotage, strikes, and violence increase. Armed conflict is imminent or actually arrives. Then the imperialist power bows to the inevitable, makes a settlement, and withdraws—sooner, with less resistance, and more gracefully than had been expected.

But much trade with the old governing country continues. Much Western capital remains. For more rapid industrial development, however, the government of the old imperial power extends grants and easy long-term credits to the new national government for technicians and capital developments.

Marxist sympathy and cooperation with the Communists ebb. The leaders of the new nation are now repelled by the drastic nature of totalitarian economics and the police state, and besides, with the economic help of the government of the old imperial power and other Western powers, particularly the United States, they see alternative and less painful ways to achieve fairly rapid industrialization. Moreover, the leaders have now become vested nationalists, nationalists in power, and they view communism's theoretical internationalism and its actual satellitism as threats to their own position and their country's independence.

With the lapse of time the leaders and the intellectuals begin to put their revolution into perspective. They see that while the economic exploitation of colonialism undoubtedly played a part in their drive for independence, at bottom there was something broader and more basic— resentment of a people reduced to a subordinate place and at best second-class citizenship in their own homeland and a yearning for equal rights, individual respect, and human dignity.

When national independence has been won, the old animosity toward the former governing country subsides. The cultural impact of that country continues in myriad ways, some obvious and others more subtle. The attitudes of the indigenous people toward the people who once governed them soften, and with more time become mellow and even sentimental.

In short, after the revolution has been accepted, a reaction in favor of the old governing power usually sets in. Already this is quite marked in India, Burma, Ghana, and Nigeria with respect to Britain, and Tunisia and most of Equatorial Africa with respect to France. The attitude of most people in the Philippines toward Americans is now downright affectionate.

However, it should be emphasized that this post-revolutionary reaction does not always take place, and under certain circumstances it should not be expected. It has not been strong in the countries carved from old French Indo-China, for the French resistance to national independence movements in this area was needlessly prolonged and obstinate, and the Communists have been the gainers. (However, good will toward the French in Cambodia, Laos, and South Vietnam is not entirely lacking, and the peoples of these countries cannot escape French cultural influences.) . . . Algeria, in spite of the long and bloody struggle for independence there, will not be able to eliminate the cultural influences of over a century of French rule, which penetrated deeply and often beneficently, and it is probable that within the next decade, with independence achieved, Algeria's good will toward France will equal that of Tunisia.

A friendly reaction has taken place or is taking place among most of the peoples of the new nations which have emerged from the old French and British empires. It is particularly noticeable in most of the new African states. By the time the British and the French had to deal seriously with nationalist movements in Negro Africa they had learned the high art of liquidating empire. Time-tables for self-government and then independence were deliberately worked out, and colonial administrators cooperated with nationalist leaders to these ends.

The independence of additional new states is now in the offing, and for some the dates for independence have already been designated. There are a few anti-colonial revolutions yet to come. In Portugal's African colonies such revolutions are now gathering momentum. In Algeria such a revolution has long been under way and is now apparently reaching a successful climax.

However, the vast majority of the revolutions for national independence are now behind us. In most cases we are already in the post-revolutionary period—in the afterglow of Western imperialism—in which the cultural influences and the reservoir of good will left by the old imperialism will operate to the advantage of the West. . . .

. . . many—though not all—of the leaders of the new nations have passed through moderately Marxist phases. With national independence achieved or within sight, most of these have dropped their Marxism. Almost without exception the leaders have had Western educations, as have the classes from which the leaders have mostly been drawn. Even the local and primary schools in the old colonies have radiated Western culture. And even those large segments of the population which have had little or no formal education know something of the language of the old governing power, are accustomed to dealing in terms of that country's monetary unit, are used to the make and style of goods from that country, and continue in considerable measure to buy from and sell to that country. Political institutions and ideals have been greatly influenced by the old governing power. These are only the more obvious manifestations of the continuing impact of the old imperialism on the new countries, for that impact asserts itself in innumerable and subtle ways.

The old imperialism continues to manifest itself in even the political combinations the new countries make. All but one of France's former colonies in Negro Africa are either members of the French Community or closely associated with France through bilateral treaties. Most of Britain's former colonies are members of the Commonwealth. After all the discussion of a West African federation, it seems likely that if an effective federation in that area is achieved it will take the forms of a West African federation of French-oriented nations and a West African federation of British-oriented nations. Among the difficulties of the abortive United Arab Republic was the fact that for many years Egypt was in the British colonial orbit and Syria in the French.

Most of the economic collectivism in the underdeveloped nations—

that is, government initiating and financing of enterprises basic to in-dustrialization—is not Marxist. It is indigenous, and it grows out of pragmatic necessity. Where there is a social philosophy behind it, as in India and Burma, it approximates Fabian socialism, borrowed from Brit-ish thinkers.

Had the more thorough-going socialism envisaged by the pre-World War I Socialists or had communism ever come to power in a European country with important overseas colonies, there is little doubt that so-cialism or that communism would have had a most powerful impact on the colonies and would have influenced them in the building of their institutions after independence. The miscarriage of the Socialist revolu-tion and of the Communist revolution in Western Europe has had decisive consequences in the former colonial areas.

In this sense the older Marxism was much more realistic than the younger Leninism. Marxism expected a thorough-going socialism or communism to triumph first in the advanced industrial countries of Western Europe and then from Europe to influence the colonial areas. Leninism gave rise to the belief that communism could win the West through a prior victory in the colonial areas. We now see that the mis-carriage of Marxism in Western Europe resulted in leaving Marxism with insufficient prestige and too few Western cultural carriers to win in the colonial areas.

Now, there is no doubt that the peoples emerging from colonialism resent the continuation of colonialism in such places as . . . Angola, and Mozambique. They are also irritated by vestiges of imperialism, whether these are foreign air bases, oil and other special business con-cessions to foreign nationals, formal economic preferences for the old imperial power, or enclaves or near-by territory they regard as still nationally unredeemed. They also bristle at the still all-too-frequent assumption that their foreign policies are for sale or are susceptible of "management" by the West. These peoples, too, have an admiration for the industrial and technological achievements of Soviet Russia, and they are willing, often eager, to take economic aid from both the West and the Communist powers.

Nor can the West afford to take the friendship of the new nations for granted. They want socially effective technical and economic aid for their industrial developments. (Western economic aid which is adminis-tered by oligarchic national governments and which fails to result in an increase in wealth-producing enterprises and a rise in mass living stand-ards is worse than useless; it backfires and causes disillusionment.) They want understanding and respect. They are sensitive to racism and quickly detect inconsistencies between the West's democratic profes-sions and its practices. They abhor the intensification of the power conflict, the nuclear arms race, and the mischief done to outsiders by atomic testing.

It is true that most of the new nations are neutralist, refuse to line up with either of the opposing power blocs. Some, organized into a distinct bloc of their own, assert a positive neutralism. Others are opposed to all permanent and formal blocs, and among the new African nations only Ghana has aligned definitely with the Nehru-Sukarno-Nasser-Tito combination.

Because most of the new nations are neutralist in international politics we tend to overlook the fact that they are preponderantly Western in their orientation. They are not Communist. They are not police states. Even those which seriously abridge democratic rights and civil liberties cannot accurately be termed totalitarian. Their economic systems are not monolithic but mixed and fluid. Their intercourse is far more with the West than with Communist countries. The outside cultural influences continue to be far more Western than they are Russian or Chinese.

Now, of course, it is quite possible that some of the new nations now non-Communist may eventually go Communist. Whether this does or does not happen will depend largely on the adequacy and wisdom of Western policies with respect to the underdeveloped peoples. At this juncture in their history most of these peoples are putting their faith in their new governments and their new nationalism. Should these fail them, some might seek more drastic social and economic changes and turn to communism. There is the likelihood that additional new nations, failing to fulfill national expectations in a hurry, will fall into the hands of transparently non-popular, anti-democratic oligarchic-military governments (like the one in South Korea today), and that this in turn will increase the chances of ultimate Communist take-overs in such nations.

However, all of this departs widely from the way Lenin envisaged the historical process. We now know that after their anti-imperialist revolutions most of the old colonial peoples did not turn their backs on the old imperialist powers and that they did not join an international proletarian society. Instead, their revolutions became national revolutions and after independence had been won the former colonial peoples looked to the West for help and stability. They gave the West another chance.

Of this we may be sure: all of the new non-Communist countries will not go Communist, and if in the future some should go Communist, their new revolutions, their Communist revolutions, will take national forms and be conditioned by their national cultures. And those national cultures, in turn, have been durably affected by Western civilization during the long period of imperialism.

In most of the new nations, nationalist parties, largely peasant in mass composition, have come or are coming or will in the future come to power. These parties sometimes use Marxist terminology to justify indigenous collectivist necessities, but in practice what they do or propose to do is so far removed from a genuine Marxism that Communists do not recognize it as Marxist at all. These parties invariably emphasize a revival of indigenous language and culture, and from now on Western cultural influences will be muted and modified.

However, these Western influences cannot be eradicated; the nationalist parties tacitly accept much of the West's cultural impact; indeed, the passionate drive of the underdeveloped peoples to nationalism, industrialism, and rational living standards dramatically attests the continuing vitality of Western values. The Communists, of course, accept and exaggerate Western industrial and rational values; what they reject are other aspects of the Western heritage such as democracy, civil liberties, and intellectual freedom. But the old colonial areas have been exposed to many aspects of Western culture, including the non-material, and the non-material aspects are also having a continuing effect. Gandhi's life exemplifies a blend of the deep spiritual experiences of both the East and the West, and Nehru has been profoundly influenced by the West's humane values as well as its rational ones. The record up to now shows that most underdeveloped peoples clearly prefer to achieve industrialization and modernization in a non-totalitarian and humane way and that only if this way demonstrably fails will they resort to drastic Communist economies.

For the underdeveloped peoples, their leaders, and their nationalist mass parties, there is magic in the Western term democracy, but the achieving of effective democracy must necessarily be difficult. Democracy will suffer many ups and downs along the way. It is easy to sneer at Nasser's "presidential democracy," at Ayub Khan's "basic democracy," and at Sukarno's "guided democracy," but such slogans more often than not exemplify honest and realistic attempts to move in the direction of democracy. Even India's Congress Party and its government must be highly paternalistic at this stage of India's journey to democracy.

Western imperialism, then, left among the old colonial peoples both material and non-material Western values, and these, blended with a new emphasis on indigenous languages and folkways, constitute the chief dynamics of their contemporary history.

It is indeed strange that so many Westerners still take for granted that the Communists have the current advantage over the West among peoples recently emerged from colonialism, still believe essentially in the "realism" of the Leninist doctrine of imperialism, with its monistic economic interpretation of the "inevitable" trend of history in the old colonial areas and its prediction that the former colonial peoples would carry over into the post-revolutionary world an implacable hatred of the "bourgeois" civilization of the West. One explanation for the persistence of this myth is that many Americans think that a mixed economy, which combines indigenous collectivism, state enterprise, private enterprise, and state welfarism, is the same thing as communism; they see the spread of mixed economies as the spread of communism, whereas of course these fluid mixed economies differ sharply from totalitarian Communist economies. The actual course of the anti-imperialist revolutions since 1945 strongly indicates that it is the West which has the advantage, and the most basic reason for that advantage is the continuing vitality of Western culture and the permanent cultural impact left by Western imperialism itself in the old colonial areas.

Throughout history, long political rule has almost always resulted in lasting cultural influences. These influences have generally been more obvious when the colonies or provinces ruled were largely composed of people transplanted from the governing country itself, but sheer conquest of a people of one culture by people of another, when the period of imperial rule covers considerable time, produces significant and enduring cultural changes.

The anti-imperialist revolutions of the late eighteenth and early nineteenth centuries—the Anglo-American and the Latin-American revolutions—severed the political ties of the American colonies from their European rulers, but cultural affinities remained. In spite of the War of 1812 and the propensity of Americans during the nineteenth century to "twist the lion's tail," American-British relations in economic and cultural matters remained close, and after over a century of political separation, common cultural ties were among the most important forces bringing the United States and Britain together in twentieth-century world politics. Even among the Indians and mestizos of Latin America today, the Spanish culture largely prevails, and most of the educated among them find their spiritual homes in Rome and Madrid and in Spanish humanism.

The tenacity of the cultural impact left by the historical imperialisms is impressive. Even at the beginning of this century the influences of the Greek colonies of antiquity in Asia Minor and the Black Sea area were discernible. Stendhal, in his delightful accounts of his travels in Italy, noted as late as the early nineteenth century that in the southern part of the peninsula—in old Magna Graecia—Italian life and attitudes still revealed marked Greek influences. Even today some of the significant characteristics which distinguish European peoples from one another have their origins in the extent of the Roman conquests and the length of time the various areas were under Roman occupation.

European imperialism, which began with the Age of Discovery and Exploration in the late fifteenth century, is now drawing to its close. Unlike the other major imperialisms of history, it has in the main been liquidated with a minimum of violence and bloodshed. But like the other major imperialisms, its cultural influences will be felt through the centuries.

Today, in its struggle with the Communist powers, the West, notwithstanding a stereotype to the contrary, is the beneficiary of cultural linkages it forged with the colonial peoples during its long years of imperial rule.

GEORGE H. T. KIMBLE

Colonialism: The Good, the Bad, the Lessons

Professor George H. T. Kimble, although recognizing the dark side of some colonial practices, points out in the article presented here the principal benefits which, he believes, non-Western peoples derived from their association with Western rule.

Born in London in 1908, Professor Kimble was educated at King's College and at the University of Montreal. After teaching at the University College of Hull and the University of Reading in Britain, and at McGill University in Canada, he became professor of geography and chairman of the department at Indiana University in 1957. Among his many books is a comprehensive two-volume work on Tropical Africa, 1960, which he prepared, with the collaboration of other experts, for the Twentieth Century Fund.

ALTHOUGH Africa was never as dark as our ignorance of it, some of the news coming out of it these days is far from bright. And not only from the still-colonial territories either. Dispatches from the Congo tell of grave social disorder and political instability, and of leaders who are seemingly unwilling or unable to do anything about either. In Algeria,

From The New York Times Magazine, August 26, 1962. Copyright © by The New York Times. Reprinted by permission.

formation of a government to lead the newly independent nation has been delayed by power struggles while economic conditions have deteriorated and violence, though sporadic, continues. From Ghana and elsewhere come other intimations that the accolade of independence is no magic wand. It confers dignity—but not prosperity, peace or even, alas, order.

The quick and easy diagnosis of the continent's continuing trouble is that it is the fruit of colonialism: that colonialism was poor soil for the growth of independence—worse, that it was poor seed, and poor seed is incapable of producing good fruit. As developed by the people concerned, it is a plausible diagnosis, and one that is supported by many doctors of the African body politic, both in and out of the United Nations. But how accurate is it? Was colonialism the unmitigated evil it is so often represented to be? Was trouble its only bequest? Let us take a look at the colonial record, which by now is clear for all to see.

As practiced in its heyday by every European power, colonialism was a conceit wrapped in a concern that was frequently less religious than sanctimonious and less charitable than mercenary. It proceeded on the premise that it was dealing with, as Kipling wrote, "lesser breeds without the Law," or, as a Southern Rhodesian administrator put it in 1925, that "we are in this country because . . . we are better men." It employed methods that were bossy, when not dictatorial, or worse. It was everlastingly telling people what was good for them, and what was bad. And all too often it failed to practice the good it looked for in others or to eschew the bad it abhorred in them.

Granted, there have been vast differences in the records of the various colonial powers. Not all of them have made the same mistakes. Thus, the French did not mistakenly classify people by the color of their skins and build separate and unequal schools, churches, park benches and washrooms for those not of their color.

On the other hand, the British did not presume to think that their wards wanted to speak English and to live like Englishmen, or that the chief end of man was to glorify the British Constitution and enjoy it forever. Of course, they did not stand in the path of those who wished to adopt British ways. Indeed, they eagerly helped them to attain this end, but the matter was not one on which they insisted. They assumed, almost from the start, that sooner or later most educated people want to be themselves and manage or mismanage their affairs in their own way.

And neither the French nor the British made the mistake of supposing that it was possible—in the words of a Governor General of the former Belgian Congo—"to live together with the African, while remaining ourselves," or, as the Portuguese did, that nobody should be allowed to remain himself but, rather, that every African should be exhorted (if need be, by methods more punitive than persuasive) to live in an orderly, regimented society purged of the old tribal excesses and hostilities.

Then, not all of them have made equally serious mistakes. Thus, the French, for all their sense of mission, interfered surprisingly little with African customary law and its enforcement. Further, they took the view that some of the higher values of African culture were not incompatible with those looked for in a community of civilized men. Wherever the organization of a group was found to be reasonably efficient, they sought to protect and strengthen it. As a result, they had fewer lawbreakers on their books, and fewer enemies, than the Spanish and Portuguese.

Again, not all of them were equally slow to learn from their mistakes. For example, as deeply attached as the British are to precedent and tradition, they have not hesitated to ignore both when the occasion served and, instead, either to take their cue from their critics or to sit down in front of a piece of blank paper and wait for a new idea to strike them.

Some of these ideas, such as indirect rule (whereby indigenous systems of government were called into the service of the colonizing authority) may not always have been any more to the liking of their critics. However, none can doubt that the willingness of the British to try almost anything once, has won them more friends than were won by the Belgians who, it is to be feared, did little trying and did it too late.

Where all the colonial powers failed, it seems to me is in the following respects:

First, they failed to forecast the rising of the "winds of change." In a recent book, Margery Perham, one of Britain's most highly respected students of colonialism, confessed that she was "taken by surprise" by these winds, and that as late as 1939 the feeling about West Africa in the "official world," that is, the British Colonial Office, was pretty much that "we can be sure that we have unlimited time in which to work." As things turned out, the British had less than twenty years in which to work.

Many French people, we may assume, were taken even more by surprise, since down to the mid-Nineteen Fifties the common official view seems to have been that France would stretch from the Rhine to the Congo. As for the Belgians, as recently as 1958 they were still affirming their intention to stay in the Congo—because "the Congo needs us even more than we need the Congo."

Yet, for those with eyes to see them, there had long been signs of the coming change. From World War I onward there had been international conventions devoted to the subject of "African liberation." From the Nineteen Twenties there had been African student organizations (notably in the United Kingdom) that served as seedbeds for the germination of nationalist ideas and programs.

From the Nineteen Thirties there had been political congresses, parties and undercover organizations that worked to the same end in several British and French territories. From about the same time there had been African newspapers which sought to form—and sometimes to inflame—public opinion. And for a generation or more there had been Africans who journeyed to Moscow and other unpatriotic places.

As the colonial powers now see, they failed to understand African nationalism—both the source of its strength and passion, and the reasons for its surging discontent with servitude in any guise.

In the second place, they failed to provide the African with sufficient "protection" when the winds did rise. None of the newly independent countries had enough skilled African administrators to run their own show; not infrequently, independence meant an increased, rather than decreased, reliance on outsiders. (As one wit put it, "It takes a lot of Europeans to Africanize a place.")

None of the countries had enough African technicians to keep their public utilities working smoothly, or enough African professional men to ensure that the health of their people would be protected and their economic and legal interests adequately served. Somalia had no indigenous doctors when it became independent; Nigeria less than one dentist for every million people; Tanganyika only two engineers; the Congo one engineer, and no doctors, dentists, lawyers or public accountants.

And no country had an electorate that knew what independence was all about or what the keeping of it would cost in self-discipline, or cold cash.

Third, the colonial powers failed either to understand the nature of the African's environment or to live up to their understanding of it. They underestimated the difficulty of getting the environment to "go to work" for the African, and so of establishing economies that were at once strong enough to take the strain of independence and durable enough to keep those who worked them independent.

All too frequently they regarded the African's land as a bank to be robbed for their profit rather than as a trust to be husbanded for his. Only belatedly did they come to perceive the delicacy of Africa's physical and biological balance: the hunger of its soils, the variability of its rainfall, the scourge of its heat and humidity, and its hostility to sustained effort and large-scale enterprise.

Today, roughly half the lands of Africa are in poorer shape than they were fifty years ago. In at least one-third of the continent wind and water are removing topsoil faster than it is being replaced, and ground water levels are receding because of the consequently increased evaporation and run-off. In at least one-half of the forest country timber is being cut for fuel, lumber, wood ash and a dozen other purposes faster than it is growing.

The agricultural picture is scarcely brighter. In many areas the rest period given to land that has been cropped—as most of it periodically is—to the point of exhaustion, is now shorter than it used to be. While this is partly because of growing population pressure on the cultivated land, it is also because in many areas the farmers are now restrained from following their traditional "bush fallowing" system of soil conservation, under which sections of land are allowed to return to "bush" for a number of years. The Government feels that this method removes too much acreage from cultivation.

Needless to say, there are ways of stabilizing the soil and of increasing its yield of water, wood and crops; but up to now these have been more often talked about than tried. When tried, they have more than once been on the wrong scale or in the wrong place.

Perhaps the colonizers' greatest failure of all was their failure to understand the African—his hopes and fears, his capacities, needs and sensibilities. True, they did much better by him in the Nineteen Fifties than in the days of H. M. Stanley and Joseph Conrad. But they (and, for that matter, we) have lost little of the old-time zeal to make over (if not to take over) his economy—to convert him to Western ways of running farms and ruining the soil, of making money and creating unemployment, and of arousing desires that cannot be satisfied.

Neither have they (or we) lost much of the old-time zeal to teach him Western ways of organizing academies and armies, of behaving toward God and neighbor, of marrying and raising a family, of dressing, drinking and dying. (Already in some territories the automobile kills more people than the anopheles mosquito.)

All this has quietly undermined, when it has not destroyed, the African's self-respect, his sense of being valued for what he is and not merely for what he can do. It has also forced him to do virtually all of the taking and none of the giving. If we are to believe Laurens van der Post, the writer-explorer, who has lived closer to the African than most, it is this denial of the African's creativeness that has embittered his spirit, inflamed his passion and been responsible for much of the continuing "darkness" of his continent.

This is not to say that the colonial powers are called upon to renounce their record, let alone to stand trial for it. As George F. Kennan observed in his Reith Lectures in England in 1957: "The establishment of the colonial relationship did not represent a moral action on somebody's part; it represented a natural and inevitable response to certain demands and stimuli of the age. It was simply a stage of history." To judge the colonial powers in the light of the standards of a later age is unfair.

Furthermore, some of the things to come out of the "colonial relationship" are cause more for praise than for shame. To begin with, independence came out of it. The fact that there are independent states in Africa today is very largely the result of the European "presence." Without this, it is hard to see how the people living there could have bridged the gap between tribaldom and nationhood, between anarchy and order in so short a time.

For all its faults, colonial government was a hundred times better than the unregulated dealings of men like Conrad's Kurtz, who were armed with power to destroy and corrupt and had no scruples about using it. It provided security of person and property in lands that had known little of either, and so, enlarged the borders of the world in which a man could wander and work, live and die. It also provided experience in the running of business, industry and civil services for people who had hitherto shown few signs of developing these for themselves.

Then, too, it provided education (little enough, to be sure) that enabled men to know of Jefferson and Burke, the Magna Carta, the Bill of Rights and the no less revolutionary doctrines of the New Testament. In other words, it provided the grain of opportunity on which the pearl of independence could be cultured.

It did more than this. It provided much of the sustenance for the growing pearl. For it was the colonial powers who were largely responsible for the opening of the region to the lumberman, miner, planter and other men of means without whom its wealth would have continued to lie fallow.

Before colonial times, almost the only tropical African "goods" to command an overseas market were slaves, ivory and gold. There was a little trade in hardwoods such as ebony, and in kola nuts, spices and incense, but none at all in cocoa, coffee, rubber, peanuts, sisal and a dozen other commodities that are now indispensable revenue-earners in as many countries.

The colonial powers were also responsible for a great deal of development that was not, and could not have been, financed from export revenues. The French Investment Funds for Economic and Social Development, the Belgian Funds for Native Welfare, the British Colonial Development and Welfare Grants and the Portuguese Colonial Development Fund—to name only four sources of such development money—provided the means, and often the ways, by which people could learn to overcome the handicaps imposed on them by a difficult environment and by centuries of isolation and apathy. In pre-colonial times there were no high schools or colleges in tropical Africa, nor any hospitals, clinics, dispensaries or other health services, and no roads or railways.

A number of uncovenanted gains also have come out of the colonial relationship. Among these is the mutual esteem—affection is not too strong a word—which has frequently developed between the colonial administrator and those he administered. Many Africans have been frank to admit that, if they have to be shoved around by somebody of another tribe, they would just as soon he was of a European "tribe."

Among them, too, is the interest taken in the African and his world by philanthropic and social agencies; and the realization by those who have gone to the African as tutors that they, also, have much to learn.

Which brings me to what the colonial relationship has done for the colonizers. It has shown them that, in many respects, they were not so good as they thought they were; that they didn't always know what was best for others; and that, not infrequently, their best—including, as it did, parliamentary democracy, paper work and plumbing—held little appeal for others.

It has shown them that the African was, in many respects, better than they thought he was; that his own ways of raising crops and family, of dealing with offenders and having fun were frequently as sensible as their own, and much less costly.

Again, it has shown them—the British and French, at any rate, and perhaps even the Belgians—that the only kind of power worth wielding is the one that decreases rather than grows with exercise. And it has encouraged them to believe that dying empires can be transformed into living commonwealths.

At the moment, it is true, this transformation is little more than a possibility in most parts of Africa; in some it is scarcely even that, for Ghana, Guinea and the Congo show no sign of wanting to be transformed into anything that can be taken for a family likeness to those who sired them. Yet none of the new states is unaware of the impossibility of being a standout in a world where the trend is increasingly toward "togetherness." After all, none of them has enough revenues, skills, experience or manpower to "go it alone."

What, then, will happen to the new states? Will they form durable regional federations among themselves, complete with common markets, common laws, armies and so on? Will they seek to establish a United

States of Africa? Will they try to turn themselves into a "third world" that is independent of both East and West?

One thing we can be sure of. The new states have no intention of changing one colonial relationship for another—whether the relationship be with fellow Africans or foreigners. They have had colonialism—and the subservience, the second-class citizenship, the economic and social disabilities, the rule by outsiders that goes with it.

Henceforth they intend to go their own way, just as we in this country have gone our own way. By the look of things, their way may not be greatly to our taste, for as yet it shows little sign of coinciding with ours in such matters as order and efficiency, to say nothing of how to deal with communism. Nor does it show any sign of being comfortable to live with.

Not that there is much any of us can do about it—except one thing. When asked (and we shall be, increasingly, as we set our own house in order) we can play the almost forgotten role of servant; clearing up a mess here, giving a helping hand there, and demonstrating that we are at least as well-fitted for the role as the Russians, the Chinese and all the other people who will be playing it, too.

[2]

Impact
of Nationalism

MAMADOU DIA

The African Nations
and World Solidarity

The achievement of national independence—which the author sees as a "collective vocation . . . an affirmation, a perpetual movement, an unfinished construction" rather than a "static, definitive state"—is the goal of every people emerging from colonial domination. No sooner is this goal achieved, however, than the newly free nation begins to realize that political independence alone will not assure its stability, well-being, or even survival in a world still dominated by great-power struggles.

This is the view of Mamadou Dia, the former Prime Minister of Senegal, until 1958 a colony of France. He fears that unbridled nationalist sentiment may result, particularly in Africa, in the creation of "micronations" and "micronationalisms"—communities too small and weak to survive on their own efforts alone which then find themselves faced with complex difficulties of economic and social development. He believes that all peoples, and particularly those now emerging on the world scene, must seek their safeguard in the Community of Nations, "the final phase toward which the building of the new civilization should lead."

Mamadou Dia was born in 1910 in Khombole, Senegal. He was educated in Africa, where he worked as a teacher and as a journalist until he was elected to the French Senate in 1948. An economics expert and a gifted orator, he served as deputy to the French National Assembly in Paris from 1948 to 1958, when he returned to Senegal at the time it achieved independence. He has written several other books, all in French, among them The African Economy, Studies and New Problems, 1957.

Chapter 1

Toward a New Definition of Nation

ONE NEED NOT be a prophet to predict that in the coming years, the arrival at the United Nations of a wave of young nations, most of them African, will continue to shake the world's equilibrium. This prospect, which causes some uneasiness—admitted or not—is attributable to a nationalism over which Western Europe has lost its monopoly. Nevertheless, the nationalism that today is liberating overseas territories owes much to the West, especially to Europe, mother of nationalism and, at the same time, by a strange destiny, mother of colonialism. By linking a colonizing mission to its national vocation, the West, or more precisely Europe, provided the impact, with results that have not always been a negative influence.

Analyzing the different phases in the economic growth of nations, W. W. Rostow, an economic historian, rightly emphasizes the positive role played by colonialism in the transforming process that prepares for the take-off and subsequently for the progress toward maturity. Willingly or unwillingly, colonization carries the germ of liberation, by virtue of the transformations that it involves, the changes it introduces in ideas, institutions, and mores, and the basic services it implants, indispensable for the activity of the colonial society, which is itself obliged to evolve from the traditional to the transitional stage.

Let us not expect colonization to be more than it could possibly become, namely, an ethic. Let us agree to judge it by its results and we shall have to admit that, along with its ravages, colonization—any colonization—makes some favorable contributions. On this point, the opinion of the political historian cannot objectively differ from that of the economic historian. African civilizations have known periods of decline during which atrocious feudalisms have reigned, after eras of splendor sustained by an impeccable state organization. Why deny it, in the face of the most patent historical truth? Human societies and nations are similar: they get the fate that they deserve. African nations, like all nations torn by dissension, anarchy, and neglect of the collective welfare, have become easy prey. Colonization has provided the shock that awakened them and inspired a new spirit. It is not paradoxical to contend that colonization engendered nationalism, not only that of clans and tribes, but also doctrinal, unifying nationalism, which transforms the struggle of colonized nations into a struggle on a world-wide scale.

From *The African Nations and World Solidarity* by Mamadou Dia. English translation by Mercer Cook, copyright © 1961 by Frederick A. Praeger, Inc. Thames and Hudson, Ltd., London. Reprinted by permission of the publishers.

But how can we speak of African nations while African nationalism is still at the revolutionary stage; while it has not yet emancipated more than a tiny fraction of the population; while the few states that have been created are for the most part unable to assume national vocations? This is the moment, we believe, to attack the concept of "nation" by which Western historians tend to make of it a special "category," a notion peculiar to their society or to Western-type societies in general. Renan stepped out of character in his famous lecture when he affirmed that the nation was not only a historical fact, not just a group of men, a territory, a tradition, a "soul," but the spiritualized version of these different material elements, the whole of which is oriented toward the common good of the group, of humanity. What must be stressed in this definition is that instead of being a static, definitive state, the nation is rather an affirmation, a perpetual movement, an unfinished construction. Placing oneself in Renan's train of thought, one might define the nation as a collective vocation, depending on a common scale of values, common institutions, and, finally, common aims.

Thus we must discard racist theories that claim to base the national vocation on the race or the people. These are mere biological elements, the components of a vocation, not the vocation itself. "To be what nature makes of us is not the same as having a vocation." Increasingly numerous are the examples of historically and ethnically heterogeneous groups that share a collective national vocation. It is to be hoped that this process may become general, thus settling certain frightful dramas and making new nations centers of humanism, by the diversity of the human elements assembled. If they are willing to seize this opportunity, the emergent nations can make an invaluable contribution to the cause of world civilization. Imagine for a single instant all the power of conciliation, concord, and fraternity accumulated in the dynamic notion of an Algerian nation conceived and accepted as in Brazil, where the German immigrants have blended into the national unity.

As a vocation, the nation cannot be a rigid framework for activities: it is a stimulus. Its frontiers cannot be those of dwarf states that try to atomize it, to divide it against itself and so guarantee its failure. We must always remember this in order not to create static situations or compromise the nation's possibilities of expansion by obstructing the future. This is how we must interpret Péguy's magnificent statement: "The nation is a mission." Certainly not the mission of devouring others, of suppressing other vocations, or of subordinating them to one's own, but that of permitting, by peaceful radiation, the accomplishment of the largest possible and most human collective vocation. This is why any qualifications that one tries to attach to the right of self-determination seem to us as dangerous as the negation of that principle. They destroy the national reality by introducing a process of disintegration and making their major premise a historical error that places on the same plane elements as diversified as nation, people, and territory.

It is perfectly obvious that the nation as a collective vocation within African dimensions necessarily groups diverse countries and peoples. Hence the stupidity of certain border disputes that seem to excite African or Arab leaders who lack neither culture nor political realism. They act as if it were a question of fixing a definite form to this vast movement that will continue to seek an equilibrium not yet attained. They act as if it were a matter of launching a competition between national vocations, while nations large or small, rich or poor, in Africa and elsewhere, have real value only as instruments of world solidarity. In short, they act as if the nation were an absolute, not—as it is by definition—a contingent reality, with changing frontiers. This is particularly true of the emergent nations.

History furnishes unforgettable examples. The Venetian and Florentine national vocations, although clearly expressed, were no less happily merged in a wider and more authentically national collective vocation —the Italian vocation. The states emerging in our time have the right to set territorial limits for themselves and to remain within those limits. They would be wrong to confuse these with the boundaries of the emergent nation or nations and to try to impose their dimensions on the latter. On the other hand, one cannot refuse the various national vocations the right to exist, on the pretext of unification or supranationality. It seems evident to us that here one must be careful not to adopt the idolatry that totalitarian regimes propose—interpreting the nation grossly without pushing the analysis any further. Western Socialists who urge colonized people to abandon their national vocation in favor of socialism—without, however, renouncing their own nationalism —have to be shown the firm desire for nationhood.

Despite what is heard or written in the name of pure doctrine, nothing is less certain than the contention that class is a higher form of integration than nation, and sufficient in itself for the realization of the common good. The formation of proletarian nations on the imperialistic model is surely the most forceful argument against the alleged power attributed to class and the illusions that many try to maintain concerning it. Pierre Moussa claims that one of the essential factors impeding the revalorization of the prices of raw materials from the Tiers-Monde—and we shall see that this problem is basic for the proletariat of those countries—is the fact that the Western working class—after bitter, violent struggles, of course—turns to its advantage an important part of the profits extracted by the capitalists. This example suffices to illustrate once and for all the inadequacy of class to realize a vertical socialist integration in the concrete domain of wages and living standards, and consequently, on the moral plane, its total inability to embody such spiritual values as justice, equality, and fraternity. In the present context of historical development, it is clear that the proletarian nations would strike a foolish bargain if they renounced their own vocations for an integration that the Western nations, of whatever bloc, do not yet seem ready for. In this respect, all the nationalists of the different underdeveloped countries will endorse the following declaration of the Lebanese Socialist Clovis Maksoud:

> The nationalist struggle is not a backward step that lessens the universality of the Arab-socialist ideal. Nationalism in the context of the Arab world is the force that seeks to raise the Arabs to a rank where they will be totally engaged in universal humanist movements and where their support of internationalist objectives will be more positive and more concrete. To ask progressive Arabs to accept the current interpretation that Western socialists attach to nationalism is to invite them to act in isolation. In fact, this is asking them to entrust the leadership of the inevitable struggle for unity and liberation to opportunistic, illogical politicians, who would turn the legitimate demands of the people to ends harmful to the cause of social, economic, and political democracy in the Middle East.

Concluding this brief analysis, we readily see that the classic theories about nation, including that of scientific socialism, must at least be revised. The nations of the twentieth century are no longer defined by a historical context, by material supports, by the homogeneity of environment, of culture, but much more so by potentialities, by possibilities of synthesis, and, at the same time, by the homogeneity of the elements to be regrouped. The U.S.S.R., India, the forthcoming Confederation of Independent States of the Franco-African Community offer, each in its fashion, instructive examples. It is the mutual respect of national vocations, of national cultures, of national personalities that assures the success of the common undertaking. Far from being an obstacle to the latter or an inhibiting force against integration, the nation-vocation is characteristic of them.

We must remember that while no nation is valid without morality, it certainly cannot be valid without economic and technical efficiency in this cruel world. The nationalism of colonial and former colonial territories, if it is to attain the desired result, owes it to itself to be an active, constructive nationalism, determined to transform a state of revolt into an effective revolution. In this light, the concept of "African nations" finds theoretical and practical justification, even in the absence of an impressive past (and we know that this is not the case), even in the absence of perfectly organized institutions. What matters primarily is the consciousness of being, the will to be born, to participate in world growth, and to require justice of other nations. Such is the meaning of the revolution that is being waged before our eyes and that henceforth will take the initiative away from the West.

Nationalism in this sense is something quite different from a theory founded on racial or religious ideology. Nationalism with a racial or religious basis is an irrational construction depending not so much on a national conscience as on the collective folly of the crowd, on the destructive force of exasperated instincts. It is a blind, closed nationalism, inaccessible to the concept of nation-solidarity, and not conducive to a universal humanism. This is why those African nations destined to play any historic role whatsoever will neither be Negro, Berber, or Arab nations, nor Christian, Moslem, or animist nations. They will, of course, be strongly marked by the influence of the different biological factors and by the impact of the various philosophies of their people, but above all, they will be—if they are to be anything at all—a synthesis, or let us say, a civilization. Only on this condition will they become an active element of the post-Marxian revolution of the twentieth century.

General Conclusions
Toward a Community of United Nations

WHETHER the disguised imperialisms approve or not, the age of resignation has ended for the peoples and nations of the *Tiers-Monde*. They are no longer willing for others to think and decide for them. From now on they intend to think for themselves and make their own decisions. They are determined to take their own initiative in every field. Neither ideologies of power nor ideologies of submissiveness, proposed by illustrious apostles, can overcome their resolve. Even if gigantic forces should be mobilized to mutilate populations and plunge nations and homelands into mourning, no material force can destroy what is today the ideal of those nations and fatherlands. One may appeal to the moderating virtues of the great religions—to Christian brotherhood or to Moslem obedience. But it would be impossible to stifle the resentment of the hungry masses of the *Tiers-Monde*, Christian or Moslem, or to prevent the explosion of their anger in a world where the most modern societies, the most advanced technically, are also the most barbaric, the most inhuman.

But to be creative, the twentieth-century revolution must be something other than a revolt against hunger or a proletarian riot. It must be more than a class revolution on the scale of nations and of continents; it must be a world revolution, affecting the totality of nations and continents. Naturally, neither the classical Marxist formulas, nor even less the models of the capitalist system, permit such a prospect, which requires a complete break with the distorted analyses to which the leading orthodoxies have accustomed us. In this phase of historical change, it is necessary to renovate everything: prospects, concepts, and methods of attacking problems, including the dialectical method, which must undergo a healthy readaptation. The revolution in question is, above all else, an intellectual revolution, challenging the ideological system and the results it has produced. Technological successes registered here and there are unfortunately too technical and, in any case, too limited for one to judge their effectiveness as instruments of universal progress. Perhaps it would be better to have, I shall not say less intelligence, but certainly less technological success and more human progress.

This may be the moment to remind Intelligence of the respect that she owes man, if she wishes to survive her present glory. This is also the moment to remind the great modern civilizations that their permanence, or simply their continuance, does not depend on their brilliance, but rather on their human content, on their capacity for human progress. "Civilizations," notes Gabriel Ardant, "have always perished because of their narrowness—physical or intellectual; in other words, from their failure to include the more numerous masses of men, with whom they have been unable to share their progress." Failing to understand this, despite the glory that they have known, mercantile civilizations, from the Roman Empire to Carthage, have crumbled one by one. Modern civilizations will not experience a better fate, notwithstanding technical advancement and extraordinary scientific contributions, if they remain narrowly limited physically and intellectually. But why prophesy, since they already show so many signs of decline, precisely because they lack the necessary breadth of vision and do not provide themselves with a framework of world-wide dimensions?

It is symptomatic that our era, which is that of guided missiles, is also the era of the greatest crisis the world has known; and the most technically advanced nations are far from secure. Science will really become a boon to all mankind only when it stops being an instrument enabling some to dominate others. Technical development will really become a crucial factor for progress only when it is within the reach of every nation, large or small, rich or poor. In short, the fundamental law of the new world is essentially co-operative. The civilization to be born will only know durable progress through scientific co-operation that will ban monopolies of national states and restore science to its universal status; and through technical co-operation that will place the most modern techniques of development at the disposal of the most backward countries by utilizing appropriate formulas of assistance. Without this co-operation between the nations of all continents, of all ages, of all ideological formations, making inventions and discoveries the property of all humanity and not exclusively that of particular nations, the progress of science and technology will only be able to hasten world disintegration by increasing the disparities and disequilibriums.

There is no reason to be pessimistic if one is determined to play the game, to use the advantages at one's disposal, to build on the ruins of the dying mercantile civilization a new one, more human, better balanced. Furthermore, it is essential that rivalry in a tormented, torn universe give way to co-operation; not verbal co-operation interested only in propaganda, but effective, sincere co-operation that—eliminating the causes of conflicts and armed disputes—would convince everyone of the uselessness of expenditures on armament, which divert so many resources from tasks of collective creation. From this will to collaborate must emerge a unanimous agreement to co-operate, especially in the peaceful use of the new nuclear science, which, under these conditions, remains the great hope of our century, the one tool powerful enough to solve the problems of our time. Thus it will be less a question of discrediting science and technology than of requiring the powers that wish to monopolize scientific and technological progress to submit to the law of solidarity. This law expropriates from individual nations for the profit of the Community of Nations.

The Community of Nations is, in short, the ultimate stage of the evolution now appearing faintly here and there in the form of communities restricted by affinities. This is the final phase toward which the building of the new civilization should lead. In various places, dialogues are fashioning this new civilization, the vocation of which is to be "a civilization of solidarity." We shall stress forcefully the fact—without indulging in demagoguery—that the nations of the *Tiers-Monde*, especially the emergent African nations, are required, as much as the old nations, to obey this fundamental law of our age, at the risk of having only a very brief history.

WILLIAM L. HOLLAND

Asian Nationalism
and the West

Often when we talk or write about non-Western areas, we are apt
to make sweeping generalizations. We may refer to "Asian nationalism," for example, as if it has taken the same form in Japan as
in Burma, in China as in India.

The more we study these areas, however, the more we see that
behind what at first sight seemed a common experience, there is as
vast a variety of national character, tradition, philosophies, and ways
of life in Asia (or Africa or the Middle East) as we find in Europe.
This becomes strikingly clear to us when we examine the widely different forms that nationalism has taken in Asia in the past century.
It has ranged from the authoritarian, militarized regime of Japan before World War II to India's democracy, which represents a synthesis of Indian traditions and British practices; and from China's
communism to Japan's postwar democratization.

The variety of nationalisms in Asia, and the problems nationalist
leaders face there once independence has been achieved, are described in this selection by William L. Holland. Born in New Zealand in 1907 and educated in that country and in Britain, Mr.
Holland has long been concerned with the study of Asian affairs.
He served as general secretary and research director of the Institute
of Pacific Relations, 1946–60, and as co-editor of the Far Eastern
Survey, 1953–60. Since 1961 he has been professor and head of the
department of Asian Studies at the University of British Columbia,
as well as editor of the magazine, Pacific Affairs. He is the editor of
the volume from which his own chapter, included here, is drawn, as
well as of several other books on Asia.

Introduction
New Trends in Asian Nationalism

NATIONALISM has become a force of such magnitude and persistence in
the contemporary Asian world that it is hard to exaggerate its importance for the future stability and development of that region. Whether

From Asian Nationalism and the West by William L. Holland. The Macmillan Co.
Copyright 1953 by International Secretariat, Institute of Pacific Relations. (Footnotes have been omitted.)

in India or Indonesia, where it was the ideological and emotional spearhead of a movement for the elimination of Western colonial rule; or in China, where it became a powerful tool of a militant Communist movement; or in Japan, where it was for a time corrupted by potent factors contributing to the spectacular decline of Western power in the Far East.

In the five years since the end of World War II the whole political balance of power in Asia has been dramatically altered. After decades or centuries of subjection to Western control, eight new nations (India, Pakistan, Ceylon, Burma, Indonesia, Vietnam, the Philippines, and Korea) have suddenly come into existence. All of them have inherited immense economic and social problems and many operate under serious handicaps of internal disunity, administrative inefficiency and the ever-present threat of economic deterioration.

Dramatic as all these changes have been, it is doubtful whether the long-term consequences in this shift of power vis-à-vis the Western world have yet been fully appreciated by either Asian or Western leaders. This arises in part from the fact that the very concept of nationalism in Asia is a changing one. Its earlier and most widely accepted meaning was crystallized during a period of active struggle against Western colonial rule or Western economic domination, but in most parts of Asia that phase has now ended. This is not to say that nationalist movements themselves have disappeared or are becoming less important as operative political forces in Asia. On the contrary, in many areas it can be argued that they are only now beginning to manifest themselves in their true colors. Only now can the political observer begin to analyze their distinctive qualities and to see whether they hold within themselves the capacity for flexible and progressive development in the interests of the mass of the people in the various new nations of Asia, or whether (as in Nationalist China) they will become ossified and discredited.

Powerful though the nationalist forces have been, it is important to remember that the political changes which have come over the face of the postwar Far East are not attributable solely to nationalism. It must never be forgotten that the Japanese played an immense catalytic role in energizing and accelerating movements which might otherwise have remained weak and unsuccessful for many years to come. The Japanese occupation of Southeast Asia and their attacks on the eastern frontiers of India automatically advanced the cause of the various nationalist movements by destroying the authority and prestige of the Western colonial administrations. In addition, the Japanese, as a deliberate part of their anti-Western policy, utilized and encouraged many of the nationalist leaders and occasionally gave them at least the appearance of exercising authority in the administration of their countries. The nationalists were often bitterly disillusioned in the subsequent failure of the Japanese to give them either authority or economic assistance, but they had had at least a taste of self-government and had been fed a steady diet of anti-Western ideas.

More important still, many of them acquired some military training and, after the Japanese surrender, also obtained quantities of Japanese arms and ammunition. This fact was to have decisive importance when the Western nations attempted to restore their control at the end of 1945, and it still remains a factor of great significance in explaining the strength and persistence of rebellious factions in Malaya, Burma, Indonesia, Indochina, and the Philippines. Even India, though not occupied by the Japanese, was affected by the Japanese policy of organizing in Malaya a so-called Indian National Army and of winning the support of the Indian nationalist leader, Subhas Chandra Bose.

Asian nationalism may be pictured as a huge and often uncontrolled source of energy. It is often not clearly formulated either in ideological slogans or in concrete economic and political programs. It is, rather, a huge emotional reservoir which can be tapped and used for good or ill depending on the kind of leadership which captures it. In recent years and especially since the victory of communism in China, there is a natural, though sometimes oversimplified, tendency on the part of Westerners to think of Asian nationalism chiefly as a possible alternative to communism. Recognizing (often belatedly) that the Chinese Communists owed much of their success to their skill in taking over the leadership of Chinese nationalism, leaders of the Western democratic nations are deeply concerned that the nationalist emotions of southern and southeastern Asia shall not be similarly captured by a militant communism now reinforced by the new military and political prestige of Communist China.

In the hope of averting this disaster, the United States has embarked on considerable programs of economic, technical, and military assistance to this part of the world. On a smaller scale, this effort has been paralleled by the similar programs of the United Nations agencies and by the Commonwealth countries in the Colombo Plan for the economic development of India, Pakistan, Ceylon, Burma, and Malaya. It is, of course, still too soon to know how far these measures will in themselves succeed in preventing the spread of communism in this area.

Hitherto, most Western analysis of Asian nationalism, and indeed most Asian preaching and thinking about it, has been concentrated on the "liberation" or anti-colonial phase, the throwing off of alien rule and the struggle of competing factions within the nationalist movements to achieve power. In most areas, with the partial exception of Indochina and the decided exception of Malaya, this phase has now passed and the problem of nationalism has taken on a wholly different aspect. But one of the ironies in the situation is that the full significance of this change seems not yet to have been fully realized by many of the nationalist leaders themselves. Their writings and speeches still tend to be dominated by ideas and slogans which had validity in the pre-liberation stage but have increasingly little relevance to the problems of today. This intellectual and political lag is a phenomenon of decided importance and some real danger.

What is the new phase of Asian nationalism? Few serious attempts have thus far been made to define it. Partly it may be described as a search by the new nationalist leaders to find a distinctive content to their own particular nationalism, to discover (and in some cases to invent or deliberately fabricate) a body of national ideals, institutions, attitudes, myths, traditions, history, literature, and even language. Partly also it consists of efforts to consolidate the political power and privileges of dominant political factions or vested interests. Sometimes it is the struggle to provide the bare minimum machinery of government needed to maintain and operate the modern state and to prevent it from falling into anarchy or dictatorship. Part of it is the effort, still not a proved success, to adapt to a very different and uncongenial Asian background the peculiar Western political forms of democracy and especially (in most areas) the even more specialized forms of parliamentary government.

The need for much more intensive study of all these phases, not merely by outside scholars but even more by Asian students and political leaders, can hardly be overemphasized. The difficulties, however, are formidable. Most Asian nationalist leaders have been too busy struggling to achieve their primary aims of getting rid of foreign rule and the vestiges of foreign economic control to become self-conscious or introspective about the special characteristics of whatever political system and set of ideals they would like to establish and persuade their peoples to adopt. Even after the attainment of power, the desperate shortage of educated people has meant that the more articulate and thoughtful nationalists have often had to become bureaucrats or diplomatic officers abroad. Few have had the time to devote themselves to formulating a code of national ideals or of giving specific political and economic content to the vaguely expressed slogans and aspirations which their leaders have hitherto used to arouse popular support.

One result is that many of the new nationalisms remain in a very nebulous state and are hard to describe in concrete terms. The people, even the more educated groups, have only dim and sometimes contradictory ideas of what is comprised in their present-day nationalism (in terms of educational aims, objects of patriotic veneration, national heroes, religious and social institutions, or aspirations). In this fact there lurks a considerable potential risk. On the one hand extremist or chauvinist groups of either the right or the left may try to seize positions of emotional and sometimes quasi-religious dominance, even though such groups are only small minorities and not yet powerful in over-all political influence. Examples of this are to be found in the Darul Islam movement in Indonesia, the R.S.S. in India, some of the Moslem extremist groups in Pakistan, and the ultra-nationalist societies which are beginning to revive on a small scale in Japan.

On the other hand there is real danger in the fact that in Asian eyes great prestige does not always attach to that special combination of political democracy with capitalism, private property, and individualism which much of the Western world has so long extolled and preached in its propaganda against the Communists. To the extent that these ideas were associated in the mind of the Asian nationalist with alien rule and economic exploitation (real or imagined), they tend to be regarded with suspicion or at least with little enthusiasm. By the same token, some of the latter-day forms of Western totalitarianism, whether of the Communist or the Fascist variety, often find a ready response in the new Asian nations where there have been long traditions of autocracy and obedience and where individual liberty and democratic majority rule have been little understood or venerated by the mass of the people.

It is worth noting that in all the countries, with only the partial exception of the Philippines, there is a widespread but ill-defined acceptance of Socialist or near-Socialist ideas in economic and social policy. There has been a far-reaching permeation of Marxist and Communist, as well as Socialist, concepts and clichés. These have become an essential part of the intellectual equipment of not merely the intelligentsia but also the political leaders and curiously enough, many of the businessmen. This body of ideas is seldom based on any intensive study of the Marxian classics or of Western Socialist thought. It can often be criticized as superficial and unrelated to the cultural traditions and the political environment of the new Asian countries. Nevertheless, it has a considerable hold on the articulate sections of these nations. This is one of several reasons why Communist propaganda, which utilizes the familiar jargon and philosophical assumptions of Marxism and socialism, finds such a ready response throughout these areas.

Another important factor in the development of Asian nationalism is religion. Its influence has differed greatly, both in strength and in the forms of its political manifestations, and in many areas it is not easy to define precisely the role it plays or is likely to play as the new nations evolve. In some countries, for example Pakistan, which is formally dedicated as a nation to the Moslem faith and tends to regard itself as having a special mission to preserve and strengthen that faith, religion has a prominent if not dominant political and educational role in developing the new sense of nationhood. Critics have indeed argued that Pakistan has many of the characteristics of a theocratic state—a notion which many Pakistanis, however, dispute as being a misleading simplification. Islam also plays a major role in the new Indonesian Republic where several of the main political parties (notably the *Masjumi*) are strongly influenced by Moslem ideas and practices. Mohammedanism is also a significant political force in Malay nationalism and, in a more geographically restricted form, among the Moros in the southern islands of the predominantly Catholic Philippine Republic. Buddhism, of course, exerts a profound and pervasive influence upon the national character and especially upon some of the nationalist leaders in Burma, Thailand, Cambodia, and Ceylon. In Burma and Thailand especially the educational influence of the Buddhist monasteries is far-reaching. Christianity too is a political force of some importance in several sub-areas [among such people] as the Karens of Burma, the Ambonese of Indonesia, and the large Catholic groups of Vietnam.

Overshadowing, and sometimes menacing, the stability of the new nations and the traditions of democratic and civilian control of their governments, is the continuing problem of internal disorders inspired by rebellious political or military factions. The Huks in the Philippines, the Darul Islam and other dissident groups in Java, the few thousand Communist rebels in Malaya, the Communist and the Karen insurrectionaries in Burma, and (most threatening of all) the large and Chinese Communist-aided Viet Minh armies . . . all these are serious challenges to the established governments, since all of them claim to have a nationalist mission themselves. They have also a serious secondary consequence in that they lead the new governments to depend upon military measures to control or suppress them. That, in itself, tends to strengthen the role of the military in the new governments and increases the long-term dangers of military cliques becoming politically dominant, as has happened in Thailand. Moreover, it adds enormously to the financial burdens of the new governments and thus blocks or retards many urgently needed economic and social reforms. The demoralizing and debilitating effect of militarism in Nationalist China is now well known; the burden of armaments in India and Pakistan, because of the Kashmir dispute and mutual suspicions, weigh heavily upon the economies of both countries; the political role of the armed forces and their leaders may well become a thorny problem in Indonesia.

On the other hand, it should be remarked that these new nations, despite their very different political and social backgrounds, have all chosen to establish democratic, and for the most part parliamentary, forms of government. The problem of developing this form of government in areas where the great mass of the people is illiterate and poverty-stricken and where there is a vast gap between them and the small groups of leaders at the top of the political pyramid, is a disquieting one. One need only look at the experience of Siam and the earlier failure of parliamentary democracy to take root in China to realize some of the dangers which may lie ahead. What is often puzzling and alarming to the outside observer is the fact that most of the political leaders are decidedly westernized in their thinking and methods, and it is very hard to find examples of where they have found effective ways of communicating these Western ideas to the illiterate populace or of linking Western institutions and practices to well-known and respected traditional social forms.

No doubt this gap will gradually be reduced with the spread of elementary education and by such devices as cheap radios and newspapers. For the present, however, the ordinary villager throughout southern Asia must sometimes feel that the nationalist governments are almost as remote and alien to the institutions and traditional codes of conduct which govern his daily life as were the former colonial regimes.

The new political leaders, therefore, face an urgent task in deliberately and quickly creating new symbols, slogans, precepts, patriotic ceremonies, by which the masses can more readily identify themselves with their new government. In many ways India was fortunate in having part of this task performed by Gandhi, whose distinctive way of life and set of values made a deep impress on the ordinary Indian citizen as well as on India's nationalist movement. It is hard, however, to find any real equivalent to Gandhi's role in the other new nations of Asia. President Sukarno's effort to expound the so-called Five Virtues (*Pantja Sila*) represents a recognition of this need in Indonesia. . . .

[3]

Impact of Communism

JULES MONNEROT

Sociology and
Psychology of Communism

Many answers have been given to the question of what is communism. Jules Monnerot, in the selection below, sees it primarily
as a force useful to the Russian Super-State in pursuing twentieth-
century totalitarianism and power politics in the form of an explosive ideology, which he calls the "twentieth-century Islam." He
believes this is basically a Russian development of Marxism for
expansionist purposes.

In reaching his conclusions, Jules Monnerot, French writer, sociologist, and expert on surrealism, looks at Russian communism
from various angles. He stresses in particular its emphasis on psychological warfare and, as can be seen by the excerpts drawn from
his book, he gives particular attention to the impact of communism
as a new religion.

Born in Martinique in 1908, Monnerot became active in several
anti-fascist organizations. Between 1940 and 1944 he took part in
the French Resistance. He has written fiction but has become more
and more interested recently in political science. He also has urged
that sociology be studied from the point of view of comparative history and psychology.

With André Malraux, who became President de Gaulle's Min-
·ister of Culture, and Jacques Soustelle, he was one of the originators
of what has been called "intellectual Gaullism."

Chapter 1
The Twentieth-Century "Islam"

In 1917 Russian bolshevism appeared to be a stage in the westernisa-
tion of Russia. What appeared to be triumphing in Russia was not the
specifically Russian "populist" socialism of the *narodniki*, but Marxism,
which had its origin in the West, designed for a different social order,
and imported into Russia at the end of the nineteenth century. The
most prominent Marxists were Germans; and Plekhanov, Lenin, and

From *The Sociology and Psychology of Communism* by Jules Monnerot. George
Allen & Unwin, Ltd., London, 1953. The Beacon Press, Boston, paper, 1960.

Trotsky were clearly anxious to absorb the wisdom of the German theorists, whose mastery was not disputed. It was not until Lenin published his famous polemical pamphlet *The Proletarian Revolution and the Renegade Kautsky* that the pre-eminence of the Westerners in the theoretical field was denied. But the reversal was decisive; it was no longer Europe which dictated doctrine and strategy to Russia. Henceforth it was from Russia that commands and directives were issued and from Russia that operations were conducted. Russian Marxism of the nineteenth century was at first an importation, a "loan" from Europe; but European communism of the twentieth century, from Lenin's death to the "cold war," appears more and more as an aggressive and unremitting interference by the dominant Russian oligarchy in the internal affairs of Europe, and indeed of the rest of the world. The eastward cultural expansion of Europe has been followed by a reaction, a counter-expansion, and the Marxism "returned" by Russia to Europe is strikingly different from the Marxism "lent" by Europe to Russia. Marxists have sharp eyes for "capitalist contradictions," but does not the outstanding riddle of our time (Is Communist strategy the revolutionary strategy of Marxism, or is it rather that the Marxist revolution is a strategic specialty of the Russian Super-State?) display a *Marxist contradiction*, Marxism being understood here as a broad sociological fact, a total social phenomenon, of which Marxist theory is but one aspect?

In the nineteenth century, Marx's study of Clausewitz gave him the idea of using strategy in the service of revolutionary planners. In the twentieth century the relationship seems to be reversed, revolutionary action becoming part of the strategic arsenal of the oligarchy that rules over the most formidable empire in the world. Encouragement of seditious elements within enemy States has always been one method of warfare. To embarrass the enemy by exploiting discontent and the discontented (fallen statesmen, ambitious younger sons, members of factions excluded from power, exiled partisans) was a familiar method both in the Mediterranean world in the thousand years before Christ and in the Italian cities from the thirteenth to the sixteenth centuries in dynastic and feudal Europe. The same methods, transformed by the rapidity with which "thought" can be disseminated (leaflets dropped by aircraft, communications by wireless and radar with those operating behind the enemy lines), can in the twentieth century be used on a vast scale; this makes social life today something quite different from social life in the nineteenth century. The destructive force generated by human sufferings and resentments can then be used, manipulated by specialists, in the same way and to the same purpose as material explosives. In this sense it can be said that the affective forces which determined Socialist thought and action in the nineteenth century have lost their absolute status. They are now no more than one specialised form of tactics competing with others within a wider total strategy. The "Marxist" general staff exploits or provokes discord among the enemy; it is the most up-to-date form of an old tactic. Mobilising their forces in enemy territory at the same time as their own, the great powers of today can subject their opponents to simultaneous pressure from without and from within.

The distinction between domestic policy and foreign policy is thus of the same order as that between infantry and artillery. Modern heavy industry provides the material elements for psychological warfare. As an explosive weapon the word, written or spoken, is comparable to the bomb, and psychological weapons are pre-eminent in long-range effectiveness. A few rule-of-thumb psychological prescriptions and the technical knowledge to apply them make it possible to coordinate the blows aimed at the enemy so that they converge on his weak spots. The vast extent of modern industrial organisation makes morale one of the attainable weak spots. Since an entire nation is today in effect mobilised, the active combatants can be indirectly attacked by striking at non-combatants; the front is vulnerable to attacks upon the rear, and indeed the distinction between the two is already much less clear than it used to be, and in some cases no longer exists.

•   •   •

In the Europe of the nineteenth century, in process of industrialisation, the Communist Manifesto distinguishes and sets in opposition to one another the *Proletariat* and the *Bourgeoisie*. The advantages of this simplification, which fosters the growth of a myth and also the development of a tactic, have been plain for all to see: it does violence to sociology but it pays dividends. But although both the dualism and the duel are religious myths, the existence of the proletariat was an historical fact, a real problem of a specific society: and until the twentieth century it remained an internal concern of the society which had produced it. Nineteenth-century socialism was the reaction of the Western conscience as much to the problems of industrialisation as to the drama of proletarianisation, and it inherited elements of humanism and Christianity which it transformed but did not deny. They were the world from which it was born and of which it was one aspect; but Marxism, as a comprehensive political strategy, as the art of seizing and holding power, both was and is the art of maintaining and widening the actual schism which gives a pretext for the theoretical opposition between the proletariat and the rest of society. Its purpose is to make the schism absolute and absolutely destructive. It is possible to discriminate in thought between what should be destroyed and what preserved, but

destruction takes place in reality and not in thought; its effects are experienced by thought but not controlled by it.

After the Russian Revolution, *at the very moment when the revolu-*
tionary Campaign was becoming formidably equipped for action, its
control passed out of the hands of the men who had conceived it.
These men had inherited the tradition of the Western European workers' movements and the Socialist doctrines which, having come to birth
in Germany, England, and France, *embodied elements of civilisation*
much older than themselves. In theory, the control passed from them
to an international body of picked revolutionaries—the Communist International. But it would be both un-Marxist and unhistorical to hold
that this select body could resist the magnetic attraction and the influence of the Russian Super-State which grew up rapidly after the revolution. The victims of the successive "purges" were drawn as freely
from members of the International who were unlucky enough to be in
Russia as from the Russians themselves. The Communist International
was thus progressively identified with the ruling oligarchy of the new
Empire in proportion as this new Empire and dominant minority became established in fact. The executive committee of the Communist
International was composed of men who, being Russian, must by
hypothesis be identified with the State interests of the new State, and of
men who, although not Russian, made no distinction or else distinguished badly between the interests and aims of the disinherited of the
countries they represented and those of the new State and the men in
whom it was incarnated. Marxism might reject such a dualistic distinction, but reality does not. What in fact happened was that Russia
gradually *obtained control over the interpretation of world history,*
which was at first effective only in some sectors and for practical purposes inoperative in others. . . .

The increasing standardisation of mankind's material conditions is
accompanied by a religious theory of the division of mankind into two
camps. This duality is a duel, and according to Communists there can
be no future for humanity unless their side wins—though it is difficult
for the unbeliever to conceive what meaning this statement can have for
them. In any case, the separation of humanity into two camps is not the
work of capitalists but of Marxists.

Whereas the nineteenth-century European Socialist wanted to create
a just society in Europe, the twentieth-century European Communist
works for the absorption of Europe by a totally alien system which includes non-European factors and was designed to meet uniquely Russian problems. It is as though the Christian Church had worked within
the Roman Empire for the success of the Parthian monarchy, or as if

every Christian in the Mediterranean world had been an agent of the Persian bureaucracy. Persia bordered on the Roman world as Russia borders on Europe, and Rome never succeeded either in absorbing Persia or in eliminating her.

There is, moreover, a resemblance between the use made of Marxism by the present masters of the totalitarian worlds and the conversion of nomadic barbarians, such as the Goths of Alaric and the Turkish mercenaries of Mahmud of Ghazna, Togrul Beg, and Alp Arslan, to the universal religion of the civilisations they treated, namely Christianity in the first case and Islam in the second. Like Stalin's Marxism, their conversion gave them the pretext for disrupting civilisation *from within*; as converts they were able to attack in the name of the true Faith the very societies which had brought the Faith to them. In the same way the Marxist chiefs of totalitarian Russia attack Western society from within, attempting to destroy the social structure of European countries for the sake of the socialism to which these countries themselves gave birth. There is no need to question the sincerity of the Bolshevik leaders' conscious motives. We may observe, however, that in the remote depths of Russia and central Asia the conception of Marxism and communism is probably comparable to the conception of Christianity entertained by the Germanic tribes (Frisians, Saxons, Chamaves, Thuringians), who were subjected to "mass conversion" after Charlemagne's victories.

The first object in the West is to prevent the integration into the society of the proletariat. The mere existence of the "Communist" Campaign, *as it is today*, implies that Western society is unfit for the task of integrating its own proletariat. *But the continued existence of Western society depends upon the accomplishment of this allegedly impossible task.* It is a precarious and alarming situation, indeed, for any nation if its "lower" classes and all the disintegrating and unattached elements that adhere to them can be mobilised at the command and for the profit of a neighbouring empire.

The Communist design can be seen to comprise in fact a two-fold campaign: to destroy one society and to construct another. In many countries the society marked for destruction is on a higher material and cultural level than Russia. The society "for construction" begins in the Super-State known as Soviet Russia, and spreads outward from it. *This dual significance of the Campaign is revealed in its very structure and anatomy, in the fact that the privileged ruling oligarchy of the Russian Super-State is theoretically the leader of the disinherited outside the frontiers of Russia.* This is the age of general staffs, and the general staff in question is composed of the "leaders" of the world revolution, who scrutinise the schisms and divisions of the Western world and do all they can to perpetuate, extend, and exploit them. But other members of this same general staff are concerned with constructive work inside Russia, which proceeds concurrently with the destruction abroad. There is social construction: the stabilising and reinforcing of the social stratification which set in after the revolution. And there is material construction: the industrialisation of Russia—building, machinery, factories and factory products, agriculture. This type of society is founded upon service, labour, hierarchy, and a *secular religion*, unlike the nineteenth-century liberal capitalist society of the West, which was founded upon profit, property, risk, and personal initiative and independence. The twofold destination and function of the Communist Campaign is served by two distinct groups of organs, whose separate roles were discernible from the beginning in the distinction between the Russian State and the Comintern, or Communist International. The Campaign aspires to synchronise the destruction of the "capitalist" and the construction of the "Socialist" world. Without counting the cost (in terms of lives), it works for a unified and homogeneous world; exalting Russia and casting down everything that is not Russia, cresting within Russia a hierarchical social system to be extended uniformly over the whole world, undermining by every available means the existing systems and hierarchies and also any which are developing or potentially developing in independence of her own system. This Campaign recognises no worse enemies than those who resist its authority and yet call themselves Socialist; and the war against the heirs of the nineteenth-century working-class movement, in so far as their loyalty to their traditions inspires them with a repugnance for Stalinism, is conducted as implacably as the rest of the Campaign. It is clear indeed that the struggle today is not only a vertical one between classes but at least equally a horizontal one between two different worlds and mentalities. The Communist Campaign appears, if one discounts such "justification" for it as the Marxist ideology can afford, to be an attempt to destroy outside Russia all the things which it is constructing, in a different form, within Russia: industry, social stability, the State, the political system, hierarchy, social movements, etc. In the whole period from 1918 to today wages have been low in Russia and the standard of life inferior not only to that of the United States but also to that of Western Europe. If this state of affairs continues long enough the Campaign would become economically unjustifiable; for economically, it now rests entirely upon the thesis that a totalitarian regime, by imposing a planned economy in a part of the world that is rich enough to maintain an autarkic independence from the rest of the world, can in theory eliminate the periodic slumps which are characteristic of capitalism. The task is made easier by the fact that the consumer has no political liberty, and can therefore make no effective complaints or protests. The government is not in the least concerned to satisfy men's demands, but only to impose upon them from above what seems good from the point of view of those above. The shortcomings of Soviet planning may be the fault of the planners and their methods, but they certainly exist; and since there is no right of assembly or meeting and no free vote the people have no way of expressing any opinion that conflicts with the orders from above—a state of affairs totally foreign even to the *aspirations* of nineteenth-century Socialists, Marx and Engels included. *Many of the major sociological characteristics of the regime are censored or travestied by the official propaganda.*

Meanwhile, outside Russia, the Campaign canalises and fosters every class and mass and individual resentment, and tries to bring it to the decisive pitch of active virulence; its whole activity abroad consists in *organising* discontent and the discontented of every kind. By means of the unions it controls through Communist fractions, the Campaign can influence the methods of fixing wage rates and their fluctuations, and can thus compromise *from within* the productive capacity of capitalist countries which—in normal times—are able to assure to their working class a higher standard of life than the "Socialist" standard of Russia. At the same time, taking advantage of "capitalist contradictions in the age of monopolies and imperialism," it "works" upon the colonial "masses" and thus lowers the standard of life of the metropolitan masses. The purpose is to inflame and envenom all the contradictions of the capitalist world and at the same time either to destroy or else absorb into the Campaign every working-class and Socialist movement and also every independent movement of revolt.

By the accelerated industrialisation of Russia, Marxists have built up an economy by which the economic can determine the political; thus demonstrating at once the efficacity of their doctrine and the need to interpret it boldly. By capitalist standards of accountancy, many Russian industries have been working and still work at a loss. But the data of the problem are changed by the fact that these enterprises are totally dependent upon the State. Economic politics have been substituted for political economy.

But the ultimate aim is the most absolute tyranny ever conceived by man; a tyranny that recognises no spatial limits (except for the time being those of the planet itself), no temporal limits (Communist believers generally refuse to contemplate any post-Communist ages), and no limits to its power over the individual: its will to power claims total possession over every man it wins, and allows no greater freedom in mental than economic life. It is this claim that brings it into conflict with faiths, religions, and values, which are older than itself or developing independently; and then the battle is joined. We are the battle.

·   ·   ·

In the nineteenth century politics and religion and economics were each a distinct and separate province. They were "specialisms," separate in fact as well as in theory; and neither as subjects of study nor as activities was there much interchange or communication between them. This kind of intellectual autonomy is a characteristic feature of the liberal world; and minds formed in this tradition, even the ablest of them, will be at first perplexed by a phenomenon so complex and yet so unified as communism, which can, in a way, be described as a total social phenomenon. It is true that soldiers, historians, diplomats, and politicians, for whom imperial rivalries are a familiar subject, will have no difficulty in perceiving that this is yet another example of it: Persia and Assyria, Carthage and Rome, Habsburg and Bourbon, and now Kremlin and White House (or Kremlin and Wall Street, as Communists put it). For such observers it seems a simple struggle for power; they will read the drama as a problem, and will easily grasp both its economic and its strategic aspects. But they will fail to take sufficient account of the drama which "over-determines" the problem: the drama of the birth, development, maintenance, and transformation of a religion. Hence their conclusions will be incomplete, and any policy deduced from them may be mistaken both in foresight and in action. The economist and the strategist will need to possess "historical tact," and to combine the penetration of the "director of conscience," the historian of religions, and the psychoanalyst. This may be too much for any one man, but it is certainly possible for a group of men. It is by no means beyond human capacity.

The paralysis of production in the "bourgeois" countries, to whose destruction the Communist Campaign is vowed, is an economic effect obtained by psychological means. The internal contradictions of capitalism are a reality, but the Communists are able to aggravate them by promoting a religious schism. What is happening in the West today can be compared to what the situation would have been in the Roman world of the third century if there had been intentional and preconcerted synchronisation between the Christian refusal of obedience and the successive thrusts of barbarian invasion; in other words, if a single general staff, devoted to the ruin of the ancient world, had had command of both the Christian Church and the barbarians. The historical innovation of contemporary communism is the virtual unification of the forces of an external and an internal enemy, a combination of subversion with invasion—so that as it expands the system can absorb simul-

taneously both societies and individuals, and can make not only territorial and economic but also political and spiritual conquests. The
innovation also consists in raising an issue and persuading a certain
number of people, by various methods of intimidation and psychological
pressure, to accept it as predestined (but the word destiny is never
used; the issue is described as "necessary," "ineluctable," etc.).

If we can see in history nothing but conflicts of power between col-
lectivities we shall miss the meaning of the contemporary crisis. Not
that there are fewer of such conflicts than before, on the contrary; but
the water-tight compartments which in the liberal period preserved the
autonomy of the different spheres of human activity have begun to leak.
A religion is propagating itself in terms of political economy. If politics tries to remain nothing but itself while economics and religion are
mixed together it is in danger of becoming completely unreal. The
Communist Campaign could not exist if it were not religious; it could
not exist if it were not pervaded by religion through and through. The
leaders and strategists of the contemporary world will ignore this fact
at their risk and peril. The Campaign is what it is solely because it has
proved capable of mobilising and energising a deep and powerful fund
of affective impulses. The fate of the Campaign, and consequently the
issue of the struggle of empires, will depend less upon strategic routes
and pipelines for uranium and oil than upon the invisible pipelines by
which this modern "Islam" canalises the resentments and discontents
of the world it is vowed to destroy; even the unprecedentedly powerful
modern weapons of war can be immobilised by the slow and secret
canalisation of resentments and discontents and the draining away of
the warlike spirit.

JOHN K. FAIRBANK

The United States
and China

*The Chinese Communists established their rule over mainland
China in 1950. More than a decade later, the American public was
still deeply divided about the reasons for the success of communism
in China and about the nature of Chinese communism, as compared and contrasted with that of Russia. Though the United*

States regards the Nationalist government of Generalissimo Chiang Kai-shek on Formosa as the legitimate government of all of China, refuses to recognize the Communist regime in Peking, and opposes its admission to the United Nations, we are increasingly aware that we must understand the background of Chinese communism, its methods of operation, and Peking's role in world affairs if we are to develop a realistic policy in Asia.

Professor John K. Fairbank, author of the book from which this selection is drawn, is one of the best-informed China scholars in the United States. Born in 1907, he has been on the Harvard University faculty since 1936, and since 1946 Francis Lee Higginson Professor of History. He is also Director of the East Asian Research Center at that institution. During World War II he was on leave from Harvard in United States government service as special assistant to our Ambassador in Chungking, 1942–43; at the Office of War Information in Washington, sometimes acting as deputy director in charge of Far Eastern operations, 1944–45; and as director of United States Information Services in China, 1945–46.

He is the author of several other books, among them A Documentary History of Chinese Communism (with Conrad Brandt and Benjamin Schwartz), 1952; and China's Response to the West: A Documentary Survey, 1839–1923 (with S. Y. Teng), 1954.

Chapter 16
Communist China

STUDIES of Communist China from the outside easily fall into that ancient trap—finding the evidence one seeks. From Peking press sources one can paint a picture in which China today looks remarkably like Russia. Alternatively the historian can discern in the Communist regime many features of the old Chinese empire. Each approach, by way of the Russian model or by way of Chinese tradition, has much to offer. Neither can be disregarded, as some would like to do. The beginning of wisdom is certainly to accept both, but only as ways of approach. For in Communist China a new power-state is struggling to create a collectivized society, in which certain influences of the past and from abroad are inextricably fused. But the totalitarian product will be something new and distinctive.

Below we look first at the measures and mechanisms by which the

Chinese Communist party built up its control over the Chinese society, state, and people, and secondly at its effort to remake them. Though the two processes went hand in hand, remaking depended on first controlling.

1. Political Control

The military take-over occupied a year and a half, from the fall of Mukden on November 1, 1948, and of Peking and Tientsin in January, 1949, until the occupation of all the mainland and Hainan Island by May, 1950. The Chinese Peoples Republic was proclaimed in the midst of this process on October 1, 1949. The take-over left in office most local administrators. On the surface the Communist cadres gave it a festive air, dancing the yang-ko in the streets, proclaiming peace and liberation. The troops generally behaved scrupulously. It was a hopeful honeymoon period, devoted to military mopping-up, economic recovery, and political organization.

COALITION GOVERNMENT

The policy for this period, laid down by Mao in January and confirmed by the CCP Central Committee in March, 1949, amounted to a platform of getting rid of the Kuomintang, supplanting it with a coalition government, and reforming China's armies, foreign relations, and economic system. In order to mobilize a broad basis of support, the coalition government should be organized by a new People's Political Consultative Conference, reminiscent in name but not in membership of the multi-party conference at the time of General Marshall's mediation.

This line was developed in Mao's statement of July 1, 1949, "On the people's democratic dictatorship." Echoing Lenin's theory of a "democratic dictatorship of workers and peasants," Mao propounded the thesis that the new government should be a democratic coalition under Communist leadership at the same time that it was a dictatorship directed against the reactionary classes or "enemies of the people." Thus the "people's democratic dictatorship" would attempt to line up the broadest possible support for the regime and at the same time eliminate its foes within the Chinese world. The "people" were defined as composed of four classes: proletariat, peasantry, petty bourgeoisie, national bourgeoisie. For the peasantry there was a prospect of maintaining, at least temporarily, private property in land, and for the bourgeoisie, a sector of privately owned industry. This carried out the original idea of the New Democracy.

Since any individual could be transferred by a stroke of the pen to the category of reactionaries or enemies of the people, this framework was completely flexible as a basis for sifting out dissident members of the population. The power of class imputation remained with the Communist party, and a reformed "reactionary" could be declared by it to be a member of the "people." Leaving this mechanism at first in the background, Mao Tse-tung called upon his countrymen, in this moment of hope and general relief, to take the first step on a 10,000 mile march, to wipe out domestic and repulse foreign enemies and to remake Chinese society, without help from abroad except that of the Soviet Union, using the means at hand but learning from all quarters.

After several months' preparation, the Preparatory Committee of the People's Political Consultative Conference was set up at Peking in June, 1949, nominally representing 23 parties or groups. The PPCC itself was convened in September for 10 days, with 662 delegates. It passed the *Common Program*, a general statement of aims of the new coalition government, and the *Organic Law* of the Central People's Government, which made the working class the leader of the republic. Since the CCP was the vanguard which represents the working class, this meant that the government was to be its administrative arm. The new administration was given complete executive, legislative, and judicial powers on a centralist basis, with no strings attached. Four committees and 30 ministries were set up, 15 of them connected with economic affairs. In the top committee, 31 out of 56 seats were occupied by Communists.

This powerful autocratic administration by Communist desire left the minor parties in existence, though without much following, and gave posts of prominence to non-Communists in order to carry out the idea of coalition government, that the talents of all the people must be used in building the new society. It was essential for Communist China to use the training and ability of that major part of the upper class which had never been Communist. These people, like the peasantry in the preceding 20 years, now formed a social group not susceptible to complete remaking into Communists but nevertheless essential for the time being as part of the Communist structure and program. Liberal intellectuals were therefore catered to, given scope for their talents and placed in high position, interlarded in the new ministries with party members who lacked their abilities but were more disciplined. . . . The larger part of the Western-returned scholars, including those educated in the United States, appear to have been in this category. As patriots, they were devoted to their country's future. Long since estranged from the Kuomintang, they saw no alternative. The Communist party also had long since developed its methods for manipulating and utilizing liberal intellectuals.

The constitution adopted in 1954 did not appreciably remake the governmental structure except for the further concentration of authority in Peking. The Communists, in short, like the Kuomintang, set up a tripod of power—party, government, and army, each forming a separate echelon but all three tied together by the Communist leadership. The party grew to twelve million in 1957.

Communist organization went far, far beyond the Kuomintang, however. On a territorial basis, People's Representative Congresses, modeled on the Russian soviets, were set up in a hierarchy from the village level on up to the People's Congress at the top, which was first convened in 1954. These congresses have quasi-legislative functions and are used mainly as sounding boards and transmission belts, to maintain a facade of democratic procedure and an arena for popular participation but without final power.

THE MASS ORGANIZATIONS

Cutting across the structure of congresses, there were set up the new nation-wide mass organizations on a functional basis. The All-China Federation of Trade Unions had been founded in 1922 and by 1956 claimed a membership of over 13 million. In 1949 there was created a full panoply of parallel bodies: an All-China Federation of Democratic Women (76 million members in 1953), of Democratic Youth (34 million in 1957), of Cooperative Workers, i.e., peasants in cooperatives (162 million in 1956), and of Literature and Art, under the prolific writer Kuo Mo-jo, to mobilize intellectuals. In addition there were an All-China Students Federation (4 million in 1955), a Children's Pioneer Corps (30 million in 1957) and many comparable bodies more specialized in nature, dealing with science, art and learning, welfare activities, or international relations—for example, the Sino-Soviet Friendship Association (68 million members in 1953) and similar associations for Sino-Indian and Sino-Burmese friendship. Finally in 1953 was established the All-China Association of Industry and Commerce, for the national bourgeoisie, who at that time still existed. (Three years later they had ceased to exist, as we shall note.)

These mass organizations, as studied by Dr. K. C. Chao, reach the individual in his professional or social role, among his peers, in ways that the government cannot. Each is controlled from the top by "democratic centralism" though authority is nominally vested in a national congress meeting at long intervals. Party members of course predominate in key posts but through them reach out to mobilize the general public. Each organization has broadly defined purposes and programs and an extensive administrative apparatus. Something like half the adult Chinese population is thus brought into one or another action group and involved in its program of meetings, study, and agitation.

The mass organizations have developed big training programs with schools and indoctrination centers, and serve as recruiting agencies for talented and activist personnel. Their welfare and cultural work has included such things as labor insurance, leave and pension systems, literacy classes, maternity hospitals and midwife training, or recreational activities, accompanied by a large output of books, magazines, and pamphlets circulated through libraries. Their members can also be used in the security system or in nation-wide campaigns like that against reactionaries. Their representatives can participate in the similar international bodies of the Communist world.

The mass organizations stand out as institutions of a new type in China, fulfilling primarily political functions as quasi-governmental agencies that bridge the immemorial gap between populace and officialdom. They receive government aid and even representation in the structure of People's Congresses. Their function is mainly to indoctrinate, working closely among the populace with meetings, demonstrations, and protests on demand as well as propaganda through mass media. The result is to mold and manipulate the climate of opinion. The mass organizations have a comprehensive coverage of the population and recruit its more able members. They can work also through the local street committees, which have the duty of promoting welfare measures, mutual surveillance and denunciation among neighbors and within families in every street. The mass organizations, when coordinated in each locality, can thus bring to bear upon every individual a completely pervasive and overwhelming public pressure.

The control mechanism for the application of this pressure is the campaign or drive. Campaigns may seem to start spontaneously once the Party has decided upon them. They are led generally by enthusiasts in each locality. Several may go on at the same time. Campaigns, in short, can quickly set in motion the enormous new apparatus of party, state, and mass organizations and direct its hammer blows against one target after another among the various classes and their institutions.

Standing behind this apparatus are well-paid security forces. In the forefront is the hierarchy of courts, also an arm of the central administration. Western jurist observers have found the kind of justice administered in open court less objectionable than the fact that cases normally come to trial only after the accused has fully confessed and denounced any others concerned in the crime with which he has been charged.

2. Economic Reconstruction

The intensive program of political organization sketched above was carried on concomitantly with a vigorous economic effort. Early in

1949 Mao announced a "shift to the cities" as the focus of effort, re-affirming the primacy of the urban proletariat in a party which was now about 90 per cent of peasant origin.

The first industrial objective set in 1949 was to get production back to its prewar level within about three years. Japan's industrial build-up in Manchuria had been reduced in 1945 by Russian removal of more than half the capital equipment, with an estimated replacement value of at least two billion American dollars. In China proper, railroads had been torn up by civil war, urban labor demoralized by hyperinflation. After the Communist victory it took some time to convince the city worker that Liberation had brought him first of all the opportunity to work harder. Wartime blockades between city and country had increased rural self-sufficiency; market crops like cotton had to be revived. Meanwhile inflation was still a major problem. With military operations still continuing in 1949–50 and some 9 million persons on government rations or payrolls (including minor Nationalist administrative and military personnel who had been taken over), the substitution of a new "people's currency" for Nationalist banknotes, even at favorable rates, left the regime still obliged to expand its note issue steadily to meet a budget deficit of perhaps 75 per cent. Shanghai prices rose 70 times in nine months, from May, 1949 to February, 1950. All this demanded strenuous measures.

The first move toward quelling the inflation was to get the budget more or less balanced by increasing revenue, first in the countryside by collecting agricultural taxes in kind, then in the cities through devices like a sales tax on each major commodity and business taxes set by "democratic appraisal" of trade associations to meet quotas previously set by government. The result of the latter was to squeeze money out of the more monetized sector of the economy. Secondly, the entire fiscal administration was reorganized and rationalized to give the central government control over formerly local taxes, to eliminate private banks' handling of official funds and generally to reduce expenditures, licit and illicit. The regime gradually made the collection process more efficient, got control of money and credit, and set up six government trading corporations to dominate prices in major consumer commodities.

One device for restoring confidence was to express wages, salaries, bank deposits, some government payments and bond issues in terms of commodity units, linked to quantities of goods of daily use rather than to monetary prices. A typical unit might be composed of 6 catties (8 lbs.) of rice, 1½ catties of flour, 16 catties of coal, and 4 feet of white shirting. As prices rose, the commodity-based unit would rise accordingly in money terms. Paid in this unit, one could save by making bank deposits or buying bonds in similar units; either way, one was protected against further inflation. Thus by a variety of methods designed to achieve a balance between the supply of goods and the flow of money income, the inflation was conquered by mid-1950.

Another achievement of the first year was an extensive reopening of railway track, to get most of China's 13,500 miles into operation. Economic recovery was aided by three good harvests in 1950–51–52. By 1952, the pre-1949 peaks of production had been equalled or surpassed in pig iron, cement, steel and oil (all very modest in China), and in coal, electric power, flour, and cotton cloth, but production was still short of the pre-1949 peak in some consumer goods such as sugar. Most important, by 1952 the national economy had been given greater unity than it had ever had before. Railway track had expanded to 15,000 and highways to 75,000 miles. A centralized banking system and single uniform currency now covered the country. Budgeting could be attempted realistically for the first time.

Peking's long-term economic aim was to mobilize China's resources and reallocate them for purposes of industrialization. This required a gradual extension of government control over all segments of the economy. Private enterprise was permitted to continue in form but in fact it was brought increasingly under state control through numerous devices —taxation and capital levies, rationing of credit, competition by state enterprise, demands of labor unions—so that businessmen practically became bureaucrats. By controlling credit and raw materials and monopolizing key commodities, the state could now dominate production and commerce, in addition to its outright control of most heavy industry, railways, and foreign trade. The other requirement was a traditional one brought up-to-date—control of the surplus product of the land.

LAND REFORM

In the history of Chinese communism there had been several shifts of land policy, exemplified by the severity of the Kiangsi period, when many landlords were exterminated, and the moderation of the Yenan period, when they were guaranteed a reasonable rent. As Communist power expanded after 1946, land reform had proceeded on a piecemeal and often violent basis, sometimes with more peasant violence than the party claims to have desired.

The nation-wide land reform, begun in mid-1950 and completed by late 1952 or early 1953, was not merely economic but also social and political in aim. A work team of cadres coming to a village first identified out-and-out enemies, if necessary got them out of the way, and then explained the desirability of land reform to the poor peasantry in particular, who would theoretically be the main beneficiaries. By this means active elements were selected who had the motivation and the capacity to lead the forthcoming movement. After this preparation a period of "class struggle" was inaugurated. In a series of "struggle meetings" the accumulated grievances of the populace could be brought forth in "speaking bitterness" or "settling accounts." Hatred could be fanned into mob violence in public "trials." Unpopular landlords or "local despots" chosen for public denunciation were either killed, expelled, or brought to confess and reform, while the entire community by taking violent measures committed themselves to the new order.

The next phase was to create the peasants association, which by a process of community assent could work out the definition of class status for each individual as landlord, rich peasant, middle peasant, poor peasant or farm laborer and could carry on the classification, confiscation, and redistribution of landholdings. The resulting "equalization of land tenure" was in the old tradition of peasant rebellions. Through Communist direction of this process, the activists were usually favored, the well-to-do reduced, and the remnants of the landlord gentry wiped out either in person or in status, while the Party representatives established their authority over the village. The tiller now had title to his land, at least for the moment.

While this New Democracy phase of private ownership had been advertised in 1950 to last for a "rather long time," in fact it lasted no longer for the farmer than it had for the capitalist. To supplant the old order the Communist regime moved without delay toward the construction of the new collectivist agrarian system beginning with a first stage of cooperatives.

Cooperation could achieve greater efficiency of production: six donkeys could go to market with one donkey-driver, not six. One housewife at a time could cook for several families. Since there were fewer draft animals than households, their use could be shared. Joint savings could buy a pump or a tool no individual could afford. In particular, handicraft cooperatives could use scattered local materials and unemployed farm labor in the off season to increase the production of consumer goods with rather little state investment. As larger units of operation, they could create a division of labor, with specialization. With organization might come literacy, health, technology, and higher productivity. Rural supply and marketing cooperatives meanwhile promoted exchange between farm and factory, handling state purchases and making available a wider variety of manufactures than the villages had seen before.

In agriculture the reform program for increased production, as it was termed, moved gradually from north to south through a series of planned phases, first setting up temporary, usually seasonal, small-scale mutual-aid teams, then larger permanent ones, and then agricultural producers' cooperatives. In the latter the peasants began to cultivate in common and share a common product in proportion to their pooled contributions of land, equipment, and labor.

The drive for agricultural producers' cooperatives which got under way in 1953 was still posited on private ownership of land and voluntary cooperation for mutual benefit. However, the goal began to shift. The regime had heretofore argued that land redistribution in itself, by eliminating landlordism (though without much increase of acreage), would release the peasantry's "productive energy." Now it was admitted that only eventual collectivization could effect the increase in agricultural product necessary to pay for industrialization. The effort was to lead the inveterately property-conscious peasant, through propaganda, practice, and steady pressure, to become (as the French agronomist, René Dumont, records it) "a Socialist without knowing it."

SOVIET AID

In most of their changes the CCP followed the Soviet example, which was plainly their greatest inspiration both in theory and in practice. Mao Tse-tung spent nine weeks in Moscow (December, 1949–February, 1950) and signed a Sino-Soviet Treaty of Friendship, Alliance, and Mutual Assistance, valid until 1980, against aggression by Japan or any power joined with Japan. Russia gradually gave up her position in Manchuria, turning Dairen back to China in 1950, ending her joint control of the main railways at the end of 1952, and withdrawing from the Port Arthur naval base in May, 1955. By a 1950 agreement she loaned China $60 million a year in economic aid for five years, all to be repaid—a meager sum compared to our largesse to the Nationalists. Russian engineers, by the thousands, have been a greater help. Later agreements called for Soviet credits and technical aid in building or renovating some 211 old and new projects, as the chief centers of the industrial program.[1]

Although the exact total of such economic aid remains unknown to us, Russian blueprints and technicians have evidently been a priceless ingredient in Communist China's performance. In addition, very extensive Soviet military assistance made it possible to build up the Chinese army without burdening the economy unbearably. But much of the Soviet industrial aid has been paid for by Chinese exports of agricultural and mineral products.

Whether or not Peking expected to participate in the Russian-armed North Korean aggression of June, 1950, rather than seizing Taiwan and

---

[1] Note: 141 such projects were announced in September, 1953; 15 more in October, 1954; and 55 in April, 1956.

expanding her influence southward, she undoubtedly gained military strength from the Korean War. In her intervention from October, 1950 a million or so Chinese "volunteers" benefited from the use of Russian tanks, planes, and artillery. By the time of the truce in July, 1951 the battle-hardened Chinese army was boasting of "glorious victories" over the superior armament of the greatest "imperialist" power. Military modernization with Russian help continued thereafter. In 1955 compulsory military service began to draw upon the five million young men who reach the age of 20 each year to create history's largest reservoir of military man power.

3. Social Reorganization

TERROR AND ENTHUSIASM

The Korean War provided a useful sanction for heightened anti-Americanism, extirpation of irreconcilables, and popular mobilization. Two major campaigns were mounted, to "Resist America, Aid Korea" and to "Suppress Counter-revolutionaries." They called for patriotic spying on neighbors and relatives, public denunciation of parents by their children, and consignment of enemies of the people, reactionaries, and counter-revolutionaries to "reform through labor." Together with the results of "people's courts" in the land reform, executions in 1951–52 evidently ran into the hundreds of thousands (some say millions). The regime benefited by extensive confiscations of property. It showed its claws and teeth, and the effect was not lost upon the populace, who became more amenable to discipline and direction.

In this context of terror on the one hand and patriotism on the other, foreign missionaries were denounced as spies and jailed or expelled. A "three-self" movement was set going, for "self-government, self-support, and self-propagation" of the Christian church in China, free of the missionaries' alleged "cultural imperialism." Uncooperative church leaders were gradually eliminated from positions of leadership and "national churches" free of foreign ties were finally set up to give Chinese Christians a religion subservient to the Communist state.

Minor campaigns were also pursued to secure a more effective payment of taxes and greater regularity in economic life. Victory bond and war donation drives mopped up public funds in order to counteract inflation. Another program was designed to raise the social status of the soldier, another to increase output and labor efficiency through the Stakhanovite system of work quotas and team competition.

The pressures and dangers of a war with the United States, whose power had bulked so large in the Chinese mind, were thus turned to purposes of totalitarian social reorganization and industrial efficiency.

The germ warfare hoax was also elaborately fabricated and publicized, with the approval of an international board of left-wing scientists and a mass of circumstantial evidence, to blacken the American name. Yet even here a subsidiary aim was also realized, since the germ warfare theme stimulated public health measures all over the country.

The mechanisms for mobilizing public pressure against designated types of individuals were used more and more plainly for refashioning China's social structure. A new height in this effort came with the Three-anti and Five-anti movements of 1951–52. These were organized very thoroughly and proceeded through well-defined phases with standardized methods.

The Three-anti campaign was directed against officialdom, in the government, in state industries, and in the party. The movement was anti-corruption, anti-waste, and anti-bureaucratism—plainly an attempt to weed out and invigorate the vast administrative apparatus inherited from the Kuomintang and rapidly added to since 1949. The Three-anti movement permitted replacement of administrative personnel by new blood, as fast as it could be developed for the purpose, and brought the enlarged bureaucracy more thoroughly under central control by keeping the bureaucrat insecure in his new power. Like many major drives, it began in Manchuria, the most advanced area under the new regime. Special committees and an apparatus were soon formed to promote the movement countrywide with spectacular denunciations, public "trials," and great publicity.

The Five-anti movement was a similarly well organized and concerted attack on merchants and manufacturers, the bourgeoisie or middle class in general. Nominally it was against bribery, tax evasion, theft of state assets, cheating in labor or materials, and stealing of state economic intelligence. Employees were inspired to accuse employers, customers accused shopowners, and there was a general screening of all persons in urban trade and industry. As in all campaigns, the public were mobilized, committees established, and appearances created of great popular initiative, righteous anger, and enthusiasm for the triumph of virtue. Confessions, apologies, and the reform or elimination of culprits by suicide, execution, or labor camp followed. But it is evident that one immediate aim in this anti-middle-class program was financial. Large sums were squeezed out of the business class, probably somewhere between one and two billion United States dollars. From this time the national bourgeoisie existed on sufferance; those who remained in business were thereafter thoroughly amenable to the continued pressure for socialization of private enterprise. (Eventually they were all expropriated and in January, 1956 dutifully celebrated, with firecrackers and dancing, their own demise as a social class.)

All these manipulations of the body politic squeezed out great numbers of enemies of the regime. Forced labor camps were the natural result, built both on the Soviet model and on the ancient corvée or labor-service tradition of China. Muscle-power has always been the country's chief natural resource. The modern use of labor armies of 4 million persons on one project of public works, like the much-publicized Huai River dikes and dams, was no great innovation except for its increased scope and the edifying moral exhortation which accompanied it. Whether the millions of Chinese who now perform forced labor on short rations are more numerous than the millions who have normally starved and still starve while farming every year, no one can say. The difference is that the grinding down and slow extinction of life through prolonged and ill-equipped labor, always a part of the Chinese scene whether planned or purely circumstantial, is now well organized.

Another imponderable to the outsider is the degree to which the revolutionary ardor which inspired the tremendous exertions of the early years of "liberation" still continues to burn. The Communist attempt is to institutionalize ardor and self-sacrifice, as well as terror and compulsion, so that hope and fear together may build a new order. Since the youth of China are an inexhaustible resource, the inspired example of selected young people, the principles of emulation and competition, the leadership of party cadres may keep the new order operating on a partially voluntary basis. It is impossible, at any rate, to understand Communist China by either extreme approach. It seems to be neither a vast prison nor a new Jerusalem but some kind of mixture, depending on who you are and where you function in the new order. This viability of totalitarianism is what makes it so ominous.

Pre-Communist China was pre-modern and particularistic in many ways—in the neglect of punctuality, the lack of civic-consciousness and public neatness, in putting family before community and personal interests before national, in all those attitudes and habits that the futile New Life Movement had condemned in 1935. The Confucian order having been eroded away, China was truly "a sheet of loose sand" as Dr. Sun complained, a country that our G.I.'s felt "ought to be cleaned up." In the old days, everyone haggled over prices, took note of manners, and treated every situation ad hoc and every person according to the circumstances if not on his merits. All this was quite contrary to the efficient impersonality of modern, universalistic market relations. This pre-modern character of Chinese society, its "medieval" traits, had fascinated foreigners and humiliated patriots for a century. The Confucian scholars who sought a panacea in gunboats, then technology, and finally in the reform of institutions have now been succeeded by revolutionists who condemn old ways as "feudal" and seek to remake their cosmos by applying the allegedly universal, abstract principles of a new Marxist-Leninist "science" of society. With reforming zeal their Leninist party, once thoroughly in control, has applied itself to remaking not only the economy and social order but also the individual.

4. *Thought Reform*

The Communist achievement in organization, among a people so recently famous for their lack of it, has depended upon the inspiring, coercing, or manipulating of individual personalities. Building upon methods used in Yenan to Leninize the party (as well as to convert Japanese war prisoners), Liu Shao-ch'i and other organizers developed empirical procedures to deal with every type of enemy or supporter. When American P.O.W.'s in Korea "confessed" to germ warfare and collaborated with their Chinese captors, they were responding to techniques developed through use with Chinese of all sorts, including party members. As a result of these methods capitalists and rich peasants smilingly gave their property to the state, professors scathingly denounced their Western bourgeois education, middle school students devotedly gave their lives to party work.

These diverse phenomena represent the real Communist effort at revolution, to change Chinese thinking and behavior. This is far more significant than the material efforts in technology and industry and at the same time is a prerequisite for their material success. Though very diverse, thought reform generally has had certain common features: control of the environment, both of the person physically and of the information available to him (this is now true of the whole country); the stimuli both of idealism and of terror, intermixed; and a grim psychological experience, undergone with guidance through successive phases and intensified by the manipulation of one's sense of guilt and shame. The Chinese slang term "brainwashing" imparts perhaps too much mystery to a process faintly visible elsewhere in religious crusades of the past, only now more thoroughly organized. Modern psychologists can explain how privation, prolonged insecurity and tension, combined with exhausting fatigue and repetitive indoctrination can shatter the individual's sense of inner identity and create pressures from which the only escape for many is submission to authority and acceptance at least temporarily of new attitudes and concepts. This coercing of the human mind, quite different in degree from the mild voluntary form of American advertising methods, is still only partially understood and exploited. Spread over the world it would create the ultimate crisis of individualism. Perhaps it is not surprising that in China, where the practical art of human relations has been more fully developed than anywhere else, these psychological methods should be most advanced.

For the Chinese student class, from whom the CCP must get its cadres, this intellectual-emotional reconditioning was carried out in the big revolutionary colleges set up through the reorganization and expansion of the educational system. Thousands of trainees went through indoctrination courses of several months duration. A center of this type containing 4,000 students might be subdivided into classes of one or two hundred and then into study groups of six to ten persons. A psychiatrist who has analyzed the procedure, Dr. Robert Lifton, divides a typical six-months course of thought reform into three stages—first, group identification, a period of togetherness and considerable freedom and enthusiasm. During this stage major Marxist-Leninist-Maoist concepts are studied and systematic rational indoctrination is delivered, partly in lectures but mainly in small group discussions. A free exchange of views, with a high *esprit de corps* and feeling of common effort, leads the trainee to expose himself freely and engage wholeheartedly in a "thought mobilization."

The second phase is one of induced emotional conflict within each individual. The daily schedule continues to be physically exhausting. The milieu, which is carefully controlled behind the scenes, now seems to close in. The individual submits his first summary of his own life and thought. He begins to feel under pressure as criticism and self-criticism intensify and the dangers of being rejected become apparent. The evils within the old individual are now attacked, not merely the old society in the abstract, and the student strives to dig up his failings and correct them. Group pressures are focussed by experienced leaders so that each individual becomes heavily involved emotionally, under assault. His failings may be labelled with any one of dozens of terms. He may struggle with himself and be "struggled with" by his group-mates over an excess of subjectivism or objectivism, of opportunism or dogmatism, bureaucratism or individual-heroism, and so forth. The individual who attempts to hold back and resist the process cannot win and suffers a psychological beating. Each participant, whether or not he resists, is completely alone, isolated within himself like all his fellows. Under this pressure, which is similar to that used against prisoners, the individual soon feels guilt—he has sinned and should be punished—and also a sense of shame—he has lost face and self-esteem, which creates intense humiliation. In attacking himself, he is thus prepared to achieve through confession and self-condemnation a psychological catharsis, feeling as though he were mentally ill and needed a cure.

The third phase is that of submission and rebirth. When his final thought summary or confession has been gone over from every angle and is accepted by the group and the authorities, the individual is likely to feel exhilarated, cleansed, a new person. This months-long process constitutes on a larger scale a sort of induced religious conversion, like those of our own revival meetings, but with added elements of pressure and psychotherapy. The individual has been manipulated so that the well-springs of his own nature have put him under intense emotional pressure and the relief from this self-induced tension is associated with the external authority of the group and the Party, on whom he should henceforth be dependent. For the Party's aim is not only to secure control over disciplined activists but also to raise the quality of their performance by changing their idea of themselves, their goals and values. They renounce family and father, and accept the Party and the revolution in their place.

In the case of older intellectuals, particularly returned students from the West, criticism, self-criticism, and confession cannot take place as in a malleable young mind but only as an overlay of the formative experience of a now mature person. The statements put out by Peking professors seem to be somewhat *pro forma*. They denounce the corrupting influence of the bourgeois West and their former subjection to it, possibly with some sense of guilt at having been seduced or alienated from their native culture. But the net effect of their self-criticism is probably less to change these individuals than to align them properly in the public eye as supporters of the new order. Thus the one class who might represent a Western non-Communist influence neutralize themselves and present no model for youth.

COMMUNISM AND CONFUCIANISM

Few who have lived in China will assume that a revolution, however irresistible, can quickly alter the immovable Middle Kingdom. The new marriage law of 1950, which attacked the family by proclaiming equal rights between the sexes, seems not to have been vigorously pushed. Substitution of the ancient ideographic script by an alphabet—the greatest literary project in all history—has been held up and modified from time to time. Our schematic account of thought reform should not imply that communism has as yet remade the Chinese personality. However, the strategy is long-term, to maintain a controlled environment of lip-service if not love for the regime until the new Socialist generation can take over.

Out of the Chinese inheritance, moreover, authoritarian traditions can be invoked for modern purposes. Thus Confucianism in one of its aspects has a certain resonance with Marxism. This is not an identity, only a partial overlap; nor is it surprising, for Confucianism is almost as broad and various as Christianity.

One point of resonance is in the important concept of the unity of theory and practice. The Bolshevik emphasis on putting theory into revolutionary practice contended that theory was no good in itself but must be applied in activity, as part of an effort not only to understand the world but to change it. Marxism as a "science of history" when put into practice must become an ethic, a personal philosophy animating one's entire thought and conduct. Self-criticism is a necessary part of discipline for this purpose. It is also a Communist doctrine that Marxist-Leninist theory should be applied according to the content of each national background, blending Communist ideas with the local tradition. As Mao says, "We must unify appropriately the general truth of Marxism with the concrete practice of the Chinese revolution."

Now it happens that Communist self-criticism is in some degree reminiscent of the Confucian doctrine of self-cultivation in the form which is associated particularly with the sixteenth century philosopher, Wang Yang-ming (1472–1529). Wang attacked the dualism of knowledge and action. In Wang's view, as David Nivison puts it, "To know is to know how and to know that one ought." The completely sincere man must express his moral perceptions in equally moral conduct. Wang and others therefore urged self-cultivation as a process by which the true philosopher can bring his thought and conduct into consonance, so that knowledge is realized in action and action contributes to knowledge. This idea was echoed in Sun Yat-sen's "Knowledge is difficult, action is easy" and later by Chiang Kai-shek.

. While Confucian self-cultivation was not a group affair, it stressed the moral improvability of human nature, the ancient Chinese belief that through proper ethical instruction and exhortation, man can be made into a more social being. The gap between individual self-cultivation and group self-criticism is a very broad one in fact but the two have something in common. Thought reform at Yenan and since has made use of traditional Chinese terminology and invoked Confucian sanctions. The good Communist, according to Liu Shao-ch'i, must discipline himself through self-cultivation, through "watching himself when alone," so as to become flexibly and resourcefully obedient to the Party's leadership. Through greater consciousness of the historical influences playing upon him, it is argued, he may indeed achieve a certain feeling of freedom within the confines of the historical process. Thus where Confucianism instilled loyalty to father and Emperor, Maoism now diverts it to the Party and the people. The classics are quoted for this totalitarian purpose. This makes Marxism-Leninism seem less outlandish.

CRITICISM, LITERARY AND POLITICAL

In the process of thought reform, the Chinese intellectual and literary world has been agitated by ideological struggles, in which Mao Tse-tung's dictum on literature and art of 1942, that literature is a political tool in the class struggle and thoroughly subordinate to politics, has provided a major premise. The full force of meetings, denunciations, and special publications was assembled to attack Hu Shih as the symbol of decadent bourgeois pragmatism. One campaign was against his inter-pretation of the famous eighteenth century novel, *The Dream of the Red Chamber*, as an autobiographical work. Communists preferred to see in it the inner collapse of China's feudal society, thus salvaging this fascinating book from China's heritage as belonging to "the people," like other selected heroes, poets, and cultural inheritances. The cam-paign simultaneously discredited Western-type literary criticism based on historical research, as part of the effort to stamp out the "worship America" tendency and the intellectual freedom associated with the West—in short, as part of the attack upon Chinese liberalism and its foreign allies.

It is a neat trick to foster intellectual vitality within a framework of uncritical loyalty to the Communist leadership. Creative ideas are still needed from the 10,000 or so higher-level non-Communist intellectuals. In the aftermath of Russia's blood bath in Hungary, which coincided with student and peasant discontent in China, Mao announced in 1957 his latest doctrine of contradictions—some "antagonistic" as between the regime and its enemies abroad or at home, and some "non-antago-nistic," normal and arguable, as between the bureaucracy and the people. Here was a framework within which it was evidently hoped that a con-tinuing struggle over policy could be healthily pursued and yet con-tained. As in the *cheng-feng* movement of the Yenan period, this dialectical process would call for criticism and then would meet it, let-ting extreme views emerge to be dealt with through open argument, in order to discover faults and correct them and also to discover fault-finders.

The campaign of 1956–57 for freer criticism of the bureaucracy under the classical slogan "Let a hundred flowers bloom together, let the hundred schools of thought contend" was not a clarion call for free speech except within the carefully enunciated limits of complete devo-tion to the Party's final authority. It was designed to resolve "non-antagonistic" contradictions between populace and government and stimulate a public catharsis through a degree of criticism. (This would be in the imperial censor's tradition of "loyal remonstrance," pointing out the ruler's errors on the basis of the ruler's assumptions, not like a "loyal opposition" which in the West would be free to attack the regime's aims and policies on a basis of continued loyalty to the state.)

Repeated invitations eventually released a surprising torrent of publicly expressed dissatisfaction with the CCP's totalitarian political system, its ideas, aims, and methods. This torrent simultaneously disclosed the minor-party and Western-educated critics of the regime, who were soon brought under attack as "rightists." Many observers felt that in the beginning Mao had honestly wanted some liberalization of thought and expression. But the widespread and basic criticism which had resulted required harsh suppression. The recent critics were soon publicly accusing themselves and condemning one another. The resulting pressure on the non-Communist press and the minor-party leaders was to make the so-called coalition more closely subservient to the dominant party, and also no doubt to destroy the position of non-Communists with a Western background.

The campaign method of revolutionary development is undoubtedly dynamic. The enormous apparatus which encourages activists to attack certain heterodox ideas or undesired activities develops a high momentum and easily overshoots the mark, achieving "excesses." One campaign therefore gives rise to another, to check, redirect, or supersede the previous one. No doubt this comparatively non-violent but total manipulation of political life is particularly feasible when the peasant masses are still just moving into literate public activity. In time, the tempo may slacken or more concrete coercion may have to supplement the publicity and "persuasion."

Behind the Party decisions, its campaigns and shifts of line, one may discern some faint echo of the bureaucratic politics of the imperial era. Parties as organized factions (tang) were anathema to the imperial ideal of harmony (a bit like the minor parties today) and were generally proscribed as treason, yet it is evident that official cliques or personal groupings have been an immemorial pattern among Chinese officialdom. Indeed, if policies are to be reasoned out in party councils, such groupings seem inevitable, even if the traditional concern for personal loyalty is now lacking. Observers have often, if too hopefully, seen the potentialities of rivalry between the theoretician and disciplinarian Liu Shao-ch'i, who studied in Moscow and is listed as second to Mao, and Chou En-lai, who studied in Paris and has had vastly more contact with the outer world.

VERA MICHELES DEAN

Red China:
Leap into Famine

When Mao Tse-tung and his associates, whose political ideas and methods are described in the selection by Professor John K. Fairbank, were engaged in their struggle to oust the government of Chiang Kai-shek and to establish Communist rule in China, they often referred to themselves as "agrarian reformers."

Once they had achieved power, they sought not only to reorganize agriculture, by establishing a system of peasant communes far more drastic than the collective farm system of the U.S.S.R., but also to start industrial development. Peking's aspirations for rapid changes in China's economy were expressed in 1958 in the phrase "the great leap forward." As events turned out, its agrarian reforms proved to be a leap backward in terms of food resources for a rapidly growing population, and by 1962 Peking had admitted that the country had suffered agricultural setbacks and would have to postpone its industrial plans. The reasons for the setbacks, and prospects for China's agriculture, are discussed in this article.

In 1961, twelve years after the Communists took power on the China mainland, and three years after proclamation of "the great leap forward" in agriculture, one Western observer with first-hand experience in China reported: "Never since the inauguration of the Communist regime in 1949 has poverty been so widespread as it is this year."

The author of this statement was Bernard Ullmann who in February, 1961 had just returned to Paris from a two-year tour of duty as Peiping bureau chief for the *Agence France-Presse*. Mr. Ullmann, who had made a number of extended trips covering much of China's countryside as well as its major cities, found that "there seems to be just one thought in the minds of pedestrians—to go on from queue to queue, from the one that stretches behind the bus stop to the one that lines up in front of a stubbornly shut shop window, where dried fish may or may not eventually be dispensed. . . .

197

"In towns and villages alike, 'tickets' must be surrendered for every purchase. For the past few months, Chinese restaurant patrons have even had to give up their day's quota of grain coupons for meals—except in a few luxury establishments whose prices are out of reach of the public. And the ration coupons are usually kept by one's factory or block eating hall, which surrender them only on official authorization.

"Eggs, poultry, and fish have almost completely disappeared from the market. The monthly meat ration is seven ounces for city dwellers, who find, moreover, that it is not always available. For peasants, as in the past, meat is a rare holiday dish. . . . Signs posted in eating establishments blare out the message: 'You don't need your "whole" ration. Eat no more than will keep the hunger away.'"

Other danger signals have been flashed by the actions of the Peiping government itself. Communist newspapers, as well as radio comments monitored in Hong Kong, frequently mention serious food shortages, which are attributed to "natural disasters" such as droughts and floods. Families which have relatives in other Asian countries are not only permitted but apparently encouraged to write abroad and ask for food parcels—a request which a few years ago would have been regarded by the authorities as an unpardonable admission of the nation's difficulties. (The Chinese of Hong Kong are reported to have sent 13 million food parcels in 1961.) The government has gone into the world market to purchase large quantities of wheat, from Burma, Canada, and Australia.

Most significant of all, the system of village communes has been drastically altered, although Peiping once boasted that they would surpass the farm collectives of the U.S.S.R. in productivity. The communes were supposed to solve the economic and social problems of the countryside, where 80 per cent of China's people live, and to serve also as an example for underdeveloped countries.

All this is a far cry from the rosy picture of the future painted by Communist leaders in 1958 when they described the anticipated consequences of "the great leap forward." According to Peggy Durdin, a writer with considerable experience in the Far East, ". . . the peasant —600 million strong—was to become an exemplary 'Communist man,' feed the big cities and the huge Red Army, provide most of the materials for light industry and give Peiping an agricultural surplus to exchange with Russia for capital goods."

What are the reasons for the dramatic reversals which have occurred on the agricultural front in Communist China? And what may be the consequences of these changes?

The four main reasons are: a spectacular increase in population since

1950; a series of genuine natural disasters in 1959 and 1960 such as have often afflicted China in its millennial history; overemphasis on rapid industrialization; and, most important of all, the acknowledged failure of the communes not only to solve the food problem, but even to maintain a survival diet.

The population explosion in China—with an estimated increase from 583 million in 1953 to 725 million in 1962, or some 142 million in a decade—is due to the same causes which are found in other underdeveloped countries from India to the nations of Latin America: the coincidence of a rising birth rate with a declining death rate.

In the opinion of India's leading population expert, S. Chandrasekhar, director of the Indian Institute for Population Studies in Madras, the rise in the birth rate has been due in part to the new marriage law, passed in 1954. Professor Chandrasekhar states: "This piece of legislation guaranteed individual and free choice of marriage partners, raised the age of consent from eighteen to twenty for males and from sixteen to eighteen for females, enforced monogamy, and outlawed concubinage. . . . In Communist China, economic considerations do not act as a deterrent or delay to marriage, because work is compulsory and everyone is guaranteed a minimum of basic economic security, even if it is only a bowl of rice and a blue boiler suit. And children are the responsibility of the state. The overall effect of the new marriage law was that marriage became more prevalent than ever, and the nation's birth rate rose to about forty per thousand, one of the highest rates in Asia."

Meanwhile, "there has been a definite decline in the nation's death rate. In 1959, the latest year for which official figures are available, it was twelve per thousand, an incredibly low figure for an Asian country." The infant mortality rate was around fifty per thousand births a year, as compared with two hundred before the Communist revolution. According to Professor Chandrasekhar, this striking decline in the mortality rate is due to remarkable improvements in public sanitation and hygiene, among them the virtual disappearance, as a result of government-staged campaigns, of flies and vermin, and the introduction of underground drainage and protected water supplies in every town. "In a word, the impossible has happened. China has been physically cleaned up, and the result is an understandable decline in the death rate."

The tragic thing is that the improvement in health conditions which, under different circumstances, would have been regarded as a great boon for the nation, proved to be a mounting threat to its stability and even to the survival of many newcomers because the mouths to be fed rapidly exceeded the food produced. Inspired by the conviction that in Communist countries poverty was impossible, and convinced that China's enemies in the West would like nothing better than to see its population diminish in numbers, Peiping at first opposed measures of population control, as Russia had done in the 1930s on the eve of World War II.

In 1956, in order to close the gap between population growth and shortage of food resources, Peiping launched a nationwide campaign for birth control. . . . At this stage, Communist China adopted patterns similar to those of Japan, which practices birth control and abortion, and India, where planned parenthood and sterilization are urged by the government. Then, at the end of 1958, the government called off the campaign "without a word of explanation," apparently, in part at least, for ideological reasons. Mao Tse-tung and his associates, it is believed, could not reconcile their conviction that communism can and will triumph over all obstacles with their short-lived decision that strong measures would be taken to prevent population growth. But they may also have been influenced by their determination to build a strong industrial and military power on the China mainland which could withstand alleged plans by the United States to conquer China, and also undertake penetration of Southeast Asia, where Peiping appears to be engaged in growing competition with Russia.

The incidence of "natural disasters" has been frequently cited by Peiping as the principal explanation for China's agricultural difficulties. Peiping asserts that 1960 was the worst year for natural calamities in a century, admitting that it "cannot yet control nature completely." Such an admission is something of a heresy, contends Peggy Durdin. "In the days of Great Leap Forward fervor . . . Socialist man could conquer anything."

Mrs. Durdin, however, along with some other observers, believes that "the Communists have exaggerated undoubtedly real blows from floods and droughts . . . of 1959 and 1960 to cover up party errors of long-standing and recent origin. . . ."

Among the errors and miscalculations, according to critics, has been the third reason for the current food crisis—the frenzied drive to endow China with heavy industry, which Mao Tse-tung described as "the fundamental goal and basis of the national economy."

Like Russia, with its ruthlessly imposed austere standard of living, China, to quote Mrs. Durdin, "neglected and sacrificed agriculture while using it to support light and finance heavy industrial development." It gave the peasants "a beggar's share of essentials like fertilizer or vital farm and irrigation equipment." Agricultural products were used to pay the U.S.S.R. and other Soviet bloc countries "for imports of heavy industrial machinery and the materials and technicians to plan, build and supervise its great new industrial complexes." To accomplish its goal, Peiping kept the entire population at "minimum rations of everything from food and clothing to paper and soap."

This harsh method of trying to force a whole people to move quickly from a backward agricultural society to a modern industrial nation is in direct contrast to India's approach to the same problem. The Peiping government drove the Chinese peasant to produce more and more while eating less and less and to join in the industrialization campaign by producing steel in small backyard forges. India, on the other hand, is improving living standards by gradual development of both agriculture and industry through the *voluntary* efforts of its people.

As late as 1958 Peiping's vast undertaking appeared to be headed for success. Theodore Shabad wrote in the *Far Eastern Survey* of July, 1959: "The Chinese (in 1958) reported the doubling of yields per unit area in many crop categories, arousing the skepticism of some Western observers. . . ." Peiping's accomplishments were due to a frantic pace achieved in 1958—a pace Chinese planners assumed would be continued in 1959 and subsequent years. By 1961, however, the Communist party was declaring that agriculture—not "simultaneous development of industry and agriculture"—was the basis of China's economy. Steel was dropped to second place in economic priority. Increase in agricultural production became a chief task, as Mrs. Durdin puts it, "not just of the rural population but of the whole people and the whole party."

This sharp change in the Communist party's economic line was precipitated by the fourth reason for Peiping's agricultural headaches—the breakdown of the communes.

These communes went far beyond the peasant collectives established by Stalin in the U.S.S.R. In the early stages of Russian communism, Soviet leaders had thought of transforming all peasants into the equivalent of factory workers who would labor on state farms (*sovhoz*), punch the clock, and be paid money wages by the government. This plan, however, promptly met with insuperable opposition, and the Soviet government settled for collective farms (*kolhoz*) which are now the accepted pattern, with a few state farms operating as experimental farms only.

In the U.S.S.R. all land is owned by the state, but the members of the collectives have a say in their management, are assigned by the boards of collectives to specific tasks, and are paid on the basis of work accomplished out of the earnings of the farms, which are obliged to sell their produce to the state at prices fixed by the government. In response to peasant demands, however, all members of the collectives have their own homes, as well as small garden plots on which they can grow vegetables and raise chickens, pigs, and rabbits. The peasants can sell the produce of their garden plots in the open market, at whatever prices they can get through bargaining, and can keep their earnings for the use of their families. This system, where private ownership of land has been abolished but the individual family can make money out of garden-plot production for private use, does not involve communal living, and has some of the features of the old *mir*, or village community ownership of land in tsarist Russia. . . .

In Communist China, however, the Communists undertook a revolution in agriculture untried in any other Communist-ruled country. "No venture in recorded human history," wrote Albert Ravenholt in the American Universities Field Staff report in 1961, "has quite matched the extent and thoroughness of this change. Essentially, it has served to transform the highly individualistic family-oriented and largely subsistence economy of the Chinese peasant into a scheme of activity where Communist managers dictate all efforts: they determine the type of meals to be served for breakfast in commune mess halls; methods of child care in the improved nurseries; when and how rice seedlings are to be transplanted and the time for harvesting. Theoretically, a commune that today disposes of the life activities of anywhere from ten thousand to fifty thousand persons should be an extraordinarily effective device for introducing technical innovations. No longer need the Chinese peasant be persuaded to adopt techniques for improving production; he can simply be ordered, on threat of being denied his ration. And he can be made to work to and sometimes beyond the limit of human endurance. China's tragedy and the specter that stalks Mao Tse-tung's empire is that in practice this has not worked out as planned."

What has happened in Communist China . . . is reminiscent of peasant opposition to enforced collectivization in Russia in the 1930s. In Russia the peasants did not sow, or if they sowed, they did not reap. Their passive resistance could not be broken even by the most ruthless punishment, up to and including exile to forced labor camps and executions. The Russians have reversed themselves but not as completely as the Yugoslavs, who have abandoned collectivization and turned to a system of cooperative farming. To them the Chinese communes, where men and women are kept apart in dormitories assigned to them, and children are placed under the care of the state, would be utterly abhorrent.

This also seems to have been the reaction of the Chinese, who by millennial tradition had been accustomed to family ownership and intensive cultivation of small farms. Reports from mainland China indicate that peasants are suffering from lassitude due to meager rations, and feel resentment against the regime because of the destruction of their accustomed way of life. Their passive resistance to bureaucratic control and restrictions, perhaps more than any other factor, has forced Peiping to revise its agricultural policy.

Today, writes Mrs. Durdin, the commune is little more than a name. "Authority belongs to the brigade . . . which delegates most of it to work teams of about twenty-five people each. A definite piece of land is assigned to the teams for long-term use. The brigade discusses and settles with the teams their production quotas. But the teams decide what to grow and how to grow it, guided by local conditions and the experience of older peasants.

"No one now can suddenly take away from the farmers the good earth, the jointly used tools, and the work animals their teams have been assigned. Loud-speakers blare out and cadres obediently emphasize to the peasants the principle of 'more work, more pay,' through both graded wages and bonuses.

"In a radical reversal of the old commune policies of collective care of livestock, cadres recently have been urging and helping . . . peasants to keep their own chickens and pigs. Cadres have allotted each household a tiny plot of private land, encouraging its members to grow there and on any other scrap of earth, such as sides of roads, fields, or canals, whatever they wish, in spare time after collective work is done. If it likes, the family can consume this produce.

"Government agents buy the grain or pork, but the remainder, along with home-made handicrafts, can be sold to other peasants at village markets or fairs, at prices reached through bargaining, in the old-fashioned way."

Thus, under pressure from the peasants, and with the population fast outstripping food resources, Peiping is making "a leap backward." Not all the way back to the pre-Communist village economy based on the family unit in the output both of food and handicrafts, but to a "mixed economy" of private and state organization and production which resembles that of the U.S.S.R. This at a time when the Chinese Communists vigorously assert their differences with the Russian Communists, and claim that they, and not the Russians, practice simon-pure communism. In China, as earlier in Russia, realities have disproved the Communists' doctrinaire theories.

But it would be a mistake—and a mistake that could prove very costly to the West, as well as to the U.S.S.R.—to assume that Peiping's leap backward spells the failure of mainland China's economy, which is still predominantly agrarian. Peiping, under the pressure of circumstances and of its own mistakes, is backing now so that it can jump better at a later date.

The experience of Communist China is like that of all technologically underdeveloped countries in the twentieth century, including Communist Russia and democratic India. The countries of Western Europe had the historical good fortune of first improving their agriculture and then, at the leisurely pace of several centuries, proceeding with the Industrial Revolution, and this occurred at a time when European countries had small populations as well as outlets for emigration and exports to overseas territories in Asia, Africa, and Latin America, where they obtained cheap raw materials for industrial expansion. In contrast, the newly emerging nations of the non-Western world, late-comers on the world scene, must telescope their agrarian and industrial revolutions, with the resulting social and political transformations, into a painfully brief span of time.

This telescoping process can involve untold hardships for human beings, as did the breakup of the manor economy and the harsh early days of the Industrial Revolution in Europe. Only a very few underdeveloped countries, such as Thailand, which have a favorable ratio of resources to population, have avoided such difficulties. Communist China, with an even greater sense of urgency than Russia, attempted to proceed with industrialization before it reorganized its agriculture. But a backward agrarian economy cannot be modernized without the tools, insecticides, and fertilizers which twentieth-century industry can provide.

In the twelve years of Communist rule, villagers hitherto isolated from modern technology have been exposed to new scientific ideas and new tools. Farms have been linked to factories. Farm mechanization has been introduced, and rural electrification is being vigorously pushed. Agricultural production has been diversified. The Chinese countryside will never be the same again. But the Communist reforms, particularly the communes, have been repugnant and grievous to the Chinese peasants.

What will be the consequences of Communist China's agricultural upheaval for its role in world affairs, and particularly for its relations with the West and with the Soviet bloc? Some observers believe that Peiping, faced with the urgent need to improve its food output, would hesitate to embark on any adventures in Asia in the immediate future. Others, however, contend that food shortages will spur the Communists to advance into South and Southeast Asia, with the hope of obtaining access to the resources of rice-growing areas like Burma and Thailand.

Whatever militant plans may be brewing in the minds of Mao Tse-tung and Chou En-lai, it seems doubtful that the vast demands for food of China's growing population could be adequately met from the output of the small countries of Asia, unless Peiping intends to turn these countries into vassals—thereby risking the danger of a clash with the United States.

It seems more likely that, until such time as current concessions to the peasants have brought increased agricultural productivity, Communist China will have to rely on food-producing countries of the West, notably Australia and Canada, for the additional resources it needs. To pay for its wheat purchases in hard currency—dollars or pounds sterling —Peiping may turn increasingly toward the West not only for food purchases, and purchases of manufactured goods, as it has just done in ordering airplanes from Britain, but also for export markets. If this should prove to be the case, Peiping might, through force of circumstances, find it necessary to depend increasingly on trade relations with the Western countries. In world affairs, as in agriculture, the Chinese Communists will find that Marxist dogmas are undermined by realities.

W. Z. LAQUEUR

The Appeal of Communism in the Middle East

The countries of the Middle East for the most part achieved national independence only after World War II. At that time Britain and France relinquished their League of Nations mandates over former portions of the Turkish Empire, which had been dissolved at the end of World War I. In these technologically developing countries, impoverished villagers and herdsmen, ruled by authoritarian governments, live side by side with the few wealthy and powerful families which benefit by the Middle East's great oil wealth. This political, economic, and social situation seemed ready-made for Communist infiltration. Yet contrary to the expectations of both the Western nations and of Moscow, communism has so far had little or no influence on Middle Eastern nations, although some of them, notably the United Arab Republic, trade with and accept financial and/or military aid from the Soviet bloc.

How communism arose in the Middle East, what its appeal has

*been, and what the chances are for its success, are discussed by an
expert on that area, Walter Z. Laqueur, editor of the British
periodical, Soviet Survey. His article, reproduced here, appears in
somewhat enlarged and altered form in a book he subsequently
published, Communism and Nationalism in the Middle East, 1956.
Mr. Laqueur, born in Breslau (Wroclaw) and now a British subject,
is the author of several other books, among them The Soviet
Union and the Middle East, 1959.*

FOUR broad periods in the history of Middle Eastern communism may
be distinguished. In 1919–20 the first Communist groups came into
being in Turkey, Palestine, and Egypt. But these attempts were doomed
from the outset: the Communists of that era put themselves into deliberate and radical opposition not only to the governments of the day
but also to all political, religious, and social institutions and traditions.
They wanted to create proletarian mass parties in countries without an
industrial proletariat. They also launched a frontal attack against Islam
at a time when its hold on the public had not yet weakened.

By 1923 this failure was obvious. The Communist parties in Turkey
and Egypt had ceased to exist; the party in Palestine lingered on but
only precariously and without any hope of gaining mass support. Yet it
was only in the middle '30's that a break was made with the "radical"
past. This break came as a concomitant of the popular front tactics of
the Comintern in Europe and the United States, but it was the line
which came to stay in the Middle East, with certain important modifications (the change into a "national," anti-imperialist front, etc.). Now
all radical Socialist demands were dropped, as was the enmity to Islam
and the unwillingness to collaborate with other parties. In countries
such as Iraq, Syria, and Lebanon, Communist parties grew up, and in
the latter two, at least, attained a certain importance. Their main competitors were the semi-Fascist groups, whose power of attraction was
still frequently the greater.

Next, World War II brought a great upsurge in Middle Eastern
communism. One of the main reasons for this growth in influence appears to be, in retrospect, the emergence of the Soviet Union as one of
the two great world powers and the downfall of Nazi Germany and
Fascist Italy. It is true that the war also brought economic, and especially industrial, progress to the Middle East and the emergence of
stronger workers' organizations than before. But it was not the class
struggle which gave communism its main impetus, rather a general

feeling that the Middle East was at last moving after many years of stagnation. Communist parties made considerable progress in Egypt and Palestine, in Syria, Lebanon, and Iraq, and even in Turkey. The social group most closely connected with communism in all these countries was the intelligentsia, for although the feeling prevailed that things were in motion, the intelligentsia had almost nowhere in the Middle East attained full political emancipation.

The fourth period began almost immediately after the war with the deterioration in relations between the Arab countries and the West. The popular front of 1935–37 was now continued as an "anti-imperialist" front in which there was room for all "honest patriots without distinction of class, political or religious convictions." The Arab world became an experimental ground for all kinds of Communist front organizations; the number of party members, on the other hand, remained comparatively small, for many sympathizers could not put up with the strict party discipline. Communist achievements in Turkey and Israel were less spectacular for several reasons. Feudalism in these two countries was no problem; westernization (or modernization) had proceeded relatively far; the politically active elite was on the whole more mature; and last but not least, Russia had been threatening directly Turkey's independence and had launched a campaign against the "cosmopolitans" in Russia and the satellites which, though discontinued after Stalin's death, was not easily forgotten in Israel. But in the Arab world, a political, social, and spiritual crisis had been developing since World War I, and into the void created as the result of the breakdown of traditions, communism entered as a strong competitor for political leadership.

The sources of Communist strength are manifold. The decay of Islamic society and its values on the one hand, the absence of liberal and democratic-Socialist forces on the other (for which in the specific conditions of the Middle East there was but little room), made Communist successes easier than in Europe, where the party faced political and spiritual competition. Resistance to communism was confined to feudal forces, vested interests, and certain religious dignitaries, but there was no body of opposition to communism among the intelligentsia. Such opposition could only have been based on the defense of freedom and the liberty of the individual, but these prerequisites were not given one of the first places in the Middle Eastern hierarchy of values.

Basis of Communist Appeal to the Intelligentsia

If class interests are indeed of paramount importance in history, a convincing case on this basis could probably be made for the large measure of fascination which Soviet society has for the intelligentsia, or the "wording intelligensis," or the managerial class (in its widest sense) in the Middle East. The turn of events in the Soviet Union and the satellite countries has shown them that in Communist regimes the status of the technical intelligentsia is one of the most privileged, and a perpetuation of its privileges appears to be a likely development for the coming years. But it is extremely doubtful whether such considerations of class interest were really decisive for the political orientation of a large segment of the intelligentsia. All that can be taken for granted is that from a class angle there was certainly nothing to repel them.

Attention has frequently been drawn to academic unemployment or underemployment in the Middle East countries, notably Egypt. On the whole, however, it must be said that the Arab states have succeeded in absorbing a larger part of the intelligentsia (and in higher posts too) than most other Asian countries. The support for the Communist in Cairo and Beirut, the old City of Jerusalem and Baghdad, often comes from well-to-do lawyers and physicians; they may be déclassé, spiritually "strangers in their own country," but certainly not socially, and their economic roots are fairly firm.[1] It should be noted, incidentally, that the leadership of the Comintern as far back as 1928 recognized this trend of the prevalence of intellectual cadres and said in one of its resolutions that "an important if not predominant part of the Party ranks is recruited in the first stage of the movement from the petty bourgoisie, and in particular from the revolutionary-inclined intelligentsia, very frequently students."[2] The implication was apparently that in the second and later stages of the development leadership would pass to other hands. But exactly the opposite has occurred. The Communist leaders have drawn the necessary lesson in practice, if not in theory, and adjusted their policy and propaganda to consumption by the intelligentsia. The West has suggested various gradual reforms, such as Point IV, which may bring economic relief to the masses and be welcomed by

---

[1] As a few examples of the predilection of the lawyers of Cairo, Beirut, Damascus, Baghdad, and Arab Jerusalem for Communists, we may cite the following: 39 Baghdad lawyers volunteered to defend 4 Communist leaders (3 of them lawyers themselves) in Baghdad early in 1947; several months later 25 Baghdad lawyers wanted to defend their prominent colleague Aziz Sharif, the head of the People's party, a Communist front. According to the newspaper Alif Ba, 200 Damascus and Beirut lawyers volunteered to defend the Lebanese Communist leader Mustafa Aris at his trial at Beirut in December, 1949: 57 Lebanese lawyers announced that they would come to defend the first secretary of the Jordan Communist party, Fuad Nasir, at his trial in Amman in January, 1951.

[2] Theses on the Revolutionary Movement in the Colonies and Semi-Colonies, Adopted at the Sixth Congress of the Communist International, Press Correspondence, vol. 8 (Dec. 12, 1928), pp. 1659–76.

them in accordance with their interests, but which are not likely to catch the imagination of the key group, the intelligentsia. The Communists, on the other hand, turn almost exclusively toward the intelligentsia. "A program of seizing political power followed by prolonged industrialization, economic planning, recasting of the social structure, realignment of a country's international position in favor of the U.S.S.R. —these are considerations of the type which can attract intellectuals only."[3]

There is, of course, as G. L. Arnold has pointed out, in all this an element of self-deception. The privileged Soviet elite, whose status appears so enviable to impoverished Middle Eastern and Latin American intellectuals and civil servants, is hagridden with fears and repressions unknown elsewhere. But this dark side of the moon is invisible to people living in a pre-revolutionary society where an efficient totalitarianism can hardly be imagined.[4]

In European countries such as France and Italy, a *secessio plebis* gave the Communists a real proletarian mass basis. Elsewhere, they have appeared in the role of a national party spearheading the fight against outside rulers (as in Yugoslavia or Indochina) or have headed and exploited agrarian revolts. But in the Middle East and Southeast Asia, in view of the absence of an urban proletariat or agrarian unrest, the Communists have become the party of the intelligentsia par excellence. This has been noted by Sjahrir, the leader of the Indonesian Socialists. Given the still strongly surviving heritage of a "feudalist" authoritarian mentality among many Indonesians, he believes that his grounds for these fears are very real. The Communists were able to exploit this authoritarian heritage by building a powerful party along authoritarian lines. The Communist leaders themselves, he says, exemplify the effect of this totalitarian heritage. "Most of them come from the old aristocratic families and a paternalistic authoritarianism is ingrained in them."[5] The same phenomenon has been noted by M. R. Masani in India, who found that Communist propaganda was more successful among the well-to-do, the managers, educators, and scientists, than among the workers and peasants. This led him to the conclusion that not poverty and not starvation were the main reasons for the spread of communism but psychological and emotional factors; the void caused as a result of

---

[3] Morris Watnick, "The Appeal of Communism to the Underdeveloped Peoples." Bert F. Hoselitz, *The Progress of Underdeveloped Areas*, ed. (Chicago, 1952), p. 165.

[4] G. L. Arnold, "The Cold War," *Twentieth Century*, vol. 153 (April 1953), pp. 165–79.

[5] Quoted in George McT. Kahin, "Indonesian Politics and Nationalism." William L. Holland, ed., *Asian Nationalism and the West* (New York, 1953), p. 92.

the decay of the traditional religions, being in the process of replacement by some new religion of materialism.[6]

The situation in the Middle East in this respect is highly illuminating too. The main spokesman of pro-communism in Egypt is one of the ten biggest landowners in the country. All prominent Arab Communist leaders in Syria, Lebanon, Israel, and Jordan (with one exception) hail from well-to-do families. In Turkey the Party has won comparatively many followers among the poets, but very few among the industrial workers. The militants of the Iraqi party are almost exclusively intellectuals. Recent events have shown that the Tudeh party in Iran has many well-wishers among the army officers, but hardly any among the non-commissioned officers and privates. In Israel, the Communist party obtained a lesser percentage at the Histadrut (trade union) elections than at the parliamentary elections.

Communism in the Middle East has functioned widely as a movement of a middle class revolt against feudal rule. But this does not mean that the intelligentsia, having attained its political emancipation, will automatically cease to be Communist. They believe probably in the essential goodness of the fellahin and workers, but they also think them incapable of managing their own affairs; the masses will need tutelage by the enlightened vanguard for many years. In the meantime a revolution will have to take place, and they see no better theory of revolution from above than communism.

The roots of the values of the West have been skin deep. The impact of communism as a technique for modernizing the Middle East, of overcoming its present backwardness in the shortest possible time, is therefore of the greatest importance. Capitalism is identified with imperialist rule and democracy is something the imperialist powers allegedly practice at home. Democracy has not been a militant creed and it has not provided the answers to many questions of Asia. Democracy could not inspire the masses and has not given firm spiritual support to the elite. It has not been able to promise a much better life in the immediate future, or make a spectacular effort in which everybody was to be told what to do; on the other hand, communism has had all the force of a secular religion—in Asia even more than in Europe.

Nor must it be assumed that nationalism in the Middle East is a

---

[6] M. R. Masani, "The Communist Party in India," Pacific Affairs, vol. 24 (March 1951), pp. 18–38. See also his The Communist Party of India: A Short History (New York, 1954). Eugene Staley, in The Future of Underdeveloped Countries (New York, 1954), says that in their attempts to influence the peoples of underdeveloped countries, the Communists put great emphasis on appeals not to the material wants of man but rather "to the human desire for status, equality, freedom from domination or oppression, especially by foreigners" (p. 384).

force opposed to communism. On the contrary, at the present time it has paved the way for and occasionally collaborated with it. Communism, more often than not, just as nineteenth-century liberalism in Europe, has grown together with nationalism and for many years a conflict between the two was not considered possible.[7] What nationalism meant had been very clear under foreign rule: it was independence, home rule, evacuation of foreign forces. But once independence had been achieved, cynicism and disillusionment prevailed and today nationalism can be given no clear formulation.

Effective Strength of Communist Parties

The following estimated numerical strength of Communist parties in the Middle East might not appear impressive to the American or Western European observer:

Egypt	8,000	Jordan	1,000–2,000
Israel	5,000	Iraq	3,000–5,000
Lebanon	10,000	Sudan	1,000–1,500
Syria	10,000	Turkey	3,000

It may be argued that the Communist parties in Holland and Belgium have more than 30,000 members each and in Austria even 60,000. All these countries are less populous than Egypt, and not much bigger than Syria or Iraq. Nevertheless, the power of communism in Belgium, Holland, and even Austria is negligible. But such comparisons are misleading: Austria may have far more Communists than the whole Middle East, and yet the Austrian Communists can never compete with the two main parties in that country, the Social Democrats and the Christian Socialists, which have party apparatuses more loosely knit, but much larger than, the Communist cadre. The decisive issue in the Middle East is that no party in Syria and Lebanon has more than 10,000 militants apart from the Communists, and only the Muslim Brotherhood has more than the Communists in Egypt. The situation should be compared with the state of affairs in underdeveloped countries where political parties do not exist or are only feebly developed. A comparison with Russia in 1917 would be far more to the point. Party membership in Russia on January 1, 1917, was 23,600; one year later, after the Bolsheviki had attained state power, it numbered only 115,000 in a country of 160 million!

The decisive test, however, is not in figures—above a certain vital

---

[7] This situation may of course change should the Soviet Union become directly and actively involved in Middle Eastern affairs.

minimum, of course—but elsewhere. How strong is state power rooted? Has the Communist party any serious rivals? Would it be sufficient for it to conquer a few urban centers? How many sympathizers does the party have, how strong are its "front" organizations? What chance is there that in a state of anarchy, a local Communist party will decide to go ahead without waiting for the green light from Moscow? Again, the reply to these and several other pertinent questions would obviously differ widely if we compare the situation in some Western European country with that in a Middle Eastern state (apart from Turkey and Israel)—or in Russia in 1917. In addition, local differences make generalizations and predictions difficult, if not impossible.

What are the Soviet intentions with regard to the Middle East for the near future? Here we face conflicting trends and interests. On a short-term view, the present Soviet policy of avoiding any involvement in Middle Eastern affairs in counteraction to a "Western imperialism" wishing to "organize the area," is undoubtedly promising and will be continued for the time being. But this will take the Communists only up to a certain point, and from that point onward the policy of non-intervention is unlikely to bear fruit. It is not impossible, of course, for local Communist parties to come to power in the Arab states within the framework of popular fronts, but historical experience has shown that without active outside intervention they are not likely to get the impetus necessary to attain state power. Their task in the age of "revolution from above" is definitely not to engage in a "leftist deviation," i.e., to try their luck in a revolution. Strategically, their assignment is that of the fifth column which is not to strike before the other four are on the march.

Chances of Communist Success

For the time being, all that can be safely predicted is that it will not be too difficult for Soviet foreign policy to achieve its minimum target: to neutralize at least the Arab countries of the Middle East. This is comparatively easy because public opinion in the Arab countries is strongly in favor of neutralism. Even among the rulers, support of the West is not very strong. There have been and are now a few politicians and even army officers genuinely in favor of an alliance with the West. But the pro-Western elements are in the minority, and the rest believe that the community of interests with the West is not large enough to warrant support and close relations. Most take Middle Eastern security for granted, and though they may be ready occasionally to admit that the Middle Eastern countries alone are not able to defend this part of the world against outside attack, they agree on the following two basic assumptions: that the Communist bloc will be in favor of peaceful co-existence if only "Western imperialism" gets out of the area; and in the unlikely case of Communist aggression, that the West will help to defend the Middle East anyway.

If a dispassionate review of the political trend in the Middle East appears to show that the question whether or not these countries will become Communist has not yet been decided, it also tends to show that there is no reason for optimism. Even if there were more political wisdom on the part of the West in its present and future dealings in the Middle East than there is now, it is doubtful whether the West can decisively influence the course of events in the area. It can merely create the prerequisites for success. The West can give money, supply agricultural machinery and even jets and tanks, but it cannot quickly provide what is needed most: a competent native elite with a high degree of political maturity. There is little sense in closing one's eyes to the reality: the absence of such a group is the main source of the permanent Middle Eastern crisis—insofar as it depends on these countries.

What then remains to be done by the West? We have stressed that the possibilities of action are fairly limited, for the key is in the hands of the native elite. The development of political awareness of the nature of the Communist threat among the nations of Asia is indeed as vital a condition for containing it as the creation of a military counter-weight.

But will they be ready to defend their own cause? Will they be able to distinguish between social reform on the one hand and totalitarianism on the other? The Turks will defend their independence because they know the danger from close quarters; the Arab governments doubt the very existence of a danger. Some of these countries are ruled by conservative and even reactionary regimes which see their main task in the prevention of social change. Reform movements have been branded "Communistic" in these countries and there is hardly reason for surprise that the Soviet Union and the Communist party have become the symbol of social justice and progress. It is very nearly hopeless to try to convince citizens of these countries that they are likely to lose human freedom and basic liberties under communism; they are little afraid of losing what they do not have anyway.

The obvious course of action for the West would be, therefore, to support the forces of reform against the reactionary powers who lead their countries toward a catastrophe. Western policy has let many opportunities slip by. At the same time, it would be unjust not to admit that there exist serious difficulties: in some countries these forces do not exist at all and in others they are as yet too weak to constitute an alternative to the present regimes. Elsewhere, these forces have taken a very critical or hostile stand vis à vis the West. Nevertheless, there is no good reason to accept the defeatist conclusion that the West must continue backing reactionary forces to the bitter end. In some countries there is an alternative, and elsewhere the West can contribute much toward its creation.

This is no attempt to advise Western statesmen. Many excellent suggestions have been made in the last few years by experts for under-developed countries, and a vast new literature on the subject is coming into being. The major problem at this time is not the absence of good advice but rather the chasm between the policy which most people agree should be followed and what is being done in practice.

Ten and even five years ago, it was almost universally believed in the West that economic and technical assistance was the most efficient way to stem the flood of communism in backward countries. It is most interesting to note that many people who resent very much the teach-ings of the late Karl Marx became all of a sudden fervent believers in historical materialism, seeing in economic progress the key to the whole situation. By now it has been realized by most concerned that "eco-nomic development doesn't necessarily make nice people," nor does it create believers in the principles of Western democracy. This does not mean, needless to say, that economic and social progress leads toward communism, but it certainly means that in the process of making head-way underdeveloped countries are more likely to be affected by it, at least temporarily, than before. This clearly shows that the appeal of communism is far more wide and complex than believed by the eco-nomic determinists.

Communism has never found a favorable breeding ground in very poor countries unaffected by outside influence. Nor do very poor people resent their poverty so long as their fellow citizens share their lot. The Egyptian fellah and the Syrian workers feel their poverty acutely only when they have seen that a far higher standard of living is possible. The Arab intellectual feels it even more strongly because he knows better than the other classes what life can be in a more developed society. At this point the competition starts between communism, which promises to work wonders, and the West, which promises slow progress at best.

In fact, despite political propaganda to the country, economic prog-ress has not been a Communist monopoly. The classical Communist argument and example for the Middle Eastern countries is the develop-ment of the Central Asian republics during the past twenty years. If we compare these results with the state of affairs in countries which have been stagnating, this may appear very impressive indeed. But if we compare achievements there with the headway made, for example, by Turkey, the thesis of Communist superiority becomes rather difficult to maintain. But most of the Middle Eastern countries have not made such progress, and, more important, there is no upward trend in sight. Great development schemes have been planned in Iraq and the means are available to implement the program, but the living standard of the majority of the population has not risen nor is it likely to rise during the immediate years which may be decisive for the future of the Middle East.

Need for a Creed

The power of attraction of communism as a creed should never be underrated, and it is nowhere so strong as in underdeveloped countries, such as those of the Middle East. In the Soviet Union everybody has a first-hand opportunity to compare ideals with realities: he can see for himself how much social justice and freedom there is in the Soviet and satellite society. In the countries of the West, much information on Soviet realities is available too, and Leninism has great difficulty in standing the competition in the free market of ideas and ideologies. But the intelligentsia of the Middle East receives Leninism uncontaminated. Next to nothing is known about Soviet conditions; and anyway, the *idea* is the important criterion. They want to receive Leninism as if it had not yet been tried anywhere in the world.

Even if rapid economic development were the main attraction to Middle Easterners, communism would still be a formidable threat. But the religious elements in communism and its ethics have been of far greater importance, and that at a time when the quest for a universal creed has been stronger than for many years and traditional religion sterile and losing appeal. Any attempt to understand or counteract the power of attraction of communism in the Middle East which disregards the very existence of its moral concepts and the sources of its fervor and ideals is doomed from the outset. This goes for all underdeveloped countries and is not an observation particular to the Middle East. Specific for the Middle East situation is the fact that for the majority of the intelligentsia of the Arab countries, Islam has ceased to be a living force. A detailed investigation of whether Islam is aiding or arresting the growth of communism would be a question of undoubted speculative interest but of little practical importance—so far as the intelligentsia is concerned. For the masses in the Arab countries, Islam continues to be of importance, but the authoritarian character of Islamic society, in disintegration even more than in its early stages, makes an easy transition to the Communist ideology a possibility and in some cases a probability. Traditional Islamic autocracy rests, as Bernard Lewis has pointed out, on three pillars: bureaucracy, the army, and the religious hierarchy.[8] And it is quite true that in this pattern only the third factor —the religious hierarchy—need be changed in order to prepare the way for a Communist state.

Successful resistance to communism is possible on the basis of a society which is either very developed or untouched by what is commonly called civilization. Unfortunately the societies of most Middle Eastern countries are far from modern and even further from finding their internal balance—but they have proceeded too far from the primitive state to put the clock back. A rational exposition of the mistaken basic tenets of communism presupposes fairly extensive philosophical, psychological, and historical studies on such questions as the nature of man, the will to power, social progress, and kindred subjects which even to the intelligentsia of these countries appear highly abstract if not altogether irrelevant. We shall come to that, they say, but first things first. What we need now, they explain, is economic development to overcome backwardness; later, we shall cope with the nature of man. But by then, one fears, it will be too late, not perhaps from the point of view of the astronomer, but for the social scientist and the ordinary mortal concerned with the present time and the foreseeable future.

Yet it would be wrong to end this discussion on a completely pessimistic note. Observers in the Middle East frequently call attention to mob rule and xenophobia, to referendum on the pattern of the Cairo "Black Saturday" and to recall by bullets. What is frequently forgotten is that the situation in the most developed countries of the West was not altogether dissimilar a mere 150 years ago. The London "mob" of the time was very nasty yet also a major political factor; the fishmongers from St. Antoine played an outstanding role in the French Revolution; and it would not be too difficult to find parallels in American history for riots and xenophobia, up to Locofocoism and the "Know Nothings." Everything depends now on whether these countries will be able to make the social, political, and economic progress made by the West in one hundred years in a far shorter period—and how much time remains for such vital experimenting. It depends on whether there will be the men to head that immense task and whether the masses will cooperate, whether there will be inner sources of strength for an effort unparalleled in many centuries of Middle Eastern history.

---

[8] Bernard Lewis, "Communism and Islam," *International Affairs*, vol. 30 (January 1954), pp. 1–12.

FRED WARNER NEAL

Tito's Communism,
Independent and Moderate

Since the establishment in Moscow of the Communist International (Comintern) in 1919, many Americans assumed that world communism, directed by the Russian Communist party on a global scale, would always be a monolithic movement, free from the fissures and conflicts which are regarded as inevitable and, in fact, desirable features of democracy as practiced in the West.

This concept was seriously shaken in 1948, when Marshal Tito, Yugoslavia's Communist leader, challenged what he regarded as Stalin's attempt to dictate his policy both in domestic and foreign affairs. Vigorously asserting Yugoslavia's right to follow its own pattern of "socialism," and rejecting what he regarded as "imperialism" on Moscow's part, Tito set out to create at home a political, economic, and social system which, in his opinion, was based on the genuine communism of Marx and Lenin. Russia under Stalin, in his opinion, had deviated from this policy. In world affairs Tito inaugurated a policy of non-alignment comparable to that adopted by India in 1947, and subsequently followed by Egypt and many other non-aligned nations. In 1962, however, both Moscow and Belgrade sought to heal the rift that had developed under Stalin in an attempt to counteract the policy of Peking.

The main features of Tito's communism are described here by Fred W. Neal, professor of international relations and government, Claremont Graduate School, Claremont, California. Professor Neal was formerly a Washington and foreign correspondent for The Wall Street Journal. He has served as a consultant on Russian affairs and chief of foreign research on Eastern Europe in the State Department. He has traveled extensively, and has worked, in Yugoslavia. His most recent publication, with George W. Hoffman, professor of geography, University of Texas, is a comprehensive study, Yugoslavia and the New Communism, 1962, prepared for the Twentieth Century Fund.

LOOKING BACK at Yugoslavia during the past five years or so, two mutually contradictory but related sets of forces emerge. On the one hand,

From The Foreign Policy Bulletin, December 1, 1959. The Foreign Policy Association.

there is the urge for maintaining national independence versus the desire for close collaboration with the rest of the Communist world. On the other hand, there is the drive for "more complete socialism" versus a desire for the moderation and liberalization which distinguishes Titoism from Russian communism.

The most important fact about Yugoslavia today is that independence and moderation have proved the stronger forces, although the counterforces are still very much alive.

There probably was never any real basis for doubting Yugoslavia's determination to preserve its independence. But Tito went so far in the interests of "internationalism" during the period 1955–58 that there were widespread fears—both inside and outside Yugoslavia—that he would be unable to call a halt when the time came. He did call a halt, however, when he refused to sign the declaration of Communist unity in Moscow in the autumn of 1957 and thus set in motion a reaction which led to a new rupture of relations with Moscow.

In the process, Yugoslavia suffered a major diplomatic setback, one none the less serious because it was the first in a foreign policy generally executed with finesse. Tito and his associates committed two errors: first, they believed that they could influence the Russians and, second, they ignored the hard, cold fact that the *sine qua non* of Soviet foreign policy is the maintenance of hegemony over Eastern Europe.

'Active Coexistence'

Yugoslavs are wont to describe their foreign policy as "active coexistence." Between 1950 and 1955 this meant being neutral in the cold war, but neutral for the West and against the U.S.S.R. Between 1955 and 1958 Yugoslav neutrality tended to be neutral less for the West than for Moscow. Now there is an effort to keep "active coexistence" on dead center. Whether this can be done will depend in part on how far the Soviet Union, as well as Bulgaria and Albania, its most anti-Yugoslav satellites, goes in threatening activities against Belgrade. For the time being, emphasis is on collaboration with the uncommitted underdeveloped non-Western nations like India and Egypt, whom the Yugoslavs regard, along with themselves, as constituting a third force, although in the moral rather than the power sense.

It is far from clear what all this means in terms of future Yugoslav-Soviet relations. The split is neither as deep nor as wide as it was after 1948. It is likely that Tito and his comrades would again respond favorably to an olive branch offered by Moscow. It is far less certain, however, that they would risk concessions of the type made in the 1955–58 period. For one thing, there is sufficient opposition to any orientation to Moscow among a wide segment of the Yugoslav Communist party—to say nothing of the public at large—to make Tito more careful about any move he makes the next time. The marshal, chief architect of Yugoslav policy toward the U.S.S.R., is 67 years old. If a new Soviet peace overture were made, it might have to be dealt with, not by *Stari* (The Old One), as the marshal is called by close comrades, but by his successor.

'Hard' vs. 'Soft'

Differences between potential successors exist not only in attitudes toward the U.S.S.R. but also in the conflict between "hard" versus "soft" socialism. Generally speaking, those who favor concessions to Moscow in order to be more a part of the international Communist movement also favor more rather than less central controls, and restriction rather than expansion of political freedom. Their leading spokesman is Aleksandar Rankovic, Tito's top party aide and head of UDBA, Yugoslavia's secret police. The leader of forces placing less emphasis on relations with Moscow and favoring more rather than less liberalization at home is Edward Kardelj, chief ideologist and top man in governmental administration. The differences between them consist of shading and emphasis rather than substance. But in a system like that of Yugoslavia, which balances like a teeter-totter between East and West and between totalitarianism and democracy, shading and emphasis can be of great importance.

The fact is that the problem of succession in Yugoslavia is more important than is generally recognized, either there or abroad. Tito has achieved the status of a national leader, more popular than his regime. Not one of the potential successors has anything like either his popularity or his dramatic qualities of leadership. More significantly, the choice among them involves the question of the ethnic rivalries which split Yugoslavia asunder before the war.

The Tito regime has had outstanding success in overcoming the bitter and historic differences between the Serbs and Croats, but it has not eliminated them altogether. Indeed there has been some sharpening of ethnic tensions in recent years as the more developed parts of the country—Slovenia and Croatia—have opposed the financial demands on them to help build up the less developed areas.

The succession of Rankovic, or any other Serb, to Tito's dominant position in Yugoslavia would be certain to exacerbate these tensions, while Kardelj, a Slovene, would be more acceptable in Slovenia or Croatia, the most westernized areas of the country, which, before the creation of Yugoslavia in 1918, had been part of the Austro-Hungarian

Empire. However, whether or not as a result of easing of relations with the Soviet Union, in recent years Rankovic appears to have gained in power over Kardelj. Belgrade expects that when Tito dies Rankovic will take over his job as secretary-general of the Yugoslav League of Communists, while Kardelj will succeed to the presidency. As things are now, there is no doubt that party power is more important than government power. There seems to be no acute personal rivalry between Kardelj and Rankovic, and any overt struggle over the succession is unlikely. But what happens in this respect may well affect the course of events at home and abroad.

Generally speaking, in the same way that the Yugoslavs have clung to their independence abroad, they have maintained their moderate course at home. While there has been some perceptible tightening up, especially in the economic sphere, much of it resulted more from the fact that Yugoslavia had initially gone too far with decentralization than from the impact of *rapprochement* with Moscow.

Laissez-faire Marxism

The laissez-faire approach to Marxist economics which characterizes Titoism has by no means been abandoned. True, there is now a Five-Year Plan, but it still relies almost entirely on indirect controls and has little if anything in common with Soviet planning. The management of industry by workers' councils in factories—the keystone of the Yugoslav industrial system—continues by and large successfully, although various steps have been taken to whittle down workers' council autonomy. These steps are designed to cope with two major economic problems— "economic particularism," with attendant monopolistic practices and wasteful investment, and inflation, resulting from increases in wages without increases in production.

One significant check on the autonomy of workers' councils is found in the growing role of the nongovernmental associations of various branches of economic activity, known as *komora*. The *komora* now help fix industry-wide wage norms, allocate investment funds, and influence prices. The labor unions, under the high-powered leadership of Svetozar Vukmanovic-Tempo, are also increasingly occupied with efforts to restrain workers' councils from improving their own lot at the expense of the country as a whole.

Similarly, although price competition is still the rule, price fixing of a sort has entered the picture. Industrial price increases not accompanied by production increases must be justified before a federal price board, and local governments have been given similar authority to curb boosts in prices of consumer goods. Cereal prices are indirectly limited by restricting sales to grain buying cooperatives. Direct price fixing, however, only applies to steel, refined lead, aluminum, electric power, transportation, sugar, and tobacco.

Perhaps more important are federal laws giving the government the right to sequester surplus funds of workers' councils which were previously used as the workers' councils saw fit. This, plus high taxes on enterprise income, in many cases goes far to nullify the right of workers' councils to dispose of their surpluses on the basis of their own decisions.

Prices during the past year remained comparatively stable, and real wages rose for the second year by 8.2 per cent. The annual rate of increase in national income was 10 per cent in 1957 and 1958, while industrial production, with an average annual rate of increase of 13.6 per cent in the 1953–58 period, rose to twice the 1952 volume in 1958.

A big gap still remains, however, between wage and price levels, and this poses a serious dilemma for the government. If it permits a too rapid increase of wages, inflation will push prices steadily upward. But at the same time popular resentment about low wages raises a thorny political problem. A hint of how serious this can be was indicated by the 1958 strikes in the Slovenia coal mines, and by the fact that a great many Yugoslavs work at two jobs—one in the so-called socialist sector between 7 A.M. and 2 P.M. (the official working day) and the other, after lunch, in the "private sector." In the latter, this usually consists of work as a carpenter, painter, mechanic, etc., or in handicrafts for sale to the public. The result is that the inflationary pressure ensues in any event, and, in addition, there is a widespread tendency to loaf on the first, socialist, job in order to conserve energy for the second, private, one.

Nevertheless, the past three years have seen a marked increase in the standard of living in Yugoslavia. The overt forms of economic privation have disappeared, even in the underdeveloped sections, and from the Danube to the Julian Alps, from the Sava to the Adriatic, people look better fed and clothed than at any time since World War II.

The improved standard of living in Yugoslavia has been accompanied and stimulated by the introduction of consumer credit on a wide scale. Houses, furniture, fuel, washing machines, refrigerators, and even automobiles can be and are obtained on credit. Indeed, such credit has reached dangerous proportions. The National Bank has several times raised the terms, but consumer credit continues to expand.

Agricultural Improvements

In 1959 the Yugoslav economy was buoyed by a good agricultural crop, due to a combination of good weather, extensive use of United

States hybrid corn and resistant Italian wheat, vastly stepped-up investment in agriculture and better peasant cooperation, which is evidenced also by the new farm buildings that dot the countryside.

It took the regime, once it decided to abandon collectivization, a long time to stop discriminating against the private peasants, on whom it must rely. Although progress toward this end continues—the private peasants have recently, for instance, been covered under a health insurance plan—there is still a long way to go. In the meantime, since the farms are so small, the advantages of mechanization are strictly limited. Short of encouraging larger landholdings or paying higher prices for produce—both of which go against the Communist doctrine—there will continue to be troubles in agriculture for a long time.

These agricultural difficulties account in large part for Yugoslavia's serious balance-of-payments position. The deficit was about 18 billion dinars ($60 million at the official rate of exchange) in 1958. Further complications ensued when the Soviet Union withdrew a promised $285 million credit. The present bumper crop means that wheat will not have to be imported this year [1959], but until Yugoslavia is assured of being a regular agricultural exporter, the way out of the balance-of-payments morass is not clear. According to Yugoslav plans, which may be overly optimistic, foreign trade will be balanced by the end of 1961. In the meantime, continuing United States aid fills most of the gap. Thus far, this aid has amounted to nearly $2 billion, including the now eliminated military aid portion.

In the area of political freedoms one might say that during recent years the democratic part of Yugoslav "socialist democracy" either stood still or contracted, but its substance—such as it is—was preserved. In particular, some Yugoslav Communist officials who had never favored the liberalization utilized the period of *rapprochement* with the U.S.S.R. to crack down on dissidents. The inexplicable trial of the three elderly and politically impotent Socialists last winter was not so much an illustration as were the general increase of UDBA activity and the high-handed legal action against those who one way or another had run afoul of the party bureaucracy. Djilas in jail and Dedijer out of a job and, until November, denied a passport, continue to testify to the limits on freedom of expression.

Important as the backtracking proved, it was of a limited nature, and now the balance appears to be righting itself. The sharp condemnation of abuses of party prerogatives issued by the Executive Committee (Politburo) more than a year ago has had its effect, and since the rupture with Moscow the UDBA has pulled in its horns again.

At the same time there has been a rapid expansion of genuine popular participation in public affairs at the local level in connection with the "commune" and "social management." The Yugoslav commune, now the basic unit of local government, has been accorded wide economic responsibility, while, as a part of social management, boards of private citizens preside over a whole gamut of activities ranging from schools and hospitals to radio stations and semiautonomous housing neighborhoods.

The question is often asked whether the Yugoslavs can continue in their half East, half West, half totalitarian, half democratic, position. The evidence shows that, although this may mean defying the laws of political and economic gravity, the Yugoslavs have a good chance of doing just that. Meanwhile, the impact of Titoism outside Yugoslavia has been apparent not only in the revolutionary events which swept Eastern Europe in 1956 and after, but also in the continued bitter attacks on "revisionism" emanating from the Soviet camp. Titoism is not the only headache the Kremlin has, but it is one of the most painful and persistent.

[4]

Impact
of Democracy

CLINTON ROSSITER

The Paradox
of India's Democracy

Until the emergence of new nations in the non-Western world, American political scientists had worked on the assumption that, as Professor Rossiter says in this article, democracy can "grow from a delicate shoot to a tough-fibered plant" only under certain conditions. Yet after Professor Rossiter had lectured and participated in university seminars in India in 1961–62 under the auspices of the Department of State, he reached the conclusion that "to all the great rules we have tried to abstract from our studies of political history, there can be astounding exceptions." From this visit to India, where none of the "certain conditions" are fulfilled, Professor Rossiter returned, in his own words, "a chastened political scientist and exhilarated democrat"—and he explains why in this article.

Since 1959 the author has been John L. Senior Professor of American Institutions at Cornell University, where he has taught since 1946. He is the author of many books, among them Conservatism in America, 1955; and Marxism: The View from America, 1960.

A STANDARD lecture in the introductory course in political science at many American colleges is called "The Prerequisites of Democracy." Solemnly and even didactically—I know, because I have given this lecture more times than I want to count—the professor ticks off the social, economic, cultural and spiritual conditions under which popular, representative, constitutional democracy has flourished at different times in different parts of the world.

After pointing to the existence of all these conditions in the United States, Great Britain, Canada, Sweden, Switzerland and Israel and to the absence of most of them in China, Spain, Guinea, Paraguay, Bulgaria and Afghanistan, he then finishes off by framing the general rule: only in societies where conditions are favorable can men even hope that democracy will arise and flourish.

From The New York Times Magazine, June 3, 1962. Copyright © by The New York Times. Reprinted by permission.

Having recently spent some weeks on a lecture-study tour of India, I have returned home a chastened political scientist and an exhilarated democrat. Reluctantly but firmly I have decided never to give that standard lecture again or at least to throw away my old notes and start in afresh on this fascinating and indeed fateful subject of the prerequisites of democracy. India has taught me a lesson I am not likely to forget: that to this rule, as to all the great rules we have tried to abstract from our studies of political history, there can be astounding exceptions.

If I have not been totally misled by the evidence presented for my consideration, India may well be the most astounding exception of all time. The truth is that one who goes in search of the real and the possible in modern India comes away impressed by two overpowering and apparently contradictory facts about its political life: first, that almost none of the alleged prerequisites of democracy exists to any marked degree in that country; second, that democracy itself does exist, and shows remarkably few signs of giving way to any other form of government.

Political scientists, an independent breed, disagree warmly over the weight to be assigned to each of the prerequisites of democracy, yet few would deny the primary importance of these six:

A productive economy that raises the mass of men above the level of exhausted privation; a progressive society that offers these men both the satisfactions of security and the delights of opportunity; a literate citizenry that has been given the tools of learning and taught how to use them in passing judgment on the issues of the day; the will and means to perpetuate this literacy from generation to generation in the form of a well-supported scheme of universal education; a system of values that gives primacy to notions of opportunity, equality, self-reliance, morality and personal liberty; and a deep-rooted consensus about this system of values and about the institutions that embody them.

Only in soil that is fertile, we have been telling ourselves for years, can democracy grow from a delicate shoot to a tough-fibered plant.

The visitor to India learns in short order—principally from Indians who know their country intimately and fondly—that the social and economic soil is anything but fertile, that most of the prerequisites simply do not exist, and that India is therefore about the last place in which one would expect democracy to flourish.

An economy in which the average annual wage is something like $70, a society upon which the phenomenon of caste has barely loosened its immemorial grip, a citizenry only 25 per cent of which can be classed as literate, a system of education that has performed miracles and yet leaves millions of children untouched, a venerable tradition that makes room for many splendid values but most certainly not for political liberty and social equality—these are not exactly the foundations of a great experiment in democratic government.

Three harsh realities of contemporary India strike the hopeful visitor with particular force, and about all of them I found most of my hosts to be both knowledgeable and despairing.

The first is the familiar fact of overpopulation, a fact that one senses crudely by walking through any village or city and understands perhaps more sharply by digesting this simple statistic: there are today within the boundaries of India perhaps *one hundred million* more persons than there were at the time of independence fifteen years ago. The problems that these persons—or would it be more dramatic to say these children? —represent in terms of food, housing, health, education and jobs would stagger even the most efficient of democracies or hard-fisted of dictatorships.

The second is the existence of vast areas of discontent and despair among the people. Paul Grimes, New York Times correspondent in India, has described the poverty of the majority of Indians as "suffocating," and one can read three or four meanings, all of them unfavorable to the prospects of democracy, into this well-chosen word. I found no one in India who could be certain of the number of the unemployed; I found dozens of men who were certain that a majority of Indians were underemployed—and also, in the biting words of one of them, "underfed, underclothed, undereducated and underhoused."

And the third is the existence of at least five mighty forces of disunity —language, caste, class, regional loyalty, religion—that threaten relentlessly to tear India apart. To those who love to boast, as I once did, of the "wondrous diversity" of American life, I can say only: Go to India and discover a nation whose diversity is so wondrous as to be stupefying —a nation of men divided into 3,000 subcastes, a nation that recognizes fourteen regional languages in its constitution, a nation whose very consciousness of nationhood is still at best a surface phenomenon. India is, as W. H. Morris-Jones has written, "a fragmented society, a society with an absence of basic consensus."

Here, then is a country from which the committed democrat, overpowered by evidence of poverty and illiteracy and dissension, should return to his own country in a mood of despair. And so he would return if he had not also been overpowered by evidence of the second great fact of Indian political life: democracy ought not exist, yet it does; it ought not to survive, yet it may.

In a part of the world where every other country is governed under some form of dictatorship, ranging from the benevolent to the malevolent by way of the merely feckless, India is governed as a recognizable form of democracy.

It has a responsible Prime Minister and cabinet, a freely elected and by no means docile Parliament, an independent and learned judiciary, a civil service that is the envy of Asia, and a collection of state governments that are at least as faithful imitations of the Government in New Delhi as ours are of the Government in Washington. Elections are largely unrigged, parties sprout like weeds (although one party remains ascendant) and the press is uncontrolled and of infinite variety.

Two overt signs of the health of Indian democracy struck me with particular force: the jails are virtually free (as are the jails of very few countries these days) of political prisoners; the Army takes orders from, rather than gives them to, the elected leaders of the people.

In hundreds of thousands of villages, to be sure, life goes on just as slowly and unimaginatively as it has for centuries, which is evidence enough to support the generalization that political democracy is something imposed upon Indian society from the top down—and not too far down at that. Yet from these villages, as from the bustling cities, come the votes—more than 130 million in the elections of 1962—that give legitimacy to the most broadly based parliament in the history of the world.

India is an imperfect democracy, as Indians are the first to admit, but a democracy nevertheless, and who are we to smile or sneer over the imperfect results of this great experiment? We should, rather, remember our own imperfections, contrast the successes of democracy in India with its failures in the half-dozen countries grouped around it, and give thanks that at least one people in that part of the world has made the democratic gamble in good faith and with high hopes.

We are left with a jumble of questions about the nature, extent, condition and prospects of Indian democracy, and in particular with the leading question: how does India manage to defy the rules and govern itself democratically in circumstances that are supposed to be fatal to democracy?

This is a question to which even professionals in Indian studies have returned only tentative answers, and mine, the answers of an amateur, must be so very tentative as to be little better than hunches. Here, in any case, would be my list of the elements or influences in Indian society that have helped so far to redress and maintain the balance of social forces in favor of democracy:

Faith in democracy. Anyone who doubts that ideas are important, and can often be determining, in the destiny of a nation, should go to India and talk to some of the men who govern it, who teach its children and who are helping to build its future. I have heard experts on India—Britons, Americans and Indians themselves—argue all day about the sources of this faith, yet I have never heard one deny its power and tenacity.

While India has its full share of cynics, skeptics and "practical men who care not for doctrine," it also has men at every level of responsibility —and for the time being enough such men—to whom concepts of stern dictatorship or benevolent autocracy or even "guided democracy" are wholly foreign.

A leader who has kept this faith. Nehru is, by any standard, a rather difficult man for Americans to understand and deal with. He is cranky, preachy and imperious; he looks at the world too often with the eyes of an arrested Socialist of the Nineteen Twenties; he has failed as badly as Franklin Roosevelt to encourage the development of men in his party who can take over the burdens of national leadership.

Yet, he is, also by any standard, a very great man—and a man who, however unsettling his manner and moods, is committed deeply to parliamentary democracy. It is, surely, a fact of immense importance that this living demonstration of the influence of "the hero in history," whose hold upon the mass of men is powerful beyond belief, would not dream of giving up on democracy and taking command as a dictator.

"We have definitely accepted the democratic process," Nehru said to his colleagues in 1957, "because we think that in the final analysis it promotes the growth of human beings and of society."

A party that embodies this faith. It is easy to poke fun at the ruling Congress party or, when one wearies of poking, to rake it with caustic fire. Like its charismatic leader, it is cranky and imperious; and, to go further with this comparison of man and movement, it is torn by internal stresses and is something less than immortal. Yet one is bound to grant three points in its favor: it was the driving force in the struggle for independence; it never drove so hard that it abandoned permanently either the ideals or practices of democracy; it has given India a special kind of political stability in these critical years.

Whatever else it has been, the Congress party has been as democratic as a party of revolution and national liberation could ever be, and thus quite different in organization and procedure and spirit from those movements organized by such as Castro, Nasser and Nkrumah.

The British influence. The visitor from the West is doubtless more likely than Indians themselves to be impressed by the good effects of British rule, which he can see without straining, and to overlook the bad effects, about which he has to be instructed. Yet almost every Indian I met was quick to acknowledge that his masters had left behind a goodly heritage: schools, universities, factories, cities, railroads, ports, a famous civil service and a crack Army led by men who respect civilian authority.

More than that, they left behind a language in which educated Indians could talk to one another, the machinery with which they could govern themselves democratically, and even some splendid buildings in which to do the talking and governing.

The elites. The most important of all legacies inherited by the new India, in part a gift from its masters but in even larger part a consequence of its own struggle for dignity and independence, is the pool of trained and competent men in politics and public administration, commerce and industry, the professions and the armed forces. The contrast between India and, let us say, Indonesia in this respect goes far to explain the different political paths they are traveling.

India was almost uniquely privileged among the emergent nations of the post-war era to begin its new life under the guidance, not merely of what Paul Appleby has rightly described as an "extraordinary national leadership," but, at the next level down, of thousands of men who knew their jobs. It is especially encouraging for the visitor to learn that new men are pushing their way up into these levels of responsibility in respectable numbers, and that most of the new men, like most of the old, are democrats by nature as well as by nurture.

The policy of neutrality. While Americans cannot be expected to be entirely happy about Nehru's foreign policy, especially when he makes use of a double standard that is harder on us than it is on the Communists, we ought to recognize that, were India to move decidedly closer to the West or to the East, the consequence would be a severe strain on national unity. We, who so wisely took refuge in a policy of nonalignment in our early years should be able to understand better than most peoples how much tension India is spared by pursuing a similar policy.

The mixed economy. India is pre-eminently the underdeveloped country in which public control and private initiative coexist peacefully in a rather judicious balance. There is enough activity going on in what Indians call "the public sector" to give men a rough sense of economic and social justice; there is enough room for the operations of private enterprise to give a real lift to the rate of economic growth in the area of consumer goods.

The secular state. Nehru's flat insistence, in the words of Norman Palmer, that "free India should be a noncommunal, secular state" has also served to reduce tensions that could easily tear India apart. The integration into Indian life of a Moslem community that numbers more than forty million persons has certainly been aided materially by this wise and, in some ways, brave decision.

I do not mean to give too genial a picture of Indian society or to appear too sanguine about the prospects of Indian democracy. The society is beset by staggering problems, and the democracy might be said to flourish only because it has not really come to grips with most of them—because, for one example, it has not yet reached down into the villages and tried to shake the mass of men loose from the routines and prejudices of a thousand years.

The processes of democracy, I heard a wise man argue in Madras, simply cannot make and enforce the decisions needed to raise the Indian economy to the level of the Japanese. The processes of democracy, I heard another wise man answer, should not be expected to do for a people what it has no will to do for itself; whereupon I recalled for their edification the sobering fact that the processes of American democracy had failed utterly to produce a solution to the two greatest problems of our first century as a free people: the preservation of the Union and the elimination of slavery.

We, the lucky Americans, were able to solve these problems on the field of battle without doing permanent damage to the processes of our democracy. India, however, can hardly expect history to be as tolerant of her departures from constitutional propriety as it was of ours.

Democracy, I feel, will be given only one throw of the dice in India, and that throw is being chanced at this very moment. To mix the metaphor, it must now be proved whether this graft called democracy can be made a permanent and integral part of the living body of Indian society.

In the end, of course, it will be for the Indians themselves—especially for those great masses of village-bound men and women who have thus far been heard from only faintly—to decide whether their legitimate economic and social goals should be pursued through more autocratic methods than those now being employed. For the time being, however, we ought to look with more admiration than we have hitherto expressed at the miraculous existence of Indian democracy, and perhaps convert some of that admiration into the hard coin of increased economic and technical assistance.

We, after all, can have something to say about the ultimate decision of life or death for Indian democracy, and it strikes me as a tough-minded rather than soft-minded policy for America to extend all the help that India can absorb in its historic effort to create the prerequisites of democracy after the fact.

India is a splendidly defiant exception to all our generalizations about these prerequisites, a country that has endured for fifteen years, and will certainly endure for some years to come, as an example of the power of faith in democracy to overcome the most adverse environment.

But it will not endure forever, not without the support that comes from improving social and economic conditions. Since either a transition to dictatorship or, as seems more likely, a dismemberment of the nation itself would be a tragedy for our cause, indeed for all mankind, we must do what we can to help Indian democracy to survive and prosper. It remains to be decided whether modern India will appear as a sad footnote or a rousing chapter in the history of democracy.

TANAKA KOTARO

In Search of
Truth and Peace

When Japan, in the mid-nineteenth century, opened its gates to Western technology, the West thought it would also open them to Western-type democracy. This, however, did not turn out to be the case. True, Japan before World War II had established parliamentary institutions, but these proved merely a facade for authoritarian governments dominated in the years preceding the war by the military. It was not until Japan's defeat and its occupation by American forces that such economic and social reforms as land reform, the break-up of industrial cartels, and changes in the status of women, all urged by General of the Army Douglas MacArthur and his staff, laid the ground for a new constitution, proposed and drafted by the Occupation authorities.

So far, there has been little discussion in Japan about the philosophical premises of democracy. The Japanese, who throughout their history have lived under authoritarian governments, have had little experience in defining political concepts. The question asked today is whether Japan has merely acquiesced in changes introduced under United States guidance, or has genuinely accepted the ideas and practices of Western democracy.

Here we present the views of a Japanese jurist, an outspoken anti-Marxist and a convert to Catholicism, one of the few Japanese leaders who has discussed democracy. Tanaka Kotaro, a graduate of

Tokyo University, served as Chief Justice of the Supreme Court in the postwar period. In that office he gained prominence as an interpreter of the new constitution and as a critic of Marxism, which has appealed to many Japanese, particularly among the young generation. In these selections Tanaka discusses the main trends of thought in modern Japan as they affect the prospect for success of democratic institutions.

Selections

Ethics and Politics

SURVEYING the general trend of political thought in the modern world, and particularly in Japan, we may observe that its most striking characteristic is its ethical indifference. This reflects the domination of humanistic studies in the nineteenth century by the dogmas of natural science. After the Meiji Restoration, with the introduction into Japan of European and American culture, we ignored the ethical and religious bases of that culture, and sought only to adopt its natural science, its material technology, and its external institutions. The subsequent trend of Japanese political thought has further intensified that tendency. The only thing that has lent any ethical character at all to our political life has been the consciousness of our "national polity" and a sense of reverence for the emperor; but in recent times not only did these attitudes lead to superstition and a loss of sanity, but they developed into a form of ultranationalism which recognized no ethical restraints upon the nation's conduct and justified immoral policies of imperialistic aggression.

The Japanese people cannot be considered traditionally unethical. The enlightened leaders of the early Meiji Period themselves had faith in Buddhism and were trained in Confucianism, but the generation which followed them was exposed neither to the discipline of Oriental moral codes nor to the influence of that Christian faith which underlies Western culture. As a result they lapsed into ethical indifference or lack of conviction. Even among those who held certain moral convictions, the majority were politically uneducated. Consequently they were unable to rise above the narrow limits of nationalism and radicalism, and accepted without question the irreconcilability of individual morality and political morality. Since the war, though nationalism and racialism

From *Sources of Japanese Tradition* by William T. De Barry. Columbia University Press, 1958.

have been overcome, the same kind of inconsistency prevails among political leaders.

One serious weakness in our political thinking which has not yet been corrected is the attitude of relativism. In the postwar period, with the adoption of the new constitution, democracy and pacifism have been loudly acclaimed; but do our people today really have faith in these fundamental principles? Do they, in the bottom of their hearts, realize how greatly they have erred in the past, or do they take the attitude that, having been beaten, there is nothing else they can do? Do they not subscribe to these principles because, from the practical standpoint, they find themselves incapable at the moment and for the indefinite future of competing militarily with the other powers? Are there not some who, so long as Japan herself was not involved or devastated by a catastrophic war, would perhaps hope for other countries to become engaged in a war from which Japan might profit, like the proverbial fisherman who watches the birds fighting over their prey and then seizes it for himself?

One form of relativism devoid of any genuine conviction is a naive and uncritical historicism. More than ten years ago, when the political party system began to lose the confidence of the people, one powerful party figure made the following comment: "The corruption of political parties is a natural outgrowth of their having reached a stage of maturity. As history spirals upward, the corruption of party politics inevitably develops as a natural phenomenon, and its very development contributes to our future political health." Those who view things historically often speak of history repeating itself, or moving in spirals or cycles, or progressing in dialectical fashion; or of "life inevitably ending in death," or of "disappointment being the rule of life," and so on. However, many people who argue thus fail to realize that each historical situation must also be judged in its own particularity. They do not recognize that history should be evaluated in terms of the true and false, the good and bad. This is because historicism does not admit the absoluteness of Truth.

From such a standpoint both individuals and peoples are absolved of any moral responsibility. The denial of moral responsibility ultimately means the denial of that freedom which constitutes the reverse side of responsibility. And by the denial of freedom man is completely deprived of his moral dignity.

* * *

In the same way man must control the blind, instinctual, and animal forces within him, and not be himself controlled by them. Where there is emancipation from instinct there is the freedom spoken of by Kant which is the true source of personal dignity. We cannot, however, be satisfied with an emancipation from the instincts which is purely negative, but must seek the meaning of human life so that the instincts can be made positively to serve the final end of human life. Man, freed from the compulsions of instinct, is not free in relation to the final end of human life. As distinct from animals, man purges instinct by raising it to higher levels; he sublimates it. And this relationship of man to instinct also exists in the relationship of the individual to history and environment.

This same relationship may also be seen in man's relation to economics. In the economy the economic activity of every individual constituting it is a manifestation of free will—just as in the case of history and environment—and yet in relation to the individual it may be looked upon in a sense as a law of necessity, being a phenomenon which derives in the main from man's most primitive instinct—the desire for self-preservation. Thus on the one hand, man drifts in the stream of the economy, and on the other he possesses the freedom to direct that stream toward the ultimate end of human life. In this sense, the economy is not the master of man, but man the master of the economy. [Marxian] historical materialism, however, turns this relationship upside down. All ideologies, according to this view, are no more than superstructures on the substructure of economics, and any economic change in the substructure must bring a change in the ideological superstructure. Man can do nothing to modify such a law of necessity. . . . So strictly speaking, to cry "Workers of the World Unite!" is contradictory. A union must be predicated upon some kind of aim, but as long as man is governed by the laws of necessity his adoption of some aim and his striving to realize it are inconceivable. . . .

Out of indignation over the evils produced by the capitalistic system and in particular by capitalist exploitation, as well as out of sympathy for the pitiful conditions of the working class, men uncritically embrace Marxism as the only way of salvation. They feel a conscious attraction to the "scientific" character of Marxism, and unconsciously they are drawn by its apocalyptic vision of the society to come. But they fail to realize that it is only partially scientific, or to ask what possible connection with "science" there can be in this Utopia appearing as if from Heaven at the end of history. Most followers of Marxism, and particularly the young, having no fundamental knowledge of Marxism, and simply being dissatisfied with society as it is, do not stop to consider whether or not there may be some more rational and natural way to reform society in accordance with human nature. Rather they put blind faith in this as the only means of solution, or uncritically accept the dictates of a press which is drunken with the power it has to exploit the weaknesses of human passions. There is no difference, fundamentally, between this and the attitude which allowed great numbers of people to be dragged along by Nazism. . . .

So to the common good which is the aim of government, though the material and economic life is by no means negligible, the most essential thing is morality and all else is at best secondary in significance. . . . Our new Constitution is permeated with the "lofty ideals which govern human relationships," based on the universal principle of humanity, the laws of universal political morality, equity, good faith, justice, peace, freedom and order. Thus the primacy of morality is recognized in the conduct of both our domestic and foreign affairs. Moreover, those who discuss politics today, almost without exception, acknowledge the necessity for a moral transformation of our political life. But to achieve this will require of our political analysts that their whole world-view be reintegrated in this direction. That is, they can no longer insist upon the importance of morality while permitting themselves the contradictory view that, in fact, economics and military power take precedence over morality. . . . To think that democracy and freedom can exist apart from morality is the greatest error of our times. In politics, in economics, in education, in culture—in every aspect of life, the firm establishment of moral authority must take precedence over all else. . . .

On Authority

An utter denial of the idea of authority could well be called the characteristic of our present era of transition. It had been thought that authority was the most essential property of militarism and extreme nationalism. Now that they have been driven to the wall and face extinction, it is thought that authority too must be banished with them.

Authority, however, is not the special property of militarism or extreme nationalism. Like "rights" or "freedom," it is not intrinsically either good or bad but ethically neutral. It works for good or ill depending upon the end it is made to serve. If authority is put in the hands of those to whom it does not rightly belong or conferred on those whose authority should not be recognized, evil and injustices will arise. Furthermore, authority is both absolute and relative, constituting a hierarchical relationship. When one with relative authority usurps absolute authority, evils and injustices also arise.

Let us consider first the government. In the old Constitution the supreme authority in government was the emperor, but in the new Constitution it is what is called "the people as a whole." . . . The Meiji Constitution was adopted unilaterally by the will of the emperor; it was a so-called "constitution by imperial grant." The new Constitution, however, was adopted by the Diet, that is, by representatives of the people. The people's right to adopt the supreme law of the land, or constitution, derives from their possession of sovereignty.

Even assuming that the people possess absolute authority in the matter of government, can the Diet in fact decide anything and everything by majority vote? There are some things which not even the English Parliament, which is recognized as having absolute authority, can do, such as change males into females. The majority vote of the people is likewise limited by the laws of nature and the principles of things, which may take the form of natural laws or the ethical laws of human society. The constitution adopted by majority vote may not be in conflict with such fundamental principles. . . . When an actual law does conflict with them, then whether it be an ordinance, an edict or even a constitution, it becomes invalid.

If this interpretation is correct, then while the Constitution is the supreme law in relation to other actual laws, still . . . as an actual law itself, there stands above it, behind it and under it as a base, the natural law which represents truth and order in the universe. This natural law is what defines the limits of actual laws. It demonstrates that even the will of the people, though having the supreme authority in the adoption of a constitution, nevertheless is not absolute but is relative to and governed by a higher principle. Whether sovereignty rests with the majority of the people or with the emperor makes no difference. The question was never raised under the Meiji Constitution, but it should be understood that even the supreme will of the emperor cannot be in conflict with the natural law.

The third article of the Preamble [to the new Constitution] states that "the laws of political morality are universal," and the eleventh article asserts that "the basic rights of man are enduring and inviolable." Such laws—such natural laws—are not confined to one nation or one period of time. They endure, and they do so because they are founded on the true nature of man.

Therefore, to say that the people possess sovereignty and supreme authority is true in a formal sense, but intrinsically the people are limited by what in a true sense is the supreme norm: the natural law. To put it another way, it is truth itself which governs social life. In truth itself rests true authority. . . .

. . . Faced by the urgent need to fashion a centralized state, to develop the material prosperity of the nation, to revise the unequal treaties which had humiliated us internationally, Japan could not help but take a superficial and imitative approach to the adoption of Western culture. What we imported was, in a word, the individualism of the Enlightenment and the material technology—the natural science—of the West.

Such tendencies were quite characteristic of the exponents of Euro-
peanization in the Meiji Era [1868–1912], who believed that this type
of culture actually represented Western civilization. Therefore it was
not at all surprising that in reaction to this there should have appeared
the exponents of Japan's "national polity." They mistook individualism
and materialism for Western culture, and opposed to it a Japanese culture stressing collectivism and the national spirit. . . . The surprising
thing is that the exponents of Japan's national polity, who started out
by upholding our traditional "spirit" and condemning the materialism
of Western culture, should have become in practical politics the spokes-
men for militarism and state power. . . .

At the beginning of her history Japan kept her doors completely open
to the world. Today Japan finds herself thrown completely into the
maelstrom of world politics and world culture. Because of this, we
should remember, we have acquired new responsibilities to the peoples
of the world and to our times. To fulfill these responsibilities is the
highest destiny of the Japanese people. . . . Japan must not only fulfill
her own peculiarly creative mission among the peoples of the world, but
realize her universal mission. Japan possesses her own characteristic
moral convictions and fine social traditions which are a legacy from
Buddhism and Confucianism. Of these she must preserve all that is
good. The Oriental peoples, including the Japanese, have always recognized the natural [moral] law. This [recognition of] natural law is the
common spiritual basis uniting the cultures of East and West. To raise
this natural morality to the supernatural plane is the high mission of
Catholicism. Faith in her own national moral virtues, as perfected in
Christianity, could be for a reborn Japan her qualification as a member
of the world community of peoples, giving us for the first time in our
history a sense of Japan's place and mission in the world, and providing
a spiritual bond between East and West, as well as a firm basis for
world peace. . . .

SAUL K. PADOVER

Japan Puts
Democracy to the Test

An American's view of Japan is presented here by Saul K. Padover, writer and historian, who was born in Austria in 1905 and came to the United States in 1920. He received his A.B. at Wayne University, his M.A. and Ph.D. at the University of Chicago. He has served in many government posts at home and in Europe. In 1949 he joined the faculty of the New School for Social Research as professor of political science, and was dean of the School from 1950 to 1955. He has been a visiting professor at several institutions in this country and during 1960 was Fulbright professor at the University of Tokyo, revisiting Japan as a State Department lecturer in 1961.

Dr. Padover is the author of numerous books, among them Living U.S. Constitution, 1954; and editor of several compilations, notably The Genius of America, 1960, which was published in a Japanese translation in 1961.

THE STRANGE behavior of Japanese democracy raises doubts about its durability. Socialists, for example, use physical force to prevent the Speaker from taking the chair in the Diet; Liberal Democrats bring in police to enforce order on the floor. The majority party acts as if the minority had no legitimate rights; the minority, when outvoted, shouts that it has been the victim of "the tyranny of the majority." Trade unionists take to the streets in violent demonstrations for purely political purposes. Organized students riot against the police and politicians, and think nothing of disrupting both traffic and the ordinary operations of government.

All this is done in the name of democracy, and sincerely so. A relatively small group among the organized students may be Communists, trade union leaders may be Communist sympathizers with sinister objectives of their own, but the overwhelming majority of Japanese are neither Reds nor fellow travelers. They are, rather, believers in the ideals of democracy and freedom, often motivated by a deeply emotional hatred of dictatorship and police brutality. But the fact is that the Japanese have simply not yet learned how to use the machinery of democracy without doing violence to its spirit.

"I think I had better confess," a student wrote me in an essay explaining the political situation, "that Japanese people did not know what is democracy till the end of the last war. Therefore our experience of democracy is not so deep as Americans'. Japanese people, especially young people, mistake license for democracy or liberty. They think they can do whatever they want." And he added with a touch of pathos that is not uncommon: "I confess that I also don't know what is real democracy."

This is a problem of supreme importance not only for Japan but also for the United States and the free world. The stakes in Japan are monumental. Here is the most industrialized and most prosperous nation in the Far East. The four main islands of Japan are one vast workshop, producing more than the rest of Asia combined. The whole place is now booming—and it is one of the ironies of the situation that amid unprecedented prosperity there are disturbing political undercurrents that lead to violence.

In Japan, a country so exemplary in its discipline, inventiveness, ingenuity and fabulous adaptability, a stable democracy could serve as both an anchor and model for the tens of millions of Asians still struggling to emerge from feudalism and ignorance. But if democracy could not work successfully in the most educated and progressive country in the Far East, then it would probably be doomed in this whole part of the world.

An objective analysis of the political situation in Japan does not justify any undue pessimism—nor warrant any smugness. There are lights and shadows. Modern Japan is a political democracy having all the institutions connected with such a polity. There is a two-chamber legislature, freely elected by the people, which enjoys a plenitude of power. The Diet selects the Prime Minister who, together with his Cabinet, wields full executive authority.

The Emperor, sacrosanct until World War II, is specifically referred to in the Constitution as the "symbol" of the nation. Except for this symbolic position, he is totally shorn of power, possessing much less of it than the British monarch. There is also an incorruptible and unfettered judiciary. There are popularly elected mayors and governors. The country enjoys virtually absolute freedom of speech and opinion. All these institutions and blessings derived from the Constitution which, in effect, the United States occupation "gave" to Japan in 1947.

It is, in a way, an ideal Constitution, largely modeled after the best American examples. Herein, however, lies a difficulty with a subtlety of its own. For the Constitution, although loyally accepted by the Japanese, still carries with it an alien flavor. Unlike the American, the Japanese Constitution is clearly neither an outgrowth of Japan's historic experience nor the creation of its indigenous mind. The Japanese are therefore slightly uneasy about it; they seem to feel as if they were driving an automobile which, although it runs quite well, is nevertheless borrowed.

Intelligent Japanese are not only aware that democracy was more or less "imposed" upon them; they also recognize that their nation has no genuine democratic background. Japan's long history has been one of authoritarianism in government and in family. The country leaped from feudalism into the modern age without that experimentation in self-government undergone by Americans and some other Western peoples.

From the Meiji period, when Japan opened its doors to the currents of modernism about a century ago, Japan had no genuine democratic representation or widespread popular participation in government until after World War II. Parliamentarism, put into effect in the Meiji period, struck no democratic roots and created no heritage of freedom. Whatever democratic elements did exist in Japan were largely destroyed by the militarists in the Nineteen Thirties.

Japan entered the contemporary world with a cartelized industrial plant operated on authoritarian, practically feudal, principles; a labor movement thoroughly enfeebled; a parliamentary system gutted and discredited; and a family structure, including the subservient position of women, that had hardly changed since the Middle Ages. All this was scarcely a solid basis for the kind of democracy which the American Occupation brought to Japan and persuaded the Japanese people to accept.

It is a matter of astonishment that, given this background, the Japanese did embrace the democratic ideology and put into effect the institutions of democracy. Viewing Japan's current political scene, one is reminded of Samuel Johnson's comparison between a woman preaching and a dog walking on his hind legs: "It is not done well; but you are surprised to find it done at all."

Where the doubts come in is in the knowledge and practices of democracy. Leading Japanese, including many members of the Diet and the Socialist party, seem to have no sense of the inner spirit of democracy. Without a proper appreciation of the meaning of freedom and its integral relationship to democratic procedures, they tend to injure the mechanisms that safeguard democracy.

The lack of trust in and identification with democracy is tied up with some of its salient features, which the Japanese view from a special angle. I will mention three: individualism, Christianity and capitalism. These are most troublesome to the Japanese.

From the available literature on democracy, particularly the translated writings of Jefferson, the Japanese conclude that individualism is the core of the democratic ideal. This is, of course, an essential truth and accepted in the West, but it is disturbing to a people whose traditions are neither rooted in nor revolve around the individual person. Western-style individualism is alien to the East in general and it is particularly so to the Japanese mentality. The Japanese people are among the most homogeneous in the world. Their homogeneity is so ancient and entwined that it has left no room for the flourishing of individuals.

As an illustration one may mention the paucity of biographic writings in Japan. The art of biography does not flourish here. Japan's outstanding figures, among them political leaders and artists, have not had their Boswells or Stracheys.

Nor, with rare exceptions, is there autobiography. When this writer suggested to an eminent Japanese, who had played an important role in World War II, that he write his autobiography, the elderly gentleman blushed and threw up his arms in protest. In Japanese literature one finds neither a Cellini nor a Franklin, neither a Rousseau nor a Henry Adams.

For the Japanese, the concept of individualism that lies at the base of democracy, with its stress on personal rights, personal opinions, and personal amelioration, is a novel importation. This does not mean that the Japanese reject individualism—in fact, many admire it—but that it is as yet unfamiliar psychological territory, so to speak.

Similarly, the question of Christianity. On one level it is tied up with individualism and on another with the core meaning of freedom. The Christian religion has become identified with the West and, especially where Anglo-American missionaries were active, with democracy. The Japanese have no particular antipathy to Christianity; they are, in fact, easy-going and tolerant in matters of religion. But, they are troubled by the notion that in order to be a good democrat one must be a Christian. Since Japan is a non-Christian nation, this tends to raise doubts about the possibilities of democracy.

Confronted with the question of the relation between democracy and Christianity by many audiences, this writer's answer has been that the two are not necessarily integrated. While it is true that democracy derives some of its moral ideas from the Judeo-Christian heritage, it does not logically follow that to be a democrat one has to be a member of a Christian church.

Periclean Athens and modern Israel are examples of non-Christian democratic societies. In regard to Japan, it is a disservice both to democracy and to religion to stress identification between the two.

A somewhat similar problem arises in connection with capitalism. For a time, especially soon after World War II, there was a tendency on the part of Washington to talk to the world in terms that made economic freedom and political freedom interchangeable.

Americans referred to "free enterprise" as being the bone and sinew of democracy, and the outside world concluded that the two had an inseparable relationship. But to a good many people, including underpaid Japanese intellectuals and workers, "free enterprise" was equated with capitalism, a term and institution not particularly attractive to them.

The identification between capitalism and democracy has been taken up by Marxists, and is being stressed not only in Communist but also in non-Communist circles. The prevalence of Marxism among Japanese students and intellectuals has been too long ignored by Americans, who have been inclined to dismiss it as merely another aspect of the Communist conspiracy. But this is an error. Marxist theory appeals to impressionable minds not necessarily in sympathy with the Communist state as it exists in the Soviet Union or Red China.

In Japan, Marxism, which was introduced in the Nineteen Twenties and thus predates Mao Tse-tung's revolution in China, has gained widespread acceptance for at least two reasons.

First, it offers a plausible theory of history and society. It stresses the class element of government and politics in a way that makes sense in the highly structured and hierarchical Japanese society.

Second, the Marxist theory of history, with its emphasis on "inevitable" developments, provides a feeling of both excitement and security to people who, like the contemporary Japanese, have seen their traditional political and familial foundations destroyed by the last war.

Marxism has penetrated crucial areas of Japanese life, including journalism, publishing and literature. Marxist intellectuals have a potent influence on the nation far out of proportion to their numbers or position. Hence, the current equation between democracy and capitalism helps undermine the trust in democracy and, specifically, America's whole position in Japan.

The situation calls for a dis-identification between the political system of freedom and the economic system of private enterprise. It is necessary to stress that freedom has its own individual existence that may or may not be connected with any particular economic system.

In many lectures, this writer has pointed out that the great thinkers and leaders of democracy—Jefferson and Lincoln, for example—were not capitalists in the Marxist sense; that it is possible to have democracy without capitalism, and vice versa; that democracy can and does exist in societies which enjoy large-scale social benefits without necessarily losing their freedom.

This approach is helpful in countering the insidious Marxist propaganda—the Japanese call it social theory—that only a rich capitalistic country like America can afford democracy.

There remains the question of identification with government. In a democracy, proper identification requires at least two conditions. One of them is an active public opinion; the other, confidence in the leaders and in the political machinery. In Japan, both of these conditions are feeble.

Public opinion implies the existence of the habit of discussion, and the Japanese have no such tradition. Anyone who has taught in Japan knows how difficult it is to get students to ask questions, to challenge, or to formulate provocative ideas. The Japanese are great readers but poor conversationalists. The ingrown national tendency is to avoid direct verbal challenges and to accept the words of authority, especially such intellectual authority as is personified by the writer and teacher. The habit of obedience and followership is deeply ingrained.

In consequence, there does not exist a vigorous public opinion in the Western, especially American, sense. There are many newspapers and an excellent radio-TV network, but few discussion groups. Organizations for the achievement of national consensus are unknown. Among the common people, long accustomed to obedience, apathy is widespread. Like many Americans, they are more interested in baseball than in politics. The concept of personal participation and responsibility for governmental decisions is still relatively rare.

This helps to explain why the second basic condition for democracy, namely, trust in the government, is not extensive. In the past, the Japanese gave universal fealty and unquestioning obedience to their Emperor. This extended to the shoguns, generals and politicians who ruled or pretended to rule in his name. With the shattering of the Emperor's august position, there came a fragmentation of Japanese loyalties.

Today the people of Japan are not even sure what Japanese patriotism means. Nowadays, only a comparatively small group of Rightist fanatics passionately preaches "patriotism" and traditional loyalty to the Emperor, but their appeal is limited, not only because they are prone to use the weapon of assassination—as they did in the case of the Socialist leader Asanuma last year—but primarily because the Japanese people know that the imperial system is dead.

To whom, then, can they attach their loyalties? Not, certainly, to the

Constitution, which, as we have seen, is viewed as a somewhat alien importation. Not to the existing political institutions, which have as yet struck no deep roots in the affections of the people. There remains only the group of politicians who run the country—and their prestige is not of a nature to inspire respect.

Japan's politicians, particularly the members of the Diet, are little esteemed primarily because they are felt to be bought creatures or party hacks. This image of the politician is fairly close to reality. The structure of party politics is such that it mitigates against individual integrity and independence.

A member of the Diet receives a monthly salary of slightly more than 100,000 yen (roughly $300), which barely covers living and travel costs. Election campaigns, however, including banquets, entertainment and the relentless Japanese habit of gift-giving, cost millions and sometimes tens of millions of yen.

Where does the money come from? Obviously it comes from the only source that has it—namely, industry and business. Funds are not handed out indiscriminately but are given to selected politicians who are particularly influential. These powerful politicians in turn subsidize lesser politicians who become their followers.

Thus Japan's parliamentary politics is dominated at the top by men of real power and at the lower levels by factional groups, each ruled by a leader, which are at the disposal of the highest or best bidder, the bids including not only money but also Cabinet positions and other posts of influence or power. This situation is hardly conducive to the creation of the kind of respect that the Japanese people used to have for their traditional leaders, including the Emperor.

In sum, the Japanese practice democracy with many misguided notions and some misgivings. What is astonishing is, as I say, that the system has worked as well as it has. Given continued prosperity, one may expect the democratic structure to be improved and strengthened.

There are hopeful features in the situation. Not the least of them is the fact that Japan has no organized Fascist or militarist movements. The totalitarians of the Right are few in number, and those of the Left lack the power (the Communists have only two members in the Diet) to do anything more effective than to promote rioting.

However they conceive it, or misconceive it, the Japanese people today are, in the main, committed to the ideals of democracy. This is hearteningly true of the youth, which has an idealistic predisposition to justice and liberty. One of my students wrote me:

"The true meaning of democracy, of government by the people and of universal suffrage, are not recognized completely among the people of Japan. I think, however, we should fight for it perseveringly. We should persistently promote democracy in Japan because it is the best way to promote our happiness and world peace."

Democracy does have a future in Japan. Continued prosperity; a more equitable distribution of material well-being; the sympathy and respect of the outside world, particularly the United States; and, above all, patience and understanding for this volatile and dynamic Far Eastern people—all these will enhance the stability of freedom in Japan.

[5]

Social
and Psychological
Adjustments

CYRIL E. BLACK

The Transformation
of Russian Society

For over half a century, many Americans—scholars, diplomats, political leaders, newspaper commentators, educators—have sought to understand Russia. Some have succeeded brilliantly in this undertaking, but many still agree with Winston Churchill, who said that Russia, to him, was "a riddle wrapped in a mystery inside an enigma."

Yet when one has a clue, a riddle can be solved and a mystery penetrated. In the case of Russia, an important clue to bear in mind is that Russian society has in the past been little affected by the forces that shaped Western civilization, and thus cannot be intelligibly appraised by the traditions and modern standards of the West, particularly of the United States. Although Russia has undergone a great transformation since the emancipation of the serfs in 1861, Professor Black points out that, "Seen in a world-wide spectrum of modernizing societies, the Russian pattern resembles somewhat that of Turkey, Iran, Japan, and China." Russia's values and traditions, he contends, are different from those of Western Europe in sufficient degree to be significant, and are likely to remain so for the foreseeable future.

The main aspects of Russia's transformation are analyzed in this selection from a book to which many experts on Russia have contributed. Cyril E. Black, one of the best-informed American students of Russia and Eastern Europe, is the editor of this book, and he contributed an introduction as well as the conclusion presented here. Dr. Black, born in 1915, is professor of history at Princeton University, where he has taught since 1939. He also served as member of the United States delegation to observe Soviet elections in 1958. He has edited several books, among them Challenge in Eastern Europe, 1954.

Conclusion
The Modernization of Russian Society

I

IN INTERPRETING the transformation of Russian society since 1861, it is useful to think in terms of the broad pattern of social change which is now commonly known as "modernization." Modernization is the process of change from an agrarian to an industrial way of life that has resulted from the dramatic increase in man's knowledge of and control over his environment in recent centuries. In Europe this process has been evolving for half a millennium or more, and in modern times the influence of European knowledge and institutions has spread to most other parts of the world.

Modernization in this general sense has come to be accepted as a desirable, if not indeed inevitable, change in human affairs. Yet it must be recognized that the transformation of traditional societies has been in many ways a vastly destructive process. Not only have governments, ruling classes, and systems of knowledge and belief been destroyed, but social institutions, personal values, and not infrequently the psychological security of the individual have been undermined. Even in the societies which were the first to modernize, where change took place gradually over a period of many generations, the destructive aspects of modernization have been apparent. In societies that have modernized more recently, under great pressure to compete with the earlier modernizers, one frequently has the impression that traditional institutions and values have been destroyed before their modern replacements were available. Now that mankind has discovered the means to destroy itself, many will no doubt question to what extent modernization can be equated with progress. In any event, it is clear that what is involved is a vastly complex and universally pervasive process of change.

What concerns us here, however, is not the destiny of mankind but the much more limited question of social change in Russia in the century since the emancipation of the serfs in 1861. It is significant that Russia was not one of the early modernizers, and that the new ideas and institutions came to Russia from Central and Western Europe in forms which the Russian government believed to be as much a threat to its security as an opportunity for the development of the peoples under its

From *The Transformation of Russian Society*, edited by Cyril E. Black. Harvard University Press. Copyright © 1960 by the President and Fellows of Harvard College. Reprinted by permission of the publishers.

rule. The influence of the more modern societies was felt in Russia with rapidly increasing force from the seventeenth century on, and to the extent that their institutions were adopted it was rather for the purpose of protecting the traditional Russian way of life against foreign intrusions than for undertaking a fundamental modernization of Russian society. Indeed, in Russia as everywhere else, modernization seems to have come in two phases: the first defensive and superficial, and the second aggressive and more thoroughgoing.

Insofar as borrowings from the West could contribute to strengthening the autocracy and increasing state power, they were accepted with alacrity. The armed forces and bureaucracy were reconstructed, mines and factories were established, an academy of sciences was created, and the nobility was transformed into a class of higher civil servants. But care was taken not to disturb the condition of the great mass of the peasants, who lived in some form of service to the state or bondage to the nobility—and on whose labor, directly or indirectly, the welfare of their owners was based. Even the emancipation in 1861 was not intended to inaugurate an era of thoroughgoing modernization, although it very soon became clear that this would be its effect. The significance of 1861 for Russia, as far as such comparisons are valid, was thus somewhat similar to the change of pace which took place in Central Europe in the first half of the nineteenth century, in France and the United States at the end of the eighteenth century, and in England somewhat earlier. To the extent that one can construct a general pattern of modernization as a yardstick for social change in Russia, it must be based primarily on the European and American experience. Something can doubtless also be learned by comparing Russian developments with those in Japan and Turkey, which modernized at about the same time and under somewhat similar circumstances, the former at first more rapidly and the latter more slowly.

Although any generalizations about the course of social change in Russia must be regarded as highly tentative at this stage, in view of the shortcomings both of our knowledge about Russia and of the theoretical bases available for the interpretation of such knowledge, it nevertheless seems worthwhile to attempt answers to three rather general questions. To what extent has the course of social change in Russia since 1861 followed more or less universal trends, as far as these can be established on the basis of what we know about other societies? To what extent can Russian deviations from such universal trends be explained by certain historically formed traditions of Russian society? And, finally, to what extent can the course of modernization in Russia be attributed to contingent circumstances, and more specifically to individual leaders, political parties, and state policy?

Any attempt to suggest brief answers to sweeping questions must of necessity omit much of the detail which provides the richness and variety of history. Such an attempt also runs the risk of neglecting important distinctions of degree and emphasis which may account for significant contrasts within superficially consistent trends. This risk is particularly great when one is discussing general trends in a very controversial period of Russian history. Indeed, some maintain that tsarist autocracy and Soviet totalitarianism are so different that any attempt to find continuities will meet with insuperable obstacles, whereas others see them as essentially similar. In any event, a particular burden is placed on the reader to distinguish between the secular trends under consideration here and the short-term developments which are equally important and were no doubt much more real to the participants. For these essential distinctions one must look to the more detailed discussion of individual aspects of social change. The reader will also recognize that "Russia" is used here as a general term embracing the wide variety of nationalities and cultures within the changing boundaries of the Russian Empire and the U.S.S.R. It is a measure of the shortcomings of our understanding of this country that it is so difficult to give due weight to the differences which characterize its many peoples.

II

In measuring social change in Russia by the yardstick of universal trends, it is useful to start with the area of government, since so many of the changes characteristic of modernization have taken place within a framework of political action. In this realm, the most characteristic feature of modernization has no doubt been the growth of the functions and scope of authority of governments. Governments which once performed no more than a few political and military functions are now engaged in a vast number of activities involving not only the maintenance of order on the provincial and local levels, but also the education and welfare of the individual, the administration of communications, and the regulation of commerce and industry, wages and prices. If it were possible to construct a table showing the proportion of the gross national product that has been administered more or less directly in recent centuries by governments, it would no doubt reflect the growth in the functions which they perform. Even in the United States, which started out with a very decentralized federal structure, a main theme of its political and legal history has been the accumulation by the federal government of a wide variety of functions. Although the American political system is still relatively decentralized, the federal budget is now equivalent to about one fifth of the gross national product.

This growth in the role of government has been accompanied by an increasing identification of the government with the people, and this has been reflected in the development of political democracy in those societies where the prerogatives of the government traditionally have been limited and the dignity of the individual has been held in high respect. In these countries the rule of law, equality before the law, and representative government have been accepted as the goal of political development. This identification of government with the people has been accompanied by sentiment favoring national self-determination, particularly in the dynastic empires, and movements for national independence and unification have been a dominant theme of modern history.

Russia had a long tradition of autocracy at the time the serfs were emancipated, but there also the functions of the government grew rapidly after 1861. The areas of local administration which had been left to the landowning nobility under serfdom were now assumed in part by the government, and in addition it soon became involved in general education, the regulation of labor, economic development, and many other activities. Until 1917 important aspects of local affairs were left to the zemstvos, the local government organizations created in 1864. The central government kept a sharp and jealous eye on the zemstvos, but the latter expanded their activities steadily until 1917 when local authority was swept away in all but name. What had been an autocracy, in considerable degree restrained by custom and by circumstance, now became a totalitarian government concerned at least in theory with every aspect of Russian life. With the inauguration of the five-year plans and the increasing urbanization of Russian life, theory has been converted into practice. The Soviet government has now achieved a more total control over society than has any other modern government and in fact administers more or less directly some three quarters of the gross national product of the U.S.S.R.

In Russia also there has been an increasing identification of the government with the people and a growth of nationalism in these years, although to a much lesser degree than in Europe. Contemporary Western observers expected Russia to follow the European example fairly promptly once the serfs were emancipated, and indeed in a moment of exuberance the New York Times assured its readers that "Russia is on a sure, steady career of progress and reform. With the new provincial bodies, and the spread of common schools and newspapers (of which we hear such encouraging accounts), she will soon educate a mass of intelligent and orderly citizens who will be fully capable of governing themselves." In actual fact, the zemstvos were representative only to a limited extent, and the Constitution of 1906 and the accompanying

electoral law made reluctant provision for only a modest degree of representative government at the national level. A system of almost universal
representation was prepared in 1917 by the Provisional Government for
the elections to the Constituent Assembly, but this proved to be an end
rather than a new beginning for representative government in Russia.

The struggle of the national minorities of the Russian empire for
autonomy and independence followed a course somewhat parallel to
that in the West, and after the revolution of 1905 substantial gains were
made in the recognition of local rights. The First World War brought
the liberation of some of the principal minorities, although at the end
of the Second World War all these except the Poles and the Finns—
along with some new territories—were once more annexed. The identification of government and people in the Soviet Union is reflected in the
attention devoted to the forms and symbols, as distinct from the substance, of representative government and minorities' rights.

In the economic realm, modernization has meant a rapid increase in
production as a result of technical improvements, a parallel growth in
capital investments, the division of labor, expansion of trade, and a
greater mobility of the factors of production. In general terms Russian
economic development fits this pattern, although it has been interrupted by formidable changes in policy. In the periods of most rapid
expansion—1890–1900, 1906–1917, and since 1928—the rate of growth
of industry has equaled or surpassed that of Russia's rivals. Agriculture
and domestic trade, on the other hand, have been relatively neglected.
Also, throughout the period the state has played a much more active
role in economic life than has been the case in most other societies.

Similarly, in the intellectual sphere Russian developments in the past
century have in significant respects followed the course pioneered by the
societies that modernized earlier. Scholarship in the humanities and
social sciences expanded rapidly in the latter half of the nineteenth century, and Russia became part of the community of Western scholarship. There was an active interchange of ideas with the rest of the
learned world, and Russian thought made numerous original contributions. In many aspects of literature and the arts, Russian achievements
were unsurpassed. In the natural sciences, applied research was held
back by the relatively low level of technology, but in theoretical work
Russian scientists were productive. Intellectual activity was to a considerable degree interrupted by the revolution, and after the inauguration of the five-year plans it was increasingly harnessed to the needs of
the state as interpreted by the Communist party. Under this policy
selected branches of science and technology flourished, and the performing arts were generously provided for; but creative thought in the humanities, in the social sciences, and in some of the natural sciences

worked under ever-tighter restrictions and in significant measure lapsed into silence.

Primary and secondary education were less immediately sensitive to changes in policy and grew steadily throughout the period when not interrupted by war or civil strife. Under the empire the government was slow to take up the idea of universal education, and much of the initiative was left to the zemstvos. Very substantial progress was made after 1905, however, and this was continued by the Soviet regime. By 1960, the literacy rate was rapidly approaching that of the most advanced countries, and educational facilities were available for universal primary and secondary education. The content of education was throughout the century subject to political control. Neither tsarist nor Soviet educational policy favored freedom of thought, although the controls exercised by the latter were immeasurably tighter. With the exception of a decade of experimentation in the immediate post-revolutionary period, since 1861 emphasis has been placed on languages, literature (carefully screened), mathematics, and the natural sciences—the latter particularly stressed in the Soviet period—and on political orthodoxy based largely on the official version of history and on the approved religious or social doctrine. The content of political orthodoxy has of course changed radically as a result of the revolution, but the relationship of state to education, while greatly intensified since 1917, has been a constant theme. To this extent Russian educational policy has resembled in form but with far greater intensity, that of the continental European states.

The social structure of Russia has in the past century also evolved in a manner that is in many ways similar to that of the societies which modernized earlier. During the past century what may loosely be called Russia's elite, for want of a better term, has grown in size from perhaps two or three million to some fifteen million and has changed substantially in composition. These changes began in the latter part of the nineteenth century, when a rising generation of professional men and technicians was added to the traditional elite of noble landowners and state officials. This process was greatly accelerated in the first decades of the twentieth century, and at the same time the influence of the nobles declined even though they retained most of their formal privileges. The revolution of 1917 brought an end to these privileges, and perhaps as many as several hundred thousand members of the elite went into exile in the course of the civil wars. The Bolsheviks and their followers were now catapulted into a position of leadership, but many members of the pre-revolutionary elite at the level of the bureaucracy and the professions continued to work in their old positions. It took another generation before an essentially new elite, educated under the Soviet regime and greatly enlarged to meet the needs of industrialization, was created. In the meantime the urban population has grown from 12 per cent of the population in 1861 to almost 50 per cent today, reflecting the fundamental impact of industrialization on the way of life of the mass of the population.

The family was much affected by these changes, in Russia as elsewhere. In size it has tended to shrink to the nuclear family, authority within the family has been more equally distributed, and women have gained greater freedom to work outside the home. The family has become more mobile, less bound by traditional social customs, and more closely reflects the values of the state and the developing mass society. There has also been an increasing social mobility as the requirements of industrialization have drawn more and more people into urban and professional life, as well as a gradual reduction in the differences among social strata as to opportunities for general education and technical training.

In the realm of values there has been in Russia, as in other modernizing societies, a gradual adjustment to the new knowledge and to the urban and industrial way of life. A traditional fatalism has given way to the belief that life can be mastered and society transformed. Perhaps because the Russian Orthodox Church was a state institution until 1917, it was slower than most Western churches to adjust to the challenge of modern ideas. In the last decades of the empire this challenge took the form within the church of support on the part of some priests of political liberalism and of reform of the church administration. The Provisional Government, during its brief existence, took the first steps toward separating church and state and curtailing the influence of the church on education. The Soviet government, for its part, has followed a policy of thoroughgoing secularization, undermining the church through a wide variety of indirect attacks and doing its best to win over the younger generation to atheism. At the same time, the Communist party has recognized the continuing influence of the Russian Orthodox Church and, since its establishment as an autonomous institution in 1943, has employed it increasingly as an instrument of policy at home and abroad. The church has thus regained its formal status to a considerable degree. The government has also been relatively lenient with the Moslem religious bodies, although it has been less compromising in its treatment of the other minority faiths. It seems likely that popular religious feeling has declined somewhat more rapidly in Russia than in other modernizing societies, although it still retains a significant influence even among members of the younger generation.

There has likewise been an increasing attention paid to the welfare of the individual in Russia since 1861. This has been reflected not only in the steady growth of educational facilities, but also in the provisions of social insurance. Since the latter part of the nineteenth century the Russian state has also been active in regulating the pay and working conditions of industrial labor. Under the empire these measures were taken in part by a paternalistic government and in part by the zemstvos which reflected local needs; in the Soviet period they have been expanded to meet the requirements of the continued growth of industry and adapted to the needs of the Communist party. There has also been a growing recognition at the level of official policy of the desirability of greater cosmopolitanism in the treatment of national, political, and religious minorities. This trend was reflected especially after 1905 in the easing of the restrictions on public activities on the part of the minorities and under the Provisional Government and in the Soviet period in the formal legal provisions for civil liberties. At the level of practice, on the other hand, in Russia as elsewhere, the strains of social change have brought to the surface deep-seated tensions—as evidenced by the pogroms under the empire and the extreme forms of political persecution in the Soviet period.

Scarcely less impressive than the development of Russia along the lines suggested above has been the destruction accompanying it. Not only have many customs and techniques become outmoded and left behind, but values and traditions that had stood the test of centuries have been cast aside. Indeed, it is in the realm of human values that the destructiveness of modernization has been most striking. In a manner parallel to that in other societies undergoing social change, but in a more extreme form, material values were deified at the expense of the dignity of the individual. The impulse of the nihilists in the 1860's to reject traditional values in the name of reason proved to be only the beginning of a growing tendency to believe that the goal of building a new world was important enough to justify any sacrifice. This phenomenon of people committing crimes in the name of ideals was one of the central preoccupations of Dostoevsky's thought, and he recognized that Russia was sharing in a widespread occurrence. "This . . . happens not only in our midst but throughout the world," he wrote in 1873; "it has been so from time immemorial, during transitional epochs, at times of violent commotions in people's lives—doubts, negations, scepticism and vacillation regarding the fundamental social convictions. But in our midst it is more possible than elsewhere, and precisely in our day. . . ."

The belief that the end justifies the means formed an important element in the Leninist version of Marxism, which regarded the allegedly inexorable laws of a historically determined destiny as the only guides to action. This attitude has its natural culmination in a political system which did not balk at destroying millions of human lives in the name of "building socialism." As Dostoevsky noted, this attitude is by no means a uniquely Russian phenomenon. "There has been a slipping off of ancient restraints; a real *decivilization* of men's minds," wrote H. G. Wells in 1920, and this is no doubt one of the fateful consequences of modernization. The examples of Nazi Germany and Communist China illustrate the extent to which the deification of a historically rationalized ideology can result in the destruction of human values.

These various ways in which social change in Russia during the past century has paralleled developments in countries that modernized earlier or at about the same time are trends of such a general character that they could hardly have been avoided by any regime in Russia, although they might have been delayed or accelerated in one respect or another. They deserve consideration, however, as the setting for a discussion of the more interesting question of the ways in which the course of Russian modernization has been unique.

III

The question of the role of Russian historical traditions in the course that social change has taken in that country is both simpler and more controversial than that of the relationship of Russian to general modernization. It is simpler because Russian historical traditions differ from those of the West in certain major respects on which there is fairly general agreement; more controversial because it involves seeking out continuities between the tsarist and Soviet eras which the adherents of both find odious. It is nevertheless an essential exercise, for it is clear that the form a modern society takes is in a substantial measure dependent on the nature of its traditional values and institutions. The things that a society does may change very rapidly, but the way in which they are done continues to bear the imprint of age-old beliefs.

The special character of Russian modernization, which sets it somewhat apart from the Western pattern, can perhaps best be discussed in terms of three interrelated circumstances, not in themselves unique yet scarcely matched elsewhere in this particular combination: the predominant role of the state, Russia's backwardness and defensiveness in relation to the more modern societies, and certain characteristic attitudes and values.

The role of the state is no doubt the most obvious continuing trait of Russian society, and in the century since 1861 it has manifested itself in many ways. Throughout this period the state has had a virtual monopoly of political power, except for brief transitional phases of anarchy. The state has made provision for the organization and regulation of social groups. Through the instrumentality of legal institutions and of the political policy it has kept a close control over all social, intellectual, and spiritual activities that might challenge its position. It has taken the primary initiative in economic growth through investment, ownership, supervision, and fiscal policy. Under its auspices, education, scholarship, and the performing arts have been developed. Indeed, it is difficult to point to a significant area of human activity in which the state has not participated throughout the century. The quality and purposes of this participation have of course varied significantly with policy and circumstance, but its existence and acceptance has been a continuing reality.

This dominant role of the state in modern Russia has deep roots and may be explained by a variety of historical circumstances. Geography played its role in giving Russia a land without natural frontiers—at least in its populated areas—and without significant mountains or other internal barriers. External influences also had some effects, for Byzantine autocracy was the principal political model for Russian statesmanship in its formative years, and for over two centuries Mongol rule exerted pressures both direct and indirect which tended to weaken resistance to central authority. In more modern times the poverty of Russia's land and the strength of her neighbors to the West have also played a role, for through the centuries Russian statesmanship has learned that domestic division can only lead to defeat and control by foreigners. After periods of profound civil strife, Vasily II, Ivan IV, and finally the Romanov dynasty emerged with successively increased authority, and a formula of statesmanship was hammered out which gave the tsar and his government authority over all in the realm. While Europe was moving from feudalism through various forms of limited monarchy and enlightened despotism to constitutional and representative government, Russia was evolving a form of autocracy which was in some degree limited only in the turbulent years from 1905 to 1917.

It is not difficult to describe the role that the state has played in Russian affairs, but to explore this role in all of its ramifications would go beyond the limits of this essay. One aspect, and it may indeed be one of the most important, is nevertheless pertinent to our problem. This is the role of the state in protecting a Russia that was backward by comparison with its principal neighbors, and in trying to redress the balance by means of a disproportionate exertion of national effort.

As a relative latecomer, Russia was confronted with the problem of modernizing on the basis of institutions and ideas borrowed from the very Western states with which it was competing and under circumstances in which failure might mean national defeat. Serfdom was one answer, for it served to mobilize the principal source of national wealth on terms considered at the time to be most favorable to the state. Reform of the army, bureaucracy, and nobility was another, for it provided the state with the technical means of playing a successful role in European affairs. Although Russia had one of the lowest per-capita national incomes in Europe, the size of the population and the manner in which its resources were concentrated in the hands of the state provided a solution to Russia's problem during the era in which agriculture and commerce were still the major sources of wealth. The turning point came in the first half of the nineteenth century, and the Russia which had turned back Napoleon was unable forty-three years later to prevent Anglo-French force from seizing Sevastopol. European industrialization is by no means the only explanation of this change in fortune, but from this defeat the conclusion was drawn that serfdom was no longer a sound basis for the autocracy.

Throughout the period since 1861, Russia has been under the pressure of competition felt by all the later modernizers, and the fact that it had a long tradition of national greatness only served to make this pressure more urgent. This position as a latecomer was not an unmitigated disadvantage, for it permitted Russia to import techniques and institutions which had been developed elsewhere as a result of many years of experimentation and at great expense. With the aid of massive infusions of state support, Russia was able to make rapid progress and in isolated fields of endeavor has surpassed its tutors. At the same time, the necessity of borrowing from its rivals has presented the state with a continuing challenge to its security. Alexander II is reported to have remarked that to wait until the serfs liberated themselves from below was the only alternative to liberating them from above, and throughout the century since emancipation the Russian state has felt the hot breath of history upon its neck. The tsar and his bureaucracy themselves undertook to serve as the modernizing elite and up to a point succeeded in maintaining their initiative. But the burden of tradition and of vested interests was too heavy to sustain this initiative, and neither Alexander III nor Nicholas II was capable of playing the role of autocrat-modernizer. Even such conservative and loyal modernizers as Witte and Stolypin came to be regarded as a threat to the autocracy, and the relations between ruler and ruled were strained to the breaking point during the First World War. The various potential heirs of the tsarist system in 1917 all regarded themselves as modernizers, and after a brief struggle the succession was seized by the leaders best able to harness the popular desire for peace and land reform.

The course of social changes in Russia has also been marked by certain characteristic attitudes and values, stemming in part from tradition and in part from the circumstances of modernization itself. Of the traditional attitudes, no doubt the most persistent has been the messianic belief, which can be traced back to the doctrine of the Third Rome formulated in the sixteenth century, in the rightness of Russian values. The belief that the Russians are a "God-bearing" people with attributes of human universality was perhaps most vigorously expressed by Dostoevsky, but it has been shared in one form or another by many Russians of whom the Bolsheviks are only the most recent. No doubt all peoples tend in some measure to become convinced of the universal validity of their views, but the Russian version of messianism has had deeper roots and more powerful political support than most.

Equally deep-rooted and no doubt much more widely held in Russia are the attitudes which seem to spring from the traditional way of life of the Russian peasant patriarchal family. In an era in which many millions of Russians have been transferred within a generation or two from the countryside to all levels of urban life, it can hardly be doubted that the attitudes and values characteristic of the former peasantry continue to have a powerful impact. Their patience and patriotism, their ambivalence with regard to neighbors and foreigners, their submissiveness when confronted by authority despite their frequent hostility to it—elements such as these give the Russian national character its distinctive features. It is indeed as though there were two Russias: the official Russia, powerful and implacable, and popular Russia, submissive but frequently resentful. When studies have been made of the attitudes characteristic of a wider range of national groups, it will no doubt be possible to identify with greater accuracy the qualities that are peculiarly Russian.

Other attitudes may be traced more directly to Russia's position vis à vis the West in modern times, although in some instances these also have a traditional basis. The fear of foreign encirclement, a recurrent theme in Russian official thought, can be found in the writings of Ivan the Terrible. The assertion by Khrushchev that encirclement is a thing of the past, and that the Soviet Union is now becoming the encircler, may properly be regarded as a milestone in the Russian outlook if it proves to be genuine and lasting. The desire to match the West, in technology and productivity if not necessarily in values and institutions, is also a recurrent theme. If the victory over Napoleon gave the Russian government a certain complacency in the era of Nicholas I, his successors turned again to the West with almost the same unrelenting vigor as did the Russia of Peter the Great. This is particularly true of the Communists, who have systematically drawn on the experience of the West and have made "overtake and surpass" a major national slogan. This desire to borrow the technology of the more modern societies while rejecting their political and social values is by no means a purely Russian phenomenon, and indeed the virulently anti-Western modernizer is one of the more common types of leader in the newer states. With the exception of the short-lived Provisional Government, no Russian regime has given serious consideration to reproducing on Russian soil a political culture of a West European type.

Equally characteristic of Russia has been the position of the intelligentsia—deeply attached to their country, profoundly concerned with social problems, and yet in considerable measure alienated from the state. The intelligentsia was in fact defined as that group of intellectuals, the most productive in terms of the public discussion of Russia's problems, who did not have responsible official positions. They relied for their living on their literary and critical skills, if they did not have an inherited income, and not infrequently they lived in Siberian exile or abroad. As is so commonly the case with intellectuals in societies relatively late to modernize, they were torn between the European standards which they had set as their model and the reality which they saw around them. To follow uncomprisingly in the Western path meant in some degree to abandon Russia, and indeed not a few went to Europe to live as distinguished citizens of the world, returning to Russia only occasionally if at all and then usually under police surveillance. To accept Russian reality and to enter public service, on the other hand, meant to become an accomplice in some measure to the policing and censorship of free intellectual inquiry and to work within the relatively narrow framework of officially approved ideas.

If one defines intellectuals as those with higher education—as distinct from the special category of intellectuals known in Russia as the intelligentsia—it must be recognized that many intellectuals achieved distinction and influence in public service in the period of the empire. They also were keen students of the West and, while they did not leave a comparable treasure of creative writing, their memoirs and public documents frequently reflect a profound and responsible concern for the modernization of Russia.

In the Soviet era this dichotomy between the large number of university-educated officials and the small group of independent thinkers has persisted, although the issues are somewhat confused by the Soviet use of the term "intelligentsia" to describe the entire white-collar class which now numbers perhaps fifteen million. If one adheres to the earlier definitions, however, one can distinguish a continuing if limited intelligentsia of free-thinking individuals, critical of officially approved doctrines and standards, irked by the constant harassment of party hacks and security officers, and on occasion willing to take the risk of expressing their views in a variety of ways. The members of this intelligentsia are primarily writers and artists, but there is also evidence of unorthodoxy among natural scientists and other scholars. In many cases they are direct survivors or descendants of the pre-revolutionary intelligentsia, but the group is also being replenished from new sources. In the 1920's they had a modicum of freedom, but in the 1930's many ended their days in labor camps. The Communist party nevertheless values their prestige and skills, and is engaged in a continuous battle of wits and of numerous more or less subtle pressures to keep at least their publicized works within the narrow channel of orthodoxy.

The members of this small intelligentsia appear to have worked out a variety of viable compromises with the state authorities, by whom they are of necessity employed since there is no other source of livelihood except for the few who can be supported by friends and relatives. Their attitudes are not easy to evaluate, however, because little is known of their writings except as they are by chance published abroad or occasionally seen in unpublished form. To this group of free-thinking intellectuals must be added the many distinguished Russians who have sought freedom in exile, in some respects an equally difficult compromise, and who in the course of forty years have stimulated the intellectual life of the Western world with their acute appreciation of both Western and Russian attitudes. These, like their pre-revolutionary forerunners, can trace their ancestry back to Prince Kurbsky, who in 1578 from his self-exile in Poland taunted Ivan the Terrible with having "shut up the kingdom of Russia—in other words, free human nature—as in a fortress of hell."

Of the many controversies that have engaged Russian thought in modern times, the one that most concerns us here is the debate over the relationship of Russia to Europe. Was Russia bound to follow in the footsteps of Europe, as the reforms of Peter the Great seemed to imply, or did she have a parallel but distinct destiny? While the arguments in this prolonged debate, which has lasted in one form or another for some four centuries, are too intricate to be summarized here, it is of interest to touch briefly on the main themes as they have developed since 1861.

Of the principal participants in this debate, only the various branches of the liberal movement and the Menshevik wing of the Social Democratic party can be said to have looked to Europe more or less unconditionally as the model for Russia to follow, although they differed in the theoretical basis of their reasoning. The other participants, again for a variety of reasons, saw Russia developing along its own distinct lines. The tsarist government expected that the autocracy, supported by a modernizing bureaucratic elite, would continue to rule the masses in a paternalistic fashion. Conservative modernizers regarded Prussia and Japan as possible models. The Populists, and their successors in the Socialist Revolutionary party, envisaged a modern society arising from a socialized peasantry without an intervening period of free-enterprise industrialization. The Bolsheviks, finally, employed the methods of the extremist wing of the Russian revolutionary movement in implementing what they considered to be a Marxist program. The Soviet state has worked out a formula for modernization that is in many respects quite distinct from European precedents, although it employs in a more drastic form some of the methods of exploiting labor which were characteristic of early capitalism.

In these various ways Russian traditions and attitudes have differed from those of the earlier modernizers and have confounded those who persist in interpreting Russian developments in terms of West European political and social values. These are no doubt only differences of degree, but they nevertheless comprise a distinctive political and social culture. Seen in a world-wide spectrum of modernizing societies, the Russian pattern resembles somewhat that of Turkey, Iran, Japan, and China. As societies with a tradition of vigorous, independent, and relatively centralized governments; modernizing at first defensively but in due course aggressively, and to a marked degree at the initiative of the state; borrowing wholesale from the West, but with a characteristically ambivalent attitude toward Western values and influences—they bear a certain resemblance to each other. This pattern of modernization is distinct not only from that of the West but also from that of the newer states of Asia and Africa.

IV

To say that the modernization of Russia has in very important respects followed the same course as in other societies, but that its style and manner have been significantly affected by certain characteristic Russian institutions and values, does not account for the many specific policies that have marked the course of social change since 1861. These must be explained rather by interests, points of view, and circumstances expressed ultimately through the medium of political leaders, and they may be regarded as contingent influences in the sense that the particular direction and emphasis of policy was the outcome of unpredictable human choices.

That the system of serfdom would at some point have to be changed, for instance, was generally recognized; but the timing and terms of the emancipation were the result of negotiations and decisions not immediately related to broader historical trends. Emancipation had been under discussion for half a century and was given serious consideration by Nicholas I; and the possibility existed of a variety of compromises between landowner and peasant interests. Once the decision was taken, it set the course of social change for a generation or more. The serfs were emancipated, but they were left poorer than before and confined within the communal framework of the mir under circumstances which gave them little mobility. Indeed, the decision to emancipate was not a decision to modernize, although the government soon found it necessary to take further measures which had unforseen consequences for social change. Once the noble landowners were removed from their traditional responsibilities, new institutions had to be established to take their place, and there ensued a chain reaction of reforms. Organs of local administration were created, the judiciary was reformed, the representative basis of municipal government was broadened, and universal military service was introduced. Public opinion was infused with a new spirit, and most educated Russians felt that their country was finally moving along the trail blazed by Western Europe.

The exhilarating atmosphere of reform was nevertheless deceptive, for thoroughgoing modernization was as yet scarcely under way. The hopes aroused by Alexander II were of West European dimensions, but his performance was quite modest insofar as it affected the mass of the population. Under these circumstances the extremists became increasingly disaffected, and the reign that ushered in a new era was terminated by an assassin's hand. The successors of Alexander II did not have his vision, but they reaped some of the benefits of his reforms and were advised by abler statesmen. The personality of Witte dominates this period, and his skill in using the Ministry of Finance to prime the pump of industrialization marked a new phase in the economic development of the country. The rate of growth of Russian industry was among the highest in the world in the 1890's, and the social consequences of this rapid expansion soon made themselves felt. This dynamic industrial growth, however, was not matched in other spheres. Self-government institutions were increasingly restricted in this period, and harsh censorship stifled public opinion. The decade or two which culminated in the revolution of 1905 were thus marked by a combination of economic boldness and political caution which has few parallels among the societies that modernized earlier, although it resembles rather closely the policies of Japan, Turkey, and perhaps also China in their earlier phases. Here again, the origins of these specific policies must be sought in men rather than in trends and forces.

When the government's authority collapsed as a result of the Japanese victory in 1905, it had to make concessions on a wide front. Once the government regained its equilibrium, however, it worked out a modification of the earlier formula which again sought to provide for economic growth within a traditional framework of autocracy and censorship. The plan of Stolypin to make the transition from communal to independent agriculture was comparable in its implications to the economic measures of Alexander II and Witte, and had it not been for the war it would have had a profound effect on Russian society. The rapid change since the late 1880's was continued in those aspects of society that reflected more or less directly the introduction of modern technology—intellectual ferment, education, industrialization, urbanization, and the erosion of the social traditions based on the peasant patriarchal family—but not in other aspects. In particular, political power remained very largely in the hands of the autocracy, which drew upon itself all the blame for the inequities that seem inevitably to result from rapid social change.

Another emperor, or other advisers, working with the same materials, could have evolved a very different policy. As it is, the political collapse of the empire during the First World War has cast a shadow over all of its policies and has led many to neglect the rapid social change that occurred in Russia in the generation or two before 1917. Indeed, a good case can be made for the proposition that if the rate of change experienced in the later years of the empire had been continued for a generation or so without the burdens of war, revolution, and civil strife, the results might not have differed very greatly from what was actually achieved after 1917. Since no such calculation can be tested, one must satisfy oneself with the realization that Russia was a dynamic society after the 1860's, however different the pattern of change may have been from that of European societies.

The tenure of office of the Provisional Government in 1917 was so brief and stormy, and under such insistent pressure from the Petrograd Soviet, that it is difficult to evaluate its impact on social change. Such influence as it exerted must in fact be judged more as an indication of already existing trends which had been suppressed by the autocracy, or of goals which liberal Russians hoped to achieve, than in terms of its actual accomplishments. The abolition of discrimination on legal and religious grounds, the separation of church and state, and the establishment of electoral procedures for the Constituent Assembly stand as its principal achievements, and its general outlook probably fitted the West European pattern more closely than that of any other Russian government. The measures which the Provisional Government adopted were nevertheless not concerned with the most urgent problems of the moment—peace, land reform, and vigorous administration. It favored a continuation of the war and postponement of land reform until after the war; and it recognized rather helplessly that it had little control over what was going on in the country.

To many, Lenin's victory in 1917 seems to be as much a result of the shortsightedness of his rivals as of his own perspicacity, but few will deny his skill in manipulating the mood of the masses and his grasp of the essentials of politics. As a political event, the Bolshevik seizure of power was as decisive a revolution as has occurred in modern times. In terms of social change, however, it had few immediate results. It was not until 1928 that the 1913 level of production in agriculture and industry was regained, and the trend toward urbanization and a growing working class was in fact temporarily reversed. Modernizing experiments were carried on in education and the arts, but their influence did not extend far beyond a few major urban centers. While efforts were made to educate groups of the population which had hitherto been under-privileged, the quality of general education suffered. The family, youth, public health, intellectual work—all suffered during the first decade after the revolution and recovered only gradually.

By contrast with 1917, 1928 is the dramatic turning point in the Communist program to modernize Russia. The inauguration of the five-year plans, and the use of the vast power at the disposal of the government to mobilize the resources of the country in the drive for industrialization, produced social consequences out of all proportion to those of the political revolution in 1917. No aspect of society was left untouched by this great effort, and in technology and in the aspects of social change directly affected by industrialization Russia again began to move rapidly along the course set by the more modern societies. In many respects the social scene resembled that of the 1890's, although change was now more rapid and more all-embracing. It may seem paradoxical that, in the realm of technology and related matters which were his principal concern, Stalin rather than Lenin should appear as the initiator of the Soviet phase of Russian modernization. This is no doubt more for reasons of circumstance than of policy, for the five-year plans would not have been possible without the preparatory work of the preceding decade. At the same time, it is from 1928 that one must date the purposeful and thoroughgoing totalitarian methods which today characterize the Soviet pattern of social change.

Whether a change of similar significance has occurred since Stalin's death is problematical. As striking as many of the innovations undertaken by Khrushchev are, they are in fact little more than variants of the pattern set a generation earlier. The essentials of the Stalinist formula—emphasis on heavy industry and on those aspects of social change directly related to industrialization, at the expense of almost everything else—have not altered. The somewhat easier way of life and the relatively relaxed methods of government that have marked Khrushchev's administration seem to be more the result of a need for greater efficiency and of differences in the personalities of the two leaders than of any fundamental change in the philosophy of modernization.

V

In reviewing the ways in which the course of social change in Russia has run parallel to that of societies that modernized earlier or at about the same time, the extent to which traditional social institutions and values peculiar to Russia have influenced its development, and the impact of specific leaders and policies, one is struck by the complexity of this process and impressed by the caution that must be exercised in drawing conclusions and making generalizations.

The comparative study of modernization is still in its infancy, and it will be a long time before an understanding of social change in Russia can overtake (let alone surpass) the level it has reached with regard to West European societies, for instance. Yet even now it seems reasonably safe to make two rather elementary generalizations. The first is that Russian social traditions and values are different from those of Western Europe—certainly only in degree, but sufficient degree to be significant—and are likely to remain different for the foreseeable future. The pattern of social change set by the early modernizers in the West has had such a powerful influence on men's minds that it has become the standard by which all modernization is judged. Many believe that modernization will have a universally homogenizing effect in creating a more or less uniform world society. Yet the evidence would seem to point in a different direction, toward a uniformity of scientifically verifiable knowledge and of its technological applications but a continued diversity of social institutions and values. Just as a language may become modernized without losing its distinctive features, so also other aspects of group behavior—in varying ways and degrees—are likely to preserve their unique styles and characteristics for some time to come. Apart from the countries of Europe and those settled primarily by Europeans, Russia and Japan are the only ones where social change has gone as far as in the societies that have modernized earlier, and it will therefore be a long time before this generalization can be tested. In any event, the evaluation of social change in Russia must be based on a careful consideration of what is universal and what is relative, and a recognition that there is likely to be significant distortion when one judges Russia (or other societies) only by European standards.

The second generalization is that within the framework of traditional Russian social institutions and values there is a wide range of choice available to the individuals and groups involved in the myriad of decisions that make up social change. The state, for example, is likely to play a predominant role in social change in Russia for a long time to come, but it need not be a totalitarian state. The state is likely to be purposeful and task-oriented, but there is no historical necessity that requires it to place the real income of the average citizen near the bottom of its scale of values. The differences between the policies of Stalin and Khrushchev provide evidence of the range of choice inherent in the Soviet system, and one can imagine many other concessions that could be made to the desire for an easier way of life without significantly affecting the party and state as the source of authority.

HENRY V. DICKS

Some Notes on the
Russian National Character

One of the most interesting pursuits in the field of international relations is that of trying to identify the national characteristics of a given people. Because Russia has long mystified many Western observers, a study of the Russian character is of particular concern in an era dominated, at one and the same time, by the "cold war" and by "peaceful coexistence."

In this selection, Dr. Henry V. Dicks points out that the most significant events which have affected the modern Russian, such as the end of agrarian serfdom, the coming of industrialization with resulting social mobility, and the secularization of a society long dominated by the Russian Orthodox Church, are comparable to those which have shaped other recently developing societies. Certain traits, however, he believes, are peculiar to the Russians. One of them is that "the Russian can vary between feeling that he is no good and that he is superior to the rest of mankind." Another is that Russian peasants regard their friends as though they may become their enemies (although some observers point out that others besides the Russians have held this attitude).

Dr. Dicks is a consulting psychiatrist at the Tavistock Clinic in London. He is the author (with others) of The Case of Rudolf Hess: a Problem in Diagnosis and Forensic Psychiatry, 1947; and of "Observations on Contemporary Russian Behavior," Human Behavior, V, 1952.

III

. . . the peasant family as it existed on countless small-holdings and, from available evidence, as it still exists today . . . is typically a patriarchal family of grandfather and grandmother with their sons, wives, and children, as well as any unmarried daughters and sons, living incredibly close together, farming the holding by joint labor. There is little privacy and the children participate in all that goes on in this living space. At the head of the household the child perceives a composite authority figure, a blend of both grandparents, of which one is the almost wholly awe-inspiring and arbitrary father-figure, shouting commands from his seat of power on the stove or at the head of the table. The other is an equally unpredictable, on the whole indulgent but also nagging and dominant, mother-figure, who inculcates prayer and demonology. Both claim divine sanction for their right to rule and chastise all their dependents, adults and children alike, and they are also the prescribed objects of love and pious duty. (One cannot help making the analogies: tsar and church; state and party.)

The typical prevailing feeling of terrified reverence for authority is best denoted by the Russian word *strakh*. In the family setting its presence leads to the phenomenon of marked duplicity in behavior. On the one hand, there is an astonishing degree of priggish, dutiful lip service and subjection to the grandfather; on the other hand, in his absence, something not far short of conspiracy of the adult sons against their father. This ambivalence is well described by Gladkov in the following words, speaking of his father's relation during his childhood to the grandfather: "He nourished in himself a constant resentment against grandfather. . . . He bore himself with contempt toward grandfather in his absence, but to his face he expressed devotion and unconditional subordination."

Periodically there occur violent outbursts against the authority of the grandfather by the grown-up sons in fits of sudden desperation, more often than not terminated by remorseful and self-humiliating contrition (such as prostration at his feet) and begging for forgiveness. The motive ascribed to these revolts is the sons' wish for freedom to leave home because the old man will not make over to them their independent plot of land, their inheritance. But it is also moral outrage and hurt dignity as a result of his tyranny. It is no accident that parricide forms such a prominent theme in Russian literature. The child's own image of immediate adults is of people subject to higher authority and filled with ambivalent resentment and submissive love for the authority figure. A little later he learns that even grandfather is but a serf and can be bullied and humiliated by his *barin* (landowner, lord) or the police. There is indeed a series of infinite regress, leading via grandfather to the barin and so to the tsar and to God.

A correlate of this situation is the frequency with which the sons identify themselves with grandfather's arbitrary power and play their own role in due course in a like manner. Aggression passes down the echelon of the family structure: the grandmother, herself under her husband's heel, coerces and torments her daughters-in-law; the adult sons assert their status and dignity by beating or bullying their wives, children, or younger brothers. Lowest in rank order is the daughter-in-law, as a "stranger." At all levels of this group, obedience is exacted by beating, threats of expulsion from the homestead, and invocation of terrible sanctions based on a near-medieval religious and demonological system of beliefs, followed by contrition, tears, and forgiveness. Emotion of every kind flows fully and unrestrainedly in comparison to, say, a nineteenth-century English family.

In sum, then, the typical childhood of a Russian peasant, including many a prominent Russian now in his prime, was spent in a helpless participation in scenes of his elders' crude emotional oscillations between tenderness and brutality. He received an ambivalent perception of his own father as strong and good as well as cowardly and weak, his mother (grandparents' daughter-in-law) as lovable but despised, and himself as powerless and dependent. A rich if chaotic inner world of emotional potentials is thus created. The experience also develops a capacity to tolerate silently the most contradictory and powerful emotions. The nature of the identifications made is highly paradoxical. The little boy will tend to idealize and to identify himself in part with the victim position—with the tender, persecuted, suffering mother. There is evidence that this theme is later elaborated into the hero fantasy of rescuing the oppressed, suffering mother-figure.[1] But it makes for a kind of despair about weak, tender emotions which can never lead to happy endings. These are covered over by a defensive identification with the power and cruelty of the male line, by repression of the inner "mother's boy" in favor of rugged, swaggering "masculine" behavior. The mother-figure is treated with sadistic contempt in fantasy—for instance, the unprintable standard oath of Russian men—and also revered, pitied, and

---

[1] For example, the fairly tale of the prince who delivers the maiden from the evil sorcerer, Koshchei "The Immortal" (cf. "Firebird"). Such motivations are also one source of fervent love of the mother-country. It was remarkable how often my interviewees expressed the postwar state of Russia in terms of their "starving, neglected mother."

idealized. Girls will harbor much hostility toward men and rebellion against the marital role as a fate not much worse than death. Love is always tragic in Russia. The strong, independent woman is admired.

The young child receives a good deal of spoiling, praise, and love from the *babushka*, from aunts and neighboring women, and a special kind of intimate, almost forbidden, love from his own mother who scarcely dares show she is human. All these female figures, except perhaps the tragic mother, convey a sense of support and shield the child from the excess of paternal wrath. The child's emotional reward comes when he feels he is considered strong, a good little helper, an eager student, and above all obedient and quiet. From this source we may visualize arising some typical attitudes toward good citizenship behavior in present Russian society.

Lastly there is also a strongly marked motive to escape from the tyranny and oppression toward a distant beckoning land of freedom, equality, and opportunity, where one can be his own master and lead his own life. . . .

IV

The March 1917 revolution was made by the heirs of the epoch just sketched against authorities essentially unchanged for centuries. It was a revolt against intolerable conditions as were all the desperate anarchic spontaneous mass risings which ineffectively preceded it. There followed a brief honeymoon à la Russe—a spate of egalitarian sentiment and talking in town and village meetings, and of possession of land taken from the murdered father-figures. The authorities whom the Russians had thrown off had been weak and ineffective, men, though remote in status, too much like themselves: unorganized, lazy, greedy. Into the power vacuum stepped Lenin and his coterie of exiles, with an appeal which was thoroughly culture-congenial: a father speaking in angry peasant tones yet in the terms of Western "science," promising bread and land and revenge on oppressors, a severe order, and a material plenty. . . .

During Turgenev's time the established order was a unity and could be taken for granted by both him and his characters. As a barin himself, he could naively describe his wonderment at the human qualities he discovers among his peasants: how wise and shrewd the old men; how tender the muzhik in his friendship and how like the barins in his veneration of order. In brief, during the Victorian era there is no difficulty in transposing our concepts from the family to the social scene, except for that tiny top crust—the French-speaking upper aristocracy, almost entirely alien to their own lower orders. The peasants viewed the "infinite regress of authorities," to which allusion was made above, much as sons viewed fathers and grandfathers, with *strakh* and duplicity, but with an understanding of their authoritarian ferocities and a use of the same methods of propitiation and self-abasement toward them that they expected to receive from their own dependents. These traits were so ingrained that they persisted into the writer's own recollection of peasant behavior in the early nineteen-hundreds. Serfdom seemed like a safe order, a knowing where one stood. The barin, the village mayor (*starosta*), and the county police were near to their "children." Their impact was personal and their *izdevatel'stvo* [moral outraging] was often linked with tenderness and paternalism. The bad object that deprived could be projected into a blurred distant "They," but was also attributed to one's own sinfulness.

As serfdom is abolished there always comes a loosening of the bonds of pious tradition, felt by the older peasants as a dangerous loss of security. For what happened to the barin begins to happen to the elder's own authority over his sons. The predicament is touchingly presented by Gladkov. In a scene in which the eldest son tells his father that "times have changed" and he feels free to leave home where there is no land, the old man, in an effort to preserve his hold over his son, bursts out:

> We are the servants of God. We are *krest'iane* [peasants; *krest* means cross]. From olden times we bear the labor of the cross; but never the slaves of Anti-Christ and his angels, of priests or of German [the Russian is *nemetskii*, meaning "foreigner" in general and German in particular] authority, of heretics who smoke tobacco, of shaven men with their tinsel and badges. You young have no freedom nor sense but what comes from the elders. In them alone is order and firmness of life.

This quotation illuminates the complex feelings of the peasant in the 1890's. There is his own identification with due authority and fear of anarchy of the young. At the same time, there is total hostility to what are felt to be *alien*, bureaucratic, newfangled secular authorities and their hirelings—the clergy.[2] Long suffering and hard fate are transfigured by the sanction of the Cross which gives the dignity of moral principle both to humility and to obstinacy.

After the reforms of the 1860's, secularization evolved along with industrialization and social mobility. The almost mythical freedom and opportunity of factory work lures the emancipated landless sons to the

---

[2] Gladkov's book, published in 1949, might have been satirizing the incursion of the Communists into the life of the village. Equally, that plea could have belonged to the era of Peter the Great.

cities. They take with them their ambivalent expectations of oppression and of boundless hope. They already have a conviction that the urban dweller (*fabrichnyi chelovek*) is a smarter fellow than they. They find nothing reassuring in labor conditions which exploit and deprive, without the compensation of paternal affection. Gorky was the finest painter of these conditions. Crafty townsmen and kulaks multiply in the countryside and batten on the average peasant no less than on his barin. They are hated as "man-eaters" and "fat men." We still read of religious resignation, in Gladkov, for instance, as a valued form of defense against mounting despair and envious resentment. Peasant-saints, ambivalently preaching love and self-surrender, but also calling for the repentance of the oppressors, seem ubiquitous and revered by the population just as the people of India revere their holy men.

Another attitude is so typical that it requires mention. Gladkov describes the scene of arrival of the police inspector in his native village for the supervision of rent and debt collection. When his carriage appears, the whole population berates its children, pushes the wives around, and flogs its horses—even the chickens scatter. This behavior means: "look, we are calling our dependents to order to show due reverence." But it also means: "scatter, for the Antichrist is riding among us. We, the heads of families, show *strakh*, but see how we can control all this undisciplined rabble." In miniature, here is the quintessence of . . . Russian authority feelings as felt by the underlings: hate of the policemen who come to support and protect the exploiters—the barin and his bailiff; eagerness to show one's siding with authority by displacing the resentment down to "stupid, unruly women and children," who must be made to toe the line and punished. Scenes with similar meaning were reported to me by the defectors I interviewed, and I have also witnessed such things personally. The police or the mayor could not be seen instrumentally—only as total enemies. Some of this is, doubtless, more of a feudal than a specific Russian trait.

Closely related is the culturally prevalent mechanism of self-undoing. Caught in hopeless impotent revolt against the all-powerful creditor or oppressor, resignation and passivity fail, and smoldering hate turns against the self and its good objects. This well-documented behavior pattern of Russian life, widespread in all classes, usually takes the form of depressive apathy, neglect or desertion of work and family, wife-and-child beating, bouts of desperate, reckless drinking. Both observer and subject usually have insight that this is a symbolic attack on the authorities. In my more recent interview material there were many examples of this "throwing up the sponge," of "making of one's own ruin a stick to beat the authorities with." It is like Dostoevsky's Raskolnikov, who makes a total mad protest by murder, equivalent to suicide, accusing and expiating at one and the same time the guilt of the evil dominating persecutor with whom he also feels at one.

Scenes like those reported during the collectivization of farms under Stalin, when peasants destroyed crops and livestock rather than hand them over, knowing they would be shot or deported, occurred often during prerevolutionary days at impoundings of property for debt. Behavior under MVD interrogation as described by my interviewees followed the same pattern: "Do what you like—I am through." "All right—kill me then," and so on.

The Soviet masters of Russia with Lenin at their head have given convincing evidence of both their Russian-ness and their hate of Russian-ness in the above sense. Psychologically we may think of them as a conspiratorial band of determined parricides who were able to catalyze the release of endless paranoid hate of Russians for the bad inner authority figure; to sanction cathartic revenge against ever-present scapegoats, and so to free also the lusty, constructive omnipotence feelings. It was a psycho-catharsis on the grand scale. But how to ride this storm of anarchic, savage hate that accompanied the constructive energy? The Bolsheviks' Russian-ness was demonstrated by their wholesale, uncompromising acceptance of Western patterns of socialism but with their paranoid lack of discrimination of finer shades between black and white, by their belief that nothing was impossible, by their magical faith in the entirely "scientific," rational nature of their "system," supplanting the sense of mission of orthodox Russian Christianity, ever watchful of the least error which would enable "the devil to get in." It was thus consonant with the deepest . . . fantasies that before long they re-established the persistent authority model inherent in the Russian mind: an absolute power which is the sole repository of Truth and which cannot be questioned or deviated from. This "restoration" was well on its way by 1928 and completed during the purges and by the reintroduction of officer status with Tsarist-like accouterments and ranks during World War II. People's commissars became ministers. It is true that they still called one "comrade," a relic of the days of equality, and that some Bolsheviks were friendly fatherly persons who pitied one.

The new elite bases its goal values on the doctrine of the will—the doctrine that man can master his own nature as well as the environment. This is culture-congenial where it stresses maximum effort, achievement, and surpassing the foreigners. It is resented when it means the exercise of authority in that impersonally implacable, nemetskii, alien way which has been the most hated feature of Communist rule. Not only was increasing instrumentalism and decreasing expressiveness bound to come because of the growing complexity of industrialization and bureaucratization. It came also because of the internal conflict of the rapidly promoted men who implemented the plan. Though they came, except in the earliest days, chiefly from the people, these men had made the closest identifications with the Western-thinking Leninist group, with its proclaimed goals of mastering the backward muzhik and turning him into a disciplined Communist paragon—the ideal industrial man. This has meant incessant war by the party against the Russian peasant character in themselves and in the "masses." I believe this is what all the current trouble is about in Russia.

For Bolshevik fantasies, greed, hate, and apathy no less than unpolitical, human relations were a threat to the efforts to build, change, and control. This cursed anarchic human material was the only obstacle to a wonderful scheme. Hence, people must not be allowed to have doubts, guilt, ambivalence, or personal wishes. The mechanisms of displacement and projection, which are by nature designed to buffer the personality against excessive guilt feelings, are massively mobilized at all levels by the party elite to a degree which constitutes a qualitative change from prerevolutionary patterns. The compulsive, inhuman tempo to industrialize and build up an invulnerable military-technological empire is due, I suspect, to this paranoid dynamic. Sadistic dominance needs are projected to foreign out-groups, creating an "encirclement" situation and a siege mentality. This externalizes the "enemy" and deflects hate with its attendant guilt from the in-group authority to the "blood-sucking" imperialists, symbols of themselves, who enact the role of everyone's oppressive father-image, but also of one's own anarchic greed and hate. Internal deviation can also be projected in this way as the work of "agents" of the external enemy. Leites and Bernaut, in a notably subtle analysis of Bolshevik mentality, have shown the fantasy-thought process by which the inner split of "total submission—total hostility" can create this recurring public myth of the party leader turned enemy. A succession of these figures can then be "unmasked" as scapegoats drawing upon themselves the wrath and execration of the group and thus purging collective guilt feelings in the people for having felt traitorous toward the government as a whole.

This mechanism . . . demonstrates the power of supreme authority, the all-seeing eye, to level even the strong. It increases *strakh* with its bracing and reassuring aspects. What is uncertain is the degree to which the rulers consciously use such mechanisms, and to what extent they are impelled by unconscious forces to rely on such myths and ritual expiations. We now know that the top Nazi leaders were as much the victims as the cold-blooded exploiters of their own paranoid fantasies, not unlike some of the more fanciful Soviet ideological propaganda themes. . . .

Another, more readily understandable, mechanism of defense against typical conflicts is that of *manic denial*, observed also in tense managerial personalities of the West. This akin to the compulsive drive, seeking escape from doubt and guilt feelings by the restless urge for achievement and organizing activity. Here we find motivations for coercing the "backward masses" . . . to higher tempo and norms; for the need of more and more technical mastery over nature and machines in an effort to convince oneself that "everything is under control." The practice as well as the terminology of Bolshevism are replete with this pseudo-objective technological scientism. The all-pervading secret police, for example, are dignified by the term "apparatus."

The effect of this war by paranoid pseudo-rationality against the depressive, insightful, sensitive side of the Russian character, is clearly discernible. We do not know how deep this effect is, for the Russian is adept at lip-service conformity and dissimulation. We know something of the attitudes of men who deserted during and after World War II— and of those who refused to be repatriated from German captivity, most of them peasants, or "rural intelligentsia" in the case of my own sample, and under age thirty-five. They felt ethically betrayed by the falsity of their masters' descriptions of Western conditions. They also had put into practice what the dispossessed sons had always done—to walk away when possible as a gesture of defiance. The chief recurring reason given was the revolt against the party's *izdevatel'stvo* against the people—their own poor hungry mothers symbolizing their motherland and people. These men—and they could not all have been atypical—felt morally insulted because after a war in which they felt they had saved the country they were again mistrusted, coerced, and terrified into total compliance. Theirs was the groan of Russians through the ages. That part of them which sought love and nurturance from "their own government" felt enraged—not with what had been done but by the manner. It has been typically Russian for this situation to recur from generation to generation.

The chief changes after 1917 were: (1) the regression in thinking and feeling toward the least mature and most psychotic layer of Russian fantasy—from the humane, broad tolerance of good and evil toward an acceptance of "black and white" mythology, a need to betray and become a turncoat, to deny friends and one's real feelings; (2) impoverishment of free communication, and suspicion of one's neighbor as a possible informer; (3) limitation of privacy; (4) lack of security from terror; and (5) the conscious awareness of disappointed expectations that the government would speed a higher standard of living and of the amenities of life.

Defectors in the younger age group showed a significantly greater acceptance than the older ones of "Soviet reality," and their defection was motivated less by principle than by their chance exposure to the West and by material dissatisfactions. They seemed to demand more from their regime. This in itself is perhaps a significant achievement of the Soviets—the truly downtrodden do not aspire to rising standards.

For a time after Stalin's death, Khrushchev not only permitted execration of the archtyrant as the supreme scapegoat, but himself wept before his comrades when he reported being forced by Stalin to dance the gopak.[3] He thus not only expressed his identification with the insulted and oppressed, but on this and other occasions staked his claim as heir to idealized Little Father Lenin and displayed his own need to deny guilt as one of Stalin's leading henchmen. Since then, as we know, he has shown more tyrannical features, tempered with the gruff, jovial . . . behavior he typifies. His standing in the popular mind appears not to have been improved by the latter: it is reported that he is "not respected because he is too close to the people." This *panebratstvo* (hail-fellow-well-met) is not the modern Soviet-conditioned people's idea of a top leader any more than it would have been respected by the generations that preceded them. Such is the Russian ambivalence. Now, as ever, the Russians value sincerity and real warmth, and are quick at spotting false cordiality in a calculating confidence-trickster. A leader ought to be distant and dignified, and severe like an angry father. It remains to be seen which Khrushchev is.

V

In trying to strike a balance between change and persistence of the old, we must try and look at the available phenomena from the Russian point of view.

The Communist leaders have known how to use to the breaking point, but always stopping short of it, that contradiction in Russians which wants omnipotently to possess and achieve everything preferably by spurts of group effort, but which also counts abstinence and postponement of gratification a virtue. Within limits, they have given immense opportunities for able people to traverse the whole gamut of social mobility and economic success. They have created a literate population whose education has made them aware not only of their own history but of economic standards, of the fun of machine-mindedness into which so much dominance need has been channeled. They have

---

[3] See the story of the peasant Ovsianikov whose barin made him dance (just as Stalin did Khrushchev) as part of his sense of possession of the serf, and then praised the humiliated man; in I. S. Turgenev, *Zapiski Okhotnika* (St. Petersburg, 1883).

used xenophobia and envy of the rich neighbor to divert hate from themselves to the West, weaving healthy Russian love of country into this parricidal and near-demonological theme, and thereby adding a persecutory paranoid urgency to their people's effort.

The leadership has also played the role of authority according to the . . . stereotype. Utter devotion is demanded but really not expected— that is, there is reliance on external sanctions and controls on the tacit Russian assumption that there is a totally hostile traitor in every man. This leads one to ask: can a society be said to be maturing if it continues to treat *all* its citizens as potential traitors and saboteurs, not fit to have mental freedom? This deep "fault" in Russian unconscious imagery moreover has fostered the rise to power mainly of the most sado-masochistic, authority-identified, and insecure among the citizens, who have for lack of other inner models aped the hate-invested, rigid, and status-conscious authority models of Russian culture, minus their easygoing tolerance and laxity. These soulless party men have made a hollow mockery of the longing for spiritual freedom, justice, and equality. Perhaps they have killed the revolution. We have seen that the young generation, especially in the cities, has so far accepted and "adapted" to the cruelty and unprincipledness of this production-machine. With them lies the future. Will they, who know no other system and whose chief value seems to be, according to reliable studies, the expectancy of bigger and better careers and rewards from it, be content with this hedging in of their freedom, especially in the sphere of contact with the West, of criticism and discussion of men and policies and priorities?

There has been a great concretization of thought and action as the result of technical education. Can the strengthening of realistic thinking in the technical sphere for long be kept out of the political sphere . . . ? Again, we do not know what millions of fathers and mothers and babushkas are transmitting to their children in private. My guess is that it is not very different from Gorky's or Gladkov's nursery experiences. A young simple cowherd from Viatka oblast said this to me: "In the U.S.S.R. May 1 and November 7 are great feast days. But we in our village have a holiday called Easter . . . have you heard of it?"

It is thus not easy to guess how and in what direction this great society will develop its values and guiding goal aspirations. Perhaps with the lessening of their ancient sense of underprivilegedness through technical achievement, together with the enduring religious values still transmitted by Russian mothers—with the passing in a few years of the last remnants of the original Leninists and Stalinists and the emergence of a solid, educated middle layer of professional and managerial personalities—one can hope for a reduction in the primitive defensive, paranoid features of Soviet attitudes. They are, with us, heirs of the same deep currents of civilization and ideas. But they have yet to show that they can tolerate doubt and uncertainty of feeling and thought without excessive anxiety, which is revealed in the aggressive dogmatism of their recent behavior toward all those not in complete agreement with their notion of truth.

DANIEL LERNER

The Passing of Traditional Society

For anyone interested in human beings, the process of change in the life of an individual or of a society holds a never-waning fascination. This is particularly true during those periods of history when a traditional order is passing away and is being replaced by another, either through peaceful readjustment or through the use of force. In such a period all existing values are being re-evaluated, all beliefs are being re-examined, and all relations between individuals and groups transformed.

The stronger has been the hold of tradition on a given country or area, the more striking is the process of change. One such area embracing several ancient as well as new nations is the Middle East, where Islamic tradition is slowly giving ground to modernization as peoples from these areas come in contact with Western ideas and ways of life. Daniel Lerner, professor of sociology and international communication at the Massachusetts Institute of Technology since 1953, examines this transformation not only as a sociologist, on the basis of statistical material, but as an observer of human experience, as can be seen in his perceptive parable about the changes taking place in the traditional society of a Turkish village.

Born in 1917, Dr. Lerner has also taught sociology at Columbia University and at Stanford University. He is the author of several other books, among them The Policy Sciences *(with H. D. Lasswell), 1951; and* The Human Meaning of the Social Sciences, *1959.*

Chapter 1

The Grocer and The Chief: A Parable

THE VILLAGE of Balgat lies about eight kilometers out of Ankara, in the southerly direction. It does not show on the standard maps and it does not figure in the standard histories. I first heard of it in the autumn of 1950 and most Turks have not heard of it today. Yet the story of the Middle East today is encapsulated in the recent career of Balgat. Indeed the personal meaning of modernization in underdeveloped lands can be traced, in miniature, through the lives of two Balgati—The Grocer and The Chief.

My first exposure to Balgat came while leafing through several hundred interviews that had been recorded in Turkey during the spring of 1950. One group caught my eye because of the underlying tone of bitterness in the interviewer's summary of the village, his earnest sense of the hopelessness of place and people. These five interviews in Balgat were moving; even so, something in the perspective seemed awry. For one thing, the interviewer was more highly sensitized to what he saw than what he heard. The import of what had been said to him, and duly recorded in his reports, had somehow escaped his attention. I, having only the words to go by, was struck by the disjunction between the reported face and the recorded voice of Balgat. For another thing, the interviews had been made in the early spring and I was reading them in the late fall of 1950. Between these dates there had been a national election in which, as a stunning surprise to everybody including themselves, practically all qualified Turks had voted and the party in power—Ataturk's own *Halk* party—had been turned out of office.

Nothing like this had ever happened before in Turkey, possibly because neither universal suffrage nor an opposition party had ever been tried before. The dazed experts could only say of this epochal deed that the Anatolian villagers had done it. Since it would be hard to imagine Anatolian villagers of more standard pattern than the Balgati whose collected opinions were spread before me, I had it on top authority that during the summer they had entered History. But it was not immediately obvious by what route.

What clues existed were in a few words spoken by the villagers. These words we collated with the words that had been spoken to the interviewers by hundreds of villagers and townspeople throughout the Middle East. As we tabulated and cross-tabulated, a hunch emerged of what in Balgat spoke for many men, many deeds. Comparing cases by class and country we gradually enlarged our minature into a panorama. Our hypothesis, heavy now with vivid details and many meanings, took shape. Four years later an oversize manuscript on the modernizing Middle East was in hand. To see how close a fit to Middle East reality was given by our picture of it, I went out for a self-guided tour and final round of interviews in the spring of 1954. My odyssey terminated where my ideas originated: in Balgat, on the eve of a second national election. With Balgat, then, our account begins.

Balgat Perceived: 1950

The interviewer who recorded Balgat on the verge—his name was Tosun B.—had detected no gleam of the future during his sojourn there. "The village is a barren one," he wrote. "The main color is gray, so is the dust on the divan on which I am writing now." Tosun was a serious young scholar from Ankara and he loved the poor in his own fashion. He had sought out Balgat to find the deadening past rather than the brave new world. He found it:

> I have seen quite a lot of villages in the barren mountainous East, but never such a colorless, shapeless dump. This was the reason I chose the village. It could have been half an hour to Ankara by car if it had a road, yet it is about two hours to the capital by car without almost any road and is just forgotten, forsaken, right under our noses.

Tosun also sought and found persons to match the place. Of the five villagers he interviewed, his heart went straight out to the village shepherd. What Tosun was looking for in this interview is clear from his *obiter dicta*:

> It was hard to explain to the village Chief that I wanted to interview the poorest soul in the village. He, after long discussions, consented me to interview the shepherd, but did not permit him to step into the guestroom. He said it would be an insult to me, so we did the interview in someone else's room, I did not quite understand whose. The Chief did not want to leave me alone with the respondent, but I succeeded at the end. This opened the respondent's sealed mouth, for he probably felt that I, the superior even to his chief, rather be alone with him.

When the shepherd's sealed mouth had been opened, little came out. But Tosun was deeply stirred:

> The respondent was literally in rags and in this cold weather he had no shoe, but the mud and dirt on his feet were as thick as any boot. He was small, but looked rugged and sad, very sad. He was proud of

being chosen by me and though limited tried his best to answer the questions. Was so bashful that his blush was often evident under the thick layer of dirt on his face. He at times threw loud screams of laughter when there was nothing to laugh about. These he expected to be accepted as answers, for when I said "Well?" he was shocked, as if he had already answered the question.

His frustration over the shepherd was not the only deprivation Tosun attributed to the Chief, who "imposed himself on me all the time I was in the village, even tried to dictate to me, which I refused in a polite way. I couldn't have followed his directions as I would have ended up only interviewing his family." Tosun did succeed in talking privately with two Balgat farmers, but throughout these interviews he was still haunted by the shepherd and bedeviled by the Chief. Not until he came to interview the village Grocer did Tosun find another Balgati who aroused in him a comparable antipathy. Tosun's equal hostility to these very different men made me curious. It was trying to explain this that got me obsessed, sleeping and waking over the next four years, with the notion that the parable of modern Turkey was the story of the Grocer and the Chief.

Aside from resenting the containment strategy which the Chief was operating against him, Tosun gave few details about the man. He reported only the impression that "the *Muhtar* is an unpleasant old man. Looks mean and clever. He is the absolute dictator of this little village." Nor did Tosun elaborate his disapproval of the *Muhtar's* opinions beyond the comment that "years have left him some sort of useless, mystic wisdom." As a young man of empirical temper, Tosun might be expected to respond with some diffidence to the wisdom of the ancients. But the main source of Tosun's hostility, it appeared, was that the Chief made him nervous. His notes concluded: "He found what I do curious, even probably suspected it. I am sure he will report it to the first official who comes to the village."

Against the Grocer, however, Tosun reversed his neural field. He quickly perceived that he made the Grocer nervous; and for this Tosun disliked *him*. His notes read:

> The respondent is comparatively the most city-like dressed man in the village. He even wore some sort of a necktie. He is the village's only grocer, but he is not really a grocer, but so he is called, originally the food-stuffs in his shop are much less than the things to be worn, like the cheapest of materials and shoes and slippers, etc. His greatest stock is drinks and cigarettes which he sells most. He is a very unimpressive type, although physically he covers quite a space. He gives the impression of a fat shadow. Although he is on the same level with the other

villagers, when there are a few of the villagers around, he seems to want to distinguish himself by keeping quiet, and as soon as they depart he starts to talk too much. This happened when we were about to start the interview. He most evidently wished to feel that he is closer to me than he is to them and was curiously careful with his accent all during the interview. In spite of his unique position, for he is the only unfarming person and the only merchant in the village, he does not seem to possess an important part of the village community. In spite of all his efforts, he is considered by the villagers even less than the least farmer. Although he presented to take the interview naturally, he was nervous and also was proud to be interviewed although he tried to hide it.

All of this pushed up a weighty question: Why did the Chief make Tosun nervous and why did Tosun make the Grocer nervous? These three men, representing such different thoughtways and lifeways, were a test for each other. Looking for answers, I turned to the responses each had made to the 57 varieties of opinions called for by the standard questionnaire used in Tosun's interviews.

The Chief was a man of few words on many subjects. He dismissed most of the items on Tosun's schedule with a shrug or its audible equivalent. But he was also a man of many words on a deportment. Only when the issues involved first principles of conduct did he consider the occasion appropriate for pronouncing judgment. Of the Chief it might be said, as Henry James said of George Eliot's salon style, "*Elle n'aborde que les grandes thèmes.*" [She discusses only the great themes].

The Chief has so little trouble with first principles because he desires to be, and usually is, a vibrant soundbox through which echo the traditional Turkish virtues. His themes are obedience, courage, loyalty—the classic values of the Ottoman Imperium reincarnate in the Ataturk Republic. For the daily round of village life these are adequate doctrine; and as the Chief has been outside of his village only to fight in two wars he has never found his austere code wanting. This congruence of biography with ideology explains the Chief's confidence in his own moral judgment and his short definition of a man. When asked what he wished for his two grown sons, for example, the Chief replied promptly: "I hope they will fight as bravely as we fought and know how to die as my generation did."

From this parochial fund of traditional virtues, the Chief drew equally his opinions of great men, nations, issues. The larger dramas of international *politique* he judged solely in terms of the courage and loyalty of the actors, invoking, to acknowledge their magnitude, the traditional rhetoric of aphorism. Generations of Aanatolian *Muhtars* resonated as he pronounced his opinion of the British:

I hear that they have turned friends with us. But always stick to the old wisdom: "A good enemy is better than a bad friend." You cannot rely on them. Who has heard of a son being friends with his father's murderers?

With his life in Balgat, as with the Orphic wisdom that supplies its rationale, the Chief is contented. At 63 his desires have been quieted and his ambitions achieved. To Tosun's question on contentment he replied with another question:

What could be asked more? God has brought me to this mature age without much pain, has given me sons and daughters, has put me at the head of my village, and has given me strength of brain and body at this age. Thanks be to Him.

The Grocer is a very different style of man. Though born and bred in Balgat, he lives in a different world, an expansive world, populated more actively with imaginings and fantasies—hungering for whatever is different and unfamiliar. Where the Chief is contented, the Grocer is restless. To Tosun's probe, the Grocer replied staccato: "I have told you I want better things. I would have liked to have a bigger grocery shop in the city, have a nice house there, dress nice civilian clothes."

Where the Chief audits his life placidly, makes no comparisons, thanks God, the Grocer evaluates his history in a more complicated and other-involved fashion. He perceives his story as a drama of Self versus Village. He compares his virtue with others and finds them lacking: "I am not like the others here. They don't know any better. And when I tell them, they are angry and they say that I am ungrateful for what Allah .has given me." The Grocer's struggle with Balgat was, in his script, no mere conflict of personalities. His was the lonely struggle of a single man to open the village mind. Clearly, from the readiness and consistency of his responses to most questions, he had brooded much over his role. He had a keen sense of the limits imposed by reality: "I am born a grocer and probably die that way. I have not the possibility in myself to get the things I want. They only bother me." But desire, once stirred, is not easily stilled.

Late in the interview, after each respondent had named the greatest problem facing the Turkish people, Tosun asked what he would do about this problem if he were the president of Turkey. Most responded by stolid silence—the traditional way of handling "projective questions" which require people to imagine themselves or things to be different from what they "really are." Some were shocked by the impropriety of the very question. "My God! How can you say such a thing?" gasped the shepherd. "How can I . . . I cannot . . . a poor villager . . . master of the whole world."

The Chief, Balgat's virtuoso of the traditional style, made laconic reply to this question with another question: "I am hardly able to manage a village, how shall I manage Turkey?" When Tosun probed further ("What would you suggest for *your village* that you cannot handle yourself?"), the Chief said he would seek "help of money and seed for some of our farmers." When the Grocer's turn came, he did not wait for the question to be circumscribed in terms of local reference. As president of Turkey, he said: "I would make roads for the villagers to come to towns to see the world and would not let them stay in their holes all their life."

To get out of his hole the Grocer even declared himself ready—and in this he was quite alone in Balgat—to live ouside of Turkey. This came out when Tosun asked another of his projective questions: "If you could not live in Turkey, where would you want to live?" The standard reply of the villagers was that they would not live, could not imagine living, anywhere else. The forced choice simply was ignored.

When Tosun persisted ("Suppose you *had* to leave Turkey?) he teased an extreme reaction out of some Balgati. The shepherd, like several other wholly routinized personalities, finally replied that he would rather kill himself. The constricted peasant can more easily imagine destroying the self than relocating it in an unknown, i.e., frightful, setting.

The Chief again responded with the clear and confident voice of traditional man. "Nowhere," he said. "I was born here, grew old here, and hope God will permit me to die here." To Tosun's probe, the Chief replied firmly: "I wouldn't move a foot from here." Only the Grocer found no trouble in imagining himself outside of Turkey, living in a strange land. Indeed he seemed fully prepared, as a man does when he has already posed a question to himself many times. "America," said the Grocer, and without waiting for Tosun to ask him why, stated his reason: "because I have heard that it is a nice country, and with possibilities to be rich even for the simplest persons."

Such opinions clearly marked off the Grocer, in the eyes of the villagers around him, as heterodox and probably infidel. The vivid sense of cash displayed by the Grocer was a grievous offense against Balgat ideas of tabu talk. In the code regulating the flow of symbols among Anatolian villagers, blood and sex are permissible objects of passion but money is not. To talk much of money is an impropriety. To reveal excessive *desire* for money is—Allah defend us—an impiety.

Balgati might forgive the Grocer his propensity to seek the strange rather than reverse the familiar, even his readiness to forsake Turkey for unknown places, had he decently clothed these impious desires in pious terms. But to abandon Balgat for the world's fleshpots, to forsake the ways of God to seek the ways of cash, this was insanity. The demented person who spoke thus was surely accursed and unclean.

The Grocer, with his "city-dressed" ways, his "eye at the higher places" and his visits to Ankara, provoked the Balgati to wrathful and indignant restatements of the old code. But occasional, and apparently trivial, items in the survey suggested that some Balgati were talking loud about the Grocer to keep their own inner voices from being overheard by the Chief—or even by themselves.

As we were interested in knowing who says what to whom in such a village as Balgat, Tosun had been instructed to ask each person whether others ever came to him for advice, and if so what they wanted advice about. Naturally, the Balgati whose advice was most sought was the Chief, who reported: "Yes, that is my main duty, to give advice. (Tosun: What about?) About all that I or you could imagine, even about their wives and how to handle them and how to cure their sick cow." This conjunction of wives and cows, to illustrate all the Chief could imagine, runs the gamut only from A to B. These are the species that the villager has most to do with in his daily round of life, the recurrent source of his pains and pleasures and puzzlements. The oral literature abounds in examples of Muhtar (or his theological counterpart, the Hoca) as wise man dispensing judgment equally about women and cows.

Rather more surprising was Tosun's discovery that some Balgati went for advice also to the disreputable Grocer. What did they ask his advice about? "What to do when they go to Ankara, where to go and what to buy, how much to sell their things." The cash nexus, this suggested, was somehow coming to Balgat and with it, possibly, a new role for the Grocer as cosmopolitan specialist in how to avoid wooden nickels in the big city. Also, how to spend the real nickels one got. For the Grocer was a man of clear convictions on which coffee-houses played the best radio programs and which were the best movies to see in Ankara. While his opinions on these matters were heterodox as compared say, to the Chief's, they had an open field to work in. Most Balgati had never heard a radio or seen a movie and were not aware of what constituted orthodoxy with respect to them. Extremists had nonetheless· decided that these things, being new, were obviously evil. Some of them considered the radio to be "the voice of The Devil coming from his deep hiding-place" and said they would smash any such "Devil's-box" on sight.

At the time of Tosun's visit, there was only one radio in Balgat owned by no less a personage than the Chief. In the absence of any explicit orthodox prohibition on radio, the Chief, former soldier and great admirer of Ataturk, had followed his lead. Prosperous by village standards, being the large landowner of Balgat, he had bought a radio to please and instruct his sons. He had also devised an appropriate ceremonial for its use. Each evening a select group of Balgati foregathered in the Chief's guest room as he turned on the newscast from Ankara. They heard the newscast through in silence and, at its conclusion, the Chief turned the radio off and made his commentary. "We all listen very carefully," he told Tosun, "and I talk about it afterwards." Tosun, suspecting in this procedure a variant of the Chief's containment tactics, wanted to know whether there was any disagreement over his explanations. "No, no arguments," replied the Chief, "as I tell you I only talk and our opinions are the same more or less." Here was a new twist in the ancient role of knowledge as power. Sensing the potential challenge from radio, the Chief restricted the dangers of innovation by partial incorporation, thus retaining and strengthening his role as Balgat's official opinion leader.

Tosun inquired of the Grocer, an occasional attendant at the Chief's salon, how he liked this style of radio session. The Grocer, a heretic perhaps but not a foolhardy one, made on this point the shortest statement in his entire interview: "The Chief is clever and he explains the news." Only obliquely, by asking what the Grocer liked best about radio, did Tosun get an answer that had the true resonance. Without challenging the Chief's preference for news of "wars and the danger of wars"—in fact an exclusive interest in the Korean War, to which a Turkish brigade had just been committed—the Grocer indicated that after all *he* had opportunities to listen in the coffee-houses of Ankara, where the audiences exhibited a more cosmopolitan range of interests. "It is nice to know what is happening in the other capitals of the world," said the Grocer. "We are stuck in this hole, we have to know what is going on outside our village."

The Grocer had his own aesthetic of the movies as well. Whereas the Chief had been to the movies several times, he viewed them mainly as a moral prophylactic: "There are fights, shooting. The people are brave. My sons are always impressed. Each time they see such a film they wish more and more their time for military service would come so that they would become soldiers too." For the Grocer, movies were more than a homily on familiar themes. They were his avenue to the wider world of his dreams. It was in a movie that he had first glimpsed what a *real* grocery store could be like—"with walls made of iron sheets, top to floor and side to side, and on them standing myriads of round boxes, clean and all the same dressed, like soldiers in a great parade." This fleeting glimpse of what sounds like the Campbell Soup section of an A&P supermarket had provided the Grocer with an abiding image of how his fantasy world might look. It was here, quite likely, that he had shaped the ambition earlier confided to Tosun, "to have a bigger grocery shop in the city." No pedantries intervened in the Grocer's full sensory relationship to the movies. No eye had he, like the Chief, for their value as filial moral rearmament and call to duty. The Grocer's judgments were formed in unabashedly hedonist categories. "The Turkish ones," he said, "are gloomy, ordinary. I can guess at the start of the film how it will end. . . . The American ones are exciting. You know it makes people ask what will happen next?"

Here, precisely, arose the local variant of a classic question. In Balgat, the Chief carried the sword, but did the Grocer steer the pen? When Balgati sought his advice on how to get around Ankara, would they then go to movies that taught virtue or those that taught excitement? True, few villagers had ever been to Ankara. But things were changing in Turkey and many more Balgati were sure to have a turn or two around the big city before they died. What would happen next in Balgat if more people discovered the tingle of wondering what will happen next? Would things continue along the way of the Chief or would they take the way of the Grocer?

Balgat Revisited: 1954

I reached Ankara in April after a circuitous route through the Middle East. The glories of Greece, Egypt, Lebanon, Syria, Persia touched me only lightly, for some part of me was already in Balgat. Even the Blue Mosque and St. Sophia seemed pallid, and I left Istanbul three days ahead of schedule for Ankara. I had saved this for last, and now here I was. I was half afraid to look.

I called a transportation service and explained that I wanted to go out the following day, a Sunday, to a village some eight kilometers south that might be hard to reach. As I wanted to spend the day, would the driver meet me at 8 A.M. and bring along his lunch?

While waiting for the car, next morning, my reverie wandered back through the several years since my first reading of the Balgat interviews. Was I chasing a phantom? Tahir S. appeared. With solitude vanished anxiety; confidently we began to plan the day. Tahir had been a member of the original interview team, working in the Izmir area. As Tosun had joined the Turkish foreign service and was stationed in North Africa, where he was conducting an inquiry among the Berbers, I had arranged in advance for Tahir to revisit Balgat with me in his place. Over a cup of syrupy coffee, we reviewed the questions that had been asked in 1950, noted the various responses and silences, decided the order in which we would repeat the old questions and interpolate the new ones.

As the plan took shape, Zilla K. arrived. She had no connection with the original survey, but I wanted a female interviewer who could add some Balgat women to our gallery. I had "ordered" her, through a colleague at Ankara University, "by the numbers": thirtyish, semi-trained, alert, compliant with instruction, not sexy enough to impede our relations with the men of Balgat but chic enough to provoke the women. A glance and a word showed that Zilla filled the requisition. We brought her into the plan of operations. The hall porter came in to say our car was waiting. We got in and settled back for a rough haul. Twenty minutes later, as we were still debating the niceties of question-wording and reporting procedure, the driver said briskly: "There's Balgat."

We looked puzzled at each other until Tosun's words of 1950 recurred to us: "It could have been half an hour to Ankara if it had a road." Now it did have a road. What was more, a bus was coming down the road, heading toward us from the place our driver had called Balgat. As it passed, jammed full, none of the passengers waved or even so much as stuck out a tongue at us. Without these unfailing signs of villagers out on a rare chartered bus, to celebrate a great occasion of some sort, we could only make the wild guess that Balgat had acquired a regular bus service. And indeed, as we entered the village, there it was —a "bus station," freshly painted benches under a handsome new canopy. We got out and looked at the printed schedule of trips. "The bus leaves every hour, on the hour, to Ulus Station. Fare: 20 Kurus." For about 4 cents, Balgati could now go, whenever they felt the whim, to Ulus in the heart of Ankara. The villagers were getting out of their holes at last. The Grocer, I thought, must be grinning over the fat canary he had swallowed.

We took a quick turn around the village, on our way to check in with the Chief. Things looked different from what Tosun's report had led us to expect. Overhead wires were stretched along the road, with branch lines extended over the houses of Balgat. The village had been electrified. Alongside the road deep ditches had been dug, in which the graceful curve of new water pipe was visible. Purified water was coming to Balgat. There were many more buildings than the 50-odd Tosun had counted, and most of them looked new. Two larger ones announced themselves as a school and a police station. An inscription on the latter revealed that Balgat was now under the jurisdiction of the Ankara district police. They had finally got rid of the *gendarmerie*, scavengers of the Anatolian village and historic blight on the peasant's existence. "These fellows are lucky," said Tahir drily. Feeling strange, we made our way along the erratic path through the old village, led and followed by a small horde of children, to the house of the Chief. Tahir knocked, an old woman with her head covered by a dark shawl appeared, the children scattered. We were led into the guest room.

The Chief looked as I had imagined. His cheeks a bit more sunken, perhaps, but the whole *présence* quite familiar. Tall, lean, hard, he walked erect and looked me straight in the eye. His own eyes were Anatolian black and did not waver as he stretched out a handful of long, bony fingers. "*Gün aydin, Bey Efendim*," he said. "Good day, sir, you are welcome to my house." I noted in turn the kindness which opens a door to strangers and the Chief responded that we honored his house by our presence. This completed the preliminary round of *formules de politesse* and steaming little cups of Turkish coffee were brought in by the Chief's elder son. The son was rather a surprise— short, pudgy, gentle-eyed and soft spoken. He bowed his head, reddening slightly as he stammered, "*Lütfen*" (Please!) and offered the tray of demitasses to me. I wondered whether he had learned to fight bravely and die properly.

As the Chief set down his second cup of coffee, signifying that we could now turn to the business of our visit, I explained that I had come from America, where I taught in a university, with the hope of meeting him. There, in my own country, I had read about Balgat in some writing by a young man from Ankara who, four years ago, had talked at length with the Chief and other persons in his village. This writing had interested me very much and I had often wondered, as the years passed by, how things were going in the village of Balgat and among its people. When I had the opportunity to come to Turkey I immediately decided that I would visit Balgat and see the Chief if I could.

The Chief heard me through gravely, and when he spoke I knew I was in. He bypassed the set of formulas available to him—for rejecting or evading my implied request—and responded directly to the point. I was right to have come to see Balgat for myself. He remembered well the young man from Ankara (his description of Tosun in 1950 was concise and neutrally-toned). Much had changed in Balgat since that time. Indeed, Balgat was no longer a village. It had, only last month, been incorporated as a district of Greater Ankara. This was why they now had a new headquarters of Metropolitan police, and a bus service, and electricity, and a supply of pure water that would soon be in operation. Where there had been 50 houses there were now over 500, and even he, the *Muhtar*, did not know any more all the people living here.

Yes he had lived in Balgat all his life and never in all that time seen so much happen as had come to pass in these four years:

It all began with the election that year. The *Demokrat* men came to Balgat and asked us what was needed here and told us they would do it when they were elected. They were brave to go against the government party. We all voted for them, as the *Halk* men knew no more what to do about the prices then, and the new men did what they said. They brought us this road and moved out the *gendarmerie*. Times have been good with us here. We are all *Demokrat* party here in Balgat now.

The Chief spoke in a high, strong, calm voice, and the manner of his utterance was matter-of-fact. His black eyes remained clear as he gazed steadily at the airspace adjoining my left ear, and his features retained their shape. Only his hands were animated, though he invoked only the thumbs and the index fingers for punctuation. When he had completed his statement, he picked his nose thoughtfully for a moment and then laid the finger alongside the bridge. The tip of the long, bony finger reached into his eyesocket.

I explained then that the young lady had come with us to learn how such changes as the Chief mentioned were altering the daily round for village women. Might she talk with some of them while Tahir Bey and I were meeting the men? The Chief promptly suggested that Zilla could speak with the females of his household. (Tosun's resentful remark that, had he followed the Chief's suggestions, "I would have ended up only interviewing his family" came back to me later that evening, when Zilla reported on her interviews with the Chief's wife and daughters-in-law. All three had identified Balgat's biggest problem as the new fashion of young men to approach girls shamelessly on the village out-skirts—precisely what the Chief had told me in answer to the same question. Tosun had been wise.) But if the Chief still used his containment tactics with the women, in other directions he had taken a decidedly permissive turn. Tahir and I, he said, could walk about Balgat entirely as we wished and speak with whomsoever it pleased us to honor —even, he added with a smile in response to my jest, some non-*Demokrat* party men, if we could find any. We chatted a bit longer and then, having agreed to return to the Chief's house, we set out for a stroll around Balgat. Our next goal was to find the Grocer.

After a couple of bends and turns, we came to a coffee-house. Here was something new and worth a detour. We stopped at the door and bade the proprietor "*Gün aydin!*" He promptly rushed forward with two chairs, suggested that we sit outdoors to benefit of the pleasant sun-shine, and asked us how we would like our coffee. (There are five ways of specifying the degree of sweetening one likes in Turkish coffee.) Obviously, this was to be on the house, following the paradoxical Turkish custom of giving gratis to those who can best afford to pay. In a matter of minutes, the male population of Balgat was assembled around our two chairs, squatting, sitting on the ground, looking us over with open and friendly curiosity, peppering Tahir with questions about me.

When our turn came, the hierarchy of respondents was already clear from the axis along which their questions to us had been aligned. Top man was one of the two farmers Tosun had interviewed in 1950. He too was tall, lean, hard. He wore store-clothes with no patches and a sturdy pair of store-shoes. His eyes were Anatolian black and his facial set was much like the Chief's. But his body was more relaxed and his manner more cocky. He sat with his chair titled back and kept his hands calmly dangling alongside. This seemed to excise punctuation from his discourse and he ambled along, in response to any question, with no apparent terminus in view. Interrupting him, even long enough to steer his flow of words in another direction, was—the obvious deference of the whole group toward him constrained us—not easy. His voice was deep and harsh, with the curious suggestion of strangling in the throat that Anatolian talk sometimes has. The content was elusive and little of his discourse made concrete contact with my notebook.

As I review my notes on that tour of monologue-with-choral-murmurs, he appears to have certified the general impression that many changes had occurred in Balgat. His inventory included, at unwholesome length, all the by-now familiar items: road, bus, electricity, water. In his recital these great events did not acquire a negative change, but they lost some of their luster. The tough old farmer did not look shining at new styles of architecture, nor did he look scowling, but simply looked. Under his gaze the new roofs in Balgat were simply new roofs. The wonder that these new roofs were *in Balgat* shone in other eyes and cadenced other voices.

These other voices were finally raised. Either the orator had exhausted the prerogative of his position (he had certainly exhausted Tahir S., whose eyes were glazed and vacant) or the issue was grave enough to sanction discourtesy toward a village elder. The outburst came when the quondam farmer undertook to explain why he was no longer a farmer. He had retired, over a year ago, because there was none left in Balgat to do an honest day's work for an honest day's lira. Or rather two lira (about 36 cents)—the absurd rate, he said, to which the daily wage of farm laborers had been driven by the competition of the voracious Ankara labor market. Now, all the so-called able-bodied men of Balgat had forsaken the natural work praised by Allah and swarmed off to the Ankara factories where, for eight hours of so-called work, they could get five lira a day. As for himself, he would have none of this. Rather than pay men over two lira a day to do the work of men, he had rented out his land to others and retired. He was rich, his family would eat, and others might do as they wished.

The protests that rose did not aim to deny these facts, but simply to justify them. Surprised, we asked whether it was indeed true that there were no farm laborers left in Balgat any more. "How many of you," we quickly rephrased the question, "work on farms now?" Four hands were raised among the 29 present, and all of these turned out to be small holders working their own land. (These four were sitting together and, it later turned out, were the only four members of the *Halk* party among the group, the rest being vigorous *Demokrat* men.)

Galvanized by the intelligence now suddenly put before us (even Tahir S. had reawakened promptly upon discovering that there were hardly any farmers left in Balgat), we started to fire a battery of questions on our own. As this created a din of responding voices, Tahir S.— once again the American-trained interviewer—restored order by asking each man around the circle to tell us, in turn, what he was now working at and how long he had been at it. This impromptu occupational census, began on a leisurely Sunday, was never quite completed. As it became clear that most of the male population of Balgat was now in fact working in the factories and construction gangs of Ankara—for *cash*—our own impatience to move on to our next questions got the better of us.

How did they spend the cash they earned? Well, there were now over 100 radio receivers in Balgat as compared to the lone receiver Tosun had found four years earlier. There were also seven refrigerators, four tractors, three trucks, and one Dodge sedan. Most houses now had electric lights and that had to be paid for. Also, since there was so little farming in Balgat now, much of the food came from outside (even milk!) and had to be brought in the grocery stores, of which there were now seven in Balgat. Why milk? Well, most of the animals had been sold off during the last few years. What about the shepherd? Well, he had moved to a village in the east a year or so ago, as there were no longer any flocks for him to tend. How was the Grocer doing? "Which one?" The original one, the great fat one that was here four years ago? "O that one, he's dead!"

Tahir S. later told me that my expression did not change when the news came (always the American-trained interviewer!). I asked a few more questions in a normal way—"What did he die of?," "How long ago?"—and then let the questioning pass to Tahir. I don't recall what answers came to my questions or to his. I do recall suddenly feeling very weary and, as the talk went on, slightly sick. The feeling got over to Tahir S. and soon we were saying goodbye to the group, feeling relieved that the ritual for leavetaking is less elaborate than for arriving. We promised to return and said our thanks. "*Güle, güle,*" answered those who remained. ("Smile, smile," signifying farewell.)

"What a lousy break," growled Tahir in a tone of reasonable indignation as we started back toward the house of the Chief. He was speaking of the Grocer. I didn't know what to say by way of assent. I felt only a sense of large and diffuse regret, of which indignation was not a distinct component. "Tough," I agreed. As we came up to the Chief's house, I told Tahir we might as well return to Ankara. We had gathered quite a lot of information already and might better spend the afternoon putting it together. We could come back the next day to interview the Chief. The Chief agreed to this plan and invited me to be his guest for lunch next day. Zilla did most of the talking, while Tahir and I listened passively. The driver said only, as I paid him, "I didn't need to bring along my lunch after all."

The Passing of Balgat

While dressing slowly, the next morning, I planned my strategy for lunch with the Chief. Had he learned anything from the Grocer? Clearly his larger clues to the shape of the future had come from Ataturk, whose use of strong measures for humane new goals had impressed him deeply as a young man. But surely he had also responded to the constant stimuli supplied by the Grocer, whose psychic antennae were endlessly *seeking* the new future here and now. The Chief, rather consciously reshaping his ways in the Ataturk image, had to be reckoned a major figure in the Anatolian transformation. But the restless sensibility of the Grocer also had its large, inadequately defined, place. Whereas the masterful Chief had been able to incorporate change mainly by rearranging the environment, the nervous Grocer had been obliged to operate through the more painful process of rearranging himself. Most villagers were closer to his situation than to the Chief's. The Grocer then was my problem and, as symbol of the characterological shift, my man. It was he who dramatized most poignantly the personal meaning of the big change now under way through the Middle East.

I recalled Tosun's unflattering sketch of him as an anxiety-ridden pusher, an "unfarming person" who "even wore some sort of necktie." What had located these details, what had made the Grocer a man I recognized, was Tosun's acid remark: "He most evidently wished to feel that he is closer to me than he is to (other villagers) and was curiously careful with his accent all during the interview." Tosun had seen this as vulgar social climbing, but there was something in this sentence that sounded to me like History. Maybe it was the eighteenth century field-hand of England who had left the manor to find a better life in London or Manchester. Maybe it was the nineteenth century French farm lad, wearied by his father's burdens of *taille* [tax] and *tithe*, who had gone off to San Francisco to hunt gold and, finding none, had then tried his hand as mason, mechanic, printer's devil; though none of these brought him fortune, he wrote home cheerfully (in a letter noted by the prespicacious Karl Marx) about this exciting new city where the chance to try his hand at anything made him feel "less of a mollusk and more of a man." Maybe it was the twentieth century Polish peasant crossing continent and ocean to Detroit, looking for a "better 'ole" in the new land.

The Grocer of Balgat stood for some part of all these figures as he nervously edged his psyche toward Tosun, the young man from the big city. I'm like you, the Grocer might have been feeling, or I'd like to be like you and wish I could get the chance. It was harsh of Tosun, or perhaps only the anti-bourgeois impatience of an austere young scholar looking for the suffering poor in a dreary village, to cold-shoulder this fat and middle-aged man yearning to be comfortably rich in an interesting city. But the Grocer had his own sort of toughness. He had, after all, stood up to the other villagers and had insisted, even when they labeled him infidel, that they ought to get out of their holes. Though dead, he had won an important victory. For the others, despite their outraged virtues, *had* started to come around, once they began to get the feel of Ankara cash, for advice on *how* to get out of their holes. Had they also acquired, along with their new sense of cash some feel for the style of life the Grocer had desired? That was what I wanted to find out in Balgat today.

I walked out of the hotel toward Ulus station, just around the corner. This time I was going to Balgat by bus, to see how the villagers traveled. We crowded into a shiny big bus from Germany that held three times as many passengers as there were seats. The bus was so new that the signs warning the passengers not to smoke or spit or talk to the driver (while the bus is moving) in German, French, and English had not yet been converted into Turkish. There was, in fact, a great deal of smoking and several animated conversations between the driver and various passengers occurred, in the intervals between which the driver chatted with a crony whom he had brought along for just this purpose.

In Balgat I reported directly to the Chief. He appeared, after a few minutes, steaming and mopping his large forehead. He had been pruning some trees and, in this warm weather, such work brought the sweat to his brow. This was about the only work he did any more, he explained, as he had sold or rented most of his land in the last few years, keeping for himself only the ground in which he had planted a small grove of trees that would be his memorial on earth. Islamic peoples regard a growing and "eternal" thing of nature, preferably a tree, as a fitting monument, and a comfortable Muslin of even diffident piety will usually be scrupulous in observing this tradition—a sensible one for a religion of the desert, where vegetation is rare and any that casts a shade is especially prized. The Chief agreed to show me his trees and as we strolled away from the house he resumed his discourse of yesterday.

Things had changed, he repeated, and a sign of the gravity of these changes was that he—of a lineage that had always been *Muhtars* and landowners—was no longer a farmer. Nor was he long to be *Muhtar*. After the coming election, next month, the incorporation of Balgat into Greater Ankara was to be completed and thereafter it would be administered under the general municipal system. "I am the last *Muhtar* of Balgat, and I am happy that I have seen Balgat end its history in this way that we are going." The new ways, then, were not bringing evil with them?

> No, people will have to get used to different ways and then some of the excesses, particularly among the young, will disappear. The young people are in some ways a serious disappointment; they think more of clothes and good times than they do of duty and family and country. But it is to be hoped that as the *Demokrat* men complete the work they have begun, the good Turkish ways will again come forward to steady the people. Meanwhile, it is well that people can have to eat and to buy shoes they always needed but could not have.

And as his two sons were no longer to be farmers, what of them? The Chief's voice did not change, nor did his eyes cloud over, as he replied:

> They are as the others. They think first to serve themselves and not the nation. They had no wish to go to the battle in Korea, where Turkey fights before the eyes of all the world. They are my sons and I speak no ill of them, but I say only that they are as all the others.

I felt at this moment a warmth toward the Chief which I had not supposed he would permit himself to evoke. His sons had not after all, learned to fight bravely and die properly. His aspiration—which had led him, four years earlier, to buy a radio so his sons would hear the Korean war news and to see movies that would make them "wish more and more their time for military service would come"—had not been fulfilled. Yet the old Chief bore stoically what must have been a crushing disappointment. These two sons through whom he had hoped to relive his own bright dreams of glory had instead become *shopkeepers*. The elder son owned a grocery store and the younger one owned Balgat's first clothing store. With this news, curiosity overcame sympathy. I rattled off questions on this subject which, clearly, the Chief would rather have changed. As we turned back to the house, he said we would visit the shops after lunch and his sons would answer all my questions.

Lunch consisted of a huge bowl of yogurt, alongside of which was stacked a foot-high pile of village-style bread, freshly baked by the Chief's wife and served by his younger daughter-in-law. Village bread fresh from the oven is one of the superior tastes that greets a visitor. As I went to work with obvious relish, the Chief suggested that I eat only the "corner" of each sheet. Village bread is baked in huge round double sheets, each about the diameter of a manhole cover and the thickness of a dime. A large glob of shortening is spread loosely around the center between the sheets, which are baked together around the circumference. These sheets are then folded over four times, making the soft buttery center into a "corner." The corner is the prerogative of the male head of the household, who may choose to share it with a favored child. To invite a guest to eat *only* the corners is, in the frugal Anatolian village, a sign of special cordiality that cannot be ignored.

As I chewed my way happily through a half-dozen corners, I wondered who was going to be stuck with my stack of cornerless circumferences. Mama and the daughters-in-law? I asked about the children and learned that, as befits the traditional extended family, the Chief now had nine descendants living under his roof. Moreover, while some were taking to new ways, *his* grandchildren had been and were being swaddled in the traditional Anatolian fashion—for three months a solid mudpack on the body under the swaddling cloths, thereafter for three months a mudless swaddle. (Geoffrey Gorer's association of Russian swaddling with *ochi chornya* [black eyes] seemed due for an Anatolian confirmation, since Turkish eyes are every bit as lustrous black as Slavic eyes.) I glanced up at the large clock on the wall, which had stood firmly at 11:09 since I first entered the room at 9:16 the preceding day. It was clearly intended only as an emblem of social standing. In the very household where swaddling continued, possibly the first clock in Balgat (as once the first radio) had won a place. And though the clock was only decorative rather than useful, yet the hourglass was no longer visible. Times had changed. The Chief noticed my glance and suggested that we could now go out to see the shops of his sons.

We went first to the elder son's store, just across the road and along-side the village "fountain," where Balgat women did the family wash as in ages past (though this would pass when the new municipal water supply became available at reasonable rates). The central floor space was set out with merchandise in the immemorial manner—heavy, rough, anonymous hemp sacks each laden with a commodity requiring no identity card, groats in one and barley in another, here lentils and there chicory. But beyond the sacks was a distinct innovation, a counter. What is more, the counter turned a corner and ran parallel to two sides of the square hut. Built into it was a cash drawer and above each surface a hygienic white porcelain fixture for fluorescent lighting. Along the walls was the crowning glory—rows of shelves running from "top to floor and side to side, and on them standing myriads of round boxes, clean and all the same, dressed like soldiers in a great parade." The Grocer's words of aspiration came leaping back as I looked admiringly around the store. His dream-house had been built in Balgat—in less time than even he might have forecast—and by none other than the Chief!

The irony of the route by which Balgat had entered history accompanied us as we walked in quartet, the Chief and I ahead, the sons behind, to the clothing store of the younger son. This was in the newer part of the village, just across the new road from the "bus station." The entrance to the store was freshly painted dark blue, a color imbued by Muslim lore with power to ward off the evil eye. The stock inside consisted mainly of dungarees, levis, coveralls (looking rather like U.S. Army surplus stocks). There was a continuous and growing demand for these goods, the Chief stated solemnly, as more and more Balgati went into the labor market of Ankara, first discarding their *sholvars* (the billowing knickers of traditional garb in which Western cartoons always still portray the "sultan" in a harem scene). In a corner of the store there was also a small stock of "gentleman's haberdashery"—ready-made suits, shirts, even a rack of neckties.

The younger son, who maintained under his smile of proprietary pleasure a steady silence in the presence of the Chief, replied to a direct question from me that he had as yet sold very few items from this department of the store. One suit had gone to a prospective bridegroom, but the Balgat males by and large were still reticent about wearing store-bought clothes. A few, indeed, had purchased in a *sub rosa* sort of way neckties which remained to be exhibited in public. But wearing them would come, now that several owned them, as soon as an older man was bold enough to wear his first. The owners of the neckties had only to get used to them in private, looking at them now and then, showing them to their wives and elder sons, and some one of them had to show the way. I remembered Tosun's rather nasty comment about the Grocer: "*He even wore some sort of a necktie.*" As one saw it now, the Grocer *had* shown the way, and it was now only a hop, skip and jump through history to the point where most men of Balgat would be wearing neckties.

The Grocer's memory stayed with me all that afternoon, after I had expressed intense satisfaction with the shops, wished the sons good fortune, thanked the Chief again and, with his permission, started out to walk among the alleys and houses of Balgat. On the way, I absently counted 69 radio antennas on the roofs and decided that yesterday's estimate of "over 100" was probably reliable. And only four years ago, I counterpointed to myself, there was but a single battery set in this village. The same theme ran through my recollection of the numbers of tractors, refrigerators, and "unfarming persons." Several of these newly unfarming persons, recognizing their interlocutor of yesterday's coffee-house session, greeted me as I strolled along. One stopped me long enough to deliver his opinion of the Turkish-Pakistani pact (strong affirmation) and to solicit mine of the proposed law to give Americans prospecting rights on Turkish oil (qualified affirmative).

Weary of walking, I turned back to the coffee-house. The ceremony of welcome was warm and the coffee was again on the house. But the conversational group was smaller, this being a workday. Only eleven Balgati appeared to praise the weather and hear my questions. The group got off on politics, with some attention to the general theory of power but more intense interest in hearing each other's predictions of the margin by which the *Demokrat* party would win the elections next month. There was also general agreement, at least among the older men, that it would be better to have a small margin between the major parties. When the parties are competing and need our votes, then they heed our voices—thus ran the underlying proposition of the colloquy. "The villagers have learned the basic lesson of democratic politics," I wrote in my notebook.

The afternoon was about over before I got an appropriate occasion to ask about the Grocer. It came when the talk returned to the villagers' favorite topic of how much better life had become during the past four years of *Demokrat* rule. Again they illustrated the matter by enumerating the new shops in Balgat and the things they had to sell that many people could buy. There was even a new barber shop, opened last month by the son of the late Altemur after going for some time to Ankara as apprentice. "How are these new grocery shops better than the old grocery shop of years ago owned by the fat grocer who is now dead?" I asked. The line of response was obvious in advance, but the question served to lead to another: What sort of man had the Grocer been?

The answers were perfunctory, consisting mainly of *pro forma* expressions of goodwill toward the departed. I tried to get back of these ritual references by indirection. How had the Grocer dressed? Why had he been so interested in the life of Ankara? The light finally shone in one of the wiser heads and he spoke the words I was seeking:

> Ah, he was the cleverest of us all. We did not know it then, but he saw better than all what lay in the path ahead. We have none like this among us now. He was a prophet.

As I look back on it now, my revisit to Balgat ended then. I went back several times, once with gifts for the Chief's grandchildren, another time with my camera (as he had coyly suggested) to take his picture. On these visits I felt less tense, asked fewer questions, than during the earlier visits. The last time I went out with the publisher of a prominent Istanbul newspaper ("The New York Times of Turkey"), a dedicated *Demokrat* man, who was eager to see the transformed village I had described to him. He was enchanted with the Chief, the stores, the bus service and electricity and other symbols of the history into which his party had ushered Balgat. He decided to write a feature story about it and asked permission to call it "Professor Lerner's Village." I declined, less from modesty than a sense of anachronism. The Balgat his party needed was the suburb inhabited by the sons of the Chief, with their swaddled children and their proud new clock, their male "corners" and their retail stores, their filiopietistic silence and their movies that teach excitement. The ancient village I had known for what now seemed only for short years was passing, had passed. The Grocer was dead. The Chief—"the last Muhtar of Balgat"—had reincarnated the Grocer in the flesh of his sons. Tosun was in North Africa studying the Berbers.

ANTON CHEKHOV

The Cherry Orchard

The gamut of emotions aroused by transition from the once cherished order of one epoch to a new order which is welcomed by some but feared and resented by others, can be more vividly portrayed by the poet, the novelist, and the playwright than by the historian, the political scientist, the economist or the sociologist who have of necessity, usually, to limit themselves to "the facts."

Many brilliant examples of such portrayals of emotion can be found in world literature. The reason for selecting scenes from The Cherry Orchard is not only that, to quote the producer Norris Houghton, this play "dramatizes the disintegration of the old order in Russia and the emergence of a new—one oriented toward hardheaded materialism," but that the picture of Chekhov paints of social transition in the Russian setting of the early 1900's has been recognized by writers in other countries, which are undergoing comparable transformations, as applicable to their own conditions. Thus a play which might otherwise have been regarded only as an example of Russian experience has acquired universal significance in non-Western countries, notably Japan, where Chekhov has profoundly affected writers of the post-World War II period, among them the novelist Osamu Dazai, author of the selections from The Setting Sun.

Chekhov, born in 1858, was a physician. He died of tuberculosis in 1904, not long after the first performance of The Cherry Orchard. Although Chekhov always had to struggle with material difficulties, his plays and short stories do not reflect a dark view of life. Chekhov had a sense of humor, a feeling of the beauty of life even amid great sadness, and a belief in the good qualities of human beings, no matter what their weaknesses. Poignant as The Cherry Orchard is, he described it as a comedy.

Characters

MADAME RANEVSKY [LYUBOV ANDREYEVNA], the owner of the Cherry Orchard
ANYA, her daughter, aged 17
VARYA, her adopted daughter, aged 24
GAEV [LEONID ANDREYEVITCH], brother of Madame Ranevsky
LOPAHIN [YERMOLAY ALEXEYEVITCH], a merchant
TROFIMOV [PYOTR SERGEYEVITCH], a student
SEMYONOV-PISHTCHIK, a landowner
CHARLOTTA IVANOVNA, a governess
EPIHODOV [SEMYON PANTALEYEVITCH], a clerk
DUNYASHA, a maid
FIRS, an old valet, aged 87
YASHA, a young valet
A WAYFARER
THE STATION MASTER
A POST-OFFICE CLERK
VISITORS, SERVANTS

The action takes place on the estate of MADAME RANEVSKY.

Act 1

A room, which has always been called the nursery. One of the doors leads into ANYA's room. Dawn, sun rises during the scene. May, the cherry trees in flower, but it is cold in the garden with the frost of early morning. Windows closed. . . .

From The Cherry Orchard by Anton Chekhov. Translated by Constance Garnett. Chatto & Windus, Ltd., London. Reprinted by permission.

LYUBOV: Can it really be me sitting here? [*Laughs.*] I want to dance about and clap my hands. [*Covers her face with her hands.*] And I could drop asleep in a moment! God knows I love my country, I love it tenderly; I couldn't look out of the window in the train, I kept crying so. [*Through her tears.*] But I must drink my coffee, though. Thank you, Firs, thanks, dear old man. I'm so glad to find you still alive.

FIRS: The day before yesterday.

GAEV: He's rather deaf.

LOPAHIN: I have to set off for Harkov directly, at five o'clock. . . . It is annoying! I wanted to have a look at you, and a little talk. . . . You are just as splendid as ever.

PISHTCHIK [*breathing heavily*]: Handsomer, indeed. . . . Dressed in Parisian style . . . completely bowled me over.

LOPAHIN: Your brother, Leonid Andreyevitch here, is always saying that I'm a low-born knave, that I'm a money-grubber, but I don't care one straw for that. Let him talk. Only I do want you to believe in me as you used to. I do want your wonderful tender eyes to look at me as they used to in the old days. Merciful God! My father was a serf of your father and of your grandfather, but you—you—did so much for me once, that I've forgotten all that; I love you as though you were my kin . . . more than my kin.

LYUBOV: I can't sit still, I simply can't. . . . [*Jumps up and walks about in violent agitation.*] This happiness is too much for me. . . . You may laugh at me, I know I'm silly. . . . My own bookcase. [*Kisses the bookcase.*] My little table.

GAEV: Nurse died while you were away.

LYUBOV [*sits down and drinks coffee*]: Yes, the Kingdom of Heaven be hers! You wrote me of her death.

GAEV: And Anastasy is dead. Squinting Petruchka has left me and is in service now with the police captain in the town. [*Takes a box of caramels out of his pocket and sucks one.*]

PISHTCHIK: My daughter, Dashenka, wishes to be remembered to you.

LOPAHIN: I want to tell you something very pleasant and cheering. [*Glancing at his watch.*] I'm going directly . . . there's no time to say much . . . well, I can say it in a couple of words. I needn't tell you your cherry orchard is to be sold to pay your debts; the 22nd of August is the date fixed for the sale; but don't you worry, dearest lady, you may sleep in peace, there is a way of saving it. . . . This is what I propose. I beg your attention! Your estate is not twenty miles from the town, the railway runs close by it, and if the cherry orchard and the land along the river bank were cut up into building plots and then let on lease for summer villas, you would make an income of at least 25,000 rubles a year out of it.

GAEV: That's all rot, if you'll excuse me.

LYUBOV: I don't quite understand you, Yermolay Alexeyevitch.

LOPAHIN: You will get a rent of at least twenty-five rubles a year for a three-acre plot from summer visitors, and if you say the word now, I'll bet you what you like there won't be one square foot of ground vacant by the autumn, all the plots will be taken up. I congratulate you; in fact, you are saved. It's a perfect situation with that deep river. Only, of course, it must be cleared—all the old buildings, for example, must be removed, this house too, which is really good for nothing, and the old cherry orchard must be cut down.

LYUBOV: Cut down? My dear fellow, forgive me, but you don't know what you are talking about. If there is one thing interesting—remarkable indeed—in the whole province, it's just our cherry orchard.

LOPAHIN: The only thing remarkable about the orchard is that it's a very large one. There's a crop of cherries every alternate year, and then there's nothing to be done with them, no one buys them.

GAEV: This orchard is mentioned in the *Encyclopœdia*.

LOPAHIN [*glancing at his watch*]: If we don't decide on something and don't take some steps, on the 22nd of August the cherry orchard and the whole estate too will be sold by auction. Make up your minds! There is no other way of saving it, I'll take my oath on that. No, No!

FIRS: In the old days, forty or fifty years ago, they used to dry the cherries, soak them, pickle them, make jam too, and they used—

GAEV: Be quiet, Firs.

FIRS: And they used to send the preserved cherries to Moscow and to Markov by the wagon-load. That brought the money in! And the preserved cherries in those days were soft and juicy, sweet and fragrant. . . . They knew the way to do them then. . . .

LYUBOV: And where is the recipe now?

FIRS: It's forgotten. Nobody remembers it.

PISHTCHIK [*to* LYUBOV ANDREYEVNA]: What's it like in Paris? Did you eat frogs there?

LYUBOV: Oh, I ate crocodiles.

PISHTCHIK: Fancy that now!

LOPAHIN: There used to be only the gentlefolk and the peasants in the country, but now there are these summer visitors. All the towns, even the small ones, are surrounded, nowadays by these summer villas. And one may say for sure, that in another twenty years there'll be many more of these people and that they'll be everywhere. At present the summer visitor only drinks tea in his veranda, but maybe he'll take to working his bit of land too, and then your cherry orchard would become happy, rich and prosperous. . . .

GAEV [*indignant*]: What rot! . . .

GAEV [opens another window]: The orchard is all white. You've not forgotten it, Lyuba? That long avenue that runs straight, straight as an arrow, how it shines on a moonlight night. You remember? You've not forgotten?

LYUBOV [looking out of the window into the garden]: Oh, my childhood, my innocence! It was in this nursery I used to sleep, from here I looked out into the orchard, happiness waked with me every morning and in those days the orchard was just the same, nothing has changed. [Laughs with delight.] All, all white! Oh, my orchard! After the dark gloomy autumn, and the cold winter; you are young again and full of happiness, the heavenly angels have never left you. . . . If I could cast off the burden that weighs on my heart, if I could forget the past!

GAEV: H'm! and the orchard will be sold to pay our debts; it seems strange. . . .

LYUBOV: See, our mother walking . . . all in white, down the avenue! [Laughs with delight.] It is she!

GAEV: Where?

VARYA: Oh, don't, mamma!

LYUBOV: There is no one. It was my fancy. On the right there, by the path to the arbor, there is a white tree bending like a woman. . . .

[Enter TROFIMOV wearing a shabby student's uniform and spectacles.]

LYUBOV: What a ravishing orchard! White masses of blossom, blue sky. . . .

TROFIMOV: Lyubov Andreyevna! [She looks round at him.] I will just pay my respects to you and then leave you at once. [Kisses her hand warmly.] I was told to wait until morning, but I hadn't the patience to wait any longer. . . .

Act 2

The open country. An old shrine, long abandoned and fallen out of the perpendicular; near it a well, large stones that have apparently once been tombstones, and an old garden seat. The road to GAEV's house is seen. On one side rise dark poplars; and there the cherry orchard begins. In the distance a row of telegraph poles and far, far away on the horizon there is faintly outlined a great town, only visible in very fine clear weather. It is near sunset. . . .

[Enter LYUBOV ANDREYEVNA, GAEV and LOPAHIN.]

LOPAHIN: You must make up your mind once for all—there's no time to lose. It's quite a simple question, you know. Will you consent to letting the land for building or not? One word in answer: Yes or no? Only one word!

LYUBOV: Who is smoking such horrible cigars here? [*Sits down.*]

GAEV: Now the railway line has been brought near, it's made things very convenient. [*Sits down.*] Here we have been over and lunched in town. Cannon off the white! I should like to go home and have a game.

LYUBOV: You have plenty of time.

LOPAHIN: Only one word! [*Beseechingly.*] Give me an answer!

GAEV [*yawning*]: What do you say?

LYUBOV [*looks in her purse*]: I had quite a lot of money here yesterday, and there's scarcely any left today. My poor Varya feeds us all on milk soup for the sake of economy; the old folks in the kitchen get nothing but pease pudding, while I waste my money in a senseless way. [*Drops purse, scattering gold pieces.*] There, they have all fallen out! [*Annoyed.*]

YASHA: Allow me. I'll soon pick them up. [*Collects the coins.*] . . .

LOPAHIN: Deriganov, the millionaire, means to buy your estate. They say he is coming to the sale himself.

LYUBOV: Where did you hear that?

LOPAHIN: That's what they say in town.

GAEV: Our aunt in Yaroslavl has promised to send help; but when, and how much she will send, we don't know.

LOPAHIN: How much will she send? A hundred thousand? Two hundred?

LYUBOV: Oh, well! . . . Ten or fifteen thousand, and we must be thankful to get that.

LOPAHIN: Forgive me, but such reckless people as you are—such queer, unbusinesslike people—I never met in my life. One tells you in plain Russian your estate is going to be sold, and you seem not to understand it.

LYUBOV: What are we to do? Tell us what to do.

LOPAHIN: I do tell you every day. Every day I say the same thing. You absolutely must let the cherry orchard and the land on building leases; and do it at once, as quick as may be—the auction's close upon us! Do understand! Once make up your mind to build villas, and you can raise as much money as you like, and then you are saved.

LYUBOV: Villas and summer visitors—forgive me saying so—it's so vulgar.

GAEV: There I perfectly agree with you.

LOPAHIN: I shall sob, or scream, or fall into a fit. I can't stand it! You drive me mad! [*To* GAEV.] You're an old woman!

GAEV: What do you say?

LOPAHIN: An old woman! [*Gets up to go.*]

LYUBOV [in dismay]: No, don't go! Do stay, my dear friend! Perhaps we shall think of something.

LOPAHIN: What is there to think of?

LYUBOV: Don't go, I entreat you! With you here it's more cheerful, anyway. [A pause.] I keep expecting something, as though the house were going to fall about our ears.

GAEV [in profound dejection]: Potted the white! It fails—a kiss.

LYUBOV: We have been great sinners. . . .

LOPAHIN: You have no sins to repent of.

GAEV [puts a caramel in his mouth]: They say I've eaten up my property in caramels. [Laughs.]

LYUBOV: Oh, my sins! I've always thrown my money away recklessly like a lunatic. I married a man who made nothing but debts. My husband died of champagne—he drank dreadfully. To my misery I loved another man, and immediately—it was my first punishment—the blow fell upon me, here, in the river . . . my boy was drowned and I went abroad—went away forever, never to return, not to see that river again . . . I shut my eyes, and fled, distracted, and he after me . . . pitilessly, brutally. I bought a villa at Mentone, for he fell ill there, and for three years I had no rest day or night. His illness wore me out, my soul was dried up. And last year, when my villa was sold to pay my debts, I went to Paris and there he robbed me of everything and abandoned me for another woman; and I tried to poison myself. . . . So stupid, so shameful! . . . And suddenly I felt a yearning for Russia, for my country, for my little girl. . . . [Dries her tears.] Lord, Lord, be merciful! Forgive my sins! Do not chastise me more! [Takes a telegram out of her pocket.] I got this today from Paris. He implores forgiveness, entreats me to return. [Tears up the telegram.] I fancy there is music somewhere. [Listens.]

GAEV: That's our famous Jewish orchestra. You remember, four violins, a flute and a double bass.

LYUBOV: That still in existence? We ought to send for them one evening, and give a dance.

LOPAHIN [listens]: I can't hear. . . . [Hums softly.] "For money the Germans will turn a Russian into a Frenchman." [Laughs.] I did see such a piece at the theater yesterday! It was funny!

LYUBOV: And most likely there was nothing funny in it. You shouldn't look at plays, you should look at yourselves a little oftener. How gray your lives are! How much nonsense you talk.

LOPAHIN: That's true. One may say honestly, we live a fool's life. [Pause.] My father was a peasant, an idiot; he knew nothing and taught me nothing, only beat me when he was drunk, and always with his stick.

In reality I am just such another blockhead and idiot. I've learnt nothing properly. I write a wretched hand. I write so that I feel ashamed before folks, like a pig. . . .

[*Enter* TROFIMOV *and* ANYA]

TROFIMOV: Humanity progresses, perfecting its powers. Everything that is beyond its ken now will one day become familiar and comprehensible; only we must work, we must with all our powers aid the seeker after truth. Here among us in Russia the workers are few in number as yet. The vast majority of the intellectual people I know, seek nothing, do nothing, are not fit as yet for work of any kind. They call themselves intellectual, but they treat their servants as inferiors, behave to the peasants as though they were animals, learn little, read nothing seriously, do practically nothing, only talk about science and know very little about art. They are all serious people, they all have severe faces, they all talk of weighty matters and air their theories, and yet the vast majority of us —ninety-nine per cent—live like savages, at the least thing fly to blows and abuse, eat piggishly, sleep in filth and stuffiness, bugs everywhere, stench and damp and moral impurity. And it's clear all our fine talk is only to divert our attention and other people's. Show me where to find the *crèches* there's so much talk about, and the reading-rooms? They only exist in novels: in real life there are none of them. There is nothing but filth and vulgarity and Asiatic apathy. I fear and dislike very serious faces. I'm afraid of serious conversation. We should do better to be silent.

LOPAHIN: You know, I get up at five o'clock in the morning, and I work from morning to night; and I've money, my own and other people's, always passing through my hands, and I see what people are made of all round me. One has only to begin to do anything to see how few honest decent people there are. Sometimes when I lie awake at night, I think: "Oh! Lord, thou hast given us immense forests, boundless plains, the widest horizons, and living here we ourselves ought really to be giants."

LYUBOV: You ask for giants! They are no good except in story-books; in real life they frighten us.

[EPIHODOV *advances in the background, playing on the guitar.*]

LYUBOV [*dreamily*]: There goes Epihodov.

ANYA [*dreamily*]: There goes Epihodov.

GAEV: The sun has set, my friends.

TROFIMOV: Yes.

GAEV [*not loudly, but, as it were, declaiming*]: O nature, divine nature, thou art bright with eternal luster, beautiful and indifferent! Thou, whom we call mother, thou does unite within thee life and death! Thou dost give life and dost destroy! . . .

Act 3

A drawing room divided by an arch from a larger drawing room. A chandelier burning. The Jewish orchestra, the same that was mentioned in Act 2, is heard playing in the anteroom. It is evening. In the larger drawing room they are dancing the grand chain. The voice of SEMYONOV-PISHTCHIK: "Promenade à une paire!" Then enter the drawing room in couples, first PISHTCHIK and CHARLOTTA IVANOVNA, then TROFIMOV and LYUBOV ANDREYEVNA, thirdly ANYA with the POST-OFFICE CLERK, fourthly VARYA with the STATION MASTER, and other guests. VARYA is quietly weeping and wiping away her tears as she dances. In the last couple is DUNYASHA. They move across the drawing room. PISHTCHIK shouts: "Grand rond, balancez!" and "Les Cavaliers à genou et remerciez vos dames."

FIRS in a swallow-tail coat brings in seltzer water on a tray. . . .

LOPAHIN [embarrassed, afraid of betraying his joy]: The sale was over at four o'clock. We missed our train—had to wait till half-past nine. [Sighing heavily.] Ugh! I feel a little giddy.

[Enter GAEV. In his right hand he has purchases, with his left hand he is wiping away his tears.]

LYUBOV: Well, Leonid? What news? [Impatiently, with tears.] Make haste, for God's sake!

GAEV [makes her no answer, simply waves his hand. To FIRS, weeping]: Here, take them; there's anchovies, Kertch herrings. I have eaten nothing all day. What I have been through! [Door into the billiard room is open. There is heard a knocking of balls and the voice of YASHA saying "Eighty-seven." GAEV's expression changes, he leaves off weeping.] I am fearfully tired. Firs, come and help me change my things. [Goes to his own room across the larger drawing room.]

PISHTCHIK: How about the sale? Tell us, do!

LYUBOV: Is the cherry orchard sold?

LOPAHIN: It is sold.

LYUBOV: Who has bought it?

LOPAHIN: I have bought it.

[A pause. LYUBOV is crushed; she would fall down if she were not standing near a chair and table. VARYA takes keys from her waistband, flings them on the floor in middle of drawing room and goes out.]

LOPAHIN: I have bought it! Wait a bit, ladies and gentlemen, pray. My head's a bit muddled, I can't speak. [*Laughs.*] We came to the auction. Deriganov was there already. Leonid Andreyevitch only had 15,000 and Deriganov bid 30,000, besides the arrears, straight off. I saw how the land lay. I bid against him. I bid 40,000, he bid 45,000, I said 55, and so he went on, adding 5 thousands and I adding 10. Well . . . So it ended. I bid 90, and it was knocked down to me. Now the cherry orchard's mine! Mine! [*Chuckles.*] My God, the cherry orchard's mine! Tell me that I'm drunk, that I'm out of my mind, that it's all a dream. [*Stamps with his feet.*] Don't laugh at me! If my father and my grandfather could rise from their graves and see all that has happened! How their Yermolay, ignorant, beaten Yermolay, who used to run about barefoot in winter, how that very Yermolay has bought the finest estate in the world! I have bought the estate where my father and grandfather were slaves, where they weren't even admitted into the kitchen. I am asleep, I am dreaming! It is all fancy, it is the work of your imagination plunged in the darkness of ignorance. [*Picks up keys, smiling fondly.*] She threw away the keys; she means to show she's not the housewife now. [*Jingles the keys.*] Well, no matter. [*The orchestra is heard tuning up.*] Hey, musicians! Play! I want to hear you. Come all of you, and look how Yermolay Lopahin will take the ax to the cherry orchard, how the trees will fall to the ground! We will build houses on it and our grandsons and great-grandsons will see a new life springing up there. Music! Play up!

[*Music begins to play.* LYUBOV ANDREYEVNA *has sunk into a chair and is weeping bitterly.*]

LOPAHIN [*reproachfully*]: Why, why didn't you listen to me? My poor friend! Dear lady, there's no turning back now. [*With tears.*] Oh, if all this could be over, oh, if our miserable disjointed life could somehow soon be changed!

PISHTCHIK [*takes him by the arm, in an undertone*]: She's weeping, let us go and leave her alone. Come. [*Takes him by the arm and leads him into the larger drawing room.*]

LOPAHIN: What's that? Musicians, play up! All must be as I wish it. [*With irony.*] Here comes the new master, the owner of the cherry orchard! [*Accidentally tips over a little table, almost upsetting the candelabra.*] I can pay for everything!

[*Goes out with* PISHTCHIK. *No one remains on the stage or in the larger drawing room except* LYUBOV, *who sits huddled up, weeping bitterly. The music plays softly.* ANYA *and* TROFIMOV *come in quickly.* ANYA *goes up to her mother and falls on her knees before her.* TROFIMOV *stands at the entrance to the larger drawing room.*]

ANYA: Mamma! Mamma, you're crying, dear, kind, good mamma! My precious! I love you! I bless you! The cherry orchard is sold, it is gone, that's true, that's true! But don't weep, mamma! Life is still before you, you have still your good, pure heart! Let us go, let us go, darling, away from here! We will make a new garden, more splendid than this one; you will see it, you will understand. And joy, quiet, deep joy, will sink into your soul like the sun at evening! And you will smile, mamma! Come, darling, let us go!

OSAMU DAZAI

The Setting Sun

In Japan, where industrialization has transformed a once feudal society into the most technologically advanced country of the non-Western world within the span of a century, the transition from the old agrarian order to the new industrial society portrayed by Chekhov is still under way. The heroine of The Setting Sun, Kazuko, daughter of an impoverished aristocratic family, trying to find her place in the new society, describes herself and those around her as "victims of a transitional period in morality." Donald Keene, translator of The Setting Sun, says that this novel, which created an immediate sensation when it first appeared in 1947, "derives much of its power from its portrayal of the ways in which the new ideas have destroyed the Japanese aristocracy." The phrase "people of the setting sun," applied to the whole of the declining aristocracy, has passed into common usage and even into dictionaries.

According to Keene, Dazai is "not only the storyteller, but a participant in the story he tells." Born in 1909 of a rich and powerful family of the north of Japan, he was a brilliant but erratic student, and had twice attempted suicide before he was twenty. He became concerned with Left-wing political activities and, in spite of a chronic chest ailment and unhappiness in love, worked hard at his writing. He continued to publish during the war, but his most outstanding works, including The Setting Sun, appeared after 1945. However, the tuberculosis from which he had suffered recurred again; and in June, 1948 he committed suicide by throwing himself into a Tokyo reservoir.

Selections

page 131

Mother did not appear in any pain as she lay there. She had not taken any food since morning, and all I had done was to moisten her lips occasionally with gauze soaked in tea. However, she was quite conscious and spoke to me from time to time in a composed tone. "I seem to recall having seen a picture of the Emperor in the newspaper. I'd like to look at it again."

I held that section of the newspaper above Mother's face.

"He's grown old."

"No, it's a poor photograph. In the photographs they printed the other day he seemed really young and cheerful. He probably is happier these days than ever."

"Why?"

"The Emperor has been liberated too."

Mother smiled sadly and said, "Even when I want to cry, the tears don't come any more."

pages 70–71

[Kazuko's brother, Naoji, keeps a notebook]

When I pretended to be precocious, people started the rumor that I was precocious. When I acted like an idler, rumor had it I was an idler. When I pretended I couldn't write a novel, people said I couldn't write. When I acted like a liar, they called me a liar. When I acted like a rich man, they started the rumor I was rich. When I feigned indifference, they classed me as the indifferent type. But when I inadvertently groaned because I was really in pain, they started the rumor that I was faking suffering.

The world is out of joint.

page 38

I began from the following day to devote my energies to working in the fields. Mr. Nakai's daughter sometimes helps me. Ever since my disgraceful act of having started a fire, I have felt somehow as if the color of my blood has turned a little darker, as if I am becoming every day more of an uncouth country girl. When, for instance, I sit on the porch knitting with Mother, I feel strangely cramped and choked, and it comes as a relief when I go out into the fields to dig the earth.

Manual labor, I suppose one would call it. This is not the first time I've done such work. I was conscripted during the war and even made to do coolie labor. The sneakers I now wear when I work in the fields are the ones the Army issued me. That was the first time in my life I had put such things on my feet, but they were surprisingly comfortable, and when I walked around the garden wearing them I felt as if I could understand the light-heartedness of the bird or animal that walks barefoot on the ground. That is the only pleasant memory I have of the war. What a dreary business the war was.

> Last year nothing happened
> The year before nothing happened
> And the year before that nothing happened.

An amusing poem to this effect appeared in a newspaper just after the war ended. Of course all kinds of things actually did take place, but when I try to recall them now, I experience that same feeling that nothing happened. I hate talking about the war or listening to other people's memories. Many people died, I know, but it was still a dreary business, and it bores me now. I suppose you might say I take a very egocentric view of it . . .

pages 119–120

. . . The porch blinds, which I had rolled up a couple of days earlier, clattered in the wind. I sat in the room next to Mother's, reading with a strange agitation Rosa Luxemburg's *Introduction to Economics*. I had borrowed this book from Naoji's room (without his permission, naturally) along with the *Selected Works of Lenin* and Kautsky's *Social Revolution*. I had left them on my desk. One morning when Mother passed beside my desk on her way to the bath, she happened to notice the three volumes. She picked them up one after another, examined the contents, and then, with a little sigh, returned them softly to the desk. She glanced at me sorrowfully as she did so. A profound grief filled her look, but it was by no means one of rejection or antipathy. Mother's chosen reading matter is Hugo, Dumas père et fils [father and son], Musset, and Daudet, but I know that even such books of sweet romances are permeated with the smell of revolution.

People like Mother who possess a Heaven-given education—the words are peculiar I know—may perhaps be able to welcome a revolution in a surprisingly matter-of-fact way, as a quite natural occurrence. Even I found some things rather objectionable when I read Rosa Luxemburg's book, but, given the sort of person I am, the experience on the whole was one of profound interest. The subject matter of her book is generally considered to be economics, but if it is read as economics, it is boring beyond belief. It contains nothing but exceedingly obvious platitudes. It may be, of course, that I have no understanding of economics. Be that as it may, the subject holds not the slightest interest for me. A science which is postulated on the assumption that human beings are avaricious and will remain avaricious through all eternity is utterly devoid of point (whether in problems of distribution or any other aspect) to a person who is not avaricious. And yet as I read this book, I felt a strange excitement for quite another reason—the sheer courage the author demonstrated in tearing apart with any hesitation all manner of conventional ideas. . . . Destruction is tragic and piteous and beautiful. The dream of destroying, building anew, perfecting. Perhaps even, once one has destroyed, the day of perfecting may never come, but in the passion of love I must destroy. I must start a revolution. Rosa gave tragically her undivided love to Marxism.

page 122

Twelve years have passed and I have yet to progress beyond the *Sarashina Diary* stage. What in the world have I been doing all this time? I have never felt myself drawn toward revolution, and I have not even known love. The older and wiser heads of the world have always described revolution and love to us as the two most foolish and loathsome of human activities. Before the war, even during the war, we were convinced of it. Since the defeat, however, we no longer trust the older and wiser heads and have come to feel that the opposite of whatever they say is the real truth about life.

page 90

[*Kazuko writes a love letter addressed to a married man, friend of her brother, whom she calls "My Chekhov. M.C."*]

No answer has come from you, and I am writing again . . . I imagine that you thought that my purpose was merely to elicit money from you to save my life. I don't deny this. However, I would like you to know, if you'll excuse me for saying so, that if my only wish was for a patron I should not have chosen you especially. I have the impression that quite a few rich old men would be willing to care for me. As a matter of fact, not long ago I had something like a proposal. You may even know the gentleman's name—he is a widower over sixty, a member of the Academy of Arts, I believe; this great artist came here to the mountains in order to ask my hand . . .

I sent my letter of refusal to the artist at his villa in the Japan Alps. Two days later he turned up without warning, having no knowledge of my answer because he had left before my letter reached him . . . I said while pouring tea, "I imagine that my letter of refusal must have reached your house by now. I carefully considered your offer, but it somehow didn't seem possible."

"Indeed?" he said with some impatience. He wiped away the perspiration. "I hope that you will reconsider. Perhaps I can't—how shall I say—give you what might be called spiritual happiness, but I can on the other hand make you very happy in a material way. That at least I can assure you. I hope I don't speak too bluntly . . ."

The artist suddenly spoke, his voice edged with spite, "I've heard a rumor that you are selling the house. I wonder if it's true." I laughed. "Excuse me, but I just remembered *The Cherry Orchard*. I suppose you would like to buy it?"

He twisted his mouth in an angry scowl and did not answer. Artist that he was, he was quick to guess my meaning.

It was true that there had been talk of selling the house to a prince, but it had never come to anything, and I was surprised that the artist had even heard the rumor. But that we should have been thinking of him in terms of Lopakhin in *The Cherry Orchard* was so distasteful that he quite lost his good humor, and after a few minutes more of small talk, he left.

What I ask of you now is not that you be a Lopakhin. That much I can warrant you. But please listen . . .

pages 186–187

[*Again Kazuko writes to "M.C."*]
I presume that since last we met you have been continuing your life of decadence or whatever it is called, drinking with the ladies and gentlemen to the tune of "Guillotine, guillotine." I have no intention of suggesting that you give that life up. It will, after all, most likely be the form your last struggle takes.

I no longer have the desire to say, "Give up your drinking, take care of your health, lead a long life, carry through your splendid career," or any of the other hypocritical injunctions. For all I know, you may earn the gratitude of later people more by recklessly pursuing your life of vice than by your "splendid career."

Victims. Victims of a transitional period of morality. That is what we both certainly are.

EDWARD A. SHILS

The Intellectual Between Tradition and Modernity

*Intellectuals have played an extraordinarily active role in the forma-
tion of modern non-Western nations. The outstanding leaders of
these countries have been drawn from the ranks of lawyers, teachers, doctors, writers, as well as from the armed forces in which, particularly in the Middle East and Latin America, many have had a
better opportunity than most of their fellow citizens to receive an
education. Lenin and Trotsky, Gandhi and Nehru, U Nu, Nasser
and Ayub Khan, to name only a few, all in one way or another had
had an opportunity to study and analyze the problems of their
countries before they started translating their ideas into practice
after their nations had achieved independence.*

*Professor Shils believes that one reason for the outstanding role
played by intellectuals in non-Western countries is that there was
practically no one else who could assume leadership. But another,
and perhaps more important reason, he points out, is that intellectuals had "a special calling from within, a positive impetus from
without." Their aspirations and contributions are summarized in
this introduction to a brief study Professor Shils wrote on the role
of intellectuals in India.*

*Edward A. Shils is professor of sociology and social thought in
the Committee on Social Thought at the University of Chicago,
and a Fellow of King's College, Cambridge. He has translated works
by Max Weber and Karl Mannheim, and is the author of several
books, among them* The Torment of Secrecy: The Background and
Consequences of American Security Policies, *1956.*

Introduction

I

THE modern intellectual—the independent man of letters, the scientist,
pure and applied, the scholar, the university professor, the journalist,

From *The Intellectual Between Tradition and Modernity: The Indian Situation* by
   Edward Shils (Comparative Studies in Society and History, Supplement I).
   Mouton & Co. N. V., The Hague.

317

the highly educated administrator, judge or parliamentarian—has not come into the world without ancestors. Nearly every section of the modern intellectual class has its prototypes in ancient and medieval European society and in the great traditional kingdoms and empires of the Near and Far East. Nonetheless, the modern intellectual class in all its elaboration is a unique historical phenomenon. It is the product of a modern society, latterly of an industrial society characterized by rational, bureaucratic administration in the state and in economic life, widespread literacy and a high standard of living, an extensive educational system with widespread participation and at its peak a university system devoted to the cultivation of truth in science and scholarship as well as to the transmission of the cultural heritage and to the training of persons for the professions of law, engineering, medicine and the service of state, church and economic life.

The culture of the modern Western intellectual is a culture which has taken the earth and the cosmos as its concerns. It has grown out of the culture and society of the West, and although it has drawn sustenance and inspiration from Asia and North Africa, and treats the problems of all the world, it has grown by a slow dialectical evolution out of the traditions and situations of its own society. However differentiated the social structure and the cultural pattern of the West have become, however intricate the intertwinement and multifarious the strands of its own traditions, they are their own—fully their own. Marxism and conservatism, agnosticism and Catholicism, scientism and traditionalism are all variants of a pattern which Western development has engendered and supported.

In the past century and a half, this Western culture has flowed beyond the boundaries of the European territories and the populations of European origin into far-off lands, the homes of cultures with their own separate histories, their own patterns of autonomous evolution. The story of the spread of the West into Asia and Africa has been told many times and in much detail. What is essential in this story is the dominion of the West over Asia and Africa. Except in Japan, Thailand, Ethiopia, Iran and China, quasi-political, administrative structures were formed in which there was little trace of indigenous sovereignty. Of the exceptions, only Japan maintained an effectively autonomous sovereignty. What is more important for our present purpose is that none of the countries, including Japan, maintained its cultural autonomy. All of them, insofar as they did not rusticate almost entirely in the backwater of archaic autocracy, came under the cultural hegemony of the West. Partly because the West was so powerful and because power always radiates its own inherent charisma, and partly because the service of authority is always positively prized—especially so in traditionally hierarchical societies—Western forms of education and certain features of Western intellectual culture became established in narrow circles of Asian and African societies. In coming to resemble the West in certain respects, the countries of Asia and Africa have done so very unevenly. Except for Japan, which has become a modern industrial society, the countries of Asia and Africa have remained predominantly agrarian, i.e., most of their national income is produced in agriculture, most of their working population works in agriculture. This rural population has not remained untouched by the Western impact on their countries, but the fundamental institutions of the rural society have withstood this impact. Religion and kinship—the two bases of strong traditional values —have held their own and exuded from their own folds an aroma which has given tone to the rest of the society. The societies of Asia and Africa have remained traditional societies—omitting for the present industrial Japan and Soviet China, where an energetic elite seeks to extirpate religion and kinship, those two seeds of traditional society.

II

Within societies enfolded in traditional beliefs and practices, there now exist states where the elites, intellectual, political, administrative, aspire to modernity. Whether this modernity be liberal, democratic or autocratic is immaterial at this point. What is significant is that the intellectual elites adhere to elements of cultural patterns which, whether they are potentially harmonious with the autochthonous traditional cultural pattern or not, are not at present actually harmonious with those traditions. The elements of the modern cultural pattern have been generated in a different tradition in another part of the world. Various parts of the content of this tradition have been assimilated by the intellectual elites of Asia and Africa. Some of the intellectuals in these countries have become creative within that tradition so that to that extent it has ceased to be a tradition which is subjectively experienced as foreign and has in fact become their own. Nonetheless, even they, in present political circumstances, are not permitted to forget its foreign origins and connections. The "foreignness" of modern intellectual culture has been rendered more emphatic by the fact that, except for Japan and, to a lesser extent, China, the language of modern culture, the language in which modern education was acquired and through which modern intellectual culture is expressed has been a foreign language.

For this reason, the intellectuals of Asian and African societies have come in varying degrees to regard themselves as disjoined from their own traditional cultures and to depend for their modern cultural sustenance on the intellectual output which emanates from metropolises located outside their own countries. Asia and Africa have in consequence been pushed, in the course of the past one and a half centuries, into a condition of provinciality *vis-à-vis* the great cultural capitals of the Western world—London, Oxford, Cambridge, Paris, Leiden, Utrecht, Berlin, New York, etc. The characteristics of provinciality within a single country have been manifested in this international provinciality. Preoccupation with the cultural products of the capital, fascination by them, resentment against them, have been the concomitants of this relationship—and even the most creative minds of this period in the countries at the peripheries of the dominant West have been unable to free themselves from it. Dostoyevski, Henry James, Tagore, Tanizaki and numerous less forceful spirits have in one form or another been enmeshed in this magnetic net. The alternatives have been either the common type of provincial smugness and ignorant indifference or, where there has been no autochthonous culture which offered any significant competition, as in science, complete and unquestioning acceptance of the standards and procedures of the West. Even in a field of intellectual effort like that of the modern scientific enterprise with a great apostolic succession and a tradition so strong and so compelling that it could engage creative minds and satisfy their needs, the tension of province and capital has been a major problem. Especially so where, as in literature and philosophy and religion, the past accomplishments of the provincial society have been very great indeed. The problem has been much more severe where there has been a great tradition of cultural achievement, thanks to the mastery of the art of writing and the formation of a differentiated specialized intellectual class which was the custodian of the written monuments. It has probably been less severe in societies where there is no written history, no written literary and philosophical religious monuments, as in Africa, which could continually call for the attention of the educated classes, and tacitly assert their claims to the loyalties and studies of the intellectuals. But even these latter societies have not been free of this tension between metropolis and province because even there the educated classes are raised in a domestic atmosphere which is full of the traditional autochthonous culture.

The strain has been aggravated by the emergence of a sense of nationality and its deepening and strengthening, where it existed earlier in a rudimentary form. The first bearers of the idea of nationality, the first to assert the argument against foreign dominance, have been the intellectuals. The main bearers of the struggle for national autonomy have been the educated classes, the classes educated by Western institutions, at home or in the West, and formed in part by Western culture. The Westernized intellectuals have not maintained a monopoly over the movement for the establishment of national sovereignty, but their preponderance in that movement has been an almost universal phenomenon.

This, too, has generated a problem for the modern intellectuals of Asian and African countries. On the one hand they have been intensely drawn to the products of a culture which is foreign to most of the historical past and to most of the population of their own society; and on the other hand they have asserted the claims of their society to autonomy. The very form of autonomy which they seek and the mode in which they would organize is foreign to their cultural traditions. The manner in which they sought to establish the claims of their society to universal respect—through "modernity," which means industry, rational administration, applied science and modern education—is of foreign inspiration. This promotion of modernity through the establishment and operation of a national state has thrown them into conflict not only with the traditional intellectual culture of their own society, in which many of them participate at least in spirit if not according to letter, but also with the living traditional institutions of their own society. However modern the intellectual culture of most of the intellectuals of the societies of Africa and Asia, most of them live their lives in a vital domestic culture of kinship, tribe and religious outlook which makes them aware of their past and of the difference of that past from the modern intellectual culture which they espouse.

III

The leaders of the states of Asia and Africa, both the new ones and the old ones, and the intellectuals who play such an important part in most of them, aspire to transform their societies according to an ideal of modernity. They wish to foster industry, to raise the standard of living and to improve the health of their people. They wish to make them literate, to inculcate in them a sense of national identity which will outweigh the sense of identity which grows from kinship, caste and religious community. They wish to establish a far-flung system of modern bureaucratic administration; they wish to benefit from the application of science. To do this, the states of Asia and Africa are in need of modern intellectuals, not just the tradition-conserving intellectuals who care for the transmission of sacred texts and the chronicles of past glories.

A modern country, with a progressively developing economic system, a literate and skilful population, a high standard of living in material and non-material goods, and efficient and reliable administrative and judicial systems, cannot dispense with a large corps of intellectuals. If it needs or desires the fruits and glories of science, if it wishes to induct its youth into the heritage of the past and to inform them about the nature of the present, if it seeks government based on assent, and assent based on opinion, it needs intellectuals.

If in addition it wishes to be a democracy which respects freedom, it must have a body of moderately well-educated legislators, and a corps of lively journalists, jealous of their own integrity, studious and trenchant in the investigation of the contemporary world, domestic and foreign.

At present, the whole intellectual world outside the West, even the most creative parts of that world, is in a state of provinciality. It is pre-occupied with Western achievements, it is fascinated and drawn to the intellectual output of the West. Even Japan, the Soviet Union and China, which in their different ways have many greatly creative intellectuals, are concerned with the West, and not just for reasons of state or for military and strategic reasons. They are transfixed by its shining light. They lack intellectual self-confidence and intellectual self-esteem. The existence of an increasingly large stratum of formally educated philistines who seek posts in state employment, who are interested in nothing beyond their immediate tasks and the immediate place and time, does not affect the truth of this generalization and it does not render it less significant. The most sensitive and the most gifted are in this situation and their gifts and sensitivity place them in positions far more important than their relative numerical inferiority to the on-coming mass of those who are intellectuals solely by virtue of their education and not by virtue of any deeper internal impulsion.

There is another aspect of the nature of the intellectuals of Asian and African countries which merits our attention. They and the military leadership—also a relatively highly educated, ideologically sensitive section of the population and by virtue of that, to some extent, intellectuals —are the elite of their countries. Their countries depend and have depended on them to an even greater extent than advanced Western countries depend on their intellectuals. The movements of political liberation have in large measure been the work of intellectuals, at least in their earlier phases, and even where populistic demagogues, themselves usually intellectuals, have pushed them aside, at the highest level of leadership, they have continued to play an important role in the newly established state. Intellectuals must play a central role, as they often did on behalf of the foreign power, at all levels of administration. In their hands must rest educational responsibilities and the responsibility for the formation of opinion, both the short-run, immediately political opinion and the longer-run, deeper opinion which provides the medium of particular policies.

In a variety of ways the modern intellectuals of Asian and African countries have been "outsiders" vis-à-vis the ruling authorities, in tradition and in government. The question is: Can they become "insiders?" Can they, in other words, overcome their inheritance of distrust of constituted authority which came easily to them in the period of foreign rule? Can they take positive responsibility in the fields of opinion and political action? Can they come to feel fully at home in their own societies, and can they become creative with the materials which their own societies and their relations with other societies provide? Can they maintain a fruitful tension between incorporation into their own societies and their newly established systems of authority and the critical detachment and autonomy which are essential to the deeper life of the intellectual everywhere in all societies?

MAX F. MILLIKAN

Education for Innovation

When we talk about development of underdeveloped countries, we most often think in terms of capital for investment, of raw materials for the construction of factories and the manufacture of industrial goods, of technical experts and skilled workers.

Until recently far less attention has been given to education as an important—perhaps the most important—factor in development. Yet, as Professor Millikan points out, education represents "investment in the stock of human capital." And observant visitors to non-Western countries quickly become aware that for the peoples of Asia, Africa and the Middle East (as had been true earlier of Russia), hunger for education often exceeds hunger for food.

The kind of education most urgently needed in underdeveloped countries is discussed in this essay by Professor Max F. Millikan, director of the Center for International Studies at the Massachusetts Institute of Technology since 1952. Professor Millikan has held many offices in the United States government, among them Assistant Executive Secretary of the President's Committee on Foreign Aid in 1947, and member of the President's Task Force on Foreign Aid in 1961. He is the author of A Proposal—Key to a More Effective Foreign Policy (with W. W. Rostow), 1957, and editor and co-author (with D. L. M. Blackmer) of The Emerging Nations: Their Growth and United States Policy, *1961.*

I. The Need to Educate for Innovation

I WOULD like to address myself as an economist, and not as a professional educator, to the problem of the relationship of education to economic development, and the implications of this relationship for the role of the more developed countries in assisting new nations attempting to make the transition from tradition into modernity. It is remarkable how recently the economics fraternity has begun to develop an awareness of the critical importance of education—or, as it is coming to be called in the jargon of my trade, "investment in the stock of human capital"—in the process of economic development. The logical structure of the economists' theory of the development process recognizes the central role of education, but their customary categories of inputs into the productive process—namely land, labor, and capital—have until recently almost excluded any serious examination of the problem of the expansion of human resources. Labor has been treated very largely as a currently available stock of undifferentiated human beings, with only grudging footnotes recognizing that labor has varying qualitative characteristics. And capital formation has been regarded as a problem of expanding the stock of physical capital, such as tools, machines, facilities, and goods.

This is the more extraordinary because education partakes of most of the classic features of capital formation. Inputs devoted to education, which produces its economic yield only over a long time in the future, must be withdrawn from the production of immediately consumable items. The period of production of human capital is longer than that of most physical plant and equipment, suggesting the need for even more careful long-range planning of human investment than of physical assets. Once produced, human capital continues to yield services over a considerable number of years. However, the stock of human capital does waste and requires replenishment through time. Properly designed, education—investment in human capital—produces a product much more flexible and adaptable than most physical capital, although, as I shall stress later, the need for greater flexibility is not adequately recognized by many educators. On the other hand, obsolete human capital cannot simply be scrapped when it is no longer productive. It can be retrained, but this too requires special educational attention. Finally, human capital embodied in an individual cannot in free societies be owned and traded by other individuals or companies as physical capital can, a fact which has profound implications for the social organization

From *Restless Nations: A Study of World Tensions and Development*. Copyright © 1962 by the Council on World Tensions, Inc. Reprinted by permission of Dodd, Mead & Company.

of investment in human capital. A few economists such as Theodore Schultz at Chicago, Richard Eckaus at M.I.T., and Frederick Harbison at Princeton have just begun to spell out some of the economic implications for development of investment in human capital.

Those of us who have been forced, because of the difficulties of explaining development in terms of the conventionally analyzed economic forces, to look upon it as a unitary economic, sociological, psychological, and political phenomenon have come increasingly to believe that for many of the countries seeking development the key factor inhibiting economic growth is the absence of an effective educational system. No matter what the availability of physical resources or financing, neither economic nor political development is possible without an educational system which is efficient in a sense I shall presently describe. While in many cases the financial resources devoted to education by the governments of underdeveloped countries constitute a large fraction of their total budgets, the imaginative attention paid to the design of an educational system to meet economic development needs has up to now been far short of what is required to make a significant dent on the problem.

From the standpoint of the developed nations, what is called for is something much more than allocation of a larger fraction of development assistance budgets to educational assistance programs. Such a reallocation is called for, to be sure, and movements in this direction are fortunately already being made. The new approach to development assistance taken by President Kennedy's administration in the United States places great emphasis on the need for devoting increased funds and attention to the development of human resources. But there is still inadequate recognition in my country of the extent to which helping the educational process in the transitional states is going to require the mobilization of forms of assistance much more difficult to come by than money. The problems are fully as much intellectual as financial. What is needed is a massive effort to focus the best and most imaginative minds of both the developed and the underdeveloped worlds cooperatively on the problems of the redesign of education for development.

I would like to stress one problem in particular which economists have neglected in their analysis of the forces at work in development and which has a special significance for education. This is the role of *innovation* in the development process. Economists, in their theoretical models of economic growth, have tended to take technology as a given factor and to explain rising levels of output as a result of the accumulation of capital in the physical sense. Recent statistical studies of growth in the United States have suggested that not more than half of our growth is attributable to physical capital formation. The balance reflects increases in the productivity of physical inputs, which are to be explained partly by the expansion of human capital accomplished by education and partly by an acceleration of invention and innovation. This acceleration has itself been enormously influenced by the educational process. It is my conviction that a similar level of innovative activity is a necessary condition for development in the underdeveloped world and that education should be more explicitly designed to promote this.

In the past we have conceived of the problem of assisting development much too narrowly as the simple transfer from the developed to the underdeveloped countries of knowledge, technology, institutions, and practices in common use in the United States and Europe. Slowly and painfully, out of the experience of ten years, we are coming to learn—in agriculture, in health, in industry, in political organization—that while the underdeveloped world has an enormous advantage in being able to draw upon the experience of the developed world accumulated since the Renaissance, an adaptation of that experience to the problems of the underdeveloped countries requires a process as creative, innovative, and experimental as any we went through.

This need for creative innovation in the development process has a double implication for education. In the first place, it suggests that one of the central goals of education in the underdeveloped societies should be a rapid expansion in the capacities of people at all levels for problem-solving and for taking a rationally inventive approach to the issues confronting them. A great weakness of traditional education in the Western world is that it is looked upon largely as a process of transmitting a body of received knowledge, information, and conventional skills from one generation to the next, and too little as a process of creating a set of attitudes and talents conducive to finding new and more effective ways of doing things—running all the way from designing simple hand tools to constructing workable administrative and political institutions for a whole society. This is not a new problem in educational philosophy, and some advances have been made on it in the West. In recent years, particularly in elementary instruction in science and mathematics, substantial strides have been made in pilot efforts to teach these subjects in ways that place more emphasis on the student's interest in and capacity for creativity and rational inquiry, and less on the absorption of received doctrine. But we have a long way to go.

However weak our efforts to design a more constructive educational process in the United States and Europe have been, the extension of Western educational techniques into the underdeveloped countries has been even less adapted to the needs there. For a variety of reasons, our export educational product has, during both the colonial and post-colonial eras, placed even more emphasis than our domestic product on rote learning, preparation for fixed subject-matter examinations, and memorization of a body of knowledge of limited relevance to local needs. Since the utilization of knowledge requires understanding adaptation to local conditions, and since economic, physical, and social conditions in the various parts of the underdeveloped world differ widely from those in the United States and Western Europe, the educational process has been even less effective in fulfilling its function there than here.

This brings me to the second implication for education of the need for creative innovation in the development process. This is for much more imaginative innovation in educational techniques themselves in order to adapt them to the needs and resources of the underdeveloped countries. The fundamental laws of physics are universal. Their application to the design of a particular piece of equipment for a particular use in a particular society with unique resources, culture patterns, psychological attitudes, and physical environment requires an intellectual effort as challenging as the discovery of the fundamental laws themselves. Similarly, some problems of educational philosophy are universal problems. But the design of appropriate and efficient educational techniques for a particular environment requires a special act of invention to accommodate education to the limitations and exploit the opportunities of that environment.

II. Some Critical Problems of Education in Underdeveloped Countries

I would like to discuss some of the crucial differences between underdeveloped and more advanced societies which suggest major variations required in the thrust and emphasis of educational policy.

1. More Economical Educational Methods

The underdeveloped countries are exceedingly poor. If they are to mount, as they must, massive educational programs, they must find ways of doing this which are much less costly than the methods in use at all levels in the United States and Europe. This can be stated in financial terms. In the United States, for instance, we spend more than $100 per capita per year on all forms of education. This is only about 4 per cent of our gross national product and about 20 per cent of our gross physical capital formation, but it is twice the entire per capita gross national product of a large part of the underdeveloped world. This comparison is of course misleading in a wide variety of ways, some of which make it an overstatement and some an understatement of the problem. Costs of teacher time of equivalent quality are several times as high in the United States as in underdeveloped countries. On the other hand, the proportion of the population of school age in most underdeveloped countries is very much larger than in the United States. Nevertheless, the orders of magnitude make it clear that an educational system of the scope and character of that of the United States (with which we Americans are not altogether happy) is wholly beyond the resources of the contemporary underdeveloped world, supplemented by any conceivable levels of international economic aid.

Where achieving an objective with presently available methods turns out to be too costly, there are two things one can do. One can restrict oneself to a more limited objective, or one can seek innovations in method which will achieve the same objective with a more manageable input of resources. In this case, the first procedure poses a series of unacceptable choices. Shall we provide primary education for only a fraction of the children of school age? Shall we abandon or sharply limit vocational training? Shall we give up the attempt to have one or more significant institutions of higher learning and research? Or shall we settle for low standards throughout the educational system? Any of these choices has a good prospect of creating limitations on economic growth which will prevent the gross national product from ever rising to the point where resources would permit a decent educational system. Faced with this dilemma, it is surely worth making serious efforts to see whether new methods, new principles, and even new gadgetry cannot be found that will make it possible to achieve the educational objectives essential to growth with inputs of resources which the underdeveloped countries can afford. These call for radical and imaginative innovation.

The kinds of innovation needed to meet this economic difference between the developed and the underdeveloped countries will become clearer if we take a look not at the financial requirements of education but at the real resources which an educational system requires. The most important of these, and the scarcest, is teachers. These, of course, must themselves be products of the educational system. In economic terms, education is an industry which requires, as one of its major inputs, a substantial fraction of its own output. This circular relationship poses limits on the feasible rate of growth of education by conventional methods. Where the number of people turned out by the educational process is very small, the number available as teachers is likewise very small and the rate of expansion of education is thus inhibited. This is particularly true in an economy just starting to develop, in which the demands for educated persons in jobs outside education are rapidly growing.

Can the rate of expansion of the educational system required by economic development be achieved in the face of the shortage of indigenous teachers, who must themselves be the product of an educational system? In part it can, and in the short run I am convinced it must be met by the import of teachers from the educationally richer countries and the export of students from the educationally poorer ones. But for a host of reasons this can solve only a tiny part of the problem.

Anything which significantly shortens the time it takes to bring a student to a given educational level will be very helpful. This reduces the input of teacher hours per pupil, and it shortens the period of production of teachers themselves and thus speeds up the cycle of expansion. There is some evidence from experiments recently under way that the learning process in certain fields could be enormously accelerated. We have not been under great pressure to do this in the United States, but it is a matter of great economic significance for the underdeveloped countries.

Furthermore, anything which increases the number of students with whom a teacher can effectively deal reduces the cost of education in teacher hours per student. There has been much talk about the possibilities of more imaginative use of some of the modern media of communication like radio and television to achieve this goal. The trouble is that the effectiveness of these devices is still uncertain, and in most cases these things too are expensive. Once effectiveness has been established, it is still necessary to make a very careful computation of the trade-off in economy between teacher hours and expensive equipment before concluding that this is a promising avenue. A perhaps more hopeful direction to explore is the development of inexpensive teaching aids which greatly increase the teaching effectiveness and productivity of a relatively inexperienced and poorly educated teacher. The conventional teaching aid of this sort is, of course, the textbook, but for a variety of reasons this is a difficult aid to employ widely, especially at the primary level. It is too expensive, it requires fluent literacy on the part of the student, and in many instances it can be made available only in a language other than the native tongue. Some interesting experiments are under way in the development of extraordinarily cheap projectors to project pictorial material on a classroom screen with the aid only of sunlight. The development of the instrument itself is not the critical part of the innovation here, which is rather the development of substantive material to be presented through such a device for a teacher with very little background education.

Other major and costly inputs in education are buildings, laboratory and other equipment, and books. Much more effective innovation is needed in the design of inexpensive items of this kind if the educational problems of the underdeveloped countries are to be made economically soluble.

2. New Needs and Methods of Language Instruction

Another critical respect in which the educational problems of most of the underdeveloped countries differ from those of Europe and the United States is the absolute requirement for training in a second language at a very early stage in the educational process. This need arises from a number of factors. First, in some underdeveloped countries substantial parts of the population have a native tongue in which there is no significant body of literature. In many cases, whatever the policy of the local government, it will simply be unfeasible economically to create such a body of literature for a long time to come. Secondly, in many underdeveloped countries there exists within the boundaries of a single state a considerable number of mutually incomprehensible languages. In such cases a national language, which for a good part of the population must be a second language, is an absolute necessity for the internal communication needed to build an economically and politically cohesive national state.

Universal mastery of the national language is essential, among other things, to ensure widespread equality of opportunity and economic and social mobility within the society. There are enormous educational advantages in the selection as the national language of one of the languages commonly used in international discourse. Where considerations of national pride or prestige or residues of anticolonial resentment prevent this from being done, it is necessary for the educational system to provide for extensive training in still a third language. The economic, cultural, and political interdependence of the various parts of the world is growing by leaps and bounds, and a nation whose educated classes do not have mastery of at least one of the four or five principal languages customarily used in international discourse is at a grave disadvantage. The effectiveness of the educational process itself is seriously limited if extensive use cannot be made of the available literature without translation, and if utilization of imported human capital in the form of teachers, researchers, advisers, and technicians is inhibited by a language barrier.

Huge strides are now being made in techniques of language instruction. Recent experiments, both with classroom methods and with a variety of mechanical aids—some of them quite inexpensive—deserve careful study by the educational authorities of underdeveloped countries. Widespread use of the best techniques currently known could immensely improve the efficiency and reduce the cost of this key aspect of the educational process. But there is a crying need for further research and continued innovation in language instruction.

3. Education to Change Attitudes Toward Nature

A third difference of profound importance to the educational process is the attitude toward nature and the physical world which is instilled at very early ages by the cultural environment in which a child grows up. In most traditional societies, the ordinary processes of life are dominated by the notion that most of what we would call natural phenomena are beyond the control of man, are unpredictable, mystical, and subject to the whims of personalized but unseen forces. There are, fortunately, and always will be elements of mystery and unpredictability about the natural world in all societies. But in the more developed countries the child grows up in an environment of repairable machines, mechanical toys manipulated according to understandable principles, medical practice based at least partly on a theory of rational inquiry into the nature of the biological world. The environment of the child, and especially of the rural child, in underdeveloped areas is quite different.

The teaching of science and of what Pareto called the logico-experimental approach in ways which will not destroy the unique nonscientific values of each culture is a challenge to educational imagination in all countries of the world. We have just recently begun to tackle this problem in a seriously innovative way in the United States with some very promising preliminary results. But the importance of finding new ways of instilling a capability for bringing a combination of reason and observation to bear on everyday problems of man's relation with the physical world is incomparably greater in the underdeveloped countries. Finding ways of doing this which are effective, which can be utilized by teachers of limited background, which are within the resources of poor countries with some assistance from the richer nations, and which have relevance to everyday problems of the common man is an urgent task, one that deserves the attention of the very best minds of all societies. Innovation in the elementary teaching of science, mathematics, and technology with transparent relevance to local conditions for both children and adults is one of the crying needs of education in the underdeveloped world.

4. Education for Problem-solving

A characteristic of the contemporary world which has implications for education everywhere but needs perhaps to be especially emphasized in designing education for underdeveloped countries, is the extraordinary rapidity and unpredictability of the changes through which these societies are going. The generation now entering school will have to cope with a world not only totally different from the one their fathers were brought into but also totally different from the one in which we now live. Thus the educational problem is not to train them to substitute our present answers for their fathers' answers, but rather to give them tools and an attitude of mind with which to work out answers of their own.

From the economist's point of view, when change is slow it is possible to predict with some confidence what for ten or twenty years ahead will be the particular knowledge and talents required by various elements of the labor force. A good deal of training can then concentrate on producing a supply of people with sufficient mastery of particular technologies to operate satisfactorily according to prescribed rules. When change is fast, such special-purpose human capital obsolesces in much less than a working lifetime, and a more flexible and adaptable labor force is required. This in turn calls for a fundamental kind of education which equips a man, through understanding what he is doing, to adapt to rapidly changing circumstances. Every society has always required a few such people. But as economic development proceeds and change accelerates, the numbers needed who have this fundamental education are enormously expanded.

Flexibility is needed not only at the top of the educational pyramid among the university-trained intellectuals. In agriculture the problem is not today to train the cultivator in the use of what is now considered the best practice, but rather to instill in him a new attitude towards continual change and a capacity to shift his methods from year to year in response to new knowledge. It is not enough to teach the mechanic to repair today's automobile or radio set. He must be equipped to grasp new technology as it comes along. Thus the key role for education at all levels is not only the transmission of a body of knowledge—though that is necessary—but also the inculcation of a spirit of inquiry, a capacity for analysis of new problems, and a willingness to set out into the unknown.

There is nothing new in this exhortation to education for problem-solving. In principle, I suspect everyone would recognize it as a desirable goal. But it carries with it heavy costs. Confronted with a choice between relatively quick training in specific subject matter and particular skills and the longer-run, inherently more difficult process of creating fundamental understanding and changing attitudes towards innovation, the emphasis is too often on the former. The educational economies of narrowly focused applied training are particularly attractive to the poorer countries, but in the world of rapid change in which we live, these economies will turn out before long to be false ones. We must achieve our economies not by limiting our goals in this fashion but by seeking greatly to increase the efficiency of a more fundamental type of education.

The rapid rate of change has another implication for educational priorities in the underdeveloped countries. For economic development to proceed rapidly, the underdeveloped countries must, as a matter of national policy, devote much more attention to adult education than is necessary in the United States and Western Europe. In the underdeveloped countries an exceedingly small fraction of the labor force possesses the education necessary to operate a modern economy. Professor Richard Eckaus of M.I.T. has estimated that in 1950 some 94 per cent of the U.S. labor force required seven years of primary education to be effective in their jobs, and some 77 per cent required the equivalent of ten years of schooling. While the figure is much lower for most underdeveloped countries, it is rising rapidly as they grow. If we were to rely exclusively on the education of school-age children to change our capital stock of educated human beings, an underdeveloped country with little education in the past, which adopted today universal primary education and extensive secondary education, would require thirty or forty years to bring its entire labor force up to the educational levels needed to operate a modern economy. This is too long to wait. Clearly special measures are needed to raise the educational level of the existing labor force. But the fundamental education of adults requires techniques in some ways quite different from those required for the education of school children. If economic development is not to be inhibited, far more resources and much more imaginative attention must be paid to new techniques of adult education.

5. EDUCATION AS A SEARCH AND SELECTION DEVICE

One final issue confronting the underdeveloped world which can be solved only through a massive educational effort is the double problem of ensuring equality of opportunity to all elements in the population and selecting from the entire population those best qualified to fill professional technical, administrative, and political roles. The first of these issues is essentially political, the second primarily economic.

There is by now a growing body of empirical evidence that political stability in the new states cannot be maintained under free institutions if both the opportunities and the fruits of economic development are concentrated in narrow segments of the population. Under the impact of modern communications there is a tendency for the aspirations to participate in the modern sector of the society—politically, economically, and socially—to spread much more rapidly than the opportunities to do so. Most new states are in principle committed to the concept of equality of opportunity for all their citizens. But whether this is accepted as a value by the leadership or not, a movement in this direction by the leadership is probably a condition for their remaining in power. The pressures of large frustrated and underprivileged classes can be held in check for a time by authoritarian measures, but ultimately the forces of change will break through constraint imposed by force. The most essential condition for equality of opportunity is universal primary and extensive secondary education. Without this, evolutionary change under democratic institutions is likely to be impossible, and political conflict disrupting economic development is probable.

Even beyond this, the purely economic need for universal education as a selection device is great. Economic growth under whatever form of political control requires for quite technical reasons an enormous broadening of the function of decision-making through all sectors of the society. The demand for competent decision-makers cannot be effectively met by relying on a small hereditary elite. Devices must be found for searching out talent through whole populations and for selecting the most promising human materials for intensive investment in training and skills. The most efficient device we have yet discovered for surveying the inherent qualities of entire populations and drawing the best qualified into responsible positions is a proper system of universal education.

There are some dangers in this process. If the educational system is universal but is designed too exclusively to select and train a top elite, the rejects from this process can, as some underdeveloped countries have already learned, form a growing pool of frustrated educated unemployables which can seriously threaten the stability of the society. There are ways of meeting this danger, which again requires innovative imagination in the design of the educational system.

III. Implications for Assistance from the Developed World

The implications for development assistance of what has been said above are fairly clear. Increased allocation of funds is called for, especially to meet the foreign exchange costs of greatly expanded educational programs. Such funds are needed for the expansion of school plant, for libraries, textbooks, other teaching aids, and perhaps especially for the hiring of people from the developed countries who can help in the reform and extension of educational systems. The provision of qualified people is a particularly critical aspect of educational assistance which will not be solved simply by the provision of funds to pay them. The fact that the most important inputs into the educational process at all levels are the products of that process, namely educated people, suggests the problem confronted by nations attempting rapidly to expand their educational systems. Many of them will require not merely technical assistance but teachers, researchers, and even administrators from abroad in considerable numbers while they are building up their stock of qualified indigenous educators.

Another requirement is education for innovation and innovation in education. This calls for serious attention to the redesign of educational methods by a large number of the quality minds of both developed and underdeveloped countries.

Let me emphasize again that the problem is not one of transferring techniques which have become conventional with us to the underdeveloped world. Just as we cannot solve the problems of agriculture, health, transport, or industry by exporting our present technology, our second-hand machines, and our second-rate people to the underdeveloped countries, so we cannot give valid help to education there by exporting our standard educational methods or our routinely trained teachers.

We need to give even more serious and more experimental intellectual attention to the design of new techniques for education in the underdeveloped world than we are giving in our own countries. The kind of thing I have in mind is illustrated by an experience I have just been through. A group of top flight natural and social scientists in the U.S. have been involved for the past several years in a basic re-examination of the teaching of science in American high schools, under the auspices of the Physical Science Study Committee. Many of these people recently assembled for six weeks with a group of leading African educators to consider in a fundamental way the whole problem of education in Africa. From this exploration a number of results emerged. The group produced proposals for curriculum change in the primary and secondary levels. They had some very imaginative ideas about teaching aids, teacher training, demonstration equipment, and the like. But their major conclusion was that much more extensive research, experimentation, and fresh thinking needed to go into educational design for Africa. More important, some of the Americans who had had no previous contact with or interest in African educational problems were so challenged by the intellectual issues raised that they indicated their intention of continuing to make this their major preoccupation for the near future. They proposed the establishment of a number of new institutes where this kind of research and experiment could be carried forward cooperatively by Americans, Europeans, and Africans on a scale sufficient to promise significant results.

If we are to help the underdeveloped countries with their mammoth educational problems in ways that will contribute to economic, social, and political development, we must allocate to this problem a substantial share of our scarcest resource, creative brain-power. In the process there is a good prospect that we will learn a good deal that will be very useful to us in dealing with our own still unsolved educational problems.

[6]

Political
Adjustments

JAMES S. COLEMAN

The Political Systems
of the Developing Areas

The study of non-Western areas is still so new to us that we are often tempted to generalize about their political systems, on the assumption that nations which have emerged on the scene only lately must be at about the same stage of development. This generalization is firmly dispelled by Professor James S. Coleman, who distinguishes five categories of political systems at present functioning not only in Asia, Africa, and the Middle East, but in Latin America, whose political conditions he perceptively compares and contrasts with those of the Afro-Asian-Arab peoples.

Dr. Coleman is professor of political science and director of the African Studies Center at the University of California, Los Angeles. He has done research in West, East, and Central Africa as a Fulbright scholar, and under Rockefeller and Carnegie Corporation awards. He is the author of Nigeria: Background to Nationalism, 1958; and of numerous articles on politics in Middle Africa. He is co-editor with Gabriel A. Almond and co-author of The Politics of the Developing Areas, the volume from which the conclusion is excerpted here.

I. Introduction

. . . A modern society is characterized, among other things, by a comparatively high degree of urbanization, widespread literacy, comparatively high per capita income, extensive geographical and social mobility, a relatively high degree of commercialization and industrialization of the economy, an extensive and penetrative network of mass communication media, and, in general, by widespread participation and involvement by members of the society in modern social and economic processes. The degree of modernization of the societies covered in this survey will be examined in greater detail in our discussion of the processes of change.

•   •   •

The political systems covered in this survey are listed in Table 1 according to the degree of competitiveness (competitive, semi-competitive, and authoritarian) and degree of political modernity (modern, mixed, and traditional). These classifications have been made with a profound awareness of the gross character of the judgments they represent, as well as of the fact that most of the systems concerned are in transition. The present classification is regarded as both tentative and disputable. Its only purpose is to bring all of the systems together in one framework for the analysis that follows.

Given the array of disparate systems shown in Table 1, it is only at the highest level of generalization that one can make statements about their common properties. At that level, at least three features stand out. One is the "mixed" character of their social, economic, and political processes. Most of the countries are still overwhelmingly rural; the majority of the populations are illiterate. Per capita income in these countries remains very low. Social and geographical mobility is relatively high in the modern sector but very low in the rest of the society. The subsistence element persists as an important factor in most of the societies, and industrialization is either just getting underway or remains only an aspiration. The central structures of government are in most instances modern in form, but the authoritative as well as the political functions tend to be performed through a variety of "mixed" structures embodying both modern and traditional elements. These admixtures of modernity and traditionality are in some instances fusional, in others, isolative in character.

A second common feature of these societies is their lack of integration. This is due in part to the ethnic, religious, racial, and cultural pluralism characteristic of the societies, in part to the limited and uneven operation of the processes of modernity. The critical fact, however, is not that these societies are pluralistic—pluralism is one of the key attributes of most modern societies—but that interests still tend to be defined predominantly in terms of tribe, race, religion, or communal reference group. The persistence and the predominance of such groups retards assimilation into the new national societies. Moreover, so long as interests are primarily rooted in and find expression through communal groups, they are far less amenable to aggregation in a competitive and bargaining process. Only in the modern sector of these mixed societies does one find the emergence of non-communal functionally specific interest groups.

A third . . . characteristic is the wide gap which exists between the traditional mass and the essentially modern subsociety of the Westernized elite. The latter controls the central structures of government

Table 1

CLASSIFICATION OF POLITICAL SYSTEMS IN UNDERDEVELOPED AREAS

Classificatory criteria		Countries by Areas				
Degree of Competitiveness	Degree of Political Modernity	Southeast Asia	South Asia	Near East	Africa	Latin America
COMPETITIVE	MODERN	Malaya Philippines	Ceylon India	Israel Lebanon Turkey		Chile Argentina Brazil Uruguay Costa Rica
SEMI-COMPETITIVE	MIXED	Burma Indonesia Thailand		Algeria Iran Jordan Morocco Tunisia	Cameroons Central African Republic Chad Dahomey Gabon Ghana Guinea Ivory Coast Mali Federation Mauritania Niger Nigeria No. Rhodesia Nyasaland Rep. of Congo Sierra Leone Somalia So. Rhodesia Tanganyika Togoland Uganda Upper Volta Union of So. Africa	Colombia Ecuador Mexico Panama Peru
AUTHORITARIAN	MIXED	Cambodia Laos	Pakistan	Iraq Libya Sudan U.A.R.	Angola Belgian Congo Liberia Mozambique Ruanda-Urundi	Bolivia Cuba Dominican Republic El Salvador Guatemala Haiti Honduras Nicaragua Paraguay Venezuela
TRADITIONAL				Afghanistan Saudi-Arabia Yemen	Ethiopia	

and essays to speak and act for the society as a whole. This elite sub-society is the main locus of political activity and of change in the society at large. The character of the principal actors and participants in the elite subsociety is variable: in the new states and colonies of Africa, and in the new states of Asia, they constitute the urbanized, Western-educated minority; in the white oligarchic states of Africa and Latin America they constitute to varying degrees a culturally defined elite. The principal differences among the societies sharing this characteristic are the degree of access to the elite subsociety, and the extent to which there is communication between the two sectors in the form of such mediators as provincial elites, or an intermediate class in transition be-tween the traditional and modern sectors. The gap between the two sectors illuminates the mixed character of the social and political proc-esses in these countries as well as the degree of malintegration on the vertical plane.

In addition to these general characteristics common to most of the . . . countries covered in this study, there are others which can be more appropriately summarized under the headings of the common out-line the area authors have employed, namely, the processes of change and their political implications, and the functions of the political system.

II. Processes of Change and Their Political Consequences

The processes of change examined in the varying contexts of the five areas are major aspects of the broader process of modernization. Analysis of the character and consequences of this process illuminates the interrelated character of the several subprocesses and supports Dan-iel Lerner's thesis that modernization as a process has a distinctive quality of its own, that the various elements in this process "do not occur in haphazard and unrelated fashion," and that they have gone together so regularly because "in some historical sense they *had* to go together."

The political consequences of the operation of the several processes of change have been many and varied. While in general the changes have brought the countries concerned nearer to the model of a modern society, their effect has by no means been uniform. At the most general level the more significant political consequences can be stated in prop-ositional form:

1. National politics tend to be primarily if not exclusively centered in urban areas; usually they are a phenomenon of capital cities. The latter are the principal political arenas because they are the centers in which the modern elite subsociety is concentrated.

2. The gap between the modern-oriented urban subsociety and the larger national society of which it is the political center is not unbridged. A substantial number of the urban dwellers maintain close ties with their rural homeland; as a consequence, they constitute a very significant medium through which modernity is pumped into rural areas and the rural population becomes involved in or identifies itself with the drama of national politics. Such participation, however, tends to be intermittent.

3. The gross disparities between the standard of living and career opportunities in the urban centers and in the village areas has accelerated a movement into the urban centers far beyond the capacity of the latter to provide employment. As a consequence there exists in most urban centers, particularly the capital cities, elements predisposed to anomic activity.

4. The processes of commercialization and industrialization of the economies of these societies have not everywhere contributed to social or political integration, or to the emergence of a politically relevant entrepreneurial or middle class. One reason is that in the initial stages at least commercial activity has been in the hands of alien groups: the Indian and Chinese middleman in Southeast Asia, the Hindu entrepreneurs in the Muslim areas of preindependence India, Lebanese and Jews in North Africa, Levantines in West Africa, Indians in South and East Africa, and various alien groups in Latin America.

5. Although modernity has introduced basic changes in the social structure of many of these countries, these changes have frequently intensified intergroup tensions. Education and economic wealth have not been acquired by nor distributed evenly among all groups, but differentially along communal, racial, or tribal lines. Thus, there is not a positive correlation between economic development and greater social and political integration.

6. Wherever the modernization process has had an impact, it has contributed to secularization, both social and political. But in most countries religion is still a factor of great significance in the political process. In the daily lives of the masses living in the traditional sector, religion is still a vital force. The new secular elites frequently feel compelled, for various reasons, to respect, or even to use, religion as a political force. In most countries there are political parties having a religious basis. The politicization of religion aggravates communal tensions; it also perpetuates the struggle between those demanding a greater role for religion in the state and those demanding a secular polity.

•   •   •

III. The Functions of the Political System

POLITICAL SOCIALIZATION AND RECRUITMENT

. . . one of the most striking features of all but a few of the . . . countries covered in this study is the fragmented character of their political cultures. Those few polities whose political culture even approximates homogeneity are quite exceptional: Argentina, Chile, Costa Rica, and Uruguay in Latin America; and Turkey, Israel, the Philippines—and, in a very special sense, Saudi Arabia and Yemen—in Africa-Asia. Elsewhere the degree of cultural fragmentation is marked, although there are wide variations in the extent to which it affects the political process and in the rate at which a homogeneous political culture is developing.

The cultural fragmentation of most of these countries is a reflection of two basic types of internal cleavage. One is the gap, previously noted, between the predominantly urban, modern subsociety of the Westernized elements, whose members are oriented toward political values and institutions representative of an exotic—usually Western—political culture, on the one hand, and the traditional societies, into the political cultures of which a large segment of the population continues to be socialized, on the other. This gap on the vertical plane is compounded by the horizontal divisions among the melange of indigenous political cultures which, by the accidents of colonialism or recent history, are included within the boundaries of larger territorial political systems. A very considerable number of persons in these countries, of course, are in a transitional stage, being subject to the socializing processes in both spheres. Where the traditional cultures are adaptive to, rather than isolative from, the modern territorial system, the task of creating a unified socialization process is obviously much easier.

The governing elites of the "new states" are engaged in the development and strengthening of system-wide secondary structures that not only impinge directly upon the individual, but also penetrate the primary socializing structures. They are seeking to create, by an act of will, an integrated process of political socialization in which at all levels there is an inculcation of positive sentiments of respect, loyalty, and pride in the new polities. Their efforts are being met with strong resistance, especially from particularistic forces—forces which modernization itself ironically tends, in many situations, to strengthen. Moreover, there are distinct limits to which a political culture can be deliberately created in a single generation; such a culture is a reflection of the ensemble of predispositions and orientations toward authority and politics, most of which are the product of socializing experiences and influences antedating the contemporary drive toward modernization.

In the remaining political systems (except for the few having fairly homogeneous political cultures) the character of the socialization process varies according to the goals of the governing elite and the nature of the cultural pluralism. Although differing in many ways, the elite in such established states as Thailand, Iran, and Ethiopia are endeavoring, through the manipulation of both old and new socializing structures, to adapt the traditional political culture to modernity. In the Union of South Africa one finds the strikingly atypical situation of the governing oligarchy deliberately bending every effort not only to maintain but to strengthen a dualistic political culture. In most of the other countries, and particularly in the culturally pluralistic states of Latin America, the dominant oligarchy is less purposive in this regard, being more inclined to let the processes of assimilation gradually bridge existing cultural discontinuities.

With these general observations regarding political socialization, it is in point to note the patterns of recruitment into the political arena and into political roles in the systems covered in this study. It is clear . . . that there are wide variations in these patterns. These variations are a reflection of several differences: (1) the character, and particularly the breadth, of the social bases from which entrants into the political arena are drawn; (2) the circumstances under which, and the avenues through which, members of the society become politically participant; (3) the degree to which the recruitment process is undergoing change; (4) the rate of political activation; and (5) motivations for entering politics.

The range of variations in the patterns of recruitment extends from the largely ascriptive patriarchal systems such as Saudi Arabia, Yemen, and Ethiopia, through the narrow-based oligarchies of Liberia and the Dominican Republic, to the broad-based competitive systems such as the Philippines and India. In most of these societies, however, the ongoing processes of social change are continuously producing, in varying degrees and at different tempos, fundamental alterations in the recruitment pattern.

In the narrow-based patriarchies and oligarchies, as well as in several of the colonial territories on the threshold of independence, the social categories from which participants are drawn reflect the mixed character of the societies. Traditional leaders are recruited by ascriptive criteria from social groups which historically have been predominant in the system (wealthy families, dominant lineages and clans, etc.). Other leaders come from the modern sector, in which university students, the urban educated classes, army officers, civil servants, and professional and business groups characteristically predominate. In the patriarchal societies professional, business, and other modern groups are largely non-participant, although the continuous increase in their numbers indicates the potentiality for change. In the other narrow-based societies modern elements are increasingly assertive and in several cases are already engaged in efforts to extinguish the influence of the traditional elements.

In those societies where political participation is broadly based, a useful distinction can be drawn, for reasons previously noted, between the countries of Latin America and of Africa-Asia (a contraction used herein to refer to Africa, the Near East, and South and Southeast Asia). In the new states and the terminal colonial systems of Africa-Asia there appears to be a fairly common pattern of development in the recruitment process. For analytical purposes four distinct periods can be distinguished: (1) the period of accommodation and petition; (2) the period of agitation and assertion; (3) the period of maneuver, characteristic of terminal colonialism, where the goal of self-government is in sight and competing groups struggle to establish a favorable position in the new order; and (4) the period of adjustment and consolidation following independence. Each of these are stages in the evolution of political participation, commencing with the initial activities of a small Westernized minority and ending with the mass popular involvement via universal suffrage and periodic elections. Not all countries have gone through all stages; indeed the terminal colonial phase has tended to be a distinctive feature of the emergence of Africa's new states. Nevertheless, in the majority of these countries there has been a progressive broadening of the social and geographical bases of recruitment.

There are at least three special features of this process which are common to most of the countries of Africa-Asia. One concerns the extreme variations in the rate of recruitment. During the age of petition the rate was comparatively slow, due to the limited degree of social mobilization, the limited horizon of political expectations, and the absence of meaningful political roles to which the ambitious could aspire. The age of agitation and assertion characteristically has been one of extremely rapid upward mobility and of a high rate of recruitment because of the heightened expectations generated by the vision of self-government. . . .

During the post-independence period of adjustment and consolidation there has been a progressive decline in the rate of recruitment into authoritative and bureaucratic roles, and a tendency toward political demobilization of large segments of the population activated during the struggle for independence. At the same time the number of new entrants into the political arena—representative of a new generation—has increased and will continue to grow as a consequence of the acceleration of the processes of change. The cleavage between generations—between the older generation of victorious nationalists holding prestigeful roles and a younger post-independence generation whose career ambitions appear thwarted—is the second special feature stressed by the authors of the chapters on the political systems of Africa-Asia.

A third common feature has been the emergence of rural or "provincial" political elites whose influence has become increasingly determinative in the political process. . . . These new rural politicians tend to be vernacular-speaking and less educated; they are also more securely rooted in the traditional social structure than are the urban-based, Western-educated politicians who constituted the vanguard in political action in the preindependence period.

INTEREST ARTICULATION

In most of the countries included in the five major areas covered by this survey there are similarities in the character of interests and in the degree and manner in which interests are articulated. Ascriptive, communal, and similar groups (i.e., those in which membership is defined by ethnic, racial, linguistic, tribal, religious, or status criteria) continue to predominate and to determine the character of political issues and the lines of political cleavage. Particular economic or occupational interests are mainly latent or in gestation and are not articulated by functionally specific associations. Where the latter exist, they have not become crucial units in the political process. In many countries, institutional interest groups (armies, religious groups, or bureaucracies) play a predominant role.

•   •   •

Armies and bureaucracies in particular tend to play a predominant role for several reasons: they have a special responsibility for the maintenance of law and order, a major *desideratum* both in the stabilization of the new states and in the maintenance of oligarchic politics. In the new states their ranks are filled mainly by statist and nationally minded modernists, including some of the most able and sophisticated elements in the Western-educated class. For special reasons linked to the rationalization of colonialism, this class supports the idea of the "divine right" of the educated to rule; and its members have not been unaffected by bureaucratic-authoritarian predispositions derived from traditional society or from the colonial experience.

This common syndrome of interests is to a large degree a reflection of the limited and uneven impact of modernity. The modernization process tends to give birth to new, functionally specific interests; yet in many cases the provocations and uneven incidence of its impact have preserved or even strengthened pre-existing tribal, communal, racial, and status cleavages, as well as the urban-rural gap. As Weiner has noted, the growth in mass communication extends and often deepens the network of communal ties, and the introduction of universal suffrage and a national political arena often pushes communal interests into politics. As the degree of functional specificity of associational interest groups is one of the key attributes of political modernity, the prevalence of this phenomenon in much of Sub-Saharan Africa and South and Southeast Asia means that in the initial stages at least the modernization process strengthens antimodern forces and institutions.

The patterning of interests in many of the countries has been partly determined by the character of the colonial experience and of the movements for national independence. In both instances, the legacy has been mixed in character. Under colonialism it was not uncommon for the colonial authorities to recognize and to deal with specific organized interest groups, particularly in the modern sector. At the same time the colonial policies of most European powers had the effect, sometimes intended, of strengthening and preserving communal, ascriptive, ethnic, and racial divisions, as well as of creating religious or status differences. Colonialism was also the medium for introducing and for habituating the mass of the population to government through highly developed structures controlled by a bureaucratic elite. The latter claimed to be responsible not only for governing in the interest of all the people but also for modernizing the society.

The legacy of movements for national independence has also been varied. In countries such as India or Nigeria, where nationalist movements acquired a mass base, the organization of all types of interests was stimulated. One of the most effective techniques employed by nationalist leaders in the mobilization of the population was to work through the network of associations which had emerged from the impact of modernity and the processes of social change. The interests that were activated, articulated, and organized in this process were both functionally specific (e.g., labor unions and student groups), and functionally diffuse (e.g., tribal unions, status associations, and other communal groupings) in character. Nationalist leaders aggregated the disparate interests of this melange of participating groups, not by compromises aimed at the immediate satisfaction or accommodations of their respective interests, but rather by subsuming the goals of all interests under the rubric of a new "national interest." When the latter was secured through independence, all specific interests, it was assumed, would automatically be satisfied. This had two consequences. As Pye has observed, it fostered the idea that national leaders, like the rulers of traditional Asian and African societies, were the embodiment of all interests of their people. It also served to create organizational linkages or identifications between interest groups on the one hand and nationalist movements or political parties on the other. Both of these developments tended to minimize and to weaken the autonomy of interest groups in pressing their demands upon the political system.

Post-independence efforts to stabilize the new political systems, to create a sense of national unity, and to accelerate the modernization of societies, have served to perpetuate the idea that the national interest not only transcends but embodies all specific interests and that public policy is not the product of competing claims of specific interests, but rather a reflection of the "national will" of the modernizing national elite. The notion of the "creative state," coupled with a statist mentality derived from traditional culture or from the colonial experience, has tended to strengthen attitudes of hostility or indifference toward special-interest economic groups (especially business and landlord groups), and, as a consequence, to minimize their role in the public policy process.

Over against these elements in the situation have been other developments in the post-independence period having different consequences. Once independence has been achieved (and in some instances even before it is achieved) functionally diffuse groups of all types (ethnic, racial, linguistic, status, and underdeveloped regions) have become activated and have asserted their claims, which in general have taken the form of implied or threatened separatism and the insistence upon safeguards to insure their continuing integrity. Moreover, even in the case of functionally specific groups linked to nationalist movements or political parties there has been a tendency for the new generation of interest-group leaders to seek greater autonomy in the articulation of the specific interests of the groups they represent.

There are other respects in which the character and articulation of interests in these countries are distinctive. One is the active and frequently crucial role played by student groups, and particularly by university students. Another is the extremely limited degree to which the economic interests of the great mass of the population—the peasantry—find associational expression. In Latin American countries, however, ideological parties (Socialist, Communist, and Aprista) are to an increasing extent articulating agrarian interests, as well as those of organized labor.

INTEREST AGGREGATION

A second attribute of a modern political system is the existence of a party system in which competing parties, broadly based in structure and pragmatic in program and tactics, perform the function of aggregating the major interests in the society. The countries most closely approximating this model of a modern party system are the Philippines and Turkey.

Elsewhere one finds an array of variant patterns, although one or more of the attributes of the foregoing model may be present. More characteristically, one finds that political groups are narrow-based and serve essentially as vehicles for competition between different elements drawn from the modern sector. *Personalismo* (the tendency for political groups to be organized in support of particularly strong personal leaders) is common not only in Latin America, where it has flourished for generations, but also in many countries of Africa, the Near East, and South and Southeast Asia. One-party systems tend to predominate, although there are important differences in this type, ranging from the comprehensive nationalist movements found in several African countries, through the broadly aggregative non-dictatorial party systems of Uruguay, Mexico, and India to such narrow-based dictatorial systems as in Paraguay, the Dominican Republic, and Liberia.

•   •   •

IV. The Authoritative Functions: Rule Making; Rule Application; Rule Adjudication

The two types of formal structure which represent the most distinctive innovation are central representative parliaments endowed with a determinative role in the rule-making function and secular independent judicial structures through which rules are authoritatively adjudicated. Most of the countries have had long experience with executive-bureaucratic government, either through traditional or colonial structures. The concepts of legislation and independent adjudication are distinctly exotic importations, which does much to explain a pattern common to all but a few of the polities concerned, namely, the under-participation by parliaments in the rule-making function, the fragility of the independent judiciary, and executive-bureaucratic predominance. For the countries of South and Southeast Asia and of Sub-Saharan Africa, particularly those which have experienced British colonial rule, this characteristic pattern is modified by a colonial experience in which great emphasis was placed upon the political neutrality of the civil service and the independence of the judiciary. In several of the new states these elements in the colonial legacy have been forces sustaining constitutional government in the post-independence period. How much they are a transitional phenomenon characteristic of the present generation has yet to be seen.

Another common feature, also in part a legacy of the traditional past and of colonialism is the tendency toward unitary government and heavy centralization of decision-making. This is true even in systems such as India and the several countries of Latin America, where federalism has been attempted. In the new and emergent states of Sub-Saharan Africa one finds Africans replacing Europeans as provincial commissioners and district officers in the role of rural agents of central government. The strong centrifugal forces pressing for separatism or greater local autonomy tend to provoke central governments to strengthen their control in terms of national unification and stabilization of the polity. Moreover, the pressures for rapid modernization perpetuate and strengthen the tendency toward centralism. The concept of strong local government, passionately encouraged by British colonial administrators, is not likely to command general acceptance. The general trend throughout the non-Western world is therefore toward centralism.

BARBARA WARD

The Rich Nations
and The Poor Nations

The attainment of independence from colonial rule by non-Western peoples marks the end of one struggle but the beginning of another, and an even more difficult, one: the struggle to create political institutions through which new governments can spur urgently needed economic development. These governments must, day after day, steer between decisions, all fraught with peril. They need aid from technologically advanced nations. If they accept it from their former colonial rulers, they run the risk of being accused of neo-colonialism by Communists at home and abroad. If they take aid from the Communists, they are criticized by the Western democracies. They must urge sacrifices on their peoples who had hoped independence would bring economic and social improvement. If these sacrifices are not made voluntarily, the governments' economic plans may fail, but if the new rulers resort to force, they are accused in the West of betraying democratic values and resorting to dictatorship.

The principal political dilemmas faced by the newly independent nations are analyzed in this chapter from a book published in 1962 by Barbara Ward, the well-known English writer long connected with the London Economist. Author and lecturer on international affairs, she was a governor of the British Broadcasting Corporation and of London's Old Vic Theatre. She has lectured extensively in the United States, has contributed articles to many magazines, and is the author of several other books, among them The Interplay of East and West, 1957; and India and the West, 1961. *In private life she is Lady Jackson, wife of Sir Robert Jackson, former Commissioner of Development in Ghana.*

Chapter 5
The Politics of Development

THE TIME has now come to look at the fourth of the great revolutions of our day: the revolution of political equality. It is everywhere at work in the underdeveloped and uncommitted nations and everywhere, too, it complicates and even exacerbates relations between the rich nations and the poor. It is an all-embracing concept of equality: equality of the nation, of the race, of the class; above all, the equality of man with man in the new world-society that is beginning to emerge.

Most of the poor and uncommitted lands have acquired this vast, almost cosmic vision of equality as a result of their colonial contact with Western societies. The ambition to modernize, to pull level with the more developed societies, has been implanted in them by their experiences as part of a Western imperial pattern. Western merchants, Western educators, Western administrators, brought the ferment of the new ideas and the new sense of the need for, and the right to, equality.

But these Western contacts brought in the new ideas by different routes. There have been positive, constructive, and creative methods of transmission; and the work of great imperial administrators—one thinks of a Monroe or an Elphinstone in India, a Lugard or a Guggisberg in West Africa—undoubtedly created a framework of order and opportunities of advance unequalled for centuries. It is in this sense that empire has proved one of the great civilizing forces in human history. But these were not the only methods by which the sense of equality was fostered. We must not forget the dark ways of dislike, exclusion, fear, and prejudice, which make imperialism one of the catastrophic forces of mankind as well.

During the West's impact on the surrounding world—an impact

From *The Rich Nations and The Poor Nations* by Barbara Ward. Copyright © 1962 by Barbara Ward. Reprinted by permission of the publishers: W. W. Norton & Company, Inc., New York; Hamish Hamilton Company, Ltd., London. This is one of the series of talks entitled 'The Rich Nations and the Poor Nations' given by the author on the Canadian Broadcasting Corporation's radio network in 1961, and subsequently published in Canada by them.

which has lasted three hundred years—there is evidence enough of both forms of transmission. We have already spoken of the great administrators who laid the foundations upon which such services as the Indian Civil Service came to be not only efficient and selfless, but even a nation-building force. Today, with the collapse of the Congo before us, we are less likely to underestimate the supreme contribution orderly administration can make to the arts of civilization.

To the administrators we must add the missionaries and the scholars. Not all missionaries came out in the spirit in which fruitful cultural contact can flourish. Too much contempt for the "heathen," too much ignorance of alien cultures diminished the effectiveness of what was done. Had more gone with the sympathy and understanding displayed by Father Matteo Ricci, the great Jesuit missionary to China, who knows what new insights might not have been achieved? Yet the influence of Christianity on great Indian reformers such as Sir Ram Mohan Roy or great leaders like Gandhi should not be forgotten. In Africa, the figure of David Livingstone, working with fortitude to end the slave-trade, towers above the greedy mob of adventurers and profiteers looking to Africa, like Pistol, for its "golden joys." And throughout West Africa, unknown heroes of the Protestant missions risked almost certain death by yellow fever to bring religion, education, and the first beginnings of modern health to the Africans. Nor should one forget the work of Western scholars who have played so great a role in piecing together from the records of monuments, temple scrolls, and archaeology the history of Asian peoples who might otherwise have lost their history, and their identity as well.

Another essential element in a developing society—a modern managerial class—was also introduced through the Western impact. There would have been no quick development of a modern middle class with effective commercial and entrepreneurial energies if colonial rule had not created a new atmosphere of peace and fostered, in great countries such as India, the development of modern commercial law, the notion of contract, a new sense of security for property, a new belief that if the merchant sets to work to develop, accumulate, and invest, his wealth should be secure.

Nor is the role of the army negligible. Elements of discipline and service were injected into traditional communities as a result of modern army training. In fact, one could argue that in some countries the officer corps had qualities of loyalty and patriotism free from any tincture of self-interest not found too generally in the community at large. To have such cadres is a positive achievement upon which much can be built.

Yet it would be a grave mistake if we in the West thought only of the constructive efforts and forgot the darker side of the record. Take first of all the most resented aspect of Western rule, particularly of British rule: we took with us in our colonial dealings an ignorant and almost irremovable racial prejudice. Now I know that most nations have had their racial prejudices; in fact, I am reminded of a Chinese proverb to the effect that God first made the African and overbaked him black, and then God made the European and underbaked him white, but then God made the Chinese and baked them exactly right—which is yellow of course. And it is an irony of history that in the nineteenth century, the Chinese called Westerners "red" barbarians; perhaps because there were so many Scotsmen among them. Prejudice, the sense of separateness and superiority, are certainly not confined to the West.

But for three hundred years the white race has enjoyed a dominant position in the world. Its members were able to stamp their prejudices across the face of the globe because they were, in fact, on top. And there can be no doubt that many white men, particularly Anglo-Saxon white men, cannot overcome a straightforward colour prejudice. And this belief that coloured people are inferior has left its mark all over the world. Perhaps one realizes how deep the wounds are only when one has lived in ex-colonial lands. Occasionally in confidential talks, late at night, when there is no longer an official front to be kept up, one hears of the insults at the hands of London boarding-house keepers or of careless wounding words from educated people: trivial incidents, perhaps, but ones which leave a mark on people's consciousness that can never be effaced.

Another whole set of problems is concerned not so much with race as with class. It seems to be a fact of life that in the early days of industrial development, the merchant, in process of turning himself into an entrepreneur, often demonstrates facets of greed and rapacity which make him a not too attractive figure to the society he raids and exploits. This of course is not a problem confined to the newly developing areas. If you read the pages of Dickens, you will meet the Mr. Merdles and the Mr. Veneerings who pursue wealth with a passion and irresponsibility that leads them to ruin others and finally themselves. Yet such men are influential. Money talks. And in a poor but developing economy it is much more likely that such men will have contacts with the colonial rulers, be consulted by them, and entertain them. There is probably no very great identification of interests. British colonial administrators tended to think of businessmen as the Victorians thought of trade. It was not quite "the thing." But there was enough contact to create some identification between colonial rule and the local magnates, and to give a social edge to nationalist criticism.

It was reinforced wherever—as was usual—the landlord system remained intact. The administrators arriving from overseas to take up their imperial appointments would not refuse the offered tiger-hunt. Again, some identification was possible between colonial rule and the local social hierarchy.

The educated groups in the new sense—the new lawyers, the new technicians, the men and women who had access to modern forms of knowledge—remained a very small group in relation to the people at large. A sense of isolation tended to weaken them and undermine their political confidence. Moreover, the environment confused them further. After a number of small hopeful beginnings, colonial economies failed to move forward to sustained momentum. The economic picture was patchy, with bits of development here and bits of development there, while social changes went forward in one sector and were quite absent in others. Young people had the feeling of belonging to a discontinuous society—a mood which increased their unease. And to all this we must add the stagnation of the twenties and the thirties.

After the First World War, the colonial powers of Western Europe entered upon a period of relative economic decline. It was followed by the appalling depression of 1929 and the chaotic conditions of the thirties. Local stagnation increased the social discontents of the colonial world and coupled rising political consciousness with social protest and economic frustration. It was no longer only the tiny educated middle class who felt the pressure. More unsophisticated people began to ask questions about the foreigner who came and lived in the big house at the top of the hill, the colonial officials with all the influential administrative jobs, the big foreign merchant and banker with something of an economic monopoly. And round these foreigners tended to cluster the few members of the local society who were doing well out of the system: the large landowner, the local merchant, the new industrialist whose wealth—old or new—cut them off more and more from their frustrated fellow countrymen.

It is therefore not surprising that the revolution of independence and national equality which has been gathering strength round the world for the last fifty years has more than one political and social overtone. There is the ambition for economic change sparked by the example of what Western society can do with its new technology. To it must be added the social unrest stirred up by the contrast between the small rich *élite*, comfortably profiting from the *status quo*, and the vast mass of the people who are beginning to resent their desperate poverty. This, in turn, fuses with anti-colonial sentiment, with the feeling that the subject nation has the right to self-government and independence. In fact, the two are often barely distinguishable; for local opinion tends more and more to see "colonial servitude" as the chief obstacle to social rights and economic development. These were the days when students like

Chou En-lai or Ho Chi-minh went to Europe for their education and found that only Leninism really seemed to describe their predicament. A stirring, uncertain, chaotic time of social, political, and economic change, all woven together—this, I think, is how we must regard the struggle of the poorer nations to get through all the sound-barriers of their life at once: the economic barrier, the social barrier, the political barrier. And if one sees the struggle in this perspective, surely it is not surprising that our days are tense. The remarkable thing is how much stability still remains in the midst of these whirling passions and ambitions for total change.

At one time, it must have seemed that the whole colonial order, battered by such pressures, would end in a violent explosion of hatred and violence. Some experiments have ended in bloodshed. The Dutch left Indonesia after war had decided the issue. The French withdrew from Indo-China under the same tragic star of conflict. Britain had to fight an ugly little war in Cyprus before a settlement could be reached. Certainly Lenin foresaw such a consummation and even suggested that the revolt of the colonial masses might be a quicker route to world communism than the milder resentments of Western workers.

But in fact, the transfer of power from the old colonial governments to the new independent states since the war has, I think, proved easier than we might have feared. We can now see that, at least in these first decades of independence, the transfer of power by Britain to India and Pakistan—the first great voluntary transfers of government—was accomplished with such restraint and generosity that a new pattern of compelling force appeared on the human scene. It was, of course, an achievement towards which British political thought had long been directed. As early as the eighteen-twenties, great British proconsuls in India had said that there could be no justification for British rule in India save to build up the conditions under which Indians would govern themselves. The evolving Commonwealth in which the white Dominions— Canada, Australia—had already found an independent place provided a structure of friendship and co-operation within which the new nations could fit without any diminution of their newly established sovereignty. But equally, the transfer was made possible by the political vision and immense personal generosity of men like Gandhi and Nehru who were ready, when the day came, to treat their former gaolers as trusted friends. For this mutual respect and conciliation there was no place in the Marxist canon, and it has had a dominant influence ever since.

Transfers of power have continued to take place with similar grace and dignity in other parts of the world—in the rest of the British Commonwealth, in French West Africa. In fact, one can say that there are perhaps only two types of ex-colonial community in which it is excessively difficult to achieve a transfer of power with anything like the goodwill that is needed to make it effective and peaceful. One type is the country where a settler problem complicates the issue—as in Algeria, in the Rhodesias, or in Kenya. In such communities, the lines of cleavage between groups—the political, social, and economic lines we have already discussed—are strengthened and exacerbated by the greatest dividers of all, the dividers of culture and race. Settlers from the metropolitan country come in and root themselves in the local community. They take the best land. Being better educated, they produce more wealth from it. They hold the best posts. They often control the administration. At the same time, internal peace and the beginnings of modernization can set in motion a violent explosion of the birth-rate among the more primitive peoples whose chief means of subsistence— the land—has nonetheless been taken away. Two societies develop. In one, the white settlers build up a more or less wealthy modern community. Around and among them the dispossessed exist, multiply, and finally begin to revolt. This has been the pattern of Algeria. In Kenya, in the Rhodesias, in parts of the Congo, acute racial differences complete the picture of separatism and hostility. Here the transfer of power presents overwhelming difficulty. The long bitter Algerian war is testimony to the vast obstacles that must be overcome.

The second category is rather more ambiguous. In some countries the transfer of power is made, but conditions prevent it from convincing the local people that a genuine transfer has in fact occurred. Lenin had these cases in mind when he argued that metropolitan powers could still exercise a preponderant influence in excolonial territories, simply by keeping all the levers of economic power in their own hands. Any form of foreign investment, particularly investment from a dominant Western or ex-imperial government, had hidden in it, he suggested, the tentacles of continued control. One cannot underestimate the degree to which the Leninist myth of power by indirection, exercised through "the monopolists and the trusts," has sunk into the distrustful minds of developing peoples. Where in fact investment from abroad seems overwhelmingly dominant and the doubt can arise whether local interests have any chance against the big foreign firms, then the Leninist pattern is not too difficult to apply and people begin to ask whether their own supposedly independent government may not.be the puppet of a foreign power. There was an element of this feeling in the Cuban reaction to Batista; and we do not yet know what sorrows have been brought upon the Congo by the decision of a separatist government to establish itself in the Katanga where Belgian mining interests are overwhelmingly strong.

Yet we are now realizing for the first time that, in spite of these difficulties, it is not in fact the moment of transfer of power that is most difficult in the emergence of the poorer nations to a sense of national equality in the modern world. After all, in the periods that lead up to the ending of the colonial régime, usually a considerable sense of common purpose unites the country. More and more people come to feel that colonial rule must be the chief target and that all differences of race or tribe or class can be subordinated to the greater struggle to achieve political equality and independence. This is the great unifying force behind such movements as India's Congress Party where the rich mill-owner and the simple peasant hand-weaver were united under the leadership of Gandhi and Nehru. This unifying force is enough to carry the country forward to the great effort of achieving independence. In fact, the greater the effort, the greater the unity. Where independence comes virtually without struggle—as in Burma or Ceylon or Nigeria— the advantages of national unity may well be lessened. It is after independence that the real troubles begin. With national equality and independence achieved, the problems of social and economic equality begin to take pride of place.

The first and obvious conflict to gather force is the fundamental conflict between rich and poor within the nation. Gone is the overriding unity of struggle. The contrasts between wealth and poverty are now all the more stark because, during the struggle, independence had been painted in millennial terms, with milk and honey for everybody.

If, as often happens, independence coincides with the early days of industrialization and economic modernization, then the conflict may take on even sharper social overtones. At this period the merchant-turned-entrepreneur is not necessarily an inspiring national leader, not often a man to whom the masses will turn with a sense that his integrity is unquestioned and his work unequivocally for the public good. A lot of the prejudice one meets in India—for example, against the Mawari trading-class—is based on the fact that the masses believe, not always without foundation, that these men will put profit before everything, even before the well-being of the community. The belief breeds acrimony, distrust, and class-hatred.

The new entrepreneur is an object of suspicion because he gets on too fast. Another dominant group—the landlords—are often disliked for the opposite reason: they do not change themselves and thus make change impossible for everyone else on the land. They are still so embedded in the past, still so set upon the old questions of status, the old attitude towards land as a way of life not as a way of development, that often it seems as though an immovable social and political lid had been clapped tightly down on the countryside, inhibiting any possibility of development and change. The unhandiness of unchanged feudal leadership for a modernizing economy can be illustrated from Japan after 1870 where the Meiji reformers found it necessary to begin their economic revolution by total land reform. In many parts of Latin America today, land reform is probably still the single most efficacious way of setting in motion the processes of economic growth.

The shortcomings of leadership based upon the old rural leaders and the up-and-coming entrepreneurs of the city are not overcome simply by introducing the formal machinery of parliamentary democracy. All too often, the present groups in power simply manipulate the democratic machine for their own purposes. They resemble in some measure the House of Commons in Britain before 1832 when the landed gentry had the margin of political strength. But Britain's parliamentary government became an efficacious instrument of social change only after several further modifications. It was widened first to include the rising middle classes including, of course, the entrepreneurs and then later, after a very considerable advance in literacy, the mass of the citizens as well.

These pre-conditions of parliamentary effectiveness often do not exist in developing economies on the morrow of independence. The entrepreneurial groups are still socially irresponsible; there are no Lord Shaftesburys, no Disraelies to express the conscience of the dominant class. In addition, the middle class is miserably small and has none of the self-confidence of the bustling Victorian world. And the mass of the people are wholly illiterate and are still overwhelmingly country folk at the mercy of local lords or bailiffs or, as in much of Africa, unaware of any leadership or change outside the tribal pattern. In such conditions the machinery of democracy is not enough to create its spirit. Parliament tends to remain an affair of cliques and manipulators. Pakistan before Ayub, Iran, the Egypt of Farouk—all are examples of systems, which though parliamentary in form, were and are in fact self-regarding, oligarchic, and to a considerable degree anti-social.

Since the old rural leaders and the new rich are so often unable to canalize the new ambitions of the people, they are often thrust aside in the years following independence. Again and again it is the army that steps in to provide new government: in the Sudan, in Egypt, in Iraq, in Pakistan. The representatives of the merchant and landlord groups are set aside, and military leaders, coming in with a tradition of service and a reputation of integrity, take over and attempt to pull the country together to face the truly daunting problems of development in the first stages of independence.

And I think we would do well to remember how daunting these problems are. The first and deepest is the dilemma we have already explored. In early days of economic development, there is no hope for expansion unless the people can be persuaded to undertake a large and expanding program of capital saving. Yet they are poor—poor by definition since the wealth-creating process has yet to begin. Saving for them entails lopping off a margin from current consumption when consumption is already so low that it is barely enough to sustain life. Even though the hope is that, five and ten years from now, conditions will be better, can the people be persuaded—least of all by free vote—to submit themselves to an even worse plight now? The dilemma, as we have seen, is absolutely inescapable because the need for saving is as unavoidable as the fact of poverty. It needs exceptional leadership, with very considerable administrative capacity and imaginative grasp, to ease the people out of this particular trap; and these qualities are not easily forthcoming in the traditional groups who make up the leadership in transitional societies.

The problem is made all the more involved by the fact that the coming of independence is precisely the hour when the hopes of the people are most acutely roused by the possibilities of achieving a modern form of society. The colonial struggle gave them political consciousness. They were told again and again during its course that only the wicked imperialists hold them back from a better life. Thus, when independence comes, they expect that better life and they expect it now. It is against this background that we should assess the pressures on their leaders.

To maintain themselves in power—the first commandment for politicians—they must be able to meet some of this rising popular pressure and to show some positive results. The chances are, however, that the turmoil of transition has lessened administrative efficiency, weakened disciplines of work, and possibly slowed down the entry of foreign capital. Economic conditions may well be worse. The pressures mount all the more rapidly as a result. These pressures are much greater than our stabler, wealthier world now finds easy to imagine. The only striking analogy that comes to mind is the pressure on any Western government if unemployment rises above a certain level. But to gauge the force of protest and discontent in the developing countries one would need to multiply the pressure a thousandfold. The issue is not simply one of being out of work for a time; it is all future possibility of work, all hope of a little wealth to come, the whole chance of moving on from stagnation and misery. Such pressure is political dynamite.

These conditions alone would be enough to tax the powers of leadership in the new state to the full and even to make the new rulers feel that they must take dictatorial powers in order to find the direction and discipline needed to face the nation's inescapable problems. But in addition to all these internal problems, they face an even more testing external difficulty. They have all come to power during the bitter international tensions of the Cold War.

They can neither change nor modify the broad struggle for power in the world in which the Great Powers maneuver to maintain their position, to extend their dominion and to achieve predominant influence. Smaller states may be able to play a part at the margin and, unhappily, as the pre-1914 crises in the Balkans showed, shifts of power at the margin can precipitate the general struggle. But the core of the fight is not theirs to influence. Dr. Nkrumah is never tired of quoting an old Swahili proverb which says that when the bull elephants fight, the grass is trampled down. In many parts of the world, the sense that the poorer, weaker nations are pawns in a bigger game, just grass to be trodden down in the struggle by the great ones, lends a tragic and, I think, moving edge to the search for neutralism. In the past, the Western Powers have often shown too little sympathetic understanding for the mood. The United States for years under the late Mr. John Foster Dulles condemned neutralism as a moral evil, forgetting its own early distaste for "entangling alliances." But the "morals" of resistance for very small states in the age of the fifty megaton bomb are at least dubious and it is not certain, in any case, whether a neutrality prepared to defend itself is not a much better safeguard than co-operation in alliances with the West.

The reason is very simple. Mass opinion still tends to become very easily anti-Western because colonial memories are so recent. To build alliances with the ex-colonial powers can easily be twisted to look like falling once again under their imperial control. This twist, it need hardly be said, is staple Communist propaganda. The royal government in Iraq fell in part because of its readiness to work with the West in a Middle-Eastern military alliance.

The blame is not all on one side. Neutralists have also earned suspicion by the way in which they have interpreted neutrality. Unfortunately the Cold War not only scares smaller powers; it also offers them temptations which very often they are unable to resist. It is, after all, very tempting for a local leader to think that he can play the Great-Power game. It gives a great sense of importance to believe himself able to play off America against Russia. The advantages at first seem greater than the risks. That by riding the tiger one may end up inside is not too obvious in the early stages of the game. If, for instance, you are having trouble with the opposition, why not turn to the Communists and get a little help? The problem of getting the Communists to stop helping afterwards belongs to a future too distant to be taken into account. In other words, the danger offered to small governments is not only a direct risk of invasion or attack but also a permanent temptation to involve themselves far out of their depth in the rapids and shoals of world politics.

I do not myself think we should meet this situation by succumbing to irritation and denunciation. It is tempting to lose one's patience and exclaim against local leaders who seem so irresponsible. But could we not try sometimes to put ourselves in their position? Are they not 'like adolescents who leave their father's house only to be involved instantly in an enormous street fight; or like children who go out into the great school of the world only to find the faculties shooting it out in just those classrooms where they had hoped to get their education? One cannot, I think, underline too much the inexperience and the sense of uncertainty which must prevail among new leaders who enter the school of the world and find the faculty throwing everything, including their desks, at each other. I confess that my own feeling is not one of irritation but rather of intense sympathy for leaders who have to take the first steps of independence over ground which gives way at every step.

However, there is no escape from the fact that for the time being the Cold War forms the environment of the modern world. The Communists' attempt at world dominion is one of the great ideological strains in their faith; however much of their tactics may vary, the underlying strategy has not yet changed. Equally, the Western powers will not abandon their desire to preserve a world in which plurality of power and capacity of choice are possible. The two aims are not compatible and all along the frontiers of the two worlds the struggle for influence and dominance cannot be evaded. We have therefore to assess the impact of the Cold War on the problems of developing states and to see how the rival ideologies influence local aspirations, particularly the great central driving aspiration to equal status and an equal chance.

We would, I think, be unwise to underestimate some of the immediate advantages which the Communists enjoy in this tough tussle for influence in the newly independent nations. For one thing, this is a time of chaotic change and hence of chaotic ideas. It is dangerously attractive to many minds to be offered a political and economic panacea as complete and apparently self-explanatory as Marxism-Leninism. It seems to tie up all their problems in a single order of explanation and to make sense of a world which they feel they do not understand and fear they never may. Another advantage enjoyed by communism is that in Asia, in Africa, in Latin America, Russia does not bear the stigma of having been a colonial power. This is paradoxical when you consider how much of Central Asia's non-Russian peoples are under Soviet control. But Russia's extension across Central Asia and Siberia to embrace so many Turkoman and Mongol peoples within its empire has the same irresistible, irreversible, almost geological force as China's imperial extension southwards or the engulfing of most of North America by the United States.

Moreover, the subject peoples—Kazakhs, Kirghiz, Uzbeks—have been drawn into the advantages of modern society as well as into its pains. The nomads from the steppes were thrown into the modernizing, industrializing process as ruthlessly as the Bantu of South Africa have been flung into the mines. But today such educational advance has accompanied the process that there are more graduates per head of population in Uzbekistan than in France. The Bantu of the Union of South Africa and the felleaga of Algeria have not fared so well. They have been left on the margins of the new modern society, unintegrated, unreconciled, the sullen proletariat of revolt. Add to this Russia's apparent freedom from racial prejudice, and its advantages in the minds of developing peoples should be clear. Then there are a number of reasons in practical politics to explain the Communists' relative advantage. When a new nation is faced with the enormous complexity and variety of economic and social problems that are inescapable after independence, the temptation to impose the rule of a single party and use hard discipline to solve them is obvious. And there stands the Communist party ready-made, offering its pattern of total obedience. Nationalist leaders looking for policies in the post-revolutionary phase are caught by the deceptive directions and vigour of the Communist solution.

It can, I think, be argued that this availability of the Soviet pattern helps to explain the unfolding paradox of the Castro régime in Cuba—a régime brought in by widespread popular revolt against the dictatorship and corruption of Batista, promising elections and civil liberties; yet degenerating almost at once into another kind of police state. There is evidence to suggest that Castro chose a Marxist pattern not because he had drawn his support from embattled peasants and workers—in fact, middle-class disgust with Batista was his strongest suit—but because it was the only pattern he knew to help him to exercise the power he had unexpectedly achieved. Faced with the multitudinous uncertainties of responsibility, he grabbed the only pattern which seemed likely to preserve his leadership and deal with his difficulties. It was Cuba's tragedy that a nation so relatively advanced in development—to give only one instance, more than half its population already lives in the cities—should be thrust back by totally inexperienced leadership to a repressive and brutal system usually associated with much earlier stages of breakthrough.

It is, of course, not only a question of communism offering ready-made solutions. Many of them seem to fit the real dilemmas very closely. At a time when changing the old leadership and bringing the masses into the new dynamic economy are pre-conditions of development, there is no doubt where communism stands. It is against the old landlord; it is against the new entrepreneur. It sides with the majority of the people whose aspirations are the motive force of change. The content of their policy also has its relevance. The Russians claim that such is their ability to achieve large rates of growth in the last forty years, that they can offer a pattern of rapid development and rapid capital accumulation in just those areas where the countries of the newly independent world need most help. They claim that their scale of capital formation has driven them forward at growth-rates of six, seven, and eight per cent a year, and the massive Communist drive for capital and production will quickly outstrip anything that the West, with its bungling experimental methods, can hope to offer. All this is heady stuff to a young government looking round desperately for policies with which to cope with all the problems of its day, and not perhaps sophisticated enough to grasp what the cost of so much "discipline" may be.

Nor do the Communists simply leave their claimed achievements to talk for themselves. Propaganda underlines them incessantly and offers of capital assistance reinforce the picture of Soviet success. Again and again missions set off to Moscow from Africa or Asia or Latin America and there receive offers of help in buying up the surpluses the West will not buy and capital assistance at very low rates of interest for a long period of time. At times it is almost as though the projects themselves— an Aswan Dam, a Volta Dam, a steel-mill for India—had become small sectors in the general fluctuating battle-front of world assistance. The building and the competition are not necessarily bad. On the contrary, more capital may be flowing into the underdeveloped areas than would otherwise be the case. But the political overtones, the sense of rivalry and pressure with which so much of the aid is beset, adds enormously to the political dilemmas of the poor nations reaching out desperately for a new way of life.

Given this context of competition, what shall we say of Western policies? Before we consider our positive aims and policies, I think we should realize soberly that the world-wide struggle is not necessarily "going our way," that we have formidable difficulties to overcome. The fact remains that the Western powers have been the colonial masters until the day before yesterday. Although the grace of making the transfers of imperial power has helped lessen colonial resentments, we still carry the ugly stigma of racialism. We are still implicated in the dangerous problem of apartheid in South Africa. We have our own Deep Souths and Notting Hills. We do not come with clean hands.

Again, the political pattern of multi-party democracy which we prefer, and often set up in colonies before we leave them, is not necessarily workable in the first turbulent days of independence. Crises at these times are not much less rigorous than our own crises of war, and we in the West usually meet such crises with governments of national union. So it is in most ex-colonies. Single-party government represents the clear-cut leadership needed when times are insanely complex and confused. Such government need not be Communist. But it is also unlikely to resemble the West's advanced political democracy. Nor is it simply a matter of crisis. A certain sophistication is also involved. If a leader has spent his life to achieve self-government from the foreigner, he cannot find it easy to give government up five years after independence because some newer leader has appeared on the scene.

Some of our economic patterns are difficult, too. Many Western governments put great emphasis on private investment as a chief instrument of economic development. But this runs into two opposite difficulties. Private capital on the scale needed to achieve "take-off" would need to be so great that it would arouse national or Leninist suspicions locally—especially if Western companies pushed their customary policy of seeking local participation not very vigorously or not at all.

The opposite difficulty is that, in fact, so much private capital is not usually forthcoming in any case and to rely on it alone would delay development indefinitely.

Of course, this difficulty has in fact been met by the great extension of Western public assistance programs in the last decade—to which the United States has made by far the largest contribution. But two things are clear about public aid. The rest of the free world has made no contribution commensurate with America's or with their own post-Marshall wealth. Certainly few have given anything like the one per cent of national income—which cannot surely be considered an excessive contribution to world development. The second point is that the aid programs have not been part of a general development strategy designed to bring the poor nations to "take-off" in the shortest time. Capital has been voted year by year in a haphazard way. Trade policies have even pulled in the other direction. There are thus new challenges to face, a new strategy to be worked out, new decisions to be taken.

Of one thing I am certain: if we continue with what is surely our greatest Western temptation, and think that in some way history owes us a solution, that we can, by pursuing our own most parochial self-interest, achieve in some miraculous way a consummation of world order, then we are heading not simply towards great disappointments, but towards disaster and tragedy as well. There has to be a new start, new places, a new approach. Otherwise we prepare for our defeat simply by default.

[7]

Economic
Adjustments

W. W. ROSTOW

The Stages of
Economic Development

Walter W. Rostow, professor of economic history at Massachusetts Institute of Technology, and chairman of the Policy Planning
Council of the Department of State, based the book from which
this selection is drawn on a set of lectures prepared and delivered
at Cambridge University in the autumn of 1958, while he was on
sabbatical leave from M.I.T. In his preface, he states that, as
student and teacher, he "found Marx's solution to the problem of
linking economic and non-economic behavior—and the solutions of
others who had grappled with it—unsatisfactory, without then feeling prepared to offer an alternative." Such an alternative—expressed
in the book's subtitle, "A Non-Communist Manifesto"—is presented in his account of economic growth based on a dynamic theory
of production and interpreted in terms of actual societies.

Professor Rostow distinguishes five basic stages of economic
growth, explains each stage in detail, and gives illustrations of his
conclusions. In particular, he takes two superficially very different
economies—those of the United States and the U.S.S.R.—and points
out in their history the same five stages of growth. He does not
subscribe to the Marxist view that history is uniquely determined by
economic forces and motives. Instead, he offers a comprehensive
and realistic alternative to Marx's theory of how societies evolve.

Chapter 2

The Five Stages-of-Growth—
A Summary

IT IS possible to identify all societies, in their economic dimensions, as
lying within one of five categories: the traditional society, the preconditions for take-off, the take-off, the drive to maturity, and the age of
high mass-consumption.

From *The Stages of Economic Growth; A Non-Communist Manifesto* by W. W.
Rostow. Cambridge University Press, 1960.

366

The Traditional Society

First, the traditional society. A traditional society is one whose struc: ture is developed within limited production functions, based on pre-Newtonian science and technology, and on pre-Newtonian attitudes towards the physical world. Newton is here used as a symbol for that watershed in history when men came widely to believe that the external world was subject to a few knowable laws, and was systematically capable of productive manipulation.

The conception of the traditional society is, however, in no sense static; and it would not exclude increases in output. Acreage could be expanded; some *ad hoc* technical innovations, often highly productive innovations, could be introduced in trade, industry and agriculture; productivity could rise with, for example, the improvement of irrigation works or the discovery and diffusion of a new crop. But the central fact about the traditional society was that a ceiling resulted from the fact that the potentialities which flow from modern science and technology were either not available or not regularly and systematically applied.

Both in the longer past and in recent times the story of traditional societies was thus a story of endless change. The area and volume of trade within them and between them fluctuated, for example, with the degree of political and social turbulence, the efficiency of central rule, the upkeep of the roads. Population—and, within limits, the level of life—rose and fell not only with the sequence of the harvests, but with the incidence of war and of plague. Varying degrees of manufacture developed; but, as in agriculture, the level of productivity was limited by the inaccessibility of modern science, its applications, and its frame of mind.

Generally speaking, these societies, because of the limitation on productivity, had to devote a very high proportion of their resources to agriculture; and flowing from the agricultural system there was an hierarchical social structure, with relatively narrow scope—but some scope—for vertical mobility. Family and clan connexions played a large role in social organization. The value system of these societies was generally geared to what might be called a long-run fatalism; that is, the assumption that the range of possibilities open to one's grandchildren would be just about what it had been for one's grandparents. But this long-run fatalism by no means excluded the short-run option that, within a considerable range, it was possible and legitimate for the individual to strive to improve his lot, within his lifetime. In Chinese villages, for example, there was an endless struggle to acquire or to avoid losing land, yielding a situation where land rarely remained within the same family for a century.

Although central political rule—in one form or another—often existed in traditional societies, transcending the relatively self-sufficient regions, the centre of gravity of political power generally lay in the regions, in the hands of those who owned or controlled the land. The landowner maintained fluctuating but usually profound influence over such central political power as existed, backed by its entourage of civil servants and soldiers, imbued with attitudes and controlled by interests transcending the regions.

In terms of history then, with the phrase "traditional society" we are grouping the whole pre-Newtonian world: the dynasties in China; the civilization of the Middle East and the Mediterranean; the world of medieval Europe. And to them we add the post-Newtonian societies which, for a time, remained untouched or unmoved by man's new capability for regularly manipulating his environment to his economic advantage.

To place these infinitely various, changing societies in a single category, on the ground that they all shared a ceiling on the productivity of their economic techniques, is to say very little indeed. But we are, after all, merely clearing the way in order to get at the subject of this book; that is, the post-traditional societies, in which each of the major characteristics of the traditional society was altered in such ways as to permit regular growth: its politics, social structure, and (to a degree) its values, as well as its economy.

The Preconditions for Take-Off

The second stage of growth embraces societies in the process of transition; that is, the period when the preconditions for take-off are developed; for it takes time to transform a traditional society in the ways necessary for it to exploit the fruits of modern science, to fend off diminishing returns, and thus to enjoy the blessings and choices opened up by the march of compound interest.

The preconditions for take-off were initially developed, in a clearly marked way, in Western Europe of the late seventeenth and early eighteenth centuries as the insights of modern science began to be translated into new production functions in both agriculture and industry, in a setting given dynamism by the lateral expansion of world markets and the international competition for them. But all that lies behind the break-up of the Middle Ages is relevant to the creation of the preconditions for take-off in Western Europe. Among the Western European states, Britain, favoured by geography, natural resources, trading possibilities, social and political structure, was the first to develop fully the preconditions for take-off.

The more general case in modern history, however, saw the stage of preconditions arise not endogenously but from some external intrusion by more advanced societies. These invasions—literal or figurative— shocked the traditional society and began or hastened its undoing; but they also set in motion ideas and sentiments which initiated the process by which a modern alternative to the traditional society was constructed out of the old culture.

The idea spreads not merely that economic progress is possible, but that economic progress is a necessary condition for some other purpose, judged to be good: be it national dignity, private profit, the general welfare, or a better life for the children. Education, for some at least, broadens and changes to suit the needs of modern economic activity. New types of enterprising men come forward—in the private economy, in government, or both—willing to mobilize savings and to take risks in pursuit of profit or modernization. Bands and other institutions for mobilizing capital appear. Investment increases, notably in transport, communications, and in raw materials in which other nations may have an economic interest. The scope of commerce, internal and external, widens. And, here and there, modern manufacturing enterprise appears, using the new methods. But all this activity proceeds at a limited pace within an economy and a society still mainly characterized by traditional low-productivity methods, by the old social structure and values, and by the regionally based political institutions that developed in conjunction with them.

In many recent cases, for example, the traditional society persisted side by side with modern economic activities, conducted for limited economic purposes by a colonial or quasi-colonial power.

Although the period of transition—between the traditional society and the take-off—saw major changes in both the economy itself and in the balance of social values, a decisive feature was often political. Politically, the building of an effective centralized national state—on the basis of coalitions touched with a new nationalism, in opposition to the traditional landed regional interests, the colonial power, or both, was a decisive aspect of the preconditions period; and it was, almost universally, a necessary condition for take-off.

There is a great deal more that needs to be said about the preconditions period, but we shall leave it for chapter 3, where the anatomy of the transition from a traditional to a modern society is examined.

The Take-Off

We come now to the great watershed in the life of modern societies: the third stage in this sequence, the take-off. The take-off is the interval

when the old blocks and resistances to steady growth are finally overcome. The forces making for economic progress, which yielded limited
bursts and enclaves of modern activity, expand and come to dominate
the society. Growth becomes its normal condition. Compound interest
becomes built, as it were, into its habits and institutional structure.

In Britain and the well-endowed parts of the world populated substantially from Britain (the United States, Canada, etc.), the proximate
stimulus for take-off was mainly (but not wholly)-technological. In the
more general case, the take-off awaited not only the build-up of social
overhead capital and a surge of technological development in industry
and agriculture, but also the emergence to political power of a group
prepared to regard the modernization of the economy as serious, high-
order political business.

During the take-off, the rate of effective investment and savings may
rise from, say, 5 per cent of the national income to 10 per cent or more;
although where heavy social overhead capital investment was required
to create the technical preconditions for take-off, the investment rate in
the preconditions period could be higher than 5 per cent, as, for example, in Canada before the 1890's and Argentina before 1914. In such
cases capital imports usually formed a high proportion of total investment in the preconditions period and sometimes even during the take-
off itself, as in Russia and Canada during their pre-1914 railway booms.

During the take-off new industries expand rapidly, yielding profits, a
large proportion of which are reinvested in new plant; and these new
industries, in turn, stimulate, through their rapidly expanding requirement for factory workers, the services to support them, and for other
manufactured goods, a further expansion in urban areas and in other
modern industrial plants. The whole process of expansion in the modern
sector yields an increase of income in the hands of those who not only
save at high rates but place their savings at the disposal of those engaged
in modern sector activities. The new class of entrepreneurs expands; and
it directs the enlarging flows of investment in the private sector. The
economy exploits hitherto unused natural resources and methods of
production.

New techniques spread in agriculture as well as industry, as agriculture
is commercialized, and increasing numbers of farmers are prepared to
accept the new methods and the deep changes they bring to ways of
life. The revolutionary changes in agricultural productivity are an essential condition for successful take-off; for modernization of a society increases radically its bill for agricultural products. In a decade or two both
the basic structure of the economy and the social and political structure
of the society are transformed in such a way that a steady rate of growth
can be, thereafter, regularly sustained.

As indicated in chapter 4, one can approximately allocate the take-off of Britain to the two decades after 1783; France and the United States to the several decades preceding 1860; Germany, the third quarter of the nineteenth century; Japan, the fourth quarter of the nineteenth century; Russia and Canada the quarter-century or so preceding 1914; while during the 1950's India and China have, in quite different ways, launched their respective take-offs.

The Drive to Maturity

After take-off there follows a long interval of sustained if fluctuating progress, as the now regularly growing economy drives to extend modern technology over the whole front of its economic activity. Some 10–20 per cent of the national income is steadily invested, permitting output regularly to outstrip the increase in population. The make-up of the economy changes unceasingly as technique improves, new industries accelerate, older industries level off. The economy finds its place in the international economy: goods formerly imported are produced at home; new import requirements develop, and new export commodities to match them. The society makes such terms as it will with the requirements of modern efficient production, balancing off the new against the older values and institutions, or revising the latter in such ways as to support rather than to retard the growth process.

Some sixty years after take-off begins (say, forty years after the end of take-off) what may be called maturity is generally attained. The economy, focused during the take-off around a relatively narrow complex of industry and technology, has extended its range into more refined and technologically often more complex processes; for example, there may be a shift in focus from the coal, iron, and heavy engineering industries of the railway phase to machine-tools, chemicals, and electrical equipment. This, for example, was the transition through which Germany, Britain, France, and the United States had passed by the end of the nineteenth century or shortly thereafter. But there are other sectoral patterns which have been followed in the sequence from take-off to maturity, which are considered in chapter 5.

Formally, we can define maturity as the stage in which an economy demonstrates the capacity to move beyond the original industries which powered its take-off and to absorb and to apply efficiently over a very wide range of its resources—if not the whole range—the most advanced fruits of (then) modern technology. This is the stage in which an economy demonstrates that it has the technological and entrepreneurial skills to produce not everything, but anything that it chooses to produce. It may lack (like contemporary Sweden and Switzerland, for example) the raw materials or other supply conditions required to produce a given type of output economically; but its dependence is a matter of economic choice or political priority rather than a technological or institutional necessity.

Historically, it would appear that something like sixty years was required to move a society from the beginning of take-off to maturity. Analytically the explanation for some such interval may lie in the powerful arithmetic of compound interest applied to the capital stock, combined with the broader consequences for a society's ability to absorb modern technology of three successive generations living under a regime where growth is the normal condition. But, clearly, no dogmatism is justified about the exact length of the interval from take-off to maturity.

The Age of High Mass-Consumption

We come now to the age of high mass-consumption, where, in time, the leading sectors shift towards durable consumers' goods and services: a phase from which Americans are beginning to emerge; whose not unequivocal joys Western Europe and Japan are beginning energetically to probe; and with which Soviet society is engaged in an uneasy flirtation.

As societies achieved maturity in the twentieth century two things happened: real income per head rose to a point where a large number of persons gained a command over consumption which transcended basic food, shelter, and clothing; and the structure of the working force changed in ways which increased not only the proportion of urban to total population, but also the proportion of the population working in offices or in skilled factory jobs—aware of and anxious to acquire the consumption fruits of a mature economy.

In addition to these economic changes, the society ceased to accept the further extension of modern technology as an overriding objective. It is in this post-maturity stage, for example, that, through the political process, Western societies have chosen to allocate increased resources to social welfare and security. The emergence of the welfare state is one manifestation of a society's moving beyond technical maturity; but it is also at this stage that resources tend increasingly to be directed to the production of consumers' durables and to the diffusion of services on a mass basis, if consumers' sovereignty reigns. The sewing-machine, the bicycle, and then the various electric-powered household gadgets were gradually diffused. Historically, however, the decisive element has been the cheap mass automobile with its quite revolutionary effects—social as well as economic—on the life and expectations of society.

For the United States, the turning point was, perhaps, Henry Ford's moving assembly line of 1913–14; but it was in the 1920's, and again in the post-war decade, 1946–56, that this stage of growth was pressed to, virtually, its logical conclusion. In the 1950's Western Europe and Japan appear to have fully entered this phase, accounting substantially for a momentum in their economies quite unexpected in the immediate post-war years. The Soviet Union is technically ready for this stage, and, by every sign, its citizens hunger for it; but Communist leaders face difficult political and social problems of adjustment if this stage is launched.

Beyond Consumption

Beyond, it is impossible to predict, except perhaps to observe that Americans, at least, have behaved in the past decade as if diminishing relative marginal utility sets in, after a point, for durable consumers' goods; and they have chosen, at the margin, larger families—behaviour in the pattern of Buddenbrooks[1] dynamics. Americans have behaved as if, having been born into a system that provided economic security and high mass-consumption, they placed a lower valuation on acquiring additional increments of real income in the conventional form as opposed to the advantages and values of an enlarged family. But even in this adventure in generalization it is a shade too soon to create—on the basis of one case—a new stage-of-growth, based on babies, in succession to the age of consumers' durables: as economists might say, the income-elasticity of demand for babies may well vary from society to society. But it is true that the implications of the baby boom along with the not wholly unrelated deficit in social overhead capital are likely to dominate the American economy over the next decade rather than the further diffusion of consumers' durables.

Here then, in an impressionistic rather than an analytic way, are the stages-of-growth which can be distinguished once a traditional society begins its modernization: the transitional period when the preconditions for take-off are created generally in response to the intrusion of a foreign power, converging with certain domestic forces making for modernization; the take-off itself; the sweep into maturity generally taking up the life of about two further generations; and then, finally, if the rise of income has matched the spread of technological virtuosity (which, as we shall see, it need not immediately do) the diversion of the fully mature

---

[1] In Thomas Mann's novel of three generations, the first sought money; the second, born to money, sought social and civic position; the third, born to comfort and family prestige, looked to the life of music. The phrase is designed to suggest, then, the changing aspirations of generations, as they place a low value on what they take for granted and seek new forms of satisfaction.

economy to the provision of durable consumers' goods and services (as well as the welfare state) for its increasingly urban—and then suburban—population. Beyond lies the question of whether or not secular spiritual stagnation will arise, and, if it does, how man might fend it off. . . .

A Dynamic Theory of Production

These stages are not merely descriptive. They are not merely a way of generalizing certain factual observations about the sequence of development of modern societies. They have an inner logic and continuity. They have an analytic bone-structure, rooted in a dynamic theory of production.

The classical theory of production is formulated under essentially static assumptions which freeze—or permit only once-over change—in the variables most relevant to the process of economic growth. As modern economists have sought to merge classical production theory with Keynesian income analysis they have introduced the dynamic variables: population, technology, entrepreneurship, etc. But they have tended to do so in forms so rigid and general that their models cannot grip the essential phenomena of growth, as they appear to an economic historian. We require a dynamic theory of production which isolates not only the distribution of income between consumption, saving, and investment (and the balance of production between consumers and capital goods), but which focuses directly and in some detail on the composition of investment and on developments within particular sectors of the economy. The argument that follows is based on such a flexible, disaggregated theory of production.

When the conventional limits on the theory of production are widened, it is possible to define theoretical equilibrium positions not only for output, investment, and consumption as a whole, but for each sector of the economy.

Within the framework set by forces determining the total level of output, sectoral optimum positions are determined on the side of demand, by the levels of income and of population, and by the character of tastes; on the side of supply, by the state of technology and the quality of entrepreneurship, as the latter determines the proportion of technically available and potentially profitable innovations actually incorporated in the capital stock.

In addition, one must introduce an extremely significant empirical hypothesis: namely, that deceleration is the normal optimum path of a sector, due to a variety of factors operating on it, from the side of both supply and demand.

The equilibria which emerge from the application of these criteria are a set of sectoral paths, from which flows, as first derivatives, a sequence of optimum patterns of investment.

Historical patterns of investment did not, of course, exactly follow these optimum patterns. They were distorted by imperfections in the private investment process, by the policies of governments, and by the impact of wars. Wars temporarily altered the profitable directions of investment by setting up arbitrary demands and by changing the conditions of supply; they destroyed capital; and, occasionally, they accelerated the development of new technology relevant to the peacetime economy and shifted the political and social framework in ways conducive to peacetime growth. The historical sequence of business-cycles and trend-periods results from these deviations of actual from optimal patterns; and such fluctuations, along with the impact of wars, yield historical paths of growth which differ from those which the optima, calculated before the event, would have yielded.

Nevertheless, the economic history of growing societies takes a part of its rude shape from the effort of societies to approximate the optimum sectoral paths.

At any period of time, the rate of growth in the sectors will vary greatly; and it is possible to isolate empirically certain leading sectors, at early stages of their evolution, whose rapid rate of expansion plays an essential direct and indirect role in maintaining the overall momentum of the economy. For some purposes it is useful to characterize an economy in terms of its leading sectors; and a part of the technical basis for the stages of growth lies in the changing sequence of leading sectors. In essence it is the fact that sectors tend to have a rapid growth-phase, early in their life, that makes it possible and useful to regard economic history as a sequence of stages rather than merely as a continuum, within which nature never makes a jump.

The stages-of-growth also require, however, that elasticities of demand be taken into account, and that this familiar concept be widened; for these rapid growth phases in the sectors derive not merely from the discontinuity of production functions but also from high price—or income-elasticities of demand. Leading sectors are determined not merely by the changing flow of technology and the changing willingness of entrepreneurs to accept available innovations: they are also partially determined by those types of demand which have exhibited high elasticity with respect to price, income, or both.

The demand for resources has resulted, however, not merely from demands set up by private taste and choice, but also from social decisions and from the policies of governments—whether democratically responsive or not. It is necessary, therefore, to look at the choices made by societies in the disposition of their resources in terms which transcend conventional market processes. It is necessary to look at their welfare functions, in the widest sense, including the non-economic processes which determined them.

The course of birth-rates, for example, represents one form of welfare choice made by societies, as income has changed; and population curves reflect (in addition to changing death-rates) how the calculus about family size was made in the various stages; from the usual (but not universal) decline in birth-rates, during or soon after the take-off, as urbanization took hold and progress became a palpable possibility, to the recent rise, as Americans (and others in societies marked by high mass-consumption) have appeared to seek in larger families values beyond those afforded by economic security and by an ample supply of durable consumers' goods and services.

And there are other decisions as well that societies have made as the choices open to them have been altered by the unfolding process of economic growth; and these broad collective decisions, determined by many factors—deep in history, culture, and the active political process—outside the market-place, have interplayed with the dynamics of market demand, risk-taking, technology and entrepreneurship, to determine the specific content of the stages of growth for each society.

How, for example, should the traditional society react to the intrusion of a more advanced power: with cohesion, promptness, and vigour, like the Japanese; by making a virtue of fecklessness, like the oppressed Irish of the eighteenth century; by slowly and reluctantly altering the traditional society, like the Chinese?

When independent modern nationhood is achieved, how should the national energies be disposed: in external aggression, to right old wrongs or to exploit newly created or perceived possibilities for enlarged national power; in completing and refining the political victory of the new national government over old regional interests; or in modernizing the economy?

Once growth is under way, with the take-off, to what extent should the requirements of diffusing modern technology and maximizing the rate of growth be moderated by the desire to increase consumption *per capita* and to increase welfare?

When technological maturity is reached, and the nation has at its command a modernized and differentiated industrial machine, to what ends should it be put, and in what proportions: to increase social security, through the welfare state; to expand mass-consumption into the range of durable consumers' goods and service; to increase the nation's stature and power on the world scene; or to increase leisure?

And then the question beyond, where history offers us only fragments: what to do when the increase in real income itself loses its charm?

Babies, boredom, three-day week-ends, the moon, or the creation of new inner, human frontiers in substitution for the imperatives of scarcity?

In surveying now the broad contours of each stage-of-growth, we are examining, then, not merely the sectoral structure of economies, as they transformed themselves for growth, and grew; we are also examining a succession of strategic choices made by various societies concerning the disposition of their resources, which include but transcend the income- and price-elasticities of demand.

JOHN KENNETH GALBRAITH

Economic Development in Perspective

Hundreds of articles and many books have been written on the most effective means of developing the economies of technologically backward countries. This array of published material reflects a wide diversity of views between those who urge that primary emphasis should be given to agriculture, those who insist on rapid, even if painful, industrialization, and those who would like to split the difference and have a little of both. Some are convinced that economic development cannot be achieved without complete control, or even coercion, by the state. Others shy away from this total—and often totalitarian—philosophy. They believe that, over the long run, more can be accomplished by persuasion than by the use of force, and that in the development of the economy of non-Western countries there is room not only for the state, but also for the private entrepreneur, and for harmonious cooperation between the two.

But however diverse may be the views of economists, Western and non-Western, "What is not in doubt," says John Kenneth Galbraith, "is the need for planning by the less developed country." In this short book, one of the best-known economists of the United States presents thought-provoking ideas based not only on theoretical work but on first-hand observation of development in non-Western nations, particularly India, where Mr. Galbraith was appointed U.S. Ambassador in 1961. Canadian-born, Mr. Galbraith has held the Paul M. Warburg Professorship of Economics at Harvard University. He served during World War II in the Office

of *Price Administration*, and after the war, before returning to
Harvard, was for some years an editor of *Fortune* magazine. He is
the author of several books, of which the most widely known is
The Affluent Society, 1958.

Chapter 3
On the Theory of Development Planning

FEW WORDS in our time are more fashionable in economic and political
discussion than "planning," or are used, one imagines, with less precision. This absence of precision was perhaps most admirably illustrated in
the early forties by the eminent British soldier and philosopher, Colonel
Blimp, who, on taking note of the current concern for postwar economic
prospects, was heard to say: "All this planning, it can lead only to chaos.
But one thing you can say for chaos; it gives real scope for free enterprise."

This imprecision was long matched by the emotions which the word
"planning" aroused. For some planning was the *sine qua non* of progress.
For others it was the quintessence of evil. Organizations and political
parties have flourished to promote planning. Others came into existence
to oppose it. Not long after the end of World War II a sizable number
of deeply concerned scholars from the United States and Western
Europe gathered on a mountain top in Switzerland to form an organization devoted to international opposition to planning. It never developed
any great influence, partly, I am told, because of an ideological schism
over whether navies should be socially owned or privately provided on a
lease-hire system by the private sector.

II

In fact one can give a good deal of precision to the notion of planning.
And as the meaning conveyed thereby has come to be better appreciated
in recent times, much of the emotion has gone out of the discussion. In
the modern and developed economy there is a certain choice as to how
resources—labor, land, capital, natural resources—will be organized for
productive purposes. The task, or a large part of it, can be entrusted to
the market; this will interpret the wants of the consumer to the producer

through the medium of higher prices and the promise of higher earnings. The market also sets in motion the investment of savings, the recruitment of labor, and the organization of the productive machinery which provides the needed and wanted products.

There is the alternative of a much more determinate organization of resources. Goals, specifying the things to be done and the goods to be produced, are proclaimed. The state then assumes the powers necessary to pursue these goals. In one way or another it ensures that the employment of labor and capital and the exploitation of other resources will contribute to, or be consistent with, the goals that have been specified. It establishes and operates the organizations that produce the goods.

The latter point is worth a further word. The theory of planning originated in close alliance with the theory of socialism—one of the reasons, more than incidentally, why the word "planning" was so long regarded in nonsocialist quarters with uneasiness. Socialist theory by its nature placed great emphasis on public ownership of natural resources and capital plant and, subject to political exigencies, of land. This was deemed necessary to prevent exploitation, ensure social justice, and ensure also that political power would not be arrogated by the owners of capital. With the development of the modern interest in planning, the public ownership and control of resources came almost implicitly to be considered both necessary and sufficient for ensuring a planned use of resources. With public ownership there could be planning; without public ownership there could be no effective planning.

In reality, as so often happens in the social sciences, we are dealing with distinctions that are far less sharp than the everyday discussion makes them out to be. Those countries that rely extensively on the market have, none the less, a substantial sector in which resources are organized by the state. If we take as the measure of the amount of planning the proportion of all current resources—gross national product—fully controlled and disposed of by the state, about 20 per cent of the American economy is planned. For India the comparable figure is 13–14 per cent. The market economy of the United States has a larger public sector than the socialist economy of India. And one could continue. While in the Soviet Union productive resources are fully owned by the state, considerable and skillful use is made of pecuniary incentives for labor and management. There is also a sizable market for privately produced agricultural products. In Poland as in Yugoslavia agriculture as a whole remains subject to market incentives.

A few weeks ago President Kennedy announced the first of a series of steps designed to carry a man to the moon. Along with most of my countrymen, and I think most men and women everywhere, I feel a sense of excitement over this adventure. But it is not a form of travel which will soon be put on a paying basis. The initial tickets will cost several billions of dollars apiece, a price which can be counted upon to discourage the average tourist. So this adventure cannot be left to the market; it can be the product only of planning. From the planned sector of the American economy also came atomic energy; from it also has come much modern electronic development. The modern jet air transport was similarly the product of planned development, a by-product of military procurement. Many of the other technical break-throughs in the unplanned economies have had a similar origin in recent times. We have public initiative in planning without public ownership. The two are no longer indissolubly allied.

III

I do not argue that the distinction between the planned and the unplanned economy is without meaning. But most of what the professional ideologists say about the distinction is without meaning. Many things must be planned even in those economic systems where the market has a major role. And the market plays an important part in the economic systems that are planned. We see a planned use of resources combined with public ownership of capital plant. We find it where the control and administration of capital remains in private hands. Clearly we must be wary of glib generalization in the discussion of planned and unplanned economies. I might add that there are few areas where it is more prevalent in our age.

What is not in doubt is the need for planning by the less developed country. For reasons I have just indicated there is much that the market can usefully encourage and accomplish. But the market cannot reach forward to take great strides when these are called for. As it cannot put a man in space so it cannot bring quickly into existence a steel industry where there was little or no steelmaking capacity before. Nor can it quickly create an integrated industrial plant. Above all, no one can be certain that it will do so in countries where development has lagged and where there is not only a need for development but an urgent demand that it occur promptly. To trust to the market is to take an unacceptable risk that nothing, or too little, will happen.

This is why in the developing country the word planning has ceased to be controversial. Five-year plans are the invention of, and were once the exclusive possession of, the Soviet Union. Now Americans and Western Europeans assemble without thought to consider how they may help finance the five-year plans of India or Pakistan. The country which does not have goals, and a program for reaching these goals, is commonly assumed to be going nowhere. This may well be so.

IV

Because planning is now taken for granted, we have been less critical of contemporary developments in its methods in recent years than would be desirable. In the last decade I have had occasion to examine a considerable number of these plans. And in the next world I face quite a few years in that well-populated part of purgatory where, it is known, economists are made to answer for all the advice they have given to governments. I am persuaded that it would be a grave error to imagine that the theory and practice of planning are completed edifices.

Earlier, I have stressed the need for accommodating our ideas of planning to the stage of development of the particular country. In the early stages of development, plan creation is not properly a matter of economic planning at all; rather it is to build basic administrative organs, to develop the educational and basic cultural structure, and to get a viable and progressive social system. In Western Europe and the United States these steps following the French and American revolutions laid the foundation for economic advance. In developing its Central Asian republics, as the visitor learns, the Soviets gave high priority to developing an effective system of provincial administration, to education, to providing a transportation system, and to getting the nomads into a settled system of agriculture. These steps were clearly regarded as prerequisites for further agricultural and industrial development.

It follows that in the early stages of development the task is not to set production targets and plan investment outlays. Rather it is to lay the administrative, social, and educational groundwork for such advance. Only in later stages is detailed planning of investment in order. This type of planning, that which is commonplace in India and Pakistan, belongs, relatively speaking, to a rather advanced stage of development. I should like now to comment on this planning.

V

The standard modern development plan is an investment plan. It reflects decisions on how best to employ scarce capital resources. Its primary goal is the thing that investment is assumed to accomplish, namely, a specified and presumably adequate rate of economic growth. In this planning a good deal of thought goes into the matching and phasing of the various segments of the plan—into ensuring that kinds and amounts of steel being produced will match requirements for steel in kind and amount and that this balance between supply and requirements is maintained over time. Equally careful attention is accorded the supply of investment resources—the question of where, internally and externally, the capital is coming from. One can find little fault, in principle at least, with the way this part of the planning task is performed. There are, however, certain other things for which a good plan must provide, and the need for these is not always so clearly perceived. Let me mention the three further and often missing elements of a good plan.

First, a good plan must provide a strategy for economic advance. In the nature of a strategy some things are central—that is, strategic, clearly separate from that which is useful or passive. Among angels, it is known, virtue goes unnoticed. Likewise if everything is held to be vital the truly vital will escape attention. By way of illustration, in an industrialized country a highly efficient transportation system, a low-cost steel supply, and an economic and reliable source of power are all indispensable. With these something is certain to happen; without them one can be less sure. Certainly other aspects of industrialization, if not unimportant, are less important. Similarly in agriculture, while many things are useful, a few things are indispensable. Water, fertilizer, and improved seed can revolutionize agriculture. Most other agricultural services can work only moderate change.

Working against these strategic forces is the pressure of individuals, departments, and regions to have their favorite enterprises included in the modern plan. This pressure is great. The desire not to overlook anything is also strong. So the plan easily becomes not a plan but a list of all the things that everyone would like to have done or that anyone believes ought to be done. Specification of the things of strategic urgency is lost.

In the American colonies prior to independence and in the early years of the Republic, there was no great surplus of food. The space between the mountains and the sea was limited and not everywhere fertile; the demands for food and fodder sometimes exceeded its capacity and food had to be imported from Europe. A plan formulated along modern lines for early American agriculture would have emphasized the need for agricultural colleges, extension services, veterinary services, plant breeding, better marketing, control of insect pests, and the provision of storage capacity for buffer stocks. Doubtless also there would have been mention of the need for improved transportation. But among the other excellent and useful ideas this could easily have been overlooked. In 1825 the State of New York opened a canal which connected the black lands of the West with the centers of population. On its completion the food shortage came to an end; there has, I am happy to say, been no sign of recurrence. This canal was the strategic factor in the plan. The importance of isolating and emphasizing the elements of strategic importance is not less in the developing country today.

VI

The second requirement of a good plan is that it emphasize both the visible and the invisible dimensions of industrial achievement. Like an iceberg, much of a modern industrial society is out of sight. And, also like an iceberg, it is its invisible part which has the greatest capacity for causing shipwreck. To get capital plant—steel mills, railway lines, coal mines, airplanes, oil rigs—into use is the visible achievement of development planning. To ensure that this plant is efficiently used—that management is independent and sound, that in consequence material costs are low, product quality good, cost-of-production low, and earnings adequate for replacement and expansion of plant—is the much larger part of the task. This part lies below the surface, and it is not sufficient that the developing country be only adequate in these respects. It must be more productive than its older competitors. It was by low cost and efficient production that Germany and Japan won their place in the industrial constellation against the competition of the earlier arrivals. New industrial countries such as Israel and Yugoslavia have recently been making their bid in the same way. It is thus that earnings for further expansion, both domestic and foreign, are won.

I think it extremely important that the modern plan set firm targets for this invisible achievement. As valuable as firm targets for steel output are firm targets for man-hour productivity, costs, and returns. Goals so set become binding on all concerned. All are challenged to meet them. All have a sense of failure if there is a falling short in performance. And there is, in addition, the highly practical fact that failure can be identified with those responsible. If there are no standards then no one fails the examination. Promotion and honor accrue to all alike. Life was not meant to be that easy, and certainly not in a developing nation.

In much of our present planning we set targets for visible physical accomplishment—for capacity in place or for production. This is possibly the easiest and certainly the smallest part of the task. Targets are equally practical for managerial performance, labor productivity, costs, and returns; all lend themselves admirably to objective measurement. It is of the greatest importance that the modern development plan be as complete in respect of these goals as of any other.

VII

The final requirement of modern development planning is that it have a theory of consumption. As I have noted, much attention has been given to the instruments for control of production. And much has been given to the means for expanding productive capacity and achieving an integrated and balanced growth. A theory of consumption—a view of what the production is ultimately for—has been surprisingly little discussed and has been too little missed. This is not a subject which I have space to deal with extensively here. But let me suggest the nature of the problem.

To say that production is planned is to say that the market has in some measure been accepted as an authority on what should be produced. The decision has passed to government.

On what grounds should government decide? How much should be withheld from present consumption to nurture increased future consumption? If today's bread is barely sufficient, can one ask for sacrifices therein so that tomorrow's people will have butter?

More important, what kind of consumption should be planned? Should it take the consumption of the more highly developed countries as a model? Should it be guided by whatever market demand exists, which in most of the underdeveloped countries will reflect a considerable inequality of incomes, with the result that production will be heavily influenced by the wants of the well-to-do minority? Or should production be tailored above all to serving as cheaply as possible the recognizable needs and desires of the average low-income consumer?

If these questions are not faced deliberately they may be answered without thought. In particular there is danger that the consumption patterns of the more developed countries will be followed as a matter of course. Prestige—the wish to show off television and multilane highways—may play a part. The theory of consumption must be more democratic than this. Prime attention must be accorded goods that are within the range of the modal income—that can be purchased by the typical family. The burden of proof is strongly on the rest.

Cheap bicycles in a low-income country are thus more important than cheap automobiles. An inexpensive electric lighting system for the villages is better than a high-capacity system which runs equipment the people cannot afford. Inexpensive radio sets are important; television belongs to another day. Above all nothing is so important as abundant and efficiently produced food, clothing, and shelter, for these are the most universal of requirements.

India, I am glad to say, has gone farther than any other developing country in testing her consumer goods production against average need. But in all developing countries we need to have much more clearly in mind the particular consumer for whom in the last analysis the planning is done.

Specification of the strategically important, concern for the invisible as well as the visible requirements of industrial achievement, and a clear view of the consumer being served—these seem to me the unfinished business of modern development planning.

[8]

Population
Problems

THOMAS R. MALTHUS

A Summary View of the Principles of Population

Of the many problems facing the newly emerged non-Western nations, that of rapid population growth is regarded in many areas as the most critical, particularly where food production and the provision of housing, clothing, educational facilities, and jobs lag far behind. This problem, however, was at one time of concern also to Western Europe.

Early in the nineteenth century, the Reverend Thomas R. Malthus wrote an essay entitled "A Summary View of the Principles of Population" for the 1824 supplement to the Encyclopaedia Britannica. This essay, which was published independently in a revised and shortened form in 1830, stirred widespread controversy in Malthus' day, and continues to be widely discussed in our times.

Malthus, basing his conclusions on developments in Western Europe, contended that populations, if unchecked, tend to grow in a geometrical progression and at a rate that would double the numbers about every twenty-five years. By contrast, food supplies, in his opinion, could increase only in arithmetical progression. Thus he foresaw dire consequences for human beings unless population growth were checked by either positive measures, such as war, civil strife, disease, starvation and so on, which he regarded as tantamount to misery and vice; or by preventive measures, which he described as "prudential restraint on marriage."

In the case of Europe, Malthus' fears that population growth would outrun food resources proved to be unfounded. In part this was due to the ravages of many wars and of civil strife. More important, however, were three major developments. First, there was large-scale emigration overseas—to the United States, Canada, Latin America, Australia and New Zealand. As a result of this emigration, there are now over 350 million people of European descent living in countries of immigration. Had this number of Europeans been added to the present population of 300 million in Europe exclusive of the U.S.S.R., this area would have today a population close to that of Communist China, and some 200 million more than contemporary India. Second, through the use of technology, most of the European countries modernized their agriculture, and thus acquired the capacity to produce more food with the labor of far fewer workers—as happened even more dramatically in the United States, where only 8 per cent of the people now feeds the largely urban population.

And, third, the growth of cities, to which peasants flocked in search of work in factories, completely altered the way of life in Britain, France, Germany, Belgium, the Netherlands, the Scandinavian countries, and northern Italy—but not in Spain, Portugal, or Italy's southland, which remained backward agrarian areas. In urban centers people found that they did not need the labor of many hands as they had done when they lived on the land, and that they could neither feed, house, nor educate a large number of children on what they earned. Through what Malthus called "prudential restraint," the number of births markedly declined after 1850 and has remained relatively stable.

Today, however, the question is being asked whether the prophecies of Malthus, which proved untrue for Western Europe, may not turn out to be tragically true for the non-Western peoples, who have no outlet for large-scale emigration, who for the most part still have a backward, relatively unproductive agriculture, and who have not yet moved in significant numbers to urban centers.

Before reading about the population problem of non-Western countries, let us re-read what Malthus said.

TAKING, therefore, into consideration the actual rate of increase, which appears from the best documents to have taken place over a very large extent of country in the United States of America, very variously circumstanced as to healthiness and rapidity of progress; considering further, the rate of increase which has taken place in New Spain, and also in many countries of Europe, where the means of supporting a family, and other circumstances favourable to increase, bear no comparison with those of the United States; and adverting particularly to the great increase of population which has taken place in this country during the last twenty years, under the formidable obstacles to its progress which must press themselves upon the attention of the most careless observer, it must appear, that the assumption of a rate of increase such as would double the population in twenty-five years, as representing the natural progress of population, when not checked by the difficulty of procuring the means of subsistence, or other peculiar causes of premature mortality, must be very decidedly within the truth.

It may be safely asserted, therefore, that population, when unchecked, increases in a geometrical progression of such a nature as to double itself every twenty-five years.

•　　•　　•

It is not in superseding the necessity of checks to population, in the progress of mankind to the full peopling of the earth (which may with truth be said to be a physical impossibility), but in directing these checks in such a way as to be the least prejudicial to the virtue and happiness of society, that government and human institutions produce their great effect. Here we know, from constant experience, that they have great power. Yet, even here, it must be allowed, that the power of government is rather indirect than direct, as the object to be attained depends mainly upon such a conduct on the part of individuals, as can seldom be directly enforced by laws, though it may be powerfully influenced by them.

This will appear, if we consider more particularly the nature of these checks which have been classed under the general heads of preventive and positive.

It will be found that they are all resolvable into *moral restraint, vice,* and *misery.* And if, from the laws of nature, some check to the increase of population be absolutely inevitable, and human institutions have any influence upon the extent to which each of these checks operates, a heavy responsibility will be incurred, if all that influence, whether direct or indirect, be not exerted to diminish the amount of vice and misery.

Moral restraint, in application to the present subject, may be defined to be, abstinence from marriage, either for a time or permanently, from prudential considerations, with a strictly moral conduct towards the sex in the interval. And this is the only mode of keeping population on a level with the means of subsistence, which is perfectly consistent with virtue and happiness. All other checks, whether of the preventive or the positive kind, though they may greatly vary in degree, resolve themselves into some form of vice or misery.

· · ·

The positive checks to population include all the causes, which tend in any way prematurely to shorten the duration of human life; such as unwholesome occupations—severe labour and exposure to the seasons—bad and insufficient food and clothing arising from poverty—bad nursing of children—excesses of all kinds—great towns and manufactories—the whole train of common diseases and epidemics—wars, infanticide, plague, and famine. Of these positive checks, those which appear to arise from the laws of nature, may be called exclusively misery; and those which we bring upon ourselves, such as wars, excesses of all kinds, and many others, which it would be in our power to avoid, are of a mixed nature. They are brought upon us by vice, and their consequences are misery.

Some of these checks, in various combinations, and operating with various force, are constantly in action in all the countries with which we are acquainted, and form the immediate causes which keep the population on a level with the means of subsistence.

A view of these checks, in most of the countries of which we have the best accounts, was taken in the Essay on Population. The object was to trace, in each country, those checks which appeared to be most effective in repressing population; and to endeavour to answer the question, generally, which had been applied, particularly, to New Holland by Captain Cook, namely, "By what means is the population of this country kept down to the number which it can subsist?"

It was hardly to be expected, however, that the general accounts of countries which are to be met with, should contain a sufficient number of details of the kind required, to enable us to ascertain what portion of the natural increase of population each individual check which could be traced had the power to overcome. In particular, it was not to be expected, that any accounts could inform us of the degree in which moral restraint prevails, when taken in its strictest sense. It is necessary, therefore, to attend chiefly to the greater or smaller number of persons who remain unmarried, or marry late; and the delay of marriage, owing to the difficulty of providing for a family, when the degree of irregularity to which it may lead cannot be ascertained, may be usefully called the prudential restraint on marriage and population. And this will be found to be the chief mode in which the preventive check practically operates.

But if the preventive check to population,—that check which can alone supersede great misery and mortality, operates chiefly by a prudential restraint on marriage; it will be obvious, as was before stated, that direct legislation cannot do much. Prudence cannot be enforced by laws, without a great violation of natural liberty, and a great risk of producing more evil than good. But still, the very great influence of a just and enlightened government, and the perfect security of property in creating habits of prudence, cannot for a moment be questioned. The principal causes and effects of these habits are thus stated in the "Principles of Political Economy Considered, with a View to their Practical Application, c. iv. p. 250."

> From real high wages, or the power of commanding a large portion of the necessaries of life, two very different results may follow; one, that of a rapid increase of population, in which case, the high wages are chiefly spent in the maintenance of large and frequent families; and the other, that of a decided improvement in the modes of subsistence, and the conveniences and comforts enjoyed, without a proportionate acceleration in the rate of increase.

In looking to these different results, the causes of them will evidently appear to be the different habits existing among the people of different countries, and at different times. In an inquiry into the causes of these different habits, we shall generally be able to trace those which produce the first result to all the circumstances which contribute to depress the lower classes of the people, which make them unable or unwilling to reason from the past to the future, and ready to acquiesce for the sake of present gratification, in a very low standard of comfort and respectability; and those which produce the second result, to all the circumstances which tend to elevate the character of the lower classes of society, which make them approach the nearest to beings who "look before and after," and who, consequently, cannot acquiesce patiently in the thought of depriving themselves and their children of the means of being respectable, virtuous, and happy.

Among the circumstances which contribute to the character first described, the most efficient will be found to be despotism, oppression, and ignorance; among those which contribute to the latter character, civil and political liberty, and education.

Of all the causes which tend to encourage prudential habits among the lower classes of society, the most essential is unquestionably civil liberty. No people can be much accustomed to form plans for the future, who do not feel assured that their industrious exertions, while fair and honourable, will be allowed to have free scope; and that the property which they either possess or may acquire, will be secured to them by a known code of just laws impartially administered. But it has been found by experience, that civil liberty cannot be permanently secured without political liberty. Consequently, political liberty becomes almost equally essential; and in addition to its being necessary in this point of view, its obvious tendency to teach the lower classes of society to respect themselves, by obliging the higher classes to respect them, must contribute greatly to all the good effects of civil liberty.

With regard to education, it might certainly be made general under a bad form of government, and might be very deficient under one in other respects good; but it must be allowed that the chances, both with regard to its quality and its prevalence, are greatly in favour of the latter. Education alone could do little against insecurity of property; but it would powerfully assist all the favourable consequences to be expected from civil and political liberty, which could not indeed be considered as complete without it.

The varying prevalence of these habits, owing to the causes above referred to, combined with the smaller or greater mortality occasioned by other customs, and the varying effects of soil and climate, must necessarily produce great differences in different countries, and at different periods, in the character of the predominant checks to population and the force of each. And this inference, which inevitably follows from theory, is fully confirmed by experience.

It appears, for instance, from the accounts we have received of ancient nations, and of the less civilized parts of the world, that war and violent diseases were the predominant checks to their population. The frequency of wars, and the dreadful devastations of mankind occasioned by them, united with the plagues, famines, and mortal epidemics of which there are records, must have caused such a consumption of the human species, that the exertion of the utmost power of increase must, in many cases, have been insufficient to supply it; and we see at once the source of those encouragements to marriage, and efforts to increase population, which, with inconsiderable exceptions, distinguished the legislation and general policy of ancient times. Yet there were some few men of more extended views, who, when they were looking to the settlement of a society in a more improved state, were fully aware, that, under the most beautiful form of government which their imagination could conceive, the greatest poverty and distress might be felt from a too rapid increase of population. And the remedies which they proposed were strong and violent in proportion to the greatness of the evil which they apprehended. Even the practical legislators who encouraged marriage, seemed to think that the supplies of children might sometimes follow too rapidly for the means of supporting them; and it appears to have been with a view to provide against this difficulty, and of preventing it from discouraging marriage, that they frequently sanctioned the inhuman practice of infanticide.

Under these circumstances, it is not to be supposed, that the prudential restraint on marriage should have operated to any considerable extent. Except in a few cases where a general corruption of morals prevailed which might act as a preventive check of the most vicious kind, a large portion of the procreative power was called into action, the occasional redundancy from which was checked by violent causes. These causes will be found resolvable almost wholly into vice and misery; the first of which, and a large portion of the second, it is always in the power of man to avoid.

In a review of the checks to population in the different states of modern Europe, it appears that the positive checks to population have prevailed less, and the preventive checks more, than in ancient times, and in the more uncultivated parts of the world. The destruction occasioned by war has unquestionably abated, both on account of its occurring, on the whole, less frequently, and its ravages not being so fatal, either to man or the means of his support, as they were formerly. And although, in the earlier periods of the history of modern Europe, plagues, famines, and mortal epidemics were not unfrequent; yet, as civilization and improvement have advanced, both their frequency and their mortality have been greatly reduced, and in some countries they are now almost unknown. This diminution of the positive checks to population, as it has been certainly much greater in proportion than the actual increase of food and population, must necessarily have been accompanied by an increasing operation of the preventive checks; and probably it may be said with truth, that in almost all the more improved countries of modern Europe, the principal check which at present keeps the population down to the level of the actual means of subsistence, is the prudential restraint on marriage.

JOSEPH MARION JONES

Does Overpopulation Mean Poverty?

Malthus' dire predictions of disaster proved false in the case of Western Europe. Can the non-Western nations hope to escape the dilemma once faced by the West? This might prove to be the case in a few areas which have a favorable ratio of food to population. Generally speaking, however, death rates in developing countries, where two-thirds of the human race live, have dropped sharply, while birth rates remain extremely high. Nor is it possible for them, where population is growing at the rate of 2 to 4 per cent annually, to find relief through large-scale emigration, as Europeans did a century or more ago.

How then, can non-Western nations solve the population problem? Possible courses of action are analyzed by Joseph Marion Jones in a pamphlet, Does Overpopulation Mean Poverty? from which this selection is drawn. Mr. Jones is a foreign policy writer and consultant with the Research and Education Committee for Free World. He has had long experience in government—in the United States Tariff Commission, the Department of State, the Economic Cooperation Administration, and as special Assistant to former Governor W. Averell Harriman of New York. Mr. Jones is the author of several books, among them The Fifteen Weeks, 1955.

Summary

The "Population Explosion"

SINCE the end of World War II a number of things have happened to bring forward the subject of population growth as World Problem Number Two—second only to the problem of preventing nuclear war:

1. Death rates in the underdeveloped countries have suddenly dropped, sharply, spectacularly, as a result of the use of newly discovered "miracle" drugs and insecticides in massive public health programs. Thus, infectious "mass killer" diseases have been brought under varying degrees of control while birth rates have remained extremely high, causing populations to increase at rates unprecedented in human history.

2. As a result of the foregoing, the world rate of population growth has doubled since 1945, from 1 per cent, which was itself an all-time historical high, to about 2 per cent a year in 1960 and is increasing steadily. At 2 per cent, our present world population of 3 billion will double to 6 billion in 35 years. In most countries in Asia, Africa, and Latin America, population is actually growing at 2 to 4 per cent annually. The highest rates of population growth in the world are found in Tropical America.

3. The people in the underdeveloped countries, where two-thirds of the human race live, have come for the first time in history to expect rapid improvements in conditions of life. Their governments, as well as the governments of the industrialized countries, are committed to help bring this about. In the underdeveloped countries per capita incomes average about $100 a year, and widespread illiteracy and malnutrition prevail. Even with increased foreign aid and investment, economic and social progress will be very slow if, indeed, possible in countries where population is increasing at today's rates. Without reduction of these rates of population increase, the hopes of two-thirds of the people on earth for a better life are doomed to frustration.

High Birth Rates Hold Back Economic and Social Development

If the world were organized in a unitary fashion without divisive political and economic boundaries, and if modern science, technology, and

From "Does Overpopulation Mean Poverty" by Joseph Marion Jones. Center for International Economic Growth, 1720 Rhode Island Ave., N.W., Washington, D.C., 1962.

statecraft were applied with sufficient intensity and on a world-wide scale to increasing production and distribution of food, certainly a mounting world population could be saved from starvation for some time to come. But we do not live in that kind of world. Hunger and malnutrition are today a major problem for two-thirds of the world's people, and it is taking considerable national and international development effort just to prevent the situation from worsening. In some countries even this effort is not succeeding.

In addition to widely prevalent hunger and malnutrition, underdeveloped countries have many conditions in common, including, (1) low per capita income, (2) a low rate of savings and investment, (3) high illiteracy, (4) a high proportion of the labor force engaged in agriculture, (5) a high percentage of dependent children, (6) low industrial output, (7) poor roads and communications, and (8) a high incidence of disease which depletes the energy of the workers. They also have in common (9) very high birth rates.

If birth rates were reduced, all the other conditions here mentioned could be much more easily improved, and this would speed up economic development and increase levels of living.

Economic development requires greater investment—in agriculture, industry, in public health, in education—and increased expenditures for public services and more efficient government administration. Increased investment requires greater savings. High birth rates operate to reduce savings: they increase the burden of mere subsistence in relation to income; they produce high percentages of dependent children; they increase the burden of education and other public services; they increase pressures on already densely settled land; and they create overcrowding, undermine health, and reduce productivity.

Development Goals Difficult or Impossible to Attain With High Birth Rates

During the 1950's development programs in the underdeveloped countries, plus a substantial volume of foreign aid and investment, succeeded in bringing about an average economic growth rate of 3 per cent a year in the underdeveloped countries as a whole. With population increasing at about 2 per cent a year in these countries, the annual increase in per capita income was about 1 per cent.

Mr. Paul Hoffman, Director of the United Nations Special Fund, has suggested as a goal for the 1960's that aid and investment from the industrialized countries be so increased as to sustain, during each year of the 1960's, an average economic growth rate of 4 per cent a year (per capita, 2 per cent) in the underdeveloped countries. The United Nations General Assembly in December, 1961, set a somewhat higher goal: the attainment by 1970 in each underdeveloped country of a 5 per cent annual growth rate.

The attainment of either of these goals will require enormous increases in domestic savings and in foreign aid and investment. It is highly doubtful that this can be done in many countries having high rates of population growth. To increase the economic growth rate from 3 per cent to 5 per cent over a period of ten years, a country would have to increase national income by 50 per cent.

Even if these over-all goals for national economic growth should be attained, the improvement in per capita income would be small in countries with high rates of population growth, because a large part of any annual increase in national income must go to provide for the annual increase in population. For a country whose population is increasing at a rate of 2 per cent each year and whose per capita income is now $100, attainment of the national economic growth rate set as a goal by the United Nations General Assembly would mean that over ten years per capita income would increase to only $123. If population is increasing at 3 per cent a year, attainment of the United Nations goal would mean an increase in per capita income to only $111 ten years hence.

Thus, even large increases in foreign aid and investment can bring only very slow and very small improvements in the life of the average worker or family in countries with high rates of population increase. With the industrialized countries growing richer, with living conditions for the average family in the underdeveloped countries improving almost imperceptibly, if at all, and with population pressures on land, living space and frontiers mounting, it is difficult to envision a peaceful, prosperous, and orderly world. In fact, because of mounting population pressures, increasing violence and war are in prospect.

Little Progress in Population Control

In all of Asia Africa, and Latin America, only in one country, Japan, have conscious efforts by the people brought about, since World War II, an effective lowering of the birth rate. The annual rate of population increase in Japan has declined from a postwar high of 2 per cent in 1947 to 1 per cent in 1961. The governments of India, Pakistan, and Tunisia recognize the problem and are moving, even though inadequately and thus far without significant numerical results, toward meeting it. But elsewhere in the three most underdeveloped continents the problem is either ignored or accorded only token recognition and action.

In the scientifically and industrially advanced countries of the world, including the United States, mature economies are able for the time being to care for increasing numbers at rising standards of living. In Europe the population growth rate is low. In the United States, Canada, Australia, New Zealand, and in the U.S.S.R., population growth rates have been quite high since World War II, though not as high as in underdeveloped countries, notwithstanding widespread family planning practices and facilities. Unless reduced they will eventually produce problems of a serious nature even in these countries.

Why So Little Progress?

Many leaders of differing faiths, throughout the world, urge full and public recognition of the true proportions of the population problem. They also urge that more extensive physiological and social research be undertaken on methods for controlling human fertility, methods acceptable to diverse cultures and creeds, and also that the results of such research be made available to such countries as may need and request it. Thus far, however, the population problem has received pitifully inadequate attention, for three principal reasons:

1. Marxism defines the causes and prescribes the cures of human poverty, and they do not include excess population growth or population control. Communism regards concern for population growth as a bourgeois excuse for the inadequacies of the capitalistic system; therefore, the Soviet Union and other Communist countries deny that a world population problem exists. Nevertheless, in varying degrees they encourage family limitation in their own countries by offering services in public facilities. In the U.S.S.R. and in the Communist satellite countries of Eastern Europe, the abortion rate is very high.

2. The Roman Catholic Church opposes as a matter of moral principle many methods of birth control, and this is widely presumed, both within the Church and outside it, to be opposition to family limitation at all times by any and all methods. It is also widely presumed that the Catholic Church opposes government expenditures for social and medical research into human fertility and all forms of government aid to other countries for dealing with their population problems. Actually, there are wide areas of agreement between Catholics and non-Catholics on these questions, as well as wide areas of disagreement; and there is no doubt that the areas of agreement could be enlarged by rational public discussion. But in many predominantly non-Catholic countries the subject is politically sensitive and assiduously avoided in official circles because of the presumed views of Catholic minorities; and in many

predominantly Catholic countries, chiefly in Latin America, a presumption that the Church opposes family limitation at all times by any method leads to official inaction and silence, and to a dearth of public discussion. Nevertheless, in every Roman Catholic country in Europe, the birth rate is so low as not to be a problem.

3. Action in the United Nations and its specialized agencies, or even thorough discussion of the subject, is delicate because of opposition by Communist countries and many Catholic countries, and of timidity by non-Catholic countries.

What Needs To Be Done

In the individual underdeveloped countries, governments should assemble the facts about population growth and analyze them in relation to their plans for economic and social development; they should start building, and training staff for, adequate maternal and child health facilities in which education and services in family planning are an integral part; and they should institute nationwide educational programs, making family planning and population planning intensive national movements.

In the scientifically and technologically advanced countries there should be:

1. Full and public recognition and discussion of the world population problem;

2. Explicit recognition of the wide areas of agreement already achieved between Catholics and non-Catholics on this subject;

3. Further explicit agreement between Catholics and non-Catholics on the essential elements of a sound and effective public policy;

4. Expanded research into all methods of fertility control that might be acceptable to people of varying cultures and creeds; and

5. Aid to any and all countries that seek to control population growth and request assistance in doing so.

There is a wide measure of agreement between Catholics and non-Catholics on the need for further research into human fertility. Yet, in the United States only about six million dollars from all sources is being spent annually on such research.

Conclusion

The problem of rapid population growth will not be ignored, for it is like a volcano erupting on a plain—building a towering mountain before our very eyes. It has erupted because modern science has suddenly in our generation brought the world "death control." It will continue to erupt, and the mountain will continue to grow, until man's will and man's conscience combine with modern science to bring population growth under comparable control. There is no time to be lost, for unless action is taken promptly, the problem of a geometrically increasing world population may soon grow beyond control. It is spreading its dominion over human affairs and in many parts of the world it is already frustrating man's prospects for self-fulfilment.

Chapter 1
The "Population Explosion"

What is Meant by the "Population Explosion"?

It has taken all the vast reaches of time for world population to reach 3 billion. It will take only 35 years to add the next 3 billion if present growth rates remain unchanged. And it will take less than 35 years after that for 6 billion people to double to 12 billion, if present growth rates persist.

Just since World War II the rate at which the population of the world is growing has doubled, increasing from 1 per cent to 2 per cent a year, and it is expected to go higher.

For every four persons on earth in 1950 there are today five, and ten years hence there will be six.

In 1961, the number of people added to the world's population was equivalent to more than the entire population of France.

Is Rapid Population Growth a New Problem?

Yes. Population growth at today's rates, and at those projected for the future, is something entirely new under the sun. According to the best possible estimates, based upon historical and archeological evidence, it took hundreds of thousands of years for world population to reach about 250 million by the time of Christ, and it took 16 centuries more for that figure to double, to 500 million, population growth being held to

---

From "Does Overpopulation Mean Poverty" by Joseph Marion Jones. Center for International Economic Growth, 1720 Rhode Island Ave., N.W., Washington, D.C., 1962.

an extremely small fraction of 1 per cent each year by starvation, disease, and violence. But about 1650 the growth rate began to move up:

In the years	The average annual increase world population was
1650–1750	0.3 per cent
1650–1950	0.5 per cent
1900–1950	0.9 per cent
1930–1940	1.0 per cent
1961	2.0 per cent

And according to a "medium" estimate of the United Nations:

In the years	World population will grow by an average
1950–1975	2.1 per cent
1975–2000	2.6 per cent

Why Is There so Much Concern Over Population Growth?

1. The earth's land space is fixed, inexpandable.

2. Population grows in geometrical progression: 2-4-8-16-32-64-128- etc. And when you get to huge numbers—billions—the results of doubling are phenomenal.

3. The time required to double a population depends upon the rate of its growth. And seemingly small percentage increases in the annual rate of population growth result in very rapid total increases in population:

If the population increases each year at	The total population will double in	And a world population of 3,000,000,000 will increase in one century to
1 per cent	69.3 years	8,200,000,000
1½ per cent	46.2 years	13,400,000,000
2 per cent	34.6 years	23,000,000,000
2½ per cent	27.6 years	36,600,000,000
3 per cent	23.1 years	60,300,000,000
4 per cent	17.3 years	163,800,000,000

4. Even a 1 per cent annual increase in population is fantastically rapid:

"One hundred persons multiplying at 1 per cent per year . . . for the 5000 years of human history, would have produced a contemporary population of 2.7 billion persons per square foot of land surface of the earth!

Such an exercise in arithmetic, although admittedly dramatic and propagandistic, is also a conclusive way of demonstrating that a 1 per cent per year increase in world population could not have taken place for very long in the past; nor can it continue for very long into the future."— Dr. Philip M. Hauser, Professor and Chairman of the Department of Sociology, and Director of Population Research Training Center, University of Chicago.

5. With a population of 3 billion people, and with the doubling time already cut below 40 years and dropping, the world is suddenly catapulted into a serious crisis—now.

The growth of world population during the next 25 years . . . is at the very heart of the problem of our existence. United Nations: THE FUTURE GROWTH OF WORLD POPULATION, Population Studies, No. 28— 1958.

Can We Rely on Population Statistics?

For general conclusions, yes—even though vital statistics for all countries are not by any means complete or accurate. The *Demographic Yearbook* for 1950 reported that about a third of the births in the world and half the deaths were not formally recorded, and this situation has not greatly improved since then. In countries with inadequate vital statistics, estimates are aided by intensive sampling. When newer and complete data become available, previous estimates usually are found to have erred on the low side.

The Mainland China census of 1953 produced a population figure of 583 million, which was 100 million more than had been estimated, but its accuracy is seriously questioned and there is no concensus as to whether the figure is too high or too low. The official Chinese indications of both birth and death rates and of rates of natural increase are believed to be far out of line on the low side. The population of Mainland China is believed by a number of experts to total about 690 million today and to be increasing at about 2.3 per cent a year.

In 1961, censuses taken in India and Pakistan revealed populations of 438 million and 95 million, there being 7 million and 4 million more people, respectively, than had been previously estimated. Following the 1961 census the Government of India, which had been reporting to the United Nations an estimated annual population increase of 1.3 per cent, now projects in its Third Five Year Plan an annual population increase of 2.4 per cent between 1961 and 1966, 2.8 per cent between 1966 and 1971, 2.7 per cent between 1971 and 1976. The estimated population increase over the next 15 years is put at 187 million people, which is slightly larger than the entire population of the United States today.

Recent studies of the population growth rate in Pakistan indicate an annual figure of 2.5 per cent rather than the 2.0 per cent previously reported.

In spite of gaps and inadequacies which still exist, vital statistics are improving, and as they improve they expose even more clearly the gravity of the population crisis.

Population Projections to the Year 2000, for the World, Continents and Regions (in millions)	1950	1960	1970	1975	2000
WORLD TOTAL	2,500	2,920	3,500	3,860	6,280
AFRICA	199	237	294	331	517
Northern Africa	43	53	67	76	147
Middle and Southern Africa	156	185	227	254	370
NORTHERN AMERICA	168	197	225	240	312
LATIN AMERICA	163	206	265	303	592
ASIA (excluding the Asian part of the Soviet Union and Japan)	1,296	1,524	1,870	2,093	3,717
JAPAN AND RYUKYU ISLANDS	84	96	110	117	153
EUROPE (excluding the European part of the Soviet Union)	393	424	457	476	568
Northern and Western Europe	133	140	148	154	180
Central Europe	128	140	151	156	183
Southern Europe	132	144	158	166	206
OCEANIA	13.2	16.3	19.4	21.0	29.3
Australia & New Zealand	10.2	12.7	14.9	16.0	20.8
Pacific Islands	2.9	3.6	4.5	5.0	8.6
SOVIET UNION (Asian and European parts combined)	181	215	254	275	379

SOURCE: United Nations, Department of Economic and Social Affairs: "The Future Growth of World Population" (Population study No. 28), New York, 1958. High estimates are used through 1975 and medium estimates for 2000.

Why Has the Rate of World Population Growth Increased so Spectacularly in Recent Years?

Chiefly because of the sudden and sharp decline in death rates, without any corresponding decline in the very high birth rates, in Asia, Africa, and Latin America, where two-thirds of the human race live. The introduction in public health programs of newly discovered insecticides such as DDT, and antibiotics, vaccines, sulfa compounds, and other "miracle drugs" have brought mass infectious and contagious diseases under varying degrees of control in most underdeveloped countries. These programs are administered at modest expense and on a vast scale, frequently by or with the assistance of technical experts from United Nations organizations, the United States, or other advanced countries. Also, in a number of countries there has been some improvement in food supply. The result has been a drastic decline in infant and child mortality, some improvement in general health, and a sharp rise in the life expectancy of entire populations.

Death rates have been reduced by more than a third in Chile and Costa Rica, and by two-thirds in Puerto Rico, in the last 30 years. And they have been reduced by a third or more in India, Malaya, Ceylon, and Pakistan just since World War II.

DECLINING DEATH RATES

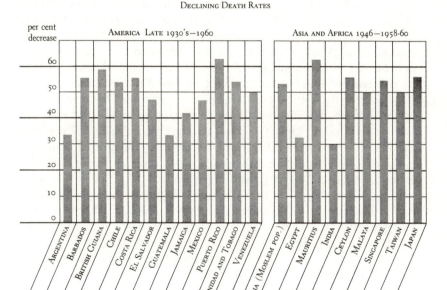

"Death control" has thus been introduced into the continents of Asia, Africa, and Latin America. It is popular, relatively inexpensive, requires little initiative on the part of the people, and meets little or no resistance from them. But birth rates are as high as before. The decline in death rates is expected to continue in the underdeveloped countries for many years to come, but there is very little prospect for a decline in birth rates, unless something is done.

Public health programs were introduced into Latin America after World War I, and declines in death rates there began somewhat earlier than in Asia and Africa.

ALDOUS HUXLEY, British Writer:
"To anyone who thinks in biological as well as in economic, political and sociological terms, it is self-evident that a society which practices death control must at the same time practice birth control—that the corollary of hygiene and preventive medicine is contraception."

Where are Birth Rates Highest? In Which Parts of the World Is Population Growing the Fastest?

Birth rates are highest in the underdeveloped areas of Asia, Africa, and Latin America. In those continents live roughly two-thirds of the world's population of 3,000,000,000; and birth rates there average between 40 and 50 per year per thousand people. Birth rates are much lower in Europe (19 per thousand); the U.S.S.R. (26); the United States and Canada (25); Australia, New Zealand (23); and Japan (19).

Rates of population increase are also higher in the underdeveloped areas of Asia, Africa, and Latin America (even though death rates there are still relatively high) than in the economically more advanced areas of the world where there are fewer people and where both lower birth rates and comparatively much lower death rates prevail. The figures are: Asia (not including Japan), 2.3 per cent per year; Africa, 1.9 per cent; Latin America, 2.5 per cent; Europe, 0.8 per cent; the United States and Canada, 1.7 per cent; the U.S.S.R., 1.8 per cent; Australia and New Zealand, 1.4 per cent; and Japan, 1.0 per cent.

There was a sharp rise in birth rates immediately following World War II in many of the developed countries—in Western Europe, North America, Australia and New Zealand—where standards of living are high and where birth control has been long and widely practiced. This was attributable largely to millions of extra marriages and births which had been deferred during the war. This "baby boom" was short-lived in Europe, but the higher rates of population increase have persisted in the United States, Canada, Australia and New Zealand, where a pattern of earlier marriage and larger families prevails amid prosperous economic conditions. At the present time the land space and the mature expanding economies of these countries accommodate rapid population growth, while permitting increases in average levels of living. Even so, the problem of providing housing, educational and health facilities, and other services is a great strain. And in the United States the problem of finding jobs is even more serious. Science and technology have nearly decimated employment in agriculture, and now automation in industry is increasingly eliminating jobs at a time when millions are being added to the labor force each year. Moreover, these annual entrants into the labor force will increase sharply for the products of the postwar "baby boom" are beginning to hit the labor market.

World Population Increase by Region	Mid-year Estimate 1950 1959 Population (millions)		1954–1958 Birth Rate Death Rate (per thousand) (annual average)		Annual Rate of Increase (per cent)
ASIA (excluding Japan)	1,293	1,529	40*	—*	2.3*
AFRICA	198	236	45	26	1.9
Northern	65	78	45	25	2.0
Middle and South	133	158	46	27	1.9
LATIN AMERICA	163	201	41	16	2.5
EUROPE	395	423	19	11	0.8
Northern and Western	133	141	18	11	0.6
Central	128	138	19	11	0.8
Southern	134	144	21	10	0.9
NORTHERN AMERICA	168	197	25	9	1.7†
USSR (Asian and European parts combined)	181	210	26	8	1.8
AUSTRALIA AND NEW ZEALAND	10.2	12	23	9	1.4
JAPAN	83	93	19	8	1.1

SOURCES: United Nations *Demographic Yearbooks* and other United Nations publications; and, Government of India Planning Commission: "Third Five Year Plan."

What Are the Rates of Population Growth in the Countries of Asia?

They vary widely, as shown in the table below. In all Asian countries except Japan birth rates are extremely high; death rates vary because of differing economic, social, and political conditions and the extent and quality of public health programs. Japan is a case apart, for widespread abortion and birth control have brought about a low birth rate; rela-

---

* United Nations publications show for Asia: Birth rate 40; death rate 22; annual rate of increase, 1.8 per cent. However, following the 1961 census of India the Indian Government revised its figures radically and in the Third Five Year Plan it estimated an average annual population growth rate, 1961–1966 of 2.4 per cent (instead of 1.3 per cent as it had previously reported). Recent studies of population growth in Pakistan indicate a figure of 2.5 per cent rather than the reported 2.0 per cent. As for Mainland China, the figure frequently used for annual population increase is 2 per cent, derived from official releases. However, more recent estimates indicate that the population of Mainland China is around 690 million and growing by 16 million a year, which means an annual increase of 2.3 per cent a year. We are therefore taking the liberty of revising accordingly the annual increase figures for Asia in this table.
† The figure for the United States, 1960–61, is 1.6 per cent.

tively good economic conditions and public health services have brought about a low death rate; and these together have operated to produce a population increase rate of only 1 per cent.

Rates of Annual Population Increase in Certain Countries in Asia
(Latest available figures)

Country	Birth* Rates	Death Rate	Annual Rate of Natural Increase (per cent)*
China (Taiwan)—1960	39.5	6.9	3.3
Malaya—1959	42.2	9.7	3.3
Singapore—1960	37.8	6.2	3.1
Philippines (est. 1953–1959)	–	–	2.6
Ceylon (est. 1953–1959)	47	22	2.5
Thailand (est. 1954–1956)	47	23	2.4
China (Mainland) (est. 1960)	–	–	2.3
Pakistan (est. 1951–1961)	–	–	2.1
India (est. 1951–1961)	–	–	2.0
Indonesia (est. 1954–1956)	43	24	1.9
Japan—1959	17.5	7.4	1.0

SOURCES: For China (Taiwan), Malaya, Singapore, Philippines, Ceylon, and Japan-United Nations *Demographic Yearbook*, 1960. For Thailand and Indonesia-United Nations Economic Commission for Asia and the Far East: "Population Trends and Related Problems of Economic Development in the ECAFE Region," June, 1959. For India and Pakistan, estimates based on 1961 census data. For Mainland China, estimates of a number of leading authorities.

What Is the Situation in Latin America?

In Latin America variations in population increase are also extremely wide. In the temperate zone countries of Argentina and Uruguay, where relatively higher standards of living prevail, birth rates are much lower than elsewhere in Latin America. The Central American countries together have the highest rates of increase of any area in the world.

Throughout Latin America there is evidence of a high degree of "death control" but nowhere except in Argentina and Uruguay is there evidence of fertility control. Latin America as a whole has the highest rates of population increase of any region.

MR. WYMBERLEY COERR, [formerly] Assistant Secretary of State for Inter-American Affairs, testifying before the Senate Committee on Foreign Relations:

---

* Birth rates and death rates are in terms of 1000 of the population per year. Rates of natural increase are in per cent of total population of the country.

"The (Latin American) area as a whole is experiencing a population increase that is outpacing the increase in its gross national product and average per capita income. . . . The long-range prospect, therefore, is that there will be more and more people to share less and less income."

Rates of Annual Population Increase in Certain Countries in Latin America (*Latest available figures*)

Country	Birth Rates (per thousand)	Death Rates (per thousand)	Annual Rate of Natural Increase (per cent of total population)
Dominican Republic (est. 1953–1958)	—	—	3.5
Costa Rica (1959)	42.8	9.0	3.4
Mexico (1960)	45.5	11.4	3.4
Nicaragua (est. 1953–1958)	—	—	3.4
El Salvador (1960)	44.8	10.8	3.4
Guatemala (1960)	50.0	17.9	3.2
Brazil (1961)	—	—	3.1
Venezuela (est. 1953–1958)	—	—	3.0
Chile (1959)	35.4	12.5	2.3
Argentina (1960)	22.3	8.1	1.4
Uruguay (est. 1953–1958)	—	—	1.3

SOURCE: For Costa Rica, Mexico, El Salvador, Guatemala, Chile, and Argentina, United Nations *Demographic Yearbook*, 1960. For Brazil, Population Reference Bureau: "Population Profile," April 2, 1962. For others, Department of Statistics, Pan American Union Release 4117a6, No. 700, July 27, 1960.

What About Africa?

Considerably less is written or known about the population problems of Africa than about those of Asia and Latin America, chiefly because vital statistics for most African countries are scarce and unreliable and population density in most African countries is relatively low. But a number of things are known: Birth rates are extremely high; infant and child mortality rates are extremely high; malnutrition is endemic, overall death rates, though lower than in the past and declining, are still high; and nevertheless, the rates of population increase are high, as shown in the table below. As public health services and nutritional levels improve, death rates are expected to continue to decline and population growth rates to increase. Thus Africa, like other underdeveloped regions of the earth seeking economic and social progress, has serious population problems.

Estimated Annual Rates of Population Increase in Certain Countries in Africa

Country	Per cent	Period Covered
Algeria	3.3	1954–1960
Libya	1.6	1954–1960
Egypt	3.5	1957–1960
Sudan	3.1	1956–1960
Kenya	1.6	1948–1960
Ghana	4.0	1948–1960
Guinea	2.9	1955–1960
Nigeria	2.0	1953–1961
Tanganyika	1.7	1957–1960
Somalia	2.4	1931–1960
Mozambique	1.1	1950–1960
Union of South Africa	2.4	1951–1960

SOURCE: *Population Index*, January, 1962—Office of Population Research, Princeton University.

MARRINER S. ECCLES, Former Chairman of the Federal Reserve Board:
". . . *nothing is more important than to understand the economic, social and political dangers of the world's failure to control its population growth. Democracy cannot survive, much less expand, unless the standard of living of the backward countries of the world is substantially improved. This is an impossible task unless the population growth is curbed.*"

What Accounts for the Wide Variations Among Countries?

IN BIRTH RATES?

The lower birth rates that prevail in one-third of the world comprising Europe, the U.S.S.R., the United States and Canada, Argentina and Uruguay, Australia and New Zealand, and Japan are the result of some form of family limitation brought about by practices ranging from abortion and contraception to late marriage and celibacy. But of course the exercise of these practices in any particular country (or group of related countries) is the product of history and tradition, social structure and culture, religion, and economics.

For example, late Hellenistic, late Hebraic, and early Christian cultures produced in Western Europe a family unit in which a man was responsible for the support only of his wife and their children (and of immediate relatives without means of support), and it was assumed he would not marry until he was in a position to discharge his responsibilities properly. There was strong social pressure against "improvident marriages." The results were relatively late marriages and also, as infant and child mortality declined in the late eighteenth century and after, family limitation in marriage and a small family pattern.

Asian cultures, on the other hand, produced the "joint family" which included brothers and their wives, and in many cases first cousins, with joint family responsibilities and pooled property and earnings. This system, in turn, gave rise to extremely early marriages and uncontrolled fertility.

These are but indications of the many factors that cause wide variations in birth rates. Full explanations require, for any country or group of related countries, extensive historical and social research and analysis.

Family planning depends upon the *will* of a couple (from whatever motivation) to limit the number of their children. Historically, where the will to limit families has existed, as for example in Europe, it has prevailed in spite of religious or government opposition and, until relatively recently, with only common sense or folk methods as aids.

In Death Rates?

Variations depend for the most part upon the relative effectiveness of different public health services, using the new products of medical research, in controlling mass infectious diseases. Beyond that, they depend upon the quality of medical services in general and their availability to the masses of the people, population density and the availability of cultivatable land, the nutritional adequacy of diets, and conditions of sanitation.

In the Rates of Population Increase?

The rate of population increase is the difference between the birth rate and the death rate. One can get various combinations of birth and death rates which produce under extremely different conditions the same rates of population increase. For example, the rate of natural increase in the United States and Indonesia are, 1.6 per cent and 1.9 per cent respectively, but the United States has a birth rate of 25 per thousand and a death rate of 9, while Indonesia has a birth rate of 43 per thousand and a death rate of 24.

Europe and North America Once Had High Birth Rates and High Rates of Population Increase. What Happened to Change the Pattern?

Before the middle of the eighteenth century Europe had high birth rates, high death rates, low life expectancy, and very slow rates of population growth. Beginning around 1750—in a setting of revolutionary advances in medicine, science and technology, growing industrialization, increasing world development and trade, improvement in transportation, and rising standards of living—there occurred a "demographic transition" of greatest importance. First, the death rate began a slow and steady decline; and then *several generations later*, after the middle of the nineteenth century, the birth rate began a similar decline, slow at first. During the early decades of this "demographic transition"—before birth rates started declining—population growth was extremely rapid. But then the accelerating decline in the birth rate began to catch up, so that by 1940 Europe had nearly stabilized its population with low death rates, low birth rates, and slow rates of population growth.

A somewhat similar demographic transition occurred in the United States, but with differences. During colonial times the United States had very high fertility but with death rates lower than in Europe; population increase was therefore rapid. But in the latter part of the eighteenth century death rates began to decline, causing an even more rapid population increase for a generation or so until about 1800 when birth rates began a steady decline. By 1930 the United States, too, had achieved low birth and death rates and a slow rate of population increase. However, the rate of population increase in the United States is now 1.6 per cent.

May We Not Expect That There Will be a Decline in Population Growth in Underdeveloped Countries of Asia, Africa, and Latin America as They Become More Developed?

It is questionable. Even if such a decline should occur, it would probably take place too late to prevent unmanageably large populations, for several reasons:

1. The *transition* in Europe and North America from high to low rates of population growth was *very slow*, beginning with small populations in relation to resources and extending over about 150 years.

2. In the early decades of the demographic transition in Europe the decline in birth rates lagged behind declines in death rates for several generations, causing during that period a very rapid increase in the rate of population growth (which nevertheless did not reach one per cent until after 1900). Death rates in the underdeveloped countries have in the last 15 to 30 years plummeted, suddenly and spectacularly, much more so than in the nineteenth century (and are continuing to decline). If declines in birth rates lag behind for generations, as in Europe, populations will grow so large as to defy all efforts in theory about that economic and social development which might in theory bring about a

decline in rates of population growth. Already, according to Mr. Eugene Black, [former] President of the World Bank, "population growth threatens to nullify all our efforts to raise living standards in many of the poorer countries."

Will Growing Population Pressures Increase the Likelihood of World Unrest and War?

The expectations among the peoples of many underdeveloped countries for a rapid rise in living levels are building up powerful pressures which can lead to violent internal revolutions (which could not in themselves change the economic situation and which would probably end in totalitarianism), or to external aggression, or to both. Uncontrolled population growth is making it virtually impossible, even with vast amounts of foreign aid and investment, to begin closing the gap between the richer and the poorer nations.

The per capita income in the underdeveloped countries as a whole is about $100; in Western Europe it is about $850; and in the United States it is about $2350. The income gap is thus extremely wide; moreover, it is growing. Whereas in ten years (1951–1960) the people in the underdeveloped countries (not including Mainland China) gained in per capita income only about $10 per person, the people in the United States gained about $225 per person in constant dollars; and in the years 1950–1959 the people living in the European Economic Community gained no less than $275 per person.

High rates of population increase which make it extremely difficult or impossible to raise per capita living standards in many of the underdeveloped countries, are thus feeding fires of violence and war. There can be little prospect of peace or world order so long as present rates of population increase persist. And ultimately there must be either a decrease in birth rates or an increase in death rates.

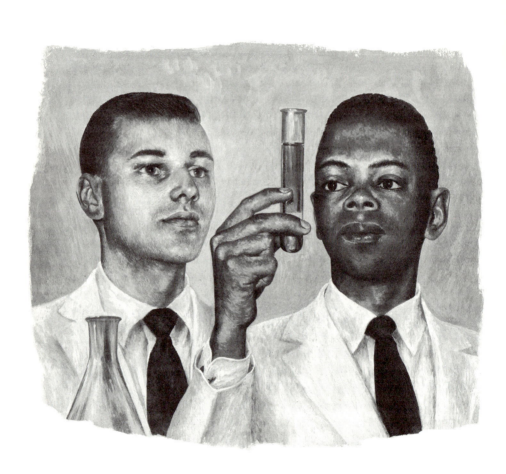

PART III

THE INTERACTION OF WEST AND NON-WEST

Introduction

IN THE SECOND HALF of the twentieth century, the nations of West and non-West are not so widely separated as they were in the past, either by such factors as geographic distance, which modern technology has significantly reduced, or by grievous hostilities engendered by colonialism and racialism. These obstacles to human communications still do exist in many parts of the globe, in latent or explicit form, but gradually they are being eroded. This erosion is caused by the rapid transmission of ideas, which in centuries past would have taken months, decades, or even centuries to spread, as ever widening exchanges between nations create common interests; and by the participation of over one hundred nations of West and non-West in the United Nations and its Specialized Agencies.

Thus today, West and non-West find that they have to deal with each other. What this involves can be listed under four main categories: efforts to comprehend each other's minds; recognition and toleration of each other's national interests; exchanges of goods and resources necessary for each other's economies; and at least a modicum of cooperation with each other in assuring our common survival on earth and the future safeguarding of our common security.

If West and non-West are to comprehend each other's minds, it is essential that both sides should no longer be satisfied merely with "scratches" inadequately and often erroneously representing the image of each, to use the phrase of Harold Isaacs. No technical expert would feel confidence in constructing a machine on the basis of flimsy and/or falsified information about the facts he must take into consideration for his task. Yet all too often, in spite of the widespread use of educational facilities, the press, the radio, and television, this is what political leaders, diplomats, and voters accept in reaching conclusions about other peoples—conclusions

414

which are then used, sometimes in fear and haste, to arrive at foreign policy decisions that may spell life or death for millions of human beings. The misleading images of China and India reflected
in the minds of well-informed and experienced Americans, as reported by Mr. Isaacs in the selection from his book, *Some Scratches
on Our Minds,* can be multiplied *ad infinitum* by comparable, or
even more erroneous, images in the minds of Russians or Chinese
about the United States; of Africans about former Western colonial
powers; of Arab countries about Israel and of Israel about Arab
countries; of the Latin Americans (whom we call "good neighbors") about the United States, which many of them call, with
both envy and resentment, "the Colossus of the North," and on
the part of North Americans who do not take the trouble to understand their neighbors to the south.

If we are to arrive at anything that resembles an accurate image
of each other, we shall have to acquire far greater knowledge of the
traditions, ideals, fears and dreams, strengths and weaknesses of the
world's various peoples—and hope that they will take the trouble
to do the same about us. But knowledge does not necessarily bring
about understanding. One may know all the available facts about a
human being, or about a nation—one can absorb all the information
to be found in encyclopedias, atlases, histories, statistics—yet fail
to perceive the thoughts and emotions which move human beings
at a given time under given circumstances. To achieve such understanding we do not need any magic formula. All we need—but it
is a lot—is to meet other people, whatever their race or color, their
religion or their ideology, with the same courtesy, the same concern
for their sensitivity, the same desire to share our ideas, not impose
them, as we display (one must hope) toward our friends, and that
we hope other people will display toward us. This is what Janheinz
Jahn shows us how to do in his account of his African experiences.

Once we have become acquainted with the problems and feelings of non-Western peoples, we shall be in a better position to
understand that they, like ourselves, have national interests, determined in the first instance not by their attitude toward us, but
by their geographic location, their natural resources, their religion
and philosophy, their historic experience, their political and economic institutions. We may then become more patient than we
have been in the past about the revulsion of non-Westerners

against remnants of Western colonialism, or their determination to avoid alignment with one great-power bloc against another. And, in turn, we shall have then earned the right to expect that they, for their part, may be more patient with us when we fear that hasty decolonization may precipitate dangerous upheavals, or that non-alignment may encourage the ambitions of militant leaders in Russia or China.

Our newly acquired sensitivity would also make us more aware than we are at present that in the years ahead it will be impossible to maintain a divided world of rich lands and poor lands, to use the phrase of the Swedish economist Gunnar Myrdal; that on the international scene, as on our domestic scene, it would be dangerous for both rich and poor to perpetuate sharp inequalities which breed resentment that sooner or later may spark rebellion. We shall come to realize that the aid we now give to non-Western peoples, calling it "foreign aid," is really aid we give ourselves in helping to create   • a more stable, more peaceful world community, of which the United States is an integral, and important, part. Then aid to non-Western developing countries may come to be seen as a form of insurance of our own present well-being, future economic growth, and social welfare. At the same time we can then hope that the non-Western countries, as some of them already do today, will increasingly want to become, not self-sufficient—in the complex world of our times self-sufficiency is impossible, even for the most powerful and richest nations—but at least in large part self-reliant.

But no nation, not even the United States or the U.S.S.R., let alone the small and weak countries of the non-Western areas, can become economically self-reliant unless they can have an opportunity to trade, to exchange the products of their labor for those of the more advanced nations, to earn their way at least in part. Aid without trade could weaken the moral fibre of recipient nations which need most of all not money, as UN Secretary General U Thant points out, but an opportunity to learn modern techniques and to take their place, however modest their natural resources, among the producers of the world, instead of being permanently treated as pensioners of the rich nations.

To effect this change in the economic role of the developing nations, a concerted effort by both rich and poor will be needed—an effort planned not only on a nation by nation scale, but on a world scale, as Dr. Myrdal recommends in his book *Beyond the Welfare State*. This vast undertaking, which may require fifty years or a century, calls for all the diplomatic skills the world can muster: not only the customary diplomacy of foreign service officers, but the diplomacy of bankers and investors, described by Eugene Black, and the people-to-people diplomacy of everyday life, illustrated by the activities of exchange teachers, doctors, technicians, and by the work of young men and women participating in such undertakings as our Peace Corps.

Once all the peoples on the globe have perceived their need of each other—psychological, political, economic, and social—we shall be better prepared than in the past to work together and to make use of all the coming wonders of science, not as master and slave, not as ruler and ruled, but as partners in a common enterprise. We shall also be better prepared to pool our efforts through the United Nations system, which, in the absence of war, could make a historic contribution toward stabilizing and strengthening relations between West and non-West.

ARNOLD J. TOYNBEE

The World and the West

One of the questions often discussed about the newly emerged nations is whether non-Western peoples must accept all of the aspects of Western life if they want to benefit by some of its advantages —notably technology, or whether they can select only those aspects which they regard as best suited for their particular traditions, conditions, and needs.

Contrary to the views of some observers, among them Professor Cyril E. Black, who believes that non-Western countries can and will be selective, Professor Arnold J. Toynbee, distinguished British teacher, government official and historian, raises the question in this chapter of whether non-Western nations can take this or that splinter of Western civilization, or must adopt it as a whole if they are to modernize successfully. Born in 1889, Dr. Toynbee has had a rich experience in comparing and contrasting the civilizations of Western and non-Western peoples. He served as director of the research department of the British Foreign Office, 1943–46; was a member of the British delegation to the Paris Peace Conference in 1919; and from 1925 to 1955 was research professor of international history at the University of London and director of studies at the Royal Institute of International Affairs.

Dr. Toynbee is the author of many books, the most famous of which are A Survey of International Affairs, published in 1929–40; and his monumental eleven-volume Study of History, published in 1934–61. In his most recent book, Between Oxus and Jumna, 1961, he assays the prospects of India, Pakistan, and Afghanistan.

Chapter 5
The Psychology of Encounters

IN THE FIRST FOUR chapters of this book we have been surveying four episodes in which our Western civilization has been encountered by some contemporary non-Western society. Russia's, Islam's, India's, and the Far East's experiences of the West have come under view. Our survey has shown that these four different experiences of being hit by a foreign civilization have had a number of features in common; and the purpose of the present chapter is to pick out, for further examination, several features that appear to be characteristic, not only of the contemporary world's encounters with the West, but of all such collisions between one civilization and another. There seems to be something like a common psychology of encounters; and this is a subject of practical interest and importance today, when the sudden "annihilation of distance," through the achievements of our Western technology, has brought face to face, at point-blank range, half a dozen societies, each of which, until yesterday, was living its own life in its own way almost as independently of its neighbors as if each society had been marooned on a planet of its own instead of living in the same world with the other representatives of its kind.

We may begin by reminding ourselves of a general phenomenon which came to our notice in the last chapter when we were taking a comparative view of our Western civilization's two successive assaults upon China and Japan. We saw that, on the first occasion, the West tried to induce the Far Eastern peoples to adopt the Western way of life in its entirety, including its religion as well as its technology, and that this attempt did not succeed. And then we saw that, in the second act of the play, the West offered to the same Far Eastern peoples a secularized excerpt from the Western civilization in which religion had been left out and technology, instead of religion, had been made the central feature; and we observed that this technological splinter, which had been flaked off from the religious core of our civilization towards the end of the seventeenth century, did succeed in pushing its way into the life of a Far Eastern society that had previously repulsed an attempt to introduce the Western way of life en bloc—technology and all, including religion.

Here we have an example of something that seems often to happen when the culture-ray of a radioactive civilization hits a foreign body social. The assaulted foreign body's resistance diffracts the culture-ray into its component strands, just as a light-ray is diffracted into the spectrum by the resistance of a prism. In optics we also know that some of the light-strands in the spectrum have a greater penetrative power than others, and we have already seen that it is the same with the component strands of a culture-ray. In the West's impact on the Far East, the technological strand in the radiation of the Western civilization has overcome a resistance by which the religious strand has been repelled; and this difference in the penetrative power of a religious and a technological culture-strand is not a phenomenon that is peculiar to the history of the relations between these two particular civilizations. We have stumbled here upon an instance of one of the "laws" of cultural radiation.

When a travelling culture-ray is diffracted into its component strands —technology, religion, politics, art, and so on—by the resistance of a foreign body social upon which it has impinged, its technological strand is apt to penetrate faster and farther than its religious strand; and this law can be formulated in more general terms. We can say that the penetrative power of a strand of cultural radiation is usually in inverse ratio to this strand's cultural value. A trivial strand arouses less resistance in the assaulted body social than is aroused by a crucial strand, because the trivial strand does not threaten to cause so violent or so painful a disturbance of the assaulted body's traditional way of life. This automatic selection of the most trivial elements in a radioactive culture for the widest dissemination abroad is obviously an unfortunate rule of the game of cultural intercourse; but this premium on triviality is not the game's worst point. The very process of diffraction, which is of the essence of the game, threatens to poison the life of the society whose body social is being penetrated by the divers strands of a diffracted culture-ray.

Analogies taken from physics and medicine may be used to illustrate this point. Since our discovery of the trick of splitting the atom, we have learnt to our cost that the particles composing an atom of some inoffensive element cease to be innocuous and become dangerously corrosive as soon as they have been split off from the orderly society of particles of which an atom is constituted, and have been sent flying by themselves on independent careers of their own. We have learnt, too— not to our own cost in this case, but to the cost of the once secluded surviving representatives of Primitive Man—that a disease which is a mild one for us, because it has been rife among us so long that we have developed an effective resistance to it, may prove deadly to South Sea Islanders who have been exempt from it before being suddenly exposed to it by the arrival among them of its European carriers.

A loose strand of cultural radiation, like a loose electron or a loose contagious disease, may prove deadly when it is disengaged from the system within which it has been functioning hitherto and is set free to range abroad by itself in a different milieu. In its original setting, this culture-strand or bacillus or electron was restrained from working havoc because it was kept in order by its association with other components of a pattern in which the divers participants were in equilibrium. In escaping from its original setting, the liberated particle, bacillus, or culture-strand will not have changed its nature; but the same nature will produce a deadly effect, instead of a harmless one, now that the creature has broken loose from its original associations. In these circumstances, "one man's meat" can become "another man's poison."

In the set of encounters between the world and the West which is the subject of this book, there is a classical example of the mischief that an institution can do when it is pried loose from its original social setting and is sent out into the world, conquering and to conquer, all by itself. During the last century and a half we have seen our Late Modern Western political institution of "national states" burst the bounds of its birthplace in Western Europe and blaze a trail of persecution, eviction, and massacre as it has spread abroad into Eastern Europe, South-West Asia, and India—all of them regions where "national states" were not part and parcel of an indigenous social system but were an exotic institution which was deliberately imported from the West, not because it had been found by experimentation to be suitable to the local conditions of these non-Western worlds, but simply because the West's political power had given the West political institutions an irrational yet irresistible prestige in non-Western eyes.

The havoc which the application of this Western institution of "national states" has worked in these regions where it is an exotic import is incomparably greater than the damage that the same institution has done in Britain, France, and the other West European countries in which it has been, not an artificially introduced innovation, but a spontaneous native growth.

We can see why the same institution has had strikingly different effects in these two different social environments. The institution of "national states" has been comparatively harmless in Western Europe for the same reason that accounts for its having originated there; and that is because, in Western Europe, it corresponds to the local relation between the distribution of languages and the alinement of political frontiers. In Western Europe, people speaking the same language happen, in most cases, to be huddled together in a single continuous and compact block of territory with a fairly well defined linguistic boundary separating it from the similarly compact domains of other languages; and, in a region where, as here, the languages are thus distributed in the pattern of a patchwork quilt, the linguistic map provides a convenient basis for the political map, and "national states" are therefore natural products of the social milieu. Most of the domains of the historic states of Western Europe do, in fact, coincide approximately with homogeneous patches of the linguistic map; and this coincidence has come about, for the most part, undesignedly. The West European peoples have not been acutely conscious of the process by which their political containers have been moulded on linguistic lasts; and, accordingly, the spirit of nationalism has been, on the whole, easy-going in its West European homeland. In West European national states, linguistic minorities who have found themselves on the wrong side of a political frontier have in most cases shown loyalty, and been treated with consideration, because their coexistence with the majority speaking "the national language" as fellow citizens of the same commonwealth has been an historical fact which has not been deliberately brought about by anyone and which has therefore been taken for granted by everyone.

But now let us consider what has happened when this West European institution of "national states," which in its birthplace has been a natural product of the local linguistic map, has been radiated abroad into regions in which the local linguistic map is on a quite different pattern. When we look at a linguistic map, not just of Western Europe, but of the world, we see that the local West European pattern, in which the languages are distributed in fairly clear-cut, compact, and homogeneous blocks, is something rather peculiar and exceptional. In the vastly larger area stretching south-eastward from Danzig and Trieste to Calcutta and Singapore, the pattern of the linguistic map is not like a patchwork quilt; it is like a shot-silk robe. In Eastern Europe, South-West Asia, India, and Malaya the speakers of different languages are not neatly sorted out from one another, as they are in Western Europe; they are geographically intermingled in alternate houses on the same streets of the same towns and villages; and, in this different, and more normal, social setting, the linguistic map—in which the threads of different colours are interwoven with each other—provides a convenient basis, not for the drawing of frontiers between states, but for the allocation of occupations and trades among individuals.

In the Ottoman Empire, a hundred and fifty years ago, before the Western institution of clear-cut, compact, homogeneous national states made its disastrous entry into this foreign arena, the Turks were peasants and administrators, the Lazes were sailors, the Greeks were sailors and shopkeepers, the Armenians were bankers and shopkeepers, the Bulgars were grooms and market-gardeners, the Albanians were masons and mercenary soldiers, the Kurds were shepherds and porters, the Vlachs were shepherds and pedlars. The nationalities were not only intermingled as a matter of geographical fact; they were also economically and socially interdependent; and this correspondence between nationalities and occupations was the order of nature in a world in which the linguistic map was, not a patchwork, but a macédoine. In this Ottoman world the only way of carving out national states on the Western pattern was to transform the native macédoine into a patchwork on the linguistic pattern of Western Europe; and this could be done only by the methods of barbarism which, for a hundred and fifty years past, have in fact been employed with devastating results in one section after another of an area extending all the way from the Sudetenland to Eastern Bengal. So great can be the havoc worked by an idea or institution or technique when it is cut loose from its original setting and is radiated abroad, by itself, into a social environment in which it conflicts with the historic local pattern of social life.

The truth is that every historic culture-pattern is an organic whole in which all the parts are interdependent, so that, if any part is prised out of its setting, both the isolated part and the mutilated whole behave differently from their behaviour when the pattern is intact. This is why "one man's meat" can be "another man's poison"; and another consequence is that "one thing leads to another." If a splinter is flaked off from one culture and is introduced into a foreign body social, this isolated splinter will tend to draw in after it, into the foreign body in which it has lodged, the other component elements of the social system in which this splinter is at home and from which it has been forcibly and unnaturally detached. The broken pattern tends to reconstitute itself in a foreign environment into which one of its components has once found its way.

If we want to see how, in the game of cultural intercourse, this process of one thing leading to another works in practice, let us look at one or two concrete examples.

In a United Kingdom blue book surveying the social and economic state of Egypt in 1839, it is mentioned that, in the city of Alexandria at this date, the principal maternity hospital is located within the precincts of the naval arsenal. This sounds odd, but we shall see that it was inevitable as soon as we retrace the sequence of events that led to this at first sight surprising result.

By the year 1839 the Ottoman governor-general of Egypt, the celebrated Mehmed 'Alī Pasha, had been working for thirty-two years to equip himself with effective armaments in the Western style of his generation. The failure of Napoleon's expedition to Egypt had opened Mehmed 'Ali's eyes to the importance of seapower. He was determined to have a navy composed of warships on the contemporary Western model; he realized that he would not be navally self-sufficient till he was in a position to have Egyptian warships built in an Egyptian naval dockyard by Egyptian hands; and he also realized that he could not provide himself with an Egyptian personnel of naval technicians without hiring Western naval architects and other experts to train his Egyptian apprentices. So Mehmed 'Alī advertised for Western experts; and suitable Western candidates were tempted to apply for these jobs in Egypt by the handsome scale of pay that the Pasha was offering. All the same, these Western applicants were unwilling to sign their contracts without being sure of being able to bring their families to Egypt with them; and they were unwilling to bring their families without being sure of there being suitable provision for the care of their health up to contemporary Western standards of medical service. So Mehmed 'Ali found that he could not hire his urgently required Western naval experts without also hiring Western doctors of medicine to attend on the naval experts' wives and children; and, as his heart was set on his ambition to create an Egyptian navy, he did hire the doctors as well. Doctors and experts and their families all arrived from the West together; the experts duly installed the arsenal and the doctors duly attended on the women and children in the new Western community at Alexandria; but, when the doctors had done all their duty by their Western patients, they found that they still had some working time on their hands; and, being the energetic and public-spirited medical practitioners that they were, they resolved to do something for the local Egyptian population as well. With what should they begin? Maternity work was obviously the first call. So a maternity hospital arose within the precincts of the naval arsenal by a train of events which, as you will now recognize, was inevitable.

The moral of this story is the speed with which, in cultural intercourse, one thing can lead to another, and the revolutionary length to which the process may go. Within the lifetime of all concerned, the traditional seclusion of Muslim women from contact with men outside their own household had still been so strictly enforced that in eighteenth-century Turkey, even when one of the Sultan's most dearly beloved wives was so ill that her life was in danger, the most that the Islamic code of manners would allow a Western doctor to do for this precious imperial patient was just to feel the pulse of a hand held out timidly between the tightly drawn curtains of the invisible lady's bed. This was the nearest that a Western physician had been permitted to approach a patient whose life was one of the principal treasures of a ruler who was deemed to be an autocrat. In those days the Sultan's autocracy had been impotent to override a traditional Islamic social convention, even in a matter of life and death which was next to the so-called autocrat's heart. And now, within the same lifetime, Muslim women were boldly venturing inside the precincts of an outlandish arsenal to avail themselves of the services of infidel Western obstetricians. This dire breach with the traditional Islamic conceptions of decency in the social relations between the sexes had been a consequence of the Pasha of Egypt's decision to equip himself with a navy in the Western style; and this undesigned and, at first sight, remote social effect had followed its technological cause within the span of less than half a lifetime.

This piece of social history, which is piquant but not unrepresentative, gives the measure of the degree to which those nineteenth-century Ottoman statesmen were deluding themselves when they imagined that they would be able to fit their country out with adequate Western armaments and then to arrest the process of Westernization at that point. It was not till the time of Mustafā Kemāl Atatürk, in our own day, that the 'Osmanlis admitted to themselves the truth that, in the game of cultural intercourse, one thing is bound to go on leading to another until the adoption of Western weapons, drill, and uniforms will inevitably bring in its train not only the emancipation of Muslim women but the replacement of the Arabic by the Latin alphabet and the disestablishment of an Islamic Church which, in Muslim countries in the past, has reigned unchallenged over the whole field of life.

In our own day in India, President Atatürk's great Hindu contemporary, the Mahatma Gandhi, did realize that in cultural intercourse one thing insidiously leads to another. Gandhi saw that a myriad threads of cotton—grown in India, perhaps, but spun in Lancashire and woven there into clothes for India's people—were threatening to entangle India with the Western world in gossamer meshes that might soon be as hard to break as if they had been steel fetters. Gandhi saw that, if Hindus went on wearing clothes made by Western machinery in the West, they would soon take to using the same Western machinery in India for the same purpose. First they would import jennies and power-looms from England; then they would learn how to build these implements for themselves; next they would be leaving their fields in order to work in their new Indian cotton-mills and Indian foundries; and, when they had become used to spending their working-time doing Western jobs, they would take to spending their leisure on Western amusements—movies, talkies, greyhound racing, and the rest—till they would find themselves growing Western souls and forgetting how to be Hindus. With a prophet's vision the Mahatma saw this grain of cotton-seed waxing into a great tree whose spreading branches would overshadow a continent; and this Hindu prophet called upon his Hindu countrymen to save their Hindu souls by laying an axe to this rank Western tree's roots. He set them the example of spending a certain time every day on spinning and weaving Indian cotton by hand, in the old-fashioned Indian way, for Indian bodies to wear, because he saw that this severance of the germinal economic ties between India and the West was the only sure means of saving the Hindu society from going Western, body and soul.

There was no flaw in the Mahatma Gandhi's insight. The Westernization of India that he foreboded and sought to avert was, and is, fast developing out of that one original grain of cottonseed; and Gandhi's remedy for India's Western infection was the right one. Only the prophet failed to induce his disciples to follow him in preserving India's cultural independence at this price in economic austerity. The wearing of machine-made cotton goods could not have been renounced by the Indian people in Gandhi's generation without lowering the Indian peasantry's already intolerably low standard of living, and without putting out of business altogether the new classes of Indian cotton operatives and Indian mill-owners that had already sprung up from India's soil in Bombay and in Gandhi's own native city, Ahmadabad. Gandhi has made an immense and perhaps permanent mark on the history of India and of the world; but the irony of history has condemned him to make this mark, not by saving India from economic Westernization, but by speeding her along the path of political Westernization through leading her triumphantly to the Western political goal of national self-government. Even Gandhi's genius was no match for the remorseless working of a social "law." In a cultural encounter, one thing inexorably goes on leading to another when once the smallest breach has been made in the assaulted society's defences.

Our inquiry will have made it evident that the reception of a foreign culture is a painful as well as a hazardous undertaking; and the victim's instinctive repugnance to innovations that threaten to upset his traditional way of life makes the experience all the worse for him; for, by kicking against the pricks, he diffracts the impinging foreign culture-ray into its component strands; he then gives a grudging admission to the most trivial, and therefore least upsetting, of these poisonous splinters of a foreign way of life, in the hope of being able to get off with no further concessions than just that; and then, as one thing inevitably leads to another, he finds himself compelled to admit the rest of the intruding culture piecemeal. No wonder that the victim's normal attitude towards an intrusive alien culture is a self-defeating attitude of opposition and hostility.

In the course of our survey we have had occasion to notice some of the statesmen in non-Western countries hit by the West who have had the rare vision to see that a society which is under fire from the radiation of a more potent foreign culture must either master this foreign way of life or perish. The figures of Peter the Great, Selīm III, Mahmūd II, Mehmed 'Alī, Mustafā Kemāl, and "the Elder Statesmen" of Japan in the Meiji Era have passed before our eyes. This positive and constructive response to the challenge of cultural aggression is a proof of statesmanship because it is a victory over natural inclinations. The natural response is the negative one of the oyster who closes his shell, the tortoise who withdraws into his carapace, the hedgehog who rolls himself up into a spiky ball, or the ostrich who hides his head in the sand, and there are classical examples of this alternative reaction in the histories of both Russia's and Islam's encounters with the West.

HAROLD R. ISAACS

Scratches on Our Minds

When the Scottish poet Robert Burns wrote, "O would that God the giftie gie us/ To see ourselves as others see us," he was expressing a wish that all of us, whether nurtured in Western or non-Western civilizations, should make in our "psychological encounters," to use Arnold Toynbee's phrase. For all too often the images that we have one of another are as distorted as those images which we see when we peer into the mirrors in amusement parks which make us appear fantastically elongated or foreshortened.

The wide range of images of India and China reflected in the minds of a panel representing a cross-section of Americans, many of them well-informed and rich in experience with Asian conditions, and the misconceptions registered by these images, are recorded and analyzed by Harold R. Isaacs. Since 1953, Mr. Isaacs has been a research associate at the Center for International Studies at the Massachusetts Institute of Technology, which sponsored the inquiry reported in this book.

Mr. Isaacs has been writing about international and mainly Asian affairs for over thirty years. He has served as an associate editor and war correspondent for Newsweek, has lived and traveled and worked in China, and has visited other areas of Asia. He is the author of several books, among them The Tragedy of the Chinese Revolution, revised edition 1961. His latest publication, Emergent Americans, 1962, deals with the reaction of students who went to live and work alongside Africans through the privately sponsored organization, Operation Crossroads Africa.

Part Four
Some Reflections

. . . We have summoned up these many images of the Chinese and the Indians. We have described them as they appeared in a number of American minds. We have traced origins, measured historical dimensions, and examined their relation to the experience and contact of individuals. This has been a many-sided exploration and, as best we

428

could, we have carried each part to its own conclusion. There are many other aspects of the matter to be explored, many observations still to pursue, and a great many questions which this inquiry has left in my own mind, and, I hope in the reader's. I would like, in the manner of a postscript, to muse about some of these in some final pages.

What is Image, What is Real?

Certain Chinese artists had a way of painting mountains which I had always taken to be an artistic convention until once, in northern Kwangsi, I came down among just such mountains as I had seen before only on parchment or on silk. They were unbelievably sorted in cones and knobs and a great host of unmountainly shapes rising at random from the flat valley floor and threaded together by fine curls of white mist. These mountains and the paintings of them come back to mind now as I think back over all the images that have crowded through these many pages and I hear a troubled reader asking: What is real? What is shadow, what is substance?

There is no tidy answer to this question. None of these images seems to me wholly a creature of pure fantasy. Each represents the effect of somebody's experience, the "truth" of somebody's perception. However fleeting, every perception is still an encounter of some kind between perceiver and perceived, one of that endless succession of interlocking observations that never quite tell the whole story. I know it would be simpler if it were otherwise, but I have no set of models, no certified genuine original portraits to which I can compare these many vignettes, no master answer sheet on which I can now tick off, true or false, any of these many images we have glimpsed through these American eyes. By unanimous—or nearly unanimous—consent, we can doubtless crop a few absurdities from the fringe, e.g., the rope trick Indian, Fu Manchu, the nerveless Chinese. But very little can really be excluded from the great host of particulars. The jeweled maharajahs were real enough, and so were the fakirs on nails, the bodies, alive or dead, on the streets of Calcutta or Shanghai, the Indian saints, and the Chinese sages. I would not be surprised to learn that there were sliding doors and secret passages in some American Chinatown establishment, and I have little doubt that somewhere, sometime, some Chinese cook did take off after juvenile tormenters with a meat cleaver in his hand. There is no end, as Ripley showed, to what can be believed or not. The trouble begins with the unwitting or witless process by which we generalize from the small fact or single experience.

The mind's bent to make much out of little is, of course, part of the secret of human genius. This is how children learn not to play with fire and how men, gradually marshaling and sharpening their wits with increasing rigor and discipline, have learned most of what they know about the universe, about the earth, about each other, and about themselves. Once in a great while, the act of the mind that turns some particular picture into a universal symbol is an act of creation: great perception, great humor, great art. Not with greatness but with a decent respect for the needs of our common understanding, many people of course employ the normal devices of generalization every day of their lives. But equally every day these are checked for relevance as validity against the realities with which they must cope. On a great many matters, however, in a great many minds, what goes on is a kind of mental trickery, a process of enlargement whereby we people our worlds with caricatures which appease some private or social needs. To distinguish between myth and reality in what we think and see requires effort and discipline. To do this we have to examine, each of us, how we register and house our observations, how we come to our judgments, how we enlarge upon them, how we describe them, and what purposes they serve for us. Even if a man discovers all this about himself, his reality need not be uniform with any other man's, for in each man substance can end and shadow begin at some different point. This point is located by the endlessly different combinations of a man's culture, education, and place in society; the time and place of his particular experience; the traits and drives of his individual personality. By examining the images we hold, say, of the Chinese and Indians, we can learn a great deal about Chinese and Indians, but mostly we learn about ourselves and about how, in each of us, this process of triangulation takes place. It is in some way unique in every man.

On this passage of inquiry through these many minds, I was heavily reinforced in my appreciation for the unending variety of individual uniqueness. But along the way I was also impressed by the influential accumulation of attitudes, images, and notions held in common by large groups or commonly attributed to others. I fear that I learned only a little about the specter of personality that makes men unique, but I was led by this experience to look at their common holdings with a new eye. There was obviously a clustering of more than one kind of uniformity among these individuals. A man can be an island, but islands are not often isolated atolls or lonely rocks. They lie mostly in archipelagos or at least in groups, and have many features alike. In this relation to each other, too, stood many members of our panel.

Some Common Holdings

It is quite plain, to begin with, that large groups in our panel of 181 Americans shared a great many biases concerning the Chinese and the

Indians. Here are the bare bones of a summary of what we found:

⟨ Ninety-eight, or 54 per cent, expressed more or less strongly negative views about Indians. Some of this antipathy was attributable to feelings over foreign policy differences. But it clearly had deeper roots, reproducing in some respects much older American reactions to Hindu life and culture. The antipathy was directed most particularly, however, toward Indians in the same professional classes as these Americans, and with but few exceptions these were Indians encountered by these Americans during the last ten years, the first decade of Indian independence.

⟨ One hundred twenty-three, or 70 per cent, expressed predominantly positive or admiring views of Chinese, applying these views to China as a nation, to Chinese culture as a whole, and to Chinese people of all sorts and classes, as known, encountered, or in some way discovered most generally in the years between 1920 and 1940. Changes reflecting the more recent circumstances have only just begun to weaken these attitudes, especially in individuals in whom they were not too strongly lodged.

⟨ Thirty-nine individuals in our panel "liked" both Chinese and Indians; 17 "disliked" both. There were 17 who "liked" Indians but did not "like" Chinese. But there were 72 who "liked" Chinese and "disliked" Indians.

⟨ This pattern of reaction held with remarkable consistency no matter how we sorted these Americans, by the kind and amount of their contact, by their policies, by their degrees of involvement in Asian affairs, or by their professional groups. In every grouping there was a predominantly positive view of the Chinese and either a roughly even division or a preponderantly unfavorable view of Indians. The Chinese stood highest in the esteem of those who had most contact with them and lowest (though never very low) among those who knew least. On the other hand, Indians scored better among those who knew them little—who tended to polarize to the extremes of "like" or "dislike"— than among those who knew them well—who tended to be more moderate or more mixed in their reactions. Thus 12 of our 16 China specialists were strongly positive about Chinese, 4 were "mixed," and none was negative. Of the 25 India specialists, 9 were positive about Indians, 9 negative, and 7 "mixed."

⟨ China-identified individuals had notably uniform attitudes about Indians. Of the 16 China specialists, 15 were strongly antipathetic, and only 1 was not. India-identified people were much less uniform in their reactions to Chinese, but there is a faint flavor of reciprocation about some of the figures. Of the 6 individuals, for example, who were most strongly admiring of the Indians, 3 distinctly did not admire the Chinese at all. Of our 25 India specialists, 7 had negative views of the

Chinese, a higher proportion (28 per cent) than appeared in any group within the panel. Of 65 panelists who had visited India but had never been to China, 13, or 20 per cent, were cool about the Chinese, while of 32 panelists who had visited both China and India, only 3 "disliked" Chinese while 21 "disliked" Indians.

From all the information and all the impressions at hand, I can say that I would expect this general pattern to be confirmed, reproduced, and reinforced by any wider or more systematically stratified inquiry in the same general milieu at this time. The evidence for this is strong and is multiplied in my own knowledge by instance after instance going far beyond the numbers of our present panel or the period of time in which these particular interviews were conducted. We are obviously confronted here with a community of views and reactions that extends far beyond these individual digits and derives from a body of common holdings covering a quite large area of experience.

Much about the character of these common holdings has already been suggested in the body of this report. It has been shown in many ways, for example, that many of these images and attitudes are products of their time and place and circumstances. It has been shown that dominant American reactions to China fluctuated widely during the 170-year history of American-Chinese contact, while American-Indian experience is connected only by thin strands to any distant past, and that this suggests that much is subject to change in the present patterns relating to Indians. True as this may be, it does not tell the whole story. For it is usually not the attributes that are changed by circumstances, but the way they are seen, a matter, again, of those lights shining at different times from different directions on different facets of what there is to see. Even under this constantly flickering and moving light, moreover, it is plain that some parts of the picture have always been in view. The lines of admiration for the Chinese, and of fear and mistrust as well, have been there from the beginning, have never been quite wholly effaced at any time since, and will not disappear wholly from any new views the future may disclose. It is similarly plain that the Westerner's capacity to be shocked and repelled by the Indian and his culture goes far, far back—there are intimations of it even in Marco Polo's brief account of his Indian travels—deeply underpinning and long antedating the irritation felt by so many Americans over so temporal a matter as Nehru's foreign policy, or by the behavior of Indians attributable to the newness of their independence.

How else may we, then, begin to define any of these common holdings? I bring no ready set of answers to this question, only some discussion. These are, by definition, large matters. They take us into a region of large and normally careless generalizations, a place where one ordinarily hunts for intellectual prey, but where now I warily seek some food for thought. One of the largest beasts rumored to be native here is now referred to in some social scientific dialects as "national character." Many hunters seek him in the belief that they will find hiding in his coat some of those bits of lively truth that are said to inhabit all popular national stereotypes. But like the Abominable Snowman, he has never yet been clearly seen, much less trapped and exhibited. The chances are that he never will be until he is much more precisely and narrowly located and identified. He may not, indeed, be like the Abominable Snowman at all, but more like the giraffe before which that man in the cartoon stood and declared: "There ain't no such animal!"

I do not propose to enter any abstract discussion about "national character," Snowman variety or giraffe. But I do want to consider here— much more seriously than I would have when I embarked on this inquiry—the possible meanings that attach to the single words "Chinese" or "Indian" or "American." All other identifying details apart, what might these adjectives alone suggest by way of common holdings of the people of all three nationalities who have figured in our study? These nationality labels are words that vibrate at many different frequencies for different people. To me they signify certain large geographic and certain very broad cultural identifications within which the possible varieties of individuality are without number. Yet I find myself now somewhat more willing than I was before to consider the possibility that they can be somewhat more descriptive, that they can suggest the presence of certain cultural traits, modes, even ideas. These can vary enormously in expression from individual to individual, but remain nevertheless in some form the common holding of large universes of people. As such, they can exert some particular effect on members of other large groups of people when contact takes place across cultural boundaries.

As one possible example, I offer the phenomenon of *li*, the Chinese code of correct manners. Our panelists gave especially high marks . . . to the special Chinese brand of courtesy, sensitivity, charming manners. Now the Chinese code of correct manners is as precise as a manual of arms or of court protocol. It is a system designed to assure within certain clearly defined limits that every man's ego is decently respected, or at least not publicly diminished. There is nothing uniquely Chinese about the business of gaining, saving, or losing "face"—it goes on in some form in every human society. But the Chinese acquired a special reputation in this matter because they acquired a high skill for it, turning it almost into an art form, full of formal convention, yet often extraordinarily satisfying in its effects. Chinese politeness was designed to smooth away all surface frictions. It established orderly priorities for almost all human relationships and the proper form of behavior for each one. Systems much like this exist in other societies but none, seemingly, with the patina and quality of the Chinese at its best. This is why Chinese amenities were always so charming, Chinese hospitality so attractive, and almost all encounters with Chinese so pleasantly memorable. In most of the ordinary business of human intercourse, this system accomplished its purpose admirably. Since over most of the period of American contact with Chinese in China, the foreigner almost automatically enjoyed high status and a high degree of deference, it was especially successful with foreigners and particularly so with Americans.

The system was fine so long as it was never tested for depth. It was based on the notion that most human contact is superficial and should be kept that way. Designed to preserve smooth surfaces, it did not allow much room for the free play of greater intimacy or interplay and expression of any deeper emotions. In times of stress, this politeness screened all sorts of unruly and unpleasant contradictions. In such circumstances, Chinese behavior could and did look to the foreigner like insincerity or downright dishonesty. This was the familiar judgment on Chinese manners in the difficult decades of the nineteenth century, and it has cropped up again in our own century whenever the going between Americans and Chinese got rough, especially during World War II, and since. The "deviousness" or "dishonesty" or "untrustworthiness" of the familiar negative stereotypes are, after all, only the undersides of good Chinese manners as they appear if the basic relationship is one of conflict. No American now is likely to mistake the well-known charm of Chou En-lai for a quality of inner virtue. But over the long period of time when the foreigner's superior status was acknowledged in fact as well as in form, it was a good deal easier for foreigners to believe in the sincerity of Chinese charm and the reality of Chinese deference. Many foreigners in China, especially teachers and scholars and masters of crafts, like ship captains or engineers, had every reason to feel they were being genuinely respected, especially in the years when so many Chinese were so seriously engaged in learning all they could about Western ways from Western tutors. This deference was, to be sure, often overdone and was associated with weakness; it sometimes became obsequious and generated contempt and patronage. This was not an uncommon form of the foreigner's experience and behavior in China, especially in the treaty ports. But in most cases, even when Chinese deference was understood to be a formal posture, I suspect that it was difficult for most Americans not to respond to it with eager self-appreciation. All other things being more or less equal, it is a rare ego that is proof against inflation, a rare man who will not believe that deference shown him is well merited. On this sure and shrewd knowledge, the Chinese built their code for interpersonal relations. As our present study and much other evidence shows, it has helped them make friends and influence people for a long, long time.

It is quite difficult to suggest any example of a similar single common holding of Indians or Americans comparable in character and effect to conventional Chinese manners. Much was said of Indian courtesy to travelers and hospitality to guests, and there was testimony to a subtle, even delicate sensitivity in many Indians met, known, and admired. But in most accounts the accent was much heavier and more frequent either on the obsequiousness of servants or the aggressiveness of Indian intellectuals, an outspokenness carried often to the point of rudeness. Now except for the item of obsequiousness, many of the things some of these Americans said about some Indians have a familiar ring, because they are the same things that some Indians (and many other foreigners) have been saying about some Americans, i.e., that they are brash, know-it-all, arrogant, unmannerly, and above all, morally self-righteous. To the extent that these qualities or manners do appear in significant numbers of individuals on both sides, the result is a collision of alikes, a repulsion between poles not because they are different but because they are the same. A meeting between two apostles of righteousness is not often the beginning of a beautiful friendship. But however unpleasant the frequency of their appearance, these are still not peculiarly "Indian" or "American" qualities. They would not on either side be enough by themselves to explain the nature of so many of our present encounters. As irritants they seem rather to compound the effect of a whole series of more important differences that have a much longer history, differences in religious and philosophic outlooks, in the manner of relatedness to other men and nature. Some of these certainly do suggest common holdings on both sides that do in profound ways mold the social character of the individual members of both cultures. But whether these holdings are distinctively "Indian" or "American" is quite another question which is not simply or quickly answered.

It does not seem at all accidental that with respect to "Chinese" it is easier to summon up such a distinctive identification, and that it turns out to be related to the Chinese system for maintaining the smoothness of surface contact, counterpart in the sphere of human relations to the Chinese preoccupation in art with exquisite form. It seems to me equally not accidental that in the attempt to summon up any comparable generalization for "Indian" or "American" we run at once into matters that are quite different, more substantial, more complicated, more difficult, and probably less truly distinctive.

Thus in seeking examples of something distinctively "Indian" and something distinctively "American," I found myself thinking of the Indian institution of *caste* and the American idea of *the totally mobile society*. I offer myself at once a dozen valid objections to accepting either one of these as truly unique attachments to the unamplified adjectives "Indian" or "American." Still, I think the collision of these elements plays so great a role in Indian-American encounters that I take the license to pursue them here at least for a short distance.

Echoes of this collision are heard from as far back in the past as we have the written record of American discoveries of India. The nine-teenth-century American traveler to India, who much resembled the twentieth-century Indian traveler to America in his thorough apprecia-tion of his own moral and political virtues, was uniformly horrified by the rigidities of Indian caste. He was likely to see it as the most com-plete antithesis of his own culture's belief in total social mobility. Caste set up for this American, and for his counterparts down into our own time, an immediate barrier of incomprehensibility, a first and powerful impulse of rejection. By the same token, this same American reacted with identifying approval to the discovery in Chinese society of a mythology akin to his own, the idea that long, long ago, the Chinese system aimed to make it possible for the lowliest farmer's son to rise by individual merit to the side of the Heavenly Throne. This won marks for the Chinese among Americans, as we have noted, all the way back to Thomas Jefferson's time.

The belief in total social mobility, the inherent right and opportunity for all to proceed through merit and achievement from rags to riches, from log cabin to White House, is a peculiarly American article of faith. It may be a myth contradicted by much in the American actuality. It may explain many American postures of self-congratulation, righteous-ness, superiority, hypocrisy. Yet, as I have suggested before in connec-tion with the American relation to Western imperialism in Asia, it has the power to overlay many of these contradictions. Every man who is a product of the American culture stands in some relation to this cen-tral dream of his society, whether in his view of himself or his view of his nation's role and behavior, in his own clusters of personal or national pride or guilt. Burdened as it may be with clichés and fatigue and failure, and despite all the great range of individual variations—one thinks of the much-caricatured American yearning after European aris-tocrats, or of the easy relish with which so many Americans adopted the modes of the lords of creation in Asia—the democratic dream still pro-vides the yardstick by which the "American" measures his experience of other cultures more formally stratified than his own.

In current American-Indian encounters the issue of caste plays a complicated role. Taken by itself as the symbol of ultrastratification and also as a symbol for all the elements in Hindu society which retard the country's advance, it arouses the traditional American reaction. Only now this reaction of rejection and bafflement is multiplied by frustration, for this American is usually interested either in helping or in seeing Indians "do something" about their problems. On the Indian side the response to this is defensive. Almost every Indian carries the mark of caste upon him, whether he counts himself a defender or a critic of the system. It is connected with the special forms of Indian caste and color prejudice, and attitudes toward status and the relation of educated Indians to their own particular groupings, to the uneducated masses, and to Indian society as a whole. If he is a conservative Indian, his response to the American reaction is a natural posture of defense. If he is a "modern" Indian, the matter grows more difficult, for every forward-looking Indian is himself today committed to ending the caste system and all its rigidities and all its extrusions in Indian life. Yet he smarts and struggles under the knowledge that he has not yet even emancipated himself from its grip. His country, like a great part of the world, has accepted, at least as a credo, the dream of a democratic society which was for so long the unique possession of the new American culture that developed from European origins. This Indian, with all his accumulated sensitivities about himself and his own culture, cannot accept this without a certain resentment. He is in much the position that Cyrano took toward comments on his nose, willing to denounce its monstrousness himself at poetic length, but quite ready to deny at sword's point any untoward word by anyone else. Unable to skewer his critic as Cyrano did, he impales him on charges of being a lyncher, a racist, a self-seeker sunk in materialism, or borrows from the fading images of his British heritage, and scorns the American as a vulgarian without art or good manners. The American, for his part, may be none of these things but still suffer from too poorly representing that great and elusive dream which he now shares with so many people all around the world.

Whatever clues these examples might offer as to the nature of the common holdings of these people, they all still remain uncomfortably large generalizations, blurred and fuzzy, like the view in a poorly focused camera's eye. The images evoked by the labels "Chinese" or "Indian" or "American" have to be more rigorously defined and more sharply seen by bringing into view the string of other identifying adjectives to which they may be attached. Much more can be said in general about such a group as "American businessmen who lived in Shanghai in the 1920's," or "Indians educated in England in the generation before independence," or "Chinese college students at the time of the Japanese invasion." These or any of a great host of other such particulars fix these

Chinese, Indians, and Americans in groups located in society, in time, in place, and often in particular circumstances. Such groups not only have a great deal of experience in common. They can also come to have many common characteristics, modes, manners, outlooks, and these are capable of producing an almost predictable effect on members of other particular groups. Among these common holdings, the nationality label adds only one meaningful item of identification to a great many others, for these are people who also share common professions, preoccupations, interests, and situations. They are people who are looking out at the world from much the same windows and who therefore tend to get much the same view of what they see.

Windows on the World

All images are shaped by the way they are seen, a matter of setting, timing, angle, lighting, distance. Images carried about by some people for a whole lifetime may have been fixed by a single exposure dating, perhaps, from an experience deep in the past. Or else they may emerge from a whole collection of pictures that a man takes with his mind over the years and which come out looking much the same because his mind's setting is fixed, like a fixed-focus box camera.

This aperture is set by the totality of what a man is. Primarily, of course, he is an individual personality with his own unique bundle of needs and forms of self-expression. These fix the most important conditions in which his images are shaped and seen. But we are trying here to see the image-shaping identities that many such individuals may hold in common as members of groups. We have suggested that the first such group identity may be the fact that he is "American" with all that may suggest or imply as to his outlook. But more graspably, he is a lot of other things too: he is a bachelor, master, or doctor of art, science, medicine, or philosophy, an editor, teacher, diplomat, businessman, writer, Congressman, or wearer of his church's cloth. These identities establish for each man the area in which he functions and expands most of his energy, the interests which govern his behavior, the kinds of satisfaction or frustration he may derive from his experience with other people. His images of the Chinese or Indian are clearly going to have quite different shapes according to whether he sees them as prospective customers, objects of his benevolence, souls to be saved, or digits in a population problem or exemplars of some sociological category. His attitude is going to be influenced to a decisive degree by what he seeks from his encounter with the Chinese or Indian (or anybody else, for that matter), by whether he wants to win acceptance of the product, the creed, or the policy he has to sell or promote, or whether he wants the person he meets to satisfy his scholarly, journalistic, acquisitive, or merely idle curiosity, or if he wants nothing at all but to meet and pass on by. All these shapes, outlooks, and purposes flickered in the many interviews of which this study is made.

•   •   •

The Specter of Personality

•   •   •

It was obvious, to begin with, that through a man's window we could discover *what* a man sees but very little of *how* he sees it. We were still left also to wonder why two men sitting at the same window, or in the same bank of windows, often saw things so differently. Why did one scholar describe Indians as "articulate" and why did another say they were "talkative"? Why did one person regard the people around him with distaste and even fear while another regarded them mostly with a relaxed and quizzical curiosity? Why did one traveler remember only the squalor and the urinal stench of city streets, and why did another call to mind the high color, vivid motion, and the "pungent odor of dung fires burning at night" in the Indian countryside? Why was one diplomat made bitter and angry by policy differences, and why did another react much more matter-of-factly, even though both held substantially the same view of the matters in dispute?

•   •   •

[One] prime example concerns two scholars, both of high repute in their respective fields. Neither is inclined to underestimate himself, both set high value on intellectual qualities and interests, both especially admire the way these values are exemplified in England, each, indeed, in his own fashion, can be said to be an Anglophile. This is a great deal for two men to hold in common. Yet one was impatiently contemptuous of Indian intellectuals and the other was warmly admiring. Both men made their first trip to India in recent years. Both came away from the experience with all their previous notions powerfully reinforced, the one more than ever convinced of the ineffably surpassing qualities of his Indian friends and acquaintances, the other full of his confirming evidence that the Indians whom he observed, with notably few exceptions, were shallow and shoddy. It is true that they had somewhat different preoccupations, but the deeper reasons for differences lie locked up in these two individuals. One could start looking for them, probably, by trying to discover the nature and sources of each one's Anglophilism and going on in from there to wherever the search might lead. But that would be another inquiry, another book, indeed another book written by someone else. I can deal here, again, only in some impressions.

• • •

Images and Politics

How, finally, do these images and attitudes relate to politics, international relations, the making of government policy, the shaping of public opinion?

The first answer is, of course, that relations between nations are determined primarily by the large and highly material considerations of geography, resources, power, economics, and the somewhat less tangible quantity of the national self-interest as conceived by governing groups. These considerations consist mostly of hard facts harshly seen, and leaders are usually effective to the degree that they keep these facts unblinkingly in view. But even these large chunks of reality can often be seen in dimensions larger or smaller than life. Great events indeed can result from such "mistaken" arrangements and images and ideas in the minds of men in power, e.g., Napoleon's views of Russia and England, the conceptions of Russia and the United States on which Hitler based his course, the ideas about China that governed the thinking of Japanese military leaders in the 1930's, the belief of certain American leaders in 1945 that Japanese fanaticism would outweigh Japan's loss of capacity to wage war, the belief of British and French leaders that they could impose their will by force on Egypt in 1956. When the issues between nations are those of war or peace, the consequences of such "miscalculations" can, as we have all seen, be quite formidable.

• • •

Generally speaking, we may assume that intelligent people who deal with problems of international politics try to distinguish between their personal feelings or reactions to nations or peoples on the one hand, and their judgment of the merits or demerits of policy decisions on the other. This effort shows up clearly in our present panel, intelligent people all, and some of them heavily burdened with policy responsibilities. In this group those who took a generally sympathetic view of India's foreign policy were about evenly divided in their reactions to Indians as people. They tended to accept Nehru's policies as sensible or wise, at least from the reasonable standpoint of Indian national interests, or even to hold that these policies for India were the better course from the American point of view as well. Among those hostile to Nehru's foreign policy, the proportion was less even. Yet even here, about one-third were individuals who were otherwise quite positively disposed toward India and Indians, but who felt that Indian foreign policy was damaging either to India or to the United States or to both.

Every government official or member of Congress who was interviewed stoutly denied that his feeling about India or Indians, whatever it was, had anything to do with his policy decisions or his votes affecting India. A conscientious public servant could hardly make any other assumption or statement about himself. Yet it is difficult not to speculate about the inner realities of the decision-making process. One government official who was a member of several interdepartmental committees in Washington confessed that whenever an India item arose, a palpable sigh would pass around the table and somebody was quite likely to say something like: "Oh God, here we go again!" Individuals operating exchange and public information programs found themselves confronted with this problem in a peculiarly acute form. They were supposed to generate good will through personal contacts which normally produced only irritation and ill will. The feeling of frustration over Indians in general and Nehru in particular became a familiar and recurring state of mind in policy-making quarters during this time in Washington. How far then, may one guess, did this feeling influence the making of critically important decisions? Perhaps the single most important one relating to India made in this period of time was the decision, made by the National Security Council and announced by President Eisenhower in February, 1954, to extend arms to Pakistan. Many factors no doubt entered into the taking of this step. But it was so obviously going to have a major effect on American-Indian relations that the issue before the policy makers really came down to a choice between the real or alleged advantages of the Pakistan aid program and the further serious alienation of India. One cannot help wondering about the role of the underlying feeling about India, expressed in a remark attributed to one of the top policy makers at the decisive meeting: "This is a good thing to do if only because it will show Nehru where to get off!"

China policy of course occupied its own special place at this time in the business of American foreign-policy making. The extraordinary role of the special images, emotions, and attitudes connected with China has already been reviewed in great detail. The watchers on these ramparts, led in Washington at this time by such figures as Senator William Knowland of California, held back for several years the public development of a more hardheaded view of American needs and interests vis-à-vis Communist China and the Nationalist remnant on Formosa. Yet by all accounts, in the summit of the Administration itself and in wide concentric circles of interested individuals, the consensus grew that Communist China was an accomplished fact of life that had to be accepted as the starting point of new American-Chinese relations, even if only for the purpose of more effectively pursuing American aims in the power struggle with the Soviet Union. In our panel, 135 individuals said that they believed that some kind of normalization of relations with Communist China was going to be required. A total of 17 believed that the United States would sooner or later get into further hostilities with Communist China—these opinions were mostly expressed at the height of the Quemoy-Matsu tension early in 1955—but only 11 individuals thought that American policy should be aimed at forcibly overcoming Communist China through isolation and blockade, and only 5 bitter-enders said that they thought that this policy should include the active preparation of Chiang Kai-shek's army for a return to the Chinese mainland. Not until the end of May, 1957, when the flare-up of an anti-American riot in Taipeh, the Formosa capital, brought a certain catharsis in the oddly artificial relations between Washington and Formosa, did the fear of offending special sensibilities on the Chinese issue seem to begin to relax. The facts of power and the needs of policy were imposing themselves. The older images and the older attitudes were being forced to give way to the new demands.

• • •

. . . Generally speaking, with notable exceptions, propagandists have found it necessary to lie more about their friends than about their foes. But not often in history have friends and foes changed places on such a large scale so swiftly as they have in the affairs of nations in the years since 1939. Never has there been such a transmogrification of so many "goodies" into "baddies" and vice versa in so short a time. Just how this process, taking place along the swollen channels of communication that now fill every man's world with sight and sound, has affected the patterns and habits of popular ideas and stereotyping in American minds is another one of the many subjects that wants more examination.

The more relevant term for politics, and perhaps for much else, is not *image* but *relationship*. In terms of relationship, especially where Chinese and Indians and Americans are concerned, something a good deal more than transmogrification is taking place. Transmogrification means change with an absurd effect, and there can be no question that such effects abound in current world affairs. But laugh, cry, or gape, what confronts us is no more speedy change of scenery, flag, costume, posture, or facial expression, no frantic flashing of new pictures on the propaganda screens. It is the beginning of a change in the underpinning of the total relationship between Western and Asian and African men. For nearly three hundred years this underpinning was the assumption of Western superiority: a whole vast political-military-social-economic-racial-personal complex was built upon it. Almost every Western image of Asian and other non-Western peoples was based on it. This assumption can now no longer be made or maintained. The whole structure based upon it is being revised. All the power relations that went with it are being changed. This is history in the large, a great continental rearrangement, bringing with it a great and wrenching shift in the juxtapositions of cultures and peoples. Western men are being relieved of the comforts and disabilities of being the lords of creation; Asian and African men can no longer merely submit, nor live on the rancors of subjection, nor revitalize their own societies by the ideas or sanctions of their own more distant past. All must move from old ground to new, from old assumptions to new ones, and as they move must constantly refocus their views. They will all be engaged, for some time to come, in more or less painfully revising the images they have of themselves and of each other.

In this revision, all the images and experiences of the past have some part. They are not effaced but are absorbed and rearranged in some new design. Much is relegated to the museums and to the memory and to the contending history books, but the greater part remains to bedevil the process of change itself. All the sounds, old and new, go on in our hearing at the same time, making the great din in which we live. All the old and new images flicker around us, giving our world and every individual mind the quality it has of a kaleidoscope. The problem for every man, be he Chinese, Indian, or American, would still seem to be to try to know the nature of this process, to sort out the sounds and distinguish among the sights, to understand their effects in his own mind and in the minds of others. It is at least barely possible that this knowledge can help make the new relationships, the new assumptions, the new images a little less unflattering to themselves and to human society. . . .

FRANCIS E. DART

The Rub of Cultures

Since World War II many Americans have had the opportunity of visiting foreign lands to bring to the so-called underdeveloped peoples the benefit of western knowledge and civilization. Such was the case with Francis E. Dart, associate professor of physics at the

University of Oregon, who went to Nepal for two years on a govern-
ment-sponsored Point Four project. His impressions of this land
long hidden away from all contact with Western civilization, and of
the impact of Western scientific culture and methods on a people
who have had no scientific tradition of their own, are recounted in
the article below.

Dr. Francis E. Dart was born at Mt. Silinda, Southern Rhodesia,
in 1914. Educated at Oberlin College and Notre Dame University,
he received his Ph.D. in physics at Cornell University. He has
taught at Notre Dame and Cornell, and has been on the faculty of
the University of Oregon since 1949. From 1960 to 1962 Dr. Dart
was on leave of absence from the University of Oregon working for
the National Academy of Science in Washington, D.C. in the
Office of Scientific Personnel, where he administered international
fellowships for graduate study in the space sciences.

THE thoughts that I record here began to take shape three years ago in a small mountain town in Nepal where my trip was interrupted by a three-day festival to Laksmi. I had been walking for eight days and was to walk nearly twenty more without once meeting a wheeled vehicle or any other evidence of mechanized civilization. Through dense tropical forests of sal a hundred feet above sea level, up steep slopes thick with rhododendron trees, along great cedared ridges cool even in the sun at 12,000 feet, I had been traveling in the only way one can in Nepal, on foot trails that are sometimes deserted, sometimes thronged with heavily burdened men and women moving in unison, their baskets weighted with new potatoes or ghee. Occasionally the trail would thread a village animated with the play of naked brown-skinned children, with cheerful old men in woolen shawls and shy dark-eyed girls carrying jars of water from the well—an irregular patch of mud-colored houses on the gold of ripening rice paddies surrounding it. With all its beauty and poverty and its growing desire for new ways, in the familiar jargon of our time, this was the underdeveloped country.

I had been asked to go to Nepal in order to teach science and to introduce new methods and equipment to the science teachers there. Soon after my arrival, however, and before I had started my project, it became clear that this was not really wanted, at any rate not by the teachers who would be most affected by my work. Equipment would certainly be acceptable, but not new methods and certainly not any direct teaching. I soon became convinced that the objections were not directed at me personally nor at American assistance and yet ran very much deeper than mere misunderstanding of words. It was more a matter of the social structure of a Nepalese college, which does not permit a professor to admit that there is anything more for him to learn, and of unwillingness to accept the changes that might result from a different sort of teaching. As a scientist or science teacher I would be very welcome, provided I did not do anything. In growing consternation, I began to see that I was to be more of a symbol than an active scientist —a sort of offering to be laid like a flower at the shrine of a modern deity. I was pretty sure I would wilt.

In the end I found many things to do, most of them inoffensive and some of them useful. During two years in this delightful country, I learned much about it and its people, but I learned on my own with practically no professional assistance. I was there as one member of a three-man team sent by the University of Oregon under contract with the International Coöperation Administration (the "point four" program of technical and economic assistance). At that time, the total American assistance to Nepal amounted to approximately $3,000,000 per year, about one-tenth of which was spent through the University of Oregon contract. The contract achieved its objectives of establishing a college of education, training Nepalese educators, setting up a press for textbook preparation, etc., and according to both Nepalese and American authorities it was among the best of all American-sponsored projects in Nepal. Nothwithstanding this, it was beset as were the other projects with much waste and delay and with much uncertainty as to its long-range effectiveness largely because of discrepancies between American and Asian ways of doing things, and because neither side could easily understand and communicate with the other.

I recount all this because it is substantially the situation in a great many of the underdeveloped countries. American aid is offered and accepted at top government levels and then met with resistance or polite evasion when it is delivered. Particularly is this true when the aid involves changes in old ways or ideas. Yet these very countries are asking for assistance because they want to change. We, in our turn, are puzzled and exasperated, yet in our puzzlement we ourselves doubt the relevance or competence of our own social science. The very development of Western science which should help us the most we are unwilling to use. Bravely we struggle ahead without it, as though to show the world that we can do it anyway—even with half our brains tied behind us.

II

Asia today is a scene of intense and rapid change. Strong winds of economic, political and social innovation are sweeping through every corner of the continent, bringing in new institutions, new industries and technologies and a whole new attitude toward Asia's part in the world ahead. Taken together, these add up to a revolution to compare with any the world has seen. Beneath all the turmoil, however, there lies a vast inertia, a great ocean of people and tradition, slow to respond to the storm at the surface, yet moving with deep and powerful currents that are hardly noticed above. The immediate revolution, one which will in time reach down to stir even these depths, is basically the same over all of Asia and is, or will be, in most of Africa too. One might almost say that it started with Marco Polo or Saint Paul; with the Western merchants and the colonial governments that followed them to exploit the rich resources of the East; or with the Christian missionaries who brought with them schools and medicine and a new concept of individual worth. Together, they sowed their seeds of resentment and hope and new knowledge, unable, surely, to guess what might be the harvest of so mixed a planting.

After World War II, these elements exploded into a drive for independence and for living standards comparable, if possible, to those in the Western world. The people of the hitherto underdeveloped countries determined now to have food enough and medicines, and yes, airplanes and wrist watches and nuclear reactors, too, and to have them on their own terms, free from Western exploitation. They wanted, also, to find and somehow adopt the concepts of equal justice, equal dignity, equal cosmic importance for all—concepts that the Westerner enjoys but has been unable to share. It is perhaps well to mention here that, in Asia at least, these things are wanted without Western religion, which is viewed with deep distrust. This is a fact of great significance, because in Asia religion is a vital and necessary part of living which, unlike Christianity, offers no strong motivation toward social change.

Not only are changes desired, they are desired in a great hurry. Generations of Western progress are to be absorbed in a decade or two and it is useless to suggest a slower, sounder pace, for the very continued existence of most political régimes depends upon their delivery of an almost impossible rate of progress; for them the fastest pace *is* the soundest. Many among their citizens know about higher standards and are unwilling to wait longer; and many of us who would help know what is possible (in a way that our forebears did not know for us), and we are eager to urge them forward. Moreover, now that a start has been made, it may well be that a rapid pace has to be maintained just to stay ahead of the expanding population. Thus, while I was in Nepal, the literacy rate was less than 5 per cent and yet, with all the nation's efforts to provide more schools and teachers, literacy was *decreasing* each year.

One is tempted, nevertheless, to question the wisdom and even sometimes the safety of proceeding so rapidly. The whole thing suggests to me an attempt to present the Bonneville Power System to St. Thomas Aquinas. One wonders just what will come of it. Yet I am sure that there is no practical use in asking whether this is good or safe. These questions are not only very complicated, but also irrelevant. It is not necessary to look very far even in Nepal (which has been isolated until very recently) in order to find convincing evidence that there is no possible turning back. People who have once learned of modern antibiotics will not be willing to go back to the "unspoiled past" with its high infant mortality. The mountain villager who showed me his new kerosene lantern with pride and asked if we had anything as good as that in America will never go back to using pine torches. The man or woman who has once attended a modern school will not be the same again, nor will his village. I met a Gurung woman who knows this. She cannot read or write two words, but she contributed three thousand rupees to her village to build a school and then herself walked five days from her village to meet me and ask if we would train teachers for the school. Shall we tell her it was only an old woman's mistaken dream? Can we refuse to train teachers for her school?

No, the revolution will not be stopped. It is of no use to ask whether it should ever have started or who started it. With or without our help it will come, and it is better by far that America should be involved, for we have much of value to offer. Better to ask how we can be a constructive force in it, how we can help make of it a renaissance instead of a new enslavement. Better for them and also better for us.

III

It is the fruits of Western technology that are most of all wanted. Everything else from America, our literature, art or "culture," could be dispensed with except only these precious apples so long forbidden. It is jeeps and tractors, hospitals and antibiotics, hydroelectric plants and refrigerators that represent the new order of civilization. It is industry (meaning wealth) and education (meaning training) which are to transform life. It is modern weapons which are to ensure national liberty and perhaps even allow a part in bigger games among the nations. Modern technology is seen as the liberator of the Western world now coming to liberate the Eastern. To be sure, there is criticism of nuclear bombs and bomb tests and a good deal of apprehension about them, but hardly anyone doubts that the less awesome products of a technological age are primary and indeed are the only primary things to be had from us. (Our interests in Asia and Africa and our fears for them are somewhat different from this view, and it is important therefore that we understand theirs.)

The costs, however, turn out to be unexpectedly high. Capital is a scarce item where the average annual income is less than $100 and the few who are wealthy would rather visit the West than bring it to the East. Where tens of millions do not have enough capital to own a pair of shoes, it is hard to promote investment, whether public or private, in expensive progress. Furthermore, the progress does not run itself and technicians brought from abroad or trained abroad are both scarce and exceedingly expensive. Fortunately, various of the more developed or most developed nations are willing "for certain reasons" (as the Indian says when he does not wish to expand on a matter) to give substantial amounts of capital and equipment and even to send trained technicians and provide training for others. Thus a start can be made.

However, this turns out to be only a beginning, a down payment, as it were, with the real and continuing payments yet to be made. Once the start has been made, of course it is hoped that the normal processes of capital accumulation and development of human resources will follow, and doubtless they will, although there is some reason to be concerned about the time required for this and also about the disruption that would attend any serious international strife. But the most serious and unexpected costs are to be measured in terms of change; the very changes that are so much desired have negative as well as positive aspects.

The introduction of new techniques, new industries and new education into a community is certain to bring far-reaching and often unforeseen changes in working habits, in work hours, in the status within the community of new sorts of workers, and in the distribution of money and power. These soon begin to affect social structures and institutions, family patterns, leadership patterns, etc. Before long, the very cultural foundation of the community may seem to be threatened, its religion called into question, its most basic philosophies of man's relation to nature and to God, of the status of women or the training of children, altered and forced to accommodate to new pressures. Of course, such changes took place in Western culture too under the impact there of the industrial-technological revolution, and even spread over generations, they seemed to be very drastic. One can only imagine what their impact must be, crowded into a few years in an Indian or African village. This is the real cost of the revolution.

It sometimes happens that the changes come too quickly for even superficial accommodation. The failures that then occur seem to be superficial or even trivial, yet they can serve to indicate the difficulty with which innovation comes. In one country steel plows are introduced where previously a pointed stick had served. The farmers accept them with polite gratitude and use them as ornaments but not for plowing. Why? These plows require two hands and the farmers are accustomed to using only one, the other being used to guide the bullock. A more productive variety of rice cannot be introduced in part of Nepal where it is needed and very well suited to climate and soil because the grains cling a bit more to the stalk and a new threshing technique would need to be used. But threshing is a family or community undertaking involving social and ritual as well as mechanical activities. Running water in people's houses is not accepted because the village well is the social center as well as a source of water. Cook stoves designed to conduct smoke out of the house through a chimney are not acceptable to Hindu housewives in place of the open smoky *chula* now in use because religion requires that all parts of the stove (including the chimney if there is one) be cleaned after each meal. It would not be difficult to put together a large list of such minor failures nor to include in it some major ones. If these seem improbable or easily overcome, the reader might review the introduction of an innovation, say the fluoridation of water, into our own technologically highly sophisticated society. He might also consider the willingness with which Christians, out of Christian motives, will help to reduce infant mortality and disease in a distant non-Christian country and how unwilling they may then be to help control the population explosion that inevitably results.

The whole process abroad is like an attempt to transplant cut flowers. Surely the changes to be introduced need to have roots in an indigenous technological revolution that will give them continuity and relationship to a whole. In the end this means that the developing nations need to have their own scientific revolutions.

IV

Far back in the hills of Nepal, seven or eight days' walk from any contact with the modern world, iron is mined and smelted and fabricated into tools. The inhabitants of the village of Those who do this use almost exactly the same process of ore-smelting which is employed in similarly remote Chokwe villages in Angola, where, as a boy, I used to admire the native-made hunting knives and arrow points. It is, in fact, the same smelting process which in ancient Greece led to the development of metallurgy and eventually to the science of chemistry. The Nepalese and the Angolans have used the process for generations, perhaps for many centuries, yet there is no hint of chemistry in Those. The men and women who operate the smelter know what to do, but they are not curious about the transformation that converts stone into metal.

They do not depend upon any understanding of it in order to keep it going or possibly improve it. For such purposes, they use a different device; into the wall of the clay smelter is molded a small image of a deity who oversees the process and to whom deference is paid before each run.

Technology is not science. Tools and the skill to make and use them are found everywhere, but science is a unique development limited almost entirely to the Western world where it has played an essential part—perhaps the most essential part—in making possible the enormous variety of innovations that collectively make up the industrial-technological revolution. Not only has the scientific revolution given the Western world the fundamental understanding of nature that makes these innovations technically feasible, but it has also fostered an attitude toward nature and natural forces that allows for their manipulation and control. The importance of this latter condition is not often appreciated, for we live and grow up from childhood in an atmosphere saturated with science. Before entering kindergarten, our children play with "scientific" toys, hear about germs, watch television and know all about automobiles and airplanes. Third graders do "research" and their parents can scarcely buy a tube of toothpaste without resort to science. As a result, we accept a scientific, a rational view of nature without question. We take it for granted that things which are not understood will some day be understood and that in understanding natural phenomena lies the way to a better life.

Such is not the case everywhere. In Nepal, as in most of Asia and Africa, children grow to adulthood in a world that is saturated not with science but with non-science—with a deep running view of nature that is essentially non-rational, non-objective. It is a world where a cholera epidemic calls for special prayer-flags no less and no more than for immunization; where a new diesel generator for the college cannot be started after installation until a blood sacrifice has rendered it safe; where only a fool would operate a bicycle or jeep without a similar ceremonial sacrifice once each year; where the timing and conduct of every new undertaking is controlled more by astrology than by technology. The important distinction here is not one of religion as such. In both East and West religion may be a mature expression of man's search to know "that of God" in his being. It is rather a question of one's view of nature, a question as to whether nature is subject to rational understanding or not. Across the street from the principal college in Kathmandu is a wall into which is built a narrow triangular window neatly framed and decorated and provided with a small shelf of flowers. One of the professors explained to me that there is a goddess living in the field beyond the wall who likes sometimes to cross the street, and it would have been discourteous to build the wall without providing a passage for her convenience. Any Westerner visiting Kathmandu who is unable to accept this goddess as a real and influential member of the community should, in my judgment, think of himself only as a tourist.

Science in such a setting is likely to be considered as a charm, practiced by the Westerner, but essentially qualitatively like the many older charms used to ward off misfortune or ensure good. The acceptance of science as a charm is clearly illustrated in medicine, where drugs and doctors are eagerly accepted, whereas public health measures are met with great reluctance and little if any understanding. The purifying of drinking water by boiling is more likely to be understood as a ritual purification than as biological. Once the ceremony is performed it may be considered as unimportant what happens thereafter to the water— what may be added, whether clean containers are used, etc. Thus our cook learned quickly that dishes were to be washed and rinsed in boiled water and he faithfully complied with this instruction. However, he saw nothing wrong with drying the dishes with a cloth he had just used to mop the floor and he could not understand my wife's distress when she discovered this. Even the native-born scientist frequently finds himself a practitioner of an alien cult uncomfortably suspended between two worlds and not fully accepted into either.

A true scientific revolution which could support technology would profoundly affect the cultures of the underdeveloped nations in their deepest traditions and not merely in the obvious things of roads and tractors and the like. It would be certain to bring about major changes in religious philosophy, ethics and social structure. Surely this is playing with fire. Surely we should stop to consider before undertaking any such program.

Yet, in fact, there is little choice, for events have moved so far and so fast that some kind of technological change is now inevitable. The real questions left are only how it will come and how much disruption can be avoided. Moreover, in the change that is surely coming, very much that is good and needed can be included. If we cannot and would not prevent the growth of science in the developing nations, we can certainly help to better its coming.

In doing so, we might well allow ourselves the luxury of good planning. For reasons of our own that few thoughtful observers would defend, we have for years limited ourselves to a one-year-at-a-time program that had to be concerned primarily with the more superficial aspects of the total revolution. Now we shall soon find that five years' planning is hardly too much, as we help the developing nations with longer-range preparation for wise introduction and use of new things. We should be even more concerned than we are to help them in the improvement and development of education in all its aspects, as distinguished from simple training for specific jobs. Training will not stand long as a substitute for education. We should help, for instance, in the introduction of science in the education of children, whose fresh curiosity and unselfconscious willingness to experiment is the same the world over. We have recently developed in America new and vital approaches to secondary school science teaching which could be of enormous significance abroad. We should urge their trial and help in the considerable work of adapting them.

There is a great opportunity to help with good science films and other teaching aids, an opportunity we have been slow to take up in our foreign aid programs. The techniques of "programmed instruction," still in the process of development in this country, might prove to have important uses in countries where there are not enough teachers and many of the existing teachers have very little training, for these techniques might speed up teacher training and can make it possible for poorly trained teachers to do a much better job than would otherwise be likely. Adaptation of these programs to children and teachers in another culture will involve much more than simple translation and in some cases they will be initially too expensive. Nevertheless, it would be worthwhile to initiate pilot studies, for the potential benefits are quite large.

At a much higher level of scientific development, while continuing and expanding the educational exchanges that have proved so valuable, we should help the developing nations solve what has become a difficult problem to many of them. This is the loss of scientists who go abroad for advanced training—often to the United States—only to find that when they have completed their degree or a period of postdoctoral study they do not wish to return to their home country, or if they do return they do not wish to stay. The research equipment back home does not compare well with what they have been using; there are few qualified scientists there with whom to collaborate; the atmosphere of the country is not conducive to scientific research; international contacts are few; publication is difficult; governments are unsympathetic; and so on. The net effect is that the less developed countries are exporting scientists to the better developed. It will take a considerable measure of international coöperation and investment to find a satisfactory solution to this problem, which, understandably enough, has not disturbed us who gain by it as much as it might.

V

Many proposals of specific foreign aid projects are being made by people who have the detailed information that is necessary for this.

I do not intend here a criticism of these projects. My purpose rather is to insist that our assistance to the developing nations, whatever its final form, must originate in clear understanding and genuine commitment. We need to have considerable understanding of ourselves as a scientifically oriented culture and of the nature of our science. We need to understand the non-scientific culture of our neighbors and to appreciate better than we now do the interaction of the two. To do so, we must place much greater reliance on our own social sciences in which we have so little faith, at least when it comes to foreign aid. It is silly for us as a scientifically mature nation to ignore our own science at just the point where it is most relevant, and we do so at our peril.

In recent months some concern for this problem has been felt by what is now named the Agency for International Development, and a small amount of research has been started to learn more about the problems connected with the introduction of change. It is to be hoped that this effort will be supported and even expanded into a serious study involving both the social and natural sciences.

When it comes to the day-to-day business of offering assistance, we should insist upon considerable skill in communication, an indispensable attribute of the good foreign technician as of any good teacher and one which we do not emphasize enough. It is never easy to be sure one understands another exactly and is exactly understood; across real barriers of language and culture, this is exceedingly difficult and requires much sensitivity and patience. When we remember that the useful foreign aid technician is not simply an observer, but a participant who must be able to teach and to criticize, with tact certainly, but without equivocation, we cannot be surprised that he sometimes fails; but we must demand a high standard of performance and we should provide him with a high quality of training.

Anyone who has traveled into a country of unfamiliar language and culture has experienced the difficulty and frustration of partial communication and has, no doubt, seen some of the attempts at escape. Many American representatives try to escape by walling themselves off and dealing with the other country only through "official" channels. They thus limit communication to what all parties are willing to have put on the record, and that is likely to be pretty thin fare. All too often those who venture farther can deal only with people who speak English and who may then be a rather special and unrepresentative group. On the other hand, to speak and hear through an interpreter puts one at the mercy not only of his skill, but also of his understanding and good will. I spent two exhausting days once walking in the wrong direction because an interpreter correctly translated the words but not the context of my inquiry about the trail to a certain village. (It was really my fault, for I had unknowingly stated my question in such a way that the reply had to transgress either the facts or local rules of courtesy. In that country courtesy takes precedence over facts.) At another extreme are those who try to escape by "doing in Rome as the Romans do," trying thereby to demonstrate their faith in the principles of equality and brotherhood. They want to dress as the native does, eat only what the poorest peasant eats and generally live at the lowest standard that the country and their stamina permit. I respect the motive behind this, but not the judgment. To dress and live like the outcast does not make us like him in anyone's sight, nor do we thus share his joys and his sorrows. It is like limping before the crippled. No, it is better to be what we are without fraud, showing from that position that we can meet, as equals before God, all men whether high or low who share with us something of His divine spirit. I do not suppose this to be always easy to do, but it is possible.

In fact, the whole undertaking is anything but easy, and, like the other great cultural revolutions, only the future can give a true measure of its cost and significance. We who are involved in it, like climbers still ascending the mountain, find that the trail is often enough steep and that perspective has its cost. Yet the effort is necessary to our future welfare as well as to that of our neighbors and we need to give it the best that we can. In the long run, wise and effective assistance to nations that are trying to develop their own scientific revolutions may be no less important than making our peace with automation or being first to reach the moon, for, in the long run, space-age nations and bullock-age nations make uncertain partners. In this century, even the "long run" is over before we know it.

JANHEINZ JAHN

Muntu
and
Through African Doors

The still relatively small number of Westerners who have become familiar with post-World War II developments in non-Western countries have usually done so from the outside—as diplomats and scholars, as traders and tourists. Few have had the time, even if they had the inclination, to become insiders by immersing themselves in the daily life of a non-Western people and learning to see it through their eyes.

This is what Janheinz Jahn, a German writer who has concerned himself for many years with African culture, especially art and literature, did for a year in Nigeria and Togo. The selections presented here are drawn from his two books. Through African Doors recounts his varied and colorful experiences with kings, villagers and city people, reported with humor and a keen eye for vivid detail. In his earlier book, Muntu, published in 1961, Mr. Jahn argued that the traditions of African culture must be preserved even while Africa develops a civilization suited to modern needs not only for the sake of the Africans, but for the sake of the Western world.

Mr. Jahn is co-editor of Black Orpheus, a periodical devoted to African and Afro-American art and literature published in the university town of Ibadan, Nigeria, and has also edited a collection of African poetry.

Chapter 1
Skokian?

V. "Muntu" (The Problem of Man)

MUNTU, the title of this book, is a Bantu word and is usually translated as "man." But the concept of "Muntu" embraces living and dead, ancestors and deified ancestors: gods. The unity expressed by the inclusive concept of Muntu is one of the characteristics of African culture, and further peculiarities are derived from it. That concept therefore seemed an appropriate title for the book. Yet at the same time the concept "Muntu" points to the fact that all differences in the nature of man have their common denominator. True, in the course of argument differences are stressed, contrasts revealed—which are necessary in order to clarify the peculiarities of a culture. But when the reader finds that these peculiarities are not so extraordinary, that much that characterizes African culture also occurs in other cultures, then the title "Muntu" may remind him that nothing superhuman can be expected of human cultures. If in places the reader is inclined to object that what we are expounding as an aspect of African culture plays a part also in other

From *Muntu: An Outline of the New African Culture* by Janheinz Jahn. Translated by Marjorie Grene. Published by Grove Press, Inc. Copyright © 1961 by Faber and Faber, Ltd., London. Reprinted by permission.

cultures, that the meaning of life is also stressed in European culture, that the spoken word has the greatest significance also in other cultures, above all in illiterate ones, that rhythm has its functions among all peoples, that even in the Christian Middle Ages the picture has also functioned as symbol, ideogram, and sensory image, and that therefore all these so emphatically African matters are not after all so original— then let him recollect that all human cultures resemble one another up to a point, that different cultures only value their common elements differently, in so far as one puts the accent here, another there, and that it is the ordering, the relation of the elements to one another that determines the difference between the cultures. The one looks for basic images, because image and idea precede the word; the other makes the word produce the image. In one rhythm is monometric, in the other polymetric. But only the sum total of all the particular ways of doing things, any one of which may also occur in other cultures, produces the big "How," the aggregate ordered by a particular philosophical conception, which constitutes the unique character of a culture.

VII. Black Souls in a White World

Millions of Afro-Americans in South America, the Antilles and the United States grow up in a European-American environment and without any knowledge of African culture. Except for the colour of their skins they are Americans like any others. Yet the others think this colour a blemish and let those in question feel it. Thus the Afro-American is constantly reminded of his origin, which has otherwise often lost all meaning for him.

Such an Afro-American, the physician and psychologist Frantz Fanon of Martinique, has presented in a stimulating book the reactions of the Afro-Americans. He explains that psychologically the majority of Afro-Americans are ill, and he shows how they react to the terrible spiritual pressure placed upon them. One group wants to become white, to liberate themselves from the burdensome memory that a more highly pigmented skin represents: in the Negro press of the United States there are countless advertisements for salves and mixtures which are allegedly able to bleach the skin. The others seek their salvation in the acquisition of the African heritage of which they have been deprived. Through an emotional stimulus a conscious step is taken—the first step into neo-African culture. The emotional need admittedly, is for an intoxicant—"Skokian" —yet when it is voluntarily sought it produces an attitude that is of interest to us here as the approach to neo-African culture. Frantz Fanon presents the psychological process in the first person:

"The knowledge of the body is uniquely negative knowledge. One is acquainted with oneself in the third person. I know that if I want to smoke, I must extend my right arm and pick up the packet of cigarettes at the other end of the table. The matches are in the left-hand drawer, so I must lean back a bit in order to reach them. I do not carry out all these movements simply out of habit, but through an implicit knowledge. The slow construction of myself as a body in the midst of a spatial and temporal world: this seems to me to be the pattern."

Fanon then shows that the basic pattern does not apply to a black-skinned person in the "white" world. The natural physical pattern is overlaid with historical-racial conceptions, with conceptions imposed by a hostile and biased world: " 'Look, a Negro!' It was an external stimulus that impinged on me as I was passing. I suppressed a smile. 'Look, a Negro!' It was true. I was amused. 'Look a Negro!' The circle narrowed more and more. I was openly amused. 'Mummy. Look, a Negro! I'm afraid.' Afraid. Afraid. So they were beginning to fear me. I wanted to split my sides laughing, but it was no longer possible. I couldn't laugh any more. For I knew that there are legends, stories, that there is history and especially historicity, as Jaspers had taught me. So the schema of normal body-experience was dissolved, attacked at several points, gave way and was replaced by a schema that is racial and epidemic. In the train I was acquainted with my body, no longer so to speak in the third person but in three persons. In the train, instead of one seat, I was left two or three. I was responsible at one and the same time for my body, for my race, for my ancestors. I looked at myself objectively, discovered my blackness, my ethnic characteristics. And I understood all that was thus being held against me: cultural backwardness, fetishism, slavery, cannibalism. I wanted to be a human being, nothing more than a human being. Nothing binds me to my forebears, enslaved and lynched as they were. Yet I decided to take them upon myself. It was on the universal level of the intellect that I understood this inner ancestry. I am the descendant of slaves just as President Lebrun is the descendant of serfs. But does anyone say, for example, to President Lebrun, 'Do you know, my friend, I have no race prejudice,' or 'But do please come in, Doctor, we have no prejudice here . . .' Or: 'So you're a doctor? I always knew there were some intelligent Negroes.' What should I do with myself? What corner could I creep into? My body seemed to be on display, dissected, inspected, put together again. The Negro trembles because he is cold. The white world, the only respectable world, denied me any share in itself. It is demanded of a man that he bear himself like a man. But of me it was demanded that I bear myself like a black man, like a Negro. How is that? Although I had every reason to hate and despise them, *they* rejected *me*. If they loved me, they said they loved me in spite of my colour. If they hate me, they tell me it is not because I am black that they hate me. So I am the prisoner of this infernal circle."

Fanon investigates the psychological consequences of this situation, the self-hatred, the disgust. He proceeds to an ever sharper analysis. "Neither my polished manner nor my literary knowledge nor my understanding of quantum theory met with favour. I complained; I demanded explanations. I was facing something irrational. The psychoanalysts say that nothing is more traumatic for a child than the contact with reality. But I say that for a human being who has no weapon but his reason, there is nothing more neurotic than an encounter with the irrational. The scientists have admitted that the Negro is a human creature; physically and mentally he has developed analogously to the white man: the same morphology, the same histology. On all fronts reason has assured our victory. But this very victory was making a fool of me. In theory it was agreed: the Negro is a human being. But what good was that to me? Too late! All the discoveries were made, the till was empty. Too late! Between them and me stood a world—a white world. For they were not capable of wiping out the past."

Fanon then describes what, in this mood, the encounter with African culture, with neo-African poetry, means: "I had rationalized my environment, but it had rejected me in the name of colour prejudice. Since there was no understanding on the basis of reason, I threw myself into the arms of the irrational. I became irrational up to my neck. The tom-tom drummed out my cosmic mission. The arteries of the world, torn open, have made me fertile. I found, not my origin, but the origin. I wedded the world! The white man has never understood this magical substitution. He desires the world and wants it for himself alone. He considers himself predestined to rule the world. He has made it useful to himself. But here are values which do not submit to his rule. Like a sorcerer I steal from the white man a certain world which he cannot identify. Above the plantations and the banana trees I gently set the true world. The essence of the world was my property. The white man suddenly had the impression that I was eluding him and taking something with me. They turned out my pockets but found there only familiar things. But now I had a secret. And if they questioned me, I murmured to myself:

"Thou Tokowaly, thou hearest the unhearable, thou explainest to me what my forebears say in the quiet of the constellations. Infinite is the milky way of the spirits in the celestial shallows, but there is the wisdom of the moon goddess and the darkness throws off her veil, thou African night, my black night, mystical and black, clear and full of splendour." I made myself the poet of the world. As an American friend said to me, I had become, "in the mechanized world of the white men, the guardian of humanity." At last I was recognized, I was no longer nothing. The whites clapped me on the shoulder, they were enchanted, in me they had recovered the fundamental, the natural, naïveté. Full of zeal I threw myself into the black past. But what did I find? Schoelcher, Frobenius, Westermann, Delafosse, white, and only white scholars had stirred up, investigated, excavated everything already. And what had they discovered? That there had been a mistake, that there never had been a primitive man. I had never been a primitive, still less a half-man. I belonged to a race which had been working gold and silver for two thousand years. Thus I could direct the white man to his proper boundaries, could demonstrate to him that I was no late comer, that my history was just as rich as his. I shouted, I jumped for joy. But he growled and muttered, he was uncomfortable. What is the point of all these historical analyses? Stop thrashing around in the past and try instead to adjust yourself to our rhythm. In our over-industrialized society there is no longer any place for your sensibility. One must be hard in order to survive. It is no longer a question of playing 'the game of the world,' but of subjecting oneself to the arrangement of integrals and atoms. Everything else is child's play. To my irrationality they opposed reason, and to my reason the 'higher reason!' "

The 'living experience of the black' which Frantz Fanon here so vividly portrays, exhibits the two facts which he emphasizes: "It is a fact that the whites think they are better than the black. And it is also a fact that the blacks want at any price to prove to the whites that their thought is just as rich, their intellect as powerful." So long as one tries to produce this proof by seeking in African culture values which correspond exactly to the standards valid for European culture, one is bound to fail. But if one measures by the standards proper to African culture—and that is what this book attempts—then this question of valuation is shown to be falsely put, since there is no universal standard for the evaluation of cultures. According to its own standard—who does not know this?—every culture is superior to every other.

Selections

I. Waiting for Mr. Odunfo

I HAD COME to Lagos from the interior, and was going to stay with a friend, Mr. Olu Odunfo, the editor of a Nigerian newspaper. I left my

From *Through African Doors: Experiences and Encounters in West Africa* by Janheinz Jahn. Translated by Oliver Coburn. Published by Grove Press, Inc. Copyright © 1962 by Faber and Faber, Ltd., London. Reprinted by permission.

luggage at the station and walked to the newspaper offices. Lagos is a very European-looking city, with large stores, shops, churches, government buildings, banks, markets, big residential quarters, and traffic comparable to that of a town like Bristol. It is the capital of Nigeria, and has a quarter of a million inhabitants.

On a Saturday afternoon the newspaper offices were as good as closed, but I was glad to find three people still in a big office on the ground floor; I will call one of them the boss and the two others clerks. One of the clerks was very young. He hardly looked up when I came in, and went on working at the twelfth lesson of an arithmetic textbook. The other was adding up the paper's order-forms and entering them in a thick book where every entry was copied in quadruplicate on to a different-coloured page. The boss wore the long colourful cotton robe of the southern region. I told him I was a friend of Mr. Odunfo's and asked if he could give me his address. He said he couldn't tell me the actual address, but he did know where Mr. Odunfo lived, and as soon as they were finished, in about an hour, he would take me to my friend's home in a taxi. So I returned by a different route, crossing the long bridge to the station—to the astonishment of passers-by, who seldom saw a European here on foot. The station was empty, and I had some trouble in finding a taxi and beating the driver down from ten shillings to five. Foreigners, of course, are fleeced in seaports all over the world.

When I got back to the paper's offices, the clerks were occupied as before, while the boss was lying on the table fast asleep. I talked the arithmetic student into summoning up the courage to wake his boss. The latter, after a short conversation in Yoruba with the taxi-driver, asked me if I had really agreed to a five-shilling fare. I said I had. He thereupon ordered the man to unload my luggage and made me pay him off.

"We'll take another taxi," he told me. "This man had two shillings too much from you. To exploit foreigners is disgraceful behaviour. After independence all that must be altered. If you would just wait till we have finished—we always have so much to do on a Saturday." After a quick glance over his shoulder at the man busily entering the order forms, he hoisted his legs up on the table, tilted over, and dropped off once more.

The order-form enterer really was industrious. When he had done a sum and found another form with twenty copies which had to be added on (as sometimes happened, because the forms were not too carefully arranged in localities), he did not simply make the 4 in 2340 into a 6, but worked it out in writing. He wrote 2340 on a piece of paper, wrote 20 under it, drew a neat line, and conscientiously added these two figures together. The result of the addition he then wrote in the book after duly crossing out the old figure with the help of a ruler. Seeing his method and looking at the heap of order forms still to be entered, I realized that it might be a matter of hours, not minutes. There was a chair outside in the courtyard, where a little breeze was blowing past to dry off my sweat a bit. I sat down and marvelled at the chief's sound sleep.

Through the open door I could also watch the arithmetic student. He was multiplying seven-figure numbers in a copy-book and then looking at the back of the textbook to see whether he had got the answer right. If it was wrong, he crossed out the sum and started again. Out of five sums he got three right first time, but there was one he had to re-do twice.

After an hour or so the chief woke up. Seeing that his bookkeeper had a lot more order forms to enter, he looked at his watch and decided to pre-sort the forms himself and help with the additions, which speeded things up. This was done for my benefit, because he knew Europeans were always in a hurry and altered his behaviour accordingly. Neither he nor the bookkeeper was in a hurry; whatever their plans for the evening might be, they would still be in time. The European considers speed an advantage, he feels he is reaching his objective sooner, in this case a friend's house. But at the same time it is a disadvantage for somebody else (a fact most Europeans never realize), in this case the arithmetic student, who was sent home earlier to an overcrowded room where he had neither enough light nor the peace and quiet to go on with his lessons.

The sun went down, and long after darkness had fallen the order forms were stuck with drawing-pins to the pages where they had been entered. The boss personally closed the book, the arithmetic student clapped his textbook shut, fetched the broom and began to sweep the room under the surveillance of the other two. When this task too was finished, the boss could send his clerks home and shut down the office. The arithmetic student carried my case and bed outside the door on his head, a distance of ten yards. The mere loading of them on his head required more effort than would have been needed to take them outside by hand—but things must be done in the correct way.

The dismissed taxi-driver had obviously been lying in wait, for we had hardly gone out in the street before he drove up and offered his services. But the boss was consistent: he warned the man never again to demand excessive fares from friends of the country, and sent him away to teach him a lesson. So we stood in the street for a quarter of an hour till another taxi came and took us for the proper fare to Yaba, the suburb where Mr. Odunfo lived.

After twenty minutes the taxi stopped in front of two big apartment houses; the one at the back could only be reached by a footpath. We went up an outside staircase, and down the central passage to the third door on the left, where Mr. Odunfo lived. The driver hoisted my luggage on his head and took it into the room; he did not ask for a tip. The boss from the newspaper office introduced me to Mrs. Odunfo, then disappeared.

She was a pretty young woman with a ready laugh, and spoke good English. She told me her husband had gone to a meeting at one, saying he would be back soon. It was now eight o'clock, so he was sure to come in a minute. "Would you like some beer while you are waiting?" she asked. I thanked her and said I would, for I was parched with thirst. She then apologized for having to leave me on my own for a moment, and went out to buy the beer. I looked round.

The Odunfos lived in a single room, with a plywood partition reaching to the ceiling. I sat in the living-room part, on one of the two wooden armchairs, opposite the wooden settee, which had cushions on it. In front of me was a round table with mementoes of Mr. Odunfo's travels: a tin Eiffel tower with thermometer, a china horse with the inscription "Düsseldorf," a picture-book of Bayreuth and another of Hamburg, and a vase containing artificial flowers. In the corner there was a small table with papers and books on it: his "study." A wireless was blaring out news, and there were personal photographs hanging on the walls: a school class symmetrically grouped with the teacher in the middle; Mrs. Odunfo in a magnificent Yoruba robe; Mr. Odunfo with parents, cousins and other relatives—a ceremonial family photo.

Mrs. Odunfo set three bottles of beer out in front of me (Beck's beer from Bremen), and disappeared into the other half of the room, where, as I could tell, cooking was in progress. She was not alone there, for I could hear the voice of an old woman, evidently toothless, since she spoke only in vowels. After I had emptied one of the bottles of beer, Mrs. Odunfo brought a plate full of sandwiches, which I devoured avidly. It was nine o'clock by now, and she said Olu was bound to come any moment. There was neither anxiety nor reproach in her voice. To help me pass the time she brought a whole stack of papers I might like to skim through while she had her supper. This she did in the other part of the room, and I could smell the dried fish in okro sauce, a greenish yellow viscous vegetable cooked in palm oil and strongly spiced with cayenne pepper. I would far rather have eaten this than the tinned sardines on stodgy white bread; but I had had no opportunity to tell her that I ate African food.

She too had altered her normal behaviour for the sake of a European guest. Not that she would ever eat at the same table as a male guest. But she had brought me European food, believing that a European could not eat African food. She had not even asked, for West African good manners do not allow you to ask a question which might oblige the visitor to admit there is something he cannot do.

This courtesy sometimes brings the African host into great difficulties. European food and drink cost many times as much as their African equivalent: a bottle of beer is 3s. 6d. [about 49 cents], the same amount of palm wine about 2d. [about 2 cents]. For a penny you get five large bananas or a whole packet of the maize-meal pudding called *eko*, cut into slices and wrapped in big leaves. Yet an African will sooner ask all his relatives for money than admit there is something he cannot do— give a European guest European hospitality. He will, however, try to get rid of the guest as soon as possible, with all the subtlety of indirect hints. The only sort of guest who will be sincerely invited to stay longer is the one who insists of his own accord, and proves it at the first meal, that he is capable of eating African food without batting an eyelid.

After Mrs. Odunfo had finished her meal, she came in with a game: something else to keep me amused. It was a version of Snakes and Ladders, the ladders taking you from Friendship to Love, from Thriftiness to Fortune, from Industry to Success, and the snakes from Envy to Poverty, etc., etc. I was rather bored after the second game, all the more when I noticed a games board under a chair in the corner. It was the board for that African game known in Yoruba as ayo; it is called something different in every part of West Africa. You play it with forty-eight nuts in the board's twelve holes, and it is a game of skill in which you have to think and move fast and work out cunning combinations. Once again Mrs. Odunfo was too polite to ask the European whether he could play it, and instead had brought a children's game imported from England.

She seemed to enjoy it herself, however, showing great delight when she went up a ladder and laughing loudly when either of us landed on a snake. At ten o'clock I asked where on earth Mr. Odunfo could be, but she answered with a laugh: "He will come." So we went on playing, and I made efforts to let out a joyful "ah" when I got on to a ladder, and a deep "oh" for a snake, which kept sending her into peals of laughter. When our counters were chasing each other, she said: "I run away from you," or quite coquettishly: "Why do you run away from me?" I told her it was the fault of the wicked dice and I would much rather stay with her all the time in the square marked Love. At this she went up and down whole scales of laughter, using every opportunity for a sort of innocent flirtatiousness.

So far as African customs prevail—everywhere, that is, even in the circles which are said to be fully Europeanized—any relationship between man and woman has erotic overtones. Buying from the woman at the market is a kind of flirting, so is serving food, asking the way, playing a game, and dancing too, at least in the towns. But flirting has very precise limits. The only male with whom the woman will eat at the same table is her husband. If he brings a guest home, whether European or African, she will serve the food and then retire into the kitchen. As long as she is married to a man, she will be absolutely faithful; but divorce is easy, and if she gets tired of him, instead of deceiving him, she will become another man's wife. So the European tourists who infer loose morals from the free and easy flirting are quite off the track.

About half past ten I had drunk almost three bottles of beer, and couldn't think of any further suggestive remarks to make about the Snakes and Ladders, hard as I tried. This must have become obvious to Mrs. Odunfo, for she suddenly said: "You don't like it any more, but I have something else." She laughed, and for an instant glanced at the game under the chair. I had almost decided to tell her how much I enjoyed playing it, when she laughed again, reached for a little box on the small cupboard, and threw it over to me. It was a sort of peepshow into which you had to push one of several cards, put it to your eyes and work a knob. Each card contained seven coloured pictures of famous scenes or places. We looked at them in turn, and I had to explain to her what she saw, such as the Black Forest, Brussels World Fair, the Three Musketeers, etc. After we had been through these, I asked rather anxiously about Mr. Odunfo. "Oh, he will come," she said once more, laughing as usual.

He came at 12:15 p.m., gave me a big hug, slapped me on the shoulder, and said there was a taxi waiting down below with two journalists from the paper. I asked if Mrs. Odunfo would come with us, but she laughed and shook her head, then wished us a good time.

We went to a night club, a big walled square with no roof. In the middle was a dance-floor, with garden-tables and chairs round it, and there was a band in the corner playing in the usual West African "Highlife" style. There were a lot of people there, the Nigerians wearing long bright-coloured robes, which made a splendid colourful scene. At some of the tables there were groups of Europeans, who periodically mingled with the dancers. Only the coloured material of the prostitutes' clothes had European cut.

More and more journalists came to our table, which had so many beer-bottles on it there was hardly room for any more. When I washed down a roast chicken with my sixth bottle of the evening, I was told I had won my host a prize: one of the bottles was marked, and whoever got it won a crate of beer. Whether by accident or design, the marked bottle was under my nose. It was getting on for four o'clock, and I was afraid the eight of us would now have to finish off the twenty-four bottles in the crate. I said I was incredibly tired, so the twenty-three bottles left were loaded into the taxi, which took home first the journalists and then ourselves. When we unloaded the bottles pretty noisily on the concrete floor, Mrs. Odunfo came out of the other part of the room with a welcoming smile and asked if she could make some coffee for us, and did we want anything to eat? I thanked her and said all I wanted was sleep. I put up my camp-bed by the wooden settee, and slept like a log.

II. A Rich Man's Responsibilities

I woke at ten, and folded up my bed. I heard Mrs. Odunfo in the other part of the room waking her husband, who presently came into my part and showed me to the washroom. It was at the end of the building's central passage. I passed a lot of doors with loud voices and wireless music coming from behind them; almost every family had only one room. There was a bucket with hot water in the washroom, so Mrs. Odunfo had already been out and fetched water from the place in the courtyard where the tap was, and heated it for me. Mr. Odunfo told me that each washroom was shared between two families.

The washroom is only for personal ablutions, laundry being done outside every day at a special place. In all the houses without running water, both in the country and in towns, the washroom is more or less similar: a room of about six foot square with a small window and slightly sloping floor, so the water can run off through a hole at the bottom of the wall. The housewife puts in a bucket full of hot water, a big cake of soap, a calabash for scooping up the water, a ball of coir for scrubbing yourself, and a small bottle of disinfectant you shake into the remains of the water, with which you swill out the room when you are finished. The West African generally takes a shower twice a day in this manner.

For breakfast there was scrambled eggs, beans and Nescafé. A visitor who introduced himself as a journalist came with his nine-year-old boy, and they had breakfast with us. The little boy had big clever eyes, looked strikingly beautiful in his Sunday suit of blue silk and white tulle, and was extremely polite—in contrast to his over-officious father. I was asked whether it would suit me to go and see Mr. Biney, and I said anything would suit me.

We went round a few corners, and came into a big estate with well-kept gardens. Seeing other people going in too—whole families walking about in the gardens—I asked who Mr. Biney was. "Oh, he is rich," I was told, "incredibly rich. You will soon see."

The house we were approaching was single-storey, erected on white piles, painted yellow, and had lots of bays and turrets in elegant "Brazilian" style. There were steps leading up to a veranda, which had a desk with a telephone. We walked straight into the lounge with its pilasters, pillars and bays, and a stuccoed ceiling; big English easy chairs and settees, enough to seat eight people; a carpet in the middle with a floral design, on a lino floor with a parquet pattern. A servant appeared, asked what we would like to drink, orangeade and beer were brought, and we made ourselves comfortable in the easy chairs. I asked Mr. Odunfo whether he was related to Mr. Biney, but before he could speak the reporter answered for him: "Oh yes, but very distantly. Mr. Biney is a lawyer, also the very rich owner of a contractor firm with thousands of workers who load and unload ships. The firm was founded in 1916 by his father, who came from Ghana."

After we had had our drinks, our host arrived, a small fat man of about thirty, wearing European clothes, with a high crowing voice. My friends explained to him that they had come to show me the zoo. Mr. Biney greeted us with little enthusiasm, the reporter asked him for a writing-pad so that I could write down what I saw, and then we got up. A servant handed me the pad requested, and was told to show us round.

For his own pleasure Mr. Biney kept a private zoo, which was open to the public. On our tour the reporter advised me to use the pad, and when I said I had a good memory, he took the pad from me and wrote down: "Chimpanzee called John, six years old, three big monkeys, two leopards," etc. We saw crocodiles of various sizes, tortoises, antelopes, porcupines, about a hundred animals altogether. After our sightseeing we returned into the lounge, where we again made ourselves comfortable. We ordered drinks and enjoyed the breeze produced by Mr. Biney's electric fans; and when our host showed himself again, about two o'clock, the reporter cross-examined him about the zoo, about his profession and family, writing down the information given on a block, which at the end of the interview he handed to me with a flourish. Mr. Biney's is the biggest of Nigeria's three zoos, and costs him £100 [about 280 dollars] a month in maintenance alone. He keeps a vet and an animal ambulance, the only one in town and free of charge for anybody's animals.

After the "interview" I felt it was definitely time for us to go, but Mr. Odunfo said he was waiting for a telephone call from his brother. Mr. Biney nodded and withdrew. His wife, a beautiful Creole from the West Indies, put gramophone records on. We made ourselves still more comfortable in our chairs, and let ourselves be lulled to sleep by music and the fans. I was dozing, my two escorts were fast asleep, and the boy was making faces. From time to time Mrs. Biney came to see if we were still there, though the picture we presented hardly suggested we were about to leave. At one point she noticed the boy looking at her with his clever eyes; she returned soon afterwards with a plate of chicken legs. He held out the plate to me, and I took one; then he offered it to Mr. Odunfo and his father. He had to wake them first, which he did gently enough, but they shook their heads and at once shut their eyes again. So he grinned and ate the remaining legs one after the other. He gave me a wink, for he had known in advance that they would both refuse the legs because they wanted to sleep.

Whenever the ten records had been played through, a servant came and turned them over. The chairs were deep and comfortable, the drinks with which the servant refilled our glasses were pleasantly refreshing, and the rotating fans, alternately blowing air at you from front and rear, produced an agreeable tiredness. I dropped off, but kept on waking up whenever a new record started. I had not yet acquired the African knack of abandoning oneself to the moment, in this case to sleep.

At six my escorts had slept their fill, we got out of our chairs and said good-bye to Mr. Biney, who had hurried along to shake hands with us. I ought to mention that he had several similar rooms in his house where other guests were sitting and enjoying his comforts. A rich man in West Africa cannot keep his wealth only to himself. It is an old tradition, quite taken for granted, that all who belong to his clan—and clans are large— may at any time find food and shelter in his house for as long as they wish. Uninvited guests stay only for hours, relatives for days, weeks and even months. In this way a large part of his wealth goes directly to the poor. When a rich man gets a poor relative a position through his connections, he is not only relieving himself of a burden but again helping the whole clan. It is the same tradition as demands that anyone asking a favour of the Oba, the king, should bring the king a present; and that the king may not keep the present but must pass it on to the poor, to his servants and his wives.

The state is in many ways successor to the kings; so hardly anyone thinks twice about bringing an official a present. The official has a high position, for which his salary, assessed on the European scale, is far from adequate. If he refuses presents, he cannot look after the poor in his clan as befits his social status. Europeans in West Africa consider nepotism and corruption the greatest evil, and many newspapers will harp on instances of it; but in fact you won't find a lot of Africans who are genuinely shocked by it. For it is simply continuing a traditional system of social distribution, involving the rich and powerful in social duties, a system which has so far stopped class-hatred and class-warfare except against European employers and firms. There are rich and poor in West Africa, but no classes, no class-consciousness, no vested interests. The rich man's bond with his clan, containing many poor people, is stronger than the interests he has in common with other rich people. Instead of teaming up with other rich people to exploit the poor, he vies with them in helping the poor of his clan.

Mr. Odunfo, the editor, was a poor man despite his modern profession, and his private life was little different from that of the peasants out in the villages. Even the urbanized life of the rich Mr. Biney, despite his modern capitalist profession, was bound up with traditional duties: he remained conscious of the social responsibility inherent in his wealth.

III. Room for All on the Bus

There are also cross-country buses, which run by timetable, such as Armel's Transport, a company which has a contract from the government to provide communications on the main routes of Nigeria where there should by rights be a railway.

Once when I was staying at Benin and wanted to go to Asaba, I was told there was a bus going there which left at eight o'clock. By the time I had had breakfast and said my good-byes it was ten to eight, and as it was a good way to the starting-point I ordered a taxi. The driver took me to the wrong place: an Armel bus was leaving from there too, but in another direction. We packed my luggage in again, and the taxi hooted its way through short cuts, which first had to be cleared, however, of humans and animals. Then the taxi stopped. "What's the matter?" I asked. "Out of petrol," was the answer. It was already a quarter past eight, so the driver loaded my luggage on his head and hurried off to our destination—to find the bus still there. It was leaving punctually at *nine* o'clock, as announced on the timetable posted.

It was a big green Mercedes bus seating fifty-five, and about thirty people were already on it. I bought my ticket, seven shillings for ninety miles, just under a penny a mile. And behold, punctually at nine, the conductor closed the door and off we went. We hadn't been going for ten minutes when we stopped, still in the town of Benin. It was a regular stop, there was a booth near it with a brass plate saying "Armel's Transport," and the conductor began shouting into the telephone. Then the driver climbed back into his seat, reversed slowly and very carefully into a track, and turned the bus; we drove back to where we had started. There was a high-school boy sitting opposite me in white sports clothes with school badge, and a portmanteau, tennis-racket and pair of football boots in his lap. He said to me: "We're going back, sir."

"So I see."

"Aren't you surprised, sir?"

"No."

Now *he* was surprised. He was familiar enough with European purposive thinking to know the sort of things that ought to surprise the average European. He called the conductor, who addressed me instead of the schoolboy, and explained that there were some people who had arrived at the starting-point and wanted to travel on the bus; that as there was now a telephone connection with that bus-stop, they had heard about it and could go back to pick them up.

The bus stopped at every crossroads, in every village. The stops were longer than the separate stretches of driving (which the powerful vehicle got through at top speed), for there were large groups of passengers waiting at every stop; mostly women with heavy baskets and crates, which had to be brought in through the narrow doors and then found room for. This took some time, but nobody ever failed to get on, remarkable as it may sound

They knew the bus would not leave without them; without pressing, jostling or argument those who got on first would take the luggage off the next comers' heads and help to stow it away, hold the babies handed to them and pass them on, until all the babies, women and luggage had been taken in. I was full of admiration for the gentleness of their movements, the tenderness and grace with which the babies were swung over people's heads. Almost all these women were short-stage travellers, getting out after a few stops, to be replaced by other women getting on. The schoolboy opposite me was nearing his destination, and when he got up he showed me his school-building, long and low, near the street; there was a very plain concrete church next to it.

The benches farther back had to be cleared to pile up the luggage. I counted fifty-five adults, and there must have been over thirty children, but I couldn't count them. I had three women sitting opposite me and two next to me. Three of the women had small children on their laps. Although they stayed in the bus over an hour, no little puddles collected in their laps, no little "packets" were pressed into nappies. The children carried a small firm leather purse tied round their naked tummies with a short string on which a few pennies chinked; they tried to stick these jingling toys into their mouths, but the string was just too short. This kept them nice and busy, without tempting them to suck their fingers and thumbs.

The women spoke only a few words of English, and I did not understand their Benin language. Amidst much laughter we communicated by signs; I threaded the children's pennies on their strings (African pennies are pierced in the middle), and ate the bean doughnuts with pepper pods offered to me. When the women got up at the stops to help with the required shifting round of the luggage, two of the babies were entrusted to me, and were quite willing to be taken up.

The journey of ninety miles took over four hours, but I never felt bored, even though there is little variety to the thickly-wooded landscape, which gradually descends to the Niger valley.

The ferries at Asaba are very big with two decks, and they also run only when full: which means when there is hardly room for another matchbox on board. Then, for sixpence, you go downstream for nearly half an hour and across to the other bank, past the long rowing-boats with their arbour of palm matting, which take yams to the market at Onitsha.

IV. The Lorries and their Slogans

At eight o'clock one morning I reached the stop for the Onitsha car-ferry, where four low-loaders and eight lorries were waiting to be taken across the Niger. All but one carried the Mercedes-Benz star, but that firm had supplied only the chassis, the engine and the radiator; the body-work was made locally of solid African wood. The bench in the cab was a narrow board with space for five or six people, and the driver himself was accustomed to sit on the far right, almost outside the car, his arms and legs very much at a slant to control steering-wheel and pedals. There was a board extending upwards from the top of the windscreen, with a roof above it rounded at the sides, to protect the broad wooden cage with its cargo of passengers and goods. The tailboard could be let down, but you could also climb in over the sides.

Every hour and a half the ferry took four vehicles to the other bank, where they could go the whole four hundred miles to Lagos via Benin, Akure, Ilesha and Ibadan. The lorries had their names or mottoes, mostly in English, painted on the board outside between windscreen and roof: such as *Trader's Friend, O Lord Help Me, Confidence, I Cannot Do Without the Lord, Fresh Lightning, Future Will Tell, Yoruba Hunter,* and *O Trust No Future However Pleasant.*

The drivers began to woo the unusual passenger. *Fresh Lightning* went straight into praising his lorry's power and speed—he was always the first to get there, as the name indicated. *O Lord Help Me* claimed that he was even faster, his lorry was new and specially powerful. I took the drivers to the backs of their vehicles, where a notice gave 35 m.p.h. as the maximum speed for safety.

They laughed. "Course those are regulations," said *Trader's Friend.* "We do what we can, but if you want get Lagos next morning, you step on it. Regulations no good for timetable."

Future Will Tell saw that I was a sceptical fellow, obviously in no great hurry to get anywhere first; he took me by the hand, showed me how new his tyres were, how well looked after his engine, and told me how large his family was, which meant he would never drive carelessly though he did not dawdle either. "So you come with me please?" he concluded.

"Future will tell," I answered, whereupon another driver responded with *his* motto 'O trust no future however pleasant.' We were all in the best of spirits, and I could see once again with what good humour and repartee the competition for passengers was carried out here.

I was taken from lorry to lorry. Almost all were new, and I could find no fault with them. The fare was the same with them all: according to whether you travelled first-class on the wooden bench by the driver or behind in the cage, you paid 2d. or 1½d. per three miles. I said I preferred to travel in the back, as I thought the cage would be safer in case of accidents.

"But you must be Christian?" said *I Cannot Do Without the Lord.* "The Lord will protect you as he protect my truck while you in it. You Europeans under the Lord's special protection." His piety, whether true or simulated, contained a distinct note of irony.

"Do you want me as a sort of mascot then?" I asked. "And if so, how much will you pay me for going with you?"

He laughed, but I persisted and held out my hand.

"White man always want money," he said to his fellow drivers. "They tell you: money for God, but God see nothing of money."

"White man his own god," said *Trader's Friend,* and we all roared with laughter.

"Well," I said to *I Cannot Do Without the Lord,* "since you cannot do without the Lord, I am not too confident of your driving. So long as the Lord is with you, I suppose everything is bound to be all right, but suppose the Lord doesn't happen to be travelling with you? In that case I would rather have a driver who trusted his own driving."

"You see, this man unbeliever," *Confidence* put in. "Confidence what he look for."

"Yes," I said, "but what do you mean by confidence—in your driving or in the Lord?"

"Best you trust in both," he answered slyly.

Confidence made a good impression on me. His lorry wasn't so very new, but was well looked after and already had its second lot of tyres; and he claimed to do the same journey regularly twice a week, which passengers confirmed. I started talking to him in private, when up came *Fresh Lightning* and asked if I wouldn't come with him, for the ferry had come back and it was his turn to go on it.

The ferry-master had already raised the barrier and beckoned the first low-loader down the ramp. After the second had gone, *Fresh Lightning* was called. I said I was in no hurry. I had said this several times already, but now I saw from the drivers' faces that they believed me for the first time. It was obviously a rare occurrence for them to meet a European who was not in a hurry. It was half past nine, and I went back to *Con-*

fidence, whose turn to cross would not come, I worked out, till about half past twelve.

Leaving the decision in the balance with him too, I watched from the high bank the path of the rowing-boats on the silvery glittering Niger, talked to the travellers who had already loaded their luggage and to the women selling various food and fruits. I lay down for a bit in the shade of two kapok trees, then returned to the drivers for some more verbal skirmishes.

While I was again sauntering round the lorries, *Yoruba Hunter*, who before had kept in the background, stood by his lorry and said: "Take mine," in a quiet, very assured tone, as if it were a matter of course; his invitation was more like a summons. I looked into wise, serious, discriminating eyes. "I'll think about it," I told him, and began inspecting his vehicle, starting with the cab. I noticed a little dog's head with pieces of iron tied to the steering-wheel. Nodding to *Yoruba Hunter*, I went on with my inspection.

Pieces of iron and dogs' heads are the symbol of Ogun, the iron-orisha, the god of hunters, blacksmiths and, in recent times, a lot of drivers too. The same process has been at work as in Cuba, where the iron-god includes among his symbols such new phenomena embodying his power as cars, tanks and aeroplanes.

It would have been futile to ask *Yoruba Hunter* whether he was a Christian. With great fervour he would have insisted he was one to me or any other European. Instead I asked what made him so sure I could trust him, and what he had confidence in. "I make good driving," he answered. "I know all rules, I expert driver."

I interpreted this to mean that he considered road safety depended on competent driving rather than on fate. Ogun, the force of iron, was good or bad according to whether you obeyed his rules. If you served him faithfully, you used the forces he gave in such a way that they did not do any harm to you or anyone else. If you misused those forces, you would have accidents. These were not an act of fate or a punishment sent by some unpredictable deity; they were your own fault, and you could only protect yourself from them by strictly observing Ogun's laws, including the local highway code, and by taking all reasonable care. Hence "I know all rules" told me a great deal about *Yoruba Hunter*'s personal convictions and was the most satisfactory answer he could have given me. "Right," I told him, "I'll come with you."

Whenever I had the choice, I always went with drivers like him and was happy in their charge; whereas with the others, who declared themselves protected by God, I never felt completely free from anxiety.

On all these forms of public transport I was invariably the only European.

EDWIN O. REISCHAUER

Wanted: An Asian Policy

It is one thing to analyze and interpret the many factors—of history, politics, economics, social change, tradition, culture and religion— which make up the foreign policy of any one nation. It is quite another, and far more difficult and delicate an undertaking, to understand the contemporary problems and prospects of several nations within a geographic region, to perceive the connections and sources, actual or potential, of conflicts or cooperation between them, and to devise a policy for the United States toward the region as well as toward the individual nations: a policy which will not only be desirable from this country's point of view, but practicable as well.

To formulate such a policy is the task undertaken by Edwin O. Reischauer, scholar, writer and diplomat in his book, Wanted: An Asian Policy. Born of American parents in Japan in 1910, Dr. Reischauer has served in the War and State Departments, and has held the post of professor of Far Eastern Affairs at Harvard University. Since 1961 Dr. Reischauer has been our Ambassador to Japan, where he has been greatly assisted by his Japanese wife, a former journalist.

Dr. Reischauer is the author of several other books, among them Japan Past and Present, rev. ed., 1953; The United States and Japan, rev. ed., 1957; and, with his Harvard colleague, John K. Fairbank, East Asia: The Great Tradition, published in 1960.

Chapter 14
Nationalism and Internationalism

In considering the means of achieving our aims in China or any other Asian country, we should not lose sight of one fundamental principle. American objectives have no real chance for ultimate success unless they are in line with what the peoples of Asia themselves desire. If our objectives run counter to the basic hopes and aspirations of Asians, we might best retire into "fortress America" and put our reliance, as some apparently advocate, in the grand strategy of sitting quietly by our dry powder with our fingers crossed. Fortunately this is not the case. In terms of fundamental aims, we see entirely eye to eye with Asians. We too look forward to the development of independent and prosperous Asian nations, living as equals with the countries of the West in an international system of law and order. Of all the peoples of the West, we probably have given the most consistent and strongest support to the peoples of the East in their efforts to achieve equality with the rest of the world. Virtually all Americans quite naturally and unselfconsciously sympathize with Asians who desire to create truly prosperous and independent nations. What else could one expect when their dream is so much our own and we have played so important a part in inspiring it in them?

The men who founded the new democracies of Asia have often drawn parallels between themselves and our own founding fathers. We should take pride in this analogy, even if it is not a very close one. The leaders of the American Revolution, as full and natural heirs to British democracy, were reacting against colonial rule in a manner wholly consistent with their British background. The new democratic leaders of Asia have faced a far greater task in breaking with their own political traditions at the same time that they were overturning colonial rule. It might be more to the point if the democracies of Asia sought for analogies in our more recent history, in our successful fight to better the lot of the common man, economically, socially, and politically, and in our slow and bitter but essentially hopeful struggle to solve our great racial problems. Here are analogies with the problems of Asia which are certainly as close as the War of Independence and considerably more relevant for the future. But, in any case, many Asians have undoubtedly drawn inspiration from our own fight for freedom, and most Americans give full emotional support to Asians in their hopes for self-respecting independence.

Our sympathy with the basic aims of Asians, however, is not merely a sentimental one born of historical parallels. It is also a matter of clear intellectual conviction. We have stood fast for the ideal of a democratic community of nations. Despite our great military power, we have specifically rejected the Russian technique of creating a power bloc by ruthless centralized control and coercion. We have in fact staked our whole future as a nation on a free association of equal allies and beyond that, on a world order in which democratic procedures of discussion and voting, rather than force, will be used to settle international disputes. Such a world order depends ultimately on the existence of truly independent and stable nations, in Asia as well as elsewhere in the world. What Asians hope to achieve in creating independent nations is an essential part of what we are hoping to achieve. Our aims are fundamentally the same.

The Russians, on the other hand, have consistently stood in direct opposition to Asian objectives. No European power was more thoroughly imperialistic in Asia than tsarist Russia throughout its history. The Communist regime in its days of initial weakness appeared at first to turn its back on the imperialist past, but with the restoration of Russian power came a re-emergence of Russian efforts to conquer and coerce neighboring lands.

Communism as a philosophy and as a practical system of organization is based on the assumption that there should be a single source of absolute authority. Human nature being what it is, such authority can be achieved only by force. There may be moments of divided authority even within the Kremlin, such as the brief period when both Malenkov and Beria sought to become Stalin's heir. An even greater division of authority may exist at present between Moscow and Peking, but if it does, it is a contradiction of all Communist theory and practice. There cannot be two different party lines even on minor matters. In the long run, there can be no place of real equality within the Communist system even for China, the colossus of Asia, much less for the smaller Asian countries.

The Russians are ultimately committed to bucking the great nationalist tides of Asia, but like any good navigator, they have sought to use these tides as best they can, even if they trend in the opposite direction. We, on the other hand, have often found ourselves battling these tides, even though they flow in general with us. Asian nationalism is perhaps the greatest potential bulwark against communism and therefore the greatest immediate support of the cause of international democracy. We, instead of the Russians, should be making effective use of these tides.

•   •   •

Our interest in the protection of Japan is very clear-cut. Japan is of vital importance to the free world not only because of military and economic considerations but also for political reasons. A democratic system operating successfully in Japan may in time serve as an invaluable precedent. On the other hand, if Japanese democracy collapses, either because of economic instability or through Communist conquest or subversion, its failure may seriously prejudice the chances for democracy throughout the non-Western world. Under these circumstances, we obviously must provide Japan with the military and economic support she needs.

But the United States cannot continue too long its indirect domination of Japan without eventually running afoul of Japanese nationalism. Naturally Americans would in any case much prefer to have the Japanese carry their own economic and defense burdens. These are two responsibilities that we are as anxious to get rid of as the Japanese are to have us relinquish them. The only difficulty is that they must be borne by some-one, and the Japanese are as yet unable to shoulder the full economic load and both unable and unwilling to undertake the military.

Because of the strong revulsion against war in any form that has swept the Japanese people, most of them are reluctant to see Japan rearm herself to any appreciable degree, and many fear that a reborn army would be a menace to their democratic institutions. They have an even stronger conviction that a native military force adequate to defend Japan would put an unbearable strain on her already shaky economy. Those elements in Japan which tend to be the most thoroughly committed to democracy have commonly embraced a dreamy pacifism and have committed themselves to the unrealistic hope that Japan can become an Asian Switzerland, forgetting that the Swiss have been able to preserve their neutrality because they have added to their strong natural defenses a proportionately heavy investment in military preparedness. This pacifistic opposition to rearmament in Japan has begun to assume the shape of a nationalistic resistance to American domination. When Americans not unreasonably urge the Japanese to assume their own defense burden, it is not hard for propagandists in Japan to distort such requests into American demands that Japan provide the cannon fodder for American imperialist ambitions.

The United States faces a delicate problem of timing in Japan. If Japan continues to be militarily and economically dependent on the United States for too long a period, we may eventually come so sharply into conflict with the nationalistic feelings of the Japanese that we shall defeat the purpose of our military defense and economic support. On the other hand, we cannot drop this economic support until effective alternatives have been developed for Japan, presumably through expanded foreign trade. Nor can we insist on too rapid a rate of rearmament without running the risk of so alienating the Japanese as to drive them toward communism. We cannot wait too long in transferring the economic and military burden to the Japanese nor can we accomplish this transfer too precipitately. We are forced to feel our way cautiously between the twin dangers of too soon and too late.

One particularly difficult aspect of the problem is that in Japanese eyes the most obvious economic alternative to American aid is trade with Communist China. While an expanded trade with south Asia would benefit all of free Asia as well as help to carry the Japanese economic burden, this does not alter the fact that before the war China and Manchuria constituted vital markets and sources of raw materials for the Japanese and still represent by all odds their greatest potential trading area. It seems altogether possible that the Communists, adopting the strategy of starving Japan economically into submission, may not be willing to trade with Japan on any significant scale, but this does not prevent the Japanese from looking toward China as the green pastures that might free them from dependence on the United States.

If Sino-Japanese trade were likely to be made up of nonstrategic materials, there would be little problem, and the United States might encourage Japan to develop what trade it could with China. But if Japanese exports do go to China in great quantity, they are certain to consist in large part of such items as rolling stock and rails, machinery and machine tools. In other words, the United States will probably face the choice of encouraging or at least permitting a Japanese trade with China that helps build up the industrial and military potential of the Communist regime there, or else of blocking such trade at the risk of turning the forces of Japanese nationalism against us.

This again is a problem that has not yet reached the critical stage, but it is definitely foreseeable. If we are to take to heart the lessons of our lack of foresight in China, Korea, and Indochina, we should certainly be preparing for future problems of this type with every possible care. If we simply wait for this particular problem to come to a head, we may find Japanese passions so aroused as to preclude any satisfactory solution. We must not dally until most Japanese angrily claim, as some do now, that we Americans are willing to sacrifice Japan's economic future to our own narrow defense plans and that we are interested only in whether the Japanese fight for us, not in whether they eat or starve. If this should happen, it may be already too late to find alternative supports for the Japanese economy or, if necessary, to reconsider an overly rigid policy toward trade with China. Our tendency in recent years to look back at past failures in Asia seems to have faced us in the wrong direction for seeing and avoiding the possible fiascoes of the future.

Actually the dilemma may not be so difficult as it at first appears. While the strengthening of Japan through Sino-Japanese trade would be all gain for our system of international democracy, the strengthening of China might merely heighten the inner contradiction of the Communist system, which cannot tolerate two equal and independent sources of authority. It is commonly assumed that Sino-Japanese trade would tend to draw the Japanese toward communism. There may be some reason for this fear, but a stronger possibility is that such trade would pull the Chinese even harder in the opposite direction. If the Chinese leaders were to discover that they could with complete safety obtain more of what they want through trade with Japan than through complete dependence on Russian industrial power, they might begin to realize the folly and dangers of their present policies. Perhaps we should be working for the development of Sino-Japanese trade rather than attempting to stifle it.

Asian nationalism is a force that creates complex problems for the United States in any colonial land or even in a country in the still somewhat ambiguous position of Japan, but it should raise no great difficulties for us in the greater part of Asia, where the national regimes are fully and indisputably independent. On the contrary, we must look to nationalism as the chief force that can preserve the freedom of these Asian nations and thus help lay the foundations for a democratic world order of independent states. We must also look to nationalism to supply much of the ardor with which Asians must tackle their many serious economic, social, and political problems.

•   •   •

In the whole sphere of our foreign relations there has been no more tragic or inexcusable blunder than our failure to utilize or at least take necessary cognizance of the tides of nationalism in developing our Asian policies. Nationalism might very well be called the nuclear weapons of the situation in Asia. Why should we be so disturbed about security lapses in the protection of the atom bomb when we have been so indifferent about letting the comparably potent weapon of Asian nationalism fall into Communist hands? Actually we have been worse than indifferent. Often enough in our ignorance we have deliberately handed this weapon over to our enemies.

A good case in point can be found in our attitude toward neutralism in Asia. We realize that for an advanced democratic country communism represents a tragic reversion into hypocritical despotism and into a terrifying brand of savagery, and so we naturally find it difficult to see how anyone can be neutral in the struggle between democracy and communism. We have small patience today with fellow Americans who cannot perceive the distinction between the imperfections in our own society and the total travesty on democracy and justice into which communism has developed.

But this does not mean that we should be equally impatient with Asian neutralists. They do not necessarily identify the cause of democracy with that of the democracies, least of all the United States. In view of the type of information and misinformation they have in their minds, it is unrealistic to expect them to share our views on the folly of neutralism or to take as clear a stand as we have on the Soviet menace.

Our policy has been unrealistic on the emotional as well as on the intellectual plane. When we demand that Asian nations follow our lead and stand up and be counted on our side or declare themselves even more decisively on the field of battle, we are undoubtedly forcing our way against the emotional currents of Asia. Asians have for the most part only recently freed themselves from Western domination. Following the lead of any Western nation is scarcely appealing to them and may appear to be a dangerous reversion to the past. They like to cite, not without some smugness, George Washington's warning to the young American Republic to avoid foreign entanglements. The parallel is historically false, invalidated by the time differential of a century and a half that has put the contemporary Asian into an entirely different international situation from that which Washington knew. But the analogy is emotionally sound. No one can blame Asians for wishing to avoid involvement in international tensions that seem more remote to them than their own pressing internal problems of economic and political survival. In any case, Asians have no more desire to follow America's lead or, as they might put it, to fight America's battles than we had in our early years as a nation to follow Britain's lead or fight her wars.

But the real tragedy of our attitude toward Asian neutralism is our entire misunderstanding of what it really signifies in the war between democracy and communism. Asian neutralism is in reality a strong assertion of independence. It is so strong as to be ultimately unwise in the world in which we live, but basically it is the assertion of a point of view with which we sympathize wholeheartedly and on which we must place our greatest reliance for the future development of Asia. The democratic world order that we envisage depends upon this strong spirit of independence; communism in the long run can triumph only if this spirit is broken. The real strength of democracy is that anyone who is not specifically against it must ultimately be for it, while communism suffers from the great tactical liability that anyone who is not specifically for it is eventually forced to oppose it. Asian neutralism runs diametrically against Communist concepts of centralized, unified control, but for us it is just one of many variations of the theme of independence that runs throughout all democracy.

Neutralism is very commonly an unconscious reflection of a nation's military weakness. Those countries which have espoused it most enthusiastically have often been those least capable of affecting the world balance of power. Many of them will be making their maximum contribution to the cause of world democracy and world peace if they can simply maintain their own independence and their democratic forms of government. This is true in varying degrees of countries such as India, Indonesia, and Japan, where neutralism is particularly strong. We should not oppose it in these countries. In Japan, for example, we might best encourage the Japanese to be realistic neutralists, capable of defending their own neutralism both externally from conquest and internally from subversion or economic collapse.

We have usually, however, fought Asian neutralism. In doing this we have saved communism from one of its most dangerous enemies and transformed neutralism instead into a potent Communist ally. A little more sympathetic understanding of the reasons why Asians seek to be neutral would do a great deal to undermine communism in any Asian country. It also would probably bring that country far more rapidly to our side both in the United Nations and on the firing line than any amount of pressure we could exert. It is not surprising that we have done so poorly in the great ideological battle in Asia when we have turned some of our best weapons over to the enemy.

The importance of nationalism in the battle of Asia can hardly be overemphasized, but it would be a mistake for us to base our strategy entirely upon this one factor. Although the Communists have made skillful use of Asian nationalism, one of their chief appeals is their claim to represent a system of international government. Even in nationally aroused Asia, more and more people are looking beyond the ideal of national independence to a still higher ideal of world peace and order. Communism is not just an international conspiracy; it also purports to be a system of international peace. We may not be able to counter the very real dangers of the international conspiracy of the Communists until we have matched their international ideal. We also should not forget that our chief reason for desiring the development of truly independent nations throughout Asia is our hope that they will become healthy members of a democratic world order.

Each time we contribute to international cooperation through democratic means we are helping to build up the democratic answer to international communism. Each time we are forced to take unilateral action we may be increasing the appeal of the Communist claims by demonstrating that a democratic world order does not yet exist. Under present conditions we cannot rely on international action to solve all of our problems in Asia, but we should exert every effort to make our policies and strategy as international as possible. Just as democracy is its own best weapon in winning the war against communism within any Asian country, so the ideal of an international democratic system of peace and justice may be the only effective weapon in combating the Communist attempt to establish a world order of ruthless dictation.

Actually our relations with Asia are in essence merely part of a greater relationship between the whole Western democratic world and the East. The individual Englishman or Dane is as much concerned in the future of Asia as the individual American. The chief difference is that there are more Americans than either Englishmen or Danes and therefore we collectively exert more influence in this relationship and have a greater responsibility for it. But it is no more a uniquely American problem than is that of European defense. There is every bit as much need for a grand alliance of the Western democracies to help solve the problems of Asia as there is for an organization like NATO to block the Russian juggernaut.

The United States clearly cannot itself carry the whole burden of external assistance to Asians. In fact, much of the burden is already being borne by European nations. Not only have French and British troops been fighting on the military battle line in Asia; the United Kingdom and the British Commonwealth nations are doing excellent work on the economic battle line through the Colombo Plan, and some other Western nations have at least small-scale economic endeavors under way. And on the ideological front we have perhaps been accomplishing proportionately less of value than have some of our Western allies.

Unfortunately we and our allies have often been working at cross-purposes. We sometimes say one thing in an Asian country and the British almost the opposite. . . . There is perhaps a greater need for the co-ordination of Western democratic efforts in the battle of Asia than in the defense of Europe, just because the battle lines in Asia are less clearly defined and our weapons so much less certain in their use.

We should also realize that our Western allies can on the whole be more effective in Asia than can we. With the exception of the Philippines, it would be hard to find a country in Asia in which an individual Swede, New Zealander, or Belgian would not be in a better position to accomplish a job in either the economic or the ideological field than an American of comparable ability. The former would labor under fewer of the suspicions or resentments that are commonly directed toward Americans in Asia. In addition, higher American wage scales and greater opportunities for jobs here make it more difficult to obtain from the United States persons with high qualifications for work in Asia than it is from our Western allies.

An even more important reason for international co-operation in our Asian policies is that prevalent fears of American domination make Asians much more reluctant to accept aid from us than from an international agency. It is true that international agencies are often clumsy and slow-moving, but these drawbacks are more than offset by the simple fact that anything done through an international body in Asia, just because of its international cachet, has more chance of accomplishing its objectives than a comparable effort by the United States alone. Our general rule should be to approach each specific project through as large an international body as seems capable of handling it at all effectively, instead of emphasizing wherever possible the uniquely American character of our actions in Asia.

It would be even more advantageous if such international bodies also embraced all those in Asia who wished to take part. The greatest advantage of the Colombo Plan is that the participating Asian nations meet with the Western members as a council of equals. Such a fully international approach to the problem gives far more promise of ultimate success than a co-ordinated but exclusively Western approach. There are many technical skills to be exchanged between Asian nations, and any agency that could make the great surplus of technical abilities now lying dangerously dormant in Japan available for use throughout Asia would be doing both Japan and the rest of Asia a great service. Even more important than these considerations, the spirit of democratic equality of such a truly international system of Western aid to Asia would itself be an important part of the war of ideas and a significant step toward the development of an effective democratic system of world peace which can match in accomplishments the glittering but false claims of the Communists.

In emphasizing this essential international ideal in our approach to Asia, we should also not forget that America too is part of a now unitary world and that our own successes or failures with democratic institutions are a vital part of the whole battle of Asia. Our enemies have been making most effective use of our shortcomings in domestic matters as well as in international affairs. Americans who disregard normal democratic ideals of fair play and due process of law or who argue that good ends justify dirty means are providing the Communists of Asia with very effective weapons. For each red or pink who may have been uncovered by McCarthyist techniques in the United States, it seems probable that ten thousand Asians have been lost to democracy's cause and many million other Asians nudged a step farther toward the Communist side. This is a miserable exchange of blows for the United States in its war with communism.

The home front is part of the struggle in Asia in still another way. In a democracy like ours, Asian policy is closely linked with the degree of understanding that the American people as a whole have of Asia and its problems. Our government's policy can only be a direct reflection of the wisdom or stupidity of the American public in such matters. We are all in the battle of Asia.

EUGENE R. BLACK

The Diplomacy of Economic Development

If we were to judge solely by newspaper headlines, we might get the impression that relations between nations in the nuclear age revolve entirely around political problems. Yet, paraxodical as it may seem, under the threat of global holocaust human beings, far from yielding to despair, have been more active than at any previous stage of history in seeking to cooperate with each other for the purpose of improving the human condition through accelerated economic development and timely social change.

One of the leading figures in worldwide efforts to spur the development of technologically backward countries has been Eugene R. Black, a banker born in Atlanta, Georgia. He has served the United States in a number of government posts, and was president of the International Bank for Reconstruction and Development (better known as the World Bank), from 1949 until his retirement in 1962. In this post Mr. Black had to exercise not only the gifts of a banker, but also those of a new kind of diplomat in negotiating delicate and controversial agreements between nations, notably the agreement between India and Pakistan about distribution of the waters of the Indus Basin. Since the bulk of aid for development now comes, and for many years ahead must continue to come, from the West—whether given on a bilateral or multilateral basis—financial experts like Mr. Black must be prepared for diplomatic negotiations with non-Western governments. The short book from which this selection is drawn contains wise and practical suggestions for this new kind of diplomacy. It consists of lectures Mr. Black delivered at the William L. Clayton Center, for International Economic Affairs at the Fletcher School of Law and Diplomacy, Tufts College.

Chapter 2
The Diplomacy of Economic Aid

I HAVE characterized what is going on in the underdeveloped world as an historic transformation. It would seem unnecessary then, to point out that it is likely to be with us for a very long while. Yet it is necessary to underline this point since so much of the discussion of economic aid today concerns a search for some simple, short-term way of turning that transformation into freedom and viability within a brief span of years.

I am afraid that much of the reason for this misdirected search stems from the blinding success of the Marshall Plan. Without detracting from that unique achievement, I am compelled to say that it bears almost no comparison to the present problem; in fact, it is useful only as a contrast.

From *The Diplomacy of Economic Development* by Eugene R. Black. Harvard University Press. Copyright © 1960 by The Fletcher School of Law and Diplomacy, Tufts University, Medford, Mass. Reprinted by permission of the publishers.

The governments participating in the Marshall Plan shared a common heritage and a common and clearly defined predicament. The political and economic aims of one nation found, if not a ready response, at least a sympathetic hearing in the others. A clear, limited, and concrete objective presented itself—that of restoring the economic strength and financial independence lost in war. It was possible to measure usefully, if not entirely precisely, the economic resources needed to achieve that objective. And there was in prospect a handy measurement, the re-establishment of substantial currency convertibility to judge when the necessary production and per capita income levels had been reached.

None of these conditions exists in the problem we are now considering. Between the rich nations and the poor nations there is little common heritage, and, in so far as there is a common predicament, it suggests no simple, short-term escape. The immediate political and economic aims of one nation in the group often compete or collide head-on with the immediate political and economic aims of the others. To the extent that there is an agreed objective for economic aid, it is to help the leaders of the poor nations to lead their countrymen out of the worst of poverty. Since this objective is neither limited nor concrete, there can be no really useful measure of the economic resources needed to achieve it. And while reasonable financial equilibrium is a necessary concomitant of orderly growth, the balance of payments is not a useful measure of how much per capita income and production will permit a tolerable order in the underdeveloped world.

The policy problem is altogether different and so are most of the operational problems. It is one thing to aid the recovery of industry, for example, in a country where there has been considerable experience with the technical and managerial problems involved. It is something else again to help launch new industries in countries that must initially import the necessary technical and managerial skills and in communities where there has not been any experience with factory life. It is no small problem just to find trained people in the world willing to undertake tasks like this, to say nothing of the many problems involved in trying to get agreement from an underdeveloped country to accept the authority of foreign technicians and managers in their special fields.

I list these contrasts—and there are more—not to belittle what was done under the Marshall Plan; it stands as one of the boldest and most imaginative diplomatic achievements in history. I list them only to show that we have before us now a brand new diplomatic problem of vastly greater dimensions.

The plain fact is that the conditions for a full integration of the political and economic aims of the rich and the poor nations in the free world community do not exist, nor is it possible to foresee a time in the future when they will. For the rich nations the problem is to live constructively with the historic transformation going on in the under-developed world, not to try to "solve" it.

The values of freedom and democracy cannot be sold like soap; nor are they the necessary result of economic development. People in the West came to respect these values only gradually over many years. If respect for them is to spread among the people of the underdeveloped world, the West must be willing to work side by side with these people and make common cause with them. For it is not by any sudden act of conversion, but only through growing together over time that the West can hope its values will take root and spread. This growing together will take constant and constructive contact and that is what the exercise of economic aid—or development diplomacy as I have called it—is all about.

Development diplomacy is such a new art in the affairs of nations that before it can earn for itself a recognizable status in the policies of the Western nations there must be a greater understanding of its specific aims and objectives. And since I will argue that economic aid cannot be effective without a separate and distinct status in the policies of these nations, let us first consider at some length just what these aims and objectives are.

The development diplomat must fill the gap between the conventional diplomat and the trader and the investor. His aim should not be commercial or strictly economic; but neither should he be concerned with the narrow political objectives which sometimes overburden the regular diplomat. The development diplomat should be a man with a vocation, rather than a man with immediate terms of reference. As an artisan of economic development he should use the tools of economics and other disciplines as best he can to place in prespective, to shed light on and to illuminate the choices before the decision-makers in the underdeveloped world.

When I say, "illuminating the choices," I refer to the problem which economists call "the allocation of resources." Now it is not economists but politicians, civil servants, and businessmen who decide, for the most part, how the resources of a country are allocated. The professional job of the economist is, or should be, to make the politician, civil servant, and businessman aware of the economic consequences of their decisions, and to provide evidence on which the decision-makers can weigh the benefits and costs of alternative courses of action. The hope the economist holds out is that there will be a "better" allocation of resources if decisions are taken with the knowledge of their economic consequences. This is the same hope development diplomacy holds out.

This may sound like a strange role for a diplomat, but as a practical matter in the modern world it promises to be the most effective way in which the free nations can exercise a constructive influence on the development of the underdeveloped countries. The task of illuminating choices goes right to the root of the development problem, which is often said to be a lack of resources, or of savings, or of education, or of entrepreneurship. These are all part of the problem, but it is more useful, I think, to look at it in terms of the decisions needed to make more of the potential for growth that already exists—decisions to organize idle time for productive work; decisions to transform unproductive investment; decisions to turn a classical, Western course of study into a course of study more relevant to an underdeveloped country, and so on. Each of these decisions involves making choices. Usually the choices must be made on the basis of very imprecise and fragmentary evidence. But it can be said that in so far as these choices are made without regard to the economic consequences, they are much less likely to yield "good" decisions in terms of growth, tolerance, freedom, and all the other aims which free nations believe in and seek beyond their shores. Thus, we can say that by illuminating the choices before the decision-makers— whether they be politicians, businessmen or bureaucrats—development diplomacy performs a very practical task and one no other kind of diplomacy is directly concerned with.

But to put some meat on the bones of these ideas let us examine this notion of development diplomacy in action.

Very often people come into my office after having visited some country or other in the underdeveloped world to tell me what they think is wrong with that country. And I am told that the trouble with country X is that the people won't work; the trouble with country Y is that there is a desperate need for outside capital; and the trouble with country Z is a lack of entrepreneurs. In each case it is some obstacle, more or less immovable, that is seen to be standing in the way of progress.

The pessimists among these visitors point to the social and political obstacles in the way of growth—whether they be India's sacred cows or the nationalistic oil policy of Brazil—and conclude that the World Bank is definitely wasting its money making loans to these countries. The optimists, on the other hand, urge the Bank to redouble its lending because they believe that all that is needed to redeem the situation is more money.

Piecing these fragmentary observations together, one gets the picture of a field strewn with obstacles, some of which are immovable and others of which can be pushed aside. So far as it goes, this is not an inaccurate picture, but it is not complete; it lacks a dynamic element. In reality the obstacles in the path of development are changing form and character all the time because in reality economic development and social change are interacting all the time. In the underdeveloped world today society is continually adapting itself to make use of existing knowledge. Development is proceeding *in spite of* the cultural attitudes, social institutions, and political conflicts which sometimes seem to be such immovable barriers. It is not a smooth, uninterrupted progression, to be sure; rather, growth appears more as a series of fits and starts. "And yet," as Galileo is supposed to have said, "it moves!"

It is really not just a lack of capital per se, of savings per se, of education per se, of entrepreneurship per se, and so forth, which stands in the way of more rapid growth in the underdeveloped world. It is more useful, I think, to consider the problem in terms of how to achieve the kinds of decisions which are needed to make more of the potential for growth. For as there is a greater awareness of the possibilities for growth in society, many of the traditional obstacles appear much less formidable.

Take entrepreneurship, for example, which is often cited as the key development component that is missing. We do not really know where entrepreneurs come from. If in England, entrepreneurs appeared among nonconformist traders, in Japan they sprang from the ranks of the petty nobility—the samurai. In India, the growth of entrepreneurship has been very complex, involving as it has the cultural background of sect and caste and the unique institution of the managing agency. There is room for a lot of speculation about where entrepreneurs come from; but it *is* speculation. All we know for certain is that once people become conscious of the possibility of economic development in their society, entrepreneurs start appearing. There has been a veritable flowering of entrepreneurs in Latin America over the past thirty years and in Pakistan and Turkey in the short period since World War II. We can confidently expect further such outbreaks as development takes hold in the underdeveloped world.

What is true of entrepreneurship is broadly true of all the requisites for economic growth. As more people become conscious of the possibility of a better material life through a different use of their time, energy, and savings, there will be more productive work and more productive savings. By illuminating the choices before the decision-makers, development diplomacy promotes such a consciousness and in this way helps to remove obstacles in the path of development.

This does not mean that direct attacks on some of these obstacles—the direct provision of development capital or the encouragement of new forms of education—are unimportant; on the contrary, they are indispensable instruments of development diplomacy. But as has been said time and time again and cannot be repeated too often, no nation can supply another nation with more than a tiny fraction of the resources needed for self-sustaining growth; the road to self-sustaining growth must be built by the poor society itself. Therefore, the most important task development diplomacy can perform is to illuminate the choices that must be made in the building of that road.

Initially, illuminating choices involves asking questions. This is easiest to illustrate in terms of specific projects. The mere fact that a river runs downhill very fast, to take a simple example, is not sufficient reason to build a power dam. First a whole lot of questions have to be asked—and some kind of answers fashioned.

One must ask whether the construction of a power dam would meet some important objective; that is, would it provide power for a market that already exists or is in prospect? Would it provide irrigation waters for land which can be made arable in this way and on which farmers might be willing to settle? Would it provide benefits in terms of flood control? Then one must ask whether a big power dam is the best way of meeting any or all of these objectives. Alternative possibilities, such as a thermal power plant or a simple irrigation barrage, or both, have to be considered as possible choices.

And there are financial questions which have to be asked. In the Bank we deal mostly with large and expensive public utilities—port facilities, power projects, railroads, and the like. Obviously, if there is to be a rational allocation of resources in terms of growth, politicians, civil servants, and utility managers must have a good idea of the real costs of these investment proposals. And since these projects can gobble up huge amounts of capital, rational decisions on whether and how to invest in them have vital importance for economic growth.

Before deciding what the real cost of capital is, it is, of course, necessary to make the best use possible of the data available. Adequate technical preparation of a project is such an obvious necessity that it hardly needs elaboration, but development diplomacy will fail if it overlooks the obvious. And often adequate preparation of a project is more a matter of good organization than of modern technology—more a matter of simply keeping separate and complete accounts than of adopting elaborate new accounting methods.

Sometimes the weight of evidence points to fairly definite answers to the questions development diplomacy must ask in project analysis; sometimes there is a clear saving in efficiency in one alternative over the other. At other times there are no very precise answers. For example, we once had a spirited argument in the Bank over whether a mining company that approached us for a loan to buy modern mining machinery would do more to increase productivity if instead it borrowed locally to build new houses for the miners. Obviously this is a question the answer to which is not subject to very precise calculation. But it is worth while asking the question nonetheless. Illuminating choices in project analysis is not just a matter of minimizing waste, though that is very important. And it is not that there is very often one, absolutely right answer. The important thing is to encourage the habit of weighing benefits and costs. When that habit becomes ingrained, society is already most of the way to becoming development-minded.

Specific development projects provide the handiest illustration of what "the illumination of choices" means. But this is just the beginning of the story. Economic development cannot be described simply in terms of a series of projects, designed in a technological vacuum and unrelated to broader economic and political issues. Economic development involves, in addition to projects, the preparation of an economic plan and the relation at the highest level of plan and projects to the formulation of a national policy of which economic policy is only one part. Unless these three sides of economic development—projects, planning, and policy—are seen, not as three separate compartments of a box, but as three aspects of a single problem the shape of which is changing all the time, nobody concerned with economic development—neither the politician, nor the businessman, nor the development diplomat—will be in a position to judge usefully the economic consequences of a given decision or of alternative decisions.

It is in the planning process that development diplomacy finds its greatest challenge. The planning process should be the place where there are the greatest opportunities for illuminating choices and where the development diplomat should make his most important contribution. But unfortunately planning is still a very new concept and there is no broad consensus about the aims and objectives of the exercise. In fact, there are few more controversial words in the lexicon of development diplomacy. The concept of planning is bedeviled equally by the suffocating embraces of its idealistic champions and the cynical shafts of its detractors.

Between the idealists, who are more interested in imposing solutions than in illuminating choices, and the cynics who distrust planning in all its interpretations, lies, I think, a rational definition of the concept which should be nourished. Planning, simply defined, should be the place where the political leader is faced with an awareness of the consequences of his decisions before he makes them instead of afterwards. Taking the definition one step further, it should be the means by which the lines of communication are kept open between those who make decisions, those who "illuminate" them, and those who carry them out.

Whatever outward form planning takes, if it does not keep these lines of communication open, there will be a mess. For example, in one country I know of a development plan was prepared simply on somebody's assumption of the rate of growth that was desirable, "needed," or otherwise divined from national income analyses. Further assumptions were made of the capital that would be needed in various sectors of the economy to produce the output that was assumed to be needed. A massive document was drawn up on these abstract assumptions, with no attempt made to find out whether the necessary finance might be forthcoming or whether the plan conformed to the realities of the many, often quite legitimate, political claims on the country's resources. When all the work was completed, the head of the local planning commission admitted that it was really just an academic exercise and could not be taken seriously.

In this case it was just time and talent wasted. But I suspect in other cases plans drawn up this way become tantamount to the law of the land and have been the cause of more than one unnecessary financial crisis. This can be dangerous.

I am not criticizing the tools of economics, but the misuse of them. Unless planning involves first and foremost a bringing together of the existing claims on a country's resources—that is, unless it is based not on a single assumption, but on an appropriate range of assumptions, some induced and some deduced—the tools of economics cannot be safely and efficiently employed as a means of illuminating choices. Neither economics nor any other academic discipline in and of itself tells us just what the shape and the magnitude of investment ought to be in a given country. These disciplines can suggest orders of magnitude and help us to judge whether plans, projects, and policy are well related to one another. But they cannot make economic development any less of a three-sided problem. Plans and projects must be checked and co-ordinated with the actual possibilities, with what people really want in the way of growth and change and with what they are prepared to sacrifice. Otherwise, planning can lead at best to waste and at worst to the encouragement of extravagant forms of coercion.

There is a fundamental principle here as well as a matter of efficiency. At any given time, in any country, rich or poor, there is a conflict between the demands of growth itself and the demands which growth is supposed to serve. At any given time there is a conflict between the demands of growth and the demands for social welfare; between the demands of growth and the demands for economic security and employment for all; between the demands of growth and the demands of national power and prestige; between the demands of growth and the demands for cultural development. In the poor countries today these conflicts are particularly acute. Leaders there, as have leaders in all developing countries in modern times, want growth so that their countries can be strong and powerful; so that their people can have more jobs, modern social services and a more equitable distribution of income; so that they can assert their cultural renaissance with visible symbols of national prestige. But always at any given time there must be a choice between more of these ends and more of growth itself. And against the background of mass poverty the choice is always agonizing.

Today the political leaders of the poor countries, besides having to reconcile traditional attitudes toward life and work, also have to reconcile most of the competing and conflicting objectives found in richer societies. Reconciling these objectives is a political, not an economic, problem. The economics of growth simply says that every time the demands of growth are overridden there is a price: the poor will remain poorer for longer. Whether planning transforms the tools of economics into useful political, as well as useful economic, tools or simply turns them into bludgeons with which to coerce society, depends fundamentally on whether planning is used as a means of illuminating choices or as a means of imposing solutions.

The use of planning largely to keep the lines of communication open among those who make decisions, those who "illuminate" them, and those who carry them out, is the most effective way to achieve a rational and democratic resolution of the conflicts and contradictions which are inherent in the growth process. If only it encourages the asking of the right questions, planning cannot help but promote better answers in terms of growth. Furthermore, it can encourage policy-makers to focus upon the necessity for engineering an escape from poverty and to make this idea a catalyst for transforming into constructive patriotism the nationalism which is rampant in the underdeveloped world.

For development diplomacy all this has rather obvious and immediate implications. Development diplomacy must recognize that if planning is regarded as a means of illuminating choices rather than of imposing solutions, then planning everywhere always involves a series of political struggles. And the development diplomat cannot be effective if he ignores this fact or tries to remain above the struggle. While he is the partisan of growth, he cannot claim any absolute authority for his criteria; he knows that no matter how poor a country may be, there will be many occasions when considerations of justice or defense will necessarily override them. And because he is in a political struggle, he knows there will be other occasions on which he will be overridden by considerations much less compelling. This means he always has to work out the economics of the second, third, or fourth "best" allocation of resources in terms of economic growth. But this does not mean that he is thereby rendered ineffective. If development diplomacy to be successful required imposing some grand design on an underdeveloped country, then the game would not be worth the candle even if it were possible to play it in this way. The strength of development diplomacy lies precisely in not becoming part of some grand design, but in illuminating choices in the real world where economic development and social change are interacting all the time.

In talking about planning, I would not want to give the impression that all decisions have to be made at some central point. Indeed, nothing can be so deadening as a process in which every "t" has to be crossed by the highest authority. Apart from anything else, it denies opportunity for local or individual initiative. Initiative is priceless. To hold it within the general lines of national policy is one thing; to treat it as though it were of purely secondary consequence is another. Initiative should be encouraged wherever it is found, whether it be the personal initiative of the entrepreneur, the group initiative of a cooperative, or the local political initiative of a town or a province.

How to achieve a consistent policy line while still leaving room for private and local initiative is one of the most difficult arts of planning. Here is no place for dogma; it is folly in the face of the wide variety of economic experience in the world to suppose that what works in one country at one stage of development necessarily will work in another country at a different stage. At the same time the kinds of choices which politicians, bureaucrats, and businessmen face in this matter can often be illuminated quite simply and dispassionately. For example, where there are private entrepreneurs willing and able to do development jobs, it is not necessary to appeal to ideology to make clear the loss which the community will suffer if they are denied their place in national plans. It is not necessary to appeal to ideology to make clear to the civil servant that both he and the private entrepreneur will have more time and energy for their respective tasks if general guidance of the private sector can be substituted for direct controls. Nor is it necessary to appeal to ideology to make clear the advantages of a development initiative by state or local government if the alternative is no initiative at all.

Again the strength of the development diplomat lies in illuminating choices, not in trying to impose solutions. If he is to succeed, he must be a man with a vocation, not a man with an ideological mission. And in no place is this more important than in the planning process, beset as it inevitably is with the most vexing of conflicts. I believe that out of today's planning procedures in many underdeveloped countries can grow a habit of resolving conflicts in a rational and democratic manner which may prove eventually the most important means of encouraging a public respect for free institutions. And development diplomacy, much more than any other kind of diplomacy, will have an important part in determining whether or not this comes to pass.

But development diplomacy needs the backing of substantial capital; unlike some other branches of the art, it is not possible to succeed in this kind of diplomacy by just talking a good game. Development diplomacy needs capital because it must be a working diplomacy, capable of pointing to visible results at any given time. Development diplomacy needs capital because it needs to point to concrete development projects, the tangible proof that it is helping to engineer an escape from poverty.

And development diplomacy needs contacts; lines of communication of its own everywhere in the underdeveloped world; contacts with men and women to whom the right kinds of development decisions are an integral part of their own professional outlook; contacts with men and women who speak the language of economics without the taint of ideology. Right now there exists a very sizable guild of these men and women in the underdeveloped world; I know, because if there were not, the World Bank would not have been able over the last fourteen years to participate in some six hundred different development projects in fifty different countries. But these people need help and encouragement; development diplomacy must build on its contacts and continually make new ones.

Finally, development diplomacy must have a status in the national policies of the Western nations—not an overriding status, but a separate and distinct status which will allow it to function in spite of the bitter controversies of our times. Just as the development diplomat is a man with a vocation, so development diplomacy, if it is to succeed, must reflect a new sense of vocation in the West towards the historic transformation going on in the underdeveloped world. This is the problem to which I will return since the kind of adventure I have in mind must start right here in the West.

PETER BRAESTRUP

The Peace Corps Thrives in First Year Abroad

In earlier centuries contacts between nations were maintained in large part by professional diplomats and by traders and bankers, and to a considerable extent by scholars and artists also, as well as by missionaries in the era of colonialism. In our times first the Communists, and more recently Western countries, have increasingly recognized the value of contacts between the youths of all lands. The United States, since World War II, has emphasized the importance of people-to-people exchanges on a non-governmental basis. It was not until 1961, however, that, under the Kennedy Administration, it was decided to create a Peace Corps recruited primarily from among young men and women who have specific skills, such as teaching, technical, or agricultural experience, for short-time' service at modest remuneration in underdeveloped countries.

The record of the Peace Corps in the first year of its activities is given in this article by Peter Braestrup, a member of The New York Times staff since 1960. A native of New York City, Mr. Braestrup graduated in 1951 from Yale University, with a degree in English literature. On active duty with the Marine Corps, he served for six months in Korea, was wounded in action, and discharged with the rank of first lieutenant in 1953.

Mr. Braestrup, who has fluent command of Danish and French, has worked for Time magazine, and from 1957 to 1960 was assistant news development editor for the New York Herald Tribune, spending his final year with that newspaper at Harvard University as a Nieman Fellow.

THE Peace Corps expects to send overseas [the week of June 24, 1962] its 1,000th newly trained volunteer.

There are no special plans to celebrate the occasion. The event is regarded as merely another sign that "the push is on" this summer, as one corps official said. "We're moving from a penny-ante operation into big business," he commented.

Sargent Shriver, the corps' director, predicted that the current total of more than 2,000 volunteers in training or overseas would climb to 5,000 by the end of 1962 to meet the mounting requests from the aided countries. The new volunteers will include retired people as well as recent college graduates.

Already, in its first year in the field, the corps has had teams of American men and women teaching school in the Philippines, surveying roads in Tanganyika, working in clinics in Malaya, and showing farmers how to raise geese on the West Indies island of St. Lucia.

Almost every week this summer and fall, new contingents will head overseas, usually for more language training in the "host country" before they go to work with local people.

A sign tacked on the door of Mr. Shriver's office says: "There is no place in this club for good losers." The corps' director is pushing his staff hard to keep recruiting, selection and training of volunteers on schedule.

Plans must be coordinated with the "host" countries (who request and assign the volunteers), the Agency for International Development, and with the colleges and private groups that do the basic training under contract.

The coordination is seldom painless. Each organization and each foreign country has its own notions of how the Peace Corps should be trained or employed. But so far the build-up has got off to a good start. . . . Mr. Shriver expects to have 10,000 volunteers by the fall of 1963.

There will be midwives in Bolivia, tractor operator (replacing Czech technicians) in Tunisia, agricultural extension workers in Chile, fisheries experts in West Africa, and thousands of college graduates of all ages teaching school in a dozen lands.

"All the countries that have thus far received volunteers," Mr. Shriver said, "have asked us to double, triple, and even quadruple the numbers."

In short, the Peace Corps, despite dark fears expressed by Congressional critics a year ago, has become a success.

The corps was first created by President Kennedy's executive order March 1, 1961, on a "temporary pilot basis" as a branch of the State Department. Congressional approval for a permanent corps came last summer. Mr. Shriver's mission is to supply volunteers to help the world's underdeveloped nations catch up in education, agriculture, health, and other fields. The first of the two-year volunteers began training June 26, 1961.

"The payoff is performance overseas," William F. Haddad, an associate director and "inspector general" of the corps said.

The organization has had a year's hard-won experience with a thirty million dollar program, which currently involves 973 volunteers overseas in sixteen countries and 1,379 more in training.

It is on the basis of this experience that President Kennedy has asked —and won Congressional authorization—for expansion of the corps to a $63,750,000-level in the year starting July 1 [1963]. The appropriations committees have yet to match the go-ahead with the actual funds, and no monetary action is expected until late in the Congressional session.

From interviews here, and from special reports by correspondents of *The New York Times* abroad, a picture emerges of the strengths and weaknesses of the corps' performance overseas since the first two groups of volunteers arrived in Tanganyika and Colombia last fall.

The first point that becomes clear is that two problems forecast last year by critics have not cropped up.

These were: that the corps would become a haven for "beatniks" and "fuzzy-minded idealists" unable to cope with spartan living and the realities of life in the bush, and that Communist agents would score easy victories in ideological debate with naive volunteers before the impressionable people of the aided countries.

On the contrary, the volunteer who emerges from the corps' training program is not a "beatnik"; if he is an idealist, he is a tough-minded one.

The corps' screening system has resulted in an 18 per cent drop-out rate among the men and women who actually started training. The training includes language and work instruction for specific projects on American college campuses ranging from Utah State to New York University. Many of the volunteers also go through a tough jungle camp in Puerto Rico. Their average age is 24 years, but seven persons older than 60 have also made the grade.

The Peace Corps volunteers come from every state in the union, and from Puerto Rico, the Virgin Islands, and Guam.

So far, corps headquarters in Washington has received 26,807 applications for duty. About 20,000 of these applicants have taken entrance tests. Of these, 4,000 have started training or are scheduled to start. Two hundred sixty-seven have been dropped from training for various reasons.

Most of the volunteers have had at least a year in college. They are reimbursed for living expenses at a rate that is intended to make them live like their local counterparts, for example, teachers or farm extension agents. This rate varies from $60 a month in the Philippines to $160 in Tanganyika. In addition, each volunteer gets $75 a month, banked for him by the corps, which is paid him after his two-year tour. In every case, the corpsman works where the host country wants to put him.

Dr. George Guthrie, a Pennsylvania State University psychologist, commented as follows on a training group bound for teaching assignments in the Philippines:

"The majority of these people were in the upper half of their class at college. But there aren't many Phi Beta Kappas. Many of their schools had no chapters of Phi Beta Kappa. They aren't Ivy League or beatnik. They come mostly from small schools and small communities. Most of them are from middle class families. More easily than some, they can afford to make the sacrifice."

This portrait does not ring true for every overseas group. The thirty-five surveyors, engineers, and geologists working in Tanganyika, for example, are far more of a professional type than the Philippine group.

The attitude overseas, once the newness has worn off, can be summed up in these words by Donald Goodyear, of Cedar Rapids, Iowa, who is teaching school in Enugu, Nigeria: "Despite all the glamorous talk and publicity, we have a perfectly straightforward job to do here. We're teachers—just as we would be at schools anywhere."

Premier Khrushchev recently denounced the Peace Corps as "imperialist." Similarly, most local Communist opposition has been limited to words, and it has been ineffectual. The Communist party in Chile earlier this year, for example, denounced Peace Corps volunteers working in rural education and health as "imperialist agents" and ordered Communist youths to "confront" the volunteers. Nothing happened.

In India's Punjab, 22-year-old Justin R. McLoughlin of Garrettsville, N. Y., recalled that an Indian farmer one day planted a hammer and sickle emblem on the chicken coop that Mr. McLoughlin was helping him build. "I persuaded him to take it down, at least until the coop was finished," the volunteer said.

In Nigeria, university students still snipe at the corps' 108 volunteers, who teach in the country's schools. It was in Nigeria that Miss Margery Michelmore, a newly arrived volunteer, created the corps' one major "incident" last fall by including adverse impressions of the local scene on a postcard, which was intercepted and made public in the African country.

"I'm convinced," said Dr. Samuel D. Proctor of Norfolk, Va., corps representative in Nigeria, "that, given a few more months, the Nigerian students will discover the Peace Corps volunteers are not here to direct their political thinking. This will reduce some of the tensions."

The Peace Corps effort has shown other strengths and weaknesses. Most of the latter stem from the hasty, experimental nature of the first dozen programs set in motion last year.

All told, only seven volunteers have been shipped home, three of them returned because of health or family reasons. Yet Mr. Shriver has pointed out that "anybody who wants can get out."

The corps' one over-all strength is that the volunteers are making friends for the United States, in places that their parents had never heard of and where few whites have ever set foot. Much of their success is simply a result of their lack of condescension or self-importance. As a result, there has been a lack of serious racial incidents.

In Ghana, for example, the fifty-one Americans teaching in British-model boarding schools do not drive cars to work. In fact, unlike other non-Africans and more prosperous Ghanaians, they ride packed "mummy lorries"—trucks used as local buses—along dusty country roads in sweltering heat.

At Kotpindas, a village outside Lahore, West Pakistan, James Mackay of Hornell, N. Y., a Peace Corps volunteer, organized his fellow volunteers and some Pakistani friends to repair a 300-year-old Moghul bridge. The middle-class Pakistanis confessed they had never used shovels, but joined in anyway. A group of villagers came up and asked: "What, no coolies?" Then, seeing the "sahibs" working, they too pitched in with cries of "shabash"—"well done."

A *Times* correspondent wrote from New Delhi, India:

"The image the corpsmen create generally is that of earnest young Americans who know what they are talking about and who are not afraid to get their hands dirty. Most volunteers here are farmers and look it. As one official said: 'Their heart is really in the Indian rural areas.' "

The real benefits of the volunteers' labor vary widely from country to country. In India, the tiny Peace Corps contingent is swallowed up in the multitudes; in other, smaller nations, the impact is less localized.

In Malaya, for example, Peace Corps nurses are helping to solve one of the biggest problems of the Health Ministry: staffing rural clinics in the "ulu," Malaya's backwoods. The thirty-six Peace Corps men and women in the team in Malaya have made a dent in several vital areas, including volunteer work in a 2,500-patient leper colony.

In Tanganyika, the thirty-six American surveyors, geologists, and engineers are not only creating goodwill, but, alongside local helpers, are doing a job that a local official described as "absolutely vital." They are working on surveying the country, and developing farm-to-market roads to open up isolated hamlets, thus enabling farmers to sell their produce at good prices.

The volunteers dismissed the old British notion that Africans would not work. On a safari, when their African helper sat down, saying he could not go on, Thomas Katus of McIntosh, S. D., and Jerry Parsons of Albany, N. Y., sat down too. "Okay," they told their friend, "it's your country, so why should we bother?" This got the team going again.

Prime Minister Rashidi Kawawa of Tanganyika paid this tribute to the volunteers: "They have done a very good job, mixing with the people and encouraging self-help measures. We hope to get more of them."

Teaching is the biggest single specialty in which the Peace Corps is engaged. In Ghana, Nigeria and Jamaica, the volunteers are especially welcome, if only because their services are relatively cheap or even free. In many cases, the volunteers serve where local teachers do not want to go.

Another major effort has been in agriculture.

In Brazil, forty-three volunteers drove jeeps into the field last month to work with the Brazilian Association for Rural Credit and Assistance on farm assistance and home economics through the local version of the 4-H Clubs.

The Peace Corps in Brazil is dovetailing its work, particularly in the country's poverty-stricken Northeast, with the Agency for International Development, which finances the two million dollar project of the rural aid association.

In Colombia, the Peace Corps has attempted one of its more ambitious assignments. Something called "community development."

Although the sixty-two men volunteers who arrived in Colombia last September have built roads and schools, set up health stations and patched up first-aid cases, their basic function has been to work with Colombian representatives to get mountain villagers to help themselves despite poverty, illiteracy and the paternalism of the landlords. The task has not been an easy one.

In Santander, Colombia, a volunteer told a village priest:

"We want to solve these problems without giving orders. We want to motivate people to work. Maybe we'll build a health center or a road, and then, when we leave, they'll tell themselves 'we need a school' and they'll shout and argue and laugh and finally build a school."

The priest replied quietly: "You will achieve that when you have economic freedom here." By this he meant freedom from malnutrition, illiteracy and the lack of opportunity for sharecroppers.

In Chitareaque, in the Colombian department of Boyacá, a hard-working Peace Corps team was pulled out three months ago to avoid its getting into a local dispute over land reform with hostile landowners, who discouraged peasants from attending community meetings.

Nevertheless, the volunteers have made do. One volunteer, Davis Grubb of Westport, Conn. took a bus into Bogotá, called on the Minister of Public Works and came back with a bulldozer, which his village used to build an eight-mile road to market.

Another volunteer, David Downing of Los Gatos, Calif., got a course in midwifery going and prevailed on his friends back home in California to send him midwifery kits.

The villagers are enthusiastic, if every harassed Colombian official is not. The volunteers, sometimes to their annoyance, are besieged with offers of coffee, liquor, or sweets.

So far, the morale of the volunteers is high. But some of them get depressed. "Maybe frustration is built within the boys themselves," said Leon Lane, deputy representative for CARE, Inc. (Cooperative for American Relief Everywhere), which is handling the project for the corps in Colombia. "They've got two years and they want to go too fast too soon. A job like this isn't going to be completed for years and years."

In Chile, forty-five men and women trained at the University of Notre Dame and local centers have been in the field since December with the long-established Institute of Rural Education. They are scattered in ones and twos for 1,000 miles in the Chilean interior. Their work is more formalized and more specialized than that of the Colombian team.

They work as carpenters, social workers, in rural husbandry, as dental assistants, home economists, nurses, home builders.

"These Peace Corps volunteers are striving for a better understanding between peoples," the Chilean newspaper La Estrella said.

More volunteers are on the way to Chile. But, as in the case of Colombia, the impact of the Americans is muted by the vastness of the problems they have tackled.

Despite such frustrations, both Latin-American officials and the Peace Corps see "rural development" as a way to make good use of young Americans with or without special talents. Several hundred counterparts of the volunteers in Colombia and Chile are being picked for work in Ecuador, Peru, Bolivia, Cyprus, British North Borneo and Sarawak.

Besides the occasional frustrations, the Peace Corps has had other problems. One of the most severe was the lack of proper language instruction—a fault that has been corrected.

For example, the first group of 128 volunteers sent to the Philippines last fall spent weeks learning Tagalog, the national language. Then they were assigned to non-Tagalog-speaking areas. Roughly the same mistake was made in training the twenty-eight volunteers sent to West Pakistan, where the state languages, along with English, are Sindhi, Punjabi and Pushto. The twenty-six men and women sent to India's Punjab just could not master Punjabi in ten weeks at Ohio State University.

A second problem has been projects that were either poorly handled or badly defined at first. Roger Ernst of New York, former corps representative in New Delhi, commented that all the volunteers sent to India should have been assigned to a single endeavor, such as agricultural work, instead of being scattered in a variety of jobs. In both India and West Pakistan, local officials were initially not quite sure what to do with the volunteers.

In the Philippines, the 128 volunteers were assigned as teachers' helpers. This aroused suspicions of local teachers that the Americans had been sent to spy on them and complaints by the volunteers that they had not been given enough work to do. In Pakistan, India and Nigeria, some unhappy volunteers were assigned initially to office jobs instead of getting out in the field.

Yet, even where the official assignments were unsatisfactory, the volunteers, with Mr. Shriver's blessing, launched a host of extracurricular projects on their own. Examples:

⟨ In the Philippines, sixteen volunteers organized a month-long summer "camp brotherhood" at Mambucal, on the island of Negros, for six hundred indigent boys. Others set up "little theatre" groups, conducted demonstration courses on the use of fertilizer and ran summer schools.

◖ In Ghana, as in other countries, the volunteers have been writing home to schools and civic organizations asking for books, and have opened their public libraries in their own cramped quarters.

◖ In East Pakistan, Robert W. Taylor of Los Gatos, Calif., invented a machine to parboil rice cheaply and efficiently, using the rice husks themselves as fuel, of which there is a critical local shortage.

In doing their varied assignments and carrying out their self-made projects, the Peace Corps volunteers have experienced few serious health and safety problems. Three corps volunteers have died—two in an airplane crash in Colombia and one under surgery in Manila.

On the happier side, there have been about twenty Peace Corps marriages—either between volunteers or between a volunteer and a citizen of the aided country. So far, all the newlyweds have continued their duties. The first Peace Corps baby was born May 16 to a young volunteer couple teaching school in Nigeria.

That the corps' problems have not been more serious is attributed here to several things, besides the hard work and the quality of the volunteers themselves.

The first is Mr. Shriver's determination not to make a bureaucracy of the Peace Corps, but to keep all hands giving top priority to people, rather than "policy" and "procedure."

The second is the work of the "inspector general" system, which provides for frequent flying trips to hear the volunteers' complaints. The language problem was unearthed early in this fashion.

"The volunteers have a very definite idea about how the corps should be run. They won't take any second-rate stuff. They keep us on our toes," an aide to Mr. Haddad said.

The greatest danger, as the corps grows, according to officials here, will be that it might lose its lively non-bureaucratic spirit. The jargon of the social scientist and bureaucrat—volunteers are "object-oriented" for example—is already creeping into ordinary speech at the corps' busy headquarters here at 806 Connecticut Avenue, across Lafayette Square from the White House.

On the other hand, as President Kennedy told the corps staff here . . .

"You have brought to Government service a sense of morale and a sense of enthusiasm and real commitment which has been absent from too many governmental agencies for too many years."

This summer [of 1962], the corps' recruiting and selection of qualified people to go overseas will continue to pose headaches as commitments increase. Some teams of volunteers will go overseas under their prescribed strength, especially where certain key skills cannot be obtained. But it is expected that, in the main, the commitments will be met.

GUNNAR MYRDAL

Beyond the Welfare State

*Economic experts who, since World War II, have had experience
with the problems of aid and trade in relations between the Western industrial powers and the developing non-Western nations, are
increasingly coming to the conclusion that aid and trade, like national development, will have to be planned and coordinated, this
time on a world scale. Only in this way will the technologically
backward countries be able to achieve the economic growth required to assure even a modicum of improvement in the lot of their
populations whose increase, in some areas, is outrunning production
facilities.*

*A leading exponent of international planning is Gunnar K.
Myrdal of Sweden, professor of economics at Stockholm University.
Dr. Myrdal, born in 1898, has long been active in public affairs,
both in his own country and on the international scene. A Social
Democrat, he is a member of the Swedish Senate, and served as
Minister of Commerce, 1945–47. For a decade, 1947–57, he was
executive secretary of the United Nations Economic Commission
for Europe, with headquarters in Geneva.*

*The volume from which the selection below is drawn is based on
the Storrs Lectures delivered by the author at Yale. Dr. Myrdal is
the author of several books, among them An American Dilemma:
The Negro Problem and Modern Democracy, 1944; International
Economy, Problems and Prospects, 1956; and Rich Lands and Poor,
1958. At present he is serving as research director for an extensive
study of economic development in Southeast Asia under the auspices
of the Twentieth Century Fund.*

Chapter 13
Towards a New World Stability

Conditions

THE international class conflict could be permitted to grow to catastrophic dimensions, and could then end in calamity for our civilization.

Or, it may be resolved by a series of gradual accommodations, approaching the establishment of a new situation of stability in the world.

No attempt will be made in this book to forecast the future development of this conflict of interests between the two classes of nations in the non-Soviet world: the powerful rich and the powerless poor, who are so many, and who are now becoming their own masters. The reason for this disclaimer of foresight is not only the conviction that prognostications on the really large and fateful issues are valueless—they have always proved grossly inaccurate in the past, and we have learned to expect the unexpected—but also the moral conviction that prognostications are in their very nature illogical and, indeed, preposterous. The future is continually our own choice. There is no blind destiny ruling history.

We are not entirely free, though. There are facts and given causal relations. In general terms, we know a good deal about what conditions would have to be established before a new world stability could be reached.

Negatively, we know that stability cannot be accomplished by a resort to force and pressure. A return to dependence of a colonial type is excluded. The poor nations will only be satisfied by an ever fuller independence.

We also know that mere political independence, without equal opportunity, economic progress, and the right to share wealth and power, will not be enough. In the end there is, in these world-wide problems, no practical alternative to international disintegration other than to initiate the development towards the democratic Welfare World, and this is the reason why these wider considerations have a bearing on the problems of economic planning in the rich countries of the Western world.

We thus know that, if a new stability is to exist in the world, the rich nations will have to be prepared to modify their economic policies in the interest of a broader sharing of opportunities. For this there is undoubtedly an ideological preparedness in the Western world. The Great Awakening is, of course, from their point of view, nothing else than the rapid spread over the globe of the old ideals of liberty, equality, and brotherhood, which are the cherished tenets of Western civilization, and which have increasingly become realized in the last two generations within the national Welfare States of the individual countries of the Western world. Very much will depend upon the rapidity and forcefulness of a positive response in the rich countries to a wider sharing of opportunities.

Finally, however, we know that the main driving force behind such a fortunate development, if it could be realized, must be the exertions of the poor nations themselves. No upper class has ever stepped down voluntarily to equality with the lower class, and as a simple consequence of a moral conviction given up their privileges and opened entrance to their monopolies. To be induced to do so, the rich and the privileged must sense that demands are raised and forcefully pressed, and that power becomes assembled behind them. At that stage, moral ideals in the upper class are given their chance to play a supporting role.

For this reason, the stronger the poor nations become, the more the attainment of a new situation of world stability is made possible. The stronger they become, the more will they be in a position to abstain from the policy measures which build up resentment against them. As always, loyalty to the community will grow as they acquire strength, assurance and a sense of belonging. This is a reason why success in their efforts towards national planning for development is such a paramount world interest.

Their Mutual Isolation

To gain strength, the poor nations also desperately need to join forces, to pool their resources, and to coordinate their policies in a planned fashion. Their similar histories and present situations should afford a basis for this. Most of them are colored and have bitter memories of segregation and discrimination practiced against them by people of European stock. In the protests which can unite them, the word "racialism" will regularly be found together with "colonialism." Above all they are poor, mostly illiterate and backward, and they are being made conscious of it. The important thing is that they are not satisfied with liberty, but demand equality of opportunity and common brotherhood as well. They describe themselves as "underdeveloped," with the clear implication that they should have economic development and a fuller share of the good things in life.

One of the most important functions of the international organizations has been to assemble representatives of the poor countries in forums where they can experience their solidarity of interests and give voice to their shared grievances. On the political plane they are already finding common ground even in specific issues, for instance in their joint support for the liberation movements in the still remaining colonial dependencies. But in economic matters they have hardly established any joint policy, other than to demand more aid and to harp in general terms on the necessity of broad reforms in the structure of international capital movements, shipping, and trade. Without more intensive economic relations among themselves, in particular more trade and division of labor within the several regions, the attempts towards forming a common front in general economic issues are bound to be largely empty demonstrations.

Their weak mutual economic ties, the lack of practical cooperation even in the regions and, indeed, the underdeveloped state of their ordinary mutual trade relations stand in dramatic contrast to the similarity of their interests and their aspirations. In the main this isolation is a result of long ages of economic stagnation, and more particularly of colonialism and other forms of foreign domination. Traditionally, the underdeveloped countries have confined their economic relations—and, indeed, their political and cultural relations too—almost exclusively to one or a few of the rich countries which used to dominate them and which had an interest in monopolizing such relations. The whole transport system had, in fact, been adapted to the old colonial and quasi-colonial matrix of forced bi-lateralism, dominated by the interests in the rich countries. Roads and railroads were built within each one of the underdeveloped countries and shipping facilities were provided for the commercial relations across the oceans. But even today—except for the new airlines which are expensive—regular transport facilities between neighboring countries, necessary for intensified commercial relations, are not available in most regions, or are inefficient and unduly expensive.

The colonial powers had also permitted, and often provoked by their policies, developments which, now the foreign domination has relaxed or disappeared, have left awkward unsolved problems, tensions and resentments between neighboring nations. Consider, for instance, the artificial boundaries created in West Asia, when the Ottoman Empire was cut up and divided between Britain and France after World War I; the Indian moneylenders and landlords in Burma; the imported Tamil laborers on the plantations in Ceylon; and, of course, the hostility between India and Pakistan in the wake of partition. After World War II, the cold war has, in some regions, caused estrangement amongst neighboring countries.

The situation of mutual isolation which the government of underdeveloped countries are inheriting is not one that can easily and rapidly be changed. To build new commercial links is under all conditions a laborious task, and particularly so in the underdeveloped regions. Greatly improved facilities for transport between neighboring countries would also require heavy investments, which would have to compete for scarce capital resources with all other development needs.

To this must be added the fact that the old established commercial relations cannot be lightheartedly severed. It is, indeed, strongly in the interest of the underdeveloped countries not to break them. They certainly need to preserve their trading relations with the rich countries that previously dominated them politically and economically. They need to widen these relations to all other rich countries, by freeing themselves from the relative monopolies held by the business interests in the metropolitan countries. It is mainly from the rich countries in the Western

world—together with the Soviet Union and the Eastern European countries—that they can buy capital equipment for economic development.
But they also need to complement these relations by breaking up the
artificial barriers amongst themselves in the regions and in the whole
world. They need to trade with each other and to cooperate in their
common interest. This would also strengthen their bargaining power in
dealing with the rich countries.

A Problem of Planning

Towards this goal of multilateralizing their trade, and in particular of
building up trade relations amongst themselves, the underdeveloped
countries have not made any real progress. The national communities
which came into being as political and economic colonialism disintegrated, had, as their first task, to consolidate the new nation-states. In
many of these countries there is still much to be accomplished in order
to reach this first goal of effectively governed national communities. The
idea of planning for development, as it spread to these countries, was
spelled out in terms of narrow national planning. The exchange difficulties had the same impact of turning economic policies in the direction of autarkic self-sufficiency.

As in the Welfare State of the rich countries, and, for various reasons,
even more than there, a tendency towards nationalism is implied in all
planning. Political power within national boundaries is its basis, and it
becomes directed towards putting the national resources to more effective use for national development. Foreign relations, including relations with neighboring countries, are the independent and uncertain
variables in planning. As in the rich countries, insofar as planning for
development became a serious matter in an underdeveloped country and
a real concern felt by its people, it tended to turn their interests inwards.

Keeping all these things in mind, it should not be surprising that the
efforts at economic planning in underdeveloped countries have been
narrowly nationalistic and, in particular, have nowhere involved any
serious attempts at overcoming the abnormal and unnatural commercial
isolation from other underdeveloped countries, even in the immediate
vicinity. On balance, it may even be a fact that this isolation, inherited
from colonial times, has in many cases become intensified. Nothing else
could perhaps have been expected under the circumstances. It would not
have been rational, practical, or even possible.

Nevertheless, I am convinced that closer commercial relations amongst
underdeveloped countries in general, and those in some region in particular, will in the future come to stand out as an eminently practical
and important problem. I am then assuming that the underdeveloped

countries in general will be reasonably successful in engendering substantial economic development. This is a very important assumption for my argument and it might not be valid, but in that case world development as a whole is bound to take a more sinister turn. I will now briefly enumerate the reasons why, under the assumption made, I expect the problem of trade and regional economic cooperation among underdeveloped countries to rise in importance.

The Future

That the levels of transport facilities and trade among underdeveloped countries are abnormally low implies that to raise these levels would be to their mutual advantage. The widespread idea, which is a spiritual heritage from the colonial era, that these countries are not complementary in their economic structures is exaggerated. Even with their present economic structures unchanged, I believe that more trade in many products would be advantageous. In many parts of the world it would be practical, for instance, to work out regional instead of national plans for agriculture and food. Some are deficit countries, but some are surplus countries, and the latter might be willing and able to increase their production and exports of food, if they were assured a regular and stable market.

The advantage of closer economic cooperation will stand out as much greater, however, if the underdeveloped countries advance in their economic development. All these countries are bent on industrialization. To build up a complete structure of industry in each country is not easily practicable and in any case not very economical. And it becomes less easy and less economical every day, as modern technology on the whole gives increasing advantages to large industrial establishments. These countries can all proceed faster in their industrial development if they can reach, through trade, a division of labor and a certain specialization amongst themselves. This holds with particular force for the smaller countries, but it is also true for the larger ones. Even India, with a population of over 400 millions, is still—and will remain for many five-year plans ahead—a rather small country economically, with an export market not very much bigger than that of one of the smaller countries in northwestern Europe, none of which would think of the possibility of expanding further on the basis of that type of national industrial self-sufficiency which is too often posited as the idea for national planning in underdeveloped countries.

As was shown, the underdeveloped countries have strong reasons for protecting their infant industries which the rich countries do not have. As their home markets are small and their resources of capital for investment scarce, as is also their supply of enterprise and managerial and technical skills, it would be in their common interest if they could arrange their industrial protection regionally and not simply nationally. These countries have much more valid economic reasons for a "common market" than the rich countries of Western Europe, which, like the United States, could and in my opinion should, have so managed their affairs that they would now be in a position to open their boundaries to the whole world for the flow of capital and commodities, instead of closing up amongst themselves in blocs. Such a "common market" would imply joint planning.

Another reason why in fifteen or twenty years' time the idea of regional instead of simply national planning and protection will enter the practical politics of underdeveloped countries lies in the increasing difficulties many of these countries may meet in raising their exports to correspond to their future import needs. Those of the underdeveloped countries which have large deposits of oil or minerals may have the right to look with confidence on their future export prospects, but hardly the others. On substantially higher levels of production, income and consumption, they will need bigger imports, however much they succeed in substituting home produce for imported goods. They will then have to enter the world market as exporters of manufactured industrial goods. If this happens on a large scale—which corresponds to the assumption that underdeveloped countries will generally have a reasonable measure of success in their strivings towards development—it will probably meet resistance in the rich countries. Wages in the poor countries will continue to be relatively low, and their exports will be looked upon as "dumping."

It would naturally be in the interest of international economic integration if the rich countries became positively interested in providing the underdeveloped countries with export outlets. They would then be systematically scrapping their protection for such industrial goods as the underdeveloped countries become prepared to export. The argument would have a particular force in regard to labor-intensive industries, because the rich countries should have better uses for their scarce labor. A determined move in this direction is a part of the adjustment of commercial policy in the Western countries, which these countries should now be prepared to undertake if they rightly appreciate the world situation and their own long-term interests. Theoretically, it would be a fully logical line of action. Practically, the temporary disturbances would not at Western levels of production and income be too difficult to meet, especially compared with, for instance, the conversions every country is prepared to undergo, and indeed to plan, in the case of a war or major recession.

It is possible—perhaps likely—that in the end such a movement towards a change in industrial structure in the rich countries will, as a market adjustment, happen unintentionally, in the hard way and with a time lag. Perhaps we have seen the beginning of such an adjustment in the textile industry, but we there also see the resistance it provokes. With the nationalistic direction of interests in the Welfare State, and particularly with the decentralization of influence to bargaining organizations on many levels, there will normally be strong attempts to withstand such an adjustment. I recall that the Welfare State has habitually won internal stability and flexibility at the price of a lower degree of international adjustability. Meanwhile the underdeveloped countries, if they really emerged as producers and exporters of industrial products on a large scale, would find themselves fiercely fighting for markets against powerful vested interests for protection in all the rich countries, supported by labor as well as business. I will return later to the problem of the commercial policies of the Western countries.

There is a possibility that the countries in the Soviet world, which have centrally controlled economic systems and can direct their trade more or less at will, would, in this situation, be prepared to preserve certain outlets for industrial exports from the underdeveloped countries. Of such a preparedness we have, as yet, no indications whatever. For underdeveloped countries that wanted to avoid becoming too dependent on the trade monopolies of the Soviet countries, the exploitation of such an outlet—if it were made available—could hardly do more than mitigate their general export difficulties somewhat.

In this situation the very fact of the underdeveloped countries' success in economic development and industrialization, if it should materialize, would greatly increase their mutual usefulness as export markets. This implies and assumes, as all trade does, division of labor and industrial specialization. In its turn, it would then make further progress in these countries' economic development easier and more possible.

•   •   •

Not Only Aid

Leaving aside this question of mutual cooperation amongst the underdeveloped countries themselves, there is now a growing consensus of opinion in the rich countries that they should be prepared to initiate economic policies in order to enable underdeveloped countries to develop economically, and to do so rapidly.

Usually the discussions about these policies have been focused almost exclusively on capital aid and technical assistance given free. This is particularly the case in the country which provides the biggest share of assistance, the United States. But capital grants and technical assistance given free of charge can never be anything but a rather minor part of the total complex of economic policies which the United States and all the other rich countries should adopt, if they really wish to help the poor countries in their struggle for economic development. This would remain true even were such aid expanded to the much larger volume that is called for on rational grounds, and even were that aid organized in a rationally justifiable, multilateral, and truly international framework.

This complex of economic policies, which the rich countries should adopt in addition to providing aid, comprises a redirection of their whole manner of doing business—or of not doing business—with each other and, in particular, with the underdeveloped countries. These countries are at the rich countries' mercy because they are poor. For their welfare and their success in engendering economic development, they depend heavily on the rich countries' policies in regard to trade and the movement over their boundaries of people, capital, enterprise, and techniques.

If the rich nations made a determined move to shape their general economic policies more in the interests of the underdeveloped ones, this would be of a vastly greater consequence to the economic development of those countries than any aid which they could ever hope to get. If instead the rich countries persist in carrying on their ordinary business with the underdeveloped world on the principle of narrow economic nationalism and adjustments to the wishes of short-sighted vested interests at home, even generous aid becomes nothing more than a palliative.

•   •   •

Trade

What would be requested of the rich countries in the field of trade would first be to recognize the rationality of the "double-standard morality" in commercial policies, which I referred to in the last chapter.

In a better integrated world the rich countries should, in the common interest, largely abstain from putting up barriers to foreign trade and, in particular, should open their markets to the underdeveloped countries. I have already given the reasons why, as industrial development gets under way in underdeveloped countries, outlets should be given them for industrial exports as well. At the same time, it should be admitted that the underdeveloped countries cannot themselves follow this principle without compromising, perhaps seriously, their ambitions for planning economic development. The rich countries, and in particular the United States, have often acted upon the opposite "double-standard morality," insisting upon following a protectionist policy on their own behalf, while preaching the virtues of free trade to the underdeveloped world.

Their commercial policies are to an astonishing extent dominated not only by such special group interests as can be understood to have a considerable weight—like, for instance, those of the textile industry and its workers in Great Britain and elsewhere, to which I have referred—but also by interests which are clearly petty. That the oil industry can move the State Department in Washington around is remarkable, but not surprising. But that, in an underdeveloped country in Southeast Asia, the American organization for technical assistance does not dare to help the country develop its fishing industry, because it would upset a few American exporters of canned fish, is perhaps shocking to the uninitiated.

Moreover, in all the commercial dealings with underdeveloped countries, business interests in the rich countries, supported by their governments, are now habitually using their superior bargaining power to press the poor countries to import commodities which they could produce themselves by putting their un-utilized manpower and other resources to work, or which they rightly consider that they cannot afford to import, at least not in the quantities and with the freedom that are urged upon them. Underdeveloped countries are everywhere pressed to import what they could do without as condition for leaving them a market for their exports for which the demand is often none too brisk. Their need for credits when they are out to buy industrial equipment is often utilized to impose upon them prices and other conditions that are unfair and burdensome. A greater consideration for underdeveloped countries in all such matters would help to bring about a very substantial improvement in their economic situation.

•   •   •

Aid

When I stress the primary importance of a readjustment of the Western countries' ordinary economic policies, and in general of their way of doing business with the underdeveloped countries, this does not imply, of course, that aid would be unnecessary or unimportant. Indeed, the permanent establishment of a considerably higher level of aid to underdeveloped countries, in cash and technical assistance, is urgently called for. It would produce, among other things, a more solid basis for a wholesome development of those ordinary economic relations which are so much more important. A sudden large income equalization on a world scale is both an impossible and, I am inclined to believe, an unimportant objective. But certainly, as part of a much wider complex of economic policies, there is a need, for economic as well as social reasons, for policy measures which imply a limited income redistribution.

My main criticism of the present state of affairs in the field of grant aid and technical assistance is that the United States has been left to pay almost the whole bill for such help. It is not difficult to explain why this has happened. The pattern was set many years ago. At the end of World War II the United States, unlike its allies, found itself not only undamaged by military action but much better off economically than at the beginning of the war. In this situation it was natural that the United States, almost single-handedly, undertook the responsibility for rendering the financial assistance that was needed for reconstruction and recovery.

•   •   •

Naturally, it has to be remembered that the United States' production and income is a very big part of the total production and income of all the rich countries taken together, and its share of the burden in any fair scheme for international aid would be a large one, even if not so large as that which the United States has carried so far. A very important moral element of every scheme for redistributing income, national as well as international, should be that the burden be shared in a just and equitable manner. It is not fair, and will never be felt to be fair, that a man who lives in Stockholm, Geneva, or Brussels should not share the burden of aid to underdeveloped countries equally with a man in the same income bracket living in Columbus, Ohio, in Detroit, Michigan, or in Denver, Colorado.

Most of the things which are imperfect and wrong in our present aid schemes spring from this lack of justice in their financing. In America, the situation is naturally felt to be unfair, even though little is said about it. This is undoubtedly a main reason why it has not proved politically feasible to raise further the level of assistance to underdeveloped countries, as well as why the suggested appropriations for aid are constantly in danger of being whittled away in Congress.

It also helps to explain why some of those who, in America, are urging higher appropriations become tempted to argue their case in terms of political or even military strategy, and, more generally, why it becomes so difficult to keep the appropriations free from political conditions. This leads naturally also to the labelling of an increasing part of legitimate economic aid as military.

When international aid becomes unilateral, and politics thus enters into its distribution, moral standards are apt to crumble. Economic standards, too, will be more difficult to uphold. A selection according to political interests is often bound to imply the diversion of aid to the less necessitous countries, or to those least capable of using it effectively for economic advancement. In the receiving countries, unilateral aid may have equally unfortunate effects. The political conditions of the aid are resented by their peoples. Indeed, political strings and the existence of ulterior motives will be suspected, even when they are not present.

The direction and control of the use of aid will also, in many cases, be less efficient. An underdeveloped country may be willing—even happy—to take from an international agency advice which it is not ready or, because of popular resentment, not able to accept under prodding by a single country, least of all when that country is very rich, powerful, and careless in its public utterances.

These are, of course, important reasons why aid is best channelled through an international agency. But it would be almost preposterous to suggest that more than a minor—indeed, almost a symbolic—part of the total flow of aid should be so handled, as long as one country pays almost all the costs. A fairer distribution of the financial burden is, therefore, a condition for transferring any substantial part of aid and technical assistance to underdeveloped countries into an institutional framework which is multilateral and truly international.

The Direction of Aid

I have felt for a long time that aid to underdeveloped countries should be placed in a definite and more rational order of priorities. This type of international cooperation, where there is not a *quid pro quo* in the ordinary way of business relations, should in my opinion be concentrated on a few fields where such aid would be particularly natural, and felt to be so, both in the countries that are given aid and in those that are receiving it.

Firstly, those underdeveloped nations who are short of food should be given what they need for attaining adequate nutritional standards. The rich countries should make up their mind that they do not want to make money out of selling food to starving peoples. In many countries, a major limitation of economic development is the valid fear that, when the unemployed and underdeveloped are set to work, they will consume more food than is available. It should be recognized that when, at the same time, other countries are laboring with the problems of food surpluses, this limitation of development is not only cruel but unnecessary and, indeed, absurd. This is, however, no reason why only those rich countries which have food surplusses should carry the burden of the costs of such aid. In any reasonable scheme of international cooperation, the costs for such a scheme should be shared by all the rich nations.

What is more, aid should never be looked upon as a permanent solution to the problems of poverty. Aid should always be a help to self-help. For that reason a definite time limit should be set to the provision of food without pay, and a condition should be made that the aid-receiving country do everything it can to raise yields in agriculture. Otherwise there is always the danger that the food aid would only buttress its complacency. Secondly, therefore, the rich countries should also decide to give, free of charge, everything that it would be practical and economic to import from abroad in terms of tools and equipment, technical assistance, and training in order to assist underdeveloped countries to raise their agricultural production of food for consumption. Insofar as surpluses of fertilizers were available, those could be part of the aid. Otherwise, aid should instead be given to set up fertilizer factories in underdeveloped countries where conditions for fertilizer production are favorable.

In a rational scheme of international cooperation, this problem of providing enough food for rapid economic development should be viewed not as a narrowly national problem, but as regional and, indeed, worldwide. Some underdeveloped countries are, and should increasingly become, food exporters, while others could concentrate more on non-food crops and manufactured industrial goods for export. The interests of the former countries should be guarded. They are not, of course, in a position to give away food as the rich countries are. They should in many cases even be aided economically to produce more food for commercial export. If their exports went to other underdeveloped countries as part of the food aid they received, the rich countries' contribution would consist in paying the former countries for their food export to the latter.

Thirdly, the rich countries should, in addition to meeting the fundamental request for more food to eat, agree to give everything that can be provided from abroad in the way of equipment, advice, personnel training, etc., for the most rapid advance the underdeveloped countries can manage to engender in sanitation, health, education at all levels, and research, including surveys of their natural resources.

There should be one general condition for aid in these three directions: that the recipient should use the aid in an economic and efficient manner. If, as I am proposing, the rich countries declared themselves willing to provide all the additional food that some underdeveloped countries need, and all financial help which they can effectively administer for raising productivity in their agriculture, and improving levels of sanitation, health, education, training, and research, the costs would not imply any substantial lowering of economic levels in the rich Western countries.

The great desirability of giving aid generously for these specific purposes would be more readily understood by the general public in the rich Western countries. If aid was given to feed hungry people, to make it more possible for them to grow more food themselves, and to raise the poor nations' levels of health and education, fewer people in the rich countries would be inclined to raise political conditions or to discriminate in giving aid. It would be less tempting to conceal aid in the twilight of "soft loans." In the underdeveloped countries themselves, there would be less suspicion of ulterior motives. Aid would be understood and accepted as the purely humanitarian effort it is, or rather should be.

If there were more funds available for aid to underdeveloped countries than are needed for these three forms, I would give the fourth priority to paying for equipment and other productive necessities from abroad, in order to speed up the formation of various types of overall capital such as irrigation and power facilities, ports, roads, storehouses, etc. Such large-scale investment is necessary in order to give the basis for development, both in industry and agriculture. It is of a particular strategic importance in economic development, as it is labor-intensive and can thus make use of the productive resources of which an underdeveloped country has surplus, labor. If food ceased to be the cruel bottleneck it is at present in many countries, and if undertaking these investments in overall capital would not compete for foreign exchange, underdeveloped countries would find it advantageous to give them a higher priority rating. A large part of the loans from the International Bank have this purpose, but it would be rational to use grant aid in order to make it possible for many underdeveloped countries to intensify their efforts in this direction.

If these forms of economic aid were made available in considerably larger quantities, industrial development, which rightly is such a paramount objective in all underdeveloped countries, could then be left with more hope to their own efforts, upon which it will anyhow have to depend. I have already referred to the fact that, at present, the lack of food, and the fear of increasing the scarcity of food in an inflationary process are often limitations to all development, and in particular to rapid industrialization. That limitation would then have been removed. In all underdeveloped countries, raising the levels of health, education, training, and research would decrease the impact of other brakes on industrialization. The widening of the basis of available social capital would have the same effect. Moreover, other favorable conditions for industrial development in underdeveloped countries would have been created if the rich countries were prepared to undertake the changes in their ordinary commercial and financial policies and business relations which I have referred to above, and which would be so much in the interests of international integration. In the final instance, those reforms in regard to trade and capital movements are, of course, more important than any grant aid for development could ever be.

It is difficult to see how these changes could be brought about, except under concerted and sustained pressure exerted by the poor countries, making the maximum possible use of the existing inter-governmental organizations. A rational organization of aid and technical assistance, and in particular the inauguration of a priority system of the type sketched above, is only possible, of course, if aid is being planned internationally by inter-governmental agencies, instead of being handed out unilaterally by individual governments. And only an internationalization of aid can provide the political and psychological basis for so raising its level that aid becomes a really important means of policy for the economic development of underdeveloped countries.

• • •

The Disentanglement of Economic Colonialism

The practical problems are of a most complicated and difficult nature: how to disentangle all these very large foreign property relations inherited from long ages of colonialism, and economic dependency; how to build up new economic relations between the rich Western world and the underdeveloped countries on the basis of the latter countries' independent nationhood; and how to do this with the minimum loss of mutual good will and the maximum protection, and even promotion, of economic values and interests on both sides in production and trade.

This is a challenge to free and constructive thinking and to statesmanship to be met both in the rich and the poor countries. The poor nations will be well advised not to take by onesided action and force what, by biding their time, they might acquire by quiet pressure and negotiation. For the rich nations, it is an equally urgent interest that they purge from their minds the untenable notion, which is a legacy from colonialism, that people in the poor countries should continue to be prepared not to think, desire, dislike, and act in the same way as they themselves do as a matter of course.

Whether it will happen peacefully and be handled with wisdom to the mutual advantage of rich and poor countries—which theoretically would be quite possible—or will mainly proceed through violent clashes and crises to the destruction of values and good will, the gradual and probably rapid disentanglement of the colonial economic enclave structures in the underdeveloped countries is an irresistible historical process, which will follow its course to the end. Basically it will be a movement along the Western way: towards national communities more akin than they are now to those of the Western countries. Only if seriously mishandled on the Western side—which, as very recent history shows, cannot be excluded—could it move the underdeveloped countries towards alliance with the Soviet bloc and thereby indirectly also influence their manner of planning in that direction. . . .

U THANT

The United Nations Development Decade

In response to a suggestion made by President John F. Kennedy when he addressed the Sixteenth UN General Assembly in September, 1961, the Assembly decided unanimously to proclaim the Development Decade in 1962. This project is intended to focus world attention on the need to mobilize all available resources—of manpower, skills, money, and raw materials—for massive economic and social development around the globe which might bring about what W. W. Rostow calls the "take-off" stage in underdeveloped countries as soon as possible.

The main objective of the Development Decade is to create conditions under which the annual rate of increase of national incomes in the developing countries would be not less than 5 per cent, and preferably would continue to expand at 6 per cent. If this can be accomplished, and if the population of the developing countries continues to rise at no more than its present rate of 2 to 2½ per cent a year, personal living standards, according to the UN experts, could be doubled within twenty to twenty-five years.

The UN report on the Development Decade, from which excerpts are given here, was presented to the Assembly in 1962 by Acting UN Secretary-General U Thant, former head of the permanent UN mission of Burma. Mr. Thant was elected in 1961 to fill the unexpired term of the late Dag Hammarskjold, and in November, 1962, was elected Secretary-General until November, 1966.

Born in 1911 to the family of a prosperous landowner and rice miller in the town of Pantanaw, near Rangoon, U Thant was educated at the local high school and at Rangoon University, where he met U Nu, subsequently Burma's Premier. He remained a teacher until 1947, when he became press and publicity director for the Anti-Fascist People's Freedom League, the strongest political group struggling for Burma's liberation from British rule. When Burma achieved independence in 1948, Mr. Thant became government press chief, and later served in a variety of posts as a personal adviser to U Nu, subsequently becoming his country's representative to the UN.

Introduction

IT is an extraordinary fact that at a time when affluence is beginning to be the condition, or at least the potential condition, of whole countries and regions rather than of a few favoured individuals, and when scientific feats are becoming possible which beggar mankind's wildest dreams of the past, more people in the world are suffering from hunger and want than ever before. Such a situation is so intolerable and so contrary to the best interests of all nations that it should arouse determination, on the part of advanced and developing countries alike, to bring it to an end. The United Nations has recognized the need for action by designating the current decade as the United Nations Development Decade. We can say with confidence that the means can be found if only there is the will to achieve the end.

At the opening of the United Nations Development Decade, we are beginning to understand the real aims of development and the nature of the development process. We are learning that development concerns not only man's material needs, but also the improvement of the social conditions of his life and his broad human aspirations. Development is not just economic growth, it is growth plus change. As our understanding of development deepens, it may prove possible, in the developing countries, to compress stages of growth through which the developed countries have passed. It may also be necessary to examine afresh the methods by which the goals of development may be attained.

During the past decade we have not only gained greatly in understanding of the development process and what it requires, but we have also achieved much. In particular, we have now at our disposal such instruments of effective action as the International Bank and the International Monetary Fund (with their newly strengthened resources), the International Development Association and the International Finance

From "The United Nations Development Decade, Proposals for Action." Report by the Secretary-General. United Nations Economic and Social Council, May 22, 1962.

Corporation, the United Nations Special Fund, the Expanded Program of Technical Assistance, special programs such as the World Food Program and the United Nations Children's Fund, and the regular programs of the various United Nations Agencies and of the United Nations itself. The resources of these various channels of proven effectiveness should be strengthened as an essential pre-condition for the success of the development decade. As new problems and new opportunities emerge, the instruments will evolve with them, as has been the case in the past.

The United Nations itself, quite apart from its own operational activities, has also proved its value as an international forum for discussion. A number of the developments, broadly described in Chapter I following, which have helped to create the conditions for the launching of the development decade, had their origin in discussions and in the gradual change of attitudes made possible by the exchange and confrontation of views in United Nations organs.

The basic problem in the present situation is to find ways in which the express desire of the advanced countries to help the developing countries can be translated into effective action. New methods of technical cooperation, added to those already well tried, will have to be found to take full advantage of the new economic and technological possibilities which have emerged in recent years.

The main economic objective for the decade is to create conditions in which the national incomes of the developing countries not only will be increasing by five per cent yearly by 1970, but will also continue to expand at this annual rate thereafter. If this can be done, and if the population of the developing countries continues to rise at its present rate of two to two and one half per cent yearly, personal living standards can be doubled within twenty-five to thirty years. If, however, the growth of population should be even more rapid by the end of the decade than it is now—and there are indications that in a number of countries the annual rate of increase is already three per cent or higher—it will take correspondingly longer to double living standards.

This objective for 1970 is within our reach, given a greater willingness among both the developing and the advanced countries to make the efforts and sacrifices required. And yet it is ambitious, for if achieved it would open up for a significant number of underdeveloped countries the prospect of a real improvement in their conditions of life. In particular, it offers hope for the younger generation of today.

•   •   •

Meanwhile, there has been increasing appreciation of the importance of a number of new approaches. These include:

1. The concept of national planning—for social as well as for economic development. This is central to all the proposals for intensified action by the United Nations system during the development decade outlined in this report. Former objections to planning, based largely on a misunderstanding of the role envisaged for the private sector in most development plans, have died away. It is now generally appreciated that the purpose of a development plan is to provide a program of action for the achievement of targets based on realistic studies of the resources available. Planning is proving to be a potent tool for the mobilization of existing and latent resources—human and material, public and private, domestic and external—available to countries for the achievement of their development aims. It has been shown that vigorous efforts are more likely to result if national and sectoral objectives are defined and translated into action programs.

2. There is now greater insight into the importance of the human factor in development, and the urgent need to mobilize human resources. Economic growth in the advanced countries appears to be attributable in larger part than was previously supposed to human skills rather than to capital. Moreover, the widening of man's horizons through education and training, and the lifting of his vitality through better health, are not only essential pre-conditions for development, they are also among its major objectives. It is estimated that the total number of trained people in the developing countries must be increased by at least 10 per cent a year if the other objectives of the decade are to be achieved.

3. One of the most serious problems facing the developing countries is increasing under-employment and unemployment. This increase is not confined to countries already experiencing population pressures, although rapidly rising population is undoubtedly a major aggravating factor. Far-reaching action will be required if the fruits of economic progress are to benefit all the inhabitants of the world.

4. The disappointing foreign trade record of the developing countries is due in part to obstacles hindering the entry of their products into industrial markets, and in part to the fact that production of many primary commodities has grown more rapidly than demand for them. It is appreciated that "disruptive competition" from low-income countries may be felt by established industries in high-income countries. Yet, precisely because they are so advanced, the high-income countries should be able to alleviate any hardships without shifting the burden of adjustment to the developing countries by restricting the latter's export markets. A related problem to be solved is that of stabilizing the international commodity markets on which developing countries depend so heavily. Progress could certainly be made if the main industrial countries were to devote as much attention to promoting trade as to dispensing aid.

5. The acceptance of the principle of capital assistance to developing countries is one of the most striking expressions of international solidarity as well as enlightened self-interest. If such assistance increases to, and maintains, a level of 1 per cent of the national incomes of the advanced countries during the development decade, as suggested by the General Assembly, this will represent yet another essential contribution to the success of the decade. At the same time, there is a need for pragmatism and flexibility in determining the forms of capital flows and aid, in relation both to the needs of the developing countries and to the shifting balance of payments position of assisting countries.

6. Towards the end of the fifties the importance of laying an adequate groundwork for large-scale investment programs came to be widely recognized. Many developing countries lack any detailed knowledge of their resources. However, even where potential investment opportunities can be identified, it may be impossible to implement them in the absence of one or more of the necessary factors of production—labour, capital, and entrepreneurial and technical skills. Within the United Nations, the Special Fund has concentrated on pre-investment work, paying special attention to surveys and feasibility studies of natural resources, technical and vocational training and the establishment of institutions for applied research. It is estimated that total expenditure on pre-investment work must rise to a level of about one billion dollars a year by 1970, if the objectives of the decade are to be reached. This is about double the present rate of expenditure.

7. A crucial area for intensified pre-investment activity is the surveying and development of natural resources, including water, minerals and power. In the development of water resources, in particular, the United Nations system may have a significant part to play. Nearly all the world's great rivers flow through several countries, and their development is a problem requiring regional and international cooperation.

8. The potentialities of modern technology and new methods of research and development for attacking the problems of the developing countries are as yet only dimly perceived. Since the Second World War it has become clear that new techniques permit the solution of most scientific and technical problems once they are correctly posed. However, too little effort has been directed towards posing or solving the problems of the developing countries, although many of them would appear to present no insuperable difficulties; for example, the problems involved in developing a sturdy piece of mechanical equipment which can be kept running with very little maintenance should be less than those involved in designing and launching a permanently operating space satellite. It also seems desirable to stimulate research on the social problems of developing countries entering upon a period of rapid social change.

9. If the skills of the advanced countries are to be successfully adapted to the problems and conditions of the developing countries, the former must be willing and able to make available the necessary resources of skilled personnel. Indeed, it may be that the shortage of such highly skilled personnel, rather than a shortage of material resources of finance, will be the greatest obstacle to action in the development decade unless new steps are taken. Technical cooperation field workers or field-teams should no longer be isolated but work in close contact with those institutions in the advanced countries which have most knowledge of the problems they will encounter. Ways must also be found for the foreign experts to participate in setting up institutions which will take over and carry forward their work when they leave.

The success of the United Nations Development Decade in achieving its objectives will depend in large part on the application of such new approaches. Precisely because they are new, all their implications cannot yet be fully seen. They may be expected to change many existing attitudes and approaches.

The report which follows contains a number of suggestions for the intensification of the existing activities of the United Nations system, together with proposals for new departures. These range over a wide area of development problems. But an attempt has been made, in every case, to identify those areas in which action by the United Nations system might be expected to have the maximum leverage effect on development as a whole, and the maximum linkage effect in promoting advances in other sectors.

Chapter 1

Setting and Problems for the Development Decade

A. The Preceding Decade—Achievements and Remaining Problems

DURING the previous decade there was valuable progress in various directions clearing the way for intensified action during the present decade. It

From "The United Nations Development Decade, Proposals for Action." Report by the Secretary-General. United Nations Economic and Social Council, May 22, 1962.

came to be generally recognized that the progress of underdeveloped countries is one of the most important problems of the world economy, and the principle of partnership of the developed and underdeveloped countries in solving this problem was accepted. This principle of international solidarity was not previously applied beyond national boundaries. The resolution adopted by the General Assembly at the beginning of the development decade on "Concerted action for economic development of economically less developed countries" signifies the acceptance of this principle. A number of other points won general acceptance.

(i) The developing countries came more and more to realize that their share of the joint responsibility would include not only great efforts and sacrifices, but also departures from traditions and the making of economic and social reforms as the price of goals which they might set themselves for more rapid improvement of their standard of living. Consequently, their efforts came to be expressed more and more in national plans for economic and social development.

(ii) The newly accepted principle of solidarity expressed itself in greater willingness to give assistance to developing countries. Actual aid rendered increased steadily year by year and constituted a slowly rising proportion of the national incomes of the wealthier as well as the poorer countries. This is also reflected in the increased rate of lending by the International Bank and the doubling of its capital. Moreover, a recognition has been growing that part of the assistance would have to be in forms adjusted to the repayment capacity of developing countries, if it were to be consistent with its primary purpose of promoting development. The creation of the IDA expresses this recognition most clearly, as do also the unanimously agreed principles of financing development formulated within the General Assembly Committee on a United Nations Capital Development Fund. There is also growing evidence of a desire to co-ordinate assistance in its various forms and sources, including plans for the mobilization of the domestic resources of the developing countries.

(iii) The need for and techniques of development planning have been greatly clarified. They are no longer confused with unrelated extraneous issues, such as the demarcation of the public and private sectors in economic life, or the policies of a country in relation to its natural resources and foreign investors. Other false issues, such as agricultural development "versus" industrialization or infrastructure "versus" the production of goods, have also largely been disposed of. The purpose of development was also clarified as including "proper regard for its human and social aspects." Thus, the ground has been cleared for a non-doctrinaire consideration of the real problems of development, namely saving, training and planning, and for action on them. In particular, the advantages of dealing with the various problems not piecemeal, but by a comprehensive approach through sound development planning, became more fully apparent.

(iv) The need for international action to solve problems arising from the structural weakness and instability of the terms of trade, and the consequent effect on export markets of developing countries, came to be recognized, and some useful experiences and proposals were gathered during the nineteen-fifties.

(v) The decade also saw the growth of the idea of international technical cooperation and pre-investment activity, and towards the end of the decade there was spreading awareness of the great potential of latent resources and latent investment opportunities. The creation of the United Nations Special Fund is an expression of this tendency.

(vi) Recently there has also been much more widespread realization of the importance of the human factor in economic development. Research and experience have indicated that the contribution of physical capital alone is by no means as dominant as had one time been imagined. This realization opened up new approaches through education, training, community development, use of idle manpower and eradication of disease to use the vast latent human resources of the developing countries. While at the beginning of the last decade the problem of developing countries was viewed essentially as a problem of producing wealth, by the end of the decade it became widely acknowledged that the crucial factor was not production but rather the *capacity* to produce, which is inherent in people.

(vii) It was also increasingly recognized that social reform and economic strategy are two sides of the same coin, the single strategy of development. This realization came about through several intermediate stages in which an original opposition of these two ideas was replaced by a parallelism expressed in such terms as "balanced economic and social development." This ultimate identity can be best expressed by saying that the problem of the underdeveloped countries is not just growth, but development. Development is growth *plus* change; change, in turn, is social and cultural as well as economic, and qualitative as well as quantitative. It should no longer be necessary to speak of "economic and social development," since development—as distinct from growth—should automatically include both. A direct corollary of this new approach to development was that the purely economic indicators of progress were seen to provide only limited insight and might conceal as much as they indicated.

(viii) Trends toward regional cooperation of developing countries became apparent and developed strongly towards the end of the decade. In this, the United Nations system played an important role.

(ix) The decade saw the building up of international administrations as instruments for international action.

(x) There was also great progress in specific directions, of which perhaps control of certain diseases was particularly striking. As a result, the gap between poor and wealthier countries has been closing in terms of life expectancy—as distinct from incomes. There was also substantial gain in education.

These are indispensable foundations on which to build for a decade of development. . . .

To state all these grounds for a cautious confidence that the basic objective of the development decade is feasible is in reality to state *tasks* which have to be completed to make our hopes come true. The very fact that these tasks have not yet been fully accomplished despite the progress made in the last ten years is an indication that they are formidable. They are:

(i) The more systematic survey, development and utilization of physical and human resources in underdeveloped countries;

(ii) The formulation of true development plans providing for maximum mobilization of domestic resources and the effective utilization of external assistance;

(iii) An improvement in the machinery of administration, in institutions and in production incentives in order to meet the new and increased demands arising from these development plans;

(iv) A redirection of science and technology to increase the attention given to specific problems of low-income countries;

(v) An increase, and subsequent more vigorous growth, of the export earnings of underdeveloped countries;

(vi) An increased and a more assured flow of capital on suitable terms to the underdeveloped countries, to be further added to if the declaration adopted in General Assembly resolution 724 (VIII) is put into effect.

These six major tasks have to be performed in a specific setting which cannot be disregarded. Prominent features of this setting are the trend towards regional organizations of countries; the fact that many countries are newly independent or will be so during the development decade, with the consequence that African problems have come strongly to the foreground in the world picture; and the greatly heightened consciousness of social as well as economic objectives and of social as well as economic policies. Some elements of these new developments could help and some may hinder the achievement of the objectives of the development decade. It will therefore also be necessary to ensure that the potential affirmative contribution of these new developments is fully realized. The following proposals for intensified action in the fields of economic and social development by the United Nations system of organizations are submitted to Governments, with confidence that the task is feasible.

J. BRONOWSKI

'1984' Could Be a Good Year

When the developing non-Western nations have obtained financial aid from technologically advanced countries and from international organizations, they have only begun the struggle to modernize their economies. As this struggle is waged, often with initially discouraging results, the question is often asked whether the newly emerged nations will have to pass through all the stages of economic development laboriously undergone by the West.

Experience to date shows that this slow process which spanned several centuries may be dramatically reduced in time element if the new nations can make prompt use of the most up-to-date scientific discoveries and technological devices the West is now producing. It is already evident, in some non-Western areas, that their peoples can, and in terms of conserving scarce financial and economic resources, should jump from the ox-cart to the modern truck or bus adapted to their particular needs; from the coal or even the more recent oil age to the use of atomic and solar energy; from school classes led by individual teachers, who are in short supply in countries with mounting populations, to teaching by TV; and skip the railway age to that of the airplane.

The West's technological advances of our times foreshadow some of the new possibilities that may be utilized by non-Western peoples. *J. Bronowski, British scientist and mathematician (see page 28), in a challenge to George Orwell's predictions of a grim "Animal Farm" and "Big Brother" era in 1984, explains in this article why he thinks 1984 could be a good year for mankind.*

A WRITER who offers to forecast the future ought to begin by showing his credentials. My credentials are that I am an optimist and a scientist. I know that it is not usual for a prophet to be an optimist; most prophets prefer to play the part of Jeremiah and Cassandra. But then, that is because most prophets have not been scientists either; they have not really been in favor of progress.

We can see this in the most popular prophets of our own lifetime: in Aldous Huxley and George Orwell. Every reader must be struck by the revulsion against science and, joined with that, by the deep-seated fear of the future, which Huxley and Orwell share. "Brave New World" and "1984" are surely the most depressing societies that have ever been imagined, because their authors are so full of self-righteousness. They seem to me to be, not works of prophecy, but Puritan works of morality, preaching on every page a fire-and-brimstone sermon of foreboding. From the first page, the authors are sure that progress must be wrong—that everything that is good is already known to them.

I do not intend to follow the social and political preoccupations of Huxley and Orwell. Certainly the political world will be very different fifty years from now, when Asia and Africa will be immensely more developed and more vigorous in world affairs. But I shall not discuss politics, and I shall not even discuss social life in the future, except in one way—the way in which they will be shaped by the scientific discoveries and the inventions which can be foreseen now. I shall stick to predictions which are rooted in technical grounds.

There are three outstanding scientific changes which, I believe, will dominate the next fifty years. One is a change in the use of energy: this change has been set in motion by the discovery that men can tap the energy in the atomic nucleus. The second is a change in the control of energy: this change has been set in motion by the development of those electronic devices which go under the general name of automation. And the third its what I call the biological revolution: the discovery, which is still unfamiliar to us, that men can remake their biological environment, including parts of the human body and mind.

Nuclear Energy

One result of the addition of nuclear power to our other resources of power is, of course, to increase the amount of energy at the command of men the world over. What I have to say on this subject is best said in strictly numerical terms; and since I have already made these calculations once before, I should like to quote them as I made them:

"Today the inhabitants of the United States command, every man, woman and child, the amount of mechanical energy each year that would be generated, roughly, by ten tons of coal. This is the backing that civilization provides now, and it is equal, again at a rough estimate, to the work that would be done by a hundred slaves. If we are no longer a slave civilization, is is because even a child in the United States has as much work done for it as would require the muscle of a hundred slaves. By contrast, Athens at her richest provided for the average member of a citizen's family—man, woman or child—no more than five slaves.

"In most parts of the world, people today still command only a fraction of the American standard. In India, for example, the average use of energy amounts to the equivalent of about half a ton of coal a year, or five slaves—the standard of Athens over 2,000 years ago. This is the figure that will rise most steeply in the next fifty years. It cannot rise to the standard of the United States in that time, but it can reach a fifth of that standard. We can expect that in the next fifty years the energy used in the poorest countries will reach at least the equivalent of twenty slaves a head each year.

"It may seem very cold to measure the lives of people by the mechanical equivalent of two tons of coal a year, or twenty slaves. But the figure is not at all cold. In the first place, it could not be achieved had nuclear energy not been discovered. All the resources of the traditional fuels in the world would not yield this figure; and the dreams of liberal minds, to raise the dark races to the standard of the white, were an illusion until nuclear energy was discovered. The standards of the West will become at least tangible to the backward countries in the next fifty years because nuclear energy can provide the power."

This is one important effect of the coming of nuclear energy; and yet, to my mind, it is not the most important. To my mind, what is most important is that energy will be more evenly distributed in the future. It will no longer be necessary to concentrate industry where either coal or oil is plentiful. We shall not need to take the industry to the fuel, but the other way about—the fuel, the nuclear fuel, to the industry. For a nuclear fuel is more than a million times as concentrated as a chemical fuel; and where we could not take a million tons of coal or oil, to South

America, to the copperbelt, to the Australian desert, we shall be able to take a ton of uranium or of heavy hydrogen.

True, it will, for example, still be proportionately cheaper to build a large nuclear power station than a small one. But there is now no longer an inherent difficulty in siting any power station far from the line of supply of its fuel. In the past, the logic of concentrating the generation of electric power in a few large stations was that it was easier to carry the current from the station in a wire than to carry the coal to the station in a truck. But if the fuel is nuclear fuel, this is no longer so; a small nuclear station can become the center of a remote township as effectively as it already drives a submarine or keeps an army camp alive under the polar ice.

Over the next fifty years, nuclear energy is also essential to the growing of food on a world scale. It is, of course, clear that if energy is cheap, then it is possible to make a substitute for any material that we need, all the way from industrial diamonds to vitamins. In this sense, then, we can count on finding a decent standard of living, in food as well as in energy, for all the six billion people who will be alive fifty years from now. And in agriculture, we shall need nuclear energy above all for the irrigation and exploitation of marginal lands, including the brackish lands now poisoned by salt water.

If energy is cheap and transportable anywhere, then irrigation is possible anywhere. In agriculture, what energy will buy fifty years from now is water; and water will be the key to growing food for the world's population, which will be twice as large as today.

Automation

Second, I want to discuss the future influence of automation. In one sense, an automatic machine is still a machine, and automation is no more than the logical use of machines. But, in fact, automation implies such a difference in outlook, such a change in the conception of the place of the machine itself, that I ought to discuss it quite fundamentally.

Two hundred years ago, the West discovered that a man's or a woman's output of work can be multiplied many times if the repetitive tasks which a handworker must do are done by a machine. Machines were invented, all the way from the power loom to the mechanical digger, that could mimic those actions of the human muscle which a man must carry out laboriously and monotonously, time and time again, in order to get a piece of work finished. The wealth of the West, and its high standard of living, derive directly from the revolution in manufacture—the Industrial Revolution—which these machines created.

Until recently, the machines of industry confined themselves to those mechanical tasks which need muscle and no more. Only in the last years have we come to see, what now seems obvious enough, that any repetitive task is really best handled by a machine. This is true, whether the repetitive task is muscular, like rolling steel sheets, or whether it demands more delicate skills of calculation and judgment, such as controlling the thickness of the steel and computing its price.

This is the real nature of automation: the discovery that repetition is a machine task, even if the repetition is in adding up a ledger or controlling the distillation of a chemical. Men and women thrive on variety, but machines thrive on monotony. Machines do not get bored (and they seldom get tired), their attention does not wander, they do not feel that their gifts are being wasted. They like nothing better than to repeat themselves.

Fifty years from now, the machine operator of any kind will be as much a fossil as the hand-weaver has been since 1830. Today we still distinguish between skilled and unskilled jobs of repetition, between office worker and factory worker, between white collar and no collar. In fifty years from now, all repetitive jobs will be unskilled.

The social implications of this change are profound, and I believe that they, more than anything else that I have forecast, will shape the community of the future. For their effect will be to change the social status of the different jobs in the community. The ability to handle a column of figures will become no more desirable than the ability to drive a rivet; and even the ability to write business letters may become less sought after than the ability to repair the machine that writes them by rote. As a result, the clerk will sink in social status, and the electrical technician will rise; and that in itself is a change as far-reaching as was once brought about by the dissolution of the monasteries.

A Social Revolution

Here I want to turn boldly to make a social prophecy. I believe that the combined effect of nuclear energy and of automation will be to revolutionize the way in which men run their industries. Today industries are concentrated in large cities. The reasons for this are twofold: we find it convenient to generate energy on a large scale, and at the same time we have to have large labor forces.

I have already shown that nuclear energy will make it possible to generate electric power in quite small units, where it is wanted. One reason for working in large cities will therefore disappear. But industry has moved to (and has created) large cities for another reason also: in the search, above all, for people. A product, whether it is a car or a can of polish, goes through many stages, so that many hands are needed to process and pass it on step by step. Is there any reason to think that industry will be able to break away from the huge arrays of semi-skilled workers which have served it hitherto?

I think that industry *is* breaking away, and that the traditional mass of factory hands *is* shrinking. The new wind in industry is automation, and I believe that it can transform industrial life in the next fifty years. There has been a great deal of technical talk about automation in recent years, but once again its more remote but important social consequences seem to me to have been missed. Yet automation is likely to revolutionize the balance between work and leisure, and the size and structure of community life, in the next fifty years.

Our industrial civilization has gone on herding people together in huge complexes of cities. Now there is a hope that the next fifty years may reverse this trend, and may begin to dissolve the ugly concentrations of the Ruhr and the Clyde, of Pittsburgh and Tokyo. In automation, joined to nuclear energy, we have the means to run industries on the scale of a small country town—a scale which does not dwarf the human sense of community.

This shift in the pattern of working life is the most far-reaching change that I foresee. The fifty years ahead of us will provide the means to create a social revolution: to create lively and efficient small communities which can hold their own in the industrial world.

There are many things to be gained by leaving the large cities. For example, we shall gain the hours (about one eighth of our waking hours) which most workers now spend in the tedium and discomfort of travel. This is a great gain in leisure, and some people will think that it will create new problems of leisure. I do not think so; I think that leisure is only a problem today in those places where tedium and discomfort have reduced everyone to a dull indifference.

I am not the first prophet, or the first dreamer, to hope that the monstrous cities of today, like glaciers of an industrial ice age, will begin to melt away. But when social reformers in the past have longed for small communities which could be self-sufficient, they have usually wanted to found them on agriculture. They have wanted to go back to the land literally—to work on the land. This is quite unrealistic, now and in the future.

In short, it is not necessary to retreat from the disaster of the metropolis into the inertia of the village. The small town of the future can be as well-equipped, physically and intellectually, as the largest modern city. It will be served physically by the new forms of travel, and intellectually by the new links of communication which we can already foresee. My guess is that it will then need to be large enough only to support those unpractical but delightful luxuries which give life to a community—a baseball club and a theatre and places where people play chess or go bowling. I think that you can do all these things in a town of about thirty thousand strong, and this is my forecast of the size of the new industrial communities in the future.

But the small community that I have sketched has no room for dullness and indifference. If thirty thousand people make an industrial town which is physically and intellectually self-sufficient, they must all be skilled. The one unpractical luxury that they cannot afford is a man with no skill.

The Biological Revolution

The third fundamental change which will, I think, shape the future is what I have called the biological revolution. We are just beginning to learn that we can mold our biological environment as well as our physical one. During the next fifty years, this will be the most exciting and, I believe, the most influential work in science.

Let me single out a few lines of work which seem to me especially interesting and promising.

There is, to begin with, the practical progress in the attack on organisms which damage us. They may be pests which damage our food supply, at one extreme, or microbes which invade our bodies at the other. Fine work has already been done in developing specific chemicals to tackle each specific enemy. I think this method of combat, the development of exact and specific chemicals, will play a growing part in making men healthier and richer.

Let me give one example. We used to think that a man could produce the antibodies which resist a virus infection (for example, smallpox) only if he were given a mild dose of the infection. Now we know that this is not necessary. We know that a virus consists of two parts—a living center of nucleic acid, and an outside covering of protein. And we know that the protein covering alone will suffice to stimulate the cells to produce the antibodies which fight the whole virus. This is how, for example, the protein in the killed polio vaccine works.

I believe in the future we shall go even further: we shall protect against a virus disease by making, in the chemical laboratory, the protein covering of that virus.

This leads me to the next outstanding field of study. We know that there are drugs which greatly sharpen a man's faculties, and others which help him to be at peace with himself. Each kind of drug helps a man to make better use of his natural (but often hidden) gifts. I am sure that there is a bright prospect here for the future and that, as a result, men and women will lead livelier and happier lives, in work and in leisure right into their old age.

Finally, I should pay tribute to the searching work that is being done in the study of biological processes on the smallest, molecular scale. This has already given us a new understanding of the nature and of the dynamics of life, and at this very moment it has opened a deep insight into the basis of all heredity. I believe that in the long run this fundamental knowledge, which still seems abstract and remote, will have the greatest effect of all in the practice of medicine.

Science for Peace

I began by saying that I am an optimist and a scientist, and you now see that the two go together. There is plenty of ground for pessimism in world affairs, and perhaps we shall not avoid the suicide of mankind. But can we not? Can we not prevent the leaders of nations from being proudest of those scientific inventions which make the loudest bang?

We must, exactly because science has so much better uses to offer for its fundamental discoveries. I have shown you the rich future that should grow out of the very discoveries that people dread most—out of nuclear energy, automation, and biological advance.

What people fear is the reach, the power of these discoveries. And there people are not foolish: they recognize that nuclear energy, automation, and biological advance are the most powerful social forces of this century. But that power can be as great in peace as in war; we can use it to create the future and not to murder it. Science promises a future in which men can lead intelligent and healthy lives in cities of a human size, and I think it is a future truly worth living for.

Glossary

These brief definitions are intended to clarify the meaning of certain difficult or unusual words that appear in the foregoing selections. The definitions are not complete in a dictionary sense; the purpose is primarily to provide meaning for words in the specific context in which they appear.

advert—to refer or allude to.

ad hoc (Latin)—concerned with a particular end or purpose with respect to this (subject or thing).

Albigenses—members of an heretical religious sect that arose in the south of France in the eleventh century and was wiped out in the thirteenth.

anomic—sociological term: a condition where there is an absence of social norms or values.

Aprista—abbreviation for the Alianza Popular Revolucionaria Americana (APRA), which means Popular Revolutionary American Alliance. It is a political party of Peru led in recent years by Victor Raul Haya de la Torre. This party, at one time regarded by the United States as Communist-inspired, came to be viewed in the 1960's as being capable of carrying out long-needed reforms in Peru. APRA failed to win in the June 10, 1962 elections, and along with other political groups was suppressed by the military junta which had seized power.

arrogate—to claim presumptuously; to assume or appropriate without right.

ascriptive—something attributed or referred to; relating or involving elements that attribute.

assimilado (Spanish)—one who is assimilated or absorbed into a group or country.

attenuate—to weaken or reduce in force.

autarkic—self-sufficient, especially in economic matters as applied to a state.

autochthonous—native, indigenous.

babushka (Russian)—grandmother.

Beghards—members of semi-monastic religious communities of laymen in Flanders in the thirteenth century which were eventually declared heretical.

Beguines—religious communities of lay women devoted to charitable purposes first founded in Flanders in the twelfth century.

cachet (French)—a seal or letter; a distinguishing mark or character.

Carbonari (Italian)—a nineteenth-century Italian secret political society of revolutionary aims.

CCP—abbreviation for Chinese Communist Party.

cheng-feng movement—the Chinese Communist party reform movement that took place in 1942–43.

Clausewitz, Karl von (1780–1831)—German military officer and writer on military strategy whose famous book On War has had great influence.

coir—prepared fiber of the husk of coconut fruit, used in making rope, matting, etc.

Colombo Plan—The plan for cooperative economic development in South and Southeast Asia adopted at a meeting of the Commonwealth foreign ministers held at Colombo, Ceylon in 1950. The original members were India; Pakistan; Ceylon; the British territories of Malaya, Singapore, and

534

Sarawak; Britain; Canada; Australia; and New Zealand. However, the plan is not restricted to members of the Commonwealth. Since 1950, Burma, Cambodia, Laos, Nepal, South Vietnam, and the United States have joined it.

concomitant—accompanying, attending.

Conrad's Kurtz—a character in Joseph Conrad's short story "The Heart of Darkness" who, while in Africa on business, went to live in the jungle and (it is suggested) became completely uncivilized, and reverted to savagery.

déclassé (French)—fallen or lowered in social class, rank, etc.

desmesne—possession (of land) as one's own; domain; as used here, the land attached to a manor house.

Durham Report—The report prepared by Lord Durham, Governor General of Canada, in 1839. This report, entitled Report on the Affairs of British North America, has been called the Magna Carta of the British colonies. It granted responsible self-government to Canada.

endemic—peculiar to a particular people or locality, as an endemic disease.

endogenous—a biological term: growing or proceeding from within.

entrepreneurs—individuals who undertake business enterprises.

exacerbate—to increase the bitterness or violence of; aggravate; embitter.

fulsome—offensive to good taste; gross, as in fulsome praise.

Gandhi cap—the white cap worn by followers of Mohandas Gandhi.

gendarmerie (French)—any corps of European police; specifically, the French police.

gestation—the incubation period in which something takes shape or form.

humanism—any system or mode of thought or action in which human interests predominate.

imputation—the act of attributing something discreditable.

indigenous—originating in and characterizing a region or country; native.

infrastructure—the underlying foundation or framework; here, those portions of a nation's economy which must either already be in existence, or else built as soon as possible if a nation is to proceed effectively with the development of its agriculture and the construction of industries.

irruption—a breaking or bursting in; a violent incursion or invasion.

juggernaut—an idol of the Hindu divinity Krishna annually drawn on an enormous car in Puri, India, under whose wheels devotees are said to have thrown themselves. Thus, anything that acts to crush men or ideas.

Keynes, John Maynard (1883–1946)—British economist and writer whose ideas were very influential during the era of the New Deal.

kulaks (Russian)—fists; a term used by the Communists in the 1930's to describe peasants regarded as rich or "tight-fists."

Kuomintang (Chinese—Kuo, nation plus min, people plus tang, party)— Chinese political party formed in 1912 by Sun Yat-sen, after the establishment of the Chinese Republic, and at present led by Chiang Kai-shek.

Laksmi—the Hindu goddess of beauty, love, and good fortune, usually portrayed as golden in color.

Lazes—a group of people in the Ottoman Empire.

loi-cadre (French)—enabling act; in this case the French act of 1956, worked out by the French government with African deputies and senators in the French Parliament and with leaders of France's colonies in Africa, which gave a considerable measure of self-government to these colonies.

macédoine (French)—a mixture, usually of fruit or vegetables, served as a salad. Derived from Macedonia, an area of the former Ottoman Empire, now part of Yugoslavia, which has a mixture of population.

mansus (Latin)—manual labor; in the Middle Ages the work obligation due to the lord of the manor.

Meiji Restoration—the period describing the reign of the Japanese emperor Mutsuhito (1867–1912). In Japanese, *meiji* means enlightened peace.

mélange (French)—mixture; medley.

mestizos—persons of mixed blood; in Latin America, persons of mixed Spanish and Indian origin.

Middle Kingdom—Chinese term for China proper.

milieu (French)—environment, setting.

mir (Russian)—the village community in pre-Communist Russia where land was held in common by the peasants and worked by them in rotation.

modal—pertaining to mode, manner, or form.

monistic—philosophical term: pertaining to one ultimate substance or principle.

mortemain (French)—inalienable possession of lands or buildings by any corporation: in the Middle Ages, usually ecclesiastical; also the condition of any property left to a corporation in perpetuity for special purposes.

muzhik (Russian)—peasant. After the Communist Revolution the word usually referred to poor peasants. *See also* kulaks.

narodniki (Russian)—members of a Russian movement in the 1870's who believed in going out to the villages to educate and organize the peasants for revolution. Term derived from narod, people.

oblast (Russian)—An administrative district in Russia.

philistine—bourgeois, materialistic; also one who is indifferent to culture, esthetic refinement, etc.; one who is commonplace in ideas and tastes.

philosophes (French)—philosophers. Specifically here, philosophers who expressed the ideas which shaped the French Revolution.

prestations—in old English law, a payment of money or performance of a service.

proximate—next, nearest; closely adjacent.

quit-rent—a fixed fee, usually small, paid by a freeholder to his overlord in the Middle Ages in substitution for his services.

R.S.S.S.—Initials of an extremist Hindu religious party whose full name is Rashtriya Swamyam Sevak Sangh.

rubric—title, heading, or the like in a book or document, originally in red.

secessio plebis (Latin)—a revolt of the common people.

sine qua non (Latin)—that without which; something essential; an indispensable condition.

soviet (Russian)—counsel; term used since the Communist Revolution for council or assembly, for example, Supreme *Soviet* of the U.S.S.R.

subsuming—classifying.

syndrome—the pattern of symptoms, in, for example, a disease.

Tiers-Monde (French)—the African colonies; literally, the third world.

travesty—any grotesque or debased likeness or imitation.

vis-à-vis (French)—face to face; with relation to.

Vlachs—a group of people in the Ottoman Empire.

yang-ko (Chinese)—a very simple Communist folk song and dance.